McGraw-Hill networks™

MEETS YOU ANYWHERE — TAKES YOU EVERYWHERE

GO online

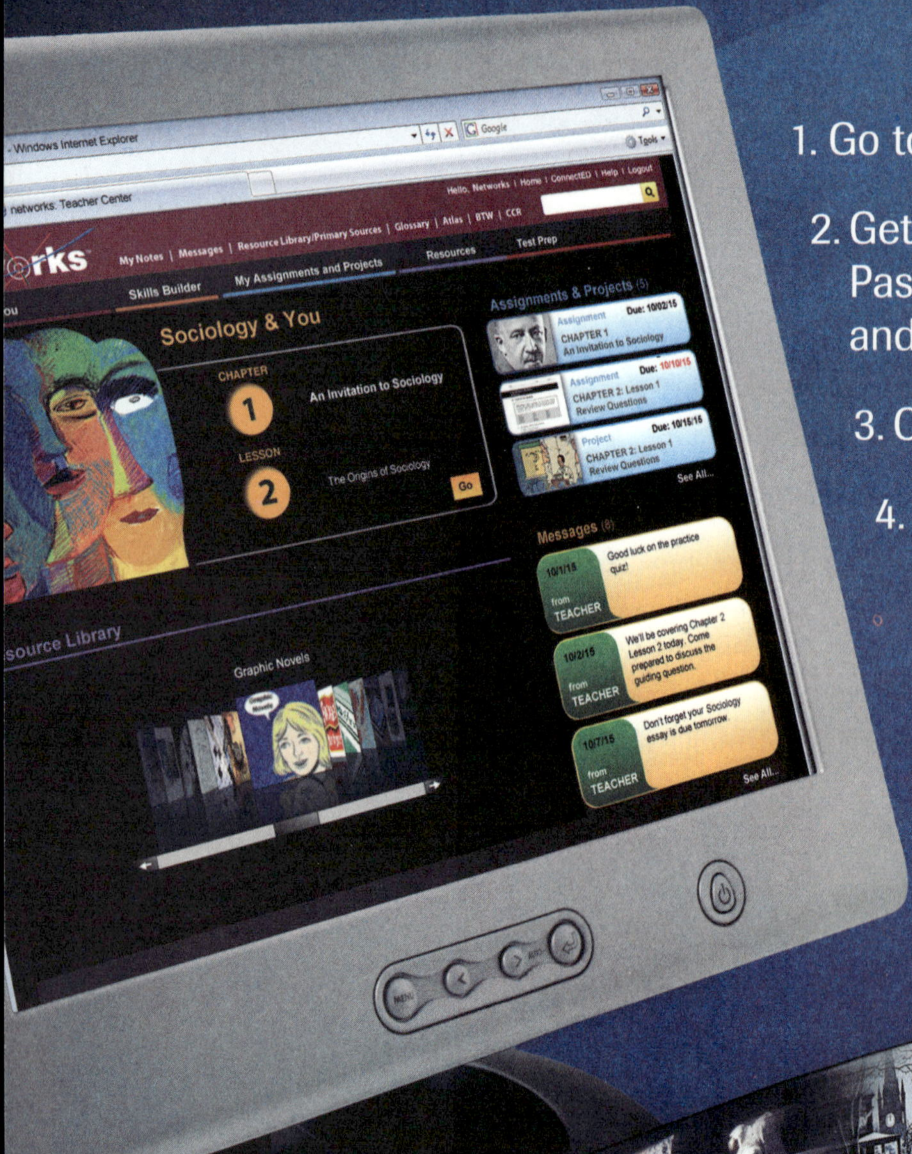

1. Go to *connected.mcgraw-hill.com*.
2. Get your User Name and Password from your teacher and enter them.
3. Click on your **Networks** book.
4. Select your chapter and lesson.

HOW do you learn?

Read • Reflect • Watch • Listen • Connect • Discover • Interact

start networking

WHAT do you learn?

Sociology Concepts • Culture • Social Awareness

start net**w**orking

M3

McGraw-Hill networks™

MEETS YOU ANYWHERE — TAKES YOU EVERYWHERE

HOW do you make Networks yours?

Organize • Take Notes • Study • Submit • Message

M4

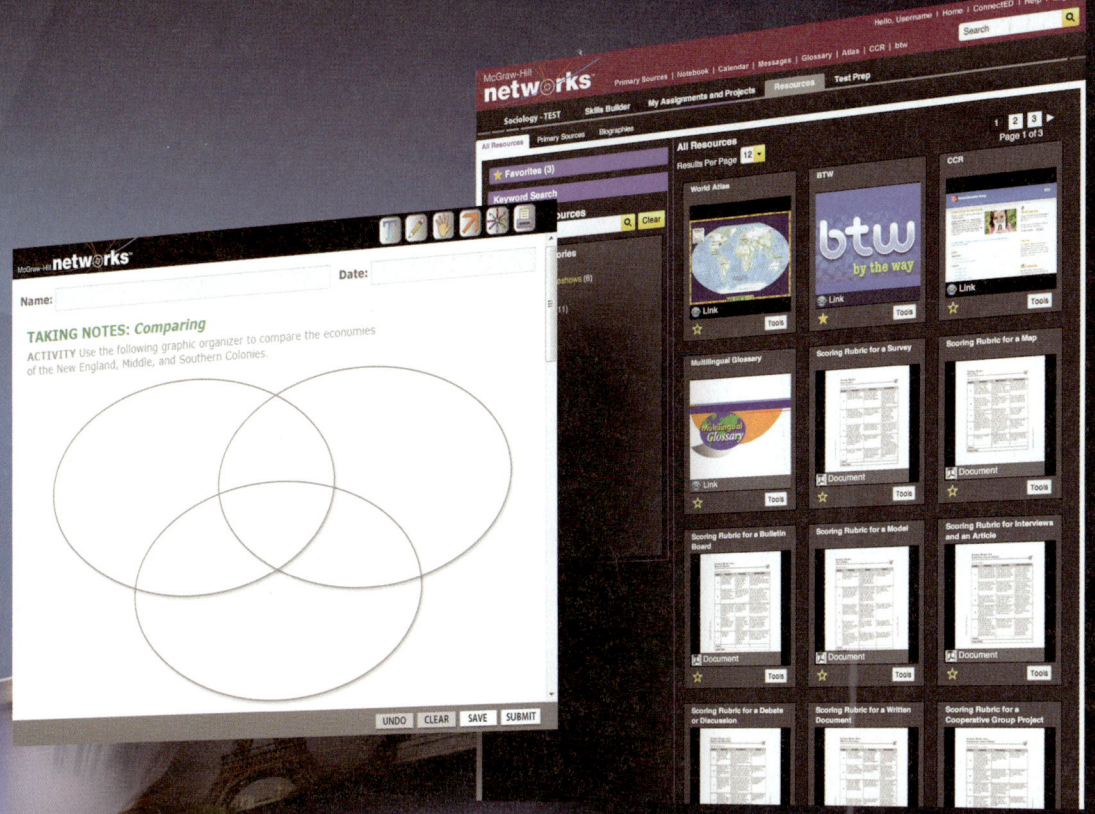

WHAT do you use?

Graphic Organizers • Primary Sources • Videos • Games • Photos

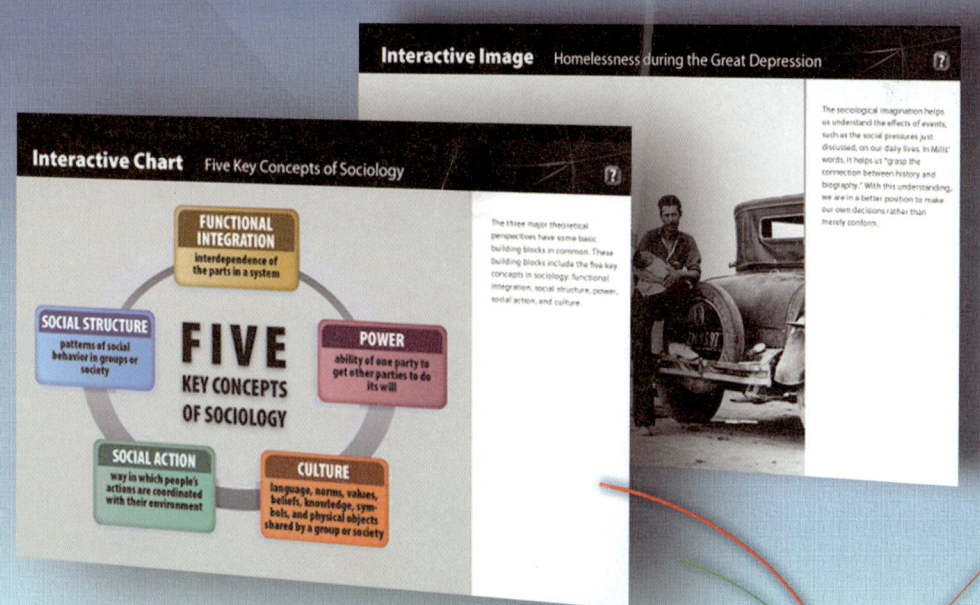

start networking

M5

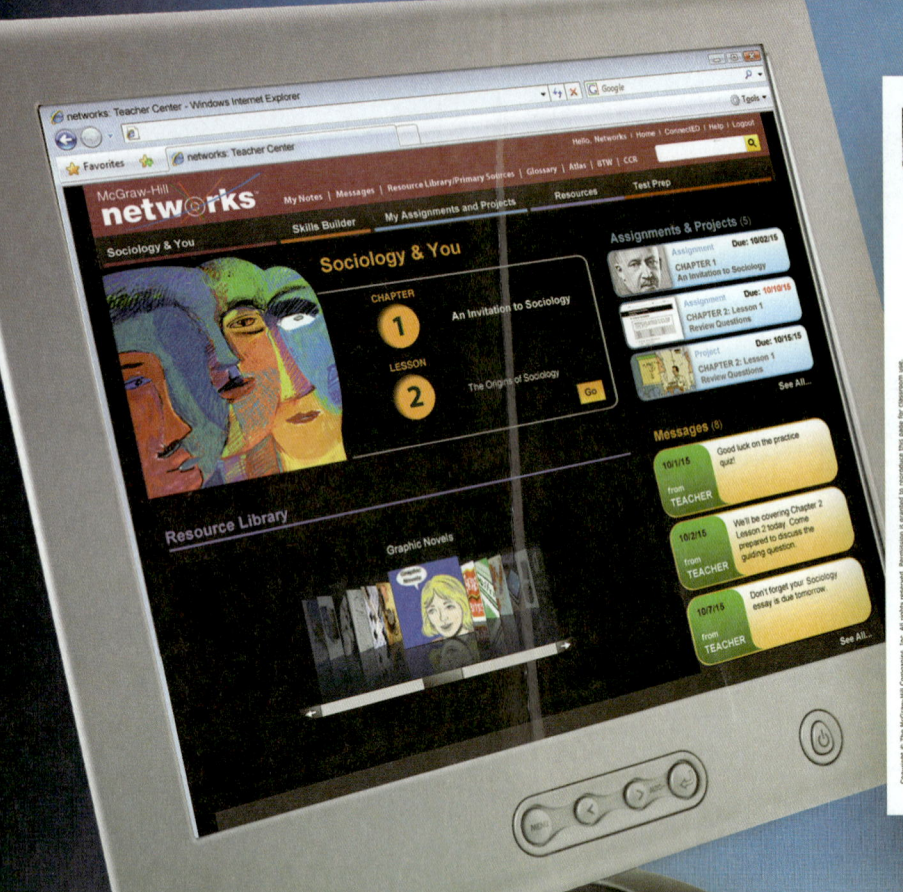

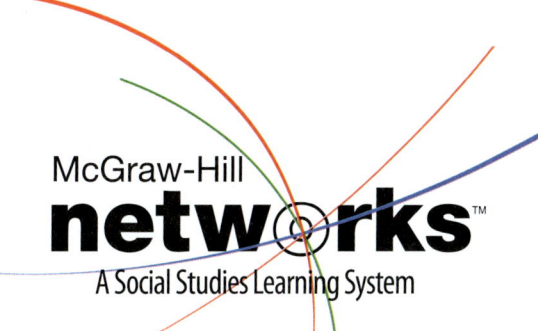

SOCIOLOGY & YOU

Jon M. Shepard, Ph.D.

Robert W. Greene

Bothell, WA • Chicago, IL • Columbus, OH • New York, NY

McGraw-Hill Networks™
A Social Studies Learning System
MEETS YOU ANYWHERE —
TAKES YOU EVERYWHERE
Go online
1. Go to *connected.mcgraw-hill.com*.
2. Get your User Name and Password from your teacher and enter them.
3. Click on your **Networks** book.
4. Select your chapter and lesson.

Cover Credits:
(Main Image) Blind Feeling, 1996, Giclee Print by artist Diana Ong, Diana Ong/SuperStock/Getty Images. (Thumbnails, top to bottom, left to right) S. Olsson/PhotoAlto; ©LWA/Dann Tardif/Blend Images/Corbis; fStop/SuperStock; Purestock/SuperStock; Tetra Images/Alamy; Image Source/Getty Images; ©moodboard/Corbis; McGraw-Hill Companies, Inc. Gary He, photographer; Design Pics/Patrick Kociniak; ©moodboard/Corbis; Library of Congress Prints and Photographs Division [LC-DIG-ggbain-07242]; ©moodboard/Corbis; McGraw-Hill Companies, Inc. Christopher Kerrigan, photographer; ©moodboard/Corbis; Hill Street Studios/Blend Images LLC; Image Source/Getty Images; Pixtal/age fotostock; Glow Images.

Credits pages M1–M6:
M1 (l to r, t to b)Apic/Hulton Archive/Getty Images, (2)Hulton Archive/Archive Photos/Getty Images, (3)Mary Evans Picture Library/Alamy, (4)Library of Congress Prints & Photographs Division [LC-USZC4-12153], (5)Library of Congress Prints and Photographs Division [LC-USZ62-52389], (6)©Stefano Bianchetti/Corbis, (7)akg-images/The Image Works, (8)Science and Society/SuperStock, (9) Official White House Photo by Pete Souza;
M2 (l to r)©Bettmann/Corbis, (2)akg-images/The Image Works, (3)India Images/Alamy, (4)Library of Congress Prints and Photographs Division [LC-USZ62-83145]
M3 (l to r, t to b)©Bettmann/Corbis, (2)Science and Society/SuperStock, (3)Lawrence Migdale/Photo Researchers, Inc., (4)James Hardy/PhotoAlto/Alamy, (5)NASA;
M5 Library of Congress Prints and Photographs Division [LC-DIG-fsa-8b38632]
cov S. Olsson/PhotoAlto

www.mheonline.com/networks

Copyright © 2014 by McGraw-Hill Education

All rights reserved. No part of this publication may be reproduced or distributed in any form or by any means, or stored in a database or retrieval system, without the prior written consent of McGraw-Hill Education, including, but not limited to, network storage or transmission, or broadcast for distance learning.

Send all inquiries to:
McGraw-Hill Education
8787 Orion Place
Columbus, OH 43240

ISBN: 978-0-07-663193-3
MHID: 0-07-663193-1

Printed in the United States of America.

2 3 4 5 6 7 8 9 QVR 17 16 15 14 13

AUTHORS

Jon M. Shepard, Ph.D., earned his Ph.D. in sociology at Michigan State University before assuming a teaching position at the University of Kentucky. The ninth edition of his popular college sociology textbook is currently being revised. He also has written extensively for academic journals and professional sociology associations. Dr. Shepard has received teaching awards at both the University of Kentucky and Virginia Tech. His love of sociology and extensive experience with introductory sociology students have motivated and guided him in the creation of this unique text for high school students.

Robert W. Greene taught high school sociology for sixteen years and in the past twelve years has taught at several Wisconsin colleges. He currently teaches courses such as Introductory Sociology, Contemporary American Society, and Social Problems at Madison and Milwaukee area technical colleges. Mr. Greene is a former president of the Wisconsin Sociological Association, having served two nonconsecutive terms, and is the only high school teacher to have served in that capacity. He also has been involved in high school sociology on the national level, serving for seven years as Chair of the Sociology Special Interest Group for the National Council for the Social Studies, and was a member of the American Sociological Association's task force to bring Advanced Placement Sociology to American high schools.

Contributing Author

Jay McTighe has published articles in a number of leading educational journals and has coauthored ten books, including the best-selling *Understanding by Design* series with Grant Wiggins. Mr. McTighe also has an extensive background in professional development and is a featured speaker at national, state, and district conferences and workshops. He received his undergraduate degree from the College of William and Mary, earned a Masters degree from the University of Maryland, and completed post-graduate studies at Johns Hopkins University.

CONSULTANTS AND REVIEWERS

ACADEMIC CONSULTANTS

Simonetta Falasca-Zamponi, Ph.D.
Professor
Department of Sociology
University of California
Santa Barbara, California

Neyooxet Greymorning, Ph.D.
Professor
Department of Anthropology, Department of Native American Studies
University of Montana
Missoula, Montana

Catherine Lee Harrington, Ph.D.
Professor
Department of Sociology & Gerontology
Miami University
Oxford, Ohio

Carol A. Jenkins, Ph.D.
Professor
Department of Social Science—Sociology
Glendale Community College
Glendale, Arizona

Elisabeth M. (Betsy) Lucal, Ph.D.
Professor
Department of Sociology and Anthropology
Indiana University—South Bend
South Bend, Indiana

Michael J. McVicar, Ph.D.
Lecturer
Department of Sociology
Ohio State University
Columbus, Ohio

Diane Pike, Ph.D.
Professor
Department of Sociology
Augsburg College
Minneapolis, Minnesota

Sally Raskoff, Ph.D.
Chair
Department of Sociology & Ethnic Studies
Los Angeles Valley College
Valley Glen, California

Kimberly S. Schimmel, Ph.D.
Associate Professor of the Sociology of Sport
Department of Sociology
Kent State University
Kent, Ohio

Jody Agius Vallejo, Ph.D.
Assistant Professor
Department of Sociology
University of Southern California

Theodore C. Wagenaar, Ph.D.
Professor, Carnegie Scholar
Department of Sociology & Gerontology
Miami University
Oxford, Ohio

Tom Daccord
Educational Training Specialist
Co-Director, EdTechTeacher
Boston, Massachusetts

Justin Reich
Educational Training Specialist
Co-Director, EdTechTeacher
Boston, Massachusetts

TEACHER REVIEWERS

Kimberly Coffelt
Sociology Teacher
Southeast High School
Wichita, Kansas

Candee Collins
Social Studies Teacher
Pine Tree High School
Kilgore, Texas

Janet DeSha
Sociology Teacher
East Nashville Magnet
Nashville, Tennessee

Terri McGill
Sociology Teacher
Edmond Santa Fe High School
Edmond, Oklahoma

Jason Orendi
Sociology Teacher
Boonsboro High School
Martinsburg, West Virginia

Jamie Reese
Sociology Teacher
Buckhorn High School
New Market, Alabama

Bill South
Sociology Teacher
Sevier County High School
Sevierville, Tennessee

Laura St. Clair
Social Studies Teacher
Farragut High School
Knoxville, Tennessee

Angela Studer
Social Studies Teacher
Northwest High School
Wichita, Kansas

Julie Sucheski
Social Studies Teacher
Twinsburg High School
Twinsburg, Ohio

Mike Wise
Sociology Teacher
Hardin Valley Academy
Knoxville, Tennessee

CONTENTS

An Invitation to Sociology 1

Essential Question
What is sociology?

TECHNOLOGY & SOCIETY Technological Change and the Birth of Sociology 2

LESSON 1 The Sociological Perspective 4
Connecting Sociology to History A Native American Perspective 8
A Diverse America Population Change 9
Applying Sociology Careers in Sociology 10

LESSON 2 The Origins of Sociology 12
Connecting Sociology to Psychology
The Pioneers of Psychology 16
Focus on Research: Field Research The Objective Value of a Social Settlement 20

LESSON 3 Theoretical Perspectives 22
A Global Perspective A Different Perspective 23
Theoretical Perspectives Assumptions of the Major Perspectives 26
Quick Case Study What Makes Us Change Behaviors? 28

Sociological Research Methods 33

Essential Questions
How do sociologists do research? •
What is ethical research?

TECHNOLOGY & SOCIETY Using Technology in Sociological Research 34

LESSON 1 Research Methods 36
Applying Sociology Evaluating Surveys 39
Theoretical Perspectives Investigating School Violence and School Funding 41
A Diverse America Percentage of Families Speaking Non-English at Home 43

LESSON 2 Causation in Science 46
A Global Perspective Cell Phone Use 47
Connecting Sociology to History
The Scientific Method 50
Focus on Research: Case Study School Talk: Gender and Adolescent Culture 52

LESSON 3 Procedures and Ethics in Research 54
Connecting Sociology to Psychology
The "Monster Study" 56
Quick Case Study How Do You Make a Research Plan? .. 57

CCSS This icon indicates where reading skills and writing skills from the *Common Core State Standards for English Language Arts & Literacy in History/Social Studies, Science, and Technical Subjects* are practiced and reinforced.

v

CONTENTS

CHAPTER 3 Culture 65

Essential Question
How does culture influence society?

TECHNOLOGY & SOCIETY Popular Culture and the Internet 66

LESSON 1 The Basis of Culture 68
Theoretical Perspectives Explaining the Role of Culture 69

LESSON 2 Language and Culture 72
Connecting Sociology to Anthropology The Nacirema . . 73
A Global Perspective Language Families 74

LESSON 3 Norms and Values 75
Applying Sociology Sociology and the Criminal Justice System 79
A Diverse America Immigration to the United States . . 80
Focus on Research: Survey Research How Do Schools and Parents Fail Teens? 82

LESSON 4 Beliefs and Material Culture 84

LESSON 5 Cultural Diversity and Similarity . 87
Connecting Sociology to History The Hippies 90
Quick Case Study How Do Stereotypes Affect You? . . . 92

CHAPTER 4 Socialization 97

Essential Question
What factors influence an individual's development?

TECHNOLOGY & SOCIETY Mass Media and Socialization . . 98

LESSON 1 The Importance of Socialization . . 100

LESSON 2 Socialization and the Self 105
Theoretical Perspectives Socialization and Mass Media . . 107
Connecting Sociology to Psychology Self-Concept 108

LESSON 3 Agents of Socialization 110
Applying Sociology Mass Media and Socialization . . . 115
Focus on Research: Case Study Black Picket Fences: Charisse Baker 116

LESSON 4 Socialization Through the Life Cycle 118
Connecting Sociology to Anthropology Rites of Passage . . 120
A Global Perspective Support for an Elderly Population 122

LESSON 5 Processes of Socialization 124
A Diverse America Rates of Imprisonment 125
Quick Case Study How Do You Compare to Your Birth Cohorts? 126

There's More Online! **EXPLORE** cyberbullying.   **SEE** status and roles.   **WATCH** a video about group behavior.

Social Structure and Society 129

Essential Questions
How is society organized? • How does the way in which a society is structured affect human relationships?

TECHNOLOGY & SOCIETY Social Structures, Roles, & Statuses 130

LESSON 1 Social Structure and Status 132
Focus on Research: Experiment
Adopting Statuses in a Simulated Prison 136

LESSON 2 Social Structure and Roles 138
A Diverse America Unemployment Rates 139
Quick Case Study What's Your Role? 140
Applying Sociology Reducing Conflict in Two-Career Families 141
Theoretical Perspectives
Illustrating Social Structure Concepts 142

LESSON 3 Preindustrial Societies 143
Connecting Sociology to Anthropology
A Preindustrial Society Today 146

LESSON 4 Industrial and Postindustrial Societies 147
Connecting Sociology to Economics
Categorizing Societies 148
A Global Perspective Agricultural Employment...... 149

Groups and Formal Organizations 153

Essential Question
How do groups function as units of society?

TECHNOLOGY & SOCIETY Teens and Cyberbullying 154

LESSON 1 Primary and Secondary Groups .. 156
Connecting Sociology to Political Science
Groups and Voting Behavior 158

LESSON 2 Other Groups and Networks 160
Applying Sociology School Violence and Social Networks 161
A Diverse America Social Networking 162

LESSON 3 Types of Social Interaction 163
Theoretical Perspectives Types of Social Interaction.. 165
Connecting Sociology to Psychology
Decision Making in Juries 166
Focus on Research: Experiment Group Pressure and Obedience 168

LESSON 4 Formal Organizations 170
Quick Case Study Bureaucracies 172
A Global Perspective Human Development 173

CONTENTS

Deviance and Social Control — 177

Essential Questions
What is deviance? • Who defines deviance?

TECHNOLOGY & SOCIETY High-Tech Crime and Deviance 178

LESSON 1 Deviance and Social Control 180
Connecting Sociology to Anthropology
Murder in Cheyenne Society 181
A Diverse America Violent Crime 182

LESSON 2 Functionalism and Deviance 184

LESSON 3 Symbolic Interactionism and Deviance 187
Connecting Sociology to History
Crime and Punishment 188
Focus on Research: Case Study
Saints and Roughnecks 190

LESSON 4 Conflict Theory and Deviance ... 192
Theoretical Perspectives
Illustrating Sociological Concepts 193

LESSON 5 Crime and Punishment 195
Global Perspective Death Penalty Policy 196
Quick Case Study Deviance and Social Control 197

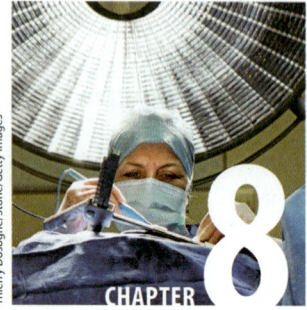

Social Stratification — 201

Essential Questions
What is "equality"? • To what extent are societies unequal?

TECHNOLOGY & SOCIETY Social Stratification and the Digital Divide 202

LESSON 1 Dimensions and Explanations of Stratification 204
Connecting Sociology to History An Outsider's View of American Society 205
Theoretical Perspectives Social Stratification 211

LESSON 2 Social Class and Poverty in America 212
A Diverse America Living in Poverty 217
Focus on Research: Field Research Nickel and Dimed .. 220

LESSON 3 Social Mobility 222
Connecting Sociology to Anthropology
India's Traditional Social System 223

LESSON 4 Global Stratification 226
Applying Sociology Nongovernmental Organizations .. 227
A Global Perspective Chronic Poverty 228
Quick Case Study What Makes a Nation Low Income or High Income? 230

There's More Online! **EXPLORE** Tejano culture. **SEE** women in the military. **WATCH** a video about inequality.

CHAPTER 9 Inequalities of Race and Ethnicity 233

Essential Questions
What challenges do minority groups face? • What are the causes and effects of racial and ethnic discrimination in society?

TECHNOLOGY & SOCIETY High-Tech Hate........234

LESSON 1 Minority, Race, and Ethnicity ... 236
A Global Perspective The African Diaspora 237
Connecting Sociology to Economics
 Attitudes Toward Minorities..................239

LESSON 2 Racial and Ethnic Relations 240
Connecting Sociology to Human Geography
 Tejano Culture............................241
Focus on Research: Survey Research
 Narratives of Mexican American Women 244

LESSON 3 Theories of Prejudice and Discrimination 246
A Diverse America Hate Groups in the United States..248
Theoretical Perspectives Prejudice & Discrimination...250

LESSON 4 Minority Groups in the United States............253
Applying Sociology Studies of Discrimination and Formation of Policy 254
Quick Case Study Race in the Media 261

CHAPTER 10 Inequalities of Gender and Age 265

Essential Questions
What are the causes and effects of discrimination in society? • How is gender discrimination reflected in the legal and economic systems? • What are the effects of age discrimination?

TECHNOLOGY & SOCIETY Technology Use Varies by Gender and Age...........................266

LESSON 1 Sex and Gender Identity 268
Connecting Sociology to Anthropology
 Gender Behavior..........................270

LESSON 2 Theoretical Perspectives on Gender 273
Applying Sociology Women in the Military 274
Theoretical Perspectives Gender Inequalities 276

LESSON 3 Gender Inequality 278
Connecting Sociology to Economics The Glass Ceiling...282
A Global Perspective Women in National Parliaments..284
Focus on Research: Survey Research Obstacles to Female Political Leadership 286

LESSON 4 Ageism........................288

LESSON 5 Inequality in America's Elderly Population.............291
A Diverse America An Aging Population 293

ix

CONTENTS

The Family 297

Essential Question
What makes a family?

TECHNOLOGY & SOCIETY Families and Technology 298

LESSON 1 Family and Marriage Across Cultures 300
Connecting Sociology to Human Geography
Family Structures Around the World 302
A Global Perspective Minimum Legal Age at Marriage for Women 304
Applying Sociology Finding a Mate 305

LESSON 2 Theoretical Perspectives and the Family 307
Theoretical Perspectives Perspectives on the Family . 311

LESSON 3 Family and Marriage in the United States 312
A Diverse America Marriage Rates 313
Connecting Sociology to Psychology
The Bobo Doll Experiment 316
Focus on Research: Case Study Family Violence 318

LESSON 4 Changes in Marriage and Family .. 320
Quick Case Study How Are Family Arrangements Alike and Different? 323

Education 329

Essential Question
What purposes does education serve?

TECHNOLOGY & SOCIETY Education and Technology .. 330

LESSON 1 Development and Structure of Education 332
A Diverse America School Expenditures 337
Applying Sociology Distance Learning 338

LESSON 2 Functionalist Perspective 340
Connecting Sociology to History The Need for an Educated Citizenry 341
A Global Perspective World Literacy Rates 342

LESSON 3 Conflict Perspective 344
Connecting Sociology to Human Geography
Dropout Rates 349
Focus on Research: Field Research Segregated Schools . 352

LESSON 4 Symbolic Interactionism 354
Theoretical Perspectives Investigating Education 355
Quick Case Study How Does the Gender Composition of a Classroom Affect Student Learning? 357

There's More Online! EXPLORE a political time line. SEE a world religions map. WATCH a video on religion.

CHAPTER 13 Political and Economic Institutions 361

Essential Question
How does the interaction between political systems and economic systems affect society?

TECHNOLOGY & SOCIETY Politics and Technology 362

LESSON 1 Power and Authority 364
Connecting Sociology to Political Science
  Constitutional Government 367
A Global Perspective Political Freedom 368

LESSON 2 Political Power in American Society 370
A Diverse America Voter Turnout in
  Presidential Elections 371
Theoretical Perspectives Two Models of
  Political Power 375
Focus on Research: Survey Research
  Consuming Politics: Jon Stewart, Branding,
  and the Youth Vote in America 376

LESSON 3 Economic Systems 378
Connecting Sociology to Economics
  The Free-Enterprise System 380

LESSON 4 The Modern Corporation 383
Applying Sociology Employee Rights 384

LESSON 5 Work in the Modern Economy ... 386
Quick Case Study Teens in the Modern Economy 390

CHAPTER 14 Religion 393

Essential Question
What roles does religion play in society?

TECHNOLOGY & SOCIETY Religion and Technology 394

LESSON 1 Religion and Sociology 396
A Global Perspective Religions of the World 397
Connecting Sociology to History
  Religious-Based Conflicts 399
Theoretical Perspectives Religion 401

LESSON 2 Religious Organization and Religiosity 402
Applying Sociology The Danger of Cults 404
Focus on Research: Survey Research
  Moral-Cultural Issues 406

LESSON 3 Religion in the United States ... 408
Connecting Sociology to Human Geography
  Religious Beliefs Around the Globe 411
A Diverse America Religiosity in the United States ... 413
Quick Case Study Should Taxpayers Fund
  Religious Schools? 414

xi

CONTENTS

Population and Urbanization ... 417

Essential Question
What is demography and why do we study demographics?

TECHNOLOGY & SOCIETY Food, Hunger, and Technology ... 418

LESSON 1 The Dynamics of Demography ... 420
A Diverse America Fertility Rate in the United States . 421
Applying Sociology Business and Demographics ... 422

LESSON 2 World Population ... 426
Connecting Sociology to Economics
Thomas Malthus: Economist ... 430

LESSON 3 The Urban Transition ... 434
A Global Perspective Urbanization ... 435
Theoretical Perspectives Urban Society ... 438
Focus on Research: Field Research Gang Leader for a Day: A Rogue Sociologist Takes to the Street ... 440

LESSON 4 Urban Ecology ... 442
Connecting Sociology to Human Geography
The Informal Housing Sector ... 444
Quick Case Study How Do Urban Environments Affect People? ... 446

Social Change and Collective Behavior ... 449

Essential Questions
What influences collective behavior? • What factors influence social change?

TECHNOLOGY & SOCIETY Social Movements and Technology ... 450

LESSON 1 Social Change ... 452
A Diverse America Geographic Mobility ... 453
Connecting Sociology to Economics
Globalization of the Economy ... 454
Focus on Research: Case Study
Globalization and Work ... 460

LESSON 2 Theoretical Perspectives on Social Change ... 462
Theoretical Perspectives Social Change ... 463

LESSON 3 Collective Behavior ... 465
Applying Sociology The 9/11 Terrorist Attacks ... 469

LESSON 4 Social Movements ... 473
Connecting Sociology to History
Leaders of Social Movements ... 474
A Global Perspective Internet Users ... 477
Quick Case Study How Would You Change the World? ... 478

Analyzing Readings in Sociology ... 481
Sociology Handbook ... 505
Glossary ... 521
Index ... 549

FEATURES

Applying Sociology

Careers in Sociology	10
Evaluating Surveys	39
Sociology and the Criminal Justice System	79
Mass Media and Socialization	115
Reducing Conflict in Two-Career Families	141
School Violence and Social Networks	161
Nongovernmental Organizations	227
Studies of Discrimination and Formation of Policy	254
Women in the Military	274
Finding a Mate	305
Distance Learning	338
Employee Rights	384
The Danger of Cults	404
Business and Demographics	422
The 9/11 Terrorist Attacks	469

Connecting Sociology to...

Anthropology

The Nacirema	73
Rites of Passage	120
A Preindustrial Society Today	146
Murder in Cheyenne Society	181
India's Traditional Social System	223
Gender Behavior	270

Economics

Categorizing Societies	148
Attitudes Toward Minorities	239
The Glass Ceiling	282
The Free-Enterprise System	380
Thomas Malthus: Economist	430
Globalization of the Economy	454

History

A Native American Perspective	8
The Scientific Method	50
The Hippies	90
Crime and Punishment	188
An Outsider's View of American Society	205
The Need for an Educated Citizenry	341
Religious-Based Conflicts	399
Leaders of Social Movements	474

Human Geography

Tejano Culture	241
Family Structures Around the World	302
Dropout Rates	349
Religious Beliefs Around the Globe	411
The Informal Housing Sector	444

Political Science

Groups and Voting Behavior	158
Minority Voting Behavior	242
Constitutional Government	367

Psychology

The Pioneers of Psychology	16
The "Monster Study"	56
Self-Concept	108
Decision Making in Juries	166
The Bobo Doll Experiment	316

FEATURES

A Diverse America

Population Change … 9	Hate Groups in the United States … 248
Percentage of Families Speaking Non-English at Home … 43	An Aging Population … 293
Immigration to the United States … 80	Marriage Rates … 313
Rate of Imprisonment … 125	School Expenditures … 337
Unemployment Rates … 139	Voter Turnout in Presidential Elections … 371
Social Networking … 162	Religiosity in the United States … 413
Violent Crime … 182	Fertility Rate in the United States … 421
Living in Poverty … 217	Geographic Mobility … 453

FOCUS on research

Case Study
- School Talk: Gender and Adolescent Culture … 52
- Black Picket Fences: Charisse Baker … 116
- Saints and Roughnecks … 190
- Family Violence … 318
- Globalization and Work … 460

Experiment
- Adopting Statuses in a Simulated Prison … 136
- Group Pressure and Obedience … 168

Field Research
- The Objective Value of a Social Settlement … 20
- Nickel and Dimed … 220
- Segregated Schools … 352
- Gang Leader for a Day: A Rogue Sociologist Takes to the Street … 440

Survey Research
- How Do Schools and Parents Fail Teens? … 82
- Narratives of Mexican American Women … 244
- Obstacles to Female Political Leadership … 286
- Consuming Politics: Jon Stewart, Branding, and the Youth Vote in America … 376
- Moral-Cultural Issues … 406

A Global Perspective

A Different Perspective … 23	The African Diaspora … 237
Cell Phone Use … 47	Women in National Parliaments … 284
Language Families … 74	Minimum Legal Age at Marriage for Women … 304
Support for an Elderly Population … 122	World Literacy Rates … 342
Agricultural Employment … 149	Political Freedom … 368
Human Development … 173	Religions of the World … 397
Death Penalty Policy … 196	Urbanization … 435
Chronic Poverty … 228	Internet Users … 477

There's More Online! EXPLORE collective behavior. SEE a map of population change. WATCH a video on socialization.

Quick Case Study

What Makes Us Change Behaviors?	28
How Do You Make a Research Plan?	57
How Do Stereotypes Affect You?	92
How Do You Compare to Your Birth Cohorts?	126
What's Your Role?	140
Bureaucracies	172
Deviance and Social Control	197
What Makes a Nation Low Income or High Income?	230
Race in the Media	261
How Is Ageism a Form of Social Inequality?	289
How Are Family Arrangements Alike and Different?	323
How Does the Gender Composition of a Classroom Affect Student Learning?	357
Teens in the Modern Economy	390
Should Taxpayers Fund Religious Schools?	414
How Do Urban Environments Affect People?	446
How Would You Change the World?	478

Technology & Society

Technological Change and the Birth of Sociology	2
Using Technology in Sociological Research	34
Popular Culture and the Internet	66
Mass Media and Socialization	98
Social Structures, Roles, & Statuses	130
Teens and Cyberbullying	154
High-Tech Crime and Deviance	178
Social Stratification and the Digital Divide	202
High-Tech Hate	234
Technology Use Varies by Gender and Age	266
Families and Technology	298
Education and Technology	330
Politics and Technology	362
Religion and Technology	394
Food, Hunger, and Technology	418
Social Movements and Technology	450

Theoretical Perspectives

Assumptions of the Major Perspectives	26
Investigating School Violence and School Funding	41
Explaining the Role of Culture	69
Socialization and Mass Media	107
Illustrating Social Structure Concepts	142
Types of Social Interaction	165
Illustrating Sociological Concepts	193
Social Stratification	211
Prejudice and Discrimination	250
Gender Inequalities	276
Perspectives on the Family	311
Investigating Education	355
Two Models of Political Power	375
Religion	401
Urban Society	438
Social Change	463

networks ONLINE RESOURCES

Technology & Society

Chapter 1	Technological Change and the Birth of Sociology
Chapter 2	Using Technology in Sociological Research
Chapter 3	Popular Culture and the Internet
Chapter 4	Mass Media and Socialization
Chapter 5	Social Structures, Roles, & Statuses
Chapter 6	Teens and Cyberbullying
Chapter 7	High-Tech Crime and Deviance
Chapter 8	Social Stratification and the Digital Divide
Chapter 9	High-Tech Hate
Chapter 10	Technology Use by Gender and Age
Chapter 11	Families and Technology
Chapter 12	Education and Technology
Chapter 13	Politics and Technology
Chapter 14	Religion and Technology
Chapter 15	Food, Hunger, and Technology
Chapter 16	Social Movements and Technology

Interactive Cartoons

Chapter 1
- Group Versus Individual Behavior
- Self-made Men
- The Power of Symbols
- Marx and Engels

Chapter 2
- Polling Practices
- Sociological Research
- A Spurious Correlation
- Ethics in Scientific Research

Chapter 3
- Informal Sanctions
- The Values of Competition
- Ideal vs. Real Culture
- Ethnocentrism

Chapter 4
- Methods of Socialization
- The Looking-Glass Self
- Socialization and the Family
- Socialization at Work

Chapter 5
- Status in Sociology

Chapter 6
- Bureaucratic Rules

Chapter 7
- The Unpopular Shirt
- The Fame Defense

Chapter 8
- Different Perspectives
- Low Status
- An Unhealthy Situation

Chapter 9
- Salad Bowl and Melting Pot
- Stereotypes in Action

Chapter 10
- Gender Identity
- Gender Roles
- Gender Inequality
- Income and the Elderly

Chapter 11
- Families and Marriages
- Boomerang Children

Chapter 12
- School Vouchers
- Intelligence Tests

Chapter 13
- Corporate Downsizing

Chapter 15
- Stress Appraisals

Chapter 16
- Rumors
- Contagion Theory

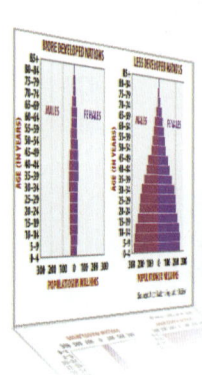

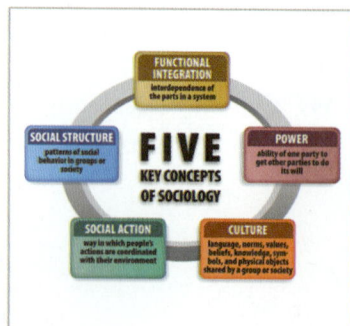

Interactive Charts

Chapter 1
Five Key Concepts of Sociology
Theoretical Perspectives: Assumptions of the Major Perspectives
Sociology and the Social Sciences

Chapter 2
Types of Survey Questions
Median Earnings in Dollars
Secondary Analysis
Summary of Research Methods
Theoretical Perspectives: Investigating School Violence and School Funding

Chapter 3
Do's and Don'ts
Cultural Universals
Theoretical Perspectives: Views on Culture

Chapter 4
Milestones in the Transition to Adulthood
Theoretical Perspectives: Socialization and Mass Media

Chapter 5
Ascribed/Achieved Statuses
Culture and Social Structure
Theoretical Perspectives: Illustrating Social Structure Concepts

Chapter 6
Cyberbullying
Group Membership by Age Range
Theoretical Perspectives: Illustrating Types of Social Interaction

Chapter 7
Crime
Theoretical Perspectives: Illustrating Sociological Concepts
Two Types of Youth Deviance

Chapter 8
American Class Structure
Distribution of Poverty in the United States
The Federal Government Dollar—Where It Goes
Global Stratification
Intergenerational Mobility in the United States
Measures of Stratification
Prestige Rankings of Selected Occupations in the United States
Theoretical Perspectives: Social Stratification

Chapter 9
Minority Population Growth
Racial and Ethnic Minority Groups in the United States
Socioeconomic Indicators for Minorities
Theoretical Perspectives: Prejudice and Discrimination

Chapter 10
Female-to-Male Earnings for the Same Jobs
Percentage of Women in Elective Offices
Poverty Rates Among Americans 65 and Over
Selected Socioeconomic Characteristics of Older Americans
Suicide Rates by Age, Gender, and Racial Group
Theoretical Perspectives: Gender Inequalities
What Women Earn Compared to Men
Women in the Labor Force
Women's Earnings as a Percentage of Men's Earnings Within Each Race

Chapter 11
Divorce and Marriage Rates
Family Violence
Single-Parent Families
Theoretical Perspectives: Family
Youths Grade Their Parents

Chapter 12
SAT Scores by Race
Theoretical Perspectives: Education

Chapter 13
Distribution of Workers by Occupational Category
Revenues of Multinational Corporations Compared to GDPs of Some Countries
Theoretical Perspectives: Two Models of Political Power
Types of Interest Groups
Voter Participation in Presidential Elections

Chapter 14
Major World Religions
Number of Members in Largest Religious Organizations in the United States
Percentage of Population Who Attend Weekly Religious Services
Religion and Technology
Religious Beliefs Around the Globe
Theoretical Perspectives: Religion
World Population By Religion

Chapter 15
City Growth Models
The Demographic Transition
Long-Range Projections of World Population
Nonmetropolitan Population Change Among 55–74-Year-Olds
Population Indicators in 2011
Population Projections Based on Family Size
Population Pyramids
Projected Populations
Theoretical Perspective: Urban Society

Chapter 16
Alexis de Tocqueville and Social Change
Social Change
Value-Added Theory of Social Movements

networks ONLINE RESOURCES

Interactive Diagrams/Graphs/Tables

Chapter 1 Sociology and the Social Sciences
Chapter 2 Median Earnings in Dollars
Positive and Negative Correlations
The Research Process
Chapter 15 Percentage of Older Population
Biggest Urban Conglomerations
Chapter 16 Value-Added Theory of Social Movements

Interactive Images

Chapter 1 Booker T. Washington
A Different Perspective
Sociological Imagination
Yesteryear's Family
Chapter 2 Ethical Standards in Research
Field Research Among Students
Galileo's Controversial Perspective
Chapter 3 Cultural Mores
DNA
Groups of the Counterculture
U.S. Material Culture
Chapter 4 Growing Up
Infant Socialization
Socialization Process: Play Stage
Chapter 5 Multiple Statuses
Postindustrial Worker
Stanford Prison Experiment
Chapter 6 Iron Law of Oligarchy
Labor Protest
Obedience
Chapter 7 Evolving Prisons
Modern Prisons
Other Systems of Punishment
Chapter 8 Alexis de Tocqueville
Caste System
Developing World
Internet at Home
Nickel and Dimed

Chapter 9 Diverse Friends
Hate
Obama as a Symbol
Organized Hate
Tejano Music
Chapter 10 Elderly Activism
Margaret Mead
Nancy Pelosi
Powerful Women
Texting
Chapter 11 Bobo the Doll
Families
Stay-at-Home Dads
Chapter 12 Families
Home Computing
Chapter 13 Dr. King
Globalized McNuggets
Politics and Technology
Semiemployment
Chapter 14 Charismatic Cultists
Religion and Technology
The Religions of Jerusalem
Separation of Church and State
Chapter 15 City Life
Food, Hunger, and Technology
Informal Settlements
Living in Poverty
Malthusian Check
A Young Population
Chapter 16 Sharing the City
Soccer Hooligans
Three Leaders of Social Movements
Voting in Egypt

Interactive Infographics

Chapter 3	Top 15 Internet Accessing Countries in Millions
Chapter 4	Major Developments in the History of the Mass Media
	Percentage of American Adults in Each Generation Who Own Each Type of Device
Chapter 5	Human Societies
	Social Networking
Chapter 16	Percentage of Population Using Facebook

Interactive Maps

Chapter 1	A Different Perspective
	Population Change
Chapter 2	Cell Phone Use
	Percentage of Non-English Speaking at Home
Chapter 3	Immigration to the United States
	Language Families
Chapter 4	Rate of Imprisonment
	Support for an Elderly Population
Chapter 5	Agricultural Employment
	Unemployment Rates
Chapter 6	Facebook America
	Human Development
Chapter 7	Death Penalty Policy
	Violent Crime
Chapter 8	Chronic Poverty
	Living in Poverty
Chapter 9	The African Diaspora
	Hate Groups in the United States
Chapter 10	An Aging Population
	Women in National Parliaments
Chapter 11	Marriage Rates
	Minimum Legal Age at Marriage for Women
Chapter 12	Dropout Rates
	School Expenditures
	World Literacy Rates
Chapter 13	Political Freedom
	Voter Turnout in Presidential Elections
Chapter 14	Religions of the World
	Religiosity in the United States
Chapter 15	The Fertility Rate in the United States
	Urban Population as a Percentage of Total Population
Chapter 16	Geographic Mobility
	Internet Users

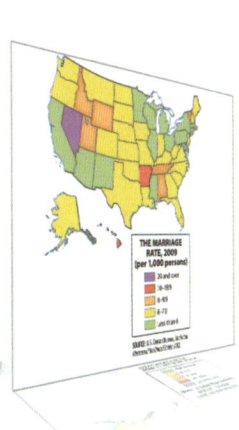

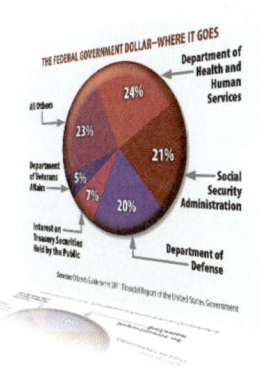
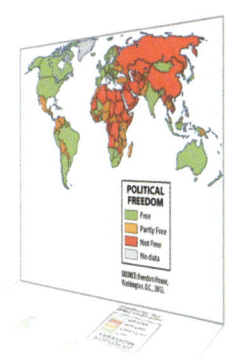

networks ONLINE RESOURCES

Interactive Self-Check Quizzes

Chapter 1: Three Quizzes, One per Lesson
Chapter 2: Three Quizzes, One per Lesson
Chapter 3: Five Quizzes, One per Lesson
Chapter 4: Five Quizzes, One per Lesson
Chapter 5: Four Quizzes, One per Lesson
Chapter 6: Four Quizzes, One per Lesson
Chapter 7: Five Quizzes, One per Lesson
Chapter 8: Four Quizzes, One per Lesson
Chapter 9: Four Quizzes, One per Lesson
Chapter 10: Five Quizzes, One per Lesson
Chapter 11: Four Quizzes, One per Lesson
Chapter 12: Four Quizzes, One per Lesson
Chapter 13: Five Quizzes, One per Lesson
Chapter 14: Three Quizzes, One per Lesson
Chapter 15: Four Quizzes, One per Lesson
Chapter 16: Four Quizzes, One per Lesson

Interactive Videos

Chapter 1 An Invitation to Sociology
Chapter 2 Sociological Research Methods
Chapter 3 Culture
Chapter 4 Socialization
Chapter 5 Social Structure and Society
Chapter 6 Groups and Formal Organizations
Chapter 7 Deviance and Social Control
Chapter 8 Social Stratification
Chapter 9 Inequalities of Race and Ethnicity
Chapter 10 Inequalities of Gender and Age
Chapter 11 The Family
Chapter 12 Education
Chapter 13 Political and Economic Institutions
Chapter 14 Religion
Chapter 15 Population and Urbanization
Chapter 16 Social Change and Collective Behavior

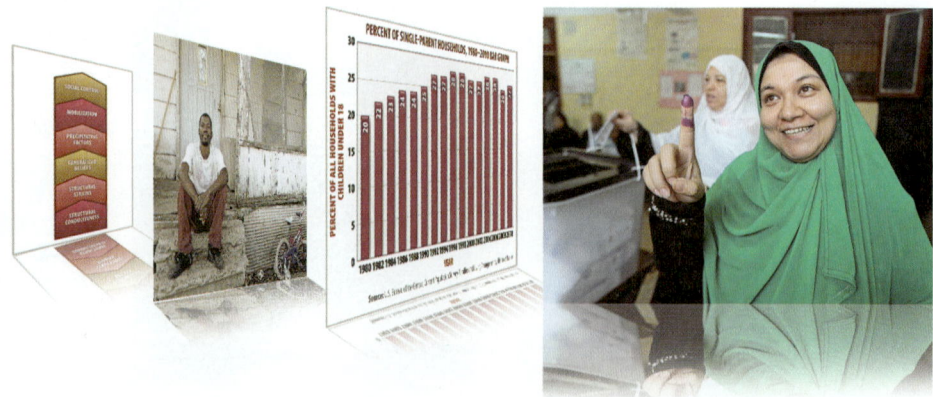

Critical Thinking Skills

How to Analyze the News
How to Analyze Primary Sources
How to Analyze Visuals
How to Compare and Contrast
How to Distinguish Fact From Opinion
How to Identify Cause and Effect
How to Make Inferences and Draw Conclusions
How to Predict

Sociology Skills

Study Skills
The Writing Process
Identifying Central Issues
Determining Cause and Effect
Separating Fact From Opinion
Making Generalizations
Line Graphs and Bar Graphs
Circle Graphs and Tables
Maps
Percentages
Mean, Median, and Mode

21st Century Skills

Analyze Political Cartoons
Creating a Bibliography: CMS Style
Creating a Bibliography: MLA Style
Getting a Job
How to Analyze the News
How to Recognize Historical Perspectives
How to Plan a Service Project
Read for Information
Social Studies Graphing Tool
Your Education: Jump-Start Your Future!

Writing Skills

Drafting: Persuasive Writing
Drafting: Creative Writing
Drafting: Expository Writing
Drafting: Narrative Writing
How to Find Main Ideas and Details
How to Find Resources on the Internet
How to Make an Outline
How to Manage Your Time
How to Paraphrase
How to Sequence Events
How to Summarize Information
How to Take Notes
How to Use What You Find on the Internet
How to Write a Letter

SCAVENGER HUNT

NETWORKS contains a wealth of information. The trick is to know where to look to access all the information in the book. If you complete this scavenger hunt exercise with your teachers or parents, you will see the textbook is organized and how to get the most out of your reading and studying time. Let's get started!

1 How many chapters and how many lessons are in this book?

2 Where do you find the glossary and the index? What is the difference between them?

3 Where can you find primary sources in the textbook?

4 If you want to quickly find all the maps, charts, and graphs about social stratification, where do you look?

5 How can you find information about sociologist Max Weber?

6 Where can you find a graphic organizer that lists issues related to gender discrimination discussed in Chapter 10?

7 Where and how do you find the content vocabulary for Chapter 2, Lesson 3?

8 What are the online resources listed for Chapter 8, Lesson 2?

9 If you want to know the Spanish word for culture, where would you look?

10 Where can you find a list of all the world maps in the book?

An Invitation to Sociology

ESSENTIAL QUESTION • *What is sociology?*

networks
There's More Online about sociology.

CHAPTER 1

Technology & Society
Technological Change and the Birth of Sociology

Lesson 1
The Sociological Perspective

Lesson 2
The Origins of Sociology

Lesson 3
Theoretical Perspectives

Sociology Matters...

We are social beings. Our social relationships influence what we think and believe, how we react to situations, and even what we wish for. The groups to which we belong or want to belong help shape our perceptions. Even groups that we do not admire influence us by providing a model of what is not acceptable.

Most of us go about our daily lives without thinking about the influences that shape our behavior and society. Sociology helps us step outside ourselves and view the social world from a new perspective. By looking at the world with a sociological eye, we can explore the forces that shape our lives and the lives of others, near and far.

◀ Sociologist W.E.B. Du Bois used sociology to study racial inequality within and outside the United States.

©Bettmann/Corbis

CHAPTER 1
Technology & Society

Technological Change
and the Birth of Sociology

**TECHNOLOGY
SOCIOLOGY**

The Industrial Revolution transformed society in Western Europe and the United States.

Sociology was born in a time of rapid social change brought on by political revolution and new technologies. The French Revolution broke European society's traditional social ties provided by the Catholic Church, craft guilds, and the family. In their place, the individual and the state took on primary importance. The Industrial Revolution put additional strain on society and traditional social ties.

New technologies led to factory-based manufacturing. Many people left their farms and moved to cities to fill factory jobs. Water and steam power led to larger machines and bigger factories. The size of cities swelled. Poor workers crowded into cheap housing. Crime, pollution, and homelessness plagued many cities. A flood of poor European immigrants added to the problems in many American cities. This shift from home to factory work further weakened the traditional social ties provided by family and community.

This greatly worried Auguste Comte. He believed that the only way to restore order to society was to restore the authority of social groups. Other early sociologists such as Herbert Spencer, Émile Durkheim, and Karl Marx were also concerned with these social changes. Influenced by advances in the natural sciences, these pioneers of sociology set out to study society and the social groups that form it.

1767 Richard Arkwright patents a water-powered spinning machine

1798 Eli Whitney develops idea of interchangeable parts

c. 1775–1800 James Watt perfects the Watt steam engine

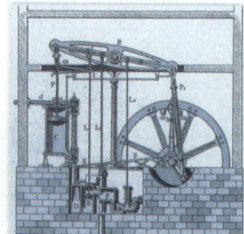

▶ **CRITICAL THINKING**

Exploring Issues What is the message of this poster in regard to industrial society in general?

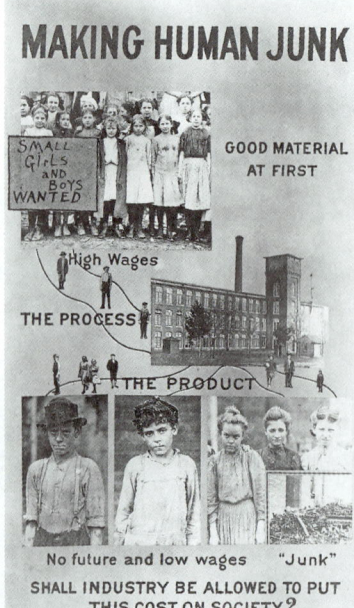

©Corbis; Mary Evans Picture Library/Alamy

TIME LINE Explore the interactive version of the time line on Networks.

Timeline

- **1813–1814** — Francis Lowell builds largest textile factory in U.S.
- **1830–1842** — Auguste Comte publishes the six-volume *Positive Philosophy*, outlining the principles of sociology
- **1832** — Samuel F. B. Morse begins work on telegraph
- **1846** — Elias Howe patents first sewing machine
- **1848** — Karl Marx and Friedrich Engels publish *The Communist Manifesto*, promoting a classless society
- **1859** — Charles Darwin publishes *On the Origin of Species*
- **1876** — Alexander Graham Bell patents telephone
- **1879** — Thomas Alva Edison invents the incandescent lightbulb
- **1892** — First U.S. department of sociology established at University of Chicago
- **1893** — Émile Durkheim publishes *The Division of Labor in Society*
- **1904–1905** — Max Weber publishes *The Protestant Ethic and the Spirit of Capitalism*
- **1913** — Model T Ford is mass produced
- **1931** — Jane Addams awarded Nobel Peace Prize

(cw from top) Apic/Hulton Archive/Getty Images; Hulton Archive/Archive Photos/Getty Images; Science and Society/SuperStock; akg-images/The Image Works; ©Stefano Bianchetti/Corbis; Library of Congress Prints and Photographs Division [LC-USZ62-52389]; Library of Congress Prints & Photographs Division [LC-USZC4-12153]

Thinking Like a Sociologist

1 Making Connections
How do you think Karl Marx would have responded to the production innovations used to mass-produce Model Ts?

2 Identifying Cause and Effect
Pick two entries on the time line and explain how they changed the way people worked.

An Invitation to Sociology 3

networks

There's More Online!

- ☑ **CARTOON** Group Versus Individual Behavior
- ☑ **CHART** Sociology and the Social Sciences
- ☑ **IMAGE** Sociological Imagination
- ☑ **MAP** Population Change
- ☑ **SELF-CHECK QUIZ**

Reading HELPDESK

Academic Vocabulary
- perspective
- conformity

Content Vocabulary
- sociology
- social structure
- sociological perspective
- sociological imagination

TAKING NOTES:
Key Ideas and Details

SUMMARIZING As you read about the field of sociology, use a graphic organizer like the one below to record details.

- The Nature of Sociology
  - Sociology and the Study of Human Behavior
  - Sociology and Social Sciences
  - Sociological Imagination

LESSON 1
The Sociological Perspective

ESSENTIAL QUESTION • What is sociology?

IT MATTERS BECAUSE
Sociology is the study of human social behavior. It assumes a group perspective rather than an individual perspective. Sociologists look for patterns in social relationships. Individuals can benefit by using their sociological imagination to look at events in their lives.

The Nature of Sociology

GUIDING QUESTION *What is the sociological perspective?*

As a newcomer to the field, you may view sociology as the study of human behavior. As you go along, however, you will acquire a more precise understanding of **sociology** as the scientific study of *social structure*. **Social structure** refers to the patterned ways in which people interact in social relationships. This focus on patterns rather than individual actions is part of the unique perspective of sociology.

A **perspective** is a particular point of view. Babies are usually brighter and better looking to their parents than they are to others. Newlyweds nearly always find their spouses much more attractive than their friends do. We all see what is happening around us through our own perspectives—our own points of view. We normally do not realize how much of our attitudes and beliefs are determined by our perspectives. Sociology looks beyond personal perspectives, however, and is interested in exposing the causes and sources of human behavior. This is known as the debunking tendency.

Sociology and the Study of Human Behavior

Sociologists, like psychologists, examine human behavior. Psychologists and sociologists, however, approach the study of human behavior from different perspectives. Whereas psychologists might be interested in the particular actions of particular individuals, sociologists never focus on the individual. The **sociological perspective** focuses on the social, or group, level. Sociologists are interested in the patterns of behavior shared by members of a group or society. They want to understand how individuals are influenced by the society and culture in which they live. They are also interested in how people's actions and beliefs help change society and culture over time.

Sociology and the Social Sciences

Social science is a branch of learning that deals with human society. It includes a number of disciplines, which we generally refer to as the social sciences. These disciplines differ, but they share enough in common to overlap. Descriptions of the major social sciences are presented in this table.

Sociology investigates human social behavior from a group rather than an individual perspective. It concentrates on patterns of social relationships, primarily in modern societies.

Social Science	Description	Contrasted With Sociology
Anthropology	Anthropology investigates culture, the customary beliefs and material traits of groups. It is the social science most closely related to sociology.	Anthropologists concentrate on the study of preliterate societies (societies that do not use writing). Sociologists focus on modern, industrial societies. When anthropologists and sociologists study the same group, anthropologists place more emphasis on artifacts (what people make), language, and kinship than sociologists do.
Economics	Economics is the study of the production, distribution, and consumption of goods and services.	Economists focus on a single part of society—the economy. Sociologists explore all parts. However, economists and sociologists share an interest in how and why people and groups make certain economic decisions.
History	History is the written record of the human past. Historians collect evidence by analyzing artifacts created during the time period being studied. These artifacts include physical objects, oral reports, and written reports and documents. Historians develop historical accounts by synthesizing and interpreting the evidence they collect.	Methodology—how historians conduct research—is one of the things that sets history apart from sociology. Unlike historians, sociologists use a wide range of research methods in addition to examining physical objects, newspapers, historical documents, and oral histories, including observation, interviews, and questionnaires.
Human Geography	Human geography examines the interaction between human populations and the places in which they live.	Human geography and human ecology in sociology share many interests. Both focus on the geographic basis of human society. Topics such as migration and economic activities are of interest to both fields.
Political Science	Political science investigates the organization, administration, history, and theory of government. For example, political scientists are concerned with voting patterns and participation in political parties.	Sociologists and political scientists share an interest in the structure of government, voting patterns, and political power. But like economists, political scientists concentrate on a single part of society—the government. Government is only one of the parts of society studied by sociologists.
Psychology	Psychology investigates human mental and emotional processes. Psychologists study the development and functioning of the individual.	Sociologists and psychologists are interested in how people adjust to the difficulties they face. Psychologists, however, tend to focus on the individual and what goes on inside people, such as emotions, decision making, and perception. Sociologists are more interested in the social forces that affect people.

▶ **CRITICAL THINKING**

1. **Contrasting** How might a sociologist and an anthropologist differ in their approaches to studying a religious sect?

2. **Drawing Conclusions** What conclusion can you draw about the scope of sociological inquiry from this chart?

sociology the scientific study of social structure; patterned social behavior

social structure the patterned interaction of people in social relationships

perspective a particular point of view

sociological perspective a view that looks at the behavior of groups, not individuals

Individual Versus Societal Problems

The person on the street might explain human behavior in individualistic or personal terms—a young man joins a gang to prove his toughness; a toddler cries inconsolably when her parents leave her with a babysitter; a factory worker loses his job when his company moves the production plant overseas; a teen commits suicide to escape depression. These are individual problems—what American sociologist C. Wright Mills called "personal troubles." They affect a particular person and the people in their immediate lives. These are private matters. Sociologists look at societal problems—at what Mills called "the public issues of social structure." Public issues deal with things that affect groups within society or society as a whole.

Sociologists do not focus on the behavior of individuals but on the patterns of behavior shared by members of a group or society. Sociologists attempt to explain these same events *without* relying on personal factors. They attempt to explain what factors lead to social problems and issues such as delinquency, child development, unemployment, or suicide. Sociologists might explain the events discussed above in the following ways:

- Young men join gangs because they have been taught by their society to be "masculine."
- It is normal for young children to go through a period of separation anxiety as they are introduced to new people and groups outside the family as part of the socialization process.
- Blue-collar jobs are lost as the United States moves from an industrial to a postindustrial society.
- Teens commit suicide because of peer group expectations of performance, material possessions, and physical appearance.

Sociologists do not speak of *a* young man, *a* toddler, *a* factory worker, or *a* teenager. They concentrate on *categories* of people—young men, toddlers, factory workers, and teenagers. Peter Berger referred to this aspect of the sociological perspective as seeing "the general in the particular." Sociologists look for general social patterns in the behavior of particular individuals.

☑ **READING PROGRESS CHECK**

Analyzing What makes the sociological perspective unique?

CARTOON ▸

GROUP VERSUS INDIVIDUAL BEHAVIOR

People often act one way in groups and another way when alone.

▶ **CRITICAL THINKING**

1. ***Analyzing*** How does the cartoon illustrate how group behavior can differ from individual behavior?
2. ***Making Connections*** How do you think this man's coworkers would react if they were told he is unhappy? Why?

The Importance of Patterns

GUIDING QUESTION *How do group behavior and individual behavior differ?*

As you know well, high school students in a classroom behave in different ways. Some students listen to everything their teacher says. Some tune in and out, and others spend much of the time daydreaming. Yet, if you visit almost any high school, you will find *patterned* relationships. Teachers walk around the room, work with students, lecture, and give tests. Students follow the teacher's lesson plan, make notes, and take tests. Although the personal characteristics of students and teachers may vary from school to school, students and teachers relate in similar patterned ways. It is the patterned interaction of people in social relationships—what sociologists call social structure—that captures the attention of sociologists.

Group Versus Individual Behavior

Sociologists assume that social relationships are not determined only by the particular characteristics of the people involved. Émile Durkheim, a pioneering nineteenth-century sociologist, helped develop the sociological perspective. He argued, for example, that we do not attempt to explain bronze in terms of its separate parts (lead, copper, and tin). Instead, we consider bronze a totally new metal created by the combination of several other metals. We cannot even predict the characteristics of bronze from the traits of its parts. Bronze is hard, while lead, copper, and tin are soft and pliable. The mixing of the individual parts creates a new whole with new characteristics. Durkheim reasoned that a similar process happens with groups of people. For Durkheim, groups are not simply a collection of individuals. They are separate from the individuals who form them.

Indeed, people's behavior within a group setting cannot be predicted from their personal characteristics. Something new is created when individuals come together. For example, in 2005 the New England Patriots won the Super Bowl championship. Following the game, a few otherwise law-abiding football fans, as a group, disrupted the peace and challenged the police in ways they would not have done as individuals.

Tragedy, as well as joy, can change group behavior. An example of this occurred in 2005 when the destructive forces of Hurricane Katrina and the subsequent breaching of the levees devastated the city of New Orleans. Large portions of the city were flooded, and many families lost everything they had. In the days following the hurricane, when help was slow in coming, some survivors turned to looting, violence, and other criminal activities, which became serious problems for law enforcement officials. Many of the looting incidents involved normally law-abiding residents gathering food, water, and other essential goods from unattended grocery stores in New Orleans.

Conforming to the Group

Groups range in size from two people to an entire society. Regardless of size, all groups encourage **conformity**. We will study conformity in more detail later. For now, you need to know only that members of a group think, feel, and behave in similar ways. For instance, Americans, Russians, and Nigerians have eating habits, dress, religious beliefs, and attitudes toward family life that reflect their groups.

Sociologists focus on patterns of behavior.

▶ **CRITICAL THINKING**

Predicting Based on normal patterns of behavior at a carnival, what do you think the boy might do?

conformity behavior that matches group expectations

An Invitation to Sociology 7

Connecting Sociology to History

A NATIVE AMERICAN PERSPECTIVE

Virginia colonists had offered to "properly educate" some young Native American boys at the College of William and Mary in Williamsburg. To the surprise of the colonists, the benefits of a white gentleman's education were not highly valued by the Native American elders. Canasatego, an Iroquois chief, offered the Native American perspective in a speech to the colonists in 1744. Benjamin Franklin printed the speech below in an essay on Native Americans.

PRIMARY SOURCE

"We know that you highly esteem the kind of learning taught in [your] colleges . . . and we thank you heartily. But you, who are wise, must know that different nations have different conceptions of things; and you will therefore not take it amiss if our ideas of this kind of education happen not to be the same with yours. We have had some experience of it; several of our young people were formerly brought up at the colleges of the northern provinces; they were instructed in all your sciences; but, when they came back to us, they were bad runners, ignorant of every means of living in the woods, unable to bear either cold or hunger, knew neither how to build a cabin, take a deer, nor kill an enemy, spoke our language imperfectly, were therefore neither fit for hunters, warriors, nor counselors; they were totally good for nothing.

We are, however, not the less obliged by your kind offer, though we decline accepting it; and, to show our grateful sense of it, if the gentlemen of Virginia will send us a dozen of their sons, we will take great care of their education, instruct them in all we know, and make *men* of them."

—Canasatego, quoted in *Memoirs of Benjamin Franklin*, 1839

Hunting was an essential skill for Native Americans. An education at the College of William and Mary would not develop this expertise.

DBQ ▶ CRITICAL THINKING

1. **Making Connections** How does Canasatego's explanation illustrate the importance of perspective in interpreting the social world?
2. **Supporting Perspectives** Describe a social encounter in which you personally experienced a "clash of perspectives" with someone from another culture.

Conformity within a group occurs, in part, because members have been taught to value the group's ways. Members generally tend to conform even when their personal preferences are not the same as the group's. Teens who start smoking only to gain group acceptance are an example of conformity. Fashion trends depend on conformity to take hold and play out.

Behavior within a group cannot be predicted simply from knowledge about its individual members. Everyone in a group might conform. Yet they might be conforming for different reasons. Some people might truly value their group's ways. Others might conform only after giving in to social pressures. Like bronze, the group is more than the sum of its parts.

✓ **READING PROGRESS CHECK**

Contrasting Why might an individual's behavior be different in a group than it might be if the person were acting alone?

Acquiring the Sociological Imagination

GUIDING QUESTION *What is gained by using the sociological imagination?*

The sociological perspective enables us to understand how social forces affect our lives. Understanding this connection can prevent us from being prisoners of those forces. C. Wright Mills called this personal use of sociology the **sociological imagination**—the ability of individuals to see the relationship between events in their personal lives and events in their society.

An important part of developing the sociological imagination is being able to look at our own society as outsiders. Viewing society in this way allows us to escape our personal perspectives and cultural beliefs and see that the problems people face reflect larger social forces and trends. Developing a sociological imagination also helps us appreciate cultural differences. By setting aside our own experiences and beliefs, we are able to understand that what one culture views as unusual might seem quite normal in another culture.

sociological imagination the ability to see the link between society and self

Using Your Sociological Imagination

People do not make decisions, big or small, in isolation. Historically, American society has shown a strong bias against childless and one-child marriages. Couples without children have been considered selfish, and an only child has often been labeled "spoiled." These values date back to a time when large families were needed for survival. Most people lived on family farms, where children were needed to help with the work. Furthermore, many children died at birth or in infancy. People responded to society's needs by having large families. Now, as the need for large families is disappearing, we are beginning to read about benefits of one-child families—to the child, to the family, and to society. This change in attitude is reflected in the decrease in family size.

A Diverse America

POPULATION CHANGE

The population of the United States increased by 9.7 percent between 2000 and 2010, rising from 281.4 million to 308.7 million people. During this time period, the South and the West grew at a much faster rate than the Midwest and the Northeast. In fact, 84.4 percent of the nation's growth occurred in these two regions. Nevada grew at the fastest rate, followed by Arizona, Utah, Idaho, and Texas. This map shows the change in population that occurred over the decade.

POPULATION CHANGE, 2000–2010
- 30% and over
- 20–29.9
- 10–19.9
- 1–9.9
- Less than 1%

SOURCE: U.S. Census Bureau, Population Distribution and Change: 2000 to 2010

Geography Connection

1. **Places and Regions** Which states had the greatest change in population? Which states experienced the least change?
2. **Places and Regions** Which regions of the country appear to have experienced the least amount of growth over the last decade?
3. **Environment and Society** How might you use your sociological imagination to explain why the West and the South experienced the greatest increase in population?

Applying Sociology

CAREERS IN SOCIOLOGY

In general, all employers are interested in four types of skills regardless of what specific career path you choose to pursue. These skills are:

- the ability to work with others.
- the ability to solve problems.
- the ability to write and speak well.
- the ability to analyze information.

Because computers have revolutionized office and business communication, for example, the ability to analyze and evaluate information from a variety of sources has become more important to managers in all types of organizations. The greater complexity of work demands strong critical thinking and problem-solving skills. Knowledge is of limited use if you cannot clearly convey what you know to others.

The study of sociology helps students develop these skills, so it is a solid career base for many career paths. For sociology majors, the following list of possibilities is only the beginning—many other paths are open to you.

- **Social services**—rehabilitation, case management, group work with youths or the elderly, child care or recreation programs, or administration
- **Community work**—fund-raising for social service organizations, community development associations, not-for-profit organizations, child-care programs, or environmental groups; research for local governmental or charitable organizations; program coordination; volunteer recruitment and training
- **Corrections**—local, state, and federal law enforcement, probation, parole, or other criminal justice work
- **Business**—advertising, marketing and consumer research and analysis, brand planning, public relations, banking and finance, communications media, law, insurance, real estate, training, or sales
- **Human resources**—human resources administration, affirmative action coordination, benefits management and analysis, employee recruitment and retention programs, and employee training
- **College settings**—admissions, alumni relations, leadership programs, academic advising, or placement offices
- **Health services**—substance abuse treatment programs, rehabilitation counseling, health planning, family planning, counseling, hospital admissions, health care policy research, and insurance companies

A sociology major might find a career helping the homeless.

- **Publishing, journalism, and public relations**—writing, research, and editing
- **Government services**—federal, state, and local government jobs in areas such as planning, public archives and libraries, military service, international relations, transportation, housing, agriculture, and labor
- **Teaching**—elementary and secondary schools—in conjunction with appropriate teacher certification, adult education, government education agencies; also in community colleges and universities, with research opportunities.

▶ **CRITICAL THINKING**

1. **Evaluating** Evaluate your capabilities in the four skill areas.
2. **Analyzing** Select a job that you might qualify for with a sociology degree and explain why sociology is a good preparation.

The sociological imagination helps us understand the effects of events, such as the social pressures just discussed, on our daily lives. In C. Wright Mills' words, it helps us "grasp the connection between history and biography." With this understanding, we are in a better position to make our own decisions rather than merely conform.

The Promise of the Sociological Imagination

Mills viewed the sociological imagination as more than just a concept or theory. He saw it as a "promise" that allows people to understand their places in society and history. This social awareness permits us to read the newspaper with a fuller understanding of the events. Instead of interpreting a letter opposing welfare as an expression of someone with no compassion, we might instead see the writer as a person who places great importance on independence and self-help. The sociological imagination questions common interpretations of human social behavior. It challenges conventional social wisdom—ideas people assume are true.

According to Mills, keeping the promise of the sociological imagination is at the heart of all good social analysis. Those who are imaginatively aware consistently ask three sets of questions that help uncover the connection between history and biography:

1. What is the structure of the society as a whole? What parts of the society are essential and how are the parts related? How is the society different from other social orders? How do the parts contribute to continuity and change?
2. Where does the society fit into human history? How is the society changing? What effect is it having on the development of humanity as a whole? How do the society's individual features and the historical time period affect each other? How is the time period different from other periods in history?
3. What are the characteristics of the people who live in the society? How are they shaped by the society? What kinds of "human nature" are revealed by studying the society?

This Mexican migrant farmworker stands outside his shack during the Great Depression of the 1930s.

▶ **CRITICAL THINKING**

Drawing Conclusions How could using your sociological imagination help you better understand this photograph?

✓ **READING PROGRESS CHECK**

Assessing How can using your sociological imagination help you in everyday life?

LESSON 1 REVIEW

Reviewing Vocabulary
1. ***Specifying*** How is a sociological perspective different from the perspective used by psychologists?
2. ***Determining Importance*** Why are patterns important to sociology?

Using Your Notes
3. ***Summarizing*** Use your notes to write a statement summarizing why using your sociological imagination is an example of using a sociological perspective.

Answering the Guiding Questions
4. ***Identifying Perspectives*** What is the sociological perspective?
5. ***Evaluating*** How do group behavior and individual behavior differ?
6. ***Identifying Central Issues*** What is gained by using the sociological imagination?

Writing Activity
7. ***Informative/Explanatory*** Choose a social issue that interests you. Briefly describe the issue. Then explain how using your sociological imagination can help you analyze the issue.

An Invitation to Sociology

networks

There's More Online!

- ☑ CARTOON Self-made Men
- ☑ GRAPHIC ORGANIZER Origins of Sociology
- ☑ IMAGE Booker T. Washington
- ☑ SELF-CHECK QUIZ

Reading HELPDESK

Academic Vocabulary
- research
- assumption

Content Vocabulary
- positivism
- social statics
- social dynamics
- bourgeoisie
- capitalist
- proletariat
- class conflict
- mechanical solidarity
- organic solidarity
- *verstehen*
- rationalization

TAKING NOTES:
Integration of Knowledge and Ideas

DESCRIBING As you read about the origins of sociology, use a graphic organizer like the one below to record information about the theories and contributions of the field's European and American pioneers.

European	American

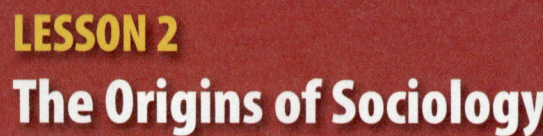

LESSON 2
The Origins of Sociology

ESSENTIAL QUESTION • *What is sociology?*

IT MATTERS BECAUSE
Sociology started with the writings of European scholars such as Auguste Comte, Harriet Martineau, Herbert Spencer, Émile Durkheim, and Karl Marx. Jane Addams, W.E.B. Du Bois, Robert Ezra Park, and other scholars helped focus America's attention on social issues. After World War II, the United States took the lead in developing the field of sociology.

European Origins

GUIDING QUESTION *What were the theories of the pioneers of sociology?*

Sociology is a relatively new science. It began in late nineteenth-century Europe during a time of great social upheaval. The social and economic effects of the Industrial Revolution and the French Revolution were touching all aspects of life. People were moving from farms to factory life, losing a sense of community. Some European intellectuals were fascinated and troubled by the sudden changes. They began to grapple with ideas for bringing back a sense of community and for restoring order. These ideas led to the rise of the science of sociology.

Auguste Comte

Auguste Comte (1798–1857), a Frenchman, is recognized as the father of sociology. Comte's main concern was the improvement of society. If societies were to advance, Comte believed, social behavior had to be studied scientifically. Because no science of society existed, Comte attempted to create one himself. He coined the term *sociology* to describe this science. Comte wanted to use scientific observation in the study of social behavior. He called this **positivism**. By *positivism*, he meant that sociology should be a science based on knowledge of which we can be "positive," or sure. Comte also distinguished between **social statics**, the study of social stability and order, and **social dynamics**, the study of social change. This distinction between social stability and social change remains at the center of modern sociology.

Comte published his theories in a book titled *Positive Philosophy*, but he died before people generally came to appreciate his work. His belief that sociology could use scientific procedures and promote social progress, however, was widely adopted by other European scholars.

12

Harriet Martineau

Harriet Martineau (1802–1876), an Englishwoman, is another important figure in the founding of sociology. She was born into a solidly middle-class home. Never in good health, Martineau had lost her sense of taste, smell, and hearing before she reached adulthood. Her writing career, which included fiction as well as sociological work, began in 1825 after the Martineau family's textile mill was lost to a business depression. Without the family income, and following a broken engagement, Martineau was forced to seek a dependable source of income to support herself. She became a popular writer of celebrity status, whose work initially outsold that of Charles Dickens.

Martineau is best known today for her translation of Comte's *Positive Philosophy*. Her English translation remains even today the most readable one. Despite being severely hearing impaired, she also made original contributions in the areas of **research** methods, political economy, and feminist theory.

In *Society in America*, Martineau established herself as a pioneering feminist theorist. Because she saw a link between slavery and the oppression of women, she was a strong and outspoken supporter of the emancipation of both women and enslaved peoples. Martineau believed women's lack of economic power helped keep them dependent. By writing about the inferior position of women in society, she helped inspire future feminist theorists.

Herbert Spencer

Herbert Spencer (1820–1903), the sole survivor of nine children, was born to an English schoolteacher. Spencer was taught exclusively by his father and uncle, mostly in mathematics and the natural sciences. He did not enjoy scholarly work or the study of Latin, Greek, English, or history, and therefore he decided not to apply to Cambridge University, his uncle's alma mater. Consequently, his higher education was largely the result of his own reading. Spencer's career became a mixture of engineering, drafting, inventing, journalism, and writing.

To explain social stability, Herbert Spencer compared society to the human body. He explained that, like a body, a society is composed of parts working together to promote its well-being and survival. People have brains, stomachs, nervous systems, and limbs. Societies have economies, religions, governments, and families. Just as the eyes and the heart make essential contributions to the functioning of the human body, religious and educational institutions are crucial for a society's functioning.

Spencer also introduced a theory of social change called *Social Darwinism*, based on Charles Darwin's theory of evolution. Spencer thought that evolutionary social change led to progress, provided people did not interfere. If left alone, natural social selection would ensure the survival of the fittest society. On these grounds, Spencer opposed social reform because it interfered with the selection process. The poor, he wrote, deserve to be poor and the rich to be rich. Society profits from allowing individuals to find their own social class level without outside help or hindrance. To interfere with the existence of poverty—or the result of any other natural process—is harmful to society. Spencer believed that the Industrial Revolution represented movement from a militaristic society to an industrial one and that violent competition would fade as industrialism progressed.

positivism the belief that knowledge should be derived from scientific observation

social statics the study of social stability and order

social dynamics the study of social change

research investigation or experimentation aimed at the discovery and interpretation of facts

Harriet Martineau.

Harriet Martineau believed that social scientists should have sympathy for the people they studied.

▶ **CRITICAL THINKING**

Speculating How might Martineau's belief in the importance of sympathy have influenced her research interests?

An Invitation to Sociology 13

CARTOON ›
SELF-MADE MEN Karl Marx examined the relationship between the bourgeoisie and the proletariat.
▶ **CRITICAL THINKING**
1. **Differentiating** Which characters in the cartoon represent the bourgeoisie and which represent the proletariat?
2. **Identifying Perspectives** What is the cartoonist's point of view?

Spencer visited the United States in 1882. Corporate leaders, who saw his ideas as moral justification for their competitive actions, warmly greeted him. Later, public support for government intervention increased, and Spencer's ideas began to slip out of fashion. He reportedly died with a sense of having failed. Spencer's contribution to sociology was a discussion of how societies should be structured.

Karl Marx

Karl Marx (1818–1883), a German scholar, did not consider himself a sociologist. Marx studied law in Bonn and Berlin. He took up philosophy after meeting like-minded intellectuals. After completing his legal studies, Marx became a journalist and eventually the editor of a radical newspaper. Nevertheless, his ideas have had a major effect on the field. Marx felt great concern for the poverty and inequality suffered by the working class of his day. His life was guided by the principle that social scientists should try to change the world rather than merely study it. Marx's friend and coauthor Friedrich Engels helped put his ideas into writing.

Marx identified several social classes in nineteenth-century industrial society. Among them were farmers, servants, factory workers, craftspeople, owners of small businesses, and moneyed capitalists. He predicted that at some point all industrial societies would contain only two social classes: the *bourgeoisie* and the *proletariat*. The **bourgeoisie** (BURZH • WAH • ZEE) are those who own the means for producing wealth in industrial society (for example, factories and equipment). The means for producing wealth are called capital. Thus, those who own them are called **capitalists**. The **proletariat** work for the bourgeoisie and are paid just enough to stay alive.

For Marx, the key to the unfolding of history was **class conflict**—a clash between the bourgeoisie, who controlled the means for producing wealth, and the proletariat, who labored for them. Just as enslaved peoples overthrew slaveholders, wage workers would overtake capitalists. Out of this conflict would come a classless *(communistic)* society—one in which there would be no powerless proletariat. Planned revolution, Marx was convinced, could speed up the change from capitalism to communism. Although he believed that capitalism would eventually self-destruct, his political objective was to explain the workings of capitalism in order to hasten its fall through revolution.

bourgeoisie class owning the means for producing wealth

capitalist person who owns or controls the means for producing wealth

proletariat working class; those who labor for the bourgeoisie

class conflict the ongoing struggle between the bourgeoisie (owners) and the proletariat (working classes)

Émile Durkheim

Émile Durkheim (1858–1917) was the son of a French rabbi. According to Durkheim, society exists because of a broad consensus, or agreement, among members of a society. In preindustrial times, societies were based on what sociologists call **mechanical solidarity**. With these societies, there was widespread consensus of values and beliefs, strong social pressures for conformity, and dependence on tradition and family. In contrast, industrial societies are based on **organic solidarity**—social interdependency based on a web of highly specialized roles. These specialized roles make members of a society dependent on one another for goods and services, such as the dependence between bankers and customers.

Although early sociologists emphasized the need to make sociology scientific, they did not have the research tools that are available today. Later sociologists developed the research methods to replace speculation with observation, to collect and classify data, and to use data for testing social theories. Durkheim was the most prominent of these later sociologists. He first introduced the use of statistical techniques in his groundbreaking research on suicide. In that study, he demonstrated that suicide involves more than individuals acting alone and that suicide rates vary according to group characteristics. Durkheim showed that human social behavior must be explained by social factors rather than just psychological ones. In *Suicide: A Study in Sociology*, originally published in 1897, he wrote:

> **PRIMARY SOURCE**
>
> "It is not mere metaphor to say of each human society that it has a greater or lesser aptitude for suicide; the expression is based on the nature of things.... These tendencies of the whole social body, by affecting individuals, cause them to commit suicide. The private experiences usually thought to be the proximate causes of suicide have only the influence borrowed from the victim's moral predisposition, itself an echo of the moral state of society. To explain his detachment from life the individual accuses his most immediately surrounding circumstances; life is sad to him because he is sad. Of course his sadness comes to him from without in one sense, however not from one or another incident of his career but rather from the group to which he belongs. This is why there is nothing which cannot serve as an occasion for suicide. It all depends on the intensity with which suicidogenetic causes have affected the individual."
>
> —Émile Durkheim, *Suicide: A Study in Sociology*, 1951

mechanical solidarity social dependency based on a widespread consensus of values and beliefs and dependence on tradition and family

organic solidarity social interdependency based on a high degree of specialization of roles

Max Weber did not begin his academic career as a sociologist, but over time he identified himself with the field.

▶ **CRITICAL THINKING**

Drawing Conclusions How might Weber's training in law and economics have influenced his work in sociology?

Max Weber

Max Weber (1864–1920) was the eldest son of a father who was a well-to-do German lawyer and politician. His mother, in stark contrast, was a strongly devout Calvinist who rejected the worldly lifestyle of her husband. Weber was affected psychologically by the conflicting values of his parents, which led at one point to a mental breakdown. As a university professor trained in law and economics, Weber wrote on a wide variety of topics, including the nature of power, the religions of the world, law, economics, rural and urban sociology, the nature of social classes, and the development and nature of bureaucracy. His most famous book is *The Protestant Ethic and the Spirit of Capitalism*, first published in 1904–1905.

Through the quality of his research and the diversity of his interests, Weber was profoundly influential in the development of sociological theory. Human beings act on the basis of their own understanding of a situation, Weber said. Thus, sociologists must discover the personal meanings, values, beliefs, and attitudes underlying human social behavior.

Connecting Sociology to Psychology

THE PIONEERS OF PSYCHOLOGY

Like sociology, psychology emerged as a recognized discipline in the late 1800s at a time when the Western world was undergoing rapid change. Industrialization and new technologies, such as electric lights and the telephone, were changing how people lived and communicated. Just as sociologists attempted to explain the impact of change on society, psychologists attempted to explain the impact on individuals.

Also like sociology, the pioneers of psychology approached the field from many different perspectives. Wilhelm Wundt (1832–1920), who is considered the "father" of experimental psychology, established the first psychology laboratory in Germany in the late 1870s. Wundt was interested in studying people's sensations and perceptions, which he thought were key to understanding the structure of the mind. He would have people perform simple activities or listen to sounds and then report their sensations. Wundt used the technique of introspection to understand people's conscious mental experiences. *Introspection* is the process of looking into one's own mind to understand what one thinks and feels about an experience.

William James (1842–1910) published the first psychology textbook, *The Principles of Psychology*, in 1890. In this book, James outlined most of the topics that are common in psychology textbooks today. James theorized that emotions are caused by physical changes in a person's body. He argued that human emotions had developed over time because they served adaptive functions that helped humans survive.

Francis Galton (1822–1911) took a more biological approach to psychology. Galton, a British psychologist, was interested in the qualities passed to offspring through heredity. His views were influenced by the work of his cousin, Charles Darwin, who outlined the theory of evolution. Galton pioneered the use of statistics and measurement in studying human behavior.

Wilhelm Wundt was a pioneer of psychology.

▶ **CRITICAL THINKING**

1. **Making Connections** What are some of the ways that the early development of sociology and psychology are similar?
2. **Comparing** Think about the approaches to research used by Émile Durkheim and Max Weber. What similarities do you see between those approaches and the approaches used by Wilhelm Wundt and Francis Galton?

---

verstehen understanding social behavior by putting yourself in the places of others

rationalization the mind-set emphasizing knowledge, reason, and planning

Weber believed that an understanding of the personal intentions of people in groups can be best accomplished through the method of **verstehen** (fehr • SHTAYUHN), understanding the social behavior of others by putting yourself mentally in their places. Putting yourself in someone else's "shoes" allows you to shed your values temporarily and see things from a different point of view.

Weber also identified *rationalization* as a key influence in the change from a preindustrial society to an industrial one. **Rationalization** is the mind-set that emphasizes the use of knowledge, reason, and planning. The influence of rationalization marked a change from the tradition, emotion, and superstition of preindustrial society. For example, agriculture became grounded in science rather than belief in luck, fate, or magic. In stressing rationality and objectivity, Weber pioneered research techniques that helped prevent personal biases from unduly affecting sociological investigations.

✓ **READING PROGRESS CHECK**

Making Connections How did the various pioneers of sociology contribute to the development of sociological theory?

Sociology in America

GUIDING QUESTION *What were the contributions of early American sociologists?*

Although the early development of sociology occurred in Europe, the greatest development of sociology has taken place in the United States. Because sociology has become a science largely through the efforts of American sociologists, it is not surprising that many of the most influential sociologists worked in the United States. The global influence of American sociologists is reflected in the fact that sociologists throughout the world use sociological writings in English.

In 1892, the first department of sociology was established at the University of Chicago. From its founding until World War II, the sociology department at the University of Chicago stood at the forefront of American sociology. Such early American sociologists as Robert Ezra Park and George Herbert Mead were members of the department. After World War II, sociology departments at eastern universities such as Harvard and Columbia, Midwestern universities such as Wisconsin and Michigan, and western universities such as Stanford and the University of California at Berkeley emerged as leaders. Sociologist Robert Nisbet, for example, earned his degree from Berkeley, while Julian Samora graduated from Washington University in Missouri.

Some early contributors to American sociology, including Jane Addams and Booker T. Washington, directed much of their efforts toward solving society's problems through social activism. Challenging racism and racial discrimination became the life's work of African American sociologists such as Washington and W.E.B. Du Bois.

Jane Addams

Jane Addams (1860–1935) was the best known of the early female social reformers in the United States. She attended the Women's Medical College of Philadelphia but had to drop out because of illness.

When she was a child, Addams saw many examples of government corruption and business practices that harmed workers. She never forgot their suffering. While on one of her European trips, she saw the work being done to help the poor in London. With this example of social action, Addams began her life's work—seeking social justice. With her college friend Ellen Gates Starr, Addams cofounded Hull House in Chicago's slums. Here, people who needed refuge—immigrants, the sick, the poor, the aged—could find help.

Addams focused on the problems caused by the imbalance of power among the social classes. She invited sociologists from the University of Chicago to Hull House to witness firsthand the effects of industrialism on the lower class. In addition to her work with the lower class, Addams was active in the woman suffrage and peace movements. As a result of her tireless work for social reform, Addams was awarded the Nobel Peace Prize in 1931—the first sociologist to receive this honor. The irony is that Addams herself suffered a sort of class discrimination. She was not considered a sociologist during her lifetime because she did not teach at a university. She was considered a social worker (then considered a less prestigious career) because she was a woman and because she worked directly with the poor.

Jane Addams believed that social action could be used to improve society.

▶ **CRITICAL THINKING**

Evaluating What are some of the ways that Addams sought to improve society?

W.E.B. Du Bois (second from the right) was one of the founders of the National Association for the Advancement of Colored People (NAACP). He was also the long-time editor of *The Crisis,* the journal of the NAACP.

▶ **CRITICAL THINKING**

Assessing How does Du Bois' work with the NAACP provide evidence of his role as a social activist?

assumption the act of taking for granted or supposing

W.E.B. Du Bois

W.E.B. Du Bois (1868–1963), an African American educator and social activist, attended an integrated high school in Great Barrington, Massachusetts, and was the first African American to receive a diploma there. Then in 1895, Du Bois became the first African American to receive a doctorate from Harvard University. He taught at a number of predominantly African American universities during his career.

Du Bois learned firsthand about racial discrimination and segregation when he attended Fisk University in Nashville, Tennessee, as an undergraduate student. Partly from this experience, and from teaching in rural, all-African American schools around Nashville, Du Bois decided to attack the "Negro problem." This racist policy was based on the **assumption** that African Americans were an inferior race. Du Bois analyzed the sophisticated social structure of African American communities, first in Philadelphia and later in other places. He published his findings in *The Philadelphia Negro*:

PRIMARY SOURCE

❝Many are the misapprehensions and misstatements as to the social environment of Negroes in a great Northern city. Sometimes it is said, here they are free; they have the same chance as the Irishman, the Italian, or the Swede; at other times it is said, the environment is such that it is really more oppressive than the situation in Southern cities. The student must ignore both of these extreme statements and seek to extract from a complicated mass of facts the tangible evidence of a social atmosphere surrounding Negroes, which differs from that surrounding most whites; of a different mental attitude, moral standard, and economic judgment shown toward Negroes than toward most other folk. That such a difference exists and can now and then plainly be seen, few deny; but just how far it goes and how large a factor it is in the Negro problems, nothing but careful study and measurement can reveal.❞

—W.E.B. Du Bois,
The Philadelphia Negro, 1899

Du Bois' concern for his race did not stop at the borders of the United States—he was also active in the Pan-African movement, which was concerned with the rights of all African descendants, no matter where they lived. While documenting the experience and contributions of African people throughout the world, Du Bois died in the African country of Ghana at the age of ninety-five.

Booker T. Washington

Du Bois' demands for African American civil rights and racial equality put him at odds with another voice of the African American community—Booker T. Washington (1856–1915). Washington had begun his life in slavery. After emancipation, he became an educator, founding the Tuskegee Institute in 1881. Washington held different assumptions than Du Bois about the best course of action for African Americans. He worked under the assumption that African Americans should accept segregation in return for promises of economic gains.

Robert Ezra Park

Robert Ezra Park (1864–1944) worked as an aide to Booker T. Washington at the Tuskegee Institute from 1905 to 1914. After he left Tuskegee, Park taught at the University of Chicago, where he specialized in race relations and human ecology, the study of the relationship among individuals, social groups, and their social environments. Park was interested in how populations grow and change. He wanted to know how groups are organized in different ways to enable them to compete and cooperate. Park, who began his career as a journalist, was also interested in the social function of newspapers as a record of public events. He believed that a sociologist was a kind of "superreporter," who chronicled the long-term trends in society.

Park used the city of Chicago as his laboratory to study collective behavior and social interaction. Although he is credited with moving American sociology toward a more objective methodology, he never completely abandoned his interest in social reform.

George Herbert Mead

George Herbert Mead (1863–1931) also taught at the University of Chicago. Mead explored how our sense of self develops. According to Mead, our sense of self develops as we interact with our world. Language, symbols, and communication are at the heart of this process. Mead's work laid the foundation for the theoretical perspective of symbolic interactionism.

Julian Samora

Julian Samora (1920–1996) became the first known Mexican American to earn a doctorate in sociology when he graduated from Washington University in St. Louis in 1953. He went on to conduct pioneering work in Mexican American studies. Samora's focus was on civil rights and discrimination, poverty, public health, and the movement of people along the Mexican-American border. While at Notre Dame University, he founded the Mexican American Graduate Studies Program and headed the Mexican Border Studies Project.

✓ **READING PROGRESS CHECK**

Generalizing How did early American sociologists change the nature of sociology?

Booker T. Washington founded the Tuskegee Institute as a training school for formerly enslaved African Americans.

▶ **CRITICAL THINKING**

Analyzing Cause and Effect How might Washington's life experiences have influenced his views on the best course of action for African Americans?

LESSON 2 REVIEW

Reviewing Vocabulary

1. *Identifying* What is the difference between social statics and social dynamics?

2. *Defining* What did Max Weber mean by *rationalization*?

Using Your Notes

3. *Describing* Use your notes to describe how both Karl Marx and Jane Addams were concerned with the issue of the imbalance of power among the social classes.

Answering the Guiding Questions

4. *Interpreting* What were the theories of the pioneers of sociology?

5. *Synthesizing* What were the contributions of early American sociologists?

Writing Activity

6. *Argument* Max Weber introduced the concept of *verstehen*. Write a brief plan for using *verstehen* to investigate the importance of money to your peers.

An Invitation to Sociology

FOCUS on research
Field Research

The Objective Value of a Social Settlement

Jane Addams was an early American sociologist and social reformer. On a trip to London, Addams visited Toynbee Hall, a settlement house in an East London slum. The residents of the settlement house provided services to the surrounding community in hopes of relieving the effects of poverty. The concept appealed to Addams, who returned to Chicago and established Hull House with the assistance of her friend Ellen Gates Starr. Hull House opened in 1889.

PRIMARY SOURCE

"Hull House is an ample old residence, well built and somewhat ornately decorated after the manner of its time, 1856.... It once stood in the suburbs, but the city has steadily grown up around it...

The streets are inexpressibly dirty, the number of schools inadequate, factory legislation unenforced, the street-lighting bad, the paving miserable and altogether lacking in the alleys and smaller streets, and the stables defy all laws of sanitation. Hundreds of houses are unconnected with the street sewer....

The houses of the ward, for the most part wooden, were originally built for one family and are now occupied by several.... Many houses have no water supply save the faucet in the back yard; there are no fire escapes; the garbage and ashes are placed in wooden boxes which are fastened to the street pavements....

This site for a Settlement was selected in the first instance because of its diversity and the variety of activity for which it presented an opportunity. It has been the aim of the residents to respond to all sides of neighborhood life: not to the poor people alone, nor to the well-to-do, nor to the young in contradistinction to the old, but to the neighborhood as a whole...

The activities of Hull House divide themselves into four, possibly more lines.... They might be designated as the social, educational, and humanitarian. I have added civic if indeed a Settlement of women can be said to perform civic duties....

There are Bohemians, Italians, Poles, Russians, Greeks, and Arabs in Chicago vainly trying to adjust their peasant life to the life of a large city, and coming in contact with only the most ignorant Americans in that city. The more of scholarship, the more of linguistic attainment, the more of beautiful surroundings a Settlement among them can command, the more it can do for them.

Perhaps of more value than to the newly arrived peasant is the service of the Settlement to those foreigners who speak English fairly well, and who have been so successful in material affairs that they are totally absorbed by them. Their social life is too often reduced to a sense of comradeship.... Perhaps the greatest value of the settlement to them is in simply placing large and pleasant rooms with musical facilities at their disposal....

Our most successful clubs are entirely composed of English-speaking and American-born young people. Those over sixteen meet in two clubs, one for young men and one for girls, every Monday evening....

To turn to the educational effort, it will be perhaps better first to describe the people who respond to it....

> "It has been the aim of the residents to respond to all sides of neighborhood life: not to the poor people alone, ... but to the neighborhood as a whole."

It is composed of people of former education and opportunity who have cherished ambitions and prospects, but who are caricatures of what they meant to be.... In addition to these there are many young women who teach in the public schools, young men who work at various occupations, but who are bent upon self-improvement and are preparing for professions. It is of these that the College Extension classes are composed....

The industrial education of Hull House has always been somewhat limited. From the beginning we have had large and enthusiastic cooking classes.... We have also always had sewing, mending, and embroidery classes. This leads me to speak of the children who meet weekly at Hull House.... There are about three hundred of them that come on three days.... We have had a kindergarten at Hull House ever since we have lived there....

Owing to the lack of a charity organization in Chicago we have been obliged to keep a sum of money as a relief fund....

The more definite humanitarian effort of Hull House has taken shape in a day nursery, which was started during the second year of our residence.... At present, we receive from thirty to forty children daily.... This nursery is not merely a convenience in the neighborhood; it is, to a certain extent, a neighborhood affair. Similar in spirit is the Hull House Diet Kitchen, in a little cottage directly back of the nursery. Food is prepared for invalids and orders are taken from physicians and visiting nurses of the district."

—Jane Addams, "The Objective Value of a Social Settlement," 1893

Working With the Research

1. **Drawing Conclusions** Why does Jane Addams describe the neighborhood surrounding Hull House in such detail?
2. **Evaluating** How would you summarize the role the settlement house plays in the neighborhood?
3. **Categorizing** Which activities would you categorize as social, educational, and humanitarian?

networks

There's More Online!

- ☑ **CARTOON** The Power of Symbols
- ☑ **CHART** Five Key Concepts
- ☑ **CHART** Theoretical Perspectives: Assumptions of the Major Perspectives
- ☑ **IMAGE** Yesteryear's Family
- ☑ **MAP** A Different Perspective
- ☑ **SELF-CHECK QUIZ**

LESSON 3
Theoretical Perspectives

ESSENTIAL QUESTION • *What is sociology?*

Reading HELPDESK

Academic Vocabulary
- symbol
- abstract

Content Vocabulary
- theoretical perspective
- functionalism
- manifest functions
- latent functions
- dysfunction
- conflict perspective
- power
- symbolic interactionism
- dramaturgy

TAKING NOTES:
Key Ideas and Details

LISTING As you read about the theoretical perspectives, use a graphic organizer like the one below to list the main assumptions or characteristics of each approach.

Functionalism	Conflict	Symbolic Interactionism
•	•	•
•	•	•
•	•	•
•	•	•

IT MATTERS BECAUSE
Sociology includes three major theoretical perspectives. Functionalism views society as an integrated whole. Conflict theory looks at class, race, and gender struggles. Symbolic interactionism examines how group members interact.

The Role of Theoretical Perspectives

GUIDING QUESTION *What is a theoretical perspective?*

Perception is the way the brain interprets an image or event. Similarly, your perspective is the way you interpret the meaning of an image or event. Your perspective is influenced by the beliefs or values you hold. It draws your attention to some things and blinds you to others. One perspective emphasizes certain aspects of an event, while another perspective accents different aspects of the same event. When a perspective highlights certain parts, it necessarily places other parts in the background.

Theoretical Perspectives

A **theoretical perspective** is a set of assumptions about an area of study. In the case of sociology, it is a set of assumptions about the workings of society. Supporters of a theoretical perspective consider it true and use it to organize their research.

But competing, even conflicting, theories usually exist at the same time. Conflicting theories can arise for many reasons. Perhaps not enough evidence exists to determine which theory is accurate, or different theories may explain different aspects of the problem.

This is even true in the so-called hard sciences such as modern physics. Albert Einstein's theory of general relativity, for example, contradicts the widely accepted Big Bang theory of the origin of the physical universe. Einstein himself never accepted quantum theory—the theory about the relationship between matter and energy at the subatomic level. Nonetheless, quantum theory has become the foundation of modern developments in such fields as chemistry and molecular biology. Today theories are being put forth that hold promise for combining relativity and quantum theory.

If theories still compete in physics and the other natural sciences, it should not be surprising that several major theoretical perspectives exist in sociology. The three theoretical perspectives most widely used by sociologists are *functionalism,* *conflict theory,* and *symbolic interactionism.* Each of these perspectives provides a different slant on human social behavior. The exclusive use of any one of these theoretical perspectives prevents our seeing other aspects of social behavior. All three perspectives together, however, allow us to see most of the important dimensions of human social behavior.

theoretical perspective
a set of assumptions about an area of study accepted as true

Five Key Concepts of Sociology

The three major theoretical perspectives have some basic building blocks in common. These building blocks include the five key concepts in sociology: *functional integration, social structure, power, social action,* and *culture.* These concepts help sociologists look beyond individual personalities and events to analyze society. While the concepts are expressed in common words, they have specific meanings in the field of sociology, meanings which will become more comprehensible as you proceed through the textbook. Different concepts are emphasized within different theoretical perspectives.

- *Functional integration* refers to the interdependence among the parts in a social system. Each part has contributions that it must make for the whole system to function well. This concept is central to functionalism, which sees integration as an essential condition for the proper functioning of society.
- *Social structure* refers to the pattern of social behavior in a group or society. It acts as a framework for society by establishing the ways that people and groups are related. These relationships are based on a person's location, or status, in the social structure. Unlike the structure of a building, social structure cannot be seen.

A Global Perspective

A DIFFERENT PERSPECTIVE

Look at this map showing the Peters Projection, an area-accurate map. Does it look like the world maps with which you are familiar? What is different? All mapmakers face the same problem: The world is round; maps are flat. Thus all maps distort the shape of Earth in some way. So it is with any perspective. When studying sociology, you will be asked to abandon the conventional perspective in favor of the sociological perspective.

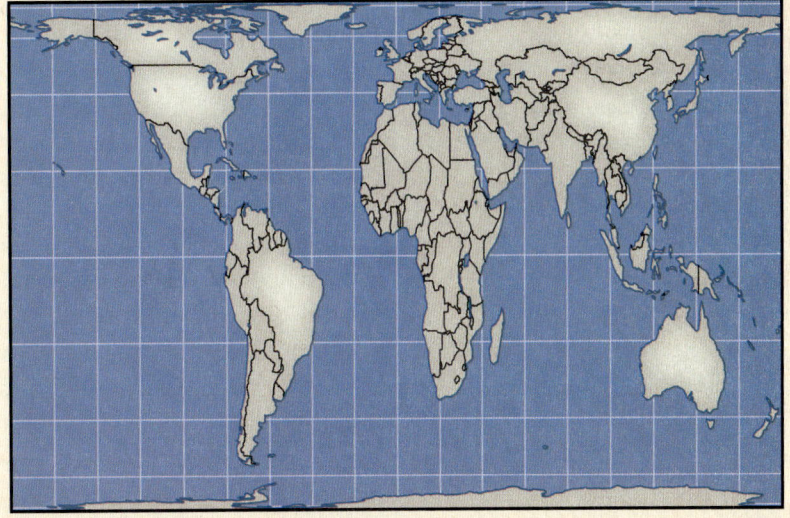

Geography Connection

1. **Places and Regions** What does your reaction to this map tell you about power of the perspective you bring to a situation?
2. **The World in Spatial Terms** Look at several different world maps. What is the size of North America and Europe relative to the other continents? What does this tell you about the perspective of the mapmakers?

An Invitation to Sociology

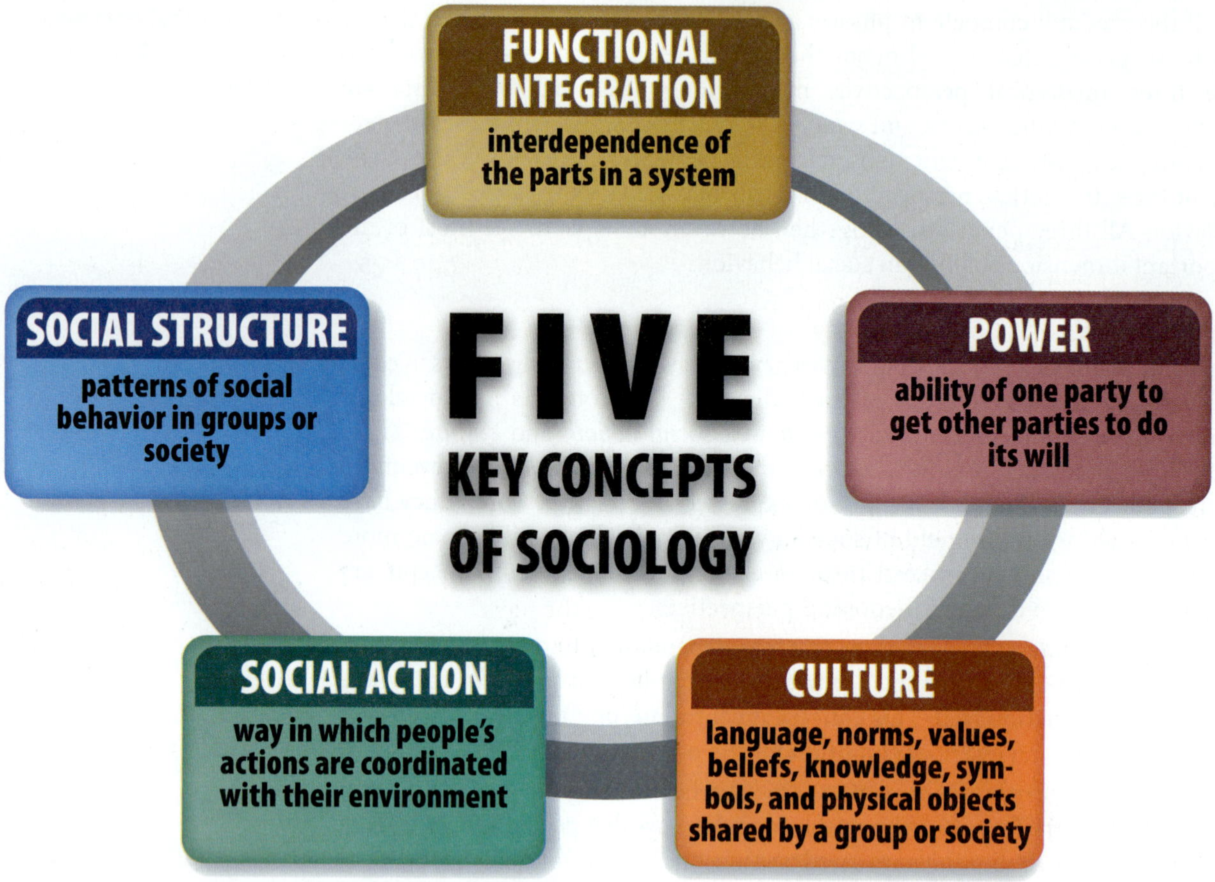

FIVE KEY CONCEPTS OF SOCIOLOGY

FUNCTIONAL INTEGRATION
interdependence of the parts in a system

SOCIAL STRUCTURE
patterns of social behavior in groups or society

POWER
ability of one party to get other parties to do its will

SOCIAL ACTION
way in which people's actions are coordinated with their environment

CULTURE
language, norms, values, beliefs, knowledge, symbols, and physical objects shared by a group or society

CHART

FIVE KEY CONCEPTS
The five key concepts of sociology serve as the building blocks of social theory.

▶ **CRITICAL THINKING**

1. **Assessing** Why are the key concepts important to building theoretical perspectives?
2. **Making Connections** Why is functional integration an important concept in functionalism?

It is inferred from people's movements and actions and from the social institutions in society. *Social institutions* are the organized ways in which a society meets its basic needs. In the United States these include the family, economy, religion, education, law, and politics. Social structure is a central concept in functionalism and conflict theory. For functionalists, social structure is the glue that holds the different parts of society together and enables functional integration. Conflict theorists, on the other hand, emphasize the imbalance of power in social relationships and social institutions.

- *Power* refers to the ability of one party to get other parties to do its will or to ensure that it will benefit from the actions of other parties. This definition mirrors Max Weber's view of power. Weber was interested in the role of power in conflict and in social stratification. He saw social class—people's economic position in society—and social status as dimensions of power. According to Weber, social class was the result of an unequal distribution of economic power, while social status was a reflection of social power. Today, power is an important concept in conflict theory.
- *Social action* refers to the way in which someone's actions are coordinated with his or her environment. Social action is a central concept in symbolic interactionism.
- *Culture* refers to the language, norms, values, beliefs, knowledge, symbols, and physical objects that are shared by members of a society or group. The concept of culture is incorporated in each of the three major theoretical perspectives.

✓ **READING PROGRESS CHECK**

Analyzing Why does sociology need more than one theoretical perspective?

Functionalism

GUIDING QUESTION *How does functionalism explain social change?*

Functionalism emphasizes the contributions (functions) of each part of a society. For example, family, economy, and religion are "parts" of a society. The family contributes to society by providing for the reproduction and care of its new members. The economy contributes by dealing with production, distribution, and consumption of goods and services. Religion contributes by emphasizing beliefs and practices related to sacred things.

Functionalism and Social Change

Functionalists see the parts of a society as an integrated whole. A change in one part of a society leads to changes in other parts. A major change in the economy, for example, may change the family—which is precisely what happened as a result of the Industrial Revolution. Before the Industrial Revolution when most people made their livings by farming, a large farm labor force was needed. Families fulfilled this need by having many children. The need disappeared as industrialization proceeded, and smaller families became the norm.

Functionalism assumes that societies tend to return to a state of stability after some upheaval has occurred. A society may change over time, but functionalists believe that it will return to a stable state. It will do this by changing in such a way that society will be similar to what it was before. Student unrest and other protests during the late 1960s illustrate this. The activities of civil rights activists, antiwar demonstrators, and other protesters helped bring about some changes:

- Many Americans became suspicious of the federal government's foreign policy.
- Schools and universities became more responsive to students' needs and goals.
- Environmental protection became an important political issue to many Americans.

Yet these changes did not revolutionize American society. They were absorbed into it. As a result, our society is only somewhat different from the way it was before the student unrest. In fact, most of the student radicals are now part of the middle-class society they once rejected.

The Nature of Functions

According to functionalism, most aspects of a society exist to promote a society's survival and welfare. It is for this reason that all complex societies have economies, families, governments, and religions. If these elements did not contribute to a society's well-being and survival, they would disappear.

Recall that a function is a contribution made by some part of a society. According to Robert Merton, there are two kinds of functions. **Manifest functions** are intended and recognized. **Latent functions** are unintended and unrecognized. One of the manifest functions of school, for example, is to teach math skills. A latent (and positive) function of schools is the development of close friendships.

Not all elements of a society are positive. Elements that have negative consequences result in **dysfunction**. Dysfunctions of bureaucracies, for example, include rigidity, inefficiency, and impersonality.

functionalism approach that emphasizes the contributions made by each part of society

manifest functions intended and recognized consequences of an aspect of society

latent functions unintended and unrecognized consequences of an aspect of society

dysfunction negative consequences of an aspect of society

Having many children meant there would be enough hands to work the family farm.

▶ **CRITICAL THINKING**

Drawing Conclusions What was the manifest function of large farm families? What might have been a latent function?

Theoretical Perspectives

ASSUMPTIONS OF THE MAJOR PERSPECTIVES
The three major perspectives in sociology hold different assumptions and ask different kinds of research questions.

Theoretical Perspective	Assumptions	Questions Asked
Functionalism	• A society is relatively stable. • A society tends to seek relative stability. • Most aspects of society contribute to the society's well-being and survival. • A society rests on the consensus of its members.	• What holds society together? • What are the major parts of society? • How are the parts of society held together? • How does each part function to help society work?
Conflict Theory	• A society experiences inconsistency and conflict everywhere. • A society is continually subjected to change. • A society involves the constraint and coercion of some members by others.	• What forces divide society? • How do people with privilege and power protect their position? • How do people without power and privilege challenge the system and seek change?
Symbolic Interactionism	• People's interpretations of symbols are based on the meanings they learn from others. • People base their interaction on their interpretations of symbols. • Symbols permit people to have internal conversations that help them gear their interaction to the behavior they think others expect of them and the behavior they expect of others.	• What meanings do people attach to their experiences? • How do people shape their own realities? • How do behaviors and meanings change from person to person and situation to situation?

▶ **CRITICAL THINKING**

1. **Identifying Central Ideas** Explain in your own words how functionalism and conflict theory view society differently.

2. **Contrasting** Describe how the three perspectives might approach the study of laws in society in different ways.

When you go to the division of motor vehicles to register your car or get your driver's license, the clerk may treat you like a "number" rather than as an individual. You may not like the clerk's bureaucratic inflexibility and impersonality.

The Role of Values

Finally, according to functionalism, there is a consensus on values. *Values* are broad ideas about what most people in a society consider to be desirable. Values are important because they influence social behavior. Most Americans, for example, agree on the desirability of democracy, individualism, action over inaction, efficiency and practicality, achievement and success, and equal opportunity. Consensus in another society might produce a different set of values. This consensus of values, say the functionalists, accounts for the high degree of cooperation found in any society. As Émile Durkheim pointed out, however, consensus is strongest in small tribal societies. As societies become more complex, consensus needs to be reinforced by more rules.

☑ **READING PROGRESS CHECK**

Identifying Cause and Effect According to the functionalist perspective, why does change in one part of society lead to change in other parts?

Conflict Perspective

GUIDING QUESTION *How does the conflict perspective explain social change?*

The **conflict perspective** emphasizes conflict, competition, change, and constraint within a society. Understanding the conflict perspective is easier when you understand functionalism because the assumptions behind these two perspectives are the reverse of each other.

The Role of Conflict and Constraint

Functionalists see a basic agreement on values within a society. This leads them to emphasize the ways in which people cooperate to reach common goals. The conflict perspective, in contrast, focuses on the disagreements among various groups in a society or between societies. Groups and societies compete as they attempt to preserve and promote their own special values and interests.

Supporters of the conflict perspective see social living as a contest. Their central question is "Who gets what?" According to this perspective, it is those with the most **power**—the ability to control the behavior of others—who get the largest share of whatever is considered valuable. Those with the most power have the most wealth, prestige, and privileges. Because some groups have more power than other groups, they are able to constrain, or limit, the less powerful groups in society. In this way, they are able to maintain their power.

Conflict Perspective and Social Change

Many conflicting groups exist in a society. As the balance of power among these groups shifts, change occurs. For example, the women's movement set out to change the balance of power between men and women. Over the course of this movement, we have seen larger numbers of women in occupations once limited to men. More women are either making or influencing decisions in business, politics, medicine, and law. Gender relations are changing in other ways as well. The divorce rate has risen as women have gained more economic power. Women in earlier generations might have been forced by economic circumstances to remain in unhappy marriages. Today, economically independent women are apt to end unhappy marriages through divorce. In addition, more women are choosing to remain single, to marry later in life, to have fewer children, and to divide household tasks with their husbands. According to the conflict perspective, these changes are the result of increasing power among women.

conflict perspective approach emphasizing the role of conflict, competition, and constraint within a society

power the ability to control the behavior of others

Conflict theorists are interested in the balance of power among groups in society.

▶ **CRITICAL THINKING**

Formulating Questions What question might a conflict theorist ask about this photograph showing a slum in Mumbai, India?

An Invitation to Sociology **27**

Quick Case Study

WHAT MAKES US CHANGE BEHAVIORS?
People often change their behaviors based on how others react. How does this process take place?

Procedure
1. Interview five people about a time they changed their behavior because of the reactions of others.
2. Record each person's account. Ask questions to get at specifics about the reactions and how the person felt.

Analysis
As you read through the accounts, consider these questions.
1. In what ways did other people show their negative reaction to the behaviors?
2. How did the people you interviewed interpret the reactions of others?
3. What "internal conversations" did the people you interviewed have with themselves?

Comparing Functionalism and the Conflict Perspective

You might be asking yourself which theoretical perspective is better—functionalism or the conflict perspective? The answer is neither. There is no "better" perspective. Each perspective highlights certain areas of social life. The advantages of one perspective are the disadvantages of the other. Functionalism explains much of the consensus, stability, and cooperation within a society. The conflict perspective explains much of the constraint, conflict, and change. A look at how the two perspectives approach the social change brought on by the rapid spread of the Internet illustrates this point.

Functionalists see the Internet as having both positive and negative consequences. On the one hand, the linking of computers has many benefits. Parents can work at home and spend more time with their children. Individuals with physical disabilities can do jobs at home that might be denied them otherwise, thus becoming more fully integrated into society. On the other hand, there are dysfunctions. Young people may have easy access to pornographic material, which can distort their views of the opposite sex. Hate groups can be formed by strangers who live hundreds or thousands of miles apart. Their anonymity may encourage them to engage in antisocial or violent behavior that they would otherwise avoid.

Conflict theorists would agree with functionalists that the Internet is changing American society and helping speed the development of new technologies. They would be more likely, however, to focus on the negative consequences—what functionalists would consider dysfunctions. Whereas a functionalist might choose to focus on how computer links give workers more flexibility, a conflict theorist might focus on how high-speed broadband connections make it possible for American companies to lay off service workers and move their jobs to other countries where wages are lower. Each chapter, throughout the text, will illustrate both functionalism and the conflict perspective, as well as the perspective discussed next—symbolic interactionism.

✓ **READING PROGRESS CHECK**

Making Connections According to the conflict perspective, what role does power play in social change?

Symbolic Interactionism

GUIDING QUESTION *How does symbolic interactionism explain social change?*

Both functionalism and conflict theory deal with large social units, such as the economy, and broad social processes, such as cooperation or conflict among social classes. At the close of the nineteenth century, some sociologists began to change their approaches to the study of society. Instead of concentrating on large social structures, they turned their attention to the way people interact. Two sociologists, George Herbert Mead and Charles Horton Cooley, developed the insight that groups exist only because their members influence each other's behavior. These early American sociologists created **symbolic interactionism**, a perspective that focuses on the actual *interaction* among people.

The Significance of Symbols

To understand social interactionism, we need to talk first about symbols. A **symbol** is something chosen to represent something else. It may be an object, a word, a gesture, a facial expression, or a sound. A symbol is something observable that often represents something not observable, something that is **abstract**. For example, your school's team mascot is often used as a symbol of the abstract concept of school loyalty. The American flag is a symbol of the United States.

The meaning of a symbol is not determined by its own physical characteristics. Those who create and use the symbols assign the meanings to them. If people in a group do not share the same meaning for a given symbol, confusion results. For example, if some people interpreted the red light of a traffic signal to mean *go* while others interpreted it to mean *stop*, chaos would result. The importance of shared symbols is reflected in the formal definition of symbolic interactionism: the theoretical perspective that focuses on interaction among people—interaction based on mutually understood symbols.

Basic Assumptions

Herbert Blumer, who coined the term *symbolic interactionism*, outlined three assumptions central to this perspective. First, according to symbolic interactionism, we learn the meaning of a symbol from the way we see others reacting to it. For example, American musicians in Latin America soon learn that when audience members whistle at the end of a performance, they are expressing the abstract concept of disapproval. Whistling serves the same function in Latin America that booing does in the United States.

symbolic interactionism approach that focuses on the interactions among people based on their mutually understood symbols

symbol anything that stands for something else and has an agreed-upon meaning attached to it

abstract expressing a quality or characteristic apart from any specific object or instance

‹ CARTOON

THE POWER OF SYMBOLS

Symbols have shared meanings.

▶ CRITICAL THINKING

1. *Analyzing* What is the reaction of the older men to the younger people's conversation?
2. *Finding the Main Idea* What point about symbols does this cartoon illustrate?

Dramaturgy likens human interaction to a theatrical performance.

▶ **CRITICAL THINKING**

Comparing In what ways is human interaction like a play?

dramaturgy approach that depicts human interaction as theatrical performances

Second, once we learn the meanings of symbols, we base our behavior (interaction) on them. Now that the musicians know that whistling symbolizes a negative response, they will definitely avoid an encore if the crowd begins whistling.

Finally, we use the meanings of symbols to imagine how others will respond to our behavior. Through this capability, we can have "internal conversations" with ourselves. These conversations enable us to visualize how others will respond to us before we act. This is crucial because we guide our interactions with people according to the behavior we think others expect of us and we expect of others. Meanwhile, these other people are also having internal conversations. The interaction (acting on each other) that follows is therefore symbolic interaction.

Dramaturgy

In an attempt to better explain the patterns of interaction that make up social life, sociologist Erving Goffman introduced **dramaturgy**. This approach depicts human interaction as a theatrical performance. At the heart of dramaturgy is the notion that we have images of ourselves we want to present to others. We also have assigned roles we play in our everyday lives. We use these roles to present our desired images of ourselves to others. Like actors on a stage, we present ourselves through dress, gestures, and tone of voice. Goffman referred to this as the *presentation of self* or *impression management*.

According to Goffman, our theatrical presentations take place on our front stages. For example, your sociology classroom would be a front stage. The image you project in class is the one you want others to see as the real you. We also have back stages. These are the places where we can relax, discuss our performances, and plan new performances. Your bedroom with the door closed might be your back stage. Sometimes the same location serves as both a front stage and a back stage. If you are alone in your sociology classroom and use the time to brush your hair, the classroom is your back stage. The minute someone comes through the door, it becomes your front stage.

✓ **READING PROGRESS CHECK**

Inferring How do the "internal conversations" people hold help explain why people might change their behaviors?

LESSON 3 REVIEW

Reviewing Vocabulary

1. ***Examining*** What is the difference between a manifest function and a latent function?
2. ***Academic Vocabulary*** What do the supporters of symbolic interactionism mean by the term *symbol*?

Using Your Notes

3. ***Listing*** Use the lists in your graphic organizer to write a brief description of each of sociology's three main theoretical perspectives.

Answering the Guiding Questions

4. ***Defining*** What is a theoretical perspective?

5. ***Explaining*** How does functionalism explain social change?
6. ***Expressing*** How does the conflict perspective explain social change?
7. ***Interpreting*** How does symbolic interactionism explain social change?

Writing Activity

8. ***Informative/Explanatory*** Observe an event in school. Record the details. Then write a brief analysis of the event using one of the three theoretical perspectives.

CHAPTER 1 Assessment

Directions: On a separate sheet of paper, answer the questions below. Make sure you read carefully and answer all parts of the questions.

Lesson Review

Lesson 1

1. **Identifying Central Issues** Why is sociology more than just the study of human behavior?
2. **Contrasting** How is the sociological perspective different from the perspective used in economics or political science?
3. **Making Connections** How does the sociological imagination help you apply sociology to your daily life?

Lesson 2

4. **Identifying Perspectives** What does Comte's use of the term *positivism* tell you about his view of sociology?
5. **Explaining** What analogy did Herbert Spencer use to explain social stability?
6. **Interpreting Significance** How are the terms *bourgeoisie*, *capitalists*, and *proletariat* related in the work of Karl Marx?

Lesson 3

7. **Assessing** How do the differences between functionalism and conflict theory illustrate the definition of *theoretical perspective*?
8. **Categorizing** How do functionalists categorize the types of functions in society?
9. **Identifying** What contributions did George Herbert Mead and Charles Horton Cooley make toward the development of symbolic interactionism?

DBQ Analyzing Primary Sources

Use the cartoon to answer the following questions.

PRIMARY SOURCE

"Religion is the opium of the people, Fred."   "Just say no, Karl."

10. **Interpreting** In this chapter, you read about Karl Marx. In the cartoon, Marx is shown making a comment to "Fred" (Friedrich Engels, his collaborator). Research this quote on the Internet and then explain what Marx meant by it and how the cartoonist is twisting its meaning.
11. **Comparing and Contrasting** Conduct research to find another type of primary source that examines the role of religion in society. How do the two sources differ in their points of view?

Need Extra Help?

If You've Missed Question	1	2	3	4	5	6	7	8	9	10	11
Go to page	4	5	9, 11	12	13	14	28	25	29	14	14

CHAPTER 1 Assessment

Directions: On a separate sheet of paper, answer the questions below. Make sure you read carefully and answer all parts of the questions.

Exploring the Essential Question

12 *Gathering Information* Go to a public place (such as a school, cafeteria, or restaurant) and discreetly observe people for 15 minutes. Write down your observations, noting such details as types of dress, general interactions, and level of activity. Do not make value judgments, but restrict your notes to factual observations. When you return home, rewrite your observations applying the sociological concepts in the chapter. Consider and list the ways your second list is different from the first. How does sociology help you describe what you observed?

Critical Thinking

13 *Drawing Inferences* Modern theoretical perspectives in sociology have their roots in the writings of Émile Durkheim and Max Weber. Describe the influences these early sociologists had on modern sociological theory.

14 *Drawing Inferences* There are similarities in the challenges faced and contributions made by Jane Addams and W.E.B. Du Bois in the fields of sociology and social reform. In what ways did Addams and Du Bois face similar challenges? In what ways did they find other avenues for using their sociological skills? How might the situation be different today if they were pursuing careers as sociologists?

College and Career Readiness Skills

15 *Examining Information* Research one of the career options for sociology that interests you. Look for such important information as educational requirements, income expectations, and management opportunities. Write a short report on the advantages and disadvantages of the particular career in sociology.

21st Century Skills

Use the table to answer the following questions.

USING TABLES

MOBILE SUBSCRIBERS PER 100 INHABITANTS, 2010	
East Asia and Pacific	76.7
Europe and Central Asia	124.0
Latin America and Caribbean	98.4
Middle East and North Africa	97.0
North America	88.2
Sub-Saharan Africa	44.9
World	78.2

Source: World Bank, 2012

16 *Identifying Cause and Effect* How might a functionalist and a conflict theorist differ in their explanations of why Africa and Asia have lower rates of mobile phone use than the United States and Europe?

17 *Using Tables* What does the low "mark" for Africa tell you about the rate of social change in Africa versus that of the United States or Europe?

Research and Presentation

18 *Informative/Explanatory* Develop a commercial for sociology using a digital video camera. Think of sociology as a product to sell. Select one of the theoretical perspectives to use as your focus. Convince viewers that the perspective is the best way to better understand the world around us.

19 *Interpreting Significance* Use the Internet to do further research on one of the pioneers of sociology. Design a poster or multimedia presentation representing the pioneer. Describe the person's basic ideas, including his or her theories or information attained through research.

Need Extra Help?

If You've Missed Question	12	13	14	15	16	17	18	19
Go to page	24	24, 26	17–18	10	28	25, 27	25–30	12–19

Sociological Research Methods

ESSENTIAL QUESTIONS • *How do sociologists do research?* • *What is ethical research?*

networks
There's More Online about sociological research methods.

CHAPTER 2

Technology & Society
Using Technology in Sociological Research

Lesson 1
Research Methods

Lesson 2
Causation in Science

Lesson 3
Procedures and Ethics in Research

Sociology Matters...

Have you ever wondered about social behavior? Do you sometimes ask yourself why certain elements of society are the way they are? Sociologists do. But instead of just wondering, they use sociological research methods, such as case studies and surveys, to arrive at conclusions.

These conclusions help sociologists—and the rest of us—understand how and why society functions the way it does.

◀ Sociologists use data gathered in U.S. Census Bureau surveys to conduct research and draw conclusions.

Robert F. Bukaty/AP Images

CHAPTER 2
Technology & Society

Using Technology in Sociological Research

Digital Age technology offers new ways for sociologists to collect and analyze data.

The use of technology in sociological research is not new. Long before the advent of digital technologies, sociologists used telephones, tape recorders, and film to collect data. Statistical software helped researchers analyze large batches of quantitative data. Now the Internet and new digital technologies offer additional ways to collect data while sophisticated software broadens the ways in which sociologists can analyze data.

Sociologists, like other scientists, often base their theories on the foundation of earlier research. As a result, investigating the findings of other sociologists is an important part of research. The Internet speeds up the process both by enabling sociologists to use keyword searches to find books and articles and by providing access to raw data for analysis. Online text forums, personal Web pages, videos, teleconferences, and usage logs offer sociologists vast amounts of data, and email makes it possible to quickly and inexpensively disperse surveys to people across a broad geographic range.

Digital audio and video devices not only make data collection easier; they also expedite analysis. Unlike film or tape recordings, digital files can be searched, coded, tagged with metadata, and easily manipulated. Audio and video editing and analysis software enables researchers to tag data for sorting, create clips that can be sequenced for easier analysis, and search data to uncover verbal or visual patterns.

©Jimmy Collins/Corbis

Digital video and audio files are important sources of data for sociological researchers.

▶ **CRITICAL THINKING**

Problem Solving How can this videographer alleviate concerns about the privacy of the people he is recording?

DATA COLLECTION

INTERNET

👍 **Advantages:**
ACCESS TO DATA & RESEARCH PARTICIPANTS
EFFECTIVE
FAST

👎 **Disadvantages:**
NOT EVERYONE IS ON INTERNET
MAY AFFECT RESPONSES
LESS CONTROL

VIDEO

👍 **Advantages:**
INEXPENSIVE/RELIABLE
DETAILED DATA
PRESERVES UNFILTERED DATA

👎 **Disadvantages:**
PRIVACY CONCERNS CAN AFFECT RESPONSES AND DATA

AUDIO

👍 **Advantages:**
INEXPENSIVE/RELIABLE
DETAILED DATA
PRESERVES UNFILTERED DATA

👎 **Disadvantages:**
PRIVACY CONCERNS CAN AFFECT RESPONSES AND DATA

DIGITAL TECHNOLOGY

DATA ANALYSIS

MANAGEMENT

👍 **Advantages:**
DATABASE MANAGEMENT
EASY SORTING OF DATA
FAST DATA REPORTS

👎 **Disadvantages:**
REQUIRES TRAINING

MANIPULATION

👍 **Advantages:**
EASIER ANALYSIS
EASIER EDITING OF DATA

👎 **Disadvantages:**
DATA CAN BE TAKEN OUT OF CONTEXT

ANALYSIS

👍 **Advantages:**
QUICK ANALYSIS OF LARGE AMOUNTS OF DATA
SOFTWARE CAN SEARCH FOR PATTERNS OF BEHAVIOR

👎 **Disadvantages:**
ONLY SEARCHES BY PROGRAMMED CRITERIA
CAN OVERLOOK OTHER PATTERNS

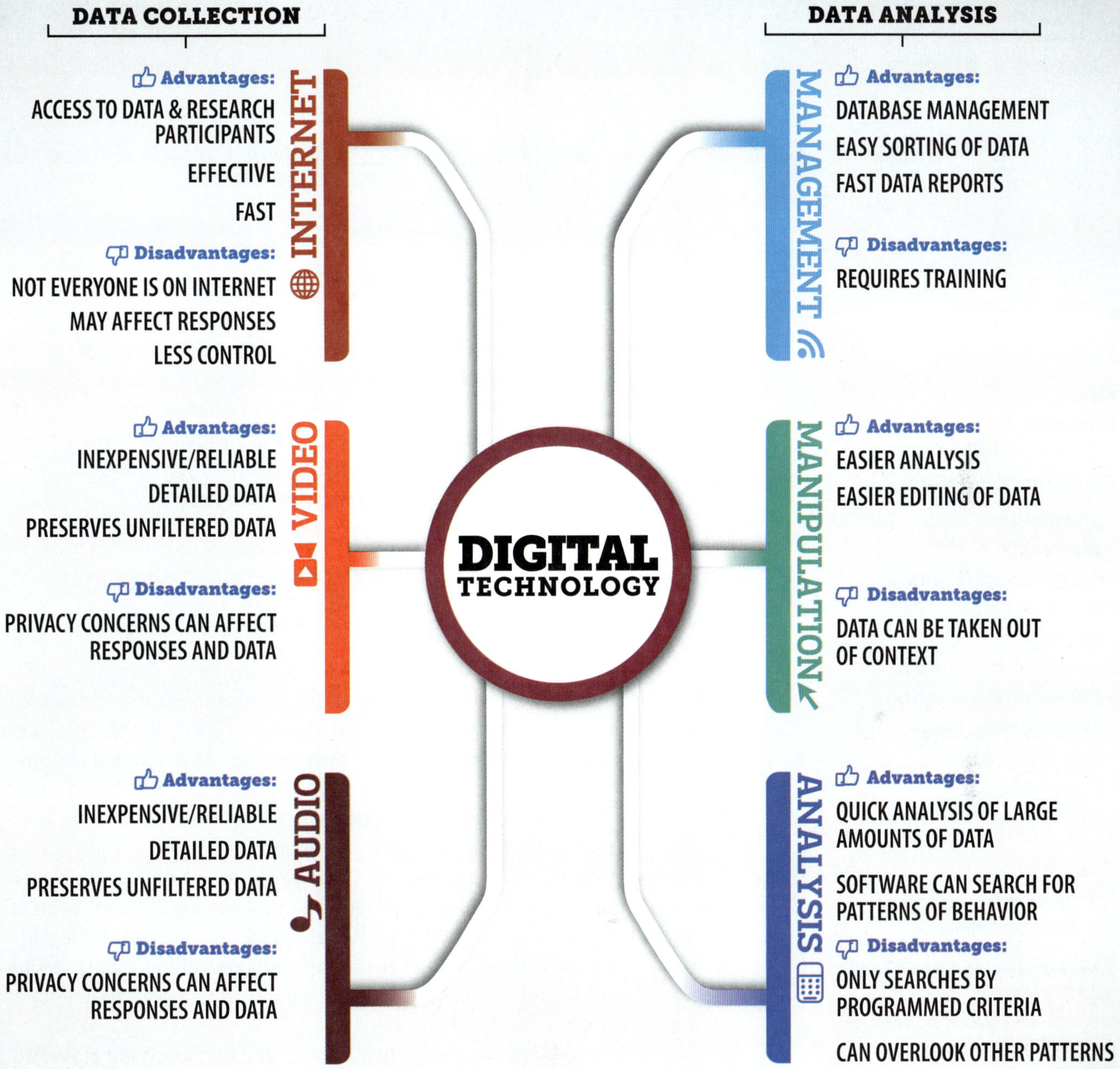

Thinking Like a Sociologist

1 Synthesizing
What are some of the advantages of using digital technologies in research? What are some of the disadvantages?

2 Considering Advantages and Disadvantages
After examining the advantages and disadvantages of using digital technologies, do you think one outweighs the other? Why?

Sociological Research Methods

networks

There's More Online!

- ☑ **CARTOON** Phone Survey
- ☑ **CHART** Research Methods
- ☑ **CHART** Secondary Analysis
- ☑ **CHART** Types of Survey Questions
- ☑ **CHART/GRAPH** Median Earnings
- ☑ **MAP** Percentage Speaking Non-English at Home
- ☑ **SELF-CHECK QUIZ**

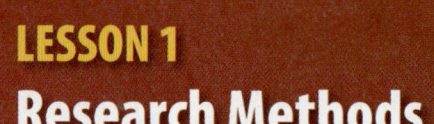

LESSON 1
Research Methods

ESSENTIAL QUESTIONS • *How do sociologists do research?* • *What is ethical research?*

Reading HELPDESK

Academic Vocabulary
- data
- survey

Content Vocabulary
- population
- sample
- representative sample
- questionnaire
- interview
- closed-ended questions
- open-ended questions
- secondary analysis
- field research
- case study
- participant observation

TAKING NOTES:
Key Ideas and Details

SUMMARIZING As you read about the different research methods in sociology, use a graphic organizer like the one below to record details about them.

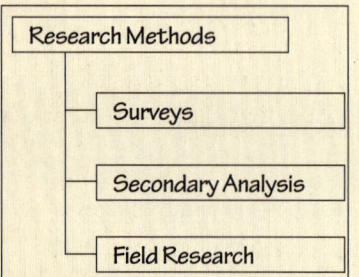

IT MATTERS BECAUSE
When sociologists do quantitative research, they generally use either surveys or precollected data. Each has its own advantages and disadvantages. Qualitative research uses descriptive rather than numerical data. Field studies are best used when interaction needs to be observed in a natural setting or when in-depth analysis is needed. The case study is the most popular approach to field research.

Doing Research in the Social Sciences

GUIDING QUESTION *What research methods do sociologists use?*

Like all scientists, sociologists gain their knowledge by doing research. The goal of sociological research is to test commonsense assumptions and replace false ideas with facts and evidence. Part of the sociological perspective is to ask "why" and "how" questions and then to form hypotheses to arrive at accurate understandings.

Social scientists differ from other scientists, however, in how they conduct much of their research. Unlike chemists, biologists, or physicists, sociologists (and often psychologists) are very limited in their ability to set up laboratory experiments to replicate real-life conditions. Even if they could reproduce conditions as they are in the outside world, the ethical issues involved in manipulating people and controlling events would prevent most sociologists from pursuing this kind of research. For sociologists, the world is their laboratory.

The methods that sociologists use to conduct research are classified as either *quantitative* or *qualitative*. Quantitative research uses numerical **data** while qualitative research rests on narrative and descriptive data. Quantitative research tools include *surveys* and *precollected data*. About 90 percent of the research published in major sociological journals is based on surveys, so this approach is discussed first.

Survey Methods
The **survey**, in which people are asked to answer a series of questions, is the most widely used research method among sociologists. It is ideal for studying large numbers of people.

In survey research, care must be taken that surveys are sent to the right number and type of people. Researchers describe the people surveyed in terms of *populations* and *samples*. A **population** is all those people with the characteristics a researcher wants to study. A population could be all high school seniors in the United States, all retired postal workers living in Connecticut, or the number of freshmen who buy school yearbooks.

Sociologists would like to collect information on all members of a population, but most populations are too large. Such a survey would cost too much and take too long for most research projects. Instead, a sample is drawn. A **sample** is a limited number of cases drawn from the larger population.

A sample must be selected carefully if it is to have the same basic characteristics as the general population—that is, if it is to be a **representative sample**. If a sample is too small or does not match the general characteristics of the population, the survey findings cannot be used to make generalizations about the entire population. For example, if you were to conduct a survey using ten students from an advanced biology class, this sample would not be representative of your school. But if you randomly selected ten students who walked into the school cafeteria, these students would probably be more representative of the student body. The sample, however, would likely be too small to give an accurate picture. The United States Census Bureau regularly uses sample surveys in its highly accurate work. The Gallup Poll and the Harris Poll are recognized as reliable indicators of national trends and public opinion because they use sufficiently large representative samples in their surveys.

The standard method for obtaining a representative sample is by random selection. Each member of the population is assigned a number, and then numbers are drawn from a container after they have been thoroughly scrambled. An easier and more practical method uses a table of random numbers. After each member of the population has been assigned a number, the researcher begins with any number in the table and goes down the list until enough subjects have been selected.

In surveys, information is obtained through either a questionnaire or an interview. A **questionnaire** is a written set of questions that survey participants answer by themselves. In an **interview**, a trained interviewer asks questions and records the answers. Questionnaires and interviews may contain *closed-ended* or *open-ended* questions.

data facts or statistics

survey research method in which people respond to questions

population a group of people with certain specific characteristics

sample a group of people who represent a larger population

representative sample a sample that accurately reflects the characteristics of the population as a whole

questionnaire a written set of questions to be answered by a research participant

interview a survey method in which a trained researcher asks questions and records the answers

◂ **CARTOON**

PHONE SURVEY
Survey researchers must guard against affecting a respondent's answer.

▶ **CRITICAL THINKING**

1. *Identifying Bias* How can you tell if a survey researcher is trying to lead you to give a particular answer?

2. *Evaluating* Why is biased questioning a poor way to obtain data?

closed-ended questions
questions a person must answer by choosing from a limited, predetermined set of responses

Closed-ended questions are those questions that a person answers by choosing from a limited, predetermined set of responses. For example, multiple choice questions are closed ended because participants are limited to certain responses. Because participants are limited in their responses, however, closed-ended questions sometimes fail to uncover underlying attitudes and opinions. On the positive side, closed-ended questions make answers easier to tabulate and compare.

CHARTS

TYPES OF SURVEY QUESTIONS

The type of question a survey researcher chooses depends on the type of data sought.

▶ **CRITICAL THINKING**

1. **Evaluating** Why might a closed-ended survey be a good research method for a study that wanted to find the relationship between level of education and annual income?
2. **Making Connections** Why might poorly worded questions be a more serious problem in closed-ended surveys than in interviews or in surveys that have open-ended questions?
3. **Contrasting** What advantage might open-ended questions have over closed-ended questions for a detailed study of a research topic?
4. **Drawing Conclusions** Why might a researcher choose the closed-ended question format for a study with a large sample population?

Closed-ended Question Survey Research

Advantages	Disadvantages
Closed-ended answers can be more precisely measured.	Surveys can be expensive to produce and distribute.
Responses can be easily compared.	Responses are limited to preset answers.
Statistical techniques can be used to make sense of the data.	Many people do not respond to surveys, resulting in low cost effectiveness.
A large number of responses can be collected.	The way a question is stated may influence the answer given. (Negatively phrased questions are more likely to get a negative answer.)

Closed-ended and Open-ended Questions

Examples of Closed-ended Questions	Strongly Agree	Agree	Disagree	Strongly Disagree
a. Most schoolteachers really don't know what they are talking about.	1	2	3	4
b. To get ahead in life, you have to get a good education.	1	2	3	4
c. My parents encouraged me to get a good education.	1	2	3	4
d. School is a lonely place.	1	2	3	4
e. Too much emphasis is put on education these days.	1	2	3	4
f. Most students cheat on tests.	1	2	3	4

Examples of Open-ended Questions

1. In your own words, please describe your view on the education you have received so far.
2. Do you think school adequately prepares you for employment? Why or why not?

Applying Sociology

EVALUATING SURVEYS

Sociologists are not the only researchers who use surveys to collect data. Surveys are a common methodology in marketing, product research, political and opinion polling, program evaluations, human resources, health care, economic and demographic analysis, and other situations in which the same types of information need to be collected from groups of people for the purposes of comparison, evaluation, or planning.

A well-planned survey presents questions clearly and does not attempt to bias or confuse the respondents. Not all surveys are soundly designed, however. Some even attempt to sway the respondents or manipulate the sample in order to influence the outcomes. When evaluating a survey that you are asked to take, think about these questions:

1. Is the sample random, or is it biased in some way?
2. Is the tone of the questions neutral, or does the wording push you toward specific answers?
3. Do the possible responses in closed-ended questions provide a reasonable range of responses, or do they force you to accept answers with which you do not agree?

▶ **CRITICAL THINKING**

1. *Hypothesizing* Why might a market researcher or a political pollster select a biased sample?
2. *Analyzing* How can the wording of questions and closed-ended responses influence the outcome of the data?

Open-ended questions require the person to answer in his or her own words. Answers to open-ended questions can reveal many attitudes. These answers are not easy to quantify or compare, however. Another problem may arise if an interviewer changes the meanings of questions by rephrasing them. The same question phrased in different ways can place the emphasis on different issues and evoke different responses. Once questions are developed, researchers must decide how to administer the survey to the sample population. The most common ways to administer a survey are through the mail or by email. A respondent is expected to complete the survey and return it to the researchers for analysis. Since the survey is self-administered, it must be clearly written and interesting enough to encourage people to take the time to reply. There is no researcher there to explain questions or urge people to respond.

Online surveys are another way to collect data. Like mail and email surveys, they are self-administered. They also share many of the same advantages and disadvantages. Like mail and email surveys, online surveys can reach large numbers of people over a vast geographic area relatively inexpensively. They can also target hard-to-locate sample populations. However, such surveys can miss key respondents. Hospital patients and adults who cannot read or have difficulty reading, for instance, often cannot complete self-administered surveys. In addition, email and online surveys have a unique disadvantage in that they require computer access to the Internet. This eliminates people without computer access from the sample.

open-ended questions
questions a person is to answer in his or her own words

Summary of Research Methods

Research Method	Definition	Advantages	Disadvantages
Quantitative Methods			
Survey Research	People answer a series of questions, usually predetermined.	• Precision and comparability of answers • Use of statistical techniques • Information on large numbers of people • Detailed analysis	• Expensive due to large numbers • Low response rate • Phrasing of questions introduces bias in favor of certain answers • Researcher's behavior can affect answers given
Secondary Analysis	Information gathered by one researcher is used by another researcher for a different purpose.	• Inexpensive • Can study a topic over a long period of time • Researcher's influence on subjects avoided	• Information collected for a different reason may not suit another researcher's needs • Original researcher may have already introduced biases • Information may be outdated
Experiment	Research occurs in a laboratory setting with a minimum of contaminating influences (not often used in social research).	• Can be replicated with precision • Variables can be manipulated • Can be relatively inexpensive • Permits the establishment of causation (rather than just correlation)	• Laboratory environment is artificial • Not suited to most sociological research • Number of variables studied is limited
Qualitative Methods			
Case Study	Thorough investigation is done of a small group, incident, or community.	• Provides depth of understanding from group members' viewpoints • Unexpected discoveries and new insights can be incorporated into the research • Permits the study of social behavior not feasible with quantitative methods	• Difficult to generalize findings from one group to another group • Presence of researcher can influence results • Hard to duplicate • Takes lots of time • Difficult to be accepted as a group member (in case of participant observation)

CHART

RESEARCH METHODS
Most sociologists use a combination of research methods.

▶ **CRITICAL THINKING**

1. **Exploring Issues** What are the advantages of experiments? Given these advantages, why do you think the method is not suited to most sociological research?
2. **Defending** Which research method would you choose if you wanted to study the effects of peer pressure to shoplift among high school students? Defend your choice with information from the chart.

Until recently, online surveys also presented special challenges to researchers. Creating online surveys required programming skills—skills that researchers might not have. The availability of survey-authoring software packages has lessened this challenge.

What is considered an acceptable response rate varies by how the survey is administered. The 2010 U.S. Census had a response rate of about 74 percent. This is a very good rate. The Census Bureau, however, uses advertising, repeat mailings, and even home visits to encourage people to return surveys. In the case of most email or mail surveys, a response rate of between 40 to 50 percent is considered average or adequate. Anywhere from 60 to 70 percent would be considered a very good response rate. Online surveys tend to have a lower completion rate, with an average of about 30 percent. Not surprisingly, researcher-administered surveys have a higher response rate. A good response rate for telephone or face-to-face surveys falls into the 80 to 85 percent range.

Secondary Analysis (Precollected Data)

When a researcher uses information that someone else has already gathered (precollected information), this is known as **secondary analysis**. It is a well-respected method of collecting data in sociology. In fact, the first sociologist to use statistics in a sociological study—Émile Durkheim—relied on precollected data. Types of precollected data include government reports, company records, voting lists, prison records, and reports of research done by other social scientists.

The U. S. Census Bureau is one of the most important sources of precollected data for American sociologists. The Census Bureau collects information on the total population every ten years and conducts countless specific surveys every year. The census contains detailed information on topics such as income, education, race, gender, age, marital status, occupation, and death and birth rates. Similarly, the U.S. Department of Labor regularly collects information on the nation's income and unemployment levels across a variety of jobs, and the U.S. Department of Commerce issues a variety of monthly economic reports.

Performing secondary analysis on existing data is a cost-effective way to do research. In addition, government data is generally more detailed, extensive, and accurate than the data an individual researcher could collect. Using precollected data does have disadvantages, though. The data may not be in the exact form that is needed for the research design. Similarly, data from different government agencies or other sources may have been collected in different ways. This may make comparing data from different sources difficult.

secondary analysis using precollected information for data collection and research purposes

Field Research

Qualitative research uses narrative or descriptive data rather than quantitative, numerical data. Some aspects of society can best be revealed by qualitative methods. Most of these methods fall under the heading of *field research*. **Field research** looks closely at aspects of social life that cannot be measured quantitatively and that are best understood within a natural setting. High school cliques and "jock" culture are examples of topics best studied by field research.

The most common method of field research is the **case study** —a thorough investigation of a single group, incident, or community. This method assumes that the findings in one case can be generalized to similar situations. For example, the conclusions of a study on drug use in Chicago should also apply to other large cities.

field research research that takes place in a natural (non-laboratory) setting

case study intensive study of a single group, incident, or community

Theoretical Perspectives

INVESTIGATING SCHOOL VIOLENCE AND SCHOOL FUNDING
This table illustrates the research method a sociologist of a particular theoretical persuasion would most likely choose to investigate school violence and school funding. Any of the three sociologists, of course, could use any of the three research methods.

Theoretical Perspective	Research Method	Approach to the Research Question
Functionalism	Survey	A questionnaire on violence in high schools is sent to a national, random sample of principals. The survey examines a possible relationship between incidence of school violence and level of school funding.
Conflict Theory	Case Study	A particular high school with low funding is studied with respect to a relationship between school violence and school funding. Researchers interview administrators, teachers, and students. Findings are then generalized.
Symbolic Interactionism	Participant Observation	Concealing her identity, a researcher takes a temporary job at a high school with low funding. She attempts to observe covertly a possible link between school violence and school funding.

▶ **CRITICAL THINKING**

1. **Assessing** Why would the survey described in the chart be an appropriate method for the functionalist perspective?

2. **Contrasting** What is one key difference between the conflict theorist's approach and the functionalist's approach?

Sociological Research Methods **41**

CHART
SECONDARY ANALYSIS
Secondary analysis involves the use of precollected data.

▶ **CRITICAL THINKING**

1. **Assessing** Why would census data be a good source of information when comparing income levels of African Americans and whites over a long period of time? Which disadvantage might census data overcome?

2. **Considering Advantages and Disadvantages** Why is it both an advantage and a disadvantage that precollected data have been collected by others?

participant observation
a case study in which the researcher becomes a member of the group being studied

Secondary Analysis

Advantages	Disadvantages
Precollected data provide sociologists with inexpensive, high-quality information.	The existing information may not exactly suit the researcher's needs because it was gathered for a different reason.
Existing sources of information permit the study of a topic over a long period of time. (With census data, for example, we can trace the changes in the relative income levels of African Americans and whites.)	Sometimes precollected data are outdated.
The researcher cannot influence answers because the data have been collected by others.	Little may be known about collection methods. The people who first collected the data or the collection methods may have been biased.

It is the researcher's responsibility to point out the factors in the study that are unique and that would not apply to other situations.

Some case studies involve participant observation. In **participant observation**, a researcher becomes a member of the group being studied. A researcher may join a group with or without informing its members that he or she is a sociologist. A compelling account of undercover participant observation appears in *Black Like Me*, a book written by John Howard Griffin that was first published in 1961. Griffin, a white journalist, dyed his skin to study the life of African Americans in the South. Although he had previously visited the South as a white man, his experiences while posing as an African American were quite different.

Barbara Ehrenreich also kept her true identity a secret when she researched what life was like for workers trying to live on the minimum wage. She disguised herself as a divorced, middle-aged housewife without a college degree to gather information. Ehrenreich published her experiences and the experiences of the low-wage workers she met in *Nickel and Dimed: On (Not) Getting By in America*, first published in 2001. Not all participant researchers keep their identities secret, however. Elliot Liebow studied disadvantaged African American males. Even though he was a white outsider, Liebow was allowed to participate in the daily activities of the men.

Combining Methods: Program Evaluations
Some sociological research combines methods. This is often the case with program evaluations. Program evaluations focus on examining the effectiveness of programs. For example, sociologists might evaluate a government-funded program that provides shelter for the homeless to determine whether it is efficient, what problems are occurring, and how the funding is being used. Program evaluation can use both quantitative and qualitative research methods. In the example above, an evaluation of a city's homeless shelters might include a statistical analysis of how many people the shelters serve, the types of services they supply, and the costs of providing those services. It might also include data collected either through questionnaires filled out by a large sample of the staff and clients or through in-depth interviews with a small number of the homeless being served by the shelters. Each method collects different types of data that are useful in evaluating the program's effectiveness.

☑ **READING PROGRESS CHECK**

Drawing Inferences Why does sociology need more than one research method to study human behavior?

Basic Skills for Sociology

GUIDING QUESTION *What skills do sociologists use?*

Conducting sociological research involves more than simply employing one or more of the available research methods. Sociologists also need to know how to work with statistics, evaluate Internet resources, and read tables and graphs.

Graphs and tables are useful for sociologists and other social scientists because they allow people to quickly see relationships and trends in the data. For example, bar graphs make it easy to compare data for men and women or data for different age groups. Line graphs make it easy to see how data change over time. Even people not trained in statistics can quickly grasp relationships and trends when the data are presented graphically. This is one reason that newspapers and magazines often use tables and graphs to present data.

Using Basic Statistical Methods

Statistics are methods used for tabulating, analyzing, and presenting quantitative data. Sociologists, like all scientists, use statistical measures. It is important to use sources of statistical data that are credible, unbiased, and verifiable. The American Sociological Association, for example, endorses data systems maintained by the National Science Foundation and the National Center for Education Statistics. Without trustworthy data, statistical methods will not produce trustworthy results. You will encounter certain statistical measures in this textbook and in periodicals. Among the basic statistical measures are averages—including modes, means, and medians.

A Diverse America

PERCENTAGE OF FAMILIES SPEAKING NON-ENGLISH AT HOME

The U.S. Census Bureau reports that the number of people who speak a language other than English at home has more than doubled in the last three decades. The most common non-English language is Spanish. However, the largest increase is among speakers of Vietnamese. More than 40 percent of families in California speak a language other than English at home. States in the Southwest and parts of the Northeast generally have a large percentage of families who speak languages other than English at home.

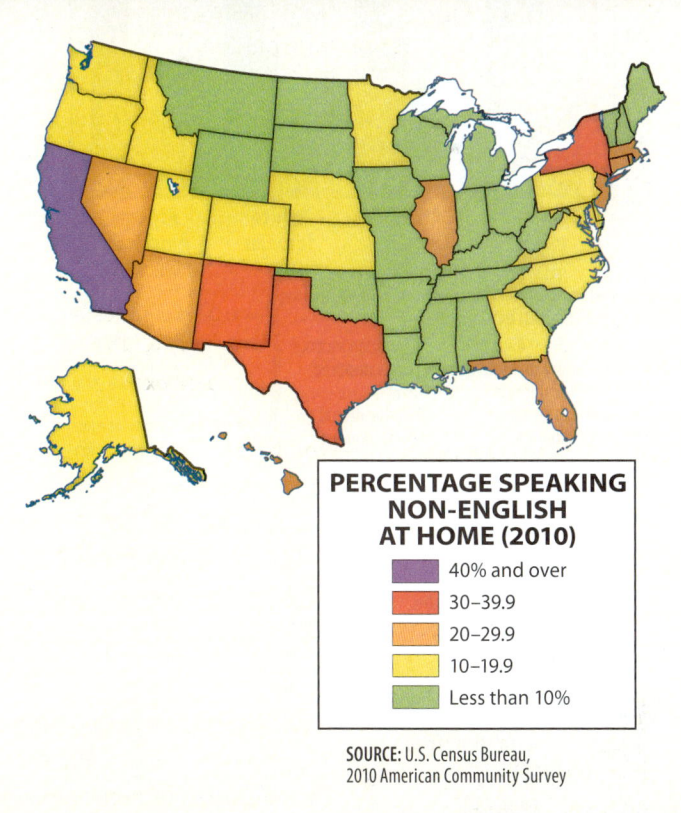

PERCENTAGE SPEAKING NON-ENGLISH AT HOME (2010)
- 40% and over
- 30–39.9
- 20–29.9
- 10–19.9
- Less than 10%

SOURCE: U.S. Census Bureau, 2010 American Community Survey

Geography Connection

1. **Places and Regions** In which states do 30 percent or more of families speak a language other than English at home?
2. **Places and Regions** In which states do less than 10 percent of families speak a language other than English at home?

Sociological Research Methods

Median Earnings in Dollars

Demographic group	Overall median earnings	Median earnings in dollars as compared with educational attainment*				
		HS degree	HS or GED	Associate's degree	Bachelor's degree	Master's degree
White males	50,000	32,000	40,000	50,000	65,000	75,500
African American males	38,000	27,000	32,000	41,000	50,000	60,000
White females	38,000	20,800	29,000	38,000	46,000	55,000
African American females	31,000	20,000	25,000	33,000	42,000	55,000

Note: These figures include the total money earnings of full-time, full-year workers, ages 25 and over, 2007
* In terms of highest degree completed.
Source: U.S. Department of Commerce, Census Bureau, Current Population Survey (CPS), Annual Social and Economic Supplement, 2008.

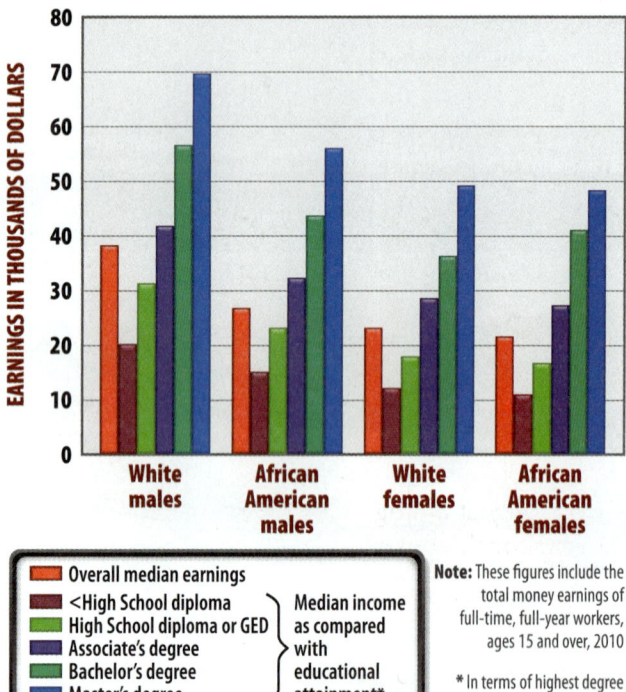

MEDIAN ANNUAL EARNINGS BY GENDER, RACE, AND EDUCATION

Note: These figures include the total money earnings of full-time, full-year workers, ages 15 and over, 2010
* In terms of highest degree completed.
Source: U.S. Department of Commerce, Census Bureau, Current Population Survey (CPS), Annual Social and Economic Supplement, 2011

TABLE AND GRAPH

This table and graph present the same information.

▶ **CRITICAL THINKING**

1. **Analyzing Visuals** Which format allows for the presentation of more precise data? Why?
2. **Evaluating** Which format makes it easier to make a quick comparison of the data? Why?

An *average* is a single number representing the distribution of several figures. For example, suppose the following figures are the salaries of the nine highest-paid major league baseball players:

$3,300,000 (catcher)
$3,600,000 (second base)
$3,600,000 (third base)
$4,200,000 (center field)
$4,300,000 (shortstop)
$4,500,000 (first base)
$4,900,000 (starting pitcher)
$5,300,000 (left field)
$6,100,000 (right field)

Three kinds of averages make these numerical values more meaningful. Each gives a slightly different picture.

The *mode* is the number that occurs most frequently. In this case, it is $3,600,000, which occurs twice. The mode is appropriate only when the objective is to indicate the most popular number. Suppose a researcher investigating these major league baseball salaries reported the mode alone. Readers would be misled, because the mode would give them no hint of the wide range of salaries ($3,300,000 to $6,100,000).

The *mean* is the measure closest to the everyday meaning of the term *average*. It lies somewhere in the middle of a range. The mean of the salary figures above—$4,422,222—is calculated by adding all of the salaries together ($39,800,000) and dividing by the number of salaries (9). The mean, unlike the mode, takes all of the figures into account. It is distorted, however, by the highest figure, $6,100,000. Although one player earns $6,100,000, most players make considerably less—the highest-paid player earns nearly twice as much as the lowest-paid player. The mean is distorted when either the high or the low end of a scale contains extreme values. The mean is more accurate when the high and low values are not widely separated.

The *median* is the number that divides a series of values in half. Half of the values lie above the median, half below. In this example, the median is $4,300,000. Half of the salaries are above $4,300,000, and half are below it. The advantage here is that the median is not distorted by extremes at either end. If the median falls between two numbers, the average of those two numbers becomes the median.

Evaluating Internet Resources

The Internet can put a library of the most current information at your fingertips. In addition to reference materials, many sociological journals are available on the Internet. In these journals, you can find reports on a wide variety of sociological research and theories. The articles in these journals have undergone strenuous review by specialists in the field. Not all information on the Internet is reliable, however. The quality of the content can range from top notch to very dubious. It is critical to evaluate the information and its source before using it.

When evaluating information on the Internet, ask yourself a series of who, what, when, where, how, and why questions: Who produces and maintains the site? Is it an established authority? What are the characteristics of the information—is it reliable, scholarly, and professional? When was the information produced? Is it up-to-date? Where did the information come from? Is it based on personal opinion, or is it based on experience, interviews, library research, questionnaires, and experiments? How is the information presented? Is it clear and accurate? Are there multiple points of view? Why is the information being presented, and who is the intended audience? Be very critical of information until you have thoroughly examined it.

Reading Tables and Graphs

Sociologists use tables and graphs to present demographic information and other statistics. *Demographics* are statistics about the characteristics of a population, such as age, sex, race, ethnicity, income, family size, and place of residence. Follow these steps to decode tables and graphs.

1. Begin by reading the title of the table or graph carefully. It will tell you what information is being presented.
2. Find out the source of the information. You will want to know whether the source is reliable and whether its techniques for gathering and presenting the data are sound.
3. Read any notes accompanying the table or graph. Not all tables and graphs have notes, but if notes are present, they offer further information about the data.
4. Examine any footnotes.
5. Look at the headings across the top and down the left-hand side of the table or graph. To observe any patterns in the data, it is usually necessary to keep both types of headings in mind.
6. Find out what units are being used. Data can be expressed in percentages, hundreds, thousands, millions, billions, means, and so forth.
7. Check for trends in the data. For tables, look down the columns (vertically) and across the rows (horizontally) for the highest figures, lowest figures, repeat numbers, irregularities, and sudden shifts.
8. Draw conclusions from your own observations. Look carefully at the figures, then write a narrative paragraph that summarizes your conclusions so that you are sure you understand what is being presented.

✓ **READING PROGRESS CHECK**

Generalizing Why must you understand basic statistical measures in order to decode the demographic information included in many graphs and tables?

LESSON 1 REVIEW

Reviewing Vocabulary
1. ***Identifying*** What is a representative sample?
2. ***Summarizing*** Why is participant observation sometimes necessary?

Using Your Notes
3. ***Examining*** Use your Key Ideas and Details graphic organizer to answer the following question: What is the main advantage of conducting field research?

Answering the Guiding Questions
4. ***Defining*** What research methods do sociologists use?
5. ***Describing*** What skills do sociologists use?

Writing Activity
6. ***Informative/Explanatory*** Choose a social issue that interests you. Briefly describe the issue and the type of research you would like to conduct on the topic. Explain which research methods you would use to conduct your research and why.

networks

There's More Online!

- ☑ **CARTOON** Sociological Research
- ☑ **DIAGRAM** A Spurious Correlation
- ☑ **GRAPHS** Positive and Negative Correlations
- ☑ **MAP** Cell Phone Use
- ☑ **SELF-CHECK QUIZ**

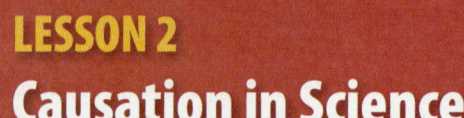

LESSON 2
Causation in Science

Reading HELPDESK

Academic Vocabulary
- variable
- intervention

Content Vocabulary
- causation
- multiple causation
- quantitative variable
- qualitative variable
- independent variable
- dependent variable
- intervening variable
- correlation
- spurious correlation

TAKING NOTES:
Key Ideas and Details

DEFINING As you read about causation in science, use a graphic organizer like the one below to record the meaning of each vocabulary word.

Word	Definition

ESSENTIAL QUESTIONS • How do sociologists do research? • What is ethical research?

IT MATTERS BECAUSE

Causation in science is the idea that one event leads to another event. Scientists assume that all events have causes, or determinants. Social events are so complex, however, that many factors may be identified as causes. Three standards must be met before causation can be proved.

The Nature of Causation

GUIDING QUESTION *Why do sociologists look for multiple causes?*

Scientists assume that an event occurs for a reason. According to the concept of **causation**, events occur in predictable, nonrandom ways. One event leads to another. Why does a ball thrown into the air return to the ground? Why do the planets stay in orbit around the sun? Today, the main goal of scientists is to discover the factors that cause events to happen. Social scientists look for the factors that cause social events to happen. This type of social research follows in the footsteps of early sociologists such as Auguste Comte and Émile Durkheim, who studied human social behavior in much the same way as a natural scientist would study the physical world. At the basis of this approach is the assumption that causation can be determined by collecting empirical evidence—evidence that can be verified through our senses.

Social events are too complex to be explained by any single factor. The concept of **multiple causation** states that an event occurs as a result of several factors working in combination. What, for example, causes crime? Cesare Lombroso, a nineteenth-century criminologist, mistakenly believed that the tendency to commit crimes was inherited and that criminals could be identified by physical traits such as large jaws or receding foreheads. Modern criminologists have shown that many factors contribute to crime, including peer pressure, the use of drugs, hopeless poverty, and poor parenting. Each of these single factors is called a *variable*.

☑ **READING PROGRESS CHECK**

Explaining Why is it important for sociologists to look for more than one cause when investigating a social event such as a crime?

46

Variables and Correlations

GUIDING QUESTION *What are variables and correlations?*

A **variable** is a characteristic—such as age, education, or occupation—that is subject to change. Variables can be *quantitative* or *qualitative, independent* or *dependent*.

Some materials have greater density than others. Some people have higher incomes than other people. Some students get better grades than other students. The literacy rate is higher in developed countries than in developing countries. Each of these characteristics is a **quantitative variable**, a variable that can be measured and given a numerical value. Because quantitative variables can be assigned numerical values, their analysis generally involves the use of mathematical operations and statistics. Quantitative analysis can be used to explain causation between variables and to make comparisons, examine relationships, test hypotheses, make forecasts, or measure change or differences.

In contrast, a **qualitative variable** is identified by membership in a category. It is an "either/or" or a "yes/no" variable. Sex, marital status, and group membership are three qualitative variables often used by sociologists. People are either male or female; they are married or unmarried; they are band members, football players, sophomores—or they are not. Qualitative variables are often used to categorize data for comparison. For example, social scientists might examine how men and women differ in their political attitudes. Similarly, they might use a qualitative variable such as marital status to compare a quantitative variable such as income.

When they conduct studies, sociologists and other scientists identify the qualitative and quantitative variables to be investigated. They then define these variables as either independent or dependent. The variable that is hypothesized to cause something to occur is the **independent variable**.

causation the belief that events occur in predictable ways and that one event leads to another

multiple causation the belief that an event occurs as a result of several factors working in combination

variable a characteristic that is subject to change

quantitative variable a characteristic that can be measured numerically

qualitative variable a characteristic that is defined by its presence or absence in a category

independent variable a characteristic that causes something to occur

A Global Perspective

CELL PHONE USE

Sometimes it seems as if everyone in the United States has a cell phone. In reality, cell phone use in the United States per 100 people ranks below that of less developed nations. In places that lack the wired networks necessary for landline phones, cell phones offer access to fast and inexpensive long-distance communication.

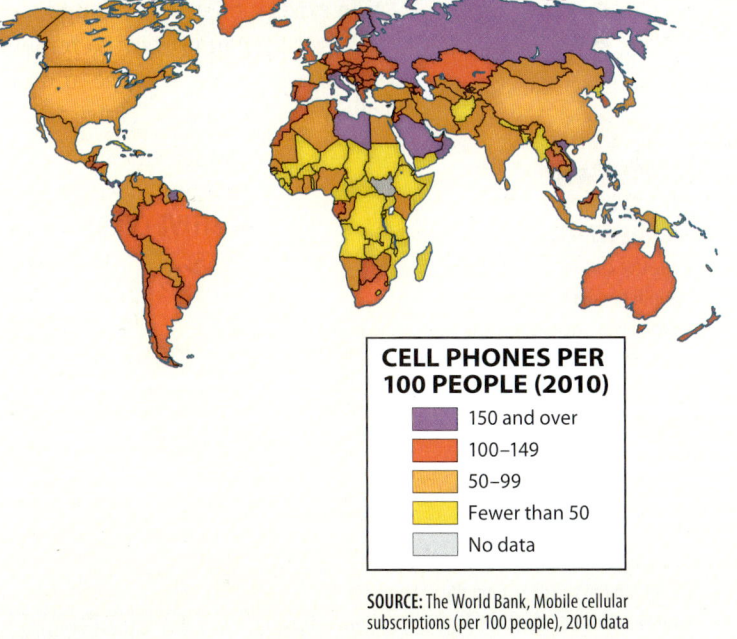

CELL PHONES PER 100 PEOPLE (2010)
- 150 and over
- 100–149
- 50–99
- Fewer than 50
- No data

SOURCE: The World Bank, Mobile cellular subscriptions (per 100 people), 2010 data

Geography Connection

1. **Places and Regions** Look at the map. In which range of use do Mexico, the United States, and Canada fall?
2. **Environment and Society** What environmental factors might make the use of cell phones a good alternative to landlines in regions such as the Caribbean and South America?

dependent variable a characteristic that reflects a change

The researcher changes, or looks for changes, in this variable. The **dependent variable** is what results from the change in the independent variable. For example, you might look at the time spent studying for a test as an independent variable that could cause a change in a grade—a dependent variable. Similarly, the independent variable of poverty is one of several independent variables that can produce a change in the dependent variable of hunger.

Whether a variable is dependent or independent can change depending on the situation. In a study of poverty, researchers might look at whether the level of poverty—the independent variable—affects the number of days a month families go hungry—the dependent variable. In this instance, the researchers are examining whether poverty causes hunger. In a study of crime, hunger might become the independent variable. In this instance, researchers might examine whether people who suffer from chronic hunger commit more crimes.

intervening variable a variable that changes the relationship between an independent and a dependent variable

intervention intervening action taken to influence the outcome of a particular event, condition, or process

An **intervening variable** influences the relationship between an independent and a dependent variable. The existence of a government support program, for example, may intervene between poverty and hunger. If a strong safety net exists, for instance, very poor parents and their children may experience no more hunger than those in the working class. Poverty is the cause of hunger but does not have to be if government **intervention** in the form of income and food exists. The poor *without* a safety net will experience more hunger. The poor *with* a safety net will not. Intervention serves as an intervening variable.

correlation a measure of the relationship between two variables

A **correlation** is simply a measure of how things are related to one another. When a change in a trait, behavior, or an event (independent variable) is tied to a change in another trait, behavior, or event (dependent variable), a correlation exists. The correlation may be positive or negative.

A *positive correlation* exists if both the independent variable and the dependent variable change in the same direction. A positive correlation exists if we find that grades (dependent variable) improve as study time increases (independent variable) or if we discover that hunger increases as the level of poverty increases.

In a *negative correlation*, the variables change in opposite directions. An increase in the independent variable is linked to a decrease in the dependent variable. A negative correlation exists if we find that grades (dependent variable) go down as time spent watching television (independent variable) increases. A negative correlation exists if the level of hunger decreases as government intervention increases.

It is very important to remember that the existence of a correlation does not necessarily mean a cause-and-effect relationship exists. People with long arms often have long legs. However, the length of a person's arms does not cause the

GRAPHS >

POSITIVE AND NEGATIVE CORRELATIONS

In a positive correlation, increases in the independent variable are associated with increases in the dependent variable. In a negative correlation, increases in the independent variable are associated with decreases in the dependent variable.

▶ **CRITICAL THINKING**

1. **Drawing Conclusions** What conclusion can you draw from the positive correlation chart?
2. **Interpreting** What does the negative correlation chart show?

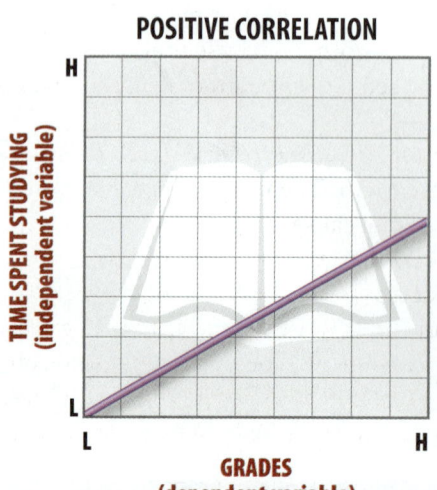
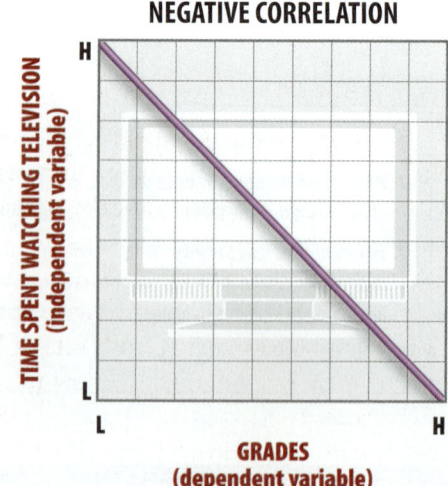

CARTOON

SOCIOLOGICAL RESEARCH The woman in this cartoon believes social science research is not very scientific.

▶ **CRITICAL THINKING**

1. **Speculating** Why do you think the woman responds to the social scientist in such a manner?
2. **Defending** If you were the social scientist, how would you respond to the woman?

legs to grow longer. Both of these variables are controlled by other factors. It is much easier to show a correlation between two variables than it is to show causation.

✓ **READING PROGRESS CHECK**

Making Connections What is the relationship between variables and correlations?

Standards for Showing Causation

GUIDING QUESTION *How do sociologists determine causation?*

In a causal relationship, one variable actually causes the other variable to occur. Three standards are commonly used to determine causal relationships. Let's look at the example of church attendance and juvenile delinquency to illustrate the three standards.

Standard 1: *Two variables must be correlated.* For two variables to be correlated, they must change together. The direction of change does not matter. One variable can increase while the other decreases, or both variables can increase or decrease. In the case of juvenile delinquency and church attendance, some researchers have found that rates of juvenile delinquency increase as church attendance declines. This is a negative correlation. Does this negative correlation mean that not attending church causes higher rates of juvenile delinquency? Not necessarily. There could be another variable that is affecting the correlation. To answer this question, the second standard of causality must be met.

Standard 2: *All other possible factors must be taken into account.* Remember that correlation is not the same thing as causation. The fact that two events are correlated does not automatically mean that one causes the other. The apparent connection between variables can actually be the result of other factors. Think about the previous example of the length of a person's arms and legs being correlated. It is obvious that having long arms does not cause your legs to grow. Other factors are causing both sets of limbs to grow. The correlation between long arms and long legs is known as a **spurious correlation**—an apparent relationship between two variables that is actually caused by a third variable affecting both of the other variables.

spurious correlation a relationship between two variables that is actually caused by a third factor

Sociological Research Methods **49**

Connecting Sociology to History

THE SCIENTIFIC METHOD

Sociologists use various research methods to make observations and develop theories about society. In the 1600s, Galileo similarly used research and observation to present new evidence that challenged traditional assumptions about the world.

Europe was an exciting place for those interested in using scientific methods in the search for truth. Copernicus was an astronomer who held that the sun was at the center of the solar system. Traditional belief at the time placed Earth at the center. Galileo sought to replace traditional myths with new knowledge based on reason and observation. This is one key aspect of the scientific method.

Galileo and his telescope

PRIMARY SOURCE

"In 1609, . . . Galileo . . . turned his recently constructed telescope to the heavens, and through his startling observations made available to astronomy the first qualitatively new evidence it had known since the ancients. And each of his observations—the craters and mountains on the surface of the Moon, the moving spots on the Sun, the four moons revolving around Jupiter, the phases of Venus, the "unbelievably" numerous individual stars of the Milky Way—was interpreted by Galileo as powerful evidence in favor of the Copernican heliocentric [sun-centered] theory.

. . . Many individuals not previously involved in scientific studies now took up the telescope and saw for themselves the nature of the new Copernican universe. Astronomy, by virtue of the telescope and Galileo's compelling writings, became of vital interest to more than specialists. Successive generations of late Renaissance and post-Renaissance Europeans, increasingly willing to doubt the absolute authority of traditional doctrines both ancient and ecclesiastical, were finding the Copernican theory not only plausible but liberating. A new celestial world was opening up to the Western mind, just as a new terrestrial world was being opened by the global explorers."

—Richard Tarnas,
from *The Passion of the Western Mind*, 1991

DBQ ▶ CRITICAL THINKING

1. **Identifying Perspectives** How do you think Galileo's view of the universe differed from mainstream views of the early 1600s?
2. **Comparing** What challenges do you think Galileo faced when presenting his ideas? How might sociologists face similar challenges?

Spotting the spurious correlation between long arms and long legs is easy. It is not always as easy to spot spurious correlations in social data. It often takes careful detective work on the part of social scientists to discover the other factors that are driving causation. One way that social scientists do this is by holding constant a variable they think might be causing a spurious correlation. If the correlation disappears when the variable is held constant, the relationship being tested is spurious. If the correlation remains, the relationship between the two variables may not be spurious.

Determining whether the relationship between church attendance and juvenile delinquency is spurious or causal is a good example of the challenges that social scientists face. Before researchers could determine the nature of the relationship, they had to take other factors into consideration. In this instance, the age variable revealed that the relationship between church attendance and delinquency is not a causal one. Age is related to both church attendance (older adolescents attend church less frequently) and delinquency (older adolescents are more likely to be delinquents). Thus, the correlation between church attendance and juvenile delinquency is spurious. Finding hidden causes and

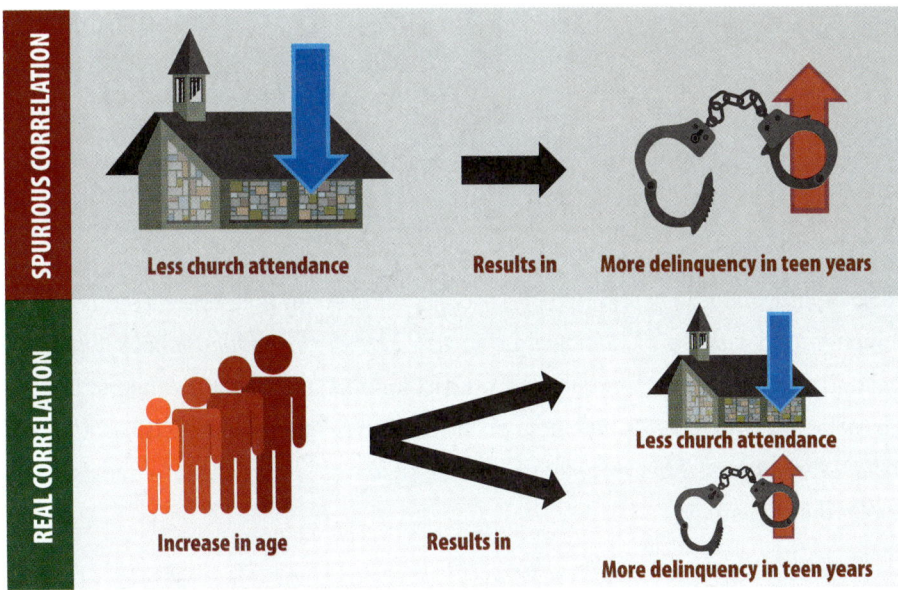

DIAGRAM
A SPURIOUS CORRELATION
The correlation between juvenile delinquency and not attending church is a spurious correlation.

▶ **CRITICAL THINKING**
1. **Analyzing Visuals** Why is the relationship spurious?
2. **Identifying** What is the actual correlation?

exposing spurious correlations is one of the greatest challenges in scientific research.

Standard 3: *A change in the independent variable must occur before a change in the dependent variable can occur.* Finding the existence of a positive or negative correlation between two variables and ruling out that the correlation is spurious are not enough to establish causation. Researchers must still establish whether the independent variable is causing the dependent variable to change. For this to be the case, the change in the independent variable must occur before the change in the dependent variable.

Consider once again the correlation between church attendance and juvenile delinquency. Forget for a moment that age is related to both level of church attendance and juvenile delinquency. Focus instead on these two questions: Do people stop attending church before they become delinquents? Or does delinquent behavior occur before people stop attending church? It is not possible to determine which comes first. Thus, even if age were not a factor in this correlation and no other factor could be found, causality could not be established, since it is not possible to determine that the independent variable changed before the change in the dependent variable occurred.

✓ **READING PROGRESS CHECK**

Defining What are the three standards for showing causation? Explain your response.

LESSON 2 REVIEW

Reviewing Vocabulary
1. **Identifying** What is a quantitative variable?
2. **Using Context Clues** What is a spurious correlation?

Using Your Notes
3. **Drawing Conclusions** Use your graphic organizer to answer the following question: Why might it sometimes be difficult to spot a spurious correlation?

Answering the Guiding Questions
4. **Explaining** Why do sociologists look for multiple causes?
5. **Defining** What are variables and correlations?
6. **Summarizing** How do sociologists determine causation?

Writing Activity
7. **Informative/Explanatory** In your own words, explain the difference between correlation and causation. Illustrate your explanation with an example not found in the text.

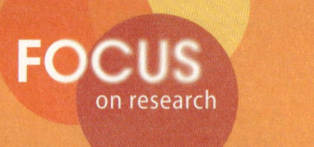

FOCUS on research

Case Study

CCSS

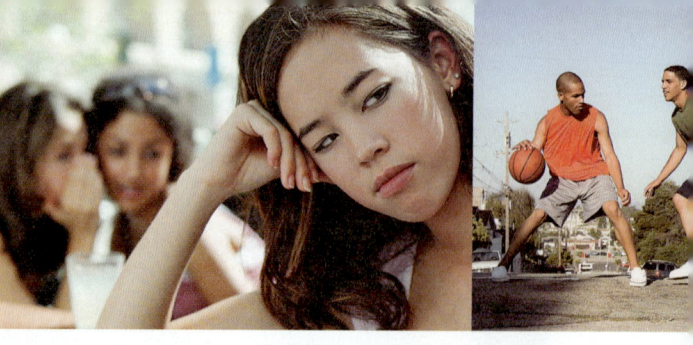

School Talk: Gender and Adolescent Culture

Sociologist Donna Eder and two of her colleagues spent three years studying the language and culture of adolescents in a Midwestern middle school. They listened to students as they exchanged gossip, insults, and teasing. The purpose of the research was to determine how peer cultures maintain and resist gender and social stereotypes. This excerpt describes research methods and ethical issues involved in the study.

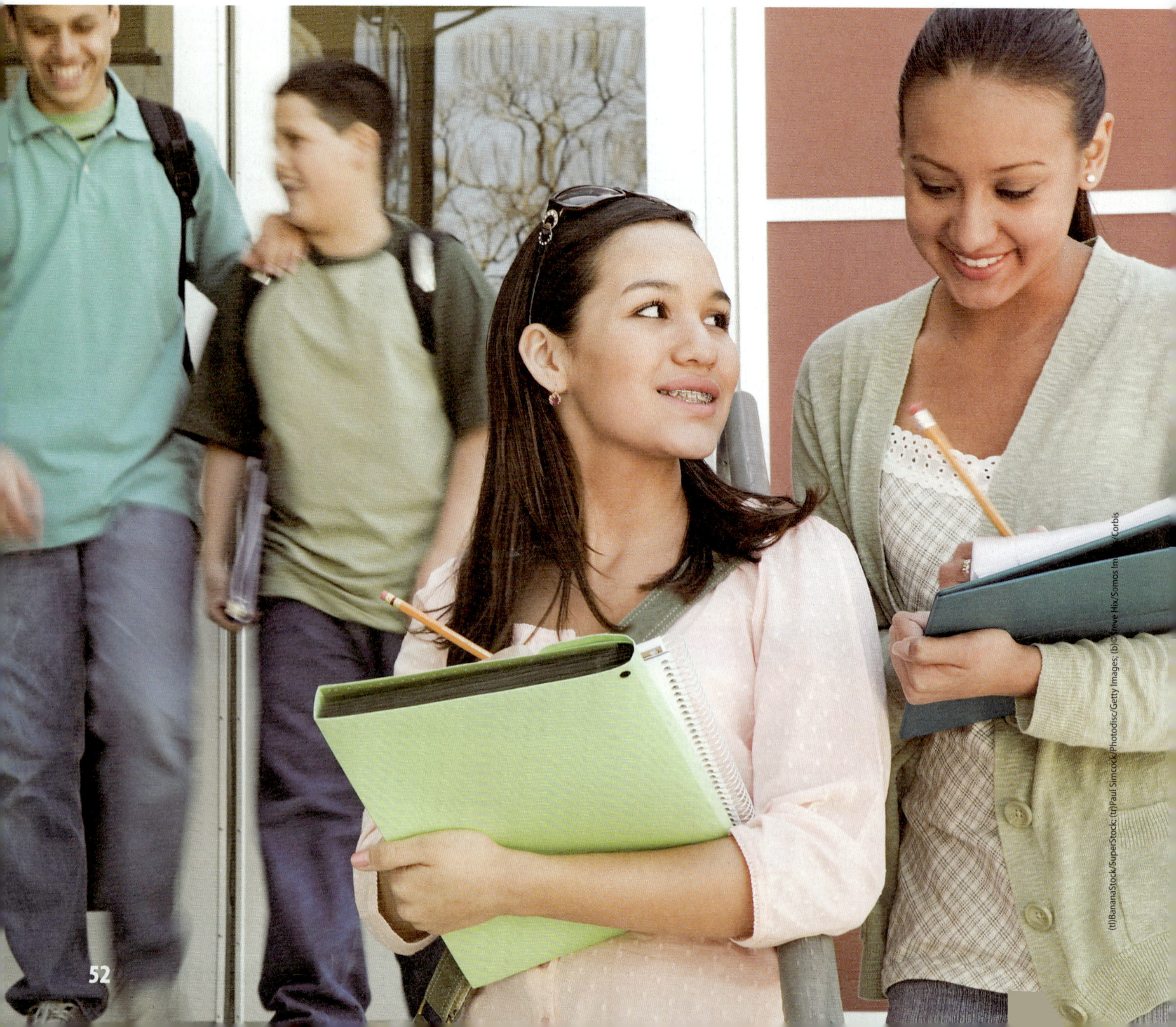

(tl)BananaStock/SuperStock; (tr)Paul Simcock/Photodisc/Getty Images; (b)Steve Hix/Somos Images/Corbis

PRIMARY SOURCE

Collecting Data on Students' Experiences

"We used a variety of means to collect data on students' experiences with peers in school. All four researchers observed lunchtime interaction at least twice weekly for periods of time ranging from five months to twelve months. We never took notes openly during the lunch period, but sometimes recorded brief notes in the bathroom or hallway between lunch sessions. These notes were expanded upon and all notes were recorded fully immediately after leaving the setting.

Donna Eder and Steve Parker also attended male and female extracurricular activities twice weekly for an entire academic year. Given the importance of athletic activities and cheerleading, we focused primarily on them. . . . In addition, we observed choir and band practices and concerts, talent shows, and the one school play. . . . We were able to take some notes during these events, since our roles were more those of observers than participants. Afterward, we expanded on these notes and recorded them fully. . . .

Once we had been in the setting for several months, we began doing informal interviews with individuals or groups of students on issues that arose from our observations. They included questions about the meaning of popularity, attitudes toward other students in the school, and views on male-female relationships. While some were so informal they were simply recorded as field notes, ten of the more extensive interviews were tape-recorded and transcribed in full.

Finally, we tape-recorded conversations in most of the lunch groups which we observed. Typically, we sat with the group members for three to seven months prior to taping them, so they were already used to our presence. We got written permission from both the students and their parents before we made a recording. On the permission forms we assured them that no one who knew them would be able to listen to or watch the tapes. We also told them that their real names would not be used in any written report. To further insure the participants' privacy, we have also changed all names of identifying locations and modified discussions about particular people or events. . . ."

Ethical issues. "When we first began the study, we openly informed all of the students that we were from Indiana University and were doing a study of middle school students. We assured students of our concern with protecting their privacy by not using their actual names or revealing private information to others who might know them. The only concern expressed by a few students was that they not get in trouble for swearing. . . . Several students again expressed a similar concern when they were first tape-recorded, asking us who would be allowed to hear the tapes. We assured them that the tapes would not be seen or heard by anyone who could identify them. . . .

We were prepared in advance for these particular ethical issues. . . . Other ethical dilemmas arose during the course of the study for which we did not have clear solutions. [Two of the researchers] . . . witnessed several incidents of verbal harassment, and . . . one incident that included physical harassment. Since we had tried from the start to minimize our roles as authority figures in the school, neither of them intervened as adults to stop these incidents. Instead they relied on non-intrusive strategies such as not participating themselves, or drawing the attention of others away from the target of ridicule to some other activity.

These incidents raise challenging questions about the role of researchers as observers of naturally occurring behavior, as opposed to interventionists who try to change the behavior of others, especially if it appears to be cruel or abusive. Had we decided to intervene more directly, we would have been seen as authority figures, and it is likely that students would no longer have acted as naturally in our presence, thus limiting the extent to which we could gain information about peer interactions. On the other hand, it was deeply disturbing to the researchers to witness these events without intervening. We struggled with the question of whether nonintervention might convey an implicit message that such behavior is acceptable to adults."

— from *School Talk: Gender and Adolescent Culture*, 1995

> "We used a variety of means to collect data on students' experiences with peers in school."

Working With the Research

1. **Drawing Conclusions** Why did the researchers avoid openly taking notes during the lunch period?
2. **Identifying Central Issues** What steps did the researchers take to protect student privacy? Why?
3. **Evaluating** The researchers chose not to intervene when they witnessed harassment. Do you agree or disagree with their actions? Explain why.

networks

There's More Online!

- ☑ **GRAPHIC ORGANIZER** Procedures and Ethics in Research
- ☑ **GRAPHIC ORGANIZER** The Research Process
- ☑ **IMAGE** Ethical Standards in Research
- ☑ **SELF-CHECK QUIZ**

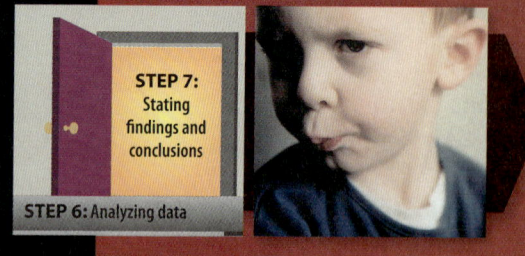

LESSON 3
Procedures and Ethics in Research

Reading HELPDESK

Academic Vocabulary
- ethics

Content Vocabulary
- scientific method
- hypothesis

TAKING NOTES:
Key Ideas and Details

LISTING As you read about procedures and ethics in research, use a graphic organizer like the one below to list the main ideas.

Procedures and Ethics in Research
- Scientific Method
  - •
  - •
  - •
  - •
  - •
- Ethical Research Measures
  - •
  - •
  - •

ESSENTIAL QUESTIONS • *How do sociologists do research?* • *What is ethical research?*

IT MATTERS BECAUSE

The research process is made up of several distinct steps. These steps represent an ideal. It is not always necessary or even possible that they be strictly followed. Researchers have an ethical obligation to protect participants' privacy and to avoid deceiving or harming them. Preserving the rights of subjects must be weighed against the value of the knowledge to be gained.

Steps for Doing Research

GUIDING QUESTION *What is the scientific method?*

Functionalist theorists view science as an important social institution that is guided by norms, or rules defining appropriate and inappropriate behavior. According to sociologist Robert K. Merton, these norms seek to ensure that science is not unduly influenced by other factors in society, such as political ideology or the pursuit of material gain. The norms help hold scientists together as a group and establish the search for reliable and testable knowledge as the primary goal of science.

The **scientific method** is a research model central to science as a social institution. One source of sociological knowledge is deductive reasoning, whereby general principles are inferred from specific examples. Another source of knowledge is inductive reasoning, in which a researcher arrives at a general conclusion based on specific observations. The following steps are commonly part of the scientific method:

1. **Identify the Problem.** Researchers begin by choosing an object or topic for study. Most topics are chosen because they interest the researcher, address a social problem, test a major theory, or respond to a government agency's or organization's needs. For example, a government agency may notice that teenage suicide rates have increased in a particular state. Alternatively, the social problem of teenage suicide might be of particular interest to a sociologist who thus chooses to study the problem.

2. **Review the Literature.** Once the object or topic of study has been identified, the researcher must find out all he or she can about any

earlier research. This process is called a *literature search*. For example, a sociologist investigating suicide will probably develop an approach related to the classic study of suicide by Émile Durkheim as well as to the work of other sociologists who have since researched the topic.

3. **Formulate Hypotheses.** The next step is to develop a *hypothesis* based on what is known. A **hypothesis** is a testable statement of relationships among well-defined variables. One hypothesis might be, "The longer couples are married, the less likely they are to divorce." The independent variable is length of marriage, and the dependent variable is divorce.

4. **Develop a Research Design.** A research design states the procedures the researcher will follow for collecting and analyzing data. Will the study be a survey or a case study? If it is a survey, will data be collected from a cross-section of an entire population, such as the Harris and Gallup polls, or will a sample be selected from only one city? Will simple percentages or more sophisticated statistical methods be used? These and many other questions must be answered so the researcher will have a sound plan to follow. Furthermore, both the hypotheses being investigated and the availability of the data will likely affect the final research design.

5. **Collect Data.** There are three basic ways of gathering data in sociological research—asking people questions, observing behavior, and analyzing existing materials and records. Sociologists studying interracial marriages could question couples about ways they communicate. They could locate an organization with many interracially married couples and observe couples' behavior. Or they could compare the divorce rate among interracially married couples with the divorce rate of the population as a whole.

6. **Analyze Data.** Once the data have been collected and classified, they can be analyzed to determine whether the hypotheses are supported. It is not unlike putting together pieces of a jigsaw puzzle. This is not as easy or automatic as it sounds, because results are not always obvious. Because the same data can be interpreted in several ways, judgments have to be made. Guarding against personal preferences for particular outcomes is especially important in this phase of research.

7. **State Findings and Conclusions.** After analyzing the data, a researcher is ready to state the conclusions of the study. It is during this phase that the methods are described (for example, a survey or a case study) and hypotheses are formally accepted, rejected, or modified. The conclusions might also suggest new avenues for research. By making the research procedures public, scientists make it possible for others to duplicate the research, conduct a slightly modified study, or go in a very different direction.

Some sociologists believe that the scientific method is too rigid to be used in studying human society. Even though most sociologists do follow the model, they do not necessarily follow it mechanically. They may conduct exploratory studies prior to stating hypotheses and developing research designs. Or they may change their hypotheses and research designs as their investigations proceed.

✓ **READING PROGRESS CHECK**

Sequencing What are the steps in the scientific method?

scientific method the recognition and formulation of a problem, the collection of data through observation and experiment, and the formulation and testing of hypotheses

hypothesis testable statement of relationships among variables

⌄ **GRAPHIC ORGANIZER**

THE RESEARCH PROCESS
The scientific method presents seven steps to guide research.

▶ **CRITICAL THINKING**

1. **Assessing** Why do you think the scientific method places literature review before hypotheses formulation?

2. **Analyzing Visuals** Do you think all of the steps have to occur in this order? Why?

THE RESEARCH PROCESS

STEP 7: Stating findings and conclusions
STEP 6: Analyzing data
STEP 5: Collecting data
STEP 4: Developing a research design
STEP 3: Formulating hypotheses
STEP 2: Reviewing the literature
STEP 1: Identifying a problem

Connecting Sociology to Psychology

THE "MONSTER STUDY"

Even well-intentioned research can cross ethical lines. In 1939 Mary Tudor, a graduate student in clinical psychology at the University of Iowa, set out to prove that stuttering was behavioral, not physiological. Wendell Johnson, Tudor's thesis director and a severe stutterer himself, held that overreactions by parents to slight stutters caused children to become full-blown stutterers. If stuttering was behavioral, it should be possible to induce stuttering in children who did not stutter. Johnson helped Tudor devise a research plan to test this theory.

Tudor selected 22 children who lived in an orphanage in Davenport, Iowa. Ten of the children had been labeled as stutterers by the orphanage staff. The remaining children did not stutter. Tudor conditioned 6 of the non-stutterers to believe that they actually stuttered and told 5 of the stutterers that they did not stutter. According to Johnson's theory, the conditioning should have caused the six non-stutterers to begin stuttering. It did not. The conditioning did, however, lead some of the children to develop behavioral problems.

The study, which came to be nicknamed the "Monster Study" because it reminded people of Nazi experiments on humans, raised serious ethical questions and eventually led to a lawsuit. Even Tudor was concerned about the effects the study had on the children. Johnson added to the ethical debate by burying the research findings that went against his own theory.

A study to try to determine if stuttering was a behavioral problem crossed ethical boundaries and caused harm to its subjects.

▶ **CRITICAL THINKING**

1. **Analyzing Ethical Issues** Why was Mary Tudor's research seen as unethical?
2. **Identifying Bias** Why were Wendell Johnson's actions biased?

Ethics in Social Research

GUIDING QUESTION *How do sociologists perform research ethically?*

Research is a distinctly human activity. Although there are principles for conducting research, such as objectivity and verifiability, scientists sometimes fail to live up to these principles. At times, they even violate the **ethics,** or the rules of acceptable conduct, of research.

Unfortunately, there is a long list of examples of lapses in ethics in medical research. Such ethics violations have occurred in the United States and throughout the world, and some of them have occurred rather recently. During the Nuremberg trials following World War II, 16 Nazi doctors were convicted of conducting sadistic experiments on concentration camp inmates. In the United States, from 1932 to 1972, the Public Health Service, an agency of the federal government, deliberately did not treat 399 syphilitic African American agricultural workers and day laborers so that biomedical researchers could study the full evolution of the disease. Federal investigators in the United States also have documented more than ten years of fraud in some of the most important breast cancer research ever done. For twenty years, researchers at Germany's University of Heidelberg used human corpses, those of adults and children, in high-speed automobile crash tests. Several universities in the United States also admitted to using corpses in crash tests, as did researchers in Austria.

ethics rules of conduct that distinguish between acceptable and unacceptable human actions

Several social scientists also have been criticized for conducting research considered unethical. In each case, subjects were placed in stressful situations without being informed of the true nature of the experiments. Sometimes the seriousness of the situation is only discovered as the research unfolds. In the Stanford Prison Experiment, for example, researchers selected young men to play the roles of prisoners and guards in a mock prison. The researchers hoped to test whether the prison setting or the character of the prisoners made prisons violent. The situation became so realistic, however, that the "guards" and "prisoners" quickly became hostile and embittered toward one another. The researchers were forced to stop the two-week experiment after the first week to protect the physical and mental health of the subjects.

More often, however, sociologists routinely protect the rights of their research subjects and avoid deceiving or harming them. Sometimes researchers must make difficult decisions about morally questionable behavior in order to act ethically. For example, Mario Brajuha, a graduate student at a major American university, kept detailed field notes while doing a participant observation study of working in a restaurant. Because of suspected arson at a restaurant where Brajuha was employed as a waiter, his field notes became an object of interest to the police and the courts. For two years, he refused to reveal the contents of his field notes, even in the face of a subpoena and the threat of imprisonment. Brajuha was protecting the privacy rights of those individuals described in his notes.

Conducting ethical research means showing objectivity; using superior research standards; reporting findings and methods truthfully; and protecting the rights, privacy, integrity, dignity, and freedom of research subjects. The American Sociological Association has published guidelines for conducting research. Briefly put, the Code of Ethics is concerned with getting the greatest possible benefit with the least possible harm.

✓ **READING PROGRESS CHECK**

Evaluating Why is a code of ethics important in social research?

Quick Case Study

HOW DO YOU MAKE A RESEARCH PLAN?
Select a topic you would like to research. Then briefly outline how you would use the scientific method to implement your research.

Procedure
1. Use the steps of the scientific method as an outline. Identify your problem, list two examples of research on the same topic, formulate your hypothesis, and describe how you would go about the rest of the steps.
2. List any ethical considerations you need to consider.

Analysis
As you read through your research plan, consider these questions.
1. How does your plan reflect the scientific method? If it deviates, how and why did you choose to do so?
2. Are there any ethical considerations? How would you handle these?

LESSON 3 REVIEW

Reviewing Vocabulary
1. ***Identifying*** What is a hypothesis?

Using Your Notes
2. ***Making Connections*** Use your graphic organizer to answer the following question: How do the scientific method and ethical research measures work together?

Answering the Guiding Questions
3. ***Describing*** What is the scientific method?
4. ***Summarizing*** How do sociologists perform research ethically?

Writing Activity
5. ***Argument*** Write a brief paragraph responding to these questions: Can secret observation of people ever be considered ethical in research? Why or why not?

American Sociological Association's Code of Ethics

> **What It Means**
> **The Preamble** The ASA's Code of Ethics consists of a preamble, five general principles, and specific ethical standards.

Preamble

This Code of Ethics articulates a common set of values upon which sociologists build their professional and scientific work. The Code is intended to provide both the general principles and the rules to cover professional situations encountered by sociologists. It has as its primary goal the welfare and protection of the individuals and groups with whom sociologists work. It is the individual responsibility of each sociologist to aspire to the highest possible standards of conduct in research, teaching, practice, and service.

The development of a dynamic set of ethical standards for a sociologist's work-related conduct requires a personal commitment to a lifelong effort to act ethically; to encourage ethical behavior by students, supervisors, supervisees, employers, employees, and colleagues; and to consult with others as needed concerning ethical problems. Each sociologist supplements, but does not violate, the values and rules specified in the Code of Ethics based on guidance drawn from personal values, culture, and experience.

> **What It Means**
> **General Principles** The second part, the General Principles, consists of five general ethical principles to which sociologists should adhere.

General Principles

The following General Principles are aspirational and serve as a guide for sociologists in determining ethical courses of action in various contexts. They exemplify the highest ideals of professional conduct.

Principle A: Professional Competence

Sociologists strive to maintain the highest levels of competence in their work; they recognize the limitations of their expertise; and they undertake only those tasks for which they are qualified by education, training, or experience. They recognize the need for ongoing education in order to remain professionally competent; and they utilize the appropriate scientific, professional, technical, and administrative resources needed to ensure competence in their professional activities. They consult with other professionals when necessary for the benefit of their students, research participants, and clients.

Principle B: Integrity

Sociologists are honest, fair, and respectful of others in their professional activities—in research, teaching, practice, and service. Sociologists do not knowingly act in ways that **jeopardize** either their own or others' professional welfare. Sociologists conduct their affairs in ways that inspire trust and confidence; they do not knowingly make statements that are false, misleading, or deceptive.

jeopardize: to put at risk

Principle C: Professional and Scientific Responsibility

Sociologists adhere to the highest scientific and professional standards and accept responsibility for their work. Sociologists understand that they form a community and show respect for other sociologists even when they disagree on theoretical, methodological, or personal approaches to professional activities. Sociologists value the public trust in sociology and are concerned about their ethical behavior and that of other sociologists that might compromise that trust. While endeavoring always to be collegial, sociologists must never let the desire to be **collegial** outweigh their shared responsibility for ethical behavior. When appropriate, they consult with colleagues in order to prevent or avoid unethical conduct.

collegial: mutually respectful

Principle D: Respect for People's Rights, Dignity, and Diversity

Sociologists respect the rights, dignity, and worth of all people. They strive to eliminate bias in their professional activities, and they do not tolerate any forms of discrimination based on age; gender; race; ethnicity; national origin; religion; sexual orientation; disability; health conditions; or marital, domestic, or parental status. They are sensitive to cultural, individual, and role differences in serving, teaching, and studying groups of people with distinctive characteristics. In all of their work-related activities, sociologists acknowledge the rights of others to hold values, attitudes, and opinions that differ from their own.

Principle E: Social Responsibility

Sociologists are aware of their professional and scientific responsibility to the communities and societies in which they live and work. They apply and make public their knowledge in order to contribute to the public good. When undertaking research, they strive to advance the science of sociology and to serve the public good.

Ethical Standards

The complete text of the Ethical Standards can be found at the ASA Web site. Excerpts from this code are reproduced here.

1. Professional and Scientific Standards

Sociologists adhere to the highest possible technical standards that are reasonable and responsible in their research, teaching, practice, and service activities. They rely on scientifically and professionally derived knowledge; act with honesty and integrity; and avoid untrue, deceptive, or undocumented statements in undertaking work-related functions or activities.

2. Competence

(a) Sociologists conduct research, teach, practice, and provide service only within the boundaries of their competence, based on their education, training, supervised experience, or appropriate professional experience.

3. Representation and Misuse of Expertise

(c) Because sociologists' scientific and professional judgments and actions may affect the lives of others, they are alert to and guard against personal, financial, social, organizational, or political factors that might lead to misuse of their knowledge, expertise, or influence.

4. Delegation and Supervision

(a) Sociologists provide proper training and supervision to their students, supervisees, or employees and take reasonable steps to see that such persons perform services responsibly, competently, and ethically.

5. Nondiscrimination

Sociologists do not engage in discrimination in their work based on age; gender; race; ethnicity; national origin; religion; sexual orientation; disability; health conditions; marital; domestic, or parental status; or any other applicable basis **proscribed** by law.

6. Non-exploitation

(a) Whether for personal, economic, or professional advantage, sociologists do not exploit persons over whom they have direct or indirect supervisory, evaluative, or other authority such as students, supervisees, employees, or research participants.

---

proscribed: forbidden

7. Harassment

Sociologists do not engage in harassment of any person, including students, supervisees, employees, or research participants. Harassment consists of a single intense and severe act or of multiple persistent or pervasive acts which are demeaning, abusive, offensive, or create a hostile professional or workplace environment. Sexual harassment may include sexual solicitation, physical advance, or verbal or non-verbal conduct that is sexual in nature. Racial harassment may include unnecessary, exaggerated, or unwarranted attention or attack, whether verbal or non-verbal, because of a person's race or ethnicity.

8. Employment Decisions

Sociologists have an obligation to adhere to the highest ethical standards when participating in employment-related decisions, when seeking employment, or when planning to resign from a position.

9. Conflicts of Interest

Sociologists maintain the highest degree of integrity in their professional work and avoid conflicts of interest and the appearance of conflict. Conflicts of interest arise when sociologists' personal or financial interests prevent them from performing their professional work in an unbiased manner.

10. Public Communication

Sociologists adhere to the highest professional standards in public communications about their professional services, credentials and expertise, work products, or publications, whether these communications are from themselves or from others

11. Confidentiality

Sociologists have an obligation to ensure that **confidential** information is protected. They do so to ensure the integrity of research and the open communication with research participants and to protect sensitive information obtained in research, teaching, practice, and service. When gathering confidential information, sociologists should take into account the long-term uses of the information, including its potential placement in public archives or the examination of the information by other researchers or practitioners.

What It Means

Harassment As with other professionals, sociologists are legally bound to avoid conduct that purposely and unjustifiably causes distress or discomfort to those they study or with whom they work.

confidential: private

What It Means

Informed Consent Like other professionals who involve human research subjects, sociologists get informed consent from their research participants before involving them in a study.

What It Means

Plagiarism, the stealing of someone else's work, is not only unethical, it is a crime if it violates copyright law.

12. Informed Consent

Informed consent is a basic ethical tenet of scientific research on human populations. Sociologists do not involve a human being as a subject in research without the informed consent of the subject or the subject's legally authorized representative, except as otherwise specified in this Code. Sociologists recognize the possibility of undue influence or subtle pressures on subjects that may derive from researchers' expertise or authority, and they take this into account in designing informed consent procedures.

13. Research Planning, Implementation, and Dissemination

Sociologists have an obligation to promote the integrity of research and to ensure that they comply with the ethical tenets of science in the planning, implementation, and dissemination of research. They do so in order to advance knowledge, to minimize the possibility that results will be misleading, and to protect the rights of research participants.

14. Plagiarism

(a) In publications, presentations, teaching, practice, and service, sociologists explicitly identify, credit, and reference the author when they take data or material verbatim from another person's written work, whether it is published, unpublished, or electronically available.

(b) In their publications, presentations, teaching, practice, and service, sociologists provide acknowledgment of and reference to the use of others' work, even if the work is not quoted verbatim or paraphrased, and they do not present others' work as their own whether it is published, unpublished, or electronically available.

15. Authorship Credit

(a) Sociologists take responsibility and credit, including authorship credit, only for work they have actually performed or to which they have contributed.

(b) Sociologists ensure that principal authorship and other publication credits are based on the relative scientific or professional contributions of the individuals involved, regardless of their status. In claiming or determining the ordering of authorship, sociologists seek to reflect accurately the contributions of main participants in the research and writing process.

(c) A student is usually listed as principal author on any multiple-authored publication that substantially derives from the student's dissertation or thesis.

DBQ ▶ CRITICAL THINKING

1. **Academic Integrity** Find a copy of your school's honor code. What parts of that code have a parallel in the ASA's Code of Ethics?

2. **Making Connections** What are the connections among nondiscrimination, non-exploitation, and harassment?

3. **Informative/Explanatory** Using the ASA's Code of Ethics as a model, write your own personal code of ethics.

CHAPTER 2 Assessment

Directions: On a separate sheet of paper, answer the questions below. Make sure you read carefully and answer all parts of the questions.

Lesson Review

Lesson 1

1. **Identifying Central Issues** Why is it important to understand research methods in sociology?
2. **Contrasting** How is quantitative research different from qualitative research? Provide at least one example of each type of research.
3. **Describing** Why do program evaluations often combine research methods?
4. **Evaluating** What are some questions you should ask yourself when evaluating Internet resources?

Lesson 2

5. **Explaining** What does the concept of multiple causation help explain?
6. **Differentiating** How is an independent variable different from a dependent variable? Provide an example to illustrate the difference.
7. **Making Connections** If a correlation exists between increasing vitamin intake and living longer, is the correlation considered positive or negative?

Lesson 3

8. **Explaining** Why do some sociologists choose not to adhere strictly to the scientific method in their research?
9. **Sequencing** What are the seven steps that guide the research process?
10. **Interpreting Significance** Why is a code of ethics important?

Critical Thinking

11. **Drawing Inferences** Think about the different types of research methods sociologists use and the skills they need to perform their research. What personal characteristics would a sociologist need to have in order to be effective at his or her job? Why?

21st Century Skills
USING GRAPHS

Use the graph to answer the following questions.

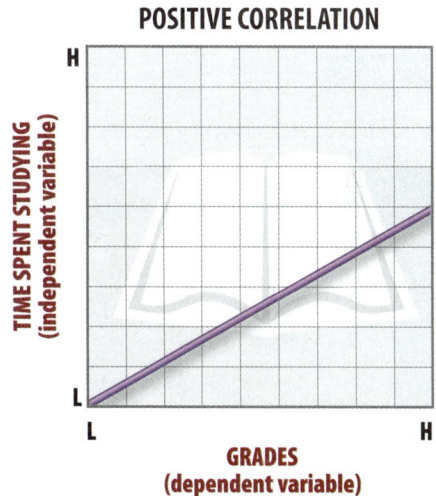

POSITIVE CORRELATION

TIME SPENT STUDYING (independent variable)

GRADES (dependent variable)

12. **Identifying Cause and Effect** What is the cause of better grades, according to this graph? What might be some additional causes?
13. **Using Graphs** What does the positive correlation reveal about the independent variable (studying) and the dependent variable (grades)?

Need Extra Help?

If You've Missed Question	1	2	3	4	5	6	7	8	9	10	11	12	13
Go to page	36	37	42	44–45	46	48	48	55	57	54	36–45	48	48

Sociological Research Methods

CHAPTER 2 Assessment

Directions: On a separate sheet of paper, answer the questions below. Make sure you read carefully and answer all parts of the questions.

Exploring the Essential Questions

14 *Gathering Information* Collect data for a research project by conducting interviews. Go to a location on campus or near your home, like a coffee shop. Interview five people for at least five minutes. Investigate how they spend their time—socializing, working at a computer, drinking coffee during a break. Take notes. Record factual observations. How much time per day do they spend there? What did you find out about who spends time there doing what kinds of activities?

DBQ Analyzing Primary Sources

PRIMARY SOURCE

Use the cartoon to answer the following question.

"The public and the scientific community can have the utmost faith that no one on our research staff would *ever* use the muscle enhancer serum to his or her benefit. And here with some further thoughts on this is our chief researcher, Dr. Small."

15 *Making Connections* In this chapter, you read the problems sociologists face when they conduct research with human subjects. In this cartoon, what position does the cartoonist take on this issue? Can you suggest who might be the supervisor of the people in the audience?

College and Career Readiness Skills

16 *Exploring the Issue* Research careers in ethics in sociology. What types of sociological studies or subdisciplines in sociology might require the most vigilance when it comes to ethical treatment of humans and animals? Look for information about who the employers are and what education is required. Write a brief report on the careers you located and advantages and disadvantages of each career. Did you find additional careers in sociology that interested you as you searched? Make a brief list of those careers to explore in the future.

Research and Presentation

17 *Gathering Information* Try this quantitative research project at home. Over the next few days, watch three television shows, each at least thirty minutes long. Choose one type of program: either prime time dramas or animated series. Record the number of times a person or animal is subjected to physical violence. Remember that physical violence can be as minimal as shoving. Then create a graph on your computer that illustrates the number of violent acts for the shows.

18 *Evaluating* Visit a website on a current events topic that interests you. Using the criteria for Evaluating Internet Resources in this chapter, determine if your site qualifies as a reliable source of information. If not, keep searching until you find one that does. Bring your recommended URL to class to create a database of reliable current events sites.

Need Extra Help?

If You've Missed Question	14	15	16	17	18
Go to page	54–57	56–57	56–57	44	44–45

Culture

ESSENTIAL QUESTION • *How does culture influence society?*

networks
There's More Online about culture.

CHAPTER 3

Technology & Society
Popular Culture and the Internet

Lesson 1
The Basis of Culture

Lesson 2
Language and Culture

Lesson 3
Norms and Values

Lesson 4
Beliefs and Material Culture

Lesson 5
Cultural Diversity and Similarity

Sociology Matters...

Celebrations are strongly shaped by the culture of the society in which they take place. A wedding, for example, symbolizes what a society considers a desirable way to live. By marrying, two people show that they are committed to upholding the society's beliefs and values.

Events such as weddings vary within a diverse and multicultural society. How do key events in your life reflect your society's culture?

◀ In many Eastern cultures, the color of choice for a bride's clothing is red, symbolizing good luck and happiness.

©Photosindia/Corbis

65

CHAPTER 3
Technology & Society

Popular Culture
and the Internet

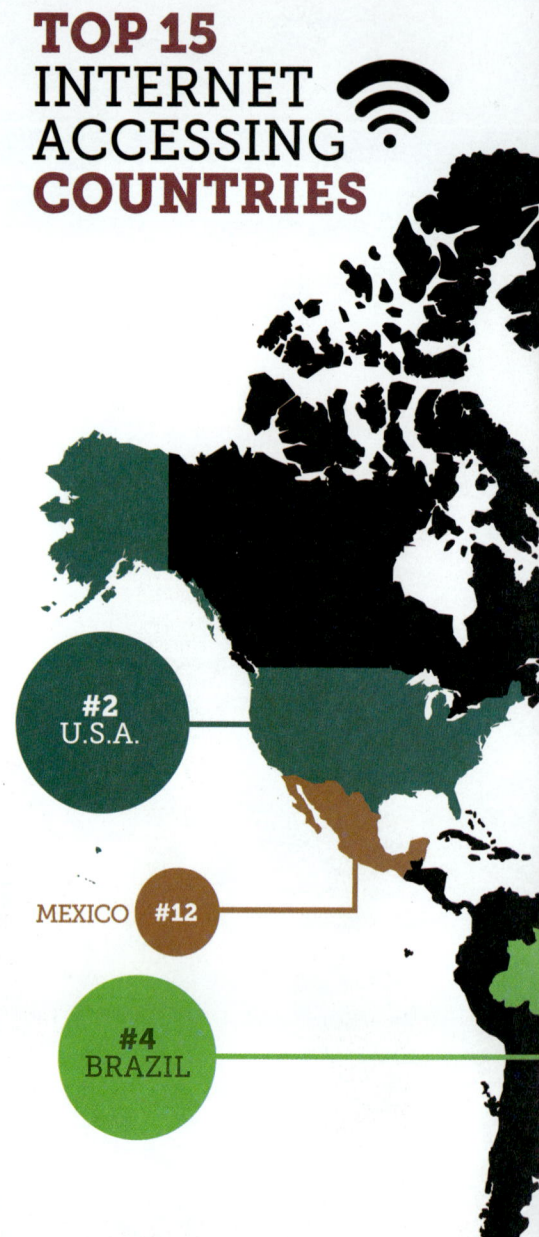

TOP 15 INTERNET ACCESSING COUNTRIES

#2 U.S.A.

MEXICO #12

#4 BRAZIL

Popular culture refers to the ideas, attitudes, and beliefs that enjoy mainstream consensus in a particular society.

Fashion styles, music, movies, comic books, video games: All these and more are part of popular culture. In the Internet age, the spread of popular culture is occurring at an ever-increasing rate. This acceleration is happening because, as a communications tool, the Internet blends text, sound, and images speedily, efficiently, and cheaply.

The advent of the interactive Web, with such tools as blogs, podcasts, and wikis, has added a distinctive new dimension to popular culture. Internet users shape popular culture even as they spread it. Today, digital communications are based largely on networks and sharing. When you publish your own blog or upload your own video on YouTube, for example, your potential audience is enormous.

Only ten years ago, English was the dominant language on the Internet. Many predictions claimed that American popular culture would come to dominate the world, crowding out other traditions. While there is no denying that American popular culture has gone global, the Internet has become more international than ever. In fact, for the period 2000–2011, five other languages showed significantly greater Internet growth than did English. They were Chinese, Russian, Arabic, Portuguese, and Spanish.

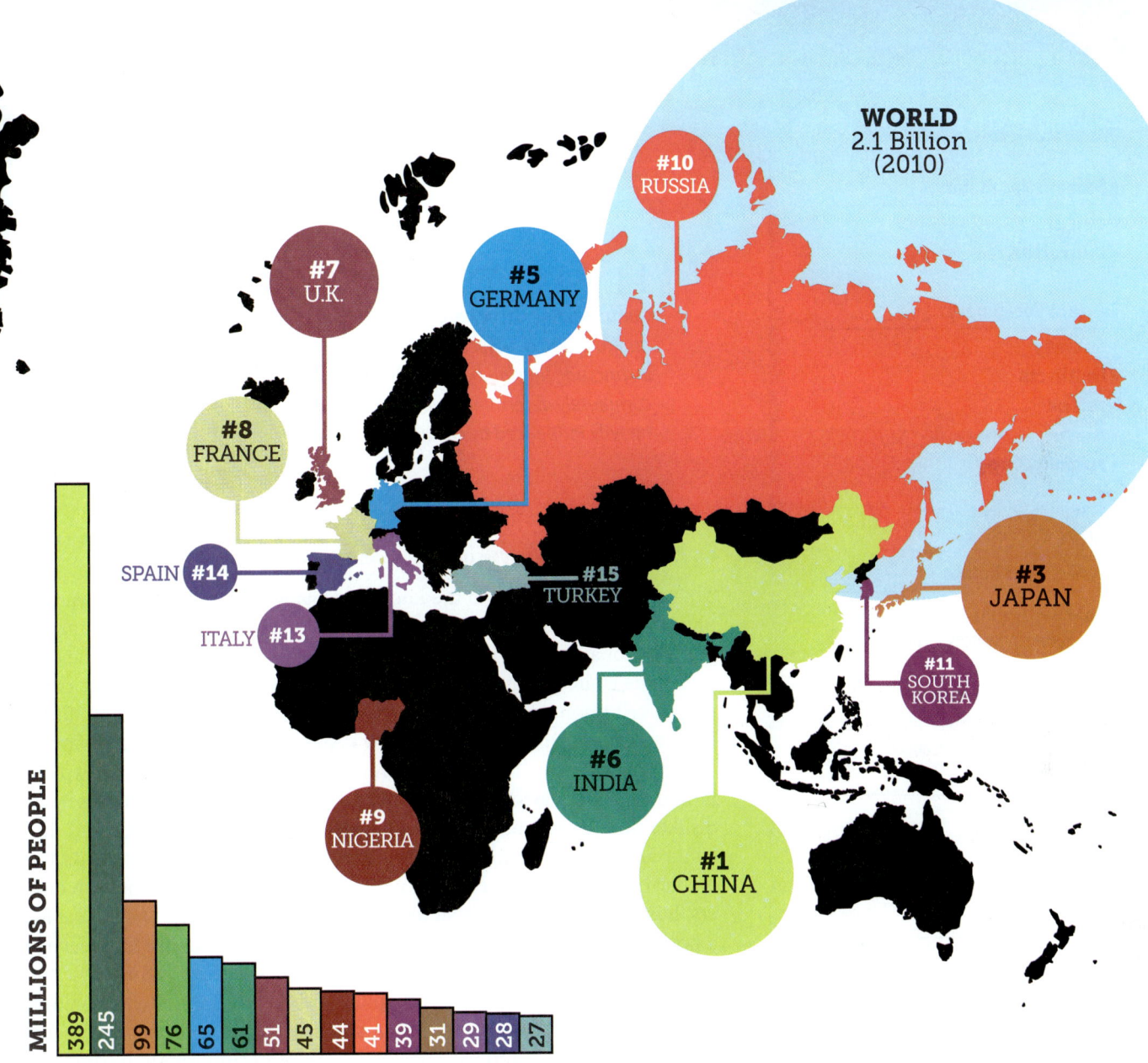

Thinking Like a Sociologist

1 Explaining
How can the Internet help make a Chinese sports hero, a film icon from Brazil, and a royal wedding in Great Britain parts of modern American popular culture? Use specific examples to support your answer.

2 Making Connections
How has the Internet significantly affected the widespread diffusion of popular culture?

networks

There's More Online!

- ☑ **CHART** Theoretical Perspectives: Views on Culture
- ☑ **GRAPHIC ORGANIZER** Society and Human Behavior
- ☑ **IMAGE** DNA
- ☑ **SELF-CHECK QUIZ**

Reading HELPDESK

Academic Vocabulary
- culture
- evolution

Content Vocabulary
- society
- instincts
- reflex
- drive
- sociobiology

TAKING NOTES:
Key Ideas and Details

QUESTIONING As you read about the ways culture influences society and human behavior, use a graphic organizer like the one below to list three questions you would like to have answered. Then write the answers as you find them in the text.

Question 1	
Answer	
Question 2	
Answer	
Question 3	
Answer	

LESSON 1
The Basis of Culture

ESSENTIAL QUESTION • *How does culture influence society?*

IT MATTERS BECAUSE

Culture defines how people in a society behave in relation to others and to physical objects. Although most behavior among animals is instinctual, human behavior is learned. Even reflexes and drives do not completely determine how humans will behave, because people are heavily influenced by culture.

Culture and Society

GUIDING QUESTION *How does culture explain human behavior?*

The term **culture** refers to the knowledge, language, values, customs, and physical objects that are passed from generation to generation among members of a group. It is a human creation. On the *material* side, the culture of the United States includes such physical objects as skyscrapers, computers, cell phones, and cars. On the *nonmaterial* side, American culture includes beliefs, rules, customs, family systems, and a capitalist economy.

What is the importance of culture? One role of culture is to help explain human social behavior. What people do and don't do, what they like and dislike, what they believe and don't believe, and what they value and discount are all based on culture. Another role of culture is to provide the blueprint that people in a society use to guide their relationships with others. It is because of culture that teenage girls are encouraged to compete for a position on the women's basketball team. It is from culture that teenage boys come to believe that "pumping iron" is a gateway to masculinity.

Culture and society are tightly interwoven. One cannot exist without the other, but they are not identical. A **society** is a group of people who live in a defined territory and participate in a common culture. All the different elements of culture—knowledge, language, values, customs, and physical objects—form a whole culture that defines that society's total way of life.

Human behavior, then, is based on culture. Since people are not born knowing their culture, human cultural behavior must be learned. People develop schemas, or mental outlines based on their experience or memory. In this lesson we will examine the influence of biology on behavior.

✓ **READING PROGRESS CHECK**

Making Connections What are some ways in which people learn culture?

Culture and Heredity

GUIDING QUESTION *How does heredity affect human behavior?*

Instincts are genetically inherited patterns of behavior. Nonhuman animals, especially insects, are highly dependent on instincts for survival. Human infants, in contrast, cannot go very far on instincts alone. Instincts are not enough to solve the problems that humans face.

Culture Versus Instinct

Most social scientists view the role of instincts in human behavior as quite limited. Cognitive psychologists—those who study how the mind works—might point out, for instance, that language would not be possible if humans did not have some predisposition—some instinct—to learn certain things. They would argue that the underlying mental rules for language are present at birth. They would not, however, argue that people have an innate ability for a specific language. People learn specific languages in a cultural context.

If humans were controlled by instincts alone, they would all behave in the same way with respect to those instincts. If, for example, women had an instinct for mothering, then *all* women would want children, and all women would love and protect their children. In fact, some women do not want to have children, and some women who give birth abuse or abandon their children.

Without instincts to dictate the type of shelter to build, the kind of food to eat, the time of year to have children, or when to mate, humans are forced to create and learn their own ways of thinking, feeling, and behaving. Even for meeting basic needs such as those involving reproduction, food, and survival, humans rely on the culture they have created.

Heredity Affects Behavior

Of course, culture is not the only influence on human behavior. Genetic inheritance plays a role too. Evidence from a variety of studies suggests that genetic factors play a role in general intelligence and in personality traits.

culture knowledge, values, customs, and physical objects that are shared by the members of a society.

society a group of people who inhabit a specific territory and share a common culture

instincts innate (unlearned) patterns of behavior

Theoretical Perspectives

EXPLAINING THE ROLE OF CULTURE

Functionalism and conflict theory examine culture on the societal—or macro—level. Symbolic interactionism focuses on the group—or micro—level. Each perspective provides different insights into how culture affects human behavior and society. This table explores some of the differences.

Theoretical Perspective	Culture Concepts	Examples
Functionalism	Values	Culture is a system for meeting basic needs. Values influence how these needs are met. For example, the Amish value hard work. They use horses to plow fields. Mainstream American culture values efficiency. Most American farmers use machines and modern technology to save time and labor.
Conflict Theory	Dominant ideology	Culture helps maintain the privileges and positions of powerful groups in society by reinforcing the dominant ideology—the cultural beliefs and practices of those in power.
Symbolic Interactionism	Social interactions	Culture is transmitted and perpetuated through social interaction. This social interaction continuously defines and redefines the culture's values.

▶ **CRITICAL THINKING**

1. **Contrasting** How do functionalists and conflict theorists differ in the way they view the role of culture?

2. **Evaluating** Which perspective would be most useful in determining how culture affects behaviors in small groups? Why?

Our DNA, or genetic code, determines our reflexes and drives.

▶ **CRITICAL THINKING**

1. **Identifying Central Issues** How can our drives form the basis for cultural interaction?
2. **Differentiating** How is a twin study based on identical twins different from one based on fraternal twins?

reflex automatic reaction to physical stimuli

drive impulse to reduce discomfort

sociobiology the study of how biology influences human behavior

For example, genetic factors have been linked to traits such as kindness, aggressiveness, sociability, drug and alcohol use, thrill seeking, depression, and anxiousness. This does not mean that individuals inherit specific personality traits and patterns of behavior. Rather, heredity sets broad parameters for the development of some behaviors and traits. People's actual behaviors and traits are formed by the interplay between genetic and environmental factors. The debate over the relative balance of these factors is sometimes referred to as the "nature versus nurture" argument.

Psychologists have used twin studies to try to determine the relative effects of genetics and environment on human behavior. Identical twins are formed when a single fertilized egg splits. Consequently, identical twins share almost 100 percent of their genes. Fraternal twins are formed from two different fertilized eggs. Thus, fraternal twins share about 50 percent of their genes—the same amount shared by siblings who are not twins. Some of the most comprehensive twin studies have focused on identical twins raised together and apart and fraternal twins raised together and apart. By including all four groups, researchers were better able to determine the influence of genetics versus environment. These studies found that about 40–50 percent of people's personality traits are influenced by genetics.

In addition, humans have **reflexes**—simple, biologically inherited, automatic reactions to physical stimuli. A human baby, for example, cries when pinched; the pupils of the eyes contract in bright light. We also have biologically inherited **drives**, or impulses, to reduce discomfort. We want to eat, drink, sleep, and associate with others.

You should remember, however, that genetically inherited personality traits, reflexes, and drives do not control human social behavior. Culture *channels* the expression of these biological characteristics. Genetics and environmental factors work together to influence behavior in a number of ways. For example, genes influence intelligence. Highly intelligent parents, however, often provide an intellectually stimulating environment for their children. This environment helps their children excel academically. Similarly, genetic factors can influence a child's tendency for antisocial behavior. Children who exhibit antisocial behavior at home or in school often meet with criticism and punishment. These responses can increase antisocial behavior.

✓ **READING PROGRESS CHECK**

Explaining What effect does culture have on biological characteristics such as personality traits, reflexes, and drives?

Sociobiology

GUIDING QUESTION *How do sociobiologists view human behavior?*

Sociobiology is the systematic study of how biology influences human behavior. It combines Darwin's theory of natural selection with modern genetics. Applying evolutionary theory to human behavior, however, is controversial and sociobiology has many critics.

How Sociobiologists View Human Behavior

According to Darwin's theory of **evolution**, organisms evolve through natural selection. Through the process of natural selection, plants and animals best suited to an environment survive and reproduce while the rest perish.

Sociobiologists apply the principle of natural selection to the evolution of social behavior. They assume that the behaviors that best help people are biologically based and transmitted in the genetic code over the course of human evolution. Behaviors that would contribute to the survival of the human species include parental affection and care, friendship, sexual reproduction, and the education of children.

Sociobiologists do not draw a sharp line between human and nonhuman animals. They claim that nonhuman animals also act on knowledge—as when baboons use long sticks to pull ants from an anthill for a meal. Many nonhuman animals, claim sociobiologists, show intelligence of a kind formerly thought to be unique to humans, such as the ability to use language.

evolution a process of change from one point of development to another

Criticisms of Sociobiology

The major criticism of sociobiology is that the importance placed on genetics could be used as a justification to label specific races as superior or inferior. Critics of sociobiology also point out that there is too much variation in societies around the world for human behavior to be explained on strictly biological grounds. They believe that the capacity for using language is uniquely human and that humans have created a social life that goes far beyond what heredity alone could accomplish.

The Search for a Middle Ground

Some common ground has emerged in this debate. A growing body of sociologists believe that genes work with culture in a complex way to shape and limit human nature and social life. They would like this relationship to be further examined.

A 1998 study found that women look for one set of characteristics in men they marry while men value a different set of characteristics in women. The researchers believe this behavior is programmed into the genetic code. Studies have also determined that stepfathers are more likely than biological fathers to abuse the children in their families. Is this because men are more protective of their own biological offspring? Because of the speed of discoveries in the field of biology, the relationships among heredity, culture, and behavior are of growing interest to sociobiologists.

✓ **READING PROGRESS CHECK**

Theorizing How might a sociobiologist explain why people make great sacrifices for their family and friends?

LESSON 1 REVIEW

Reviewing Vocabulary
1. *Identifying* How is society different from culture?

Using Your Notes
2. *Explaining* Use the questions in your graphic organizer to write a brief explanation of how culture influences society and human behavior.

Answering the Guiding Questions
3. *Finding the Main Idea* How does culture explain human behavior?

4. *Analyzing* How does heredity affect human behavior?
5. *Identifying Central Issues* How do sociobiologists view human behavior?

Writing Activity
6. *Argument* Do you think human behavior is more a result of culture or heredity? Give reasons to support your answer.

networks

There's More Online!

- ☑ **GRAPHIC ORGANIZER** Language and Culture
- ☑ **IMAGE** A Daily Cleansing Ritual
- ☑ **MAP** Language Families
- ☑ **SELF-CHECK QUIZ**

Reading HELPDESK

Academic Vocabulary
- exposure
- adjacent

Content Vocabulary
- hypothesis of linguistic relativity

TAKING NOTES:
Key Ideas and Details

OUTLINING As you read about language and culture, use the headings and text from the lesson to create an outline similar to the one below.

Language and Culture
I. Symbols, Language, and Culture
   A. Defining Symbols
      1.
      2.
   B. Language and Culture Are Related
      1.
      2.
II. The Sapir-Whorf Hypothesis

LESSON 2
Language and Culture

ESSENTIAL QUESTION • *How does culture influence society?*

It Matters Because
Humans can create and transmit culture. The symbols of language play key roles in transmitting culture and determining people's views of reality.

Symbols, Language, and Culture

GUIDING QUESTION *How do symbols and language define culture?*

If culture is to be transmitted, it must be learned anew by each generation. Both the creation and the transmission of culture, known as *cultural transmission,* depend heavily on the use of symbols. The most powerful symbols are those that make up language. In Lewis Carroll's *Through the Looking Glass,* Humpty Dumpty says to Alice, "When I use a word, it means just what I choose it to mean—neither more nor less." So it is with symbols—things that stand for or represent something else.

Symbols range from physical objects to sounds, smells, and tastes. The meaning of a symbol is not based on physical characteristics. There is nothing, for example, naturally pleasing about the sound created by hands loudly clapping together. In the United States, applause warms the heart of an entertainer, a politician, or a high school athlete, but in Latin America the same sound indicates disapproval. The Confederate flag that represents oppression for many African Americans and a proud cultural heritage for many white Southerners is a symbol with different meanings attached.

Language frees humans from the limits of time and place. The Wright brothers' successful flight did not come just from their own personal efforts. They built their airplane according to principles of flight already existing in American culture. Through language they could read, discuss, and recombine existing ideas and technology.

Equipped with language, humans can pass their experiences, ideas, and knowledge to others. Although it may take time and repetition, children can be taught the dangers of fire and heights without being burned or falling down stairs. This process of social learning, of course, applies to other cultural patterns as well, such as eating, showing patriotism, or staying awake in class.

☑ **READING PROGRESS CHECK**

Explaining How does language facilitate cultural transmission?

The Sapir-Whorf Hypothesis

GUIDING QUESTION *How does language shape perceptions of the world?*

According to Edward Sapir and Benjamin Whorf, language is our guide to reality. How we think about a thing relates to the number and complexity of words available to describe it. Our perceptions depend in part on the particular language we learn. Since languages differ, perceptions differ as well. This theory is known as the Sapir-Whorf hypothesis, or the **hypothesis of linguistic relativity**.

When something is important to a society, its language will have many words to describe it. The importance of time in American culture is reflected in the many words that describe time intervals—*nanosecond, moment, minute, hour, era, interim, recurrence, century, light-year,* and *afternoon,* to name a few. When something is unimportant to people, their language may not have even one word for it. When Christian missionaries first went to Asia, they were dismayed because the Chinese language had no word for *sin*. Other missionaries were no less distressed to learn that Africans and Polynesians had no word to express the idea of a single, all-powerful God. The Pirahã of Brazil lack words to express numbers greater than two.

hypothesis of linguistic relativity theory stating that our idea of reality depends largely upon language

Connecting Sociology to Anthropology

THE NACIREMA

In our own culture, the things we do and believe seem natural to us. Like sociologists, however, anthropologists look at cultures from a different perspective. This excerpt explores a culture that is very close to home!

PRIMARY SOURCE

A typical Nacirema shrine from the 1950s

"Nacirema culture is characterized by a highly developed market economy which has evolved in a rich natural habitat. While much of the people's time is devoted to economic pursuits, a large part of the fruits of these labors and a considerable portion of the day are spent in ritual activity. The focus of this activity is the human body....

The fundamental belief underlying the whole system appears to be that the human body is ugly and that its natural tendency is to debility and disease. Incarcerated in such a body, man's only hope is to avert these characteristics through the use of ritual and ceremony. Every household has one or more shrines devoted to this purpose. The more powerful individuals in the society have several shrines in their houses and, in fact, the opulence of a house is often referred to in terms of the number of such ritual centers it possesses. Most houses are of wattle and daub construction, but the shrine rooms of the more wealthy are walled with stone. Poorer families imitate the rich by applying pottery plaques to their shrine walls.

While each family has at least one such shrine, the rituals associated with it are not family ceremonies but are private and secret. The rites are normally only discussed with children, and then only during the period when they are being initiated into these mysteries...

The daily body ritual performed by everyone includes a mouth-rite.... This rite involves a practice which strikes the uninitiated stranger as revolting. It was reported to me that the ritual consists of inserting a small bundle of hog hairs into the mouth, along with certain magical powders, and then moving the bundle in a highly formalized series of gestures."

—Horace Miner, "Body Ritual among the Nacirema," 1956

DBQ ▶ CRITICAL THINKING

1. **Drawing Inferences** Who are the Nacirema, and what is their shrine? How do you know?
2. **Speculating** What do you think Horace Miner hopes to accomplish by describing the culture of the Nacirema?

...erspective

...up of languages that ...from one original ...re than a hundred ...milies in the world, but ...into one of 14 language families. ...p shows the worldwide distribution of these 14 language families.

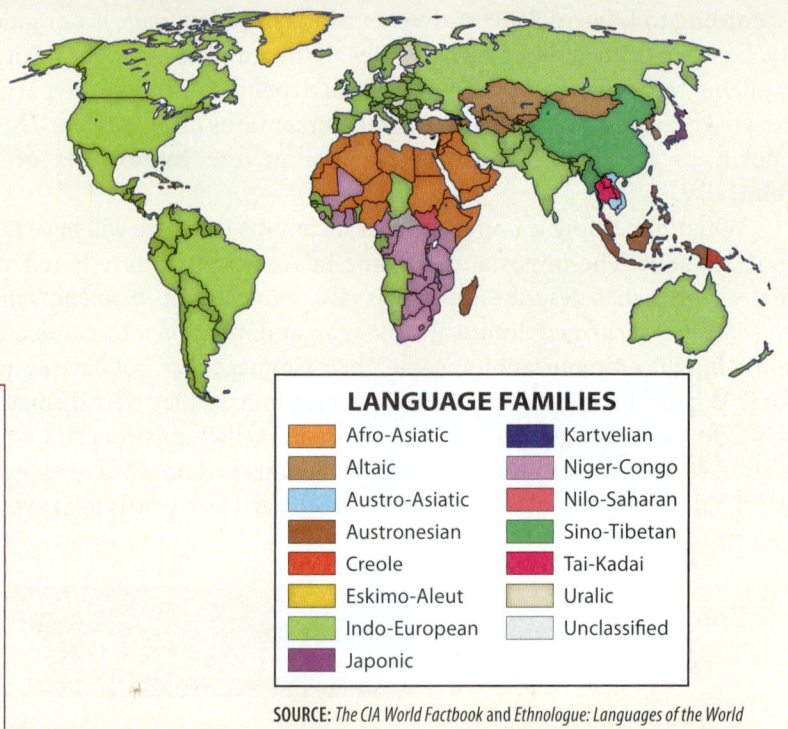

LANGUAGE FAMILIES
- Afro-Asiatic
- Altaic
- Austro-Asiatic
- Austronesian
- Creole
- Eskimo-Aleut
- Indo-European
- Japonic
- Kartvelian
- Niger-Congo
- Nilo-Saharan
- Sino-Tibetan
- Tai-Kadai
- Uralic
- Unclassified

SOURCE: *The CIA World Factbook* and *Ethnologue: Languages of the World*

Geography Connection
1. **Human Systems** What conclusion can you draw about exploration and cultural transmission of language from the distribution of these language families?
2. **The Uses of Geography** Imagine you are a marketing director for a company that is introducing a new product. How might you use the information on this map to decide how to market your product?

exposure the state of being made known

adjacent situated next to or nearby

Even if our view of the world is shaped largely by language, we are not forever trapped by language. **Exposure** to another language or to new words can alter our perception. This is one reason it is important to avoid stereotypical labels. People can begin to view the world differently as they learn a new language.

Other factors can also affect how members of a culture experience the world. The Japanese traditionally use paper walls to create the sense of privacy and are not bothered by noise in **adjacent** rooms. Americans staying at hotels in Japan complain they are being bombarded with noise because Westerners have not been *conditioned* (mentally trained) to screen out sound. Privacy is so important to most Germans that German executives generally have a "closed-door policy." Problems arise in American firms located in Germany because most American executives leave their doors open.

✓ **READING PROGRESS CHECK**

Interpreting How can learning a new language change our view of the world?

LESSON 2 REVIEW

Reviewing Vocabulary
1. **Summarizing** What does the hypothesis of linguistic relativity state about the way language affects how people perceive reality?

Using Your Notes
2. **Expressing** Use your notes to write a statement expressing the relationship of language to culture.

Answering the Guiding Questions
3. **Identifying Central Issues** How do symbols and language define culture?
4. **Theorizing** How does language shape perceptions of the world?

Writing Activity
5. **Argument** Some experts believe that without language, there is no thought. Do you agree? Write a paragraph explaining why or why not.

networks

There's More Online!

- ☑ **CARTOON** Differing Values
- ☑ **CARTOON** Odd Man Out
- ☑ **CHART** Do's and Don'ts
- ☑ **IMAGE** Cultural Mores
- ☑ **MAP** Immigration to the United States
- ☑ **SELF-CHECK QUIZ**

Reading HELPDESK

Academic Vocabulary
- norms
- violation

Content Vocabulary
- folkways
- mores
- taboo
- law
- sanctions
- formal sanctions
- informal sanctions
- values

TAKING NOTES:
Key Ideas and Details

COMPARING AND CONTRASTING As you read about norms and values, use a graphic organizer like the one below to write two statements in each circle and in the overlapping area about how norms and values are alike and different.

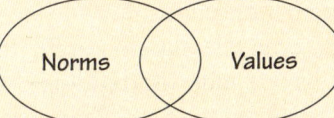

LESSON 3
Norms and Values

ESSENTIAL QUESTION • *How does culture influence society?*

It Matters Because

Two essential components of culture are norms and values. Norms include folkways, mores, and laws. Sanctions are used to encourage conformity to norms. Values, the broadest cultural ideas, form the basis for norms. Norms can change over time.

Norms

GUIDING QUESTION *What are the three basic types of norms?*

For sociologists, norms and values are a defining component of culture. **Norms** are rules that define behavior. Norms help explain why people in a society or group behave similarly in similar circumstances. For example, a young Basarwa girl in Africa might become engaged to a man she has not met in order to strengthen clan bonds. This example reflects a cultural norm—a way of behaving in specific situations.

William Graham Sumner, an early sociologist, stated that anything can be considered appropriate when norms approve of it. Once norms are learned, members of a society use them to guide their social behavior. Norms are so ingrained that they guide behavior without our awareness. For instance, you may not think of standing in the checkout line in a store as a norm until someone attempts to step in front of you. Then it registers that waiting your turn in line is expected behavior. Cutting in line violates that norm. Norms range from minor behavior, such as applauding after a performance, to extremely important rules, such as laws against stealing.

Social norms can change over time. For example, research has shown that women in college today are much more interested in earning money than they were in the 1960s. Sociologists have identified at least three factors that cause change in social norms and culture over time: (1) *invention*, the creation of new cultural elements, including both objects and ideas; (2) *discovery*, or a better understanding of something already known; and (3) *diffusion*, the spread of cultural elements from one culture to another.

William Graham Sumner identified three basic types of norms: *folkways*, *mores*, and *laws*. These norms vary in importance in a society, and their **violation**, or the breaking of them, is tolerated to different degrees.

Culture **75**

norm rules defining appropriate and inappropriate behavior

violation the breaking of a rule or law

folkways norms that lack moral significance

mores norms that have moral dimensions and that should be followed by members of the society

taboo a rule of behavior, the violation of which calls for strong punishment

At age 13, Jewish boys become part of their religious community in a ceremony called a bar mitzvah.

▶ CRITICAL THINKING

1. **Describing** How do this boy's clothing and actions reflect the norms of his Orthodox Jewish community?
2. **Making Connections** What norms does your community have for young teens?

Folkways

Rules that cover customary ways of thinking, feeling, and behaving but lack moral overtones are called **folkways**. For example, sleeping in a bed instead of sleeping on the floor is not a moral issue; it qualifies as a folkway. Because folkways are not considered vital to group welfare, disapproval of those who break them is not very great. Those who consistently violate folkways—say, by talking loudly in quiet places or wearing a different-colored sock on each foot—may appear odd. We may avoid these people, but we do not consider them wicked or immoral.

Other examples of folkways involve how members of a society adapt to their physical environments. It is extremely common to see people of all ages in Great Britain carrying umbrellas, or people in Sweden wearing shearling coats. You can imagine why they do this. Do you think people in the Sahara Desert carry umbrellas or wear fur coats? Of course not, but their cultures have adopted different folkways to adapt to their own environment.

Some folkways are more important than others, and the social reaction to their violation is more intense. Not offering a woman a seat on a crowded bus draws little notice today, but obnoxious drunken behavior at a party may bring a strong negative reaction from others.

Mores

The term *mores* (pronounced "MOR-ayz") is based on the word *moral*. Morality deals with conduct related to right and wrong. **Mores** are norms of great moral significance and are vital to the well-being of a society. Conformity to mores draws strong social approval; violation brings strong disapproval. For example, Americans believe that able-bodied men should work. Able-bodied men who do not work are scorned.

Various practices of the culture can create differences within group behavior, however. Some of these differences depend upon gender, age, or social class. In religiously conservative societies, for example, women are often required to have their heads or even their bodies fully covered in public, while men do not face such restrictions. Women might also not be allowed to talk to males who are not family members unless a male family member is present. Even in the United States, there are rules for acceptable dress. It is acceptable for adolescent boys to play basketball shirtless. Could an adolescent girl do the same?

Although following folkways is generally a matter of personal choice, conformity to mores is a social requirement. Still, some mores are more vital to a society than others. Failure to stand at attention while the national anthem is being played is not as serious a violation of American mores as using loud profanity during a religious service.

The most serious mores are taboos. A **taboo** is a norm so strong that its violation demands punishment by the group (or, some people think, even the supernatural). In India, followers of Hinduism have a taboo forbidding the killing of cows. Other taboos are related to sexual behaviors. Although definitions of incest vary from society to society, the incest taboo (forbidding sexual contact with close relatives) is generally regarded as the only taboo that is present in all societies. The "mother-in-law" taboo existing in some societies prohibits or severely restricts social contact between a husband and his wife's mother.

Do's and Don'ts

Knowing the norms and customs of other nations may prevent embarrassing moments as you travel the world.

Country	Custom
Brazil	When accepting an invitation to a Brazilian home, arrive at least a half hour late if you are coming to dinner and around an hour late if you are attending a party. Be sure to bring flowers as a hostess gift, but avoid purple flowers. They are used for funerals.
Bulgaria	Give only an odd number of gifts to a newborn baby. If dining in a Bulgarian home, take only a small portion of food for your first serving—guests show their appreciation for their host's hospitality by eating several servings. An empty glass will always be filled, so if you are done with your beverage, leave a mouthful of it in your glass.
Ghana	A Ghanaian handshake involves clasping right hands as in the United States, but then the people greeting each other twist their middle fingers and click them together. If you are not familiar with this greeting, it's best to stick to a traditional, straightforward handshake!
India	If your Indian hosts invite you to dinner, arrive on time. Etiquette demands that you remove your shoes before you enter the home. Do not accept items of food or a beverage the first time your host asks. Food and drink will be offered several times, and refusing the first time is simply good manners.
Japan	Remove your shoes when entering a Japanese home, and put on the slippers provided for guests. Make sure your shoes point away from the doorway through which you will enter. When using chopsticks, take care never to use them to point. Do not rest the chopsticks on your plate, but lay them on the rest provided by your plate when you are not using them. Never, ever cross them!
New Zealand	The Maori—the indigenous peoples of New Zealand—have an elaborate protocol for greeting guests from outside their group. It is called a Powhiri, and it involves welcoming speech making that can last up to several hours. The Powhiri is followed by a meal. After the meal, it is considered good manners to thank those who have cooked and served the meal. This may result in a request to sing. Singing a song that represents your home country is a way to show gratitude and respect.
Norway	If you are bringing flowers as a hostess gift to a Norwegian home, have the flowers sent the morning of the meal so that they can be put on display before guests arrive. Always arrange for an odd number of flowers, and never send lilies, carnations, or any white flowers, as those are reserved for funerals.
Saudi Arabia	Saudis rarely entertain those from outside their culture in their homes unless they know them very well. As a visitor to a Saudi home, you should greet the older members of the host family first. Meals are often eaten with the fingers, but use only your right hand, as Saudis believe the left hand is unclean. Sample everything that is offered, but do not be surprised if the most valued food items—such as a sheep's head—are reserved just for you!

Source: Kwintessential, *Country Profiles: Global Guide to Culture, Customs and Etiquette*

Laws

The third type of norm is law. **Laws** are norms that are formally defined and enforced by officials. Folkways and mores emerge slowly and are often unconsciously created, while laws are consciously created and enforced.

Mores are an important source for laws. At one time, the norm against murder was not written down. But as civilization advanced, the norm against murder became formally defined and enforced by public officials.

Folkways can become mores or laws. Smoking was acceptable behavior to most Americans until the 1970s. Today, many states have laws against smoking in public places. Not all mores become laws. For example, it is not against the law to cheat on an exam, although you may be suspended or punished by the teacher. Furthermore, not all laws began as mores. Fines for overtime parking and laws against littering have never been mores.

✓ **READING PROGRESS CHECK**

Explaining What is the relationship of laws to mores?

CHART
DO'S AND DON'TS
Norms differ throughout the world.

▶ **CRITICAL THINKING**

1. *Assessing* What norm do you find most unusual? Why?
2. *Making Connections* About what norms would you inform a foreign guest to your community?

law a norm that is formally defined and enforced by officials

Enforcing the Rules

GUIDING QUESTION *What are formal and informal sanctions?*

People do not automatically conform to norms. Norms must be learned and accepted. Groups teach norms, in part, through the use of *sanctions*. **Sanctions** are rewards and punishments used to encourage conformity to norms. They can be formal or informal.

Formal Sanctions

Formal sanctions are sanctions that may be applied only by officially designated persons, such as judges and teachers. Formal sanctions can take the form of positive as well as negative rewards. A soldier earns a Congressional Medal of Honor as a positive sanction for heroism. Teachers reward outstanding students with As. Of course, formal sanctions can also take the form of punishments.

Formal punishments range widely in their severity. From the Middle Ages to the Protestant Reformation, for example, it was an unpardonable sin for lenders to charge interest on money. This practice was called *usury* and was condemned in the Bible. Usury was punishable on the third offense by public humiliation and social and economic ruin.

Informal Sanctions

Informal sanctions are sanctions that can be applied by most members of a group. They, too, can be positive or negative. Informal sanctions include thanking someone for pushing a car out of a snowbank (positive) or staring at someone who is talking loudly during a movie (negative). Sanctions are not used randomly or without reason. Specific sanctions are associated with specific norms. A high school student who violates his parents' curfew is not supposed to be locked in a closet, for example.

After we reach a certain age, most of us conform without the threat of sanctions. We may conform to norms because we believe that the behavior expected of us is appropriate, because we wish to avoid guilt feelings, or because we fear social disapproval. In other words, we sanction ourselves mentally.

✓ **READING PROGRESS CHECK**

Identifying Cause and Effect How might an informal sanction become a formal sanction?

sanctions rewards and punishments used to encourage people to follow norms

formal sanctions sanctions imposed by persons given special authority

informal sanctions rewards or punishments that can be applied by most members of a group

> **CARTOON >**
> **ODD MAN OUT**
> One of these men is violating the norms of the group.
>
> ▶ **CRITICAL THINKING**
> 1. ***Drawing Conclusions*** What sanction is being applied to the man in the middle? Why?
> 2. ***Classifying*** Is the sanction formal or informal?

"Dirk, we need to have a talk."

Applying Sociology

SOCIOLOGY AND THE CRIMINAL JUSTICE SYSTEM

According to the American Sociological Association (ASA), 21st-century careers are especially well suited to students with degrees in sociology. The ASA cites these skills needed to obtain and succeed at 21st-century careers: creativity and innovation, critical thinking, analytic problem solving, communication, collaboration, multicultural and global understandings, strong math and science skills, and excellent written expression.

Many sociology majors find employment in the U.S. criminal justice system, where these and other skills are vital. Jobs filled by sociology majors (some require advanced degrees) include:

- probation/parole officer
- juvenile probation officer
- victim services specialist
- mediation specialist
- attorney
- corrections counselor
- private security/background investigation
- FBI analyst

▶ **CRITICAL THINKING**

1. **Evaluating** Choose the job you feel you would be most effective performing. What skills and characteristics do you have that would help you in this job?
2. **Analyzing** Select a job in the criminal justice system that you might qualify for with a sociology degree and explain why sociology is a good preparation.

Values—The Basis for Norms

GUIDING QUESTION *What are values, and why are they important?*

Norms and sanctions are relatively specific. Values are much more general. **Values** are broad ideas about what most people in a society consider to be desirable. Values are so general that they do not dictate precise ways of thinking, feeling, or behaving. Thus, different societies or different groups within the same society can have quite different norms based on the same value. Consider the historical example of the Soviet Union. Soviet leaders said their people were free because the leaders claimed to provide full employment, medical care, and education. Americans have different norms based on the value of freedom. These norms include the right to free speech and assembly, the right to engage in private enterprise, and the right to a representative government.

Values have a tremendous influence on human social behavior because they form the basis for norms. A society that values democracy will have norms ensuring personal freedom. A society that values human welfare will have norms providing for its most unfortunate members.

Values are so general that they are involved in most aspects of daily life. In America, for example, the influence of the value of freedom goes beyond political life. The value of freedom affects how family relationships are conducted, how people are treated within the legal system, how organizations are run, and how people worship. Values also influence our economic decisions. For example, most Americans place a high value on material comfort. Therefore, they make economic decisions that are likely to ensure material comfort, such as going to college, choosing a career that pays well, and working hard.

values broad ideas about what is good or desirable shared by people in a society

✓ **READING PROGRESS CHECK**

Evaluating Why do identical values not result in identical norms?

A Diverse America

IMMIGRATION TO THE UNITED STATES

From the earliest days of the United States, immigrants from around the world have brought their cultures to American shores. A century ago, the majority of immigrants arrived from Europe, particularly from Italy and Russia. Today, the majority of immigrants are from Mexico, China, and India. This map shows the number of people who have obtained legal permanent residence status in each state.

Geography Connection

1. **The World in Spatial Terms** What generalization can you make about the states that have received the highest number of immigrants?
2. **Human Systems** This map shows how many immigrants each state has received. What other kinds of information would make this map even more useful to sociologists?

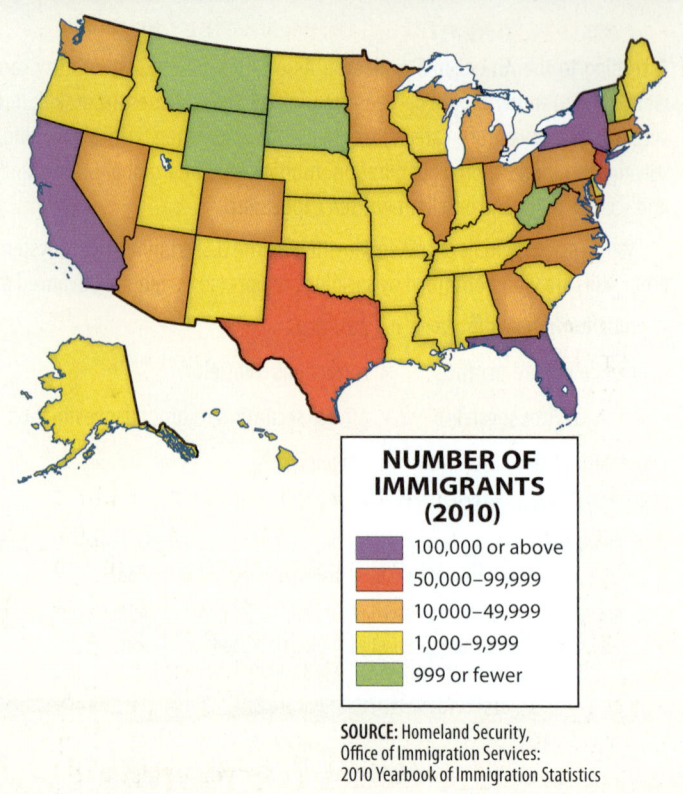

NUMBER OF IMMIGRANTS (2010)
- 100,000 or above
- 50,000–99,999
- 10,000–49,999
- 1,000–9,999
- 999 or fewer

SOURCE: Homeland Security, Office of Immigration Services: 2010 Yearbook of Immigration Statistics

Basic Values in the United States

GUIDING QUESTION *What values shape the lives of Americans?*

No single set of values is likely to hold across a country as diverse as the United States. Despite this problem, sociologist Robin Williams identified important—sometimes competing—values that have traditionally guided the daily lives of most people in the United States. A partial list includes:

- *Achievement and success.* People emphasize achievement, especially in the world of work. Success is supposed to be based on effort and competition and is viewed as a reward for performance. Wealth is viewed as a symbol of success and personal worth.
- *Activity and work.* People tend to prefer action over inaction in almost every case. For most Americans, continuous and regular work is a goal in itself. Promotion should be for merit rather than favoritism. Finally, all citizens should have the opportunity to perform at their best.
- *Efficiency and practicality.* People pride themselves on getting things done by the most rational means. We search for better and faster ways of doing things, praise good workmanship, and judge performance by the results. We love to rely on science and technology and have also learned to adapt to and influence our natural environment for our benefit.
- *Equality.* From the beginning of our history, we have declared a belief in equality for all citizens. As minority groups and women achieved citizenship, our concept of equality grew. We tend to treat one another as equals, defend everyone's legal rights, and favor equal opportunity—if not equal results—for everyone.

- *Democracy.* People emphasize that all citizens are entitled to equal rights and equal opportunity under the law. In a democracy, the people elect their government officials. Power is not in the hands of an elite few.
- *Group superiority.* Despite concern for equality of opportunity, people in the United States tend to place a greater value on people of their own race, ethnic group, social class, or religious group.

These values are clearly interrelated. Achievement and success affect and are affected by efficiency and practicality, for example. But we can also see conflicts among some values. For instance, people in the United States value group superiority while at the same time stressing equality and democracy.

Williams identified these major values more than forty years ago—about the time many of your parents were children. Although these values have remained remarkably stable over the years, some have changed. Today there is less emphasis on group superiority in America than in the past. This can be seen in the decline of openly racist attitudes and behaviors. In reality, however, it is usually norms and behavior rather than underlying values that change radically. It is probably because of the passage of civil rights laws that many Americans are now less likely to make overt racist statements. Racism, based on a belief in the superiority of one racial or ethnic group over another, however, remains part of the fabric of American culture.

The norms related to hard work and activity have also changed in recent years. Many Americans now work as hard at their leisure activities as they do at their jobs. Although Williams's analysis of major American values remains basically sound today, some sociologists believe that his list is incomplete. They would add, for example, optimism, honesty, and friendliness to the list of major values in the United States.

CARTOON

DIFFERING VALUES
These children have very different ideas about the value of athletic competition.

▶ **CRITICAL THINKING**
1. *Contrasting* How does the boy's view of the value of competition differ from the girl's view?
2. *Identifying Perspectives* Which child's view is closest to your own? Why?

✓ **READING PROGRESS CHECK**

Applying Name an important American value and explain how it affects life in our society.

LESSON 3 REVIEW

Reviewing Vocabulary
1. *Identifying* Identify an example of a formal sanction and an informal sanction and tell how they are alike and different.

Using Your Notes
2. *Comparing and Contrasting* Use your notes to write several sentences comparing and contrasting norms and values.

Answering the Guiding Questions
3. *Identifying* What are the three basic types of norms?

4. *Explaining* What are formal and informal sanctions?
5. *Discussing* What are values, and why are they important?
6. *Applying* What values shape the lives of Americans?

Writing Activity
7. *Argument* Take a position on the following statement and support it with reasons: The most important values never change.

FOCUS on research
Survey Research

How Do Schools and Parents Fail Teens?

Adolescence is often marked by drama and difficulty. In a study from the early 1990s, Jacquelynne Eccles set out to determine if there is something about this developmental period that puts adolescents at risk for difficulty. Eccles used survey research to track the experiences of American teenagers attending Midwestern junior high schools over a two-year period. She discovered that some adolescent troubles are more than hormonal—they are cultural as well.

PRIMARY SOURCE

Jacquelynne Eccles studied 1,500 early adolescents moving from sixth-grade elementary schools to seventh-grade junior high schools. The junior high schools were located in twelve school districts in middle-class Michigan communities. Students filled out questionnaires at school for two consecutive years—in the sixth and seventh grades. This procedure permitted Eccles to document changes the teenagers experienced after the first year of their transition.

The findings were not encouraging. The relationships between students and teachers tended to worsen over the year. At the very time when the young adolescents especially needed supportive relationships outside their homes, personal and positive relationships with teachers were strained by cultural and organizational changes in junior high school. Eccles described the situation this way:

"We believe that there are developmentally inappropriate changes in a cluster of classroom organizational, instructional, and climate variables, including task structure, task complexity, grouping practices, evaluation techniques, motivational strategies, locus of responsibility for learning, and quality of teacher-student and student-student relationships. We suggest that these changes contribute to the negative change in students' motivation and achievement-related beliefs assumed to coincide with the transition into junior high school."

These changes come just when young adolescents are most insecure about their status relative to their peers. As a result, student motivation and self-confidence declined. Eccles concluded that junior high school culture denies adolescents the emotionally supportive environment they need for proper social development.

Eccles's news was no better on the home front. Changes in the family paralleled those of the school system. Parental control over teenagers went up during the year, often to excessive levels. At the same time, school motivation and self-esteem of the junior high students went down. Eccles noted:

"Adolescents' relationships with their parents also undergo a stressful period during early and middle adolescence. This stress is often focused on issues of control and autonomy within the family, which are renegotiated during this developmental period. By necessity, children's relationships with their parents are asymmetrical in terms of power and authority; but as children mature, they need to take more and more responsibility for themselves until they eventually leave their natal home and take full responsibility for their own lives. In the optimal situation, parents will reinforce and stimulate this process of growing autonomy, self-determination, and independence. However, it is likely that the renegotiation processes . . . will not be smooth."

As a check on these general findings, Eccles compared students in more supportive schools and families with those in less supportive ones. In both the school and the family settings, she found more positive results in supportive environments. Students who were able to participate in school and family decision making showed higher levels of academic motivation and self-esteem than their peers with less opportunity to participate.

The solution to this problem, Eccles concludes, lies in a change in the norms and values of the schools and families. Schools and families need to develop balanced cultural expectations of young adolescents based on their developmental needs. Neither cracking down on them nor giving up control strikes the proper balance. The task is for the family and school to provide "an environment that changes in the right way and at the right pace."

—from Jacquelynne S. Eccles,
"Development During Adolescence," 1993

> "We believe that there are developmentally inappropriate changes in a cluster of classroom organizational, instructional, and climate variables . . . that contribute to the negative change in students' motivation and achievement."

Working With the Research

1. **Identifying Central Issues** According to Eccles, what in the school environment affects motivation?
2. **Identifying Cause and Effect** According to Eccles, why are adolescent-parent relationships stressful?
3. **Making Generalizations** What steps do you think might improve the transition to junior high school?

networks

There's More Online!

- ☑ **CARTOON** The Cat Did It
- ☑ **GRAPHIC ORGANIZER** Beliefs and Material Culture
- ☑ **IMAGE** U.S. Material Culture
- ☑ **SELF-CHECK QUIZ**

Reading HELPDESK

Academic Vocabulary
- contrast
- encounter

Content Vocabulary
- **nonmaterial culture**
- **material culture**
- **beliefs**
- **ideal culture**
- **real culture**

TAKING NOTES:
Key Ideas and Details

ORGANIZING As you read about beliefs and material culture, use the headings and text from the lesson to create an outline similar to the one below.

```
Beliefs and Material Culture
I. Beliefs and Physical Objects
   A.
   B.
   C.
```

LESSON 4
Beliefs and Material Culture

ESSENTIAL QUESTION • How does culture influence society?

It Matters Because
Besides norms and values, beliefs and physical objects make up culture. Ideal culture includes the guidelines we claim to accept, while real culture describes how we actually behave.

Beliefs and Physical Objects

GUIDING QUESTION *What is the difference between material culture and nonmaterial culture?*

The **nonmaterial culture** involves beliefs, ideas, and knowledge. The **material culture** is about how we relate to physical objects. Values, norms, knowledge, ideas (nonmaterial), and physical objects (material) make up a culture.

Why Beliefs Matter

Beliefs are ideas about the nature of reality. Beliefs can be true or false. The Romans believed Caesar Augustus to be a god; the Tanala, an ethnic group of Madagascar, believed that the souls of their kings passed into snakes; and many Germans believed that pictures of Hitler on their walls would prevent the walls from crumbling during World War II bombing raids. We would certainly consider these beliefs to be false. In **contrast**, other beliefs—such as the belief that the human eye can distinguish more than seven million colors and the belief that no intelligent life exists on Mars—are supported by factual evidence. We consider these beliefs to be true. Beliefs are important because people base their behavior on what they believe, regardless of whether their beliefs are true or false or how accurate they are.

Beliefs—like traditions, roles, and cultural expectations—provide a sense of continuity to a community. They help put into action the values that a culture considers important. For example, sociologist Jun Li has examined how immigrant Chinese parents use traditional Chinese beliefs and expectations to help their children adjust to life in their new homeland of Canada. Jun Li found that Chinese immigrant parents continue to stress the traditional Chinese belief in the value of education when they settle in Canada. Many expect their children to obtain degrees from top universities. They do this even though they often find that their own high levels of education have not translated into well-paying jobs in Canada. In stressing the importance of education, the parents are instilling in their own children the same expectations their parents instilled in them in China.

Material Culture

Material culture consists of the concrete, tangible objects within a culture. These can be items of popular culture such as video games or objects of high culture such as fine art paintings. Material culture also includes ordinary objects such as automobiles, books, chairs, tools, and buildings. These objects can be contrasted with the beliefs, ideas, and knowledge that make up nonmaterial culture. The physical objects of material culture have no innate—or natural—meanings or uses. Their meanings and uses are assigned by the culture that creates them.

Consider newspaper and pepper. Each has some meaning for you, but can you think of a combined use for them? One way to combine the two is in the process known as "nettling," once a common practice among some midwives. Nettling involved rolling a newspaper into a funnel shape to form a cone and then putting a liberal amount of pepper into the cone. At the height of labor, the midwife would use the pointed end of the cone to blow the pepper deeply into the expectant mother's nose. The force of the resulting sneeze would help deliver the baby. Before your introduction to the practice of nettling, the combination of newspaper and pepper had no meaning for you, even though you have **encountered** both newspapers and pepper in your daily life. You required the introduction to nettling to gain knowledge of the connection.

Material Culture Is Related to Nonmaterial Culture

The uses and meanings of physical objects can vary among societies. Although it is conventional to use a 787 jet for traveling, it is possible that a 787 downed in a remote jungle region could be used as a place of worship, a storage bin, or a home. In the United States, out-of-service buses and trains have been converted to restaurants.

The cultural meanings of physical objects are not determined by their physical characteristics but based on the beliefs, norms, and values people hold with regard to them. This is obvious when new meanings of a physical object are considered. At one time, only pianos and organs were used in church services. Guitars, drums, and trumpets were not "holy" enough to accompany a choir. Yet many churches today use these "worldly" instruments in their worship. The instruments have not changed, but the cultural meanings placed on them have.

Similarly, the objects that make up material culture can carry meanings not related to their actual uses. An automobile is designed to transport people and goods. However, the type of automobile a person drives can also have social meaning. In the United States, for instance, owning certain automobiles is seen as a sign of wealth and success. These automobiles convey this message only because people have attached this meaning to them.

✓ **READING PROGRESS CHECK**

Discussing What determines the cultural meanings of physical objects?

nonmaterial culture ideas, knowledge, and beliefs that influence people's behavior

material culture the concrete, tangible objects of a culture

beliefs ideas about the nature of reality

contrast dissimilar attributes among things with common natures

encounter to come across or meet

Consumers often line up in advance to be the first to purchase a new item.

▶ CRITICAL THINKING

1. ***Analyzing*** Are these people standing in line only to purchase the item, or does the item hold additional cultural meaning for them? Explain.

2. ***Making Connections*** What item would you stand in line to buy? Why?

CARTOON >

THE CAT DID IT.
Ideal and real culture are often at odds.

▶ **CRITICAL THINKING**

1. **Identifying Central Issues** How does this cartoon illustrate the gap between ideal and real culture?

2. **Speculating** Why do you think the boy lies about his role in painting the cat? Will the lie work? Explain.

Ideal and Real Culture

GUIDING QUESTION *How is real culture different from ideal culture?*

A gap sometimes exists between cultural guidelines and actual behavior. This gap is captured in the concepts of ideal and real culture. **Ideal culture** refers to cultural guidelines publicly embraced by members of a society. In contrast, **real culture** refers to actual behavior patterns, which often conflict with these guidelines.

One value of America's ideal culture is honesty. Yet in real culture, honesty is not always practiced. Some taxpayers annually violate both the letter and spirit of existing tax laws. Some businesspeople engage in dishonest business practices. Some students cheat on exams. These are not isolated instances. They are real cultural patterns passed on from generation to generation. We are not referring here to individuals whose violations of norms include murder, rape, and robbery. These types of antisocial behavior violate even real culture.

Does the fact that we sometimes ignore cultural guidelines make ideal culture meaningless? Absolutely not. In an imperfect world, ideal culture provides high standards. These ideals are targets that most people attempt to reach most of the time. Ideal culture also permits the detection of deviant behavior. Individuals who deviate too far from the ideal pattern are sanctioned. This helps preserve the ideal culture.

ideal culture cultural guidelines that group members claim to accept

real culture actual behavior patterns of members of a group

☑ **READING PROGRESS CHECK**

Stating What is an example of the gap between ideal and real culture?

LESSON 4 REVIEW

Reviewing Vocabulary
1. *Summarizing* Why are beliefs important?

Using Your Notes
2. *Organizing* Use your notes to write a paragraph summary of the lesson.

Answering the Guiding Questions
3. *Contrasting* What is the difference between material culture and nonmaterial culture?

4. *Explaining* How is real culture different from ideal culture?

Writing Activity
5. *Narrative* Write a short story that illustrates the conflict between ideal and real culture in everyday life.

networks

There's More Online!

- ☑ **CARTOON** We're Number One!
- ☑ **CHART** Cultural Universals
- ☑ **IMAGE** Groups of the Counterculture
- ☑ **SELF-CHECK QUIZ**

Reading HELPDESK

Academic Vocabulary
- diversity
- similarity

Content Vocabulary
- social categories
- subculture
- counterculture
- ethnocentrism
- cultural universals
- cultural particulars

TAKING NOTES: *Integration of Knowledge and Ideas*

ORGANIZING As you read about cultural diversity and similarity, use the information from the lesson to create word webs, similar to the one below, for three of the Content Vocabulary terms.

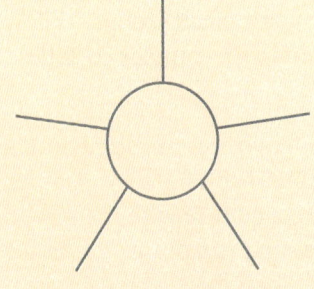

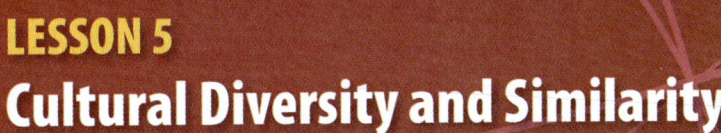

LESSON 5
Cultural Diversity and Similarity

ESSENTIAL QUESTION • *How does culture influence society?*

IT MATTERS BECAUSE

Cultures change according to three major processes. Cultures contain groups within them called subcultures and countercultures that differ in important ways from the main culture. People tend to make judgments based on the values of their own cultures. While apparently very different on the surface, all cultures have common traits or elements that sociologists call cultural universals.

Cultural Change

GUIDING QUESTION *Why does culture change?*

So far we have only talked briefly about how cultures can change. Actually the processes that govern cultural change are so important they will be discussed in more depth in another chapter. Briefly, however, all cultures experience change. Norms, values, and beliefs are relatively stable, but they do change over time. For example, many of your grandparents never went to college; as teenagers, your parents never texted friends. It was not that long ago that middle-class women with young children were discouraged from working outside the home. Interracial dating was once widely condemned in the United States, but it gradually became more widely accepted. A study conducted by the Pew Research Center found that in 2010 about 15% of all new marriages were between spouses who were of different races or ethnicities. These are aspects of culture that are changing in response to certain processes.

Culture changes for three reasons. One cause is *discovery*, the process of finding something that already exists. While the athletic abilities of females were once generally unrecognized, female participation in competitive sports grew rapidly in the late twentieth century. This began to change the perception of girls and women and the relationship between males and females.

Culture also changes through *invention*, the creation of something new. Science has led to inventions that have changed the world since the fifteenth century, from the creation of the steam engine to the personal computer, the cellular phone, and the Internet. Such inventions have greatly altered our way of life.

Culture 87

A third cause of cultural change is *diffusion*, the borrowing of aspects of culture from other cultures. One aspect of culture that diffuses rapidly is food. Tacos, pizza, and hamburgers can be found on menus all over the world. Christmas trees and piñatas are part of celebrations in many countries. Ideas are also diffused. Japanese society was fundamentally transformed as a result of the adoption of democracy and capitalism after World War II. As stated earlier, these three processes of cultural change will be examined more closely in another chapter.

☑ **READING PROGRESS CHECK**

Identifying What are three reasons culture changes?

Cultural Diversity

GUIDING QUESTION *What are subcultures and countercultures?*

Cultural **diversity** exists in all societies. Some diversity is a result of **social categories**—groups that share a social characteristic such as age, gender, or religion. Certain behaviors are associated with particular ages, genders, or religions. For example, devout Catholics are expected to attend Mass regularly.

Factors that promote cultural diversity in the United States and other countries include immigration, globalism, better and faster communications, travel, and increased cultural relevance. *Cultural relevance* means making sure that materials are appropriate for the cultures for which they are intended. For example, having information available in multiple languages may make it more culturally relevant.

Other aspects of cultural diversity include pop and folk culture. *Folk culture* refers to cultural patterns practiced by traditional groups, often in isolation, while *pop culture* refers to cultural patterns that are widespread among a society's population. Both increase the cultural diversity of a society. A third important element affecting cultural diversity is culture shock. *Culture shock* is the feeling of surprise and confusion people may feel when they encounter cultural practices different from their own.

Cultural diversity also comes from groups that differ in particular ways from the larger culture. These groups participate in the larger culture. They may speak the language, work regular jobs, eat and dress like most others, and attend recognized houses of worship. But despite sharing in the broader culture, they have some ways of thinking, feeling, and behaving that set them apart. Such groups—known as *subcultures* and *countercultures*—are usually found in large, complex societies.

Subcultures

A **subculture** is part of the dominant culture but differs from it in some important respects. The subculture of San Francisco's Chinatown is a good example. Early Chinese immigrants brought much of their native culture with them to the United States and have attempted to retain it by passing it from generation to generation. Although Chinese residents of Chinatown have been greatly affected by American culture, they have kept many cultural patterns of their own, such as language, diet, and family structure.

Several problems are associated with subcultures. Members of American subcultures can be labeled with negative stereotypes, from both within and outside the society. Some Americans associate teenagers of various ethnicities as being gang members prone to criminality and violence. Many stereotypes are promoted and reinforced through popular culture, such as the movies. American "Westerns" have popularized certain images and stereotypes of American cowboys and Native Americans around the world. People from other countries

diversity the condition of being made up of different elements, such as racial identities, ethnicities, religious beliefs, and so on

social categories groupings of persons who share a social characteristic

subculture a group that is part of the dominant culture but that differs from it in some important respects

sometimes think of Americans in terms of these stereotypes; for example, Americans can be seen as rough, untamed cowboys. Not all stereotypes are negative, however. The stereotypical American cowboy may be seen as rough and untamed, but he is also perceived as being brave and true to his convictions.

Subcultures can also be prone to social problems. For example, rates of alcoholism are higher than average for many Native American groups. Non-Latino African Americans have higher than average obesity rates.

Countercultures

A **counterculture** is a subculture that is deliberately and consciously opposed to certain central beliefs or attitudes of the dominant culture. A counterculture can be understood only within the context of this opposition. The rise of the youth counterculture in the latter 1960s—the "hippie" movement—set the stage for adolescent rebellion throughout the world. More recent examples of primarily teenage countercultures include the "goth" and the "punk" scenes. *Goth* is a shortening of the term *gothic*, meaning "dark, strangely mysterious, and remote." Punk is a philosophy of rebellion and sexual revolution popularized by the lyrics and music of punk-rock bands.

Prison counterculture surfaced at the trial of John King, a man convicted of the gruesome truck-dragging murder of James Byrd, Jr. During an earlier prison stretch, King had become a member of a white supremacist gang that promoted many forms of violence. The gang's motto was "blood in, blood out," meaning that entry into the gang demanded a violent act, and leaving the gang would result in violence as well. Delinquent gangs, motorcycle gangs, certain types of drug groups, and revolutionary or religious groups may also form countercultures.

counterculture a subculture deliberately and consciously opposed to certain central beliefs or attitudes of the dominant culture

Punks, beatniks, the Occupy Wall Street Movement, and right-wing militia are examples of American countercultures.

▶ **CRITICAL THINKING**

Comparing and Contrasting
Why do we label these groups as countercultures? How are they alike? How are they different?

☑ **READING PROGRESS CHECK**

Explaining What are social categories?

Culture 89

Connecting Sociology to History

THE HIPPIES

When many Americans hear the word *counterculture*, they think of young people in the 1960s. The 1960s were a collision of some important demographic and cultural forces. Throughout the 1930s and early 1940s, during the Great Depression and World War II, the birthrate declined. Following the war, a "baby boom" occurred, and by the 1960s, young people aged 14–25 comprised a much larger share of the population. These young people grew up in a time of strong economic growth. Some came to reject their Depression-raised parents' sturdy work ethic and social conformity and sought personal fulfillment instead.

The 1960s were a time of social and cultural upheaval. The civil rights struggle, anti-Vietnam war protests, women's liberation, and other social movements raised serious questions about American society and culture. Some young people, who came to be known as hippies, answered these questions by rejecting mainstream society and culture, which they saw as materialistic, class-based, and separated from nature.

Hippies believed that they could create a new culture, free from the pressures of material gain, the corporate "rat race," and a reliance on technology. Their new culture would be built on egalitarian principles and achieved through individual self-awareness, self-fulfillment, and self-expression. This quest was marked by nonconformity in dress, hairstyles, and personal habits. It also often led to an indulgence in drugs and sexual expression.

▶ **CRITICAL THINKING**

1. **Analyzing** How did the social movements of the 1960s influence hippies?
2. **Differentiating** Why are the hippies considered a counterculture and not a subculture?

Hippie counterculture grew in the 1960s.

CARTOON

WE'RE NUMBER ONE!
Ethnocentrism can affect the way we look at the world.

▶ **CRITICAL THINKING**

1. **Interpreting** How is ethnocentrism affecting this sports fan's reasoning?
2. **Identifying Bias** What examples of ethnocentrism have you encountered recently?

Ethnocentrism

GUIDING QUESTION *How does ethnocentrism affect perceptions?*

Once people learn their culture, they tend to become strongly committed to it. In fact, they often cannot imagine any other way of life. They may judge others in terms of their own cultural standards—a practice referred to as **ethnocentrism**. Ethnocentrism is not unique to any one country or group. Because people internalize their own culture, they often feel uncomfortable when confronted by an unfamiliar culture. Ethnocentrism is at the heart of the culture shock some people experience when they travel to new places.

ethnocentrism judging others in terms of one's own cultural standards

Examples of Ethnocentrism

Examples of ethnocentrism are plentiful. The Olympic Games are much more than an arena of athletic competition. The Games are also an expression of ethnocentrism. Political and nationalistic undercurrents run through the Olympics. A country's final ranking in this competition for gold, silver, and bronze medals is frequently taken as a reflection of the country's status on the world stage.

Ethnocentrism also exists within societies. Regional rivalries in the United States are a source of many humorous stories, but these jokes reflect an underlying ethnocentrism. Boston is said by some (mostly Bostonians) to be the hub of the universe. Texans often claim to have the biggest and best of everything. New Yorkers bemoan the lack of culture in Los Angeles. Finally, members of churches, schools, and political parties all over the United States feel that their particular ways of living should be adopted by others.

Ethnocentrism, Globalism, and Diversity

Ethnocentrism is almost always in conflict with globalism. As the countries of the world become more interconnected, cultural diffusion brings new ideas. In the United States as well as in other countries, these new ideas can cause either positive or negative reactions in societies. For example, think about how U.S. soldiers serving in Afghanistan and Iraq sometimes encountered suspicion or hostility from the local populations because of differing cultural values. But also think about what you might eat for lunch. Pizza (from Italy), tacos (from Mexico), falafel (from the Middle East), and sushi (from Japan) are just a few of the foreign foods that have met with wide acceptance in the United States. Even in a foreign country, you could probably find a hamburger or hot dog.

Culture

Quick Case Study

HOW DO STEREOTYPES AFFECT YOU?
Many of our ideas about different groups of people in different social categories are unexamined. In this experiment, you will look more closely at how people perceive other groups.

Procedure
1. With a partner, list five different social categories (groups that share a social characteristic such as age, gender, or religion). Examples are senior citizens, teenagers, women, Muslims, and evangelical Christians.
2. Read your list to another pair of students and have each of them say five words that come to mind immediately. Write down the words.

Analysis
As you read through the lists of words, consider these questions.
1. Do any of the words show stereotyping?
2. Is the stereotyping positive or negative?
3. What might be the basis or reason for each word listed?

Ethnocentrism: Advantages and Disadvantages

Ethnocentrism has two faces—it offers both advantages and disadvantages. On the positive side, ethnocentrism builds group loyalty. People feel good about themselves and about others in their group when they believe that what they are doing is right and superior to what other groups do. The patriotism that people feel for the actions of their own country during times of war is an example of this side of ethnocentrism. The belief that the actions of their own country are just helps make people more willing to accept the sacrifices necessary in war. Similarly, ethnocentrism helps maintain traditions and values that are central to a society. People are more likely to uphold traditions and values if they believe that these traditions and values are superior to the traditions and values held by other groups. By supporting traditions and values, ethnocentrism adds to the stability of a society.

If a society is too rigid, however, it becomes inflexible. Extreme ethnocentrism can prevent change for the better. Societies whose members are firmly convinced of their superiority tend not to create anything new or accept new ideas. The ancient Chinese, for example, built a series of walls to keep invaders out. The walls helped unify China, but they also kept new ideas out. As a result China's culture changed slowly over the centuries.

Extreme ethnocentrism can have a much darker side. It can divide people and lead to hatred and violence. Adolf Hitler's Final Solution was ethnocentrism at its worst. Hitler and his Nazi regime attempted to wipe out European Jewry and other minorities in an effort to establish racial purity. The result was the slaughter of some 6 million Jews and large numbers of people from other targeted groups. In the United States, racial ethnocentrism led to discrimination against African Americans and other minority populations. The civil rights movement was born to combat the effects of this ethnocentrism. Today, many states are passing laws that increase the penalties against people who commit violent acts against others based on their race, origin, or religion.

☑ **READING PROGRESS CHECK**

Discussing What are some dangers of extreme ethnocentrism?

Cultural Universals

GUIDING QUESTION *What are cultural universals, and why do they exist?*

Although it may seem that different cultures have little in common, researchers have identified more than seventy common cultural traits that exist in all cultures. Social scientists refer to these common traits as **cultural universals**. The American anthropologist George Murdock attempted to define these cultural universals in his pioneering 1945 paper "The Common Denominators of Cultures." He identified such cultural universals as sports, cooking, courtship, division of labor, education, etiquette, funeral rites, family, government, hospitality, housing, inheritance rules, joking, language, medicine, marriage, mourning, music, property rights, religious rituals, sexual restrictions, status differences, and tool making. Because all societies have these cultural universals, they are more similar than you think.

Expression of Cultural Universals

Cultural universals are not always carried out in the same way. In fact, different cultures have developed quite different ways to express universals. These are called **cultural particulars**. One cultural universal is caring for children. In the United States, women historically worked within the home caring for children, and men worked outside the home. Although this has changed, women in this country are still largely responsible for child care. Among the Manus of New Guinea, in contrast, the man is completely in charge of child rearing. Among the Mbuti pygmies and the Lovedu of Africa and the Navajo and Iroquois of North America, men and women share equally in domestic and economic tasks.

cultural universals general cultural traits that exist in all cultures

cultural particulars the ways in which a culture expresses universal traits

A smile means the same thing in every culture.

▶ **CRITICAL THINKING**

1. *Identifying* What cultural universals can you identify in this photo?
2. *Describing* What cultural particulars do you see in this photo?

Cultural Universals

Economy	Institutions	Arts	Language	Environment	Recreation	Beliefs
Trade	Family	Art	Words	Communities	Games	Values
Tools	Government	Literature	Expressions	Geography	Toys	Traditions
Technology	Education	Dance	Pronunciations	Geology	Arts	Ethnicity
Goods	Religion	Theater	Alphabets	Habitat	Media	Customs
Services	Economy	Music	Symbols	Wildlife	Holidays	Religions
Jobs		Crafts		Climates	Festivals	Morals
Business		Folktales		Resources		
Transportation						
Communications						
Food						
Shelter						
Clothing						

CHART

CULTURAL UNIVERSALS
Researchers have identified more than 70 traits that appear in all cultures.

▶ **CRITICAL THINKING**

1. Analyzing Choose one of the traits in the chart and explain how it can be applied to all cultures.

2. Contrasting How is the trait expressed differently in two different cultures?

similarity the quality of being alike

Accounting for Cultural Universals

The biological **similarity** shared by all human beings helps account for many cultural universals. If a society is to survive, children must be born and cared for, and some type of family structure must exist. Groups that deliberately eliminate the family—such as the Shakers religious sect of New England—disappear. Because people become ill, there must be some sort of medical care. Because people die, there must be funeral rites, mourning, and inheritance rules. Because food is necessary, cooking must be done. Many other similarities lead to other cultural universals.

The physical environment provides another reason for the existence of cultural universals. Because humans cannot survive without protection from the environment, some form of shelter must be created. Armies were formed to settle disputes over boundaries and important waterways.

Finally, cultural universals exist because of the similarity in the types of social problems societies face. If a society is to survive, new members must be taught the culture. Goods and services must be produced and distributed. Tasks must be assigned, and work must be accomplished. Cultures develop similar methods of solving these problems.

☑ **READING PROGRESS CHECK**

Identifying What is one factor that explains why cultural universals exist?

LESSON 5 REVIEW

Reviewing Vocabulary
1. *Identifying* What is ethnocentrism?
2. *Questioning* Why do cultural particulars exist?

Using Your Notes
3. *Organizing* Use your word webs to write a statement for each of your words telling how the idea influences cultural change. Then give an example that supports your statement.

Answering the Guiding Questions
4. *Identifying Central Issues* Why does culture change?

5. *Explaining* What are subcultures and countercultures?
6. *Theorizing* How does ethnocentrism affect perceptions?
7. *Explaining* What are cultural universals, and why do they exist?

Writing Activity
8. *Informative/Explanatory* Think of a social norm in the United States. Then write a paragraph describing how two American subcultures differ in their approaches to the social norm. The subcultures could be based on ethnicity, national origin, age, socioeconomic status, or gender.

CHAPTER 3 Assessment

Directions: On a separate sheet of paper, answer the questions below. Make sure you read carefully and answer all parts of the questions.

Lesson Review

Lesson 1

1. **Identifying Central Issues** Describe an example of an action that reflects both material and nonmaterial aspects of a culture.

2. **Comparing and Contrasting** What are the similarities and differences between reflexes and drives? Give an example of a reflex and a drive.

Lesson 2

3. **Analyzing** How does telling a friend about a trip you took last summer show how language frees humans from the limits of time and place?

4. **Explaining** How does the hypothesis of linguistic relativity relate to the large number of words connected to *work*, such as *career, job, position, labor, management, calling, post,* and *livelihood*?

Lesson 3

5. **Making Connections** What is the relationship between norms and sanctions?

6. **Specifying** What are folkways? Give three examples of folkways either in the United States or elsewhere.

Lesson 4

7. **Identifying** Give two examples each of material and nonmaterial culture in the United States.

8. **Contrasting** How does real culture differ from ideal culture? Use an example to explain.

Lesson 5

9. **Contrasting** Choose a cultural universal, such as wildlife, religion, or music. Compare and contrast how two different cultures address this cultural universal.

10. **Analyzing** How does ethnocentrism affect a person's perceptions of others?

Critical Thinking

11. **Drawing Inferences** More than any other symbol of our country, the American flag provokes powerful emotional responses. Some people are willing to give their lives for it, while others have burned it in protest. Discuss why this symbol is an example of nonmaterial culture and how people assign meaning to it.

12. **Considering Perspectives** All societies have cultural universals, as discussed in this chapter. Why, then, are so many groups in conflict? Think of examples of groups in this country that seem to be in conflict, such as animal rights activists and fur shop owners, and examine the reasons for these conflicts.

13. **Evaluating** Some Amish parents have gone to jail rather than enroll their children in public schools. What does this say about Amish cultural values?

21st Century Skills

CREATING AND USING GRAPHS, CHARTS, DIAGRAMS AND TABLES

14. **Creating Graphs and Charts** Think about what you have learned about folkways, mores, laws, norms, sanctions, and values. Then design a chart, diagram, or other visual that explains how these six ideas are related. The chart below provides one example. You might redraw this chart and fill it in or design a different visual.

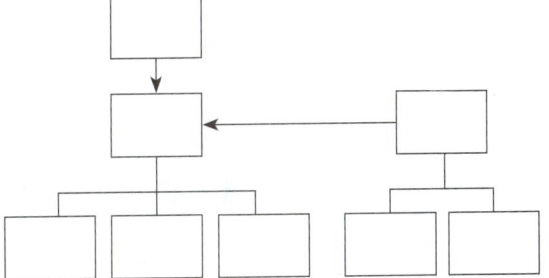

Need Extra Help?

If You've Missed Question	1	2	3	4	5	6	7	8	9	10	11	12	13	14
Go to page	68	70	72	73	78	76	84–85	86	93–94	91–92	84–85	93	79–81	75–81

Culture 95

CHAPTER 3 Assessment

Directions: On a separate sheet of paper, answer the questions below. Make sure you read carefully and answer all parts of the questions.

Exploring the Essential Question

15 *Defending* A letter to the editor of your local newspaper states that the success or failure of children in school is completely determined by whether their parents succeeded or failed in the same grade level in school. Write a response supporting or opposing this letter, using what you have learned in this chapter.

DBQ Analyzing Primary Sources

PRIMARY SOURCE

16 *Analyzing* The sport shown in the photograph is popular in several countries, most notably Spain. Supporters of this sport claim it is an ancient and honorable art and part of their nation's cultural heritage. Why do you think this sport has never become popular in the United States, as have many foreign sports such as soccer, ice hockey, and rugby (the ancestor of football)? Use what you have learned about ethnocentrism and cultural norms, beliefs, and values, along with the photograph, to discuss why the sport has not become popular in the United States.

College and Career Readiness Skills

17 *Personal and Group Identities* You work in a government agency that provides social services to recent immigrants to this country. Your supervisor has asked you to prepare a memo to your coworkers on the topics of ethnocentrism and culture shock and how your agency should address problems that might arise because of them. Use what you have learned in this chapter to write the memo.

Research and Presentation

18 *Simulating* You and your team are archaeologists of the future, and you have just uncovered a civilization called "America." Find at least one item from three of these aspects of culture: economy, religion, sports, science/technology, education, families, and politics/government. For example, you might uncover an ATM card as an example of the economy. Prepare a presentation for the class in which your group shows your objects and shares your ideas about the civilization from which they come. Be sure to examine how these objects represent the material and nonmaterial culture of "America."

19 *Multicultural Societies* You are a Peace Corps volunteer in an African, Asian, or Middle Eastern country. To what elements of culture do you think will be most difficult for you to adjust? What characteristics of your own culture and society will the people of the country you are assigned to find most surprising? Why? Research the culture you will work in as a Peace Corps volunteer. Then write a report to your Peace Corps supervisor and present it to the class.

Need Extra Help?

If You've Missed Question	15	16	17	18	19
Go to page	68–71	75, 76, 79–81, 90	88, 91–92	84, 85	88, 91–92

Socialization

ESSENTIAL QUESTION • *What factors influence an individual's development?*

networks
There's More Online about socialization.

CHAPTER 4

Technology & Society
Mass Media and Socialization

Lesson 1
The Importance of Socialization

Lesson 2
Socialization and the Self

Lesson 3
Agents of Socialization

Lesson 4
Socialization Through the Life Cycle

Lesson 5
Processes of Socialization

Sociology Matters...

Have you ever visited a community or another country where the culture is very different from your own? Did you feel lost or unsure of what to say or how to act? We are not born knowing the rules of our culture, what is expected of us in various situations, or how to interact successfully with other people. We learn these things through the lifelong process of socialization.

◀ The family is responsible for teaching many lessons of socialization.

Blend Images/John Lund/Marc Romanelli/the Agency Collection/Getty Images

CHAPTER 4
Technology & Society

Mass Media and Socialization

Along with family, school, and peer groups, the mass media are primary agents of the lifelong socializing process.

The mass media may be defined as communications technologies intended to reach a large audience. Such media are often separated into two categories. *Broadcast media* transfer content electronically and include television, radio, film, CDs, and DVDs. *Print media* employ physical objects to diffuse content. Examples are newspapers, magazines, books, pamphlets, posters, and brochures.

Ever since the mid-1400s, when Johannes Gutenberg invented the printing press, the mass media have had an enormous impact on people's lives. Today, the media are powerful shapers of socialization. To take only two examples, magazine advertisements and television programs transmit influential, persuasive (and sometimes unwritten or unspoken) messages and stereotypes relating to style, personal goals, political choices, and gender roles. In many respects, the media shape how we see ourselves and others.

The media are also in a continuous state of flux. In the mid-1900s, newspaper and television were two of the most powerful forms of mass media in the United States. Today, both are in sharp decline. The reason for the decline: the explosive growth of the Internet. People are forsaking newspapers for other sources of news. And young people are deserting the TV screen for other screens, primarily computer monitors, tablet displays, and the miniature displays on mobile phones.

MILLENNIALS
Born between 1977 and 1993

GEN X
Born between 1965 and 1976

YOUNGER BOOMERS
Born between 1955 and 1964

OLDER BOOMERS
Born between 1946 and 1954

SILENT GENERATION
Born between 1937 and 1945

G.I. GEN
Born before 1936

Source: Pew Research Center, 2011

Many people today receive news and other information electronically rather than through print media.

▶ **CRITICAL THINKING**

Drawing Conclusions In what ways do you think these brothers are being socialized? Explain.

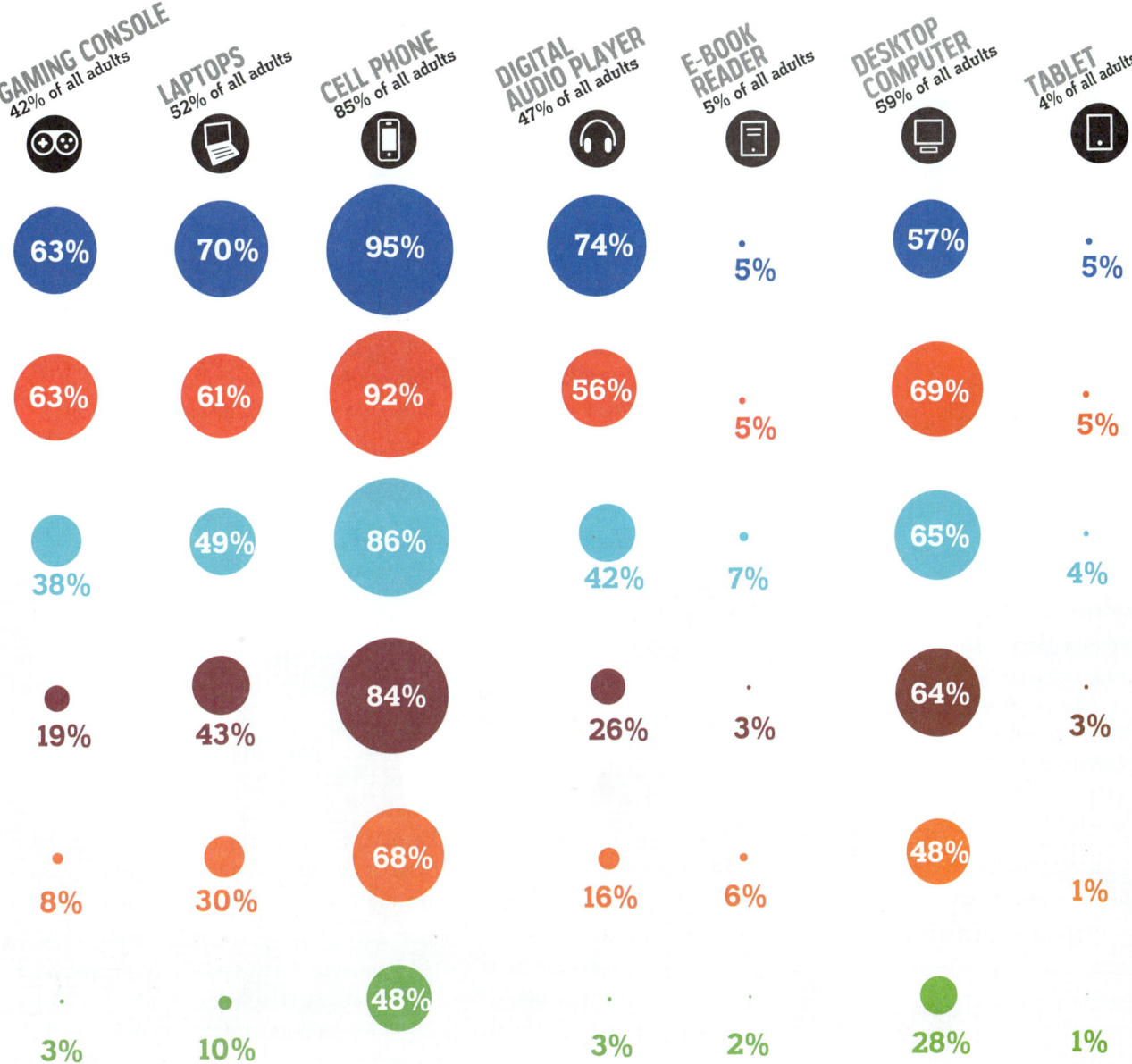

Thinking Like a Sociologist

1 Evaluating

Review the infographic. What does it tell you about the state of mass media today?

2 Interpreting

Why do you think that television and newspapers are in decline as favored forms of mass media?

networks

There's More Online!

- ☑ **CARTOON** Social Interaction
- ☑ **GRAPHIC ORGANIZER** Importance of Socialization
- ☑ **IMAGE** Infant Socialization
- ☑ **IMAGE** Well-Socialized Children
- ☑ **SELF-CHECK QUIZ**

LESSON 1
The Importance of Socialization

ESSENTIAL QUESTION • *What factors influence an individual's development?*

Reading HELPDESK

Academic Vocabulary
- transmission
- isolation

Content Vocabulary
- socialization

TAKING NOTES:
Integration of Knowledge and Ideas

CAUSE AND EFFECT As you read about the importance of socialization, use a graphic organizer like the one below to record details about the effects of socialization versus isolation.

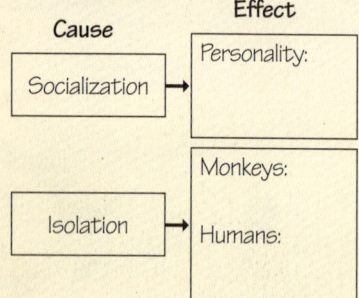

IT MATTERS BECAUSE

Socialization is the cultural process of learning to participate in group life. Without it, we would not develop many of the characteristics we associate with being human. Studies have shown that animals and human infants who are deprived of intensive and prolonged social contact with others are stunted in their emotional and social growth.

Socialization and Personality

GUIDING QUESTION *Why is socialization important?*

Nearly all the human social behavior we consider natural and normal is learned. It is natural to us in the United States for husbands and wives to walk along side-by-side. In many places in India, however, it seems natural for wives to walk slightly behind their husbands. In fact, nearly all aspects of social life (including walking patterns) are not natural but learned through the process of socialization. Human beings at birth are helpless and without knowledge of their society's ways of thinking, feeling, and behaving. If a human infant is to grow and participate in cultural life, much learning has to take place. This is the role of socialization. **Socialization** is the cultural process of learning to participate in group life. Such learning takes place through cultural **transmission**.

Socialization begins at birth and continues throughout life. Successful socialization enables people to fit into all kinds of social groups. Socialization must occur if high school freshmen are to adjust to a new situation, if graduating seniors are to look for employment, and if the president of the United States is to govern successfully.

Psychological case studies point out the importance of socialization early in life. Without prolonged and intensive social contact, children do not learn such basics as walking, talking, and loving. Without socialization, a human infant cannot develop the set of attitudes, beliefs, values, and behaviors associated with being an individual in society. Without socialization, infants and children cannot develop the capacity for language. Without language, they cannot understand human relationships. Without this understanding, they cannot form bonds.

Researching the Effects of Social Isolation

Suppose you wanted to design an experiment to see how socialization affects infants. You would have to set up an experiment that compared a group of normally socialized infants (the *control* group) with a group of isolated infants—infants with little or no human contact (the *experimental* group). For obvious reasons, such experiments are not conducted with human infants. Such experiments have been done with monkeys, however.

Psychologists Harry Harlow and Margaret Harlow devised a famous set of experiments that showed the negative effects of social **isolation** on rhesus monkeys. In one experiment, the Harlows isolated infant monkeys for different lengths of time before introducing them to group life. They found that monkeys that had been isolated for around three months were able to learn to play and to adjust to group life. The monkeys that had been isolated for six months or more never adjusted to group life and were rejected by the other monkeys. The Harlows reported that infant monkeys raised in isolation became withdrawn, hostile adults. They never exhibited normal sexual patterns. As mothers, they either rejected or ignored their babies. Sometimes, they even physically abused them.

In another experiment, the Harlows separated infant monkeys from their mothers at birth. They then exposed the infants to two artificial mothers. Both artificial mothers were wire dummies of the same approximate size and shape as real adult monkeys. One of the substitute mothers had an exposed wire body. The other was covered with soft terry cloth. Free to choose between them, the infant monkeys consistently spent more time with the soft, warm mother. Even when the exposed wire dummy became the only source of food, the terry cloth mother remained the favorite. Closeness and comfort seemed to be more important to these monkeys than food. When the researchers frightened the monkeys with a mechanical toy bear or a rubber snake, they consistently ran to their cloth mothers for security and protection. This led the Harlows to conclude that infant-mother bonding is not the result of feeding. Rather, it is the result of close physical contact, what in humans we would call *cuddling*.

Generalizing from Monkeys to Humans

Rhesus monkeys are not humans. Thus scientists are careful when drawing conclusions about human behavior from animal studies. Yet many experts on human development believe that—like the rhesus monkeys in the Harlows' experiments—human infants have emotional needs for affection, intimacy, and warmth that are as important as their physiological needs for food, water, and protection. Contact and communication appear to be essential to normal human development. Human babies denied close human contact usually have difficulty forming emotional ties with other people. According to classic studies by René Spitz and Lawrence Casler, the developmental growth rate of institutionalized children—who generally receive less physical contact than children raised in family settings—can be improved with only twenty minutes of extra touching a day.

✓ **READING PROGRESS CHECK**

Analyzing How does research on the social isolation of rhesus monkeys show the importance of socialization?

socialization the process of learning to participate in a group

transmission the act or process of conveying information from one person to another

isolation the condition of being set apart from others

The rhesus monkeys in the Harlows' experiment on isolation consistently ran to their terry cloth "mothers" when frightened.

▶ **CRITICAL THINKING**

Determining Cause and Effect
Why do you think the monkeys preferred the cloth mother over the wire mother?

Case Studies on Isolated Children: Anna, Isabelle, and Genie

GUIDING QUESTION *How can a lack of socialization affect children?*

To understand more about how socialization affects development, we will look at the case histories of three children—Anna, Isabelle, and Genie—who were socially and emotionally abused. Anna, Isabelle, and Genie had traumatic childhoods. Although these children were born many years ago, similar situations still occur today, unfortunately.

Anna

Anna was found tied to a small chair in a second-floor storage room on a farm in Pennsylvania in 1938. According to an article in the *New York Times* published at the time of her discovery, the chair was tilted back, and Anna's arms were tied above her head.

Anna was born on March 6, 1932, the second child born to her unmarried mother. For the first six to ten months of her life, Anna lived at a children's home or in the care of a practical nurse. Those who cared for her then said that she seemed to be a normal baby. Then, when outside agencies refused to pay for her care, Anna was returned to her mother's home. Anna's mother feared that the sight of the child would anger her father, so she kept Anna confined to a small upstairs room in the family farmhouse. For five years, Anna received only milk to drink. When finally found, she was barely alive. Her legs were skeleton-like, and her stomach was bloated from malnutrition. Apparently, Anna had seldom been moved from one position to another, and her clothes and bedding were filthy. She did not know what it was like to be held or comforted. At the time of her discovery, Anna could not walk or talk and showed few signs of intelligence.

Sociologist Kingsley Davis visited Anna soon after her discovery. He noted that three days after arriving at the county home where she was being cared for,

---

CARTOON

SOCIAL INTERACTION
We learn to participate in group life through interaction with others.

▶ **CRITICAL THINKING**

1. **Analyzing** Prior to their conversation, how do you think the two "cavemen" were interacting?
2. **Drawing Conclusions** How does this cartoon illustrate the importance of language in human relationships?

Anna begin to show slight improvement. When she first arrived, she had lain motionless and expressionless. By the time Davis saw her on the third day, Anna could sit up if she was placed in a sitting position, and she could move her arms, legs, and head. Davis attributed these changes to the fact that Anna had been given attention, a high-vitamin diet, and massages. She liked food, but she could not chew solid food or drink from a cup. She had to be fed with a spoon or a bottle. Although she did not cry or smile, she lost her temper when people tried to restrain her. When Davis returned ten days after his first visit, he noted some additional progress. For example, she had begun to smile and handle her toys.

During the first year and a half after being found, Anna continued to live at the county home for children. She learned to walk, to understand simple commands, and to feed herself. She could recall people she had seen. But her speech was that of a one-year-old.

Anna was then transferred to a school for learning disabled children where she made further progress. Still, at the age of seven, her mental age was only nineteen months, and her social maturity was that of a two-year-old. A year later, she could bounce and catch a ball, participate as a follower in group activities, eat normally (although with a spoon only), attend to her toilet needs, and dress herself (except for handling buttons and snaps). At this point, she had acquired the speech level of a two-year-old. By the time of her death at age ten, she had made additional progress. She could carry out instructions, identify a few colors, build with blocks, wash her hands, brush her teeth, and try to help other children. Her developing capacity for emotional attachment was reflected in the love she had developed for a doll.

Social interaction is critical to a child's emotional growth.

▶ **CRITICAL THINKING**

Making Connections How does playing with others help a child develop?

Isabelle

Nine months after Anna was found, Isabelle was discovered in Ohio. Kingsley Davis reported on Isabelle's case, too. Isabelle, like Anna, had been hidden away because her mother was unmarried. Isabelle's mother had been deaf since the age of two and did not speak. She stayed with her child in a dark room, secluded from the rest of the family. Isabelle's mother eventually escaped from her parents' house and took Isabelle with her. When Ohio authorities found them, Isabelle was six. She was physically ill from an inadequate diet and lack of sunshine. Her legs were so bowed that when she stood the soles of her shoes rested against each other, and her walk was a skittering movement. Some of her actions were like those of a six-month-old infant. Unable to talk except for a strange croaking sound, Isabelle communicated with her mother by means of gestures. Like an animal in the wild, she reacted with fear and hostility to strangers, especially men.

At first, Isabelle was thought to be severely learning disabled. Her initial IQ score was near the zero point. Nevertheless, an intensive program of rehabilitation was begun. After a slow start, Isabelle progressed through the usual stages of learning and development at a faster pace than normal. Within a few months she was speaking in complete sentences. Less than a year later, she could identify words and sentences. It took her only two years to acquire the skills mastered by a normal six-year-old. By the time she was eight and a half, Isabelle was on an educational par with children her age. By outward appearances, she was an intelligent, happy, energetic child. At age fourteen, she participated in all the school activities normal for other children in her grade.

Studies have shown that children raised under extremely isolated conditions have little or no chance of ever being socialized.

▶ **CRITICAL THINKING**

Interpreting Significance How does the case of Genie support the theory that the effects of prolonged isolation are difficult to overcome?

To Isabelle's good fortune, she, unlike Anna, benefited from intensive instruction at the hands of trained professionals. Her ability to progress may also have been because she was confined with her mother for company and comforting.

Genie

Isabelle was the exception not the rule. Genie's fate was more typical. Genie was found in 1970 in California, when she was 14 years old. From the time she was nearly two, Genie's father had kept her in a locked room, believing that she was mentally disabled. She was tied to a potty chair and forced to sit alone with no one to talk to and little to look at.

When Genie was discovered, she weighed only 59 pounds. Her mental capacity was that of a one-year-old. Much of her behavior was subhuman. Because Genie's father severely punished her for making any sounds, she never sobbed when she cried or spoke when angry. Because her father never gave her solid food, she could not chew. Her social behavior was primitive. She had a strange bunny walk, and she sniffled, clawed, and spat. If another person had something she liked, she would take it without asking.

A team of doctors and rehabilitation specialists studied Genie and worked to help her overcome the effects of isolation. They tested her brain waves and found they were abnormal. They worked to teach her to speak. Speech was a special interest of some of the researchers. Linguists had put forth the theory that language is more than simply learned behavior. Some argued that there was a window within which people needed to learn to speak and if language was not achieved by puberty, it might not be attainable. A year into therapy, Genie had learned some words and phrases, but her language ability resembled that of an 18-month-old. Although she made further progress, she never achieved complete language ability.

Implications

The implication of the cases of Anna, Isabelle, and Genie is unmistakable. The personal and social development associated with being human is acquired through intensive and prolonged social contact with others.

✓ **READING PROGRESS CHECK**

Comparing and Contrasting How were the cases of Anna, Isabelle, and Genie similar and different?

LESSON 1 REVIEW

Reviewing Vocabulary
1. ***Summarizing*** Why does socialization continue throughout life?
2. ***Explaining*** In what ways is socialization the opposite of isolation?

Using Your Notes
3. ***Describing*** Use your notes to describe the effects of a lack of socialization on Anna, Isabelle, and Genie.

Answering the Guiding Questions
4. ***Assessing*** Why is socialization important?
5. ***Evaluating*** How can a lack of socialization affect children?

Writing Activity
6. ***Argument*** Do you think sociologists have overemphasized the importance of human contact in an individual's development? Briefly describe the sociological view. Then take a stand for or against the view. Provide reasons for your stand.

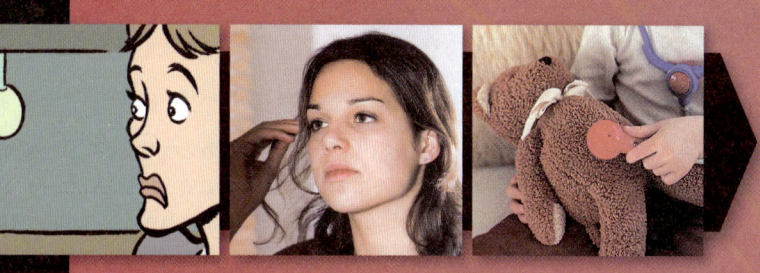

networks

There's More Online!

- ☑ **CARTOON** The Looking-Glass Self
- ☑ **CHART** Theoretical Perspectives: Socialization and the Mass Media
- ☑ **IMAGE** Socialization Process: Play Stage
- ☑ **SELF-CHECK QUIZ**

Reading HELPDESK

Academic Vocabulary
- distort
- anticipate

Content Vocabulary
- self-concept
- looking-glass self
- significant others
- role taking
- imitation stage
- play stage
- game stage
- generalized other
- "me"
- "I"

TAKING NOTES:
Key Ideas and Details

LISTING As you read about how the different theoretical perspectives view the socialization of the self, use a graphic organizer like this one to list the main assumptions of each approach.

Functionalism	Conflict Theory	Symbolic Interactionism
•	•	•
•	•	•
•	•	•

LESSON 2
Socialization and the Self

ESSENTIAL QUESTION • *What factors influence an individual's development?*

IT MATTERS BECAUSE

All three theoretical perspectives agree that socialization is needed if cultural and societal values are to be learned. Symbolic interactionism offers the most fully developed perspective for studying socialization. In this approach, the self-concept is developed by using other people as mirrors for learning about ourselves.

The Functionalist and Conflict Perspectives on Socialization

GUIDING QUESTION *How do functionalism and the conflict perspective explain socialization?*

Each of the three major theoretical perspectives provides insights into socialization. Yet functionalism and conflict theory approach socialization from a societal level. Functionalism examines how socialization helps maintain social institutions, while conflict theory focuses on its role in social control. Symbolic interactionism is interested in the role individuals and their social relationships play in socialization, so it allows for a more complete understanding than the other two.

Functionalism stresses the ways groups work together to create a stable society. Schools and families, for example, socialize children by teaching the same basic norms, beliefs, and values. If it were otherwise, society could not exist as a whole. It would be fragmented and chaotic.

The conflict perspective views socialization as a way of perpetuating the status quo. When people are socialized to accept their family's social class, for example, they help preserve the current class system. People learn to accept their social status before they have enough self-awareness to realize what is happening. Because they do not challenge their position in life, they do not upset the existing class structure. Consequently, socialization maintains the social, political, and economic advantages of the higher social classes.

☑ **READING PROGRESS CHECK**

Contrasting How do functionalists and conflict theorists differ in their explanations of socialization?

Socialization **105**

Symbolic Interactionism and Socialization

GUIDING QUESTION *How does symbolic interactionism explain socialization?*

In the early part of the twentieth century, George Herbert Mead and Charles Horton Cooley developed the symbolic interactionist perspective. They challenged the once widely held belief that human nature is biologically determined—that you are a certain way because you were born that way. For them, human nature is a product of society. Symbolic interactionism uses a number of key concepts to explain socialization. These concepts include:

- The self-concept
- The looking-glass self
- Significant others
- Role taking (the imitation stage, the play stage, and the game stage)
- The generalized other
- The "me" and the "I"

Self-Concept

self-concept an image of yourself as having an identity separate from other people

Charles Horton Cooley developed the idea of the **self-concept** from watching his own children at play. Your self-concept is your image of yourself as having an identity separate from other people. Cooley realized that children interpreted how others reacted to them in many ways. For example, young children learn quickly that causing some disturbance when adult visitors are present turns attention from the guests to themselves. From such insights, children learn to judge themselves in terms of how they imagine others *will* react to them. Thus, other people serve as mirrors for the development of the self. Cooley called this way of learning the **looking-glass self**—a self-concept based on our idea of others' judgments of us.

looking-glass self an image of yourself based on what you believe others think of you

Looking-Glass Self

According to Cooley, we use other people as mirrors to reflect back what we imagine they think of us. In this view, the looking-glass self is the product of a three-stage process that is constantly taking place:

1. We imagine how we appear to others (our perception of how others see us).
2. We imagine the reactions of others to our (imagined) appearance.
3. We evaluate ourselves according to how we imagine others have judged us.

CARTOON

THE LOOKING-GLASS SELF

According to Charles Horton Cooley, we develop our self-concept by imagining how others react to us.

▶ CRITICAL THINKING

1. **Evaluating** What perception does the man in the middle have of himself?
2. **Identifying Cause and Effect** What is the reaction of his friends? How might their reaction affect his self-concept?

Theoretical Perspectives

SOCIALIZATION AND MASS MEDIA
Each theoretical perspective has a unique view of the socialization process. This table identifies these views and illustrates the unique interpretation of each view with respect to the influence of the mass media on the socialization process.

Theoretical Perspective	Socialization Concepts	Examples
Functionalism	Stabilizes society	The Internet and television programs encourage social integration by exposing the entire society to shared beliefs, values, and norms.
Conflict Theory	Maintains status quo	Cable news shows and newspaper owners and editors exercise power by setting the political agenda for a community.
Symbolic Interactionism	Determines human nature	Through words and pictures, children's books expose the young to the meaning of love, manners, and motherhood.

▶ **CRITICAL THINKING**

1. **Differentiating** Which perspectives focus on maintaining society and which focus on how the mass media affect the development of the self?

2. **Contrasting** How do functionalists and conflict theorists differ in their explanations of the role of the media in the socialization process?

This is not a conscious process, and the three stages can occur in very rapid succession. The result of the process is a positive or negative self-evaluation. Suppose you have a new teacher you want to impress. You prepare hard for the next day's class. In class, as you are making a comment on the assignment, you have an image of your performance (stage 1). After finishing your comments, you think your teacher is disappointed (stage 2). Because you wanted your teacher to be impressed, you feel bad about yourself (stage 3).

Because the looking glass we use comes from our imaginations, it may be **distorted**. The teacher in this example may not have been disappointed at all. Unfortunately, the looking-glass process works even if we have distorted others' perceptions of us. If we incorrectly believe that a teacher, a date, or our parents dislike us, the consequences to us are just as real as if the distorted perception were true.

distort to twist out of the true meaning

Significant Others

George Herbert Mead pointed out that some people are more important to us than others. The people whose judgments are most important to our self-concepts are called **significant others**. For a child, significant others are likely to include mother, father, grandparents, teachers, and playmates. Teenagers place heavy reliance on their peers. The variety of significant others is greater for adults, ranging from spouses, parents, and friends to ministers and employers.

significant others those people whose reactions are most important to your self-concept

Role Taking

As humans, we carry on silent conversations. That is, we think something to ourselves and respond internally to it. All of us do this when we predict the behavior of others. Through internal conversation, we can imagine the thoughts, emotions, and behavior of others in any social situation. **Role taking** allows us to see ourselves through the eyes of someone else. It allows us to take the viewpoint of another person and then respond to ourselves from that imagined viewpoint.

With role taking we can play out scenes in our minds and **anticipate** what others will say or do. For example, you might want to ask your teacher for an "A."

role taking assuming the viewpoint of another person and using that viewpoint to shape the self-concept

anticipate to expect or predict

Socialization **107**

Connecting Sociology to Psychology

SELF-CONCEPT

The concept of self is important to both sociology and psychology. The two fields, however, approach the self from different perspectives. For symbolic interactionists, the creation of the self is a social process that is rooted in place and history. People develop their sense of self by interacting with other people in their environment and imagining how others perceive them. People living in different cultures or at different times in history would develop different self-concepts.

Many psychologists also believe that interactions with others in a person's environment shape a person's self-concept. Sigmund Freud, the founder of psychoanalysis, considered the self a social product. He also believed that personality is shaped by other people. Some psychologists believe that positive and negative rewards condition people to behave in certain ways. This conditioning shapes a person's sense of self. Other psychologists believe that people have an internal drive that pushes them to grow and improve. Like symbolic interactionists, these psychologists believe that the self-concept is created as people interact with others. Still other psychologists focus on genetics and environment as determinants of self. These psychologists believe that our biology and how our environment differs from the environments of others affect our temperament and how we view ourselves.

Sociologists see the creation of self as a social process.

▶ **CRITICAL THINKING**

1. **Comparing** How are symbolic interactionists and some psychologists similar in their views of the self?
2. **Contrasting** How do symbolic interactionists and some psychologists differ in the way they view the creation of the self?

---

imitation stage Mead's first stage in the development of role taking; children begin to imitate behaviors without understanding why

play stage Mead's second stage in the development of role taking; children act in ways they imagine other people would

game stage Mead's third stage in the development of role taking; children anticipate the actions of others based on social rules

If you could not mentally put yourself in your teacher's place, you would have no way to anticipate the objections that she might raise. But by role-playing her reaction mentally, you can be ready for those reactions and may justify your "A."

According to Mead, the ability for role taking is the product of a three-stage process. He called these the imitation stage, the play stage, and the game stage. In the **imitation stage**, which begins at around one and a half to two years, the child imitates (without understanding) the physical and verbal behavior of a significant other. This is the first step in developing the capacity for role taking.

At the age of three or four, a young child can be seen playing at being mother, father, police officer, teacher, or astronaut. This play involves acting and thinking as a child imagines another person would. This is what Mead called the **play stage**—the stage during which children take on roles of others one at a time.

The third phase in the development of role taking Mead labeled the **game stage**. In this stage, children learn to engage in more sophisticated role taking as they become able to consider the roles of several people simultaneously. Their games involve several participants, and there are rules designed to ensure that the behaviors of the participants fit together. All participants must know what they should do and what is expected of others. Imagine the confusion in a baseball game if young first-base players have not yet mastered the idea that the ball hit to a teammate will usually be thrown to them. In the second stage (the play stage), a child may pretend to be a first-base player one moment and a base runner the next. In the game stage, however, first-base players who drop their gloves and run to second base when the other team hits the ball will not remain in the game for very long. It is during the game stage that children learn to gear their behavior to the norms of the group.

Generalized Other

During the game stage, a child's self-concept, attitudes, beliefs, and values gradually come to depend less on individuals and more on general concepts. Being an honest person is no longer merely a matter of pleasing significant others such as one's mother, father, or minister. Rather, it begins to seem wrong *in principle* to be dishonest. As this change takes place, a **generalized other**—an integrated conception of the norms, values, and beliefs of one's community or society—emerges.

The "Me" and the "I"

Since the Protestant Reformation and the Enlightenment, Western society has emphasized the importance of the individual as an autonomous moral actor. In contrast, Asian cultures have traditionally placed a greater emphasis on the interconnectedness of people.

According to Mead, we can think of the self as having two parts: the "me" and the "I." The **"me"** is the part of the self created through socialization. It is constructed from the attitudes we develop by interacting with others. The "me" accounts for predictability and conformity in behavior. Yet much human behavior is spontaneous and unpredictable. An angry child may, for example, unexpectedly yell hurtful words at the parent whom he or she loves. To account for this spontaneous, unpredictable, often creative part of the self, Mead proposed the **"I."**

The "I" does not operate only in extreme situations of rage or excitement. It interacts constantly with the "me" in a kind of conversation as we conduct ourselves in social situations. According to Mead, the first reaction of the self comes from the "I." Before we act, however, this reaction is directed into socially acceptable channels by the socialized "me." When the "I" wants a piece of a friend's candy bar, the "me" reflects on the consequences of taking the candy without permission. Thus, the "I" normally takes the "me" into account before acting. The unpredictability of much human behavior demonstrates that the "me" is not always in control.

Mead chose the pronouns "I" and "me" because of their meanings in the English language. "I" is active—it is the self as subject: "I helped you." "Me" is the self as object: "You helped me." Mead stressed that the individual is not passive in the socialization process. The "I" evaluates other people's reactions to us and guides the "me" in better meeting expectations.

✔ READING PROGRESS CHECK

Making Connections How do the concepts developed by Cooley and Mead help explain the socialization process?

According to George Herbert Mead, the ability to take on roles is a three-stage process.

▶ **CRITICAL THINKING**

Assessing What stage of role taking is this child exhibiting? How do you know?

generalized other integrated conception of the norms, values, and beliefs of one's community or society

"me" the part of the self formed through socialization

"I" the part of the self that accounts for unlearned, spontaneous acts

---

LESSON 2 REVIEW

Reviewing Vocabulary
1. ***Paraphrasing*** What is the looking-glass self?
2. ***Describing*** What is the significance of the generalized other?

Using Your Notes
3. ***Interpreting*** Use your notes to explain why the symbolic interactionist approach allows for a more complete understanding of socialization than do functionalism and conflict theory.

Answering the Guiding Questions
4. ***Interpreting*** How do functionalism and the conflict perspective explain socialization?
5. ***Synthesizing*** How does symbolic interactionism explain socialization?

Writing Activity
6. ***Argument*** Select one of the three theoretical perspectives and defend that perspective's view of socialization. Support your choice with specifics.

networks

There's More Online!

- ✓ **CARTOON** Patterns of Socialization
- ✓ **GRAPHIC ORGANIZER** Agents of Socialization
- ✓ **IMAGE** Hidden Curriculum
- ✓ **TIME LINE** Major Developments in the History of Mass Media
- ✓ **SELF-CHECK QUIZ**

LESSON 3
Agents of Socialization

ESSENTIAL QUESTION • *What factors influence an individual's development?*

Reading HELPDESK

Academic Vocabulary
- objective
- exhibit

Content Vocabulary
- hidden curriculum
- peer group
- mass media

TAKING NOTES:
Key Ideas and Details

SUMMARIZING As you read about the agents of socialization, use a graphic organizer like the one below to record details about each agent.

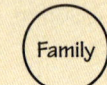

IT MATTERS BECAUSE

During childhood and adolescence, the major agents of socialization are family, religion, school, peer group, and the mass media. The family's role is critical in forming basic values, as is the role of religion. Schools introduce children to life beyond the family. In peer groups, young people learn to relate as equals. The mass media provide role models for full integration into society.

The Family and Socialization

GUIDING QUESTION *What is the family's role in socialization?*

The child's first exposure to the world occurs within the family, which is the primary agent of childhood socialization. Essential developments occur through close interactions with a few people—none of whom the child has selected. Within the family the child learns to think and speak; internalize norms, beliefs, and values; form some basic attitudes; develop a capacity for intimate and personal relationships; and acquire a self-image.

The impact of the family reaches far beyond its direct effects on the child. Our family's social class shapes what we think of ourselves and how others treat us, even far into adulthood. Author Jean Evans offers an illustration of this in the case of twenty-year-old Johnny Rocco.

PRIMARY SOURCE

"Johnny hadn't been running the streets long when the knowledge was borne in on him that being a Rocco made him 'something special'; the reputation of the notorious Roccos, known to neighbors, schools, police, and welfare agencies as 'chiselers, thieves, and trouble-makers,' preceded him. The cop on the beat, Johnny says, always had some cynical smart crack to make. Certain homes were barred to him. Certain children were not permitted to play with him. Wherever he went—on the streets, in the neighborhood settlement house, at the welfare agency's penny milk station, at school, where other Roccos had been before him, he recognized himself by a gesture, an oblique remark, a wrong laugh."

—Jean Evans, "Johnny Rocco,"
The Journal of Abnormal and Social Psychology, 1948

Families are generally the first agents of socialization to teach children the gender roles considered appropriate in the general society or in the family's culture. Because adults' gender roles tend to be deeply ingrained, parents may not even be aware that they are teaching their children about gender expectations. For example, in the United States, it seems natural to dress baby girls in pink, but most parents would never consider dressing their baby boys in pink. Parents also reinforce gender roles by the toys they buy their children. Researchers note that parents are more likely to buy their sons toy guns and action figures and buy their daughters dolls. They also note that parents reinforce gender roles through the play patterns they encourage. Parents tend to expect boys to be rough and tumble, to get dirty, and to be more defiant. They expect their daughters to be more obedient and dainty. Even today, girls who play in ways more typical of boys are often called tomboys.

Socialization varies by social class. Researchers have found that most working-class parents tend to worry about their children staying out of trouble and are more likely than middle-class parents to use physical punishment as a means of socialization. Middle-class parents, on the other hand, tend to worry more about fostering curiosity, self-control, and self-expression in their children. Sociologist Melvin Kohn and others contend that the reasons for these differences rest in the way the parents make a living. According to Kohn, working-class parents often hold jobs in which they are told what to do. They assume that their children will grow up to hold similar jobs. Thus, the parents attempt to socialize their children to be obedient. Middle-class parents more often hold jobs in which initiative is valued. Thus, they attempt to instill in their children qualities that will help them in similar jobs.

Kohn found that not all working-class and middle-class parents fit this pattern. Some middle-class parents value conformity, while some working-class parents value initiative. Kohn concluded that jobs were again the deciding factor. Middle-class parents who held office jobs in which they are closely supervised socialize their children to conform. Conversely, working-class parents who make their living doing home repairs or other jobs in which they have freedom to make decisions on their own tend to socialize their children in ways typical of most middle-class parents.

✓ **READING PROGRESS CHECK**

Classifying What do children learn within the family?

◁ CARTOON

PATTERNS OF SOCIALIZATION
Researchers have found that socialization varies by class.

▶ **CRITICAL THINKING**

1. **Differentiating** How do middle-class parents and working-class parents tend to differ in patterns of socialization?

2. **Analyzing Visuals** Which parenting style is reflected in the cartoon? Why do you say this?

Religion and Socialization

GUIDING QUESTION What is religion's role in socialization?

Sociologists recognize that religion is an important agent of socialization. In the United States, this is true even for people who do not attend religious services. Religious values have played an important role in American society from colonial times onward, and religious references are widespread in daily life. In addition, many religious values and ideas of morality have become part of American culture, and their religious roots are no longer visible. Sociologist Thomas Luckmann refers to these values and beliefs as *invisible religion*.

Religion as an agent of socialization is even stronger for people who attend religious services. By attending religious services, children learn the values, morals, and beliefs of their particular religions. But the effects are more far-reaching than that. Children also learn aspects about group life, such as proper dress and speech. In addition, sociologists have found that religion influences people's views on sexuality, proper gender roles, work, and child-rearing practices, as well as other beliefs. The socializing influence of religion can continue into adulthood, especially if an individual experiences a religious conversion.

Sociologists point out that religious participation also reduces the likelihood of divorce. This, in turn, strengthens the family, the primary agent of socialization. Places of worship also help socialize new immigrants to the ways of the community, help the poor and the sick, and bring extended families together for religious holidays and rites of passage. Similarly, religious beliefs and practices help the elderly as they prepare for their own and their peers' eventual deaths.

✓ **READING PROGRESS CHECK**

Analyzing How does religion serve as an agent of socialization for both people who attend religious services and those who do not?

objective based on facts; not distorted by personal feelings

hidden curriculum the informal and unofficial aspects of culture that children are taught in school

Teaching children proper behavior in the lunchroom is part of a school's hidden curriculum.

▶ **CRITICAL THINKING**
Applying Why is the lunchroom experience part of a school's hidden curriculum?

Socialization in Schools

GUIDING QUESTION How do schools socialize students?

In school, children are under the care and supervision of adults who are not relatives. For the first time, many of the child's relationships with other people are impersonal. Rewards and punishments are based on performance rather than affection. Although a mother may cherish any picture that her child creates, a teacher evaluates his or her students by more **objective** standards. Slowly, children are taught to be less dependent emotionally on their parents. The school also creates feelings of loyalty and allegiance to something beyond the family.

The socialization process in school involves more than reading, writing, and arithmetic. Underlying the formal goals of the school is the **hidden curriculum**—the informal and unofficial aspects of culture that children are taught in preparation for life. The hidden curriculum teaches children discipline, order, cooperation, and conformity—characteristics required for success in the adult world of work.

School also teaches children how we experience time in the real world. According to education critic John Holt, life in schools is run by the clock, as it is in the working world. A bell signals when children must move to the next scheduled event, whether or not they understand what they have been working on and whether or not they are ready to switch to a different subject. Getting through a preset number of activities within a given time period often becomes more important than learning.

Schools have rules and regulations to cover almost all activities—how to dress, how to wear one's hair, which side of the hall to walk on, when to speak in class. Teachers reward children with praise and acceptance when they recite the "right" answers, behave "properly," or **exhibit** "desirable" attitudes.

Children are isolated from the working adult society by being set apart in school for most of their preadult lives. Because they are separated from the adult world for such a long time, young people must depend on one another for much of their social life.

✓ READING PROGRESS CHECK

Evaluating How does the hidden curriculum of schools help socialize children for their adult lives?

Team sports help teach students valuable life lessons.

▶ CRITICAL THINKING

Drawing Inferences In what ways might participation in team sports be good preparation for adult life?

exhibit to show or display

peer group set of individuals of roughly the same age and interests

Peer Group Socialization

GUIDING QUESTION *How do peer groups contribute to socialization?*

The family, religion, and the school are agents of socialization organized and operated by adults. The child's **peer group**—composed of individuals of roughly the same age and interests—is the only agent of socialization that is not controlled primarily by adults. Children usually belong to several peer groups. A child may belong to a play group in the neighborhood, a clique at school, an after-school club, or a sports team.

In the peer group, young people have an opportunity to engage in give-and-take relationships. Children experience conflict, competition, and cooperation in such groups. The peer group also gives children experience in self-direction. They can begin to make their own decisions; experiment with new ways of thinking, feeling, and behaving; and engage in activities that involve self-expression. Peer groups also promote independence from adults because often the norms of the peer group conflict with those of the adult world. Children learn to be different from their parents in ways that help develop and exhibit self-sufficiency.

The peer group also provides an opportunity for children to develop close ties with friends outside the family, including members of the opposite sex. At the same time, they are learning to get along with large numbers of people, many of whom are quite different from themselves. This helps develop the social flexibility needed in a mobile, rapidly changing society.

Most Americans now live in either urban or suburban areas. In both two-income families and single-parent families, parents may commute many miles to work and spend much of their time away from home. Consequently, once children reach the upper levels of grade school, they may spend more time with their peers than with their parents.

✓ READING PROGRESS CHECK

Making Connections Why do peer groups become more important agents of socialization as children get older?

The Mass Media and Socialization

GUIDING QUESTION *What role does the mass media play in socialization?*

mass media means of communication designed to reach the general population

The **mass media** are means of communication designed to reach the general population. They include such things as television, radio, newspapers, magazines, movies, books, and the Internet. Many popular images presented in the mass media are highly distorted. For example, detective and police work are not as exciting and glamorous as depicted in books, in movies, and on television. Nevertheless, it is often through the mass media that children are first introduced to numerous aspects of their culture.

The mass media display role models for children to imitate. Learning these role models helps integrate young children into society. The mass media also offer children ideas about the values in their society. They provide children with such images and ideals as achievement and success, activity and work, equality and democracy.

On the negative side, however, consider the relationship between violence on television and real-life violence. By the age of sixteen, the average American child will have seen twenty thousand homicides on television. Social scientists have been reluctant in the past to recognize a causal connection between violence on television and real-life violence. Based on hundreds of studies involving more than ten thousand children, however, most social scientists now conclude that watching aggressive behavior on television increases aggression in society.

Consider a few examples. A two-year-old girl died when her older brother, age five, set the house on fire with matches while imitating behavior he had seen on the adult cartoon program *Beavis and Butt-Head*. Just on the basis of televised

TIME LINE

MAJOR DEVELOPMENTS IN THE HISTORY OF THE MASS MEDIA

Innovations in mass media, such as recorded music, radio, and television, have long been powerful agents of socialization.

▶ **CRITICAL THINKING**

1. **Hypothesizing** In what year did the first radio station begin broadcasting in the United States? How might radio have affected socialization?

2. **Speculating** Why might the Internet have an even greater impact than radio on socialization and the spread of culture?

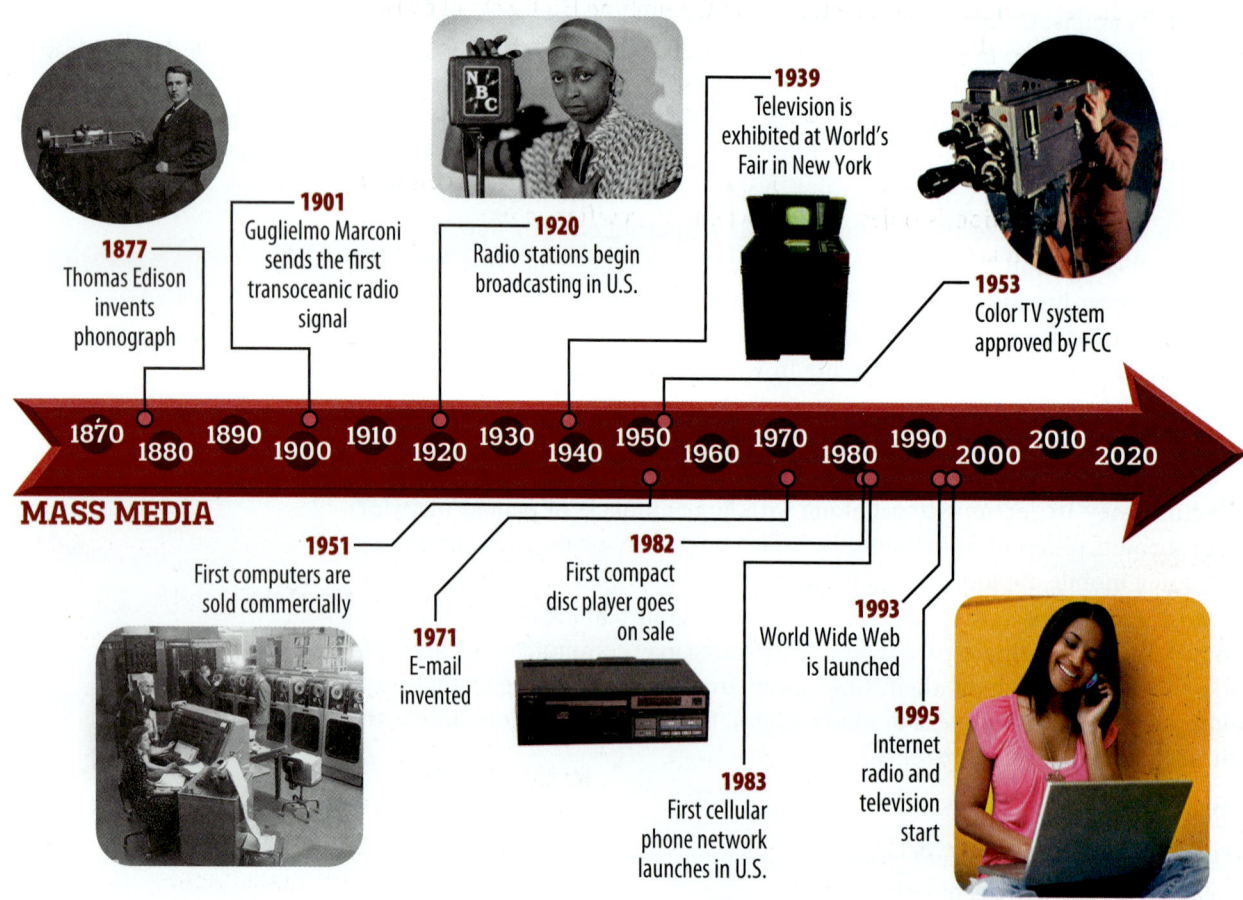

MASS MEDIA

- **1877** Thomas Edison invents phonograph
- **1901** Guglielmo Marconi sends the first transoceanic radio signal
- **1920** Radio stations begin broadcasting in U.S.
- **1939** Television is exhibited at World's Fair in New York
- **1951** First computers are sold commercially
- **1953** Color TV system approved by FCC
- **1971** E-mail invented
- **1982** First compact disc player goes on sale
- **1983** First cellular phone network launches in U.S.
- **1993** World Wide Web is launched
- **1995** Internet radio and television start

Applying Sociology

MASS MEDIA AND SOCIALIZATION

The different types of mass media are powerful agents of socialization. Because they are so powerful, they generate a great deal of research interest on the part of sociologists and other social scientists. In addition to interest in the effects of mass media on violent behavior, sociologists and other social scientists examine how mass media affect gender socialization.

Gender socialization—how we learn what is expected of us as males or females—is an important part of growing up. Television and movies present images related to gender that affect this socialization process. For example, studies have found that commercials geared toward children more often portray boys doing outdoor activities and girls doing indoor activities. Similarly, commercials are more likely to portray adult women as extremely attractive, sexy, and submissive and men as dominant and outdoorsy. Although television programs and cartoons have begun to show more forceful women and girls, male characters tend to outnumber female characters, particularly in evening shows. Sociologists point out that this reinforces the message that males are more important than females in American society.

▶ **CRITICAL THINKING**

1. **Evaluating** Why does it matter how commercials and television portray the appearance and behavior of males and females?
2. **Hypothesizing** What effect on socialization might there be if television shows and movies offered a wider range of gender traits and behaviors?

Television is a powerful agent of socialization.

reports of violence, a rash of would-be copycat crimes followed the shooting massacre of thirteen students and one teacher at Columbine High School by two students who then shot themselves.

The effects of television and other mass media are usually more hidden, subtle, and long-term. For example, sociologists point out that mass media can be used as vehicles for propaganda to influence behavior. *Propaganda* is the use of ideas, information, or rumors to influence opinion. Propaganda is not necessarily harmful, if the information is objective. But when information is presented in a one-sided manner or inaccurately, propaganda takes on a negative connotation.

✓ **READING PROGRESS CHECK**

Comparing and Contrasting How are the mass media both a positive and a negative force for socialization?

LESSON 3 REVIEW

Reviewing Vocabulary
1. **Identifying** What do sociologists mean by *hidden curriculum*?
2. **Naming** What forms of communication are considered mass media?

Using Your Notes
3. **Explaining** Use your notes to explain why socialization is the result of many factors.

Answering the Guiding Questions
4. **Assessing** What is the family's role in socialization?
5. **Making Connections** What is religion's role in socialization?
6. **Evaluating** How do schools socialize students?
7. **Interpreting** How do peer groups contribute to socialization?
8. **Synthesizing** What role does the mass media play in socialization?

Writing Activity
9. **Argument** Some psychologists believe that peer groups have more influence on later socialization than the family group. Give reasons you agree or disagree with this premise.

Socialization 115

FOCUS on research

Case Study

CCSS

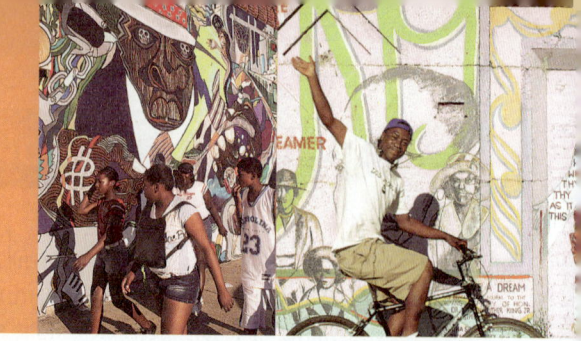

Black Picket Fences: Charisse Baker

Sociologist Mary Pattillo notes that much of the research on African Americans centers on the poor. Little attention is paid to middle-class African Americans. In an effort to shed light on their experience, Pattillo spent more than three years studying a predominantly African American middle-class neighborhood on Chicago's South Side that she calls Groveland. In this excerpt from her book, Black Picket Fences, *she focuses on Charisse Baker and the roles that her parents, neighbors, church, and schools play in her socialization.*

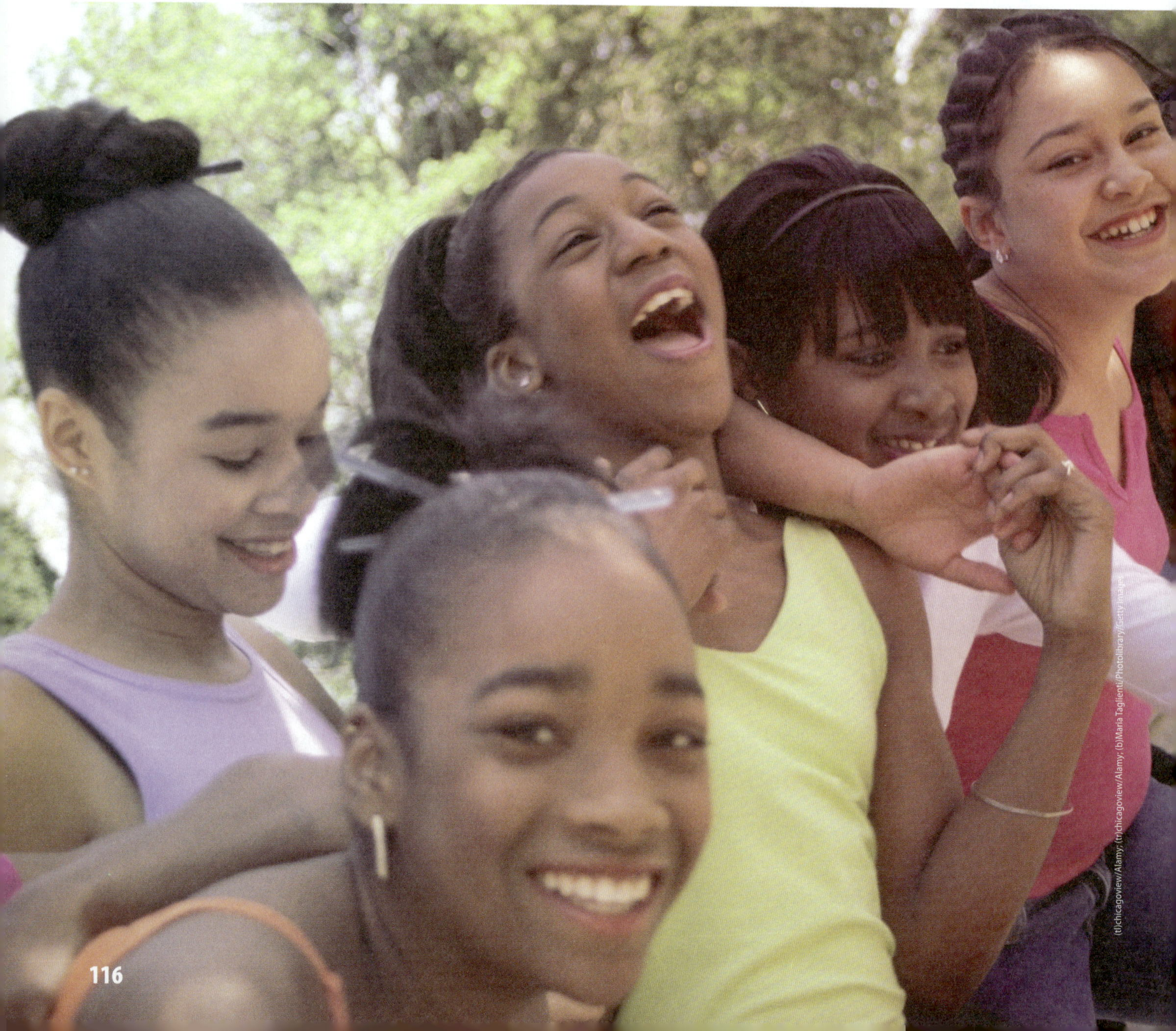

(tl)chicagoview/Alamy; (tr)chicagoview/Alamy; (b)Maria Taglienti/Photolibrary/Getty Images

PRIMARY SOURCE

"Charisse has a clear vision for her life—school, marriage, children."

"Charisse . . . is sixteen and lives with her mother and younger sister, Deanne, across the street from St. Mary's Catholic Church and School. Charisse's mother is a personnel assistant at a Chicago university, and is taking classes there to get her bachelor's degree. Mr. Baker is a Chicago firefighter. While her father and mother are separated, Charisse sees her father many times a week at the after-school basketball hour that he supervises at St. Mary's gym. He and Charisse's mother are on very good terms, and Charisse has a loving relationship with both parents. Mr. Baker is as active as any parent could be, attending the father/daughter dances at Charisse's high school, never missing a big performance, and visiting his daughters often. . . .

Charisse is a third-generation Grovelandite. . . . Her grandparents moved into Groveland with Charisse's then-teenage father when the neighborhood first opened to African Americans. Charisse's parents lived in other neighborhoods when they were first married, only to eventually settle back in Groveland a few houses down from Mr. Baker's parents. Now Charisse is benefiting from the friends her family has made over their years of residence in Groveland, especially the members of St. Mary's Church, who play the role of surrogate parents. When Charisse was in elementary school at St. Mary's, her late paternal grandmother was the school secretary, and so the Baker girls were always under the watchful eye of their grandmother as well as the staff, who were their grandmother's friends. And in the evenings Charisse's mother would bring her and her sister to choir practice, where they accumulated an ensemble of mothers and fathers.

After St. Mary's elementary school, Charisse went on to St. Agnes Catholic High School for girls, her father's choice. St. Agnes is located in a suburb of Chicago and is a solid, integrated Catholic school where 100 percent of the girls graduate and over 95 percent go on to college. Many of the students come from lower-middle-class families like the Bakers. . . .

Most of Charisse's close friends went to St. Mary's and now go to St. Agnes with her, but her choice of boyfriends shows modest signs of rebellion. From her father's perspective, the mere fact of having boyfriends is rebellious, but Charisse still manages to have a very full social life when it comes to boys. Many of Charisse's male interests are older than she, and irregularly employed—although some are in and out of school. She meets many of them hanging out at the mall. One evening, members of the church's youth choir sat around talking about their relationships. Charisse cooed while talking about her present boyfriend, who had just graduated from high school but did not have a job and was uncertain about his future. But in the middle of that thought, Charisse spontaneously changed her attentions to a new young man that she had just met. 'Charisse changes boyfriends like she changes her clothes,' her sister joked, indicating the impetuous nature of adolescent relationships.

While these young men are not in gangs or selling drugs, many of them do not seem to share Charisse's strong career goals and diligence in attaining them. Some of them would not gain the approval of her parents. However, this full list of boyfriends has not clouded Charisse's focus. In her always bubbly, fast-talking manner, she declared:

> Okay, I would like to go to the University of Illinois in Champaign–Urbana. I would like to major in marketing and I'm considering minoring in communications, because I talk a lot. And once I get a job, I get stable, then I can pursue a relationship. I'd like to get married and I want five kids. 'Cause I love children. I really do. I love children.

Charisse has a clear vision for her life—school, marriage, children. The content and order of these plans subscribe to a very traditional life sequence, perhaps more traditional than anyone ever really follows. . . Her parents have made decisions about Charisse's schooling that will prepare her for college, that have instilled in her the Christian values in which they believe, and that have steered her toward a group of like-minded friends."

—from *Black Picket Fences: Privilege and Peril Among the Black Middle Class*, 1999

Working With the Research

1. **Drawing Conclusions** In what ways is Charisse's family a strong agent of socialization?
2. **Identifying Perspectives** What might a functionalist say about the value of children growing up in a community where their family members have been active participants for several generations?
3. **Making Connections** What roles have neighbors, the church, and Charisse's schools played in her socialization?

Socialization

networks

There's More Online!

- ☑ **CHART** Milestones in the Transition to Adulthood
- ☑ **GRAPHIC ORGANIZER** Socialization Through the Life Cycle
- ☑ **IMAGE** Growing Up
- ☑ **MAP** Support for an Elderly Population
- ☑ **SELF-CHECK QUIZ**

Reading HELPDESK

Academic Vocabulary
- reorientation
- terminal

Content Vocabulary
- life cycle
- adolescence
- transitional adulthood
- rites of passage

TAKING NOTES:
Key Ideas and Details

DESCRIBING Use a graphic organizer like the one below to organize details about each stage of development.

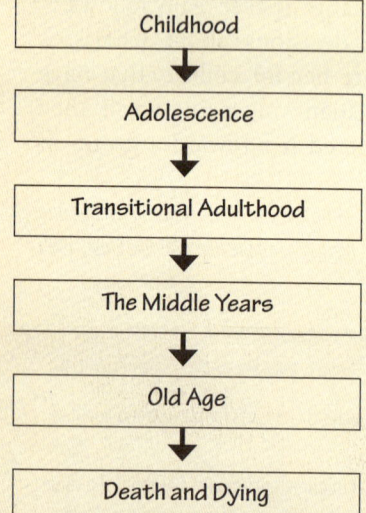

LESSON 4
Socialization Through the Life Cycle

ESSENTIAL QUESTION • *What factors influence an individual's development?*

IT MATTERS BECAUSE
Socialization continues over the course of a person's life. At each stage of the life cycle—childhood, adolescence, adulthood, and old age—people are expected to adopt different behaviors. Socialization is the mechanism through which people learn what is expected of them at each stage. Rituals known as rites of passage often mark the transitions between the stages.

Childhood and Adolescence

GUIDING QUESTION *How are childhood and adolescence different stages of socialization?*

Socialization begins at birth and continues through the **life cycle**—the stages of development individuals pass through between birth and death. Socialization continues over the course of people's lives because expected behaviors change as people age. The first two stages of the life cycle are childhood and adolescence.

Childhood

Like the other stages of the life cycle, childhood is a socially constructed concept. Depending on location, culture, and time in history, people have held quite different notions of childhood. In some societies and at some periods in history, children have been regarded as adults in miniature. In Europe during the Middle Ages and the Renaissance, for example, children were often pictured in adult clothing.

Industrialization changed the way people in Europe and the United States viewed childhood. At first even young children worked in factories. As late as the 1900 census, some 1.75 million children younger than the age of 15—6 percent of the workforce—were gainfully employed in the United States. Today, however, most industrialized nations have laws that bar children younger than a certain age from the workplace. In the United States, for instance, state and federal laws have regulated child labor since 1938. Children under the age of 16 are effectively barred from full-time employment by laws that determine what jobs they can hold and how many hours they can work.

In the United States, as children were freed from working, ideas about childhood changed. Today, we view children as dependent and in need of guidance, protection, and schooling.

Adolescence

Adolescence is the stage between childhood and adulthood—typically spanning an individual's teenage years. Developments in the United States and Europe during the 1800s contributed to the emergence of adolescence as a distinct stage in the life cycle. Among these developments were the growth of a universal education system, the gradual exclusion of children and teenagers from the labor force, the emergence of a juvenile justice system, and the decline of the apprentice system. More recently, the competition to obtain a college degree has tended to prolong the period of adolescence as a life stage.

The changes that mark adolescence are both physiological and psychological. Puberty involves noteworthy biological changes. Adolescents experience growth spurts, adding height and weight quickly at the beginning of this life stage. The growth spurts and changes in hormones cause adolescents to take on the appearances of their adult bodies. Changes in the brain also take place during adolescence. One of the effects of these changes is an increase in risk-taking behavior.

In addition, adolescence presents several psychological challenges to self-concept:

- Adolescents usually have an undefined status, somewhere between childhood and adulthood.
- Adolescents face the challenge of increased decision making. They are often expected to demonstrate responsible behavior related to study habits, dating choices, interaction with older and younger siblings, and team efforts such as school sports.
- The challenge of increased decision making often results in increased feelings of pressure.
- Finally, adolescents often appear to themselves, as well as to others, as embarked on a quest for self and identity. As they navigate this quest, they often sense a paradox. They are neither entirely dependent nor are they fully independent.

Social class affects adolescents too. Adolescents in working-class families may feel pressure to cut short their educations and join the workforce. Adolescents in more affluent families may feel pressure to achieve in school and extracurricular activities in order to gain admission to a top-ranked college or university.

Many of the concerns facing adolescents today produce stress: dating and dating violence, for example, as well as sexuality, teen parenting, drug use, eating disorders, and even suicide. Adolescents must develop the skills they need to make responsible life choices. Such skills include analyzing cause and effect, evaluating risk, listening to parents and mentors, sharpening their proactive (as opposed to reactive) behavior, resisting the myth of invulnerability, and comparing their own behavior with that of others. The nurturing of such skills is an important part of the socialization process at this stage of the life cycle.

life cycle the stages of development individuals pass through between birth and death

adolescence stage of development between childhood and adulthood

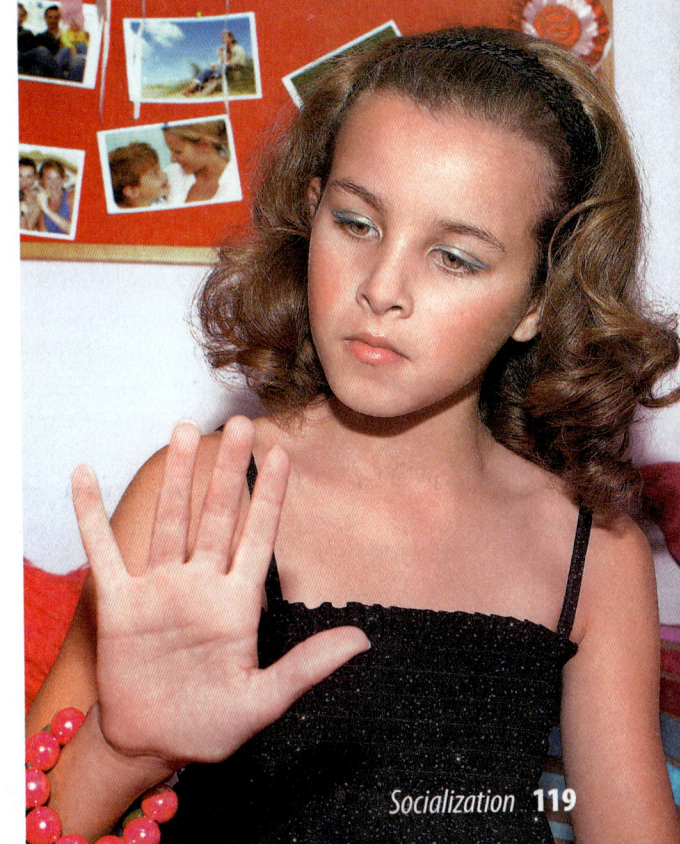

The search for personal identity is a hallmark of the adolescent years.

▶ **CRITICAL THINKING**

Making Connections Adolescents are no longer children, but they are not yet adults. How might that affect this girl's quest for self-identity?

✓ **READING PROGRESS CHECK**

Analyzing What are some of the factors that make adolescence a different developmental stage than childhood?

Connecting Sociology to Anthropology

RITES OF PASSAGE

Rites of passage are rituals that mark the transition from one stage to another in the life cycle. Examples include such things as Christian baptism, the first day of school, Jewish bar mitzvah or bat mitzvah, Latino *quinceañera* celebrations, Christian confirmation ceremonies, puberty rites, high school prom, high school graduation, college graduation, marriage ceremonies, childbirth rites, retirement, and funeral observances. Rites of passage are public recognitions of an individual's change from one position to another in the life cycle.

The Baining fire dance in Papua New Guinea, for instance, is a rite of passage with multiple associations: the birth of children, the onset of the harvest, the initiation of young men into adulthood, and the commemoration of the dead. It involves about 40 dancers and may last all night. The enormous mask, made of tree bark, is fashioned to resemble a canary.

Anthropologists began to investigate rites of passage in the early 1900s. It soon became clear that such rituals are universal. Anthropologists discovered that a rite of passage typically displays a three-part pattern. First comes separation from the society as a whole. For example, in some societies teenage boys are often sent out to the forest to make do on their own. Second, initiates undergo a transition phase, in which they adjust to their new status. This phase often involves a challenge. Finally, the initiates are reincorporated into society.

The Baining Fire Dance

▶ **CRITICAL THINKING**

1. **Making Inferences** What can you infer about the importance of the fire dance in Papua New Guinean culture? Why do you think this?
2. **Making Connections** How do rites of passage relate to stages of development in the life cycle?

Adulthood and Old Age

GUIDING QUESTION *How does socialization continue throughout adulthood?*

Adulthood may be divided into three sub-stages: early adulthood, also called "transitional adulthood" (age 18–29); the middle years (age 30–65); and old age (older than 65).

Transitional Adulthood

Millions of young people have extended adolescence beyond the teenage years by attending college. We refer to this stage of development as **transitional adulthood**. During this period, young people live apart from parental control, but they are not financially independent. Even after obtaining a college degree, some young people return to live at home for a while, as they attempt to secure full-time jobs and settle into careers. This pattern may become especially pronounced in tough economic times, such as the recession that began in 2008.

Transitional adults face the challenge of juggling different roles. There is, in particular, the task of securing and retaining a full-time job in the workforce. There is also decision making related to courtship, marriage, and parenthood—the traditional **rites of passage** that mark entry into adulthood. As is the case for adolescents, at this stage of the life cycle there is an urgent need for critical-thinking and decision-making skills that will result in wise, fulfilling choices.

Psychologist Erik Erikson referred to this period of adulthood as the intimacy versus isolation stage because of what he saw as the main challenge for young adults: entering into loving, committed relationships with others in order to partially replace parental bonds. According to Erikson, if young adults are

---

transitional adulthood a period after high school when young adults have not yet assumed the responsibilities usually associated with adulthood

rites of passage rituals marking the passage from one status to another

successful in this endeavor, they will have the intimacy skills needed to progress into adult life. If they are not successful, they will become isolated and less capable of full emotional development.

The Middle Years

During the early middle years (30–49), most adults become more confident of their life goals. The two hallmarks of adulthood—family and employment—are usually achieved by this time. Divorce, the loss of a job, and the responsibilities of parenting can cause instability, however. The early middle years can be particularly stressful for women who are faced with juggling the roles of parent and employee. In the later middle years (50–64), a **reorientation** often occurs. A person's emphasis shifts from how far he or she has come to how much time may be left. Some people at this stage enjoy an enviable living standard. They have hit the peak years in their careers, with the benefits of seniority and higher compensation. It is not unusual, however, for couples in this stage to be providing homes for their transitional adult children and one or more elderly or infirm parents. Such a double burden has led to the term "sandwich generation."

reorientation a change in attitudes and beliefs

Old Age

With increasing life expectancy, the perception of old age has changed. Many people do not view themselves, or others, as "old" until they are in their mid-70s. As a result, the period from age 65 to age 75 is sometimes referred to as "the transitional older years." Nevertheless, with the deaths of parents and friends, older people often experience a feeling of "time closing in." Both the body and the mind fail to function as sharply and flexibly as they once did. In addition, retirement may result in isolation. Widows are especially vulnerable in this respect, since women typically outlive men by four to five years in the United States. As psychologist Erik Erikson has noted, an appraisal of their own lives is often a preoccupation for the elderly. Have they accomplished what they hoped to achieve, or have they fallen short?

✓ **READING PROGRESS CHECK**

Making Connections What characteristics mark the different stages of adulthood?

Milestones in the Transition to Adulthood	
Life Event that Marks Adulthood	Percentage of People Who View Event as Extremely/Quite Important
Complete formal schooling	90.2
Full-time employment	83.9
Financial independence	81.1
Support family	82.4
Get married	33.2
Have children	28.9
Not live with parents	57.3

Source: General Social Surveys, 1972–2006

◀ **CHART**

◀ **CRITICAL THINKING**

1. **Drawing Conclusions** What do the statistics tell you about the importance of economic factors in the transition to adulthood?

2. **Analyzing Visuals** According to the survey, how does getting married and having children rank in importance as a measure of adulthood?

Death and Dying

GUIDING QUESTION *How is dying a stage of socialization?*

From a sociological perspective, death is a process, rather than an event. Psychiatrist Elisabeth Kübler-Ross conducted hundreds of interviews with people suffering from **terminal** illnesses. From these interviews she developed a theory outlining five stages of grieving associated with the process of dying:

1. **Denial.** In the first stage, the terminally ill go into denial. They cannot believe that they are going to die. They resist their terminal diagnosis by questioning the validity of the information they are given.
2. **Anger.** In the second stage, denial turns to anger. The terminally ill accept the reality of death but denounce it as unjust. They are often hostile, envious of others who are not dying, and irritable with family members and caregivers.
3. **Bargaining.** The third stage is one of negotiation. The terminally ill are not yet ready to accept that death is inevitable. During this stage, they try to strike bargains with God, with fate, or with their terminal disease. They may be willing to undergo painful treatments as part of their bargain with their illness.
4. **Depression.** In the fourth stage, reality sets in as the terminally ill realize that they are not going to escape death. They experience depression, grieving that they are powerless to change the course of events. They often feel guilty that they are going to leave loved ones behind.

terminal leading ultimately to death

A Global Perspective

SUPPORT FOR AN ELDERLY POPULATION

The age distribution in a population is important. As a population ages, it puts pressure on a society to support its elderly citizens. Working-age people—generally those aged 15–64—must provide for the elderly who are no longer working. Sociologists refer to this as the elderly support ratio—the number of potential providers of support per potential elderly dependent.

The number of elderly as a percentage of the population is growing in most industrialized nations. In Japan, Germany, and Italy, for instance, more than 20 percent of the population is 65 or older. The United States is "graying" too, but the percentage of elderly is not as dramatic. According to the 2010 census, 13 percent of the U.S. population is 65 or older. At the other end of the spectrum are less developed nations such as Afghanistan, Angola, Congo, Kenya, Sudan, and Yemen, which have elderly populations of less than 8 percent.

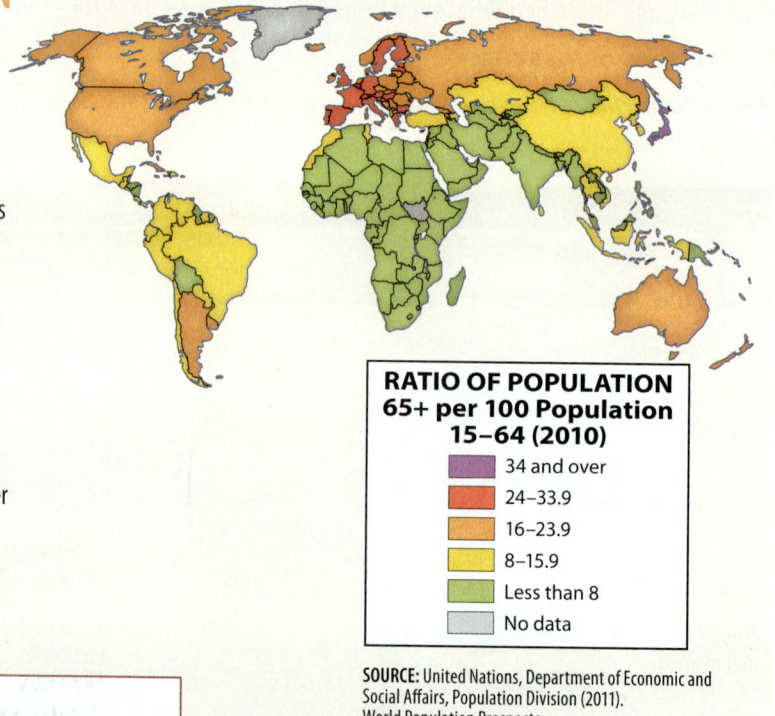

RATIO OF POPULATION 65+ per 100 Population 15–64 (2010)
- 34 and over
- 24–33.9
- 16–23.9
- 8–15.9
- Less than 8
- No data

SOURCE: United Nations, Department of Economic and Social Affairs, Population Division (2011). World Population Prospects: The 2010 Revision, CD-ROM Edition.

Geography Connection

1. **Places and Regions** In which regions of the world are the ratios the lowest?
2. **Places and Regions** In which regions of the world are the ratios the highest?

5. Acceptance. In the fifth and final stage, the depression clears and the terminally ill reach a state of acceptance. This acceptance is generally a state of emotional exhaustion rather than a state of happy acceptance. They put their affairs in order and say their farewells to family and friends.

Kübler-Ross's framework has been criticized as overly schematic. Some dying patients may not go through all five stages, or they may go through a single stage more than once. Yet her findings have been very influential in reorienting people's views of death and dying. People now talk about death far more openly than they once did. Euphemisms such as "passed away" for "died" are less common than they used to be. New approaches to dying are being pioneered.

One of these new approaches is the hospice movement. Whereas the goal of most hospitals is to prolong life if at all possible, hospices are institutions aimed at providing dignity and care—either in a dying patient's home or in a separate location. The goal of hospice is to make a terminally ill person, as well as his or her friends and family, comfortable during the living-dying interval. Hospice provides such services as pain and symptoms management; medical supplies and equipment; drugs; speech and physical therapy; patient counseling; and bereavement, or grief, care and counseling for surviving family and friends. The National Hospice and Palliative Care Organization estimates that approximately 41.9 percent of the people who died in the United States in 2010 participated in a hospice program.

Changing attitudes toward the process of death are accompanied by shifts in the process of bereavement. Mourning the death of a family member or loved one used to be relatively formal and protracted. Mourners would wear black and not attend the usual social functions they formerly enjoyed for a year or more. There is no denying that a death—particularly a sudden and unexpected one—produces intense feelings of grief and loneliness sometimes combined with guilt or anger. Today, however, there is far greater understanding of, and investment in, support groups and the achievement of closure.

From a sociological perspective, a funeral brings closure to the death process and initiates the grief process for the living.

▶ **CRITICAL THINKING**
Identifying Perspectives How might a functionalist view the purpose of a funeral?

✓ **READING PROGRESS CHECK**

Summarizing What are Elisabeth Kübler-Ross's five stages of grief?

LESSON 4 REVIEW

Reviewing Vocabulary
1. *Explaining* What do sociologists mean by the life cycle?
2. *Identifying* What are rites of passage?

Using Your Notes
3. *Listing* Use your notes to list and define the developmental stages people pass through during the course of their lives.

Answering the Guiding Questions
4. *Contrasting* How are childhood and adolescence different stages of development?

5. *Sequencing* How does socialization continue throughout adulthood?
6. *Drawing Inferences* How is dying a stage of socialization?

Writing Activity
7. *Informative/Explanatory* Choose two life-cycle stages. Then write a paragraph about a friend or family member who, in your opinion, exemplifies the process of socialization at each of the stages you have selected.

There's More Online!

☑ **GRAPHIC ORGANIZER**
Processes of Socialization

☑ **MAP** Rates of Imprisonment

☑ **SELF-CHECK QUIZ**

LESSON 5
Processes of Socialization

Reading HELPDESK

Academic Vocabulary
- unique
- voluntary

Content Vocabulary
- total institution
- desocialization
- resocialization
- anticipatory socialization
- reference group

TAKING NOTES: *Integration of Knowledge and Ideas*

GATHERING INFORMATION As you read about the processes of socialization after childhood, use a graphic organizer like the one below to record details.

```
Processes of Socialization
    ├── Desocialization
    ├── Resocialization
    └── Anticipatory Socialization
```

ESSENTIAL QUESTION • *What factors influence an individual's development?*

IT MATTERS BECAUSE
Symbolic interactionism views socialization as a lifelong process. Desocialization is the process of having to give up old norms. Resocialization begins as people adopt new norms and values. Anticipatory socialization and reference groups are concerned with voluntary change as when moving from one life stage to another.

Desocialization and Resocialization

GUIDING QUESTION *What are desocialization and resocialization?*

Whenever change occurs over the course of your life, you will learn new behaviors and skills. This learning is important to socialization. Symbolic interactionism describes four processes associated with socialization after childhood: *desocialization, resocialization, anticipatory socialization*, and *reference groups*.

Desocialization

Military boot camps, mental hospitals, and prisons are examples of what sociologist Erving Goffman called **total institutions**—places where residents are separated from the rest of society. Residents of total institutions are not free to manage their own lives. They are controlled and manipulated by those in charge. They cannot come and go as they please, and they are expected to follow all orders without question. The end purpose of this control and manipulation is to permanently change the residents by having them shed their past identities and adopt new ones. In a military boot camp, for example, recruits shed their civilian identities and adopt the norms, values, attitudes, and behaviors of soldiers.

The first step in this transformation is **desocialization**—the process by which people give up old norms, values, attitudes, and behaviors. For those in total institutions, desocialization often means the destruction of old self-concepts of personal identity. Desocialization in total institutions is accomplished in many ways. The use of serial numbers to identify people and the loss of privacy contribute to the breakdown of past identity. So too does replacing personal clothing and possessions with standard-issue items. This promotes sameness among the residents by depriving them of the personal items (long hair, hairbrushes, ball caps) they have used to present themselves as **unique** individuals. At military boot camp, for example, male soldiers have their heads shaved, and everyone dresses alike in the uniform of that branch of the military. One of the intended messages is that the recruits are not unique individuals; they are members of a team.

Resocialization

Once the self-concept has been broken down, **resocialization**—the process in which people adopt new norms, values, attitudes, and behaviors—can begin. Those in control of total institutions use an elaborate system of rewards and punishments in an attempt to give residents new self-concepts. Rewards for taking on a new "identity" can include extra food, special responsibilities, or periods of privacy. Punishments for nonconformity involve shaming, loss of special privileges, physical punishment, and physical isolation.

The concepts of desocialization and resocialization were developed to analyze social processes in extreme situations. They still apply to other social settings, including basic training in the U.S. Marine Corps and plebe year (first year) at the United States Military Academy. In much less extreme form, these concepts illuminate changes in our normal life course. Desocialization and resocialization occur as a child becomes an adolescent, when young adults begin careers, and as the elderly move into retirement or widowhood.

✓ **READING PROGRESS CHECK**

Synthesizing Why do total institutions desocialize and then resocialize people?

total institutions places in which people are separated from the rest of society and controlled by officials in charge

desocialization the process of giving up old norms, values, attitudes, and behaviors

unique like no other, distinct

resocialization the process of adopting new norms, values, attitudes, and behaviors

A Diverse America

RATES OF IMPRISONMENT

The United States has one of the highest rates of imprisonment in the industrialized world. Justice officials worry that some prisons function as "schools for crime." If prisons first desocialize and then resocialize inmates toward a criminal identity, then the U.S. prison system is unintentionally increasing the criminal portion of the population. This map shows the number of prisoners (per 100,000 U.S. residents) with sentences of more than one year.

Geography Connection

1. ***Environment and Society*** Where does your state rank in terms of imprisonment rates? Can you relate the extent of imprisonment in your state to the nature of the socialization that occurs in your state?
2. ***Places and Regions*** Do the states adjoining your state have imprisonment rates that are similar or dissimilar to your state?

RATES OF IMPRISONMENT
(sentenced to more than 1 year per 100,000 U.S. residents)

- 600 or more
- 500–599
- 400–499
- 300–399
- 200–299
- Less than 200

SOURCE: Bureau of Justice Statistics Bulletin: Prisoners in 2009

Quick Case Study

HOW DO YOU COMPARE TO YOUR BIRTH COHORTS?

Studying birth cohorts—people born in the same time period—is one way that sociologists determine patterns within developmental stages. How do you compare with your birth cohorts on anticipatory socialization?

Procedure
1. Write a paragraph titled "What I Am Doing to Prepare for the Next Stage in My Life."
2. Ask five of your classmates who were born in the same year as you to do the same.

Analysis
As you read the paragraphs, consider these questions.

1. In what ways are your paragraphs similar? In what ways are they different?
2. Why does this type of research make sense to study birth cohorts?

Anticipatory Socialization

GUIDING QUESTION *How does anticipatory socialization lead to voluntary change?*

anticipatory socialization
the voluntary process of preparing to accept new norms, values, attitudes, and behaviors

voluntary done by free choice

reference group group whose norms and values are used to guide behavior; group with whom you identify

Anticipatory socialization is the process of preparing (in advance) for new norms, values, attitudes, and behaviors. It does not generally occur in prisons or mental hospitals because it involves **voluntary** change.

Anticipatory socialization may occur in people who are moving from one stage in their lives to another. For example, because they want to resemble those their own age, adolescents may voluntarily abandon many of the norms, values, attitudes, and behaviors learned previously. This process generally begins in pre-adolescence. Preteens adopt adolescents as their new **reference group**—the group they use to evaluate themselves and from which they acquire attitudes, values, beliefs, and norms. In this situation, the new reference group is a tool for anticipatory socialization.

Seniors in college, normally seen on campus only in jeans and other casual clothing, suddenly, as graduation nears, are wearing tailored clothing and much more serious expressions. In preparing for entry into the business world, they are talking with friends who have graduated as well as company recruiters. In effect, they are preparing themselves for the resocialization they know awaits them.

☑ **READING PROGRESS CHECK**

Identifying Cause and Effect How does anticipatory socialization ease the transition between stages in life?

LESSON 5 REVIEW

Reviewing Vocabulary
1. **Identifying** What is a total institution?
2. **Observing** Describe two reference groups that are important to you now.

Using Your Notes
3. **Making Connections** Use your notes to identify how desocialization and resocialization help people adapt to changing situations.

Answering the Guiding Questions
4. **Differentiating** What are desocialization and resocialization?
5. **Analyzing** How does anticipatory socialization lead to voluntary change?

Writing Activity
6. **Narrative** Think back to your preadolescent years. Write a description of the anticipatory socialization you went through in preparation for adolescence.

CHAPTER 4 Assessment

Directions: On a separate sheet of paper, answer the questions below. Make sure you read carefully and answer all parts of the questions.

Lesson Review

Lesson 1

1. **Making Generalizations** What generalizations can you make about human needs based on the Harlows' research on rhesus monkeys?

2. **Evaluating** Do the case studies of Anna, Isabelle, and Genie support the Harlows' conclusions? Why or why not?

Lesson 2

3. **Identifying Cause and Effect** Describe an example of the three stages of a distorted looking glass and explain at least one consequence of it.

4. **Explaining** Which "self" is the first to react to a situation, the "me" or the "I"? How might it interact with the other "self"? Explain with an example.

Lesson 3

5. **Assessing** Why does the family have such strong influence on a child's socialization?

6. **Categorizing** Describe four specific peer groups a high school student might belong to and explain why each is a peer group.

Lesson 4

7. **Interpreting** Why is it not practical to give a definite age range for the beginning and end of adolescence?

8. **Categorizing** Marco has just earned his college degree but is having a hard time finding a full-time job. He moves back home to live with his parents while he accepts temporary jobs and continues to look for a full-time position. What stage of life is Marco going through?

Lesson 5

9. **Identifying** Identify the following actions as desocialization, resocialization, or anticipatory socialization.

    a. First-year students acquire a new identity during their freshman year at a military academy.

    b. Prison personnel deliberately attempt to destroy the self-concepts of inmates.

    c. High school students identify with college students.

10. **Contrasting** How does resocialization differ from anticipatory socialization?

DBQ Analyzing Primary Sources

PRIMARY SOURCE

Use the cartoon to answer the following questions.

"Doug, your 150 IQ isn't doing much good under there."

11. **Interpreting** How do you think a sociologist would diagnose the problem of the man under the table?

12. **Drawing Inferences** What does the cartoon imply about the environment of a typical workplace?

Need Extra Help?

If You've Missed Question	1	2	3	4	5	6	7	8	9	10	11	12
Go to page	101	102–104	107	109	110–111	113	119	120	124–126	125–126	100–104	110–113

Socialization

CHAPTER 4 Assessment

Directions: On a separate sheet of paper, answer the questions below. Make sure you read carefully and answer all parts of the questions.

Critical Thinking

13 *Evaluating* This chapter discusses the socializing influences of mass media. Our perceptions of ideal body types seem to be largely a product of media socialization. Girls often feel the need to be thin and boys tend to measure how muscular they are. Discuss how television, magazines, podcasts, and video games reinforce these images. Give examples from your experience of how the media have socialized Americans to admire certain figure and body types.

14 *Applying* Which group do you feel is the most influential in the present stage of your socialization—family, peers, school, or the media? Why?

15 *Analyzing* Your daily life includes many social networks or groups that regularly contribute to your socialization. They include family, friends, teachers, people at work, teammates, and so forth. Identify one of these groups and imagine your day if you suddenly lost contact with those people. What support would you be missing? What key elements are provided by this particular social network?

21st Century Skills

16 *Understanding Relationships Among Events* Describe an experience you have had with the looking-glass process. How did this experience touch or change your self-concept?

17 *Identifying Cause and Effect* One of the skills that adolescents must develop is analyzing cause and effect. Why is this an essential skill to develop? Give an example.

Exploring the Essential Question

18 *Drawing Conclusions* Consider the meaning of the song lyric "Walk a mile in my shoes." Work with a partner to create a skit that conveys this meaning and shows at least two factors that influence an individual's development.

College and Career Readiness Skills

19 *Problem Solving* Total institutions, such as prisons, presume that desocialization and resocialization occur since one of their goals is to make prisoners law abiding. Yet, more than half of the inmates released in the United States return to prison. If desocialization and resocialization really do take place, why is the recidivism rate (the number of prisoners who return to prison) so high? Propose a theory for what might be happening using the concept of resocialization.

Research and Presentation

20 *Interpreting Significance* Some children without parents or close family find themselves being moved from one foster home to another for the greater part of their childhood. Research case studies related to this topic. Present your findings to the class.

21 *Informative/Explanatory* Use the Internet to conduct additional research on the effects of social class on socialization. Collect evidence from recent studies. Then write an essay of at least two pages in which you summarize the studies and draw conclusions about how and why socialization processes vary by social class.

Need Extra Help?

If You've Missed Question	13	14	15	16	17	18	19	20	21
Go to page	114	110–114	110–113	106–107	119	107–109	124–125	110–111	110–111

Social Structure and Society

ESSENTIAL QUESTIONS • How is society organized? • How does the way in which a society is structured affect human relationships?

networks
There's More Online about social structure and society.

CHAPTER 5

Technology & Society
Social Structures, Roles, & Statuses

Lesson 1
Social Structure and Status

Lesson 2
Social Structure and Roles

Lesson 3
Preindustrial Societies

Lesson 4
Industrial and Postindustrial Societies

Sociology Matters...

How we participate in daily life is profoundly shaped by how we are socialized. Through socialization, we learn our society's social structure, which includes the roles we play.

Think about the structure and roles in a marching band. Brass and woodwind musicians play the melody. Drummers keep the beat. The conductor leads them. Learning the structure of a group helps us know how we are supposed to act with others in the group. That is true not just for marching bands but for all groups—and for all societies.

◄ In a marching band, each musician has particular movements to make as well as specific notes to play.

Stephen Dunn/Getty Images Sport/Getty Images

CHAPTER 5
Technology & Society

Social Structures, Roles, & Statuses

As access to computers and technology increases, more people are interacting with each other online and changing our social structure.

The Internet is a bustling place, and users have unique online roles and statuses. When someone joins a social networking site, he or she takes on a new status. For example, many people use social networking services to let their followers know what they are doing. So one role of a person involved in a social networking service would be the "poster" of a status update or a tweet. Users are also expected to comment on the updates or wall comments of people with whom they have connected, which makes commenter another status.

Online video-sharing sites give different roles and statuses to users and viewers. A girl who posts a video of herself acting in a short film has a new online role: actress. A boy who uploads a short documentary he filmed also has a new online role: documentarian. Anyone who watches these performances may take on the role of fan or critic. These roles may cross over into the respective offline lives of each person.

Services like email and online search engines have forced many to adopt a new, more informal social structure for correspondence and research. Sending and receiving mail instantly has led to a greater flexibility for telecommuters and business travelers, but it has also increased the pressures to respond quickly and may result in email overload, or decreased productivity due to excessive email. Managing and responding to email has become another task many people, not just professionals, must work into their daily lives. This may be offset by the ease with which one can search for information on the Internet using a search engine. With so much information so readily available, the ability to evaluate facts from online sources has become an important skill.

Thinking like a Sociologist

❶ Making Connections

Have you ever belonged to a social networking site or visited one? How does your interaction with others online differ from the in-person relationships you have?

❷ Differentiating

Refer to the infographic. Which of these do you use most frequently for personal purposes? Which do you use more in your role as a student?

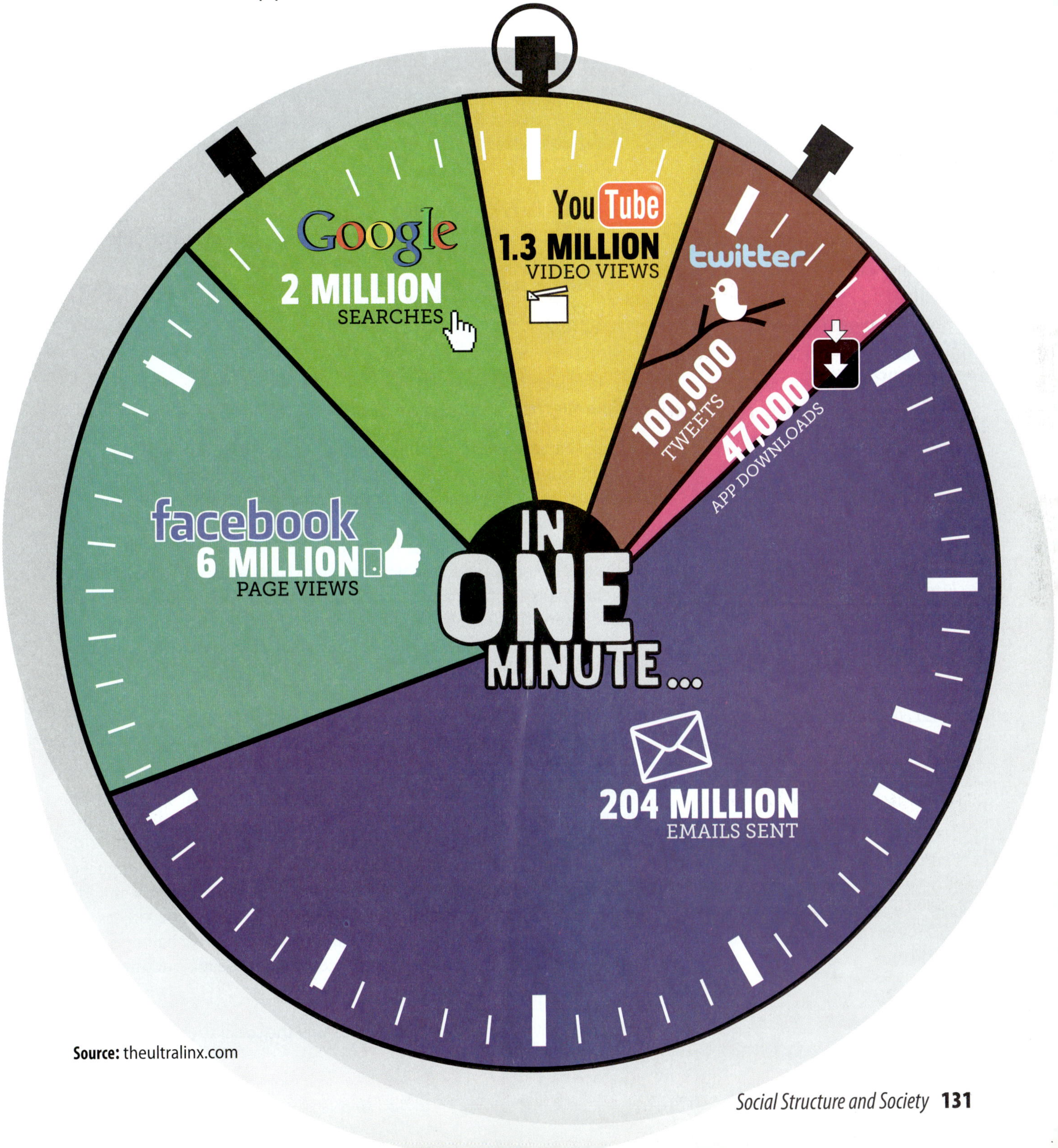

networks

There's More Online!

- ☑ **CARTOON** Status in Sociology
- ☑ **GRAPHIC ORGANIZER** Social Status
- ☑ **IMAGE** Multiple Statuses
- ☑ **INFOGRAPHIC** Sample Statuses
- ☑ **SELF-CHECK QUIZ**

LESSON 1
Social Structure and Status

ESSENTIAL QUESTIONS • How is society organized? • How does the way in which a society is structured affect human relationships?

Reading HELPDESK

Academic Vocabulary
- interact
- assign

Content Vocabulary
- social structure
- status
- ascribed status
- achieved status
- status set
- master status

TAKING NOTES:
Key Ideas and Details

ORGANIZING As you read about status, use a graphic organizer like the one below to record information about four key concepts related to status.

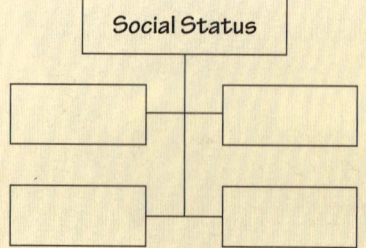

IT MATTERS BECAUSE
The underlying pattern of social relationships in a group is its social structure. Status is one very important element of social structure. Ascribed statuses are assigned at birth; achieved statuses are earned or chosen by the individual.

Social Structure Is All Around You

GUIDING QUESTION What is social structure?

Culture shapes our social behavior, guiding how we think, feel, and act. Without culture, we would have no blueprint for social living. We learn this blueprint—our culture's norms and values—through socialization.

One thing we learn is the structure of social groups. Think about a classroom. Early on, students learn that they are supposed to listen to what a teacher says and to ask permission to speak. They also realize that a teacher leads the class and teaches the lesson. If you found yourself in a class where the teacher raised his or her hand to talk and students napped on the floor, you would wonder what planet you were on. You would not know how to act.

As this example shows, to act appropriately in any group, you must understand the underlying social structure. What is social structure? In our minds, we carry a "social map" for various group situations. This map shows us the patterns of social relationships within the group—the group's **social structure**. The role of social structure, then, is to help us see how we fit into a group. The importance of social structure is that it helps people **interact**, or relate to one another, more smoothly.

We are not born with these mental maps. Just as we learn a language by picking up cues about what words mean, we develop an understanding of the social structure of different groups by watching how others act in those groups. In learning the structure of each group we belong to, we learn about statuses and roles—major elements of social structure.

☑ **READING PROGRESS CHECK**

Explaining Why do people need to understand the social structure of the groups to which they belong?

Everyone Has Status

GUIDING QUESTION *What do sociologists mean by status?*

When asked to describe themselves, people may use such terms as *web designer, doctor, mother,* or *daughter*. Each of these labels refers to a **status**—a position that the person occupies within a social structure. Some refer to the person's position in a workplace or within an industry. Others refer to his or her position within a family. Status helps us define who and what we are in relation to others within the same social structure. There are two types of social status—ascribed and achieved.

Status Can Be Ascribed or Achieved

An **ascribed status** is neither earned nor chosen but is **assigned**, or given, to us. For example, a newborn female instantly becomes a *child* and a *daughter*. She does not choose her position in the family or her gender. Instead, those statuses are given to her automatically. In some societies, social class is an ascribed status that is assigned to someone as the result of birth into a particular family or into a religious, ethnic, or racial group.

An **achieved status** is a position that a person earns or chooses. Achieving a status is possible only if people have some degree of control over their lives and a range of choices. In most modern societies, for example, an individual can decide to become a spouse or a parent. Marriage and parenthood are not mandated by society but the result of individual choices. Occupations are also achieved statuses in most modern societies, in which people are free to choose their work.

social structure the pattern of social relationships within a group

interact to relate with other people

status a position a person occupies within a social structure

ascribed status a position in a social structure that is neither earned nor chosen but assigned to a person

assign to give someone a particular social position

achieved status a position in a social structure that is earned or chosen

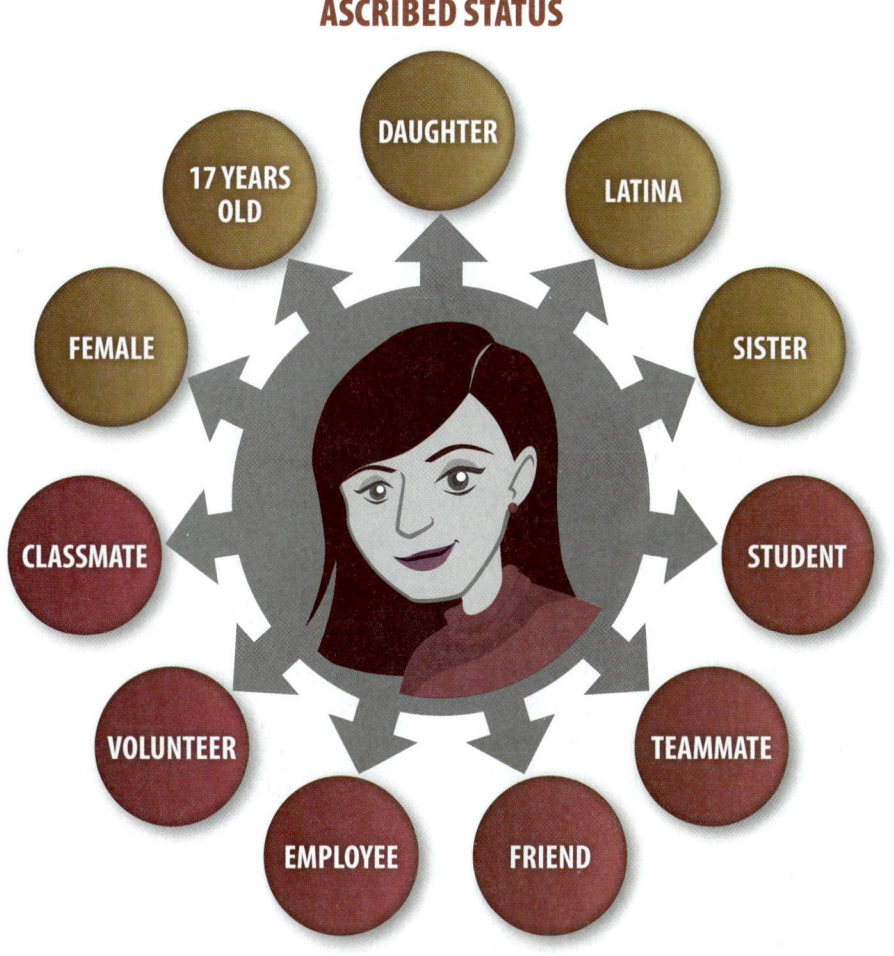

INFOGRAPHIC

SAMPLE STATUSES
All the statuses that an individual has are either ascribed or achieved.

▶ **CRITICAL THINKING**

1. **Applying** What are two ascribed statuses this girl has that she was not necessarily given at birth? Why?

2. **Drawing Inferences** Which statuses are more likely to change over time, achieved or ascribed statuses? Why?

Social Structure and Society

CARTOON

STATUS IN SOCIOLOGY
People often use the word *status* in everyday conversation. Sociologists, however, mean something very special by it.

▶ **CRITICAL THINKING**

1. **Making Connections** What do people usually mean by *status* in everyday conversation?
2. **Comparing** How does that definition differ from how sociologists use the term?

status set all the statuses a person occupies at any given time

Ascribed status is based on a person's characteristics, such as age, gender, ethnicity, or race. Ascribed status treats a person not as an individual but as a member of a group. If religion or ethnicity is linked to status in a particular society, all members of the same religion or ethnic group have the same relative status compared to members of other religions or ethnic groups, regardless of their individual differences. Achieved status, on the other hand, reflects a person's individual accomplishments or choices.

Some ascribed statuses can change over time. Age is an example. Each life stage—childhood, adolescence, young adulthood, mature adulthood, and old age—has a distinct position in society. Once a person enters that life stage, he or she is expected to interact with others in accordance with society's view of appropriate behavior for that position.

Social status is often hierarchical. Different statuses are seen by members of a group as ranking higher or lower than one another. People with higher status have the ability to control or influence the behavior of people with lower status. Think of a high-school sports team. The head coach has higher status than the assistant coaches. Those coaches have higher status than the players. Among the players themselves there are different statuses. The star player has a different position than a substitute who rarely plays. If the team has a captain, that player has higher rank than the other players. The relative ranking of different statuses within a society is a key to understanding its social structure.

People Have Multiple Statuses

Any person in society occupies more than one status. You are a child, a friend, and a student. You might also be a worker, team member, or club member.

A **status set** is all the statuses that a person occupies at any particular time. The status sets of two individuals can be very different, even if they have the same status in one particular group. For example, one social worker may be a wife, a mother, an author, and a church choir director. Another may be a single parent, a service club leader, and a jazz musician.

Each of these statuses is part of a network of linked statuses. Assume that in addition to being a social worker, someone is also a jazz musician. In this status, she might interact with people who have the status of club owner, fellow musician, singer, and customer of the club, among others. That is very different from the group of statuses she will interact with as a social worker or parent.

Master Statuses and Other Statuses

Among the many statuses an individual holds, some are more important than others. Sociologists call these **master statuses** because they influence most other aspects of the person's life. Master statuses may be achieved or ascribed.

In modern industrial societies, occupations—which are generally achieved statuses—are typically master statuses. Your occupation strongly influences such matters as where you live, how well you live, and how long you live. "Criminal" is another achieved master status. That status is not automatically assigned to someone at birth or because of membership in a group. A person has to do something to have the status of "criminal." Once earned, though, the status has a profound effect on a person's life choices. This is in part because expected behavior is often based on master statuses.

Gender, age, race, and ethnicity are all ascribed master statuses. They are ascribed because they are assigned to individuals because of their membership in a group. They are master statuses because they significantly affect the likelihood of achieving other social statuses. When will the United States have a female president? Would you want a fifteen-year-old or a fifty-year-old to give you advice on comparing colleges? Would you most likely prefer one or the other to provide tips on using a social networking site?

Studying Status

Sociologists study status for several reasons. First, social status is a major aspect of social structure. A person's ascribed status can play a huge role in determining what opportunities he or she has in life.

Another reason to study status is that sociologists are interested in the relationships among people with different statuses. Suppose a sociologist is studying how the juvenile justice system treats those accused of delinquency. The researcher might focus on how the statuses of the social worker, police officer, judge, and lawyer affect how they interact with one another.

 READING PROGRESS CHECK

Analyzing How do sociologists describe the relationship of social status to social structure?

African American and woman are both ascribed master statuses of this astronaut.

▶ **CRITICAL THINKING**

Drawing Inferences What is the achieved master status of the African American woman featured in the photograph?

master status a position that strongly influences most other aspects of a person's life

---

LESSON 1 REVIEW

Reviewing Vocabulary

1. *Explaining* How do humans make use of our understanding of social structure?

2. *Contrasting* How do ascribed and achieved statuses differ?

Using Your Notes

3. *Applying* Based on your notes, give an example from your own life of each of the four key concepts about status.

Answering the Guiding Questions

4. *Explaining* What is social structure?

5. *Finding the Main Idea* What do sociologists mean by *status*?

Writing Activity

6. *Argument* What master status—gender, age, race, occupation, or some other factor—do you think is the most important in American society? Explain why you think so in a brief essay.

FOCUS on research
Experiment

Adopting Statuses in a Simulated Prison

Social psychologist Philip Zimbardo and his colleagues designed an experiment to observe the behavior of people without criminal records in a mock prison simulation. Zimbardo and his colleagues were amazed at how quickly statuses were adopted and roles fulfilled by the college students playing the roles of prisoner and guard. This experiment reveals the ease with which people can be socialized to statuses and roles. Zimbardo's own words describe the design and the results of this experiment.

PRIMARY SOURCE

"In an attempt to understand just what it means psychologically to be a prisoner or a prison guard, Craig Haney, Curt Banks, Dave Jaffe and I created our own prison. We carefully screened over 70 volunteers who answered an ad in a Palo Alto city newspaper and ended up with about two dozen young men who were selected to be part of this study. They were mature, emotionally stable, normal, intelligent college students from middle-class homes throughout the United States and Canada. They appeared to represent the cream of the crop of this generation. None had any criminal record and all were relatively homogeneous on many dimensions initially.

Half were arbitrarily designated as prisoners by a flip of a coin, the others as guards. These were the roles they were to play in our simulated prison. The guards were made aware of the potential seriousness and danger of the situation and their own vulnerability. They made up their own formal rules for maintaining law, order and respect, and were generally free to improvise new ones during their eight-hour, three-man shifts. The prisoners were unexpectedly picked up at their homes by a city policeman in a squad car, searched, handcuffed, fingerprinted, booked at the Palo Alto station house and taken blindfolded to our jail. There they were stripped, deloused, put into a uniform, given a number and put into a cell with two other prisoners where they expected to live for the next two weeks....

At the end of only six days we had to close down our mock prison because what we saw was frightening. It was no longer apparent to most of the subjects (or to us) where reality ended and their roles began. The majority had indeed become prisoners or guards, no longer able to clearly differentiate between role playing and self. There were dramatic changes in virtually every aspect of their behavior, thinking and feeling.... We were horrified because we saw some boys (guards) treat others as if they were despicable animals, taking pleasure in cruelty, while other boys (prisoners) became servile, dehumanized robots who thought only of escape, of their own individual survival and of their mounting hatred for the guards.

We had to release three prisoners in the first four days because they had such acute situational traumatic reactions as hysterical crying, confusion in thinking, and severe depression. Others begged to be paroled, and all but three were willing to forfeit all the money

"At the end of only six days we had to close down our mock prison because what we saw was frightening. It was no longer apparent to most of the subjects (or to us) where reality ended and their roles began. The majority had indeed become prisoners or guards."

they had earned [$15 per day] if they could be paroled. By then (the fifth day) they had been so programmed to think of themselves as prisoners that when their request for parole was denied they returned docilely to their cells....

About a third of the guards became tyrannical in their arbitrary use of power, in enjoying their control over other people. They were corrupted by the power of their roles and became quite inventive in their techniques of breaking the spirit of the prisoners and making them feel they were worthless....

By the end of the week the experiment had become a reality."

— Philip G. Zimbardo, "Pathology of Imprisonment," *Society*, April 1972

Working With the Research

1. **Evaluating** If you were asked to discuss Zimbardo's experiment in light of one of the three major theoretical perspectives, which would you choose? Why?

2. **Constructing Arguments** One of Zimbardo's conclusions, not stated in the above account, is that the brutal behavior found in real-life prisons is not due to the antisocial characteristics or personality defects of guards or prisoners. Can you argue sociologically that he is right in this conclusion? How?

3. **Drawing Inferences** How did adopting different roles affect the "prisoners'" behavior? Explain.

4. **Integrating** Conduct research to find another sociological experiment that explores the ways in which people can be socialized into statuses and roles. Then write an essay comparing and contrasting the findings of Zimbardo's experiment with those of the one you found.

networks

There's More Online!

- ☑ **GRAPHIC ORGANIZER** Links Between Culture and Social Structure
- ☑ **GRAPHIC ORGANIZER** Theoretical Perspectives: Illustrating Social Structure Concepts
- ☑ **MAP** Unemployment Rates
- ☑ **SELF-CHECK QUIZ**

Reading HELPDESK

Academic Vocabulary
- encounter
- incompatible

Content Vocabulary
- role
- right
- obligation
- role performance
- social interaction
- role conflict
- role strain

TAKING NOTES:
Key Ideas and Details

ORGANIZING As you read about social structure and roles, use the headings from the lesson to create an outline similar to the one started below.

Social Structure and Roles
I. Rights and Obligations
II. Role Performance and Social Interaction
III.

LESSON 2
Social Structure and Roles

ESSENTIAL QUESTIONS • How is society organized? • How does the way in which a society is structured affect human relationships?

It Matters Because
People interact according to prescribed roles. These roles carry certain rights and obligations. Role conflict or role strain can arise when an individual has clashing expectations from more than one role.

Rights and Obligations

GUIDING QUESTION *What are rights and obligations?*

Every status carries with it a variety of roles. A **role** is simply an expected behavior associated with a particular status. The roles of a doctor, for example, include seeing patients, diagnosing illnesses, prescribing treatments, and keeping informed about new medical developments.

Think of roles as statuses in action. Whereas statuses describe *positions,* roles describe *behaviors.* These behaviors are based on the rights and obligations attached to various statuses. **Rights** are behaviors that individuals expect *from* others. **Obligations** are behaviors that individuals are expected to perform *toward* others. The rights of one status correspond to the obligations of another. Students have a right to expect that teachers will be adequately prepared to explain the material. Teachers, in turn, have an obligation to be prepared to teach lessons each day. Rights and obligations flow in both directions in social interactions. Thus, teachers have a right to expect that students will make the attempt to learn, and students have the obligation to make that effort.

In his play *As You Like It,* William Shakespeare wrote, "All the world's a stage, and all the men and women merely players." In a play, actors follow the script to say the words and perform the actions that reveal their characters' thoughts, feelings, and beliefs. In life, people with different statuses follow social scripts to act out social roles. A playwright specifies the content of an actor's performance. In the same way, culture provides the script for the roles we play in real life. Of course, different cultures have different scripts for the same role. American mothers, for instance, may promote more independence in their children than most Iranian mothers.

☑ **READING PROGRESS CHECK**

Analyzing What are the rights and obligations of a doctor and a patient?

138

Role Performance and Social Interaction

GUIDING QUESTION *What is role performance?*

Statuses and roles provide the basis for group life. It is primarily when people interact with one another that they perform in the roles attached to their statuses.

Role performance is the actual conduct, or behavior, exhibited by people as they carry out a role. Role performance can occur without an audience. For example, a student can study alone for a test and a doctor can study alone to keep up-to-date in her field. Most role performance, though, involves social interaction.

Social interaction is any of the processes by which people influence one another as they interrelate. These interactions can be as simple as the conversation when a customer orders a meal from a server at a restaurant. They can be as complicated as the back-and-forth among a group of friends trying to decide what movie to see. Whatever the situation, the same basic process of influence and reaction to others is involved in any interaction between two or more people.

Think again of the analogy of the play. Remember that statuses are like the characters in a play and roles are like the script. So social interaction represents the way actors use words and actions to cue one another and how they respond to those cues. Role performance is the performance itself.

The play analogy is helpful, but it can also be misleading if we take it too far. First, performing in real life is not the conscious process used by actors. Unlike staged performances, most real-life role performance occurs without planning.

role an expected behavior associated with a particular status

right a behavior that individuals expect from others

obligation a behavior that individuals are expected to perform toward others

role performance the actual conduct, or behavior, exhibited by people as they carry out a role

social interaction any of the processes by which people influence one another as they interrelate

A Diverse America

UNEMPLOYMENT RATES

For many Americans, occupation serves as their master status. Sometimes, however, that master status is disrupted by unemployment—a situation that occurs when a person does not have a job in spite of actively seeking one. Unemployment prevents people from fulfilling their role expectations as earners, which can also affect their performance in spousal and parental roles. This map shows the percentage of each state's civilian labor force, aged 16 and older, that was unemployed in March 2012.

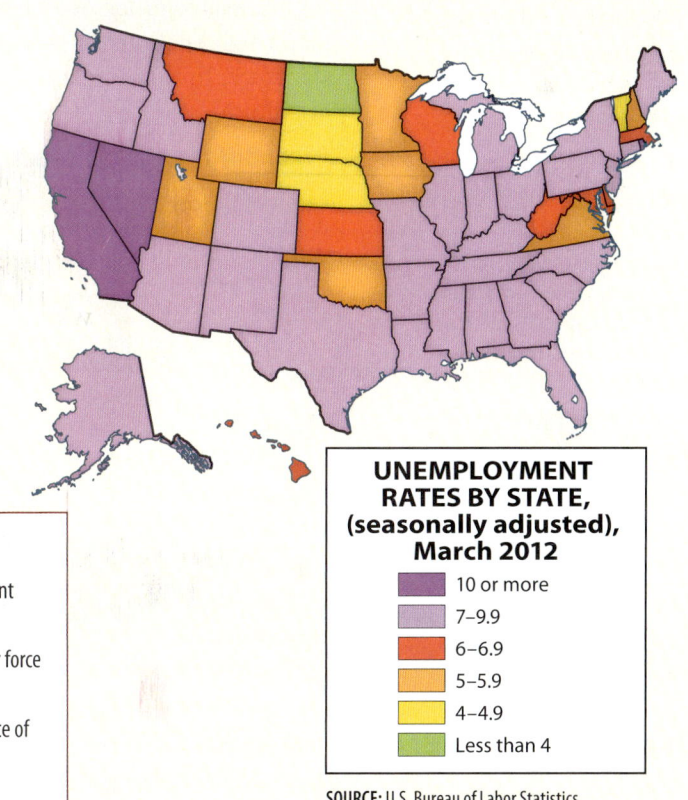

UNEMPLOYMENT RATES BY STATE, (seasonally adjusted), March 2012
- 10 or more
- 7–9.9
- 6–6.9
- 5–5.9
- 4–4.9
- Less than 4

SOURCE: U.S. Bureau of Labor Statistics

Geography Connection

1. **Places and Regions** Which states had the highest unemployment rates in March 2012? Which states had the lowest rates?
2. **Places and Regions** About what percentage of the civilian labor force in your state was unemployed in March 2012?
3. **Human Systems** How can unemployment affect the performance of spousal and parental roles?

Social Structure and Society 139

Second, although actors may sometimes ad-lib or change lines to suit themselves, overall they stick to the script. Departures are fairly easy to detect and control. This is not the case with differences between a role and a role performance. Someone's inability to perform a role may not be apparent to others or may become known only after it is too late to do anything about it. Have you ever been frustrated because a partner on a group project failed to deliver the work he or she was supposed to?

Third, a play involves a programmed and predictable relationship between cues and responses. One performer's line is a cue for a specific response from another. In life, we choose our own cues and responses. A student may decide to tell a teacher that her tests are the worst he has ever **encountered**, or come across. On hearing this, the teacher may tell the student that it is not his place to judge, or she may ask for further explanation to see if she agrees that there is a problem. In effect, the teacher can choose from among several scripts. Similarly, the student has a variety of ways of responding to the teacher's response.

The process of choosing how to perform one's roles occurs in nearly all instances of social interaction. Keep in mind, however, that the range of options is not limitless. Only certain behaviors are culturally acceptable. It is not an appropriate response for the teacher to bodily eject the complaining student from her classroom or for the student to pound the teacher's desk in protest.

The Links Between Culture and Social Structure graphic organizer illustrates the connection between culture and social structure. As you can see at the top of the figure, the first link between culture and social structure is the concept of role (behavior associated with a status). Cultural norms are transmitted via roles, which are attached to statuses (positions a person occupies within a group). Yet people do not always follow roles exactly. The manner in which roles are actually carried out is role performance, the third link in the conceptual chain. Role performance is exhibited in our social interactions when we encounter other people. Social interaction based on roles is observable as patterned relationships—and those patterned relationships make up social structure. In turn, existing social structure affects the creation of and changes to culture.

✓ **READING PROGRESS CHECK**

Analyzing How is role performance related to status and roles?

GRAPHIC ORGANIZER

CULTURE
- transmitted via roles
- attached to social statuses
- guides role performance
- through social interaction
- which may be observable as patterned relationships
- which constitute

SOCIAL STRUCTURE

LINKS BETWEEN CULTURE AND SOCIAL STRUCTURE
Culture influences the roles, statuses, and role performance that make up social interactions, which reveal a society's social structure.

▶ **CRITICAL THINKING**
1. **Explaining** Why is it significant that roles and statuses "guide" role performance?
2. **Analyzing Visuals** Why is there a connection linking social structure back to culture?

encounter to come across or meet

Quick Case Study

WHAT'S YOUR ROLE?
Throughout your day, you perform many roles. What are they?

Procedure
1. Write a paragraph on the topic "What are my roles today?" In your paragraph, describe the roles you play at different points in the day—in the morning at home, at school, and after.
2. Randomly exchange your paragraph with those of your classmates and compare your experiences.

Analysis
As you read one another's work, consider these questions:
1. What roles do you share with your classmates?
2. How do your roles change over the course of a day?
3. What role strains do you face?

Role Conflict and Role Strain

GUIDING QUESTION How does role diversity lead to conflict and strain?

The existence of statuses and roles permits social life to be predictable and orderly. At the same time, life is complicated by the fact that each individual holds many statuses, each of which involves diverse roles.

Role Diversity Creates Problems

Each role carries with it a set of expectations. These role expectations are the social script for that role—the rights someone with that role has and the obligations he or she is expected to perform. **Role conflict** exists when the role expectations for or performance of a role in one status clash with the expectations for or role performance in another status. Many teenagers, for example, are both students and employees. They may often find it difficult to balance their study and work demands. They are experiencing role conflict.

Role strain occurs when a person has trouble meeting the many roles connected with a single status. If your expectations as a high-school student require you to perform well academically, join a social organization, pursue a sport, date, and participate in other school activities, you will probably experience some degree of role strain as a result.

role conflict the situation that exists when expectations for or performance of a role in one status clash with expectations for or performance of a role in another status

role strain the situation that occurs when a person has trouble meeting the many roles connected with a single status

Applying Sociology

REDUCING CONFLICT IN TWO-CAREER FAMILIES

Families with two working adults have special strains. In 2010, nearly 60 percent of all women aged 16 or above were in the labor force (U.S. Bureau of Labor Statistics). This has resulted in role conflict for women. In a two-career family, the woman is more likely to suffer from conflict because she is still generally expected to balance her traditional homemaker roles with her career roles. Partners and children feel the effects of this conflict as well. The following are some techniques for reducing role conflict.

1. **Focus on the Positive** If both partners are working from choice rather than necessity, it can be helpful to remember some of the reasons they first made the choice for both to work. These reasons may include additional income or personal satisfaction.

2. **Put Family Needs First** Role conflict can be most effectively managed when family roles are placed ahead of working roles. Placing a higher priority on family needs helps keep the family support structure intact.

3. **Assume One Role at a Time** Leaving job-related problems at work and family issues at home is often difficult but is very effective in reducing role conflict.

4. **Find the Compromise Balance** Although many men take active roles in child care today, women still make the most compromises in their careers. With more women in better-paying careers, we should expect more equality in career compromises between husbands and wives.

▶ CRITICAL THINKING

1. **Problem Solving** Identify three ways to reduce role conflict in two-career families.
2. **Assessing** Why would assuming one role at a time be particularly difficult to do?

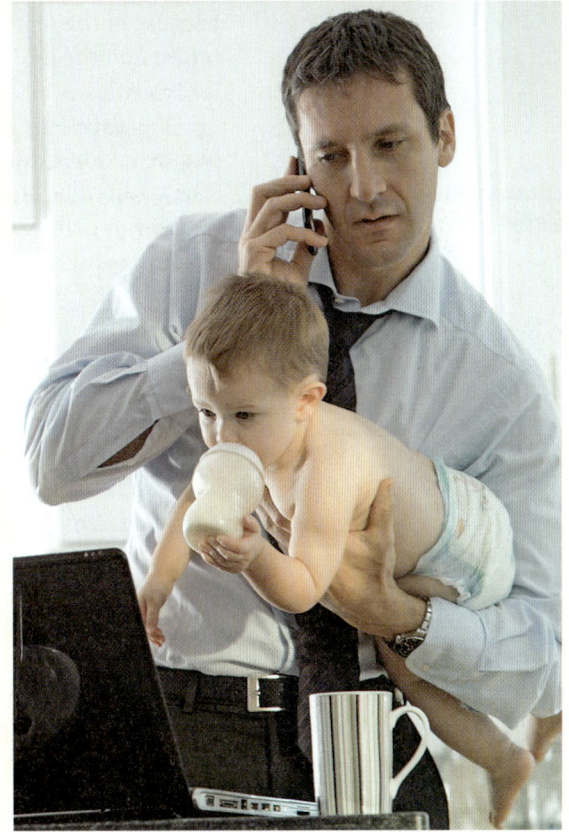

Equal participation in child care in two-career families is often a source of conflict.

Theoretical Perspectives

ILLUSTRATING SOCIAL STRUCTURE CONCEPTS
This table illustrates how each theoretical perspective might apply to the study of social structures. The concepts can be changed to any other theoretical perspective and illustrated from that perspective.

Theoretical Perspective	Social Structure Concept	Example
Functionalism	Role	Social integration is promoted by culturally defined rights and obligations honored by group members.
Conflict Theory	Ascribed master status	Ascribed master statuses, such as gender and race, empower some to subjugate others.
Symbolic Interactionism	Social interaction	Roles are performed by individuals on the basis of the symbols and meanings they share.

▶ **CRITICAL THINKING**

1. **Contrasting** Explain in your own words how functionalism and conflict theory differ in their concepts of social structure.

2. **Connecting Ideas** Associate each concept with a different theoretical perspective and provide your own example.

Managing Role Conflict and Role Strain

Role conflict and role strain create problems. We often solve these dilemmas by setting priorities. Suppose a student frequently misses school-related activities because of the demands of a job. If those activities are more important to her, she might quit the job. If the job has higher priority, she might drop the extracurricular activities.

We also segregate roles. That is, we separate our behavior in one role from our behavior in another. This is especially effective for reducing the negative effects of roles that are **incompatible**, or unable to be reconciled with one another. A college coach encountering role strain associated with simultaneously coaching and recruiting can separate the two roles. He may, for example, have an assistant do most of the recruiting until the season ends.

Because of role conflict and role strain, meeting the incompatible goals and expectations of all our roles is impossible. This poses no problem as long as our role performance falls within accepted limits. Coaches who win too few games, however, are likely to be fired at some point for failing to meet expected role performance.

incompatible unable to be reconciled

✓ **READING PROGRESS CHECK**

Analyzing What is the difference between role conflict and role strain?

LESSON 2 REVIEW

Reviewing Vocabulary
1. *Distinguishing* What is the difference between *role performance* and *social interaction*?
2. *Determining Cause and Effect* What causes role strain?

Using Your Notes
3. *Summarizing* Use your notes to write a statement explaining the relationship between roles and social structure.

Answering the Guiding Questions
4. *Defining* What are rights and obligations?

5. *Explaining* What is role performance?
6. *Making Connections* How does role diversity lead to conflict and strain?

Writing Activity
7. *Informative/Explanatory* Write a paragraph giving an example of someone experiencing role conflict or role strain and suggest how he or she might solve the problem.

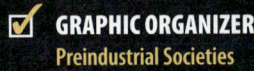

There's More Online!
- ☑ **GRAPHIC ORGANIZER** Preindustrial Societies
- ☑ **IMAGE** Yanomami Boy
- ☑ **TIME LINE** Human Societies
- ☑ **SELF-CHECK QUIZ**

Reading HELPDESK

Academic Vocabulary
- accompany
- domesticated

Content Vocabulary
- society
- hunting and gathering society
- horticultural society
- pastoral society
- agricultural society

TAKING NOTES:
Key Ideas and Details

ORGANIZING As you read about preindustrial societies, use a graphic organizer like the one below to record information about each type.

```
Preindustrial Societies
├── Hunting and Gathering Societies
├── Horticultural Societies
├── Pastoral Societies
└── Agricultural Societies
```

LESSON 3
Preindustrial Societies

ESSENTIAL QUESTIONS • *How is society organized?* • *How does the way in which a society is structured affect human relationships?*

IT MATTERS BECAUSE
The way a society provides for basic needs greatly affects its culture and social structure. Each meets these needs in different ways. Preindustrial societies include hunting and gathering, horticultural, pastoral, and agricultural societies.

Types of Society

GUIDING QUESTION *What defines a society?*

The culture and social structure of a society are greatly affected by the way the society provides for basic needs. A **society**, of course, is any group of people living within defined territorial borders and who share a common culture. All societies are composed of social structures, but their size and scale vary greatly. Members in each type of society know what is expected of them and what they can expect from others. They repeatedly engage in the same basic social patterns. That is, they share patterned and predictable social relationships that are passed from generation to generation.

Societies meet their members' basic needs, such as the needs for food and shelter, in different ways. These differences form the basis of a system anthropologists often use to classify societies. In this system, societies are classified as preindustrial, industrial, or postindustrial. This lesson distinguishes among types of preindustrial societies; the next lesson examines industrial and postindustrial societies. The preindustrial societies examined here are hunting and gathering, horticultural, pastoral, and agricultural societies. Each type is unique in important ways.

In theory, a society is independent. Its smaller social structures—family, economy, and so forth—work together so it can meet all the needs of its members. Preindustrial societies, in fact, can be independent and self-sufficient. Modern societies, however, are not. Although they are capable of caring for most members' needs, these societies must have political, military, economic, cultural, and technological ties with other societies. In fact, modern societies are rapidly moving toward the creation of a global society.

☑ **READING PROGRESS CHECK**

Identifying What distinguishes one society from another?

Social Structure and Society 143

PREINDUSTRIAL

HUNTING AND GATHERING	HORTICULTURAL GARDENING	PASTORAL HERDING
2 million to 10,000 years ago	12,000 to 10,000 years ago	12,000 to 10,000 years ago

TIME LINE

HUMAN SOCIETIES
As new types of societies appeared on Earth, older existing ones did not necessarily disappear.

▶ **CRITICAL THINKING**

1. **Evaluating** Why are older types of societies not replaced everywhere in the world when new types appear?
2. **Analyzing Visuals** How does technology change across these societies?

society a group of people living within defined territorial borders and sharing a common culture

hunting and gathering society a society that survives by hunting animals and gathering edible plants

accompany to go along with someone engaging in an activity

horticultural society a society that survives primarily through using simple tools to grow plants

Hunting and Gathering Societies

GUIDING QUESTION What are the characteristics of a hunting and gathering society?

The **hunting and gathering society** survives by hunting animals and gathering edible fruits and vegetables. Though this is the oldest solution to the problem of meeting subsistence needs, few hunting and gathering societies remain today. Among them are the Khoi-San (Bushmen) in Southern Africa, the Kaska in Canada, and the Yanomamö of Venezuela and Brazil.

Hunting and gathering societies are usually nomadic, moving as the food supply changes with the seasons. They tend to be small, with just 50 or so people. Most members are related by blood or marriage, although marriage is usually limited to those outside the family or band. They have little or no idea of private property or ownership. As a result, these societies have no social classes, no rich and poor. There is also no political authority. Without political institutions, they resolve conflict in other ways. Traditional Inuit societies of Canada and Alaska, for example, use dueling songs to settle disputes. The people involved in the dispute prepare and sing songs to express their sides in a disagreement. Their families **accompany** them. Those listening applaud their choices for victor.

☑ **READING PROGRESS CHECK**

Analyzing Why do hunting and gathering societies tend to be small?

Horticultural Societies

GUIDING QUESTION What are the characteristics of a horticultural society?

A **horticultural society** solves the subsistence problem primarily through using simple tools to grow plants. This type of society came into being about 10,000 to 12,000 years ago, when people learned they could grow and harvest certain plants instead of simply gathering them. The gradual change from hunting and gathering to horticulture occurred over several centuries. A few horticultural societies remain today, such as the Birom people of Nigeria and the Hanunóo of the Philippines.

The shift from hunting and gathering to horticulture, or gardening, led to more permanent settlements. Even without plows and animals to pull them, people could work a piece of land for extended periods of time before the soil lost its fertility and they had to move. This allowed the growth of larger societies—as many as one thousand or more people.

The family is even more basic to horticultural societies than to hunting and gathering societies. In the latter groups, survival of the group usually has top priority. In horticultural societies, primary emphasis is on the survival of family members. In fact, all family members contribute to food production.

Horticultural societies can produce a surplus of food. As a result, a more complex division of labor arises. Some members become leaders; others focus on making certain goods. From these differences, social inequality develops.

✅ **READING PROGRESS CHECK**

Explaining Why does social inequality arise in horticultural societies?

Pastoral Societies

GUIDING QUESTION *What are the characteristics of a pastoral society?*

In **pastoral societies**, food is obtained primarily by raising and caring for animals. These groups herd **domesticated**, or tamed, animals, such as cattle, camels, goats, and sheep. Examples include the reindeer-herding Saami, or Lapps, of Scandinavia and the cattle-herding Masai of East Africa.

Migration is a key feature of pastoral societies. Some, however, have long-term villages and simply move their herd animals to different pastures within a given area at different times of year. In such societies, the women usually do not accompany the men when they drive the herds but remain at home. As a result, these societies tend to be male dominated. Like horticultural societies, pastoral societies produce surpluses and have social inequality as a result.

pastoral society a society in which food is obtained primarily by raising and taking care of animals

domesticated tamed

✅ **READING PROGRESS CHECK**

Analyzing Why is migration a feature of pastoral societies?

Agricultural Societies

GUIDING QUESTION *What are the characteristics of an agricultural society?*

An **agricultural society**, like a horticultural society, subsists by growing food. Agricultural societies, however, use plows and domesticated animals, which boost productivity by digging more deeply into the ground and making it possible to farm larger areas. As a result, more people are free to engage in noneconomic activities such as education and the arts. Cities can be built, and occupations appear that are not directly tied to food production. New political, economic, and religious institutions emerge. Even though agricultural societies can have cities, they are agrarian because farming is the basis of the society. Modern agricultural societies include the cash-crop-growing areas of Southeast Asia and Central America, which are dominated by large-scale plantations.

agricultural society a society that uses plows and draft animals to grow food

✅ **READING PROGRESS CHECK**

Analyzing Why are agricultural societies considered to be agrarian?

Social Structure and Society **145**

Connecting Sociology to Anthropology

A PREINDUSTRIAL SOCIETY TODAY

Anthropology is the study of human culture. In 1964, anthropologist Napoleon Chagnon began studying the Yanomami, who live largely isolated from the outside world in the tropical forest of southern Venezuela. Chagnon's study, first published in 1968, provides a good examination of social structure in a preindustrial society.

PRIMARY SOURCE

"Social life is organized around those same principles utilized by all tribesmen: kinship relationships, descent from ancestors, marriage exchanges between kinship-descent groups, and the transient charisma of distinguished headmen who attempt to keep order in the village and whose responsibility it is to determine the village's relationship with those in other villages. Their positions are largely the result of kinship and marriage patterns; they come from the largest kinship groups within the village. They can, by their personal wit, wisdom, and charisma, become autocrats, but most of them are largely 'greaters' among equals. They, too, must clear gardens, plant crops, collect wild foods, and hunt. They are simultaneously peacemakers and valiant warriors. Peacemaking often requires the threat or actual use of force, and most headmen have acquired reputations for being *waiteri*: fierce.

The social dynamics within villages are involved with giving and receiving marriageable girls. Marriages are arranged by older kin, usually men, who are brothers, uncles, and the father. It is a political process, for girls are promised in marriage while they are young, and the men who do this attempt to create alliances with other men via marriage exchanges. There is a shortage of women due in part to a sex-ratio imbalance in the younger age categories, but also complicated by the fact that some men have multiple wives.

A young Yanomami girl

Most fighting within the village stems from sexual affairs or failure to deliver a promised woman—or out-and-out seizure of a married woman by some other man. This can lead to internal fighting and conflict of such an intensity that villages split up and fission, each group then becoming a new village and, often, enemies to each other."

—*Yąnomamö*, fifth revised edition, 1997

DBQ ▶ CRITICAL THINKING

1. **Making Inferences** Describe an activity in your culture that illustrates patterned social relationships. Explain the statuses and roles involved.
2. **Making Connections** How does the excerpt above compare with this lesson's description of the characteristics of a preindustrial society?

LESSON 3 REVIEW

Reviewing Vocabulary
1. **Differentiating** How do agricultural societies differ from horticultural societies?

Using Your Notes
2. **Organizing** Using your notes, rank the societies from the least to the most complex. Explain your reasoning.

Answering the Guiding Questions
3. **Defining** What defines a society?
4. **Characterizing** What are the characteristics of a hunting and gathering society?
5. **Characterizing** What are the characteristics of a horticultural society?
6. **Characterizing** What are the characteristics of a pastoral society?
7. **Characterizing** What are the characteristics of an agricultural society?

Writing Activity
8. **Argument** In which preindustrial society would you prefer to live? Why?

networks

There's More Online!

- ☑ **GRAPHIC ORGANIZER** Industrial and Postindustrial Societies
- ☑ **IMAGE** Postindustrial Worker
- ☑ **MAP** Agricultural Employment
- ☑ **SELF-CHECK QUIZ**

LESSON 4
Industrial and Postindustrial Societies

Reading HELPDESK

Academic Vocabulary
- complex
- consensus

Content Vocabulary
- industrial society
- mechanization
- urbanization
- gemeinschaft
- gesellschaft
- social solidarity
- mechanical solidarity
- organic solidarity
- postindustrial society

TAKING NOTES:
Key Ideas and Details

Comparing and Contrasting
As you read about industrial and postindustrial societies, use a graphic organizer like the one below to compare and contrast them.

Industrial Societies
-
-

Postindustrial Societies
-
-

ESSENTIAL QUESTIONS • How is society organized? • How does the way in which a society is structured affect human relationships?

IT MATTERS BECAUSE
The Industrial Revolution created a new type of society, called an industrial society. Characteristics that distinguish this society from all earlier ones include the growth of large cities and dependence on machines and technology. Postindustrial society has a predominately white-collar labor force concentrated in service industries. Social instability has been linked to the transition from an industrial to a postindustrial society.

Basic Features of Industrial Societies

GUIDING QUESTION What are the characteristics of an industrial society?

The Industrial Revolution, which began in Great Britain in the late 1700s, created a society dependent on science and technology to produce basic goods and services. Sociologists call this an **industrial society**.

From an Agricultural to an Industrial Society

Some fundamental structural changes occur in societies shifting from an agricultural to an industrial base. First is a move from simple, traditional technology (plows, hammers, and harnesses) toward the use of scientific knowledge to create more **complex,** or complicated, technologies. Early industrial technology included the steam engine and textile machinery. More recent technological advances include computers and lasers.

In industrial societies, animal and human labor are replaced by power-driven machines, a process known as **mechanization**. Machines are operated by wage earners, who hold increasingly complex and specialized jobs. By using farm machinery, farmers can produce enough food to support larger numbers of people than in other types of societies. This surplus allows people to move away from farms and villages to cities. **Urbanization**, then, is also a basic feature of industrial societies.

The United States became an industrial society in the 1800s. Adoption of the factory system led to urban growth. Increased immigration provided needed labor and contributed to urban growth. Societies currently shifting to an industrial economic base include Vietnam and Malaysia.

Social Structure and Society **147**

industrial society a society that depends on science and technology to produce basic goods and services

complex complicated

mechanization the process of replacing animal and human power with machine power

urbanization the shifting of the population from farms and villages to large cities

The Changing Role of the Family

In preindustrial societies, kinship is the fundamental basis of society. Kinship-based systems, however, are ineffective at solving the problems that arise in larger-scale societies. With industrialization, family functions change. Economic activities once carried out in the home move to factories. Homemade goods are replaced by mass-produced items. Education moves from the home to schools.

Families are more likely to separate socially and physically due to urbanization and the necessity of taking jobs in distant factories. Personal choice and love replace arranged marriages. Women, as a result of entering into the workforce, become less subordinate to their husbands. Individuals' social mobility increases dramatically, and social class is based more on occupational achievement than the social class of one's parents.

✅ **READING PROGRESS CHECK**

Identifying What are two key features of an industrial society?

A Conversation With Two Sociologists

GUIDING QUESTION *What were the views of Tönnies and Durkheim on preindustrial and industrial societies?*

Ferdinand Tönnies was an early German sociologist who wrote about preindustrial and industrial societies. In his writing, he distinguished preindustrial and industrial societies using the concepts of *gemeinschaft* (ga • MINE • shahft) and *gesellschaft* (ga • ZELL • shahft). **Gemeinschaft** is German for "community."

gemeinschaft a preindustrial society based on tradition, kinship, and close social ties

Connecting Sociology to Economics

CATEGORIZING SOCIETIES

Sociologists refer to societies in such terms as *preindustrial*, *industrial*, and *postindustrial*. Economists use different terms to make similar distinctions: They typically describe societies as "more developed," (such as the United States and Canada); "newly developed" (Brazil); and "less developed" (Bangladesh).

Economists do not have a set definition of what makes an economy "developed." The term is used to describe those economies that, relative to others, have a high gross domestic product (GDP). This measure of economic activity represents the total value of goods and services produced in a country in a year. People in more developed economies typically enjoy a relatively high per capita income and overall standard of living. Increasingly, economists are taking into account other measures of development, such as education and health, in measuring a country's level of development.

In the cases of the less developed countries, again, there are no set criteria or definitions. Economists, however, typically define those countries with the lowest level of income as "less developed." Measures such as nutrition, health, education, and literacy are also taken into account. Another factor is economic vulnerability—that is, how much instability exists in its agricultural sector and how dependent the nation is on a single good or service.

Countries with significant high-tech activity often enjoy high levels of income and economic output—and are designated by economists as "more developed economies."

▶ **CRITICAL THINKING**

1. **Making Connections** How do economists and sociologists differ in their views of economic activity and its effect on a country or society?
2. **Making Inferences** Why do you think economists are increasingly trying to factor in measures such as health and education into their determinations of a country's economic status?

A Global Perspective

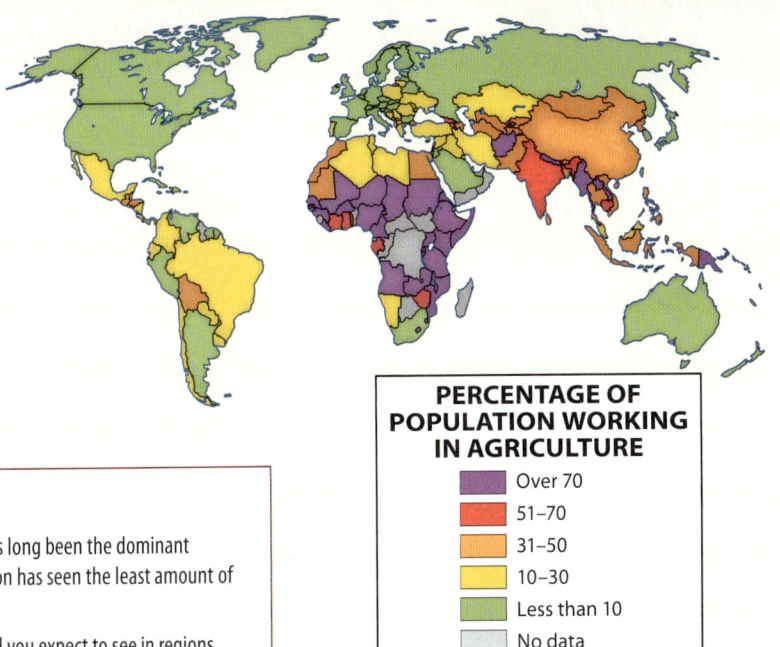

AGRICULTURAL EMPLOYMENT
As a society moves from being preindustrial to industrial and postindustrial, fewer and fewer people are required to raise food to feed the population. This is largely due to the mechanization of agriculture in industrial and postindustrial societies. This map shows the percentage of each country's population involved in the production of agricultural products.

PERCENTAGE OF POPULATION WORKING IN AGRICULTURE
- Over 70
- 51–70
- 31–50
- 10–30
- Less than 10
- No data

SOURCE: U.S. Central Intelligence Agency, *The World Factbook*, 2009.

Geography Connection

1. **Places and Regions** Assuming that agriculture has long been the dominant segment of economies around the world, which region has seen the least amount of change in the overall economic structure?
2. **Making Connections** What kind of changes would you expect to see in regions such as Africa if the shift from preindustrial to postindustrial societies continues?

It describes a society based on tradition, kinship, and intimate social relationships—as in rural preindustrial societies. **Gesellschaft** is German for "society." This concept represents urban industrial society and is characterized by weak family ties, competition, and more impersonal social relationships.

Shortly after Tönnies published his theories, Émile Durkheim made a similar argument using different terms. Durkheim distinguished the two types of societies by the nature of their social solidarity. **Social solidarity** is the degree to which a society is unified or can hold itself together in the face of obstacles. Social solidarity, Durkheim contended, is a result of society's division of labor.

In societies in which the division of labor is simple—in which most people are doing the same type of work—social solidarity arises from **mechanical solidarity**. That unity is achieved through a **consensus**, or broad agreement, on beliefs, values, and norms; through strong social pressures for conformity; and through dependence on tradition and family. Preindustrial societies have these characteristics.

In an industrial society, however, roles are increasingly differentiated. Members depend on a variety of people—factory workers, barbers, bakers, and other suppliers of services—to fulfill their needs. Such a society is based on **organic solidarity**. It achieves social solidarity through a complex network of specialized statuses that make members of society interdependent. The term *organic solidarity* is based on an analogy with living organisms. For a plant or animal of highly specialized parts to survive, its parts must coordinate. Similarly, the parts of a society based on organic solidarity must cooperate if the society is to survive.

gesellschaft an industrial society characterized by weak family ties, competition, and impersonal social relationships

social solidarity the degree to which a society is unified

mechanical solidarity a type of social unity achieved by people doing the same type of work and holding similar values

consensus a broad agreement

organic solidarity a type of social unity in which members' interdependence is based on specialized functions and statuses

✓ **READING PROGRESS CHECK**

Comparing How are Tönnies's concept of gemeinschaft and Durkheim's idea of mechanical solidarity similar?

Social Structure and Society **149**

Major Features of Postindustrial Society

GUIDING QUESTION *What are the characteristics of a postindustrial society?*

Some societies, such as the United States, have evolved into a new type of society, **postindustrial society**. In this type of society, the emphasis is on providing services and information rather than on producing goods through manufacturing. Sociologist Daniel Bell identified five major features of a postindustrial society:

1. The majority of the labor force is employed in service industries. Service industries entail performing activities—banking, medical care, food service, or entertainment—rather than producing goods.
2. White-collar employment replaces much blue-collar work. White-collar workers include office workers, sales workers, and professionals. Blue-collar workers are in manufacturing, construction, and skilled trades.
3. Technical knowledge is the key organizing feature. Knowledge is used to create innovations and as the basis for decision making. As technical expertise gains in importance, so do educational and research institutions.
4. Technological change is planned and assessed. In an industrial society, the effects of a new technology are not assessed before its introduction. For example, when the automobile engine was invented, no one asked whether it would affect the environment. In postindustrial societies, the effects—good and bad—of any innovation are analyzed before it is introduced.
5. There is a reliance on computer modeling. With modern computers, it is possible to consider a large number of interacting variables simultaneously. As a result, humans can effectively manage complex organizations.

Historian Francis Fukuyama believes that the transition to postindustrial society increases social instability. Studying that transition in North America and Europe in the mid-1960s, he noted increasing crime and the rapid decline in the importance of family. To support his claim that families were in decline, he pointed to falling marriage rates and birthrates, rising divorce rates, and the rise in children being born outside marriage. Fukuyama also believed that this transition was marked by falling trust and confidence in social institutions.

According to Fukuyama, this social instability is now lessening in these first postindustrial societies. He believes that this return to stability reflects the difficulty humans have in living without values and norms.

✓ **READING PROGRESS CHECK**

Differentiating How do service industries differ from manufacturing industries?

Computer skills and analytical skills become increasingly important in a postindustrial society.

▶ **CRITICAL THINKING**

Making Connections Which of the five features of a postindustrial society identified by David Bell is exemplified by this photograph?

postindustrial society
a society in which the economic emphasis is on providing services and information

---

LESSON 4 REVIEW

Reviewing Vocabulary
1. *Explaining* Why is the mechanization of agriculture important to the development of industrial society?
2. *Defining* What does Durkheim mean by *social solidarity*?

Using Your Notes
3. *Interpreting* Based on the notes you took, do you think the importance of families might decline further in postindustrial societies or would that trend reverse? Why?

Answering the Guiding Questions
4. *Characterizing* What are the characteristics of an industrial society?
5. *Explaining* What were the views of Tönnies and Durkheim on preindustrial and industrial societies?
6. *Characterizing* What are the characteristics of a postindustrial society?

Writing Activity
7. *Informative/Explanatory* Do you think Durkheim was right that industrial societies are similar to living organisms? Why or why not?

CHAPTER 5 Assessment

Directions: On a separate sheet of paper, answer the questions below. Make sure you read carefully and answer all parts of the questions.

Lesson Review

Lesson 1

1. **Identifying Central Issues** Why is it important to understand social structure?

2. **Drawing Conclusions** Would it be difficult or easy for most inhabitants of a preindustrial society to obtain achieved status? Explain.

Lesson 2

3. **Making Connections** How do rights differ from obligations? Other than those of a teacher and student or doctor and patient, provide an example of corresponding rights and obligations.

4. **Classifying** The range of options for acting one's roles in social interaction is not limitless. Why not? In your response, identify two instances of inappropriate cultural response in the workplace.

Lesson 3

5. **Defending** Modern societies are moving toward the creation of a global society. Explain whether—and why—you believe a global society should be viewed in a positive light or a negative light. Provide strong support for your response.

6. **Interpreting Significance** Why was the shift from hunting and gathering societies to horticultural societies important?

Lesson 4

7. **Comparing and Contrasting** Compare and contrast mechanical solidarity and organic solidarity. Other than the examples in the chapter, provide an example of each.

8. **Analyzing** Daniel Bell identified five major features of a postindustrial society. Which two of these features do you think are the strongest indicators? Explain.

21st Century Skills

USING GRAPHS

The graph below compares selected countries on the basis of how great a percentage of their manufactured exports are high-tech products, an indicator that suggests the existence of a postindustrial society or a society moving in the direction of becoming a postindustrial society. Examine the chart. Then answer the questions below.

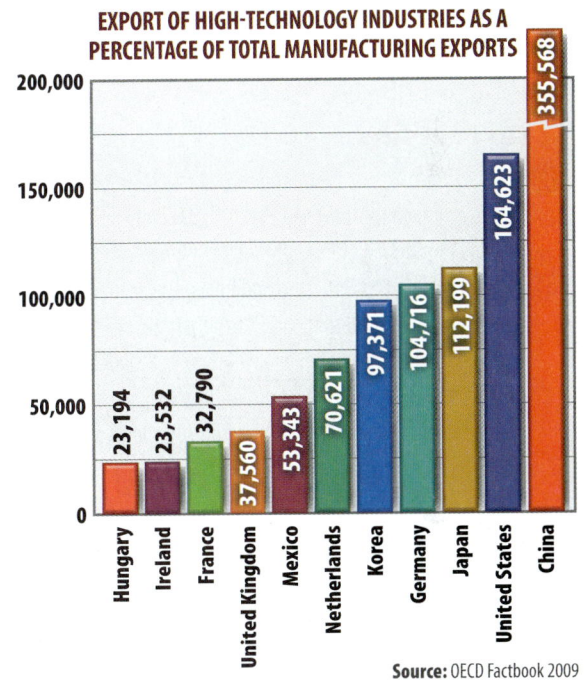

EXPORT OF HIGH-TECHNOLOGY INDUSTRIES AS A PERCENTAGE OF TOTAL MANUFACTURING EXPORTS

Hungary: 23,194; Ireland: 23,532; France: 32,790; United Kingdom: 37,560; Mexico: 53,343; Netherlands: 70,621; Korea: 97,371; Germany: 104,716; Japan: 112,199; United States: 164,623; China: 355,568

Source: OECD Factbook 2009

9. **Economics** Since Japan has long been known for its technology exports, why is the bar representing these exports so low?

10. **Identifying Cause and Effect** What does the high "mark" for Ireland indicate regarding the remainder of its exports?

Need Extra Help?

If You've Missed Question	1	2	3	4	5	6	7	8	9	10
Go to page	132	133	138	140	143	144–145	149	150	149–150	149–150

CHAPTER 5 Assessment

Directions: On a separate sheet of paper, answer the questions below. Make sure you read carefully and answer all parts of the questions.

Exploring the Essential Questions

11 *Analyzing* Collect information for this project by selecting and watching a television drama or comedy for three weeks. As you watch each week, take notes regarding social structure. Include notes regarding status, roles, rights, obligations, status set, role performance, social interaction, role conflict, role strain, and the depiction of the changing role of the family since industrialization. Write a short essay to analyze your findings. As a class, compare and contrast your analyses of the programs selected.

Critical Thinking

12 *Drawing Inferences* Imagine you are a sociologist developing content for a new university website. You have been asked to develop sections related to Social Structure and Status, Social Structure and Roles, Preindustrial Societies, and Industrial and Postindustrial Societies. Which section do you believe will require the greatest effort and the greatest amount of time to develop? The least? Write an essay, including strong support from the chapter to explain.

College and Career Readiness Skills

13 *Identifying Cause and Effect* Interview at least four students who have jobs. Develop and ask questions to determine positive and negative aspects of their employment. Then imagine you have been hired by a local restaurant owner to analyze problems with students who frequently fail to show up for their work shifts. Prepare a report for the restaurant owner, suggesting possible solutions to the restaururant's problem. As you write your report, consider the responses provided by the students who have responded to your questions. Within your report, explain whether you are focusing on role conflict or role strain.

DBQ Analyzing Primary Sources

PRIMARY SOURCE

Use the document to answer the following question.

> "The fate of our times is characterized by rationalization and intellectualization and, above all, by the 'disenchantment of the world.'"
>
> —Max Weber, *Science as a Vocation*, 1918–1919

14 *Comparing and Contrasting* In this chapter, you read that the theories of Ferdinand Tönnies and Émile Durkheim were similar. Based on the quote above, from sociologist Max Weber, does it appear that Weber's ideas regarding societies were quite similar to—or different from—those of Tönnies and Durkheim? Explain.

Research and Presentation

15 *Gathering Information* From the map in the A Diverse America feature in this chapter, select three states in addition to your own. Use Internet resources to research the most recent unemployment rates available online for these four states. On a computer, create a graph that compares the unemployment rates in 2012 with the current unemployment rates for the four states.

16 *Drawing Conclusions* Present your graph to the class and explain what you believe was the impact of the 2012 unemployment rates on status sets and master statuses of those who were unemployed. Explain your conclusions as to why the unemployment rates have or have not changed and state your supported views regarding the impact of the new rates on status sets and master statuses.

Need Extra Help?

If You've Missed Question	11	12	13	14	15	16
Go to page	138–142	129–150	141–142	148–149	132–136	132–136

Groups and Formal Organizations

ESSENTIAL QUESTION • *How do groups function as units of society?*

◀ These girls belong to a group that is part of a larger organization.

networks

There's More Online about groups and formal organizations.

CHAPTER 6

Technology & Society
Teens and Cyberbullying

Lesson 1
Primary and Secondary Groups

Lesson 2
Other Groups and Networks

Lesson 3
Types of Social Interaction

Lesson 4
Formal Organizations

Sociology Matters...

We are all members of groups and, possibly, formal organizations. Groups often make important decisions with long-term effects. One group of friends may choose to participate in a sport or volunteer activity while a different group may choose to break a law.

A group of NASA leaders chose to disregard the recommendations of engineers in 1986. The result was the *Challenger* explosion, which killed seven astronauts. Analyzing group decisions is one way sociologists help us understand human behavior.

CHAPTER 6
Technology & Society

Teens and Cyberbullying

As teenagers are increasingly in constant contact through texts, social networking, and other digital communication, a new problem has emerged: cyberbullying.

Repeatedly picking on someone with verbal or social abuse or physical contact are examples of bullying. It has been a mainstay of adolescence for centuries in the United States and abroad. Recently, the Internet—as well as cell phones and texting—has become another vehicle for bullying, in what has come to be called "cyberbullying."

With a variety of technological devices and platforms at their disposal, cyberbullies can cause severe emotional pain for their victims. What they might not realize is that cyberbullying, through the posting of pictures, blogging, commenting, emailing, and texting, is traceable and trackable. These methods are not anonymous. Once detected, offenders can be charged with a misdemeanor crime in some states. Many schools have rules against cyberbullying, with punishments that include suspension or expulsion.

Nearly half of American teenagers are affected by cyberbullying, either directly or indirectly. The victim can be a son, a daughter, a friend, a brother, a sister, or a classmate. The cyberbully and the victim can be part of the same social group. Cyberbullying often occurs over an extended period of time and can intensify over time. The effects can be damaging and range from hurt feelings to health problems, poor self-esteem, depression, and even suicide.

Teens are being counseled to report this serious behavior to a parent, teacher, guidance counselor, or another trusted adult. Teens may be encouraged to join or start a group for victims of cyberbullying, speak out against cyberbullying, or raise awareness in their community by handing out fliers. Cyberbullying is more vicious than simple teasing and the consequences are far more harmful.

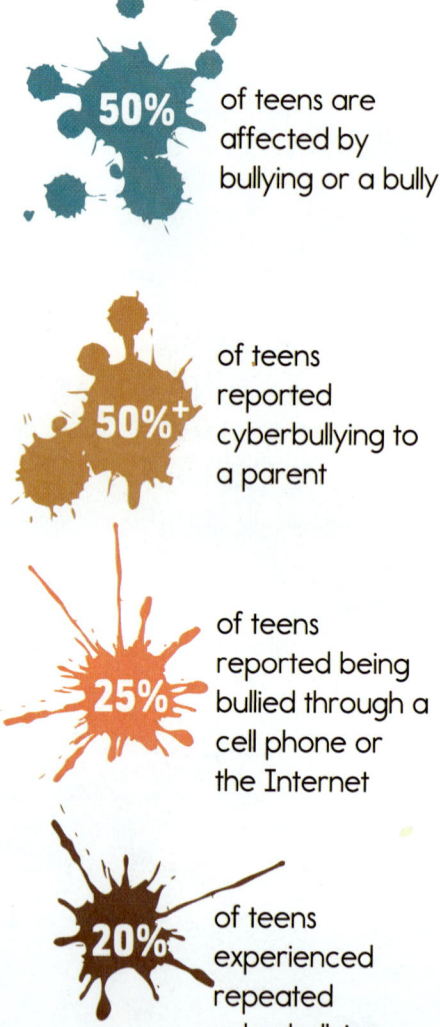

50% of teens are affected by bullying or a bully

50%+ of teens reported cyberbullying to a parent

25% of teens reported being bullied through a cell phone or the Internet

20% of teens experienced repeated cyberbullying

Source: Cyberbullying Research Center, "Cyberbullying Research from 2004–2010," 2012.

INFOGRAPHIC Explore the interactive version of this infographic on Networks.

TECHNOLOGY AND CYBERBULLYING

80% of teens used cell phones

WHERE CYBERBULLYING OCCURS

EMAILS ✉
WEBSITES
INSTANT MESSAGES
sent over the Internet

Interactions through
ONLINE GAMES

CHAT ROOMS
teens talk to each other online

@BLOGS
or web logs, which are public online journals

TEXT MESSAGES
sent to a teen's cell phone

Social networking sites, where individuals have a page about themselves where others can post messages
FACEBOOK
MYSPACE

 TWITTER
which sends short messages to a teen's online account and cell phone

Thinking Like a Sociologist

1 Analyzing
Why do you think some people use the Internet and other types of technology to cyberbully?

2 Researching
Find additional statistics to add to the infographic on cyberbullying. Note any discrepancies among sources.

Groups and Formal Organizations **155**

networks

There's More Online!

- ☑ **GRAPHIC ORGANIZER** Groups, Categories, and Aggregates
- ☑ **IMAGE** Car Full of Friends
- ☑ **IMAGE** Rebuilding a House
- ☑ **SELF-CHECK QUIZ**

Reading HELPDESK

Academic Vocabulary
- interaction
- correspond

Content Vocabulary
- group
- social category
- social aggregate
- primary group
- primary relationship
- secondary group
- secondary relationship

TAKING NOTES:
Key Ideas and Details

ORGANIZING As you read about primary and secondary groups, use a graphic organizer like the one below to record details.

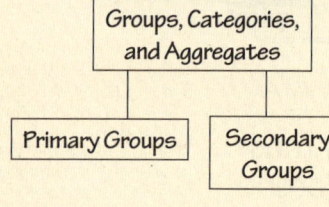

LESSON 1
Primary and Secondary Groups

ESSENTIAL QUESTION • How do groups function as units of society?

IT MATTERS BECAUSE
Groups are classified by how they develop and function. Primary groups meet emotional and support needs; secondary groups are task oriented.

Groups, Categories, and Aggregates

GUIDING QUESTION How are groups, categories, and aggregates different?

A **group** consists of at least two people who share one or more goals and think, feel, and behave in similar ways. They are also in regular contact with one another and take one another's behavior into account.

Groups play important roles in the lives of their members, as well as influencing society around them. Groups range from small and informal to large and formal. They tend to draw lines around themselves, creating insiders and outsiders. Some boundaries are tighter and more definite than others. Boundaries between groups in the South in the 1950s were rigidly enforced. African Americans were forbidden to drink from the same water fountains, use the same restrooms, or eat at the same restaurants as whites. Group boundaries may change over time, however. Since the 1960s, relations between African Americans and whites in the United States have become much more fluid.

A group is not the same as a **social category**—people who share a social characteristic. High-school seniors and women are two examples of social categories. A group is also sometimes confused with a **social aggregate**—people who happen to be in the same place at the same time, such as students waiting to get on a bus.

Although neither categories nor aggregates are groups, some members may form groups. Witnesses of a disaster (an aggregate) may work together to cope with an emergency. Citizens of a state (a social category) may band together in a political party. These people may form a group if they begin to interact regularly; share ways of thinking, feeling, and behaving; take one another into account; and share some common goals.

✓ **READING PROGRESS CHECK**

Assessing Why do groups influence a person's behavior more than categories or aggregates?

156

Primary Groups

GUIDING QUESTION *What is a primary group?*

Two principal types of groups are *primary* and *secondary*. At the extremes, the characteristics of these two types of groups—and the relationships that occur within them—are opposites. Most groups sit at different points along a continuum from primary to secondary, however.

Primary Groups

Charles Horton Cooley, one of the founders of symbolic interactionism, was the first to use the term *primary group*. A **primary group** is composed of people who are emotionally close, know one another well, and seek one another's company. The members of a primary group have a "we" feeling and enjoy being together. These groups are characterized by **primary relationships** that are intimate, personal, caring, and fulfilling. Members feel responsible for one another.

Primary groups are the most important setting for socialization. Family and childhood playgroups are the first primary groups a child experiences. Later, people participate in other primary groups. Close friends in high school and college, neighbors who keep an eye on one another's children, and friends who meet regularly for dinner are all examples of primary groups for adults.

The Development of Primary Groups

A number of conditions help primary groups form and primary relationships develop.

- **Small size.** It is hard for members of large groups to develop close emotional ties. The chances of knowing everyone fairly well are far greater in small groups. The boys or girls who play for the school basketball team are more likely to develop primary relationships than the crowd of student spectators who cheer them on.
- **Face-to-face contact.** Primary relationships occur more easily when **interaction** is face-to-face. People who can see one another and who can experience nonverbal communication such as facial expressions, tone of voice, and touch are much more likely to develop close ties.
- **Continuous contact.** A primary relationship rarely develops in a short period of time. In spite of reports of love at first sight, most of us require repeated social contact with another person to develop the closeness of a primary relationship.
- **Proper social environment.** Just seeing someone every day is not enough to form a primary relationship. You may visit your local grocery store every day and never form a relationship with the cashier. The social setting does not encourage personal relationships, and the statuses are unequal. This is why primary relationships do not usually develop between students and teachers, bosses and employees, or judges and lawyers.

group at least two people who have one or more goals in common and share ways of thinking and behaving

social category people who share a social characteristic

social aggregate people temporarily in the same place at the same time

primary group people who are emotionally close, know one another well, and seek one another's company

primary relationship interaction that is intimate, personal, caring, and fulfilling

interaction meaningful contact

Consider the members of this group and the setting.

▶ CRITICAL THINKING

Identifying What kind of group do you think is pictured here? Why?

Connecting Sociology to Political Science

GROUPS AND VOTING BEHAVIOR

Political science is a social science that dates back to ancient China and India as well as to the medieval Muslim world. Contemporary political science developed in the nineteenth century when the expansion of the social sciences grew to include new branches. The term *ideology* was introduced by two French philosophers and further refined by French socialist Henri de Saint-Simon in the early twentieth century. In fact, Saint-Simon worked closely with Auguste Comte, whom many view as the father of sociology.

Specifically, political scientists study the political struggles, attitudes, and behaviors among different groups, such as voters, interest groups, and even nation-states. Political scientists may use the scientific method to do their research and to build their arguments. For example, they may want to research how a special-interest group uses a strategy such as lobbying to influence public policy.

To better understand how political scientists work, let's examine what they have found about the influence of different groups on voting. On an election day, U.S. citizens who are at least 18 years of age can go to a designated area for voting. Outside that voting area, voters may encounter members of special-interest groups or political campaigns who try to influence their preference for a candidate, party, or issue. Inside, the voting booth is private, and a voter casts, or submits, his or her ballot seemingly alone. Political scientists, however, have learned that the voter's behavior is most commonly influenced by the voter's family members, whether intentionally or unintentionally.

Children are usually first introduced to political ideas by their parents.

▶ **CRITICAL THINKING**

1. **Making Connections** How was the early development of political science connected to sociology?
2. **Evaluating** What evidence do you think political scientists have used to support the conclusion that family members influence voting behaviors of other family members?

Functions of Primary Groups

Primary groups serve three important functions in society.

- **Emotional support.** At the end of World War II, the German army had endured years of being outnumbered, undersupplied, and outfought. These conditions should have led to desertion and surrender, but they did not. Strong emotional-support ties within German combat units kept them fighting against overwhelming odds.

- **Socialization.** For children, the family is the primary group that teaches them how to participate in social life. Primary groups also promote adult socialization—as adults enter college, take new jobs, change social classes, marry, and retire.

- **Encouragement of conformity.** Primary groups not only teach new members the appropriate norms and values but also pressure them to conform. William F. Whyte's classic study of an Italian slum gang illustrates encouragement to conform within primary groups. Whyte reported that bowling scores **corresponded** with status in the gang—the higher the rank, the higher the score. If a lower-ranked member began to bowl better than those above him, verbal remarks—"You're bowling over your head" or "How lucky can you get?"—were used to remind him that he was stepping out of line.

correspond to align with or match

✓ **READING PROGRESS CHECK**

Analyzing How can a primary group help people achieve their goals?

Secondary Groups

GUIDING QUESTION *How is a secondary group different from a primary group?*

Unlike a primary group, a **secondary group** is impersonal and goal oriented. Members' responsibilities involve making contributions toward the group's goal, but those contributions only affect a limited segment of members' lives. Secondary groups exist to accomplish a specific purpose. Work groups, volunteers coming together temporarily to respond to disasters, and environmental organizations are examples of secondary groups. Members of secondary groups interact impersonally in ways involving only limited parts of their personalities. These interactions are called **secondary relationships.** Interactions between clerks and customers, employers and workers, and dentists and patients are secondary relationships.

Groups are formed to serve a wide variety of functions.

▶ **CRITICAL THINKING**
Defining Why is this group of young people probably not a primary group?

Secondary Relationships

Members of secondary groups may be friends and identify with one another, but the purpose of the secondary group to which they belong is to accomplish a task, not to enrich friendships. In fact, if friendship becomes more important than the task, a secondary group may become ineffective. If the members of a disaster relief group became more interested in the emotional relationships among themselves than in meeting the needs of the victims, their performance could suffer.

secondary group people who share only part of their lives while focusing on a goal or task

secondary relationship impersonal interaction involving limited parts of personalities

Secondary Groups and Primary Relationships

Although primary relationships are more likely to occur in primary groups and secondary relationships in secondary groups, there are a number of exceptions. Many secondary groups include some primary relationships. Members of work groups may relate on personal terms, demonstrate genuine concern for one another, and have relationships that are fulfilling in themselves. Similarly, members of a primary group sometimes engage in secondary interaction. One family member may, for example, lend money to another member of the family with a set interest rate and repayment schedule.

✓ **READING PROGRESS CHECK**

Analyzing What is the main purpose of a secondary group?

LESSON 1 REVIEW

Reviewing Vocabulary
1. *Identifying* How is a social category different from a group?
2. *Defining* What are the most common primary groups for young people?

Using Your Notes
3. *Summarizing* Use your notes to write a statement that compares primary groups with secondary groups.

Answering the Guiding Questions
4. *Contrasting* How are groups, categories, and aggregates different?

5. *Defining* What is a primary group?
6. *Contrasting* How is a secondary group different from a primary group?

Writing Activity
7. *Informative/Explanatory* Choose a primary or secondary group you belong to, describe your rights and responsibilities within it, and explain how it affects your behavior.

Groups and Formal Organizations

networks

There's More Online!

- ☑ **GRAPHIC ORGANIZER** Other Groups and Networks
- ☑ **IMAGE** Columbine
- ☑ **MAP** Social Networking
- ☑ **SELF-CHECK QUIZ**

Reading HELPDESK CCSS

Academic Vocabulary
- initiation
- colleague

Content Vocabulary
- **reference group**
- **in-group**
- **out-group**
- **social network**

TAKING NOTES:
Key Ideas and Details

IDENTIFYING As you read about other groups and networks, use a graphic organizer like the one below to record details.

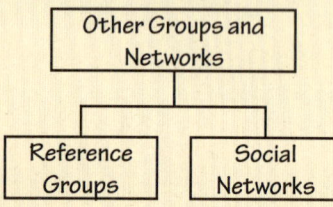

LESSON 2
Other Groups and Networks

ESSENTIAL QUESTION • *How do groups function as units of society?*

IT MATTERS BECAUSE
Reference groups help us evaluate ourselves and form identities. In-groups and out-groups divide people into "we" and "they." Social networks extend our contacts and let us form links to many other people.

Reference Groups

GUIDING QUESTION *What are reference groups, in-groups, and out-groups?*

We use certain groups to evaluate ourselves and to acquire attitudes, values, beliefs, norms, and mores. These groups are called **reference groups**.

Reference groups may include families, teachers, classmates, student government leaders, social organizations, rock groups, and professional sports teams. We may consider a group to be a reference group without being a member. You don't need to be a member of a rock band to view its musicians as a reference group. You need only evaluate yourself in terms of their standards and subscribe to their beliefs, values, and norms.

Reference groups do not have to be positive models. Observing the behavior of a group you dislike may reinforce a desire to act, feel, and behave differently. For example, a violent gang can provide a blueprint of behavior for people to avoid.

In-groups and out-groups are types of reference groups. They are like two sides of a coin—you can't have one without the other. An **in-group** requires extreme loyalty from its members. The in-group competes with and is opposed to an **out-group**. One membership role of in-group members is to feel opposition, antagonism, or competition toward the out-group. Members divide people into "we" and "they."

In-groups and out-groups may form around schools, athletic teams, racially or ethnically divided neighborhoods, or countries at war. In a high school, jocks, cheerleaders, geeks, and nerds are in-groups for some and out-groups for others.

In-groups must have boundaries to tell who is and is not "in." A boundary is often a symbol (badges, clothes, or a particular slang); it may be an action (handshake, high five); or it may involve a place. New members are often taught the boundaries at formal or informal **initiation** ceremonies.

160

Applying Sociology

SCHOOL VIOLENCE AND SOCIAL NETWORKS

The 1999 murders of 12 students and a teacher at Columbine High in Littleton, Colorado, shocked many Americans. Explanations for the attack, carried out by two students, came rapidly. Some blamed the lack of gun control, violent video games and movies, or the attackers' parents. Many sociologists thought the problem was the failure of social networks. Social networks help reduce violence in three ways:

1. Strong bonds reinforce acceptable and unacceptable behavior.
2. Members can share information about other members.
3. Networks provide members with help and social support.

In January 2012, a teenager from Roy, Utah, used social networks in one of these ways. A student from Roy High School interested in the Columbine shootings sent a text message that worried a friend. The student asked if the friend would not go to school if he asked the friend not to show up on a certain day. The worried friend alerted school administrators. An investigation uncovered the student's plan to bomb an all-school assembly and then to escape by plane. Because the student's friend shared his concerns with an adult, who responded quickly, lives were saved.

People react to the shooting at Columbine High School.

▶ CRITICAL THINKING

1. **Evaluating** Have the social networks in your school become larger and stronger or smaller and weaker in the past few years? Explain.
2. **Analyzing** Which example of how to reduce violence using social networks would be the most effective in your school? Why?

Group boundaries form an entrance barrier to outsiders. Maintaining group boundaries requires intense loyalty and commitment from members. Unfortunately, this may involve clashes with outsiders. Members of violent gangs may injure or kill an enemy gang member who has entered their "territory."

✓ **READING PROGRESS CHECK**

Identifying To what in-groups and out-groups do you belong?

Social Networks

GUIDING QUESTION *What social relationships are included in a social network?*

As individuals and as members of primary and secondary groups, we interact with many people. All of a person's relationships make up his or her **social network**—the web of social relationships that join a person to other people and groups. This network includes family members, work **colleagues**, classmates, church members, close friends, and store clerks. Social networks tie us to hundreds of people within our communities, and even around the world, in expansive networks and smaller e-communities. Your broad social network contains many smaller webs. Your close friends are only one part of your social network. Another part is composed of the people at your school with whom you have any social relationship.

The Internet has expanded the number of interactions and the flow of information within networks. Before the Internet, humanitarian relief organizations had to solicit donations using print media, telephones, and letters. Today, they can reach millions of people in just a few moments. For example, humanitarian aid began to pour in almost immediately after the 2010 earthquake in Haiti and the 2011 earthquake and tsunami in Japan. Feedback among network members can be instantaneous.

reference group group used for self-evaluation and the formation of attitudes, values, beliefs, norms, and mores

in-group exclusive group demanding extreme loyalty

out-group group targeted by an in-group for opposition, antagonism, or competition

initiation a ceremony marking entry into a group

social network a web of social relationships that join a person to other people and groups

colleague associate; fellow worker

Groups and Formal Organizations

A Diverse America

SOCIAL NETWORKING

While the population of the United States continues to increase, so has the use of social-networking sites (SNS). The number of Americans who use social-networking sites has doubled since 2008. Polls conducted by the Pew Research Center indicate that many users of social-networking sites "friend" their closest confidants to maintain social relationships, which ultimately creates a new type of social network. This map shows the percentage of Facebook users by state in 2009.

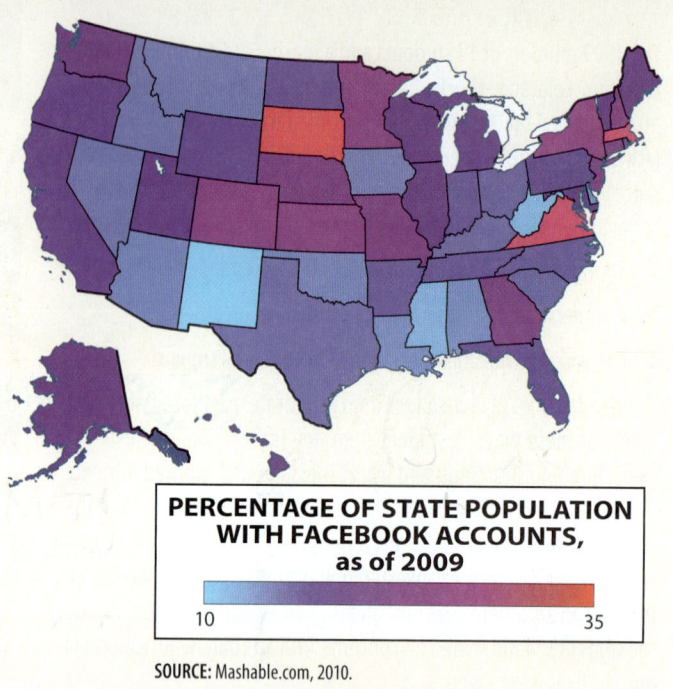

PERCENTAGE OF STATE POPULATION WITH FACEBOOK ACCOUNTS, as of 2009

10 — 35

SOURCE: Mashable.com, 2010.

Geography Connection

1. **Places and Regions** In which region does a larger percentage of the population use social-networking sites?
2. **Environment and Society** The Pew Research Center has found that nearly the same percentage of SNS users lived in urban, suburban, and rural areas. Explain.

Although a person's social network includes groups, it is not a group itself. A social network lacks the boundaries of a group, and it does not involve close or continuous interaction among all members. Thus, all members of a social network do not necessarily experience a feeling of membership because many of the relationships are too temporary for that sense of belonging to develop. On the other hand, the increased ease, speed, and frequency of social contact using computers and cell phones can promote a sense of membership in a network.

Social networks include both primary and secondary groups. Thus, the social relationships within a network involve both strong and weak ties. Social networks can serve several important functions. They can provide a sense of belonging and purpose. They can furnish support in the form of help and advice. Finally, networks can be useful tools for those individuals who are entering the labor market. Getting to know people who can help you in your career is very important.

✓ **READING PROGRESS CHECK**

Explaining How do you use the Internet to build your social network?

LESSON 2 REVIEW

Reviewing Vocabulary
1. ***Describing*** How do people use reference groups?
2. ***Explaining*** Which is larger—an in-group or a social network? Why?

Using Your Notes
3. ***Summarizing*** Use your notes to write a few sentences that describe a social network and its functions.

Answering the Guiding Questions
4. ***Defining*** What are reference groups, in-groups, and out-groups?
5. ***Defining*** What social relationships are included in a social network?

Writing Activity
6. ***Informative/Explanatory*** Identify your social network and describe some of the different types of relationships within it.

networks

There's More Online!

- ☑ **CHART** Theoretical Perspectives: Illustrating Types of Social Interaction
- ☑ **GRAPHIC ORGANIZER** Types of Social Interaction
- ☑ **IMAGE** Labor Protest
- ☑ **IMAGE** Obedience
- ☑ **SELF-CHECK QUIZ**

Reading HELPDESK

Academic Vocabulary
- uniformity
- predictability

Content Vocabulary
- cooperation
- conflict
- social exchange
- coercion
- conformity
- groupthink

TAKING NOTES:
Key Ideas and Details

IDENTIFYING As you read about types of social interaction, use a graphic organizer like the one below to record details.

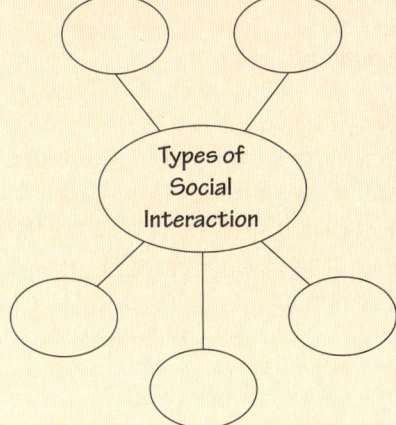

LESSON 3
Types of Social Interaction

ESSENTIAL QUESTION • *How do groups function as units of society?*

IT MATTERS BECAUSE
Social interaction is crucial to groups. Sociologist Robert Nisbet described five types of social interaction basic to groups: cooperation, conflict, social exchange, coercion, and conformity.

Cooperation

GUIDING QUESTION *Why do people cooperate?*

Cooperation is a form of interaction in which individuals or groups combine their efforts to reach a goal. Cooperation can occur in many different settings. It often occurs during a crisis when the single goal is physical survival or meeting basic physical needs. Crisis situations demand the best use of limited resources and efforts. Survivors of a plane crash in a snow-covered mountain range must cooperate to survive. Victims of natural disasters must help one another to get through their crisis.

Another type of crisis that promotes cooperation is a war of defense. During World War II, the United States was attacked by Japan at Pearl Harbor. Millions of Americans volunteered to serve in the armed forces while individuals and groups at home agreed to limit consumption of many items, donate money and materials for the war effort, and postpone individual plans to marry or continue a career or education. The goal was to win the war, and many cooperated to reach that goal.

Cooperation exists outside crises as well. Children and adults agree to a set of rules for recreational games. Many couples agree to share the duties of child care and household chores so that they can achieve the goal of an efficient and enjoyable home environment. Students agree to cooperate when they work to support or complete a community project, such as a playground or an environmental cleanup.

Without some degree of cooperation, social life could not exist. People agree to act in certain ways to achieve the goal of a peaceful and productive society.

☑ **READING PROGRESS CHECK**

Applying List three examples of interactions you have had in which you cooperated with others.

Groups and Formal Organizations 163

cooperation interaction in which individuals or groups combine their efforts to reach a goal

conflict interaction aimed at defeating an opponent

Conflict

GUIDING QUESTION *How can conflict benefit society?*

Groups or individuals who work together to obtain certain benefits are cooperating. Groups or individuals who work against one another to secure a larger share of the rewards for themselves are in **conflict**. In conflict, defeating the opponent is considered essential. It may become even more important than the overall goal. For example, consider two salespeople competing to win business contracts from the same companies. Their overall goal is to help their own company gain more profits. They might work very hard to win a very small contract that is almost insignificant to their company, however. The goal of beating their opponent has then become more important than the overall goal of gaining more profits.

Conflict is usually considered disruptive, and laws and social norms discourage it. A cooperative, peaceful society or group is generally assumed to be better than one in conflict. But conflict can be beneficial as well, depending on how it is handled. Positive ways to handle conflict include persuasion, compromise, debate, and negotiation. In most cases, using these techniques allows each side to gain something from the conflict rather than allowing for only a single winner.

According to the early German sociologist Georg Simmel, one of the major benefits of conflict is the promotion of cooperation and unity *within* opposing groups. The Revolutionary War drew diverse American colonists together even though it brought them into conflict with the British. Similarly, a labor union often becomes more united during the process of collective bargaining.

Another positive effect of conflict is the attention it draws to social inequities. Norms and values are reexamined when conflicts erupt. Civil rights activists in the early 1960s, for instance, pressured the U.S. Congress into passing laws that ensured basic rights and freedoms for all people. In the spring of 2011, conflicts in the Middle East forced the world to recognize the limited rights of citizens there.

social exchange a voluntary action performed with the expectation of getting a reward in return

Conflict may also be beneficial when it changes norms, beliefs, and values. Student protests in the late 1960s and early 1970s resulted in changes to previously accepted norms and behaviors within universities. Students were given greater representation in decision-making bodies, and university administrations became more sensitive to diverse student needs.

✓ **READING PROGRESS CHECK**

Evaluating Describe one interaction in which you have been involved when conflict had a positive effect and one in which it had a negative effect.

Supporters of several different causes marched together in Los Angeles in a collective protest in May 2012.

▶ **CRITICAL THINKING**

Hypothesizing Do you think these protests had a positive or negative effect on society? Why?

Social Exchange

GUIDING QUESTION *How is social exchange different from cooperation?*

> **PRIMARY SOURCE**
>
> "All men, or most men, wish what is noble but choose what is profitable; and while it is noble to render a service not with an eye to receiving one in return, it is profitable to receive one. One ought, therefore, if one can, to return the equivalent of services received, and to do so willingly."
>
> —Aristotle, *The Nicomachean Ethics*, circa 350 B.C.

In this passage, Aristotle touches on **social exchange**, a type of social interaction in which one person voluntarily does something for another, expecting a reward in return. If you help a friend wash her car, expecting that she will help you study for a test, the relationship is one of exchange. In an exchange relationship, the benefit to be earned, rather than the relationship itself, is key. In social exchange, when you do something for someone, he or she becomes obligated to return the favor. Thus, the basis of an exchange relationship is reciprocity, or the state of being shared, felt, or shown on both sides.

While both cooperation and social exchange involve working together, there is a significant difference between them. In cooperation, individuals or groups work together to achieve a shared goal. Reaching this goal, however, may or may not benefit all those who are cooperating. And although individuals or groups may profit from cooperating, that is not their main objective. In social exchange, however, the goal may be less important than the benefits to those involved.

For example, group members may work to build and maintain an adequate supply of blood for a local blood bank without thought of benefit to themselves. This is an example of cooperation. Suppose, though, that the group is working to ensure availability of blood primarily for its own members. In this case, it has an exchange relationship with the blood bank.

Exchange relationships are often apparent in political and legislative maneuvering. For example, members of Congress often need support for bills that benefit their home districts. To get that support, they may agree to support another member's bill, which they might have opposed or had no opinion on. A common Latin phrase describing this type of exchange behavior is *quid pro quo*, or "this for that."

Working with a friend on homework may be an example of cooperation or social exchange, depending on whether a reward is expected.

▶ **CRITICAL THINKING**

Classifying What would make the situation in the photograph a social exchange and not cooperation?

✓ **READING PROGRESS CHECK**

Analyzing Describe one action you have taken that is an example of social exchange.

Coercion

GUIDING QUESTION *Why is coercion the opposite of social exchange?*

Coercion is social interaction in which individuals or groups impose their will on other individuals or groups. Governments enforce laws through legalized punishment. Parents control children's behavior by threats to withdraw privileges.

coercion interaction in which individuals or groups are forced to behave in a particular way

Theoretical Perspectives

TYPES OF SOCIAL INTERACTION

This chart illustrates one way that the major theoretical perspectives would illustrate types of social interaction. Each perspective has an explanation or rationale for the different types of interaction, which may not agree with the explanations given by other perspectives. For example, conflict theory suggests that cooperation and social exchange are rare because two people or groups seldom have the same amount of power and that in most cases there is actually a struggle for power.

Theoretical Perspective	Type of Social Interaction	Example
Functionalism	Conformity	Team integration is promoted when baseball players accept their roles on the field.
Conflict Theory	Coercion	Conflict in prisons is controlled by the superior power of the guards.
Symbolic Interactionism	Social Exchange	Two students exchange ideas through the Internet on different school projects so each benefits.

▶ **CRITICAL THINKING**

1. *Applying* Explain how conflict theory would explain conformity and provide an example.

2. *Applying* Explain how functionalism would explain conflict and provide an example.

Groups and Formal Organizations

Connecting Sociology to Psychology

DECISION MAKING IN JURIES

American citizens who are 18 years of age and over are required by law to serve on juries if selected. Jurors listen to the case presented by both sides in a trial and study the evidence. Their main responsibility is to deliberate and to reach a unanimous verdict. In analyzing jury decisions, psychologists would most likely study the behavior and thought process of each juror; sociologists might look at how the dynamics of the group affect decision making.

Groupthink is one model that can be used to analyze how a jury reaches a verdict. Two psychologists, David H. Mitchell and Daniel Eckstein, published an article in 2009 exploring the issue. In it, they examined how a group of jurors performed their duty.

Mitchell and Eckstein explained that because juries work in isolation and do not have access to other perspectives on the case, they are susceptible to the preferences of fellow jurors. Since the decisions that jurors make may determine, at times, whether a person who is charged with a crime lives or dies, Mitchell and Eckstein suggested that actions should be taken to prevent juries from the effects of groupthink. They suggested that jurors could be trained for their duties and made aware of the conditions that often lead to groupthink.

Juries must reach a group consensus when they decide a verdict.

▶ CRITICAL THINKING
1. **Making Connections** How do sociologists and psychologists view a group of jurors?
2. **Hypothesizing** Based on the findings of Mitchell and Eckstein, what hypothesis can you form about the potential effects of groupthink on jurors who have received some training?

Coercion is the opposite of social exchange. Whereas social exchange involves voluntary actions for mutual benefit, coercion is a one-way street. Social exchange occurs between groups or individuals roughly equal in power. In coercion, one party is clearly dominant. This domination may occur through physical force, such as imprisonment, torture, or death. More often, however, it is expressed through social pressure—ridicule, rejection, or withdrawal of affection.

Conflict theory best describes this type of social interaction. When parents coerce children with a curfew, guards coerce prisoners with force, and governments coerce bad drivers with fines, obvious power differences are at work.

✓ **READING PROGRESS CHECK**

Explaining What is the relationship between groups or individuals in coercion?

Conformity

GUIDING QUESTION *What is groupthink?*

conformity behavior that matches group expectations

uniformity consistency; without variation

predictability when something can be foretold or predicted

Conformity is behavior that matches group expectations. When we conform, we adapt our behavior to fit that of those around us. Conformity is an expectation of socialization. Social life—with its **uniformity**, **predictability**, and orderliness—could not exist without it. Without conformity, there could be no churches, families, governments, or social structure. Conformity is a way to avoid conflict.

Conforming to Group Pressure

The tendency to conform to group pressure has been dramatically illustrated in a classic experiment by Solomon Asch. In this experiment, many participants publicly denied their own senses because they wanted to avoid disagreeing with majority opinion. Asch asked groups of male college students to compare lines printed on two cards. The students were asked to identify the line on the second card that matched, in length, one of the lines on the first card. In each group, all but one of the subjects had been instructed by Asch to choose a line that obviously did not match. The naive subject—the only member of each group unaware of the real nature of the experiment—was forced either to select the line he actually thought matched the standard line or to yield to the unanimous opinion of the group.

In tests of individuals in isolation, Asch had found that the error rate in matching the lines was only 1 percent. Under group pressure, however, the naive subjects conformed to the majority's incorrect opinion over one-third of the time. If this large a proportion of subjects yielded to group pressure among strangers, it is not difficult to imagine the conformity rate in groups where people are emotionally committed to the group and value the opinions of other members.

Groupthink

Because of the difficulty of going against group decisions, Irving Janis has argued that many decisions are likely to be the product of *groupthink*. **Groupthink** exists when thinking in a group is self-deceptive, based on conformity to group beliefs, and created by group pressure. In groupthink, pressures toward uniformity discourage members from expressing their concerns about group decisions.

During the administration of President John F. Kennedy in the early 1960s, for example, the president and his advisers decided to launch a planned invasion of Cuba at the Bay of Pigs. The invasion failed. Analysis by Janis revealed that during the decision-making process, because of group pressure, several top advisers failed to admit that they thought the plan would probably not succeed.

Research indicates that groupthink can be avoided when leaders or group members make a conscious effort to see that all group members participate actively in a multisided discussion. In addition, members must know that points of disagreement and conflict will be tolerated.

People in groups are also affected by the "bystander effect." Studies have shown that people are hesitant to react differently than other observers. People in a crowd are apt to walk by a person needing help while they are apt to stop when alone. One reason is that in a group they feel the responsibility is not theirs alone, but a shared one. They tend to conform to the behavior of others as a result.

People's actions are often related to the actions of a larger group. Some people feel that it's acceptable to cheat on their taxes because "Everyone else is doing it."

✅ **READING PROGRESS CHECK**

Describing Why did so many subjects in Asch's experiment choose an answer they knew to be incorrect?

groupthink self-deceptive thinking that is based on conformity to group beliefs and created by group pressure to conform

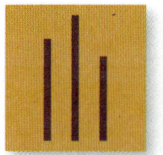

CARD A   **CARD B**

△ **DIAGRAM**

ASCH'S EXPERIMENT
Because of pressure to conform, people in Solomon Asch's experiment often chose the lines on the left or right of Card A as a match for the line on Card B.

▶ **CRITICAL THINKING**

1. ***Analyzing Visuals*** How difficult is the judgment that Asch required subjects to make? Why do you think so?
2. ***Interpreting*** One-third of Asch's subjects conformed to the group decision. Do you think that is strong or weak evidence for groupthink. Why?

LESSON 3 REVIEW

Reviewing Vocabulary
1. ***Contrasting*** How are *conflict* and *coercion* different?
2. ***Comparing*** What benefits do *cooperation* and *conformity* share?

Using Your Notes
3. ***Identifying*** Use your notes to write a sentence for each type of social interaction that describes its main characteristic or how it differs from other types of interaction.

Answering the Guiding Questions
4. ***Analyzing*** Why do people cooperate?

5. ***Assessing*** How can conflict benefit society?
6. ***Contrasting*** How is social exchange different from cooperation?
7. ***Contrasting*** Why is coercion the opposite of social exchange?
8. ***Defining*** What is groupthink?

Writing Activity
9. ***Informative/Explanatory*** Describe three different situations in which you have been involved that are examples of three different types of social interaction and explain which type of interaction is most common in your life.

FOCUS on research

Experiment

CCSS

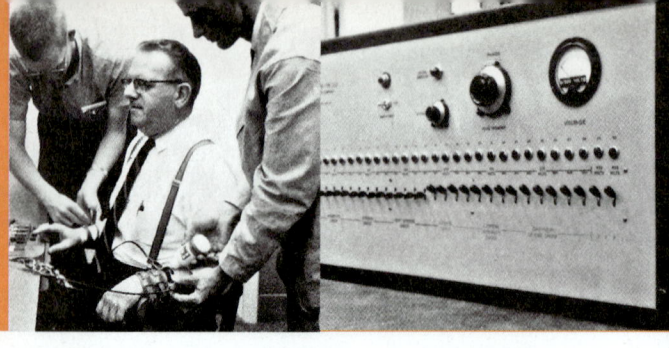

Group Pressure and Obedience

Can group pressure cause a person to physically punish a victim with increasing severity despite the victim's pleas for mercy? Researcher Stanley Milgram has shown that this can happen. In an experiment that would be condemned by today's ethical standards, Milgram demonstrated a surprisingly high level of obedience to authority among the participants in the study.

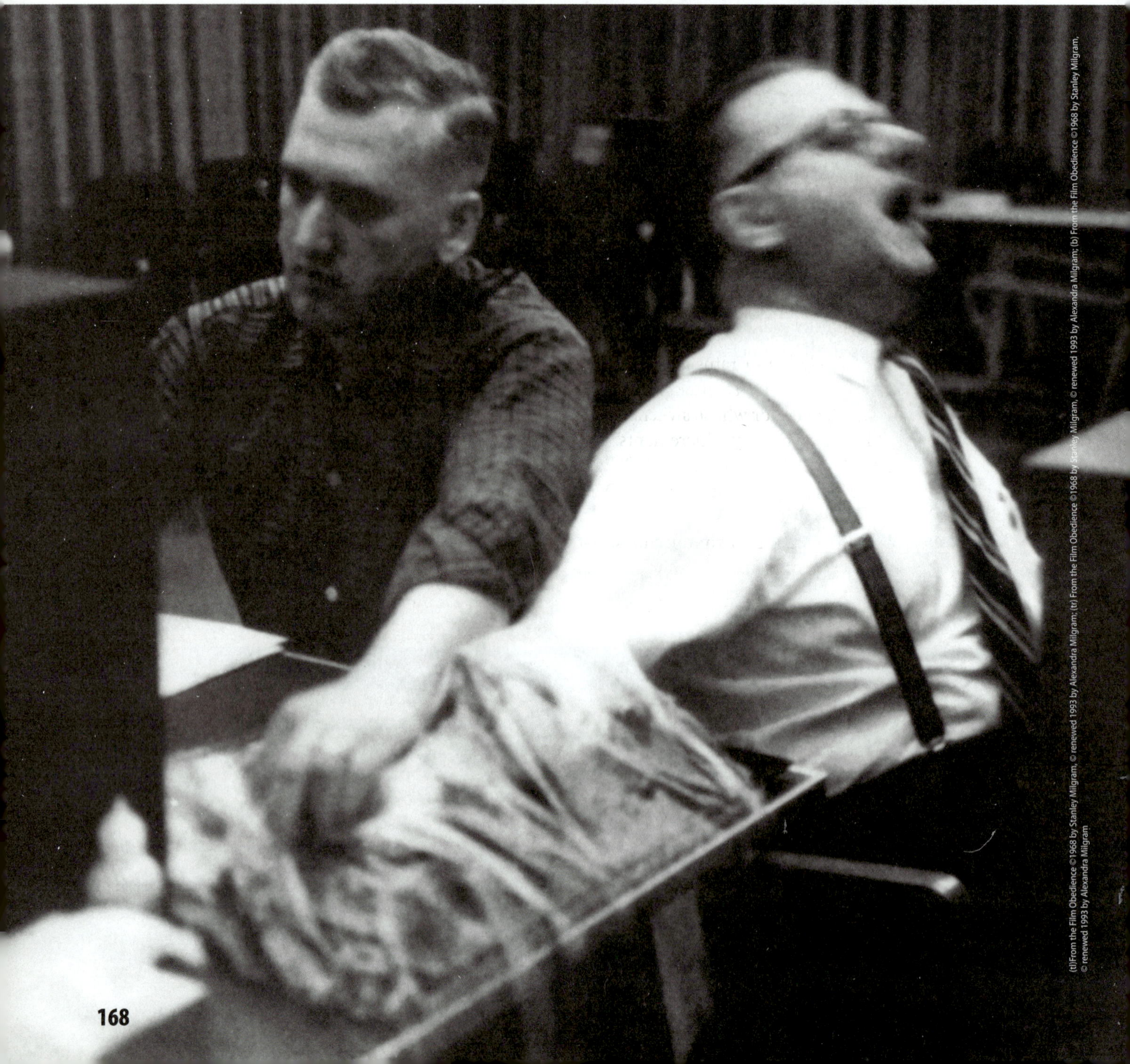

In his classic experiment, Solomon Asch demonstrated that group pressure can influence people to make false claims about what they see. Specifically, experimental subjects can be pressured to claim that two lines (drawn on a card) match in length even though they originally perceived these same two lines as different in length. Researcher Stanley Milgram wanted to know if group pressure can have the same effect on behavior. Can group pressure cause people to treat others in ways they otherwise would not?

In his experiment, Milgram asked research participants to administer increasingly stronger electric shocks to people who appeared to be in pain. He placed eighty males in an experimental situation in which a team of three individuals (two "confederates" who knew the nature of the experiment and one "subject" who did not) tested a fourth person (who was also in on the experiment) on a learning task. Each mistake by the fourth party brought an apparent electric shock from the subject. The two confederates (participants cooperating with Milgram) on each team suggested increasingly higher shock levels for successive mistakes made by the "learner" (the third confederate in the electric chair). The researcher recorded the degree to which the "operator" (the subject of the experiment) resisted or went along with group pressure to increase the voltage levels. After explaining to the subject that the purpose of the experiment was to determine the effects of punishment (electric shocks) on memory, the learner was strapped into an electric-chair apparatus in full view of the other three team members. These three were seated in front of a large shock generator whose switches were labeled from 15 to 450 volts in 15-volt increments. The lowest-level group of switches was labeled "Slight Shock"; the highest-level group of switches read "Danger: Severe Shock."

The "operator" controlled the maximum shock that could be administered. He could keep the shock level at 15 volts throughout or increase the shock level in line with the group's recommendation. It was his decision.

The learner was primed to always answer questions incorrectly. As the shocks became stronger, he grunted, protested, and finally demanded that the experiment stop. Each of these complaints was actually prerecorded and played in coordination with a given shock level. No discomfort was indicated until a 75-volt shock was administered. At 120 volts, the learner shouted that the shocks were becoming painful. Groans followed a 135-volt shock, and at 150 volts the learner cried out to be released from the experiment, complaining of a heart condition. At 180 volts, the learner cried out, "I can't stand the pain," and 285 volts was followed by an agonized scream. From 300 to 450 volts, the learner continuously shouted desperately that he would no longer answer questions.

Milgram first needed to know how far the operator would go in administering shocks without group influence. To accomplish this, an identical experiment was run minus the two confederates in the punishing group. Response to group pressure was measured by the difference in the operator's behavior in the two situations.

Group pressure heavily affected the level of shock administered by the operator. That is, the average shock level in the three-person situation was significantly higher than in the one-person situation. Perhaps most interesting are the results on maximum shock levels. When alone, only two operators went beyond the point where the learner first vehemently protested. Under group pressure, twenty-seven of the operators went beyond this point. Nineteen of the operators went above 255 volts ("Intense Shock"), and ten went into the group of voltages labeled "Danger: Severe Shock." Seven even reached 450 volts (the highest shock level possible). Milgram admitted to finding the results of the experiment "disturbing":

PRIMARY SOURCE

"They raise the possibility that human nature, or—more specifically—the kind of character produced in American democratic society, cannot be counted on to insulate its citizens from brutality and inhumane treatment at the direction of malevolent authority. A substantial proportion of people do what they are told to do, irrespective of the content of the act and without limitations of conscience, so long as they perceive that the command comes from a legitimate authority."

—Stanley Milgram, *Obedience to Authority: An Experimental View*, 1974

Working With the Research

1. **Making Connections** How might the findings by Stanley Milgram and Solomon Asch apply to social pressures young people face in school?
2. **Comparing** What books or articles have you read that provide you with a better understanding of group pressure and obedience? Explain.
3. **Evaluating** How do you think society would function without the tendency to conform? Explain.

Groups and Formal Organizations

networks

There's More Online!

- ☑ **CARTOON** Bureaucratic Rules
- ☑ **CHART** Public School District Organization Chart
- ☑ **GRAPHIC ORGANIZER** Formal Organizations
- ☑ **IMAGE** Iron Law of Oligarchy
- ☑ **MAP** Human Development
- ☑ **SELF-CHECK QUIZ**

Reading HELPDESK

Academic Vocabulary
- corporation
- submit

Content Vocabulary
- formal organization
- bureaucracy
- power
- authority
- rationalization
- informal organization
- iron law of oligarchy

TAKING NOTES:
Key Ideas and Details

SUMMARIZING As you read about formal organizations, use a graphic organizer like the one below to record details.

| Formal Organizations | Bureaucracies |
| Informal Organizations | Iron Law of Oligarchy |

LESSON 4
Formal Organizations

ESSENTIAL QUESTION • How do groups function as units of society?

IT MATTERS BECAUSE
A formal organization is created to achieve some goal. Most are bureaucratic. The existence of informal primary groups and primary relationships within formal organizations can either help or hinder the achievement of goals.

The Nature of Formal Organizations

GUIDING QUESTION How are formal organizations and bureaucracies related?

Until the 1920s, the majority of Americans lived on farms or in small towns and villages. Most of their daily lives were spent in primary groups, such as families, neighborhoods, and churches. As industrialization and urbanization advanced, Americans became more involved in secondary groups. Born in hospitals, educated in large schools, employed by huge **corporations**, regulated by government agencies, cared for in nursing homes, and buried by funeral homes, Americans, like other members of industrialized societies, now often find themselves in formal organizations.

A **formal organization** is deliberately created to achieve one or more long-term goals. A current list of types of formal organizations is extensive: educational institutions, such as high schools and colleges; business entities, such as corporations and small businesses; local, state, and federal government agencies; medical groups, such as hospitals and physicians groups; religious bodies, such as churches, synagogues, and mosques; political organizations, such as political parties and interest groups; and fraternal societies and social clubs.

To manage their affairs, most formal organizations today are also **bureaucracies**—formal organizations based on rationality and efficiency. Although many people think of them as "monuments to inefficiency," bureaucracies have proven to be effective in industrial societies. They are found everywhere from governments to corporations.

✓ **READING PROGRESS CHECK**

Analyzing Which formal organization do you think affects your life most directly?

170

Major Characteristics of Bureaucracies

GUIDING QUESTION *What are the characteristics of a bureaucracy?*

All bureaucracies possess certain important characteristics:

- **A division of labor based on the principle of specialization:** Each person in a bureaucracy is responsible for certain functions or tasks. This specialization allows an individual to become an expert in a limited area. For example, the organizational chart shown here outlines the division of labor in a public school district.
- **A hierarchy of authority:** **Power** is the ability to control the behavior of others, even against their will. **Authority** is the exercise of legitimate power—power that derives from a recognized or approved source. People **submit** to authority because they believe it is the right or necessary thing to do. Authority in bureaucratic organizations is structured like a pyramid. The greatest amount of authority is given to a few positions at the top, with decreasing amounts of authority spread out in more positions at lower levels. Those lower in this hierarchy of authority submit to the decisions of those higher.
- **A system of rules and procedures:** Rules and procedures direct how work is to be done and decisions will be made. This system provides stability by coordinating activities and providing guidelines for most situations.
- **Written records of work and activities:** Written records of work and activities are made and then kept in files. This organizational memory is essential to smooth function, stability, and continuity.
- **Promotion on the basis of merit and qualifications:** Jobs are filled on the basis of technical and professional qualifications. Promotions are given on the basis of merit, not favoritism. The norm in a bureaucracy is equal treatment for all.

✓ **READING PROGRESS CHECK**

Drawing Inferences Why do you think an organizational memory is important in a bureaucracy? Give an example to support your view.

corporation a large legal business group with its own duties, powers, and liabilities

formal organization a group deliberately created to achieve one or more long-term goals

bureaucracy a formal organization based on rationality and efficiency

power the ability to control the behavior of others

authority the legitimate or socially approved use of power

submit to yield or to surrender to the authority of another

⌄ **CHART**

PUBLIC SCHOOL DISTRICT ORGANIZATIONAL CHART

The connecting lines indicate who reports to whom and thus show relative authority.

▶ **CRITICAL THINKING**

1. **Analyzing Visuals** What two individuals or groups have authority over all the other members of the bureaucracy?
2. **Comparing** How are the responsibilities of the executive of student services and the executive of human resources similar?

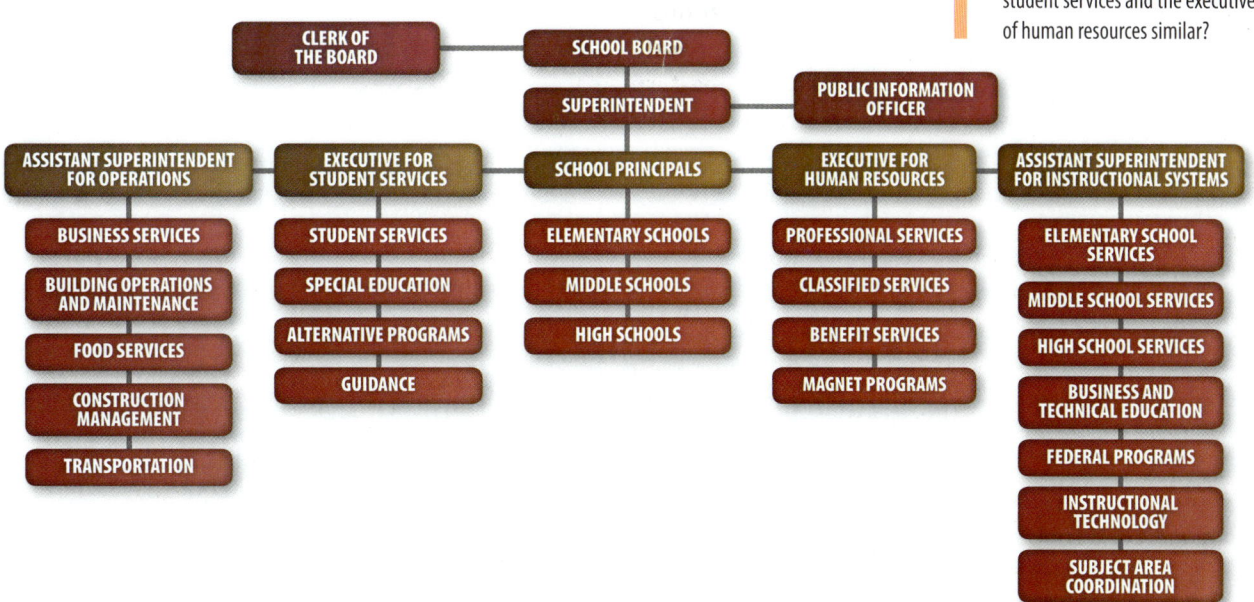

Groups and Formal Organizations 171

Quick Case Study

BUREAUCRACIES
We are all members of bureaucracies. What are their effects?

Procedure
1. Write a paragraph that names and describes the basic goal or goals of one bureaucracy to which you belong.
2. Randomly exchange your paragraph with another student.

Analysis
After reading your classmate's paragraph, answer these questions:
1. Why does this organization qualify as a bureaucracy?
2. How does this bureaucracy protect its members?
3. Does this bureaucracy dehumanize its members in any ways? How so?

Max Weber and Bureaucracy

GUIDING QUESTION What are the advantages and disadvantages of a bureaucracy?

Max Weber was the first to analyze the nature of bureaucracy. He recognized the problems inherent in bureaucracies, but overall he believed they were very efficient in meeting the needs of industrial societies.

Advantages of Bureaucracies
Weber feared the dehumanizing effects of bureaucracies. But as the values of preindustrial societies began to weaken, he also saw advantages to them. In *Economy and Society,* originally published in 1921, he wrote:

PRIMARY SOURCE

"The decisive reason for the advance of bureaucratic organization has always been its purely technical superiority over any other form of organization. The fully developed bureaucratic mechanism compares with other organizations exactly as does the machine with the nonmechanical modes of production."

—Max Weber, quoted in *Essays in Sociology,* 1948

Earlier kinds of organizations, where the decision makers were chosen on the basis of family or wealth, were just not capable of dealing with an industrial economy. A fast-moving industrial economy required steadiness, precision, continuity, speed, efficiency, and minimum cost—advantages bureaucracy could offer. **Rationalization**—a mind-set that emphasizes knowledge, reason, and planning over tradition and superstition—was on the rise in industrialized areas.

rationalization a mind-set that emphasizes knowledge, reason, and planning

How Bureaucracies Protect People
People often complain about the rules, procedures, and impersonal treatment that characterize a bureaucracy. Bureaucracies are actually designed to protect individuals, however. Without them, decision making could be arbitrary and

CARTOON >

BUREAUCRATIC RULES
Many people think of bureaucracy as something designed to make everyone's life more difficult.

▶ **CRITICAL THINKING**

1. **Applying** What is the effect of bureaucratic rules in the cartoon?
2. **Assessing** What benefit, if any, does the bureaucrat bring?

A Global Perspective

HUMAN DEVELOPMENT

Each year, the United Nations ranks the countries of the world in terms of their human development. The Human Development Index (HDI) is based on the life expectancy, educational attainment, and adjusted real income of a country's population. This map shows how the world's countries ranked on the HDI in 2011.

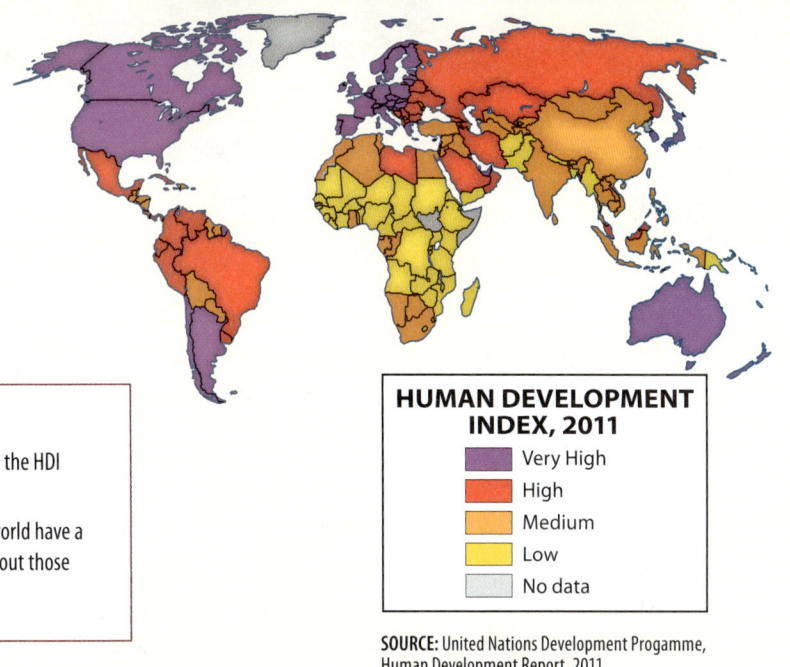

HUMAN DEVELOPMENT INDEX, 2011
- Very High
- High
- Medium
- Low
- No data

SOURCE: United Nations Development Progamme, Human Development Report, 2011.

Geography Connection

1. **Places and Regions** In what regions of the world is the HDI mostly medium to low?
2. **The World in Spatial Terms** What regions of the world have a very high HDI? What generalizations can you make about those regions?

---

without logic. For example, it might sound appealing to abolish final exams, but then grading would not be objective. A teacher might give higher grades to males or another favored group. This is not to say that favoritism never occurs in bureaucracies. But the presence of rules promises at least a measure of equal treatment.

✓ **READING PROGRESS CHECK**

Making Generalizations How did the industrial age promote the development of bureaucracies?

Informal Structures Within Organizations

GUIDING QUESTION Why do informal organizations develop?

Bureaucracies are designed to act as secondary groups but include primary relationships as well. Primary relationships emerge as part of **informal organizations**—groups within a formal organization in which personal relationships are guided by norms, rituals, and sentiments that are not part of the formal organization. Based on common interests and personal relationships, informal groups are usually formed spontaneously.

The existence of informal organizations within bureaucracies was first documented in the mid-1920s when a group of Harvard researchers studied the Hawthorne plant of the Western Electric Company in Chicago. In *Management and the Worker*, their 1939 study of 14 male machine operators in the Bank Wiring Observation Room, F. J. Roethlisberger and William Dickson observed that work activities and job relationships were based on norms and social sanctions of that particular group of male operators. Group norms prohibited "rate busting" (doing too much work), "chiseling" (doing too little work), and "squealing" (telling group secrets to supervisors). Conformity to these norms was maintained through ridicule, sarcasm, criticism, and hostility.

informal organization a group within a formal organization in which personal relationships are guided by norms, rituals, and sentiments that are not part of the formal organization

Informal groups exist to meet needs ignored by the formal organization. Informal groups offer personal affection, support, humor, and protection. The study at the Hawthorne plant demonstrated that informal organizations encourage conformity, but the resulting solidarity protects group members from mistreatment by those outside the group.

☑ **READING PROGRESS CHECK**

Contrasting How do informal organizations differ from formal organizations?

CARTOON

THE IRON LAW OF OLIGARCHY

Sociologist Robert Michels suggests that even in organizations intended to be democratic, power becomes concentrated in the hands of a few.

▶ **CRITICAL THINKING**

1. *Analyzing Visuals* In this cartoon showing combinations of corporations called trusts and U.S. senators, who is the oligarchy? Why do you think so?

2. *Analyzing* Do you think this cartoon applies to the U.S. political system today? Why or why not?

iron law of oligarchy the theory that power increasingly becomes concentrated in the hands of a few members of any organization

Iron Law of Oligarchy

GUIDING QUESTION *What is the iron law of oligarchy?*

Individuals or smaller groups must exercise power for an organization to achieve its goals. Sometimes this power may be grabbed by individuals for their own purposes. This process was formulated and described by German sociologist Robert Michels in his 1911 book, *Political Parties*. It is called the **iron law of oligarchy** and states that power tends to become more and more concentrated in the hands of fewer members of any organization. Michels observed that even in organizations intended to be democratic, a few leaders eventually gain control and other members become virtually powerless. He concluded that this increased concentration of power occurs because those in power want to remain in power.

The government in communist China is a prime example of Michels's principle. Not subject to popular election, China's leaders have been able to consolidate, or strengthen, their power. Each leader has been able to increase his power, to build a loyal staff, control money, offer jobs, and give favors.

According to Michels, three organizational factors encourage oligarchy, or rule by a powerful few. First, organizations need a hierarchy of authority to delegate decision making. Second, the advantages held by those at the top allow them to consolidate their power. They can create a staff loyal to them, control channels of communication, and use organizational resources to increase their power. Third, members of an organization tend to submit or defer to leaders.

☑ **READING PROGRESS CHECK**

Analyzing Do you think the iron law of oligarchy is inevitable? Why or why not?

LESSON 4 REVIEW

Reviewing Vocabulary

1. *Making Connections* How are *power* and *authority* related?

2. *Making Connections* How does *rationalization* promote the formation of *bureaucracies*?

Using Your Notes

3. *Identifying* Use your notes from the graphic organizer to write a few sentences that describe formal organizations and the formation of informal organizations within them.

Answering the Guiding Questions

4. *Making Connections* How are formal organizations and bureaucracies related?

5. *Listing* What are the characteristics of a bureaucracy?

6. *Evaluating* What are the advantages and disadvantages of a bureaucracy?

7. *Analyzing* Why do informal organizations develop?

8. *Defining* What is the iron law of oligarchy?

Writing Activity

9. *Argument* Write a paragraph that describes the strengths of bureaucracies and supports their use today or that describes their weaknesses and argues against their use today.

CHAPTER 6 Assessment

Directions: On a separate sheet of paper, answer the questions below. Make sure you read carefully and answer all parts of the questions.

Lesson Review

Lesson 1

1. **Analyzing** Lesson 1 provides a disaster relief group as an example of a secondary group. Explain the purpose of this example. Analyze why this is a strong example and provide another strong example of the same principle.

2. **Diagramming** Create a diagram to compare and contrast the major characteristics of primary and secondary groups.

Lesson 2

3. **Categorizing** Provide examples of in-groups and out-groups at your school. Explain why each is an in-group or an out-group.

4. **Making Connections** What is a social network? Explain whether there are students in your sociology class you would consider part of your social network. Are some of these students part of your family, work, or social groups? Explain.

Lesson 3

5. **Explaining** What is cooperation? Must a crisis arise in order for cooperation to occur? Explain.

6. **Interpreting Significance** Why is it essential to defeat the opponent in a conflict?

Lesson 4

7. **Identifying Central Issues** Why were industrialization and urbanization important to the formation of secondary groups in the United States?

8. **Identifying Perspectives** What are advantages and disadvantages of governing through the principle of the iron law of oligarchy? In your response, explain the importance of perspective—the perspective of the governing party and the perspective of those being governed.

DBQ Analyzing Primary Sources

PRIMARY SOURCE

The table below shows the percentage of the population who participate in volunteer activities, according to age and type of activity. Use the table to answer the following questions.

Organization Type	16–24 years	25–34 years	35–44 years	45–54 years	55–64 years	65 and above
Civic & Political	5.5	5.5	5.3	8.1	9.3	8.7
Educational & Youth	32.4	34.1	39.8	26.0	13.2	6.4
Environment & Animal Care	1.5	2.4	1.4	1.5	2.0	1.4
Hospital & Health	8.6	6.4	5.5	6.9	8.9	10.9
Public Safety	1.7	2.2	1.4	1.4	1.5	1.1
Religious	28.5	30.4	30.5	35.3	39.6	45.2
Social Service	13.0	11.1	9.0	12.3	15.0	16.9
Sport/Hobby	3.4	2.8	3.4	4.2	4.3	3.6
Other*	4.9	5.2	3.8	4.2	6.1	5.9

*includes undetermined
Source: *Statistical Abstract of the United States*

9. **Hypothesizing** In this chapter, you read about formal groups. As people join these groups freely, volunteer groups might provide a strong measure of personal identity and cultural trends. Study the statistics in this table. Then write two hypotheses that could be tested by research, including survey research. For example, you might hypothesize that social service volunteering dips when people are in their mid-30s and 40s because people are building careers and rearing children.

Need Extra Help?

If You've Missed Question	1	2	3	4	5	6	7	8	9
Go to page	159	157–159	160–161	161–162	163	164	170–172	174	170–174

CHAPTER 6 Assessment

Directions: On a separate sheet of paper, answer the questions below. Make sure you read carefully and answer all parts of the questions.

Exploring the Essential Question

10. *Comparing and Contrasting* For this project, recall plots of novels you have read and focus on two novels that provide strong examples of groups functioning as units of society. Write an essay to compare and contrast the ways the groups in each novel function as units of society. Support your analysis with information from the chapter.

Critical Thinking

11. *Drawing Inferences* Imagine you are a high school principal who is writing an evaluation of the school year. In your evaluation, include explanations of the following at your school: primary and secondary groups, in-groups and out-groups, social networks, types of social interaction, and bureaucracy.

21st Century Skills

CREATING AND USING GRAPHS, CHARTS, DIAGRAMS AND TABLES

12. *Creating Graphs and Charts* Consider the information you have learned about primary and secondary groups, reference groups, social networks, and types of social interaction. Then design a chart, diagram, or other visual that explains how these are related.

College and Career Readiness Skills

13. *Synthesizing* As the dean of a college campus, write a memo to professors at the beginning of a school year. Provide a list of suggestions professors should share with students in an effort to stop cyberbullying.

Research and Presentation

14. *Gathering Information* This chapter provides information about the characteristics of a bureaucracy, such as promotion based on merit rather than favoritism. In many organizations, it is argued that *merit* has become synonymous with *seniority*, which can result in time served being just as important, if not more important, than the skill and diligence exercised in performing job duties. Your task is to interview six employees of large businesses. Develop questions to determine the role these employees believe seniority should play in promotion decisions. Make certain your questions do not convey bias regarding the issue. In addition to the interviews, conduct online research to locate surveys or studies regarding the merit/seniority debate. Use search terms such as *survey, study, promotion, merit,* and *seniority*. Maintain a list to identify each survey and study, including the title of the document, the year completed, and the name of the entity completing the research and analysis.

15. *Comparing and Contrasting* On the computer, create a visual, for example, a chart, graph, or editorial cartoon. In your visual, show the results of your interviews and research. Within your visual, illustrate whether the interviews seem to show that today's employees agree or disagree with the findings of the surveys and studies you have discovered through your research. Present your findings to the class through the visual and a brief summary you have written. In your summary, include the terms *formal organization, bureaucracy, power, authority, merit,* and *seniority*.

Need Extra Help?

If You've Missed Question	10	11	12	13	14	15
Go to page	156–174	156–174	156–167	154	170–174	170–174

Deviance and Social Control

ESSENTIAL QUESTIONS • What is deviance? • Who defines deviance?

networks

There's More Online about deviance and social control.

CHAPTER 7

Technology & Society
High-Tech Crime and Deviance

Lesson 1
Deviance and Social Control

Lesson 2
Functionalism and Deviance

Lesson 3
Symbolic Interactionism and Deviance

Lesson 4
Conflict Theory and Deviance

Lesson 5
Crime and Punishment

Sociology Matters...

What image comes to mind when you hear the word *deviance*—prisoners in striped uniforms and leg irons? Protesters? Terrorists? Our ideas about deviance and its opposite, conformity, are shaped by the time and place in which we live. Sociology offers us various perspectives on deviance and can help us better understand and respond to it.

◄ Societies show how deviant they think various crimes are by the relative punishments they assign them.

Flirt/SuperStock

CHAPTER 7
Technology & Society

High-Tech Crime and Deviance

The expansion of worldwide computer networks has created a whole new environment for would-be criminals and deviant behavior.

Criminals and others who engage in deviant behavior have been quick to adapt the power of computers and computer networks to pursue criminal and deviant activities. For example, computers now serve as the means by which nearly all financial information is stored and moved. It is possible for a criminal to steal vast amounts of money by clicking keys on a keyboard rather than picking safes or breaking into buildings.

With a computer, a person can assume the identity of another person and open credit card accounts. He or she can send e-mails posing as a Nigerian prince seeking to defraud people. E-mail can also provide a criminal with a way into the computers of recipients. Skilled criminals can hack into systems, peek into private records, and then sell the information they find to other criminals or make it public to embarrass or blackmail the victim. Over the Internet, sexual predators can seek out unwary victims on social-networking sites. Dishonest spouses can carry on secret relationships that betray the trust of their families. Not opening and deleting e-mails from persons unknown to the user, installing security software, and activating spam filters are some of the commonly used methods to keep cyber criminals out of personal computers.

In short, the very features that make computers so useful in our lives create opportunities for crime and other deviant behavior. Everyone who uses a computer or smartphone is continuously made aware that there are no guarantees of anonymity or security online. Any information created, stored, or sent can be "hacked"—accessed or stolen. And, of course, those who use high technology improperly should know that authorities are finding new ways of tracing and tracking such crime.

INTERNET CRIME COMPLAINTS DEPARTMENT

Yearly Comparison of Complaints Received

Year	Complaints
2010	303,809
2009	336,655
2008	275,284
2007	206,884
2006	207,492
2005	231,493
2004	207,449
2003	124,515
2002	75,064
2001	50,412
2000	16,838

Source: Internet Crime Complaint Center, 2010 Internet Crime Report, 2011

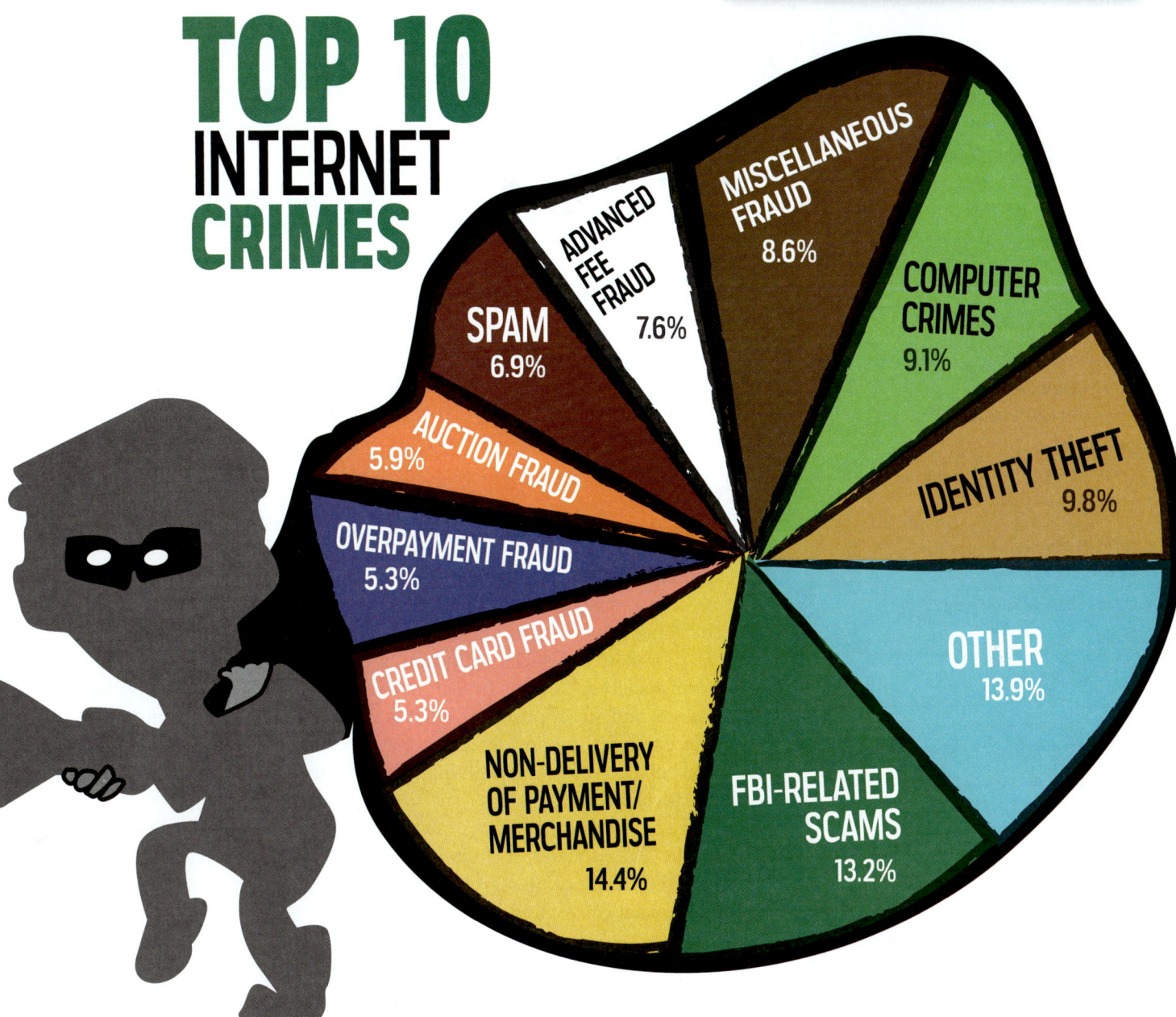

Thinking Like a Sociologist

1 Analyzing
How do you think the apparent anonymity of the Internet affects the behavior of criminals and others seeking to pursue deviant activities online?

2 Making Connections
How do you think the use of the Internet for carrying out crime or other deviant behavior relates to the practice of cyberbullying?

networks

There's More Online!

- ☑ **CARTOON** The Unpopular Shirt
- ☑ **GRAPHIC ORGANIZER** Deviance and Social Control
- ☑ **MAP** Violent Crime
- ☑ **SELF-CHECK QUIZ**

Reading HELPDESK

Academic Vocabulary
- violation
- stability

Content Vocabulary
- deviance
- negative deviance
- positive deviance
- deviant
- social control
- social sanctions

TAKING NOTES:
Integration of Knowledge and Ideas

DESCRIBING As you read about deviance and social control, use a graphic organizer like the one below to record information and ideas.

Deviance	Social Control

LESSON 1
Deviance and Social Control

ESSENTIAL QUESTIONS • What is deviance? • Who defines deviance?

IT MATTERS BECAUSE

If we want to reduce deviance, such as violent crime, we must first understand what deviance means and why it occurs. We must also understand current methods of controlling deviance to evaluate their effectiveness.

The Nature of Deviance

GUIDING QUESTION *What do sociologists mean by* deviance?

The term **deviance** refers to behavior that departs from societal or group norms. It can range from criminal behavior, such as theft and murder, to antisocial behavior, such as cheating and lying. Because deviance is subjective, or a matter of social definition, it can vary from group to group and from society to society. In fact, our ideas of deviance are relative to time, place, and social position. What is considered deviant in one time and place might be considered normal in another. Furthermore, the harmful behavior of people with high status in society might not be considered deviant in that society.

Thus, deviance is not always easy to identify. In a diverse society like that of the United States, it is often difficult to agree on what is deviant behavior. For instance, in a groundbreaking study, J. L. Simmons polled people on what constitutes deviant behavior:

PRIMARY SOURCE

❝The sheer range of responses predictably included homosexuals, prostitutes, drug addicts, radicals, and criminals. But it also included liars, career women, Democrats, reckless drivers, atheists, Christians, suburbanites, the retired, young folks, card players, bearded men, artists, pacifists, priests, prudes, hippies, straights, girls who wear makeup, the President of the United States, conservatives, integrationists, executives, divorcees, perverts, motorcycle gangs, smart-alec students, know-it-all professors, modern people, and Americans.❞

—J. L. Simmons, *Deviants*, 1969

To this list, researcher Leslie Lampert would add obese people. For a week, she wore a "fat suit," adding 150 pounds to her normal body weight, to experience firsthand what it feels like to be an overweight woman in American society. She concluded that American "society not only hates fat people, it feels entitled to participate in a prejudice that at many levels parallels racism and religious bigotry."

Deviance may be either *negative* or *positive*. **Negative deviance** involves behavior that fails to meet accepted norms. People expressing negative deviance either reject the norms, misinterpret the norms, or are unaware of the norms. This is the kind of behavior popularly associated with the idea of deviance. There is, however, another type of deviance. **Positive deviance** involves over-conformity to norms, which leads to imbalance and extremes of perfectionism. Positive deviants idealize group norms. In its own way, positive deviance can be as disruptive and hard to manage as negative deviance. Think about the norms related to personal appearance in American society. The mass media are constantly telling young women that they can never be too thin. Negative deviants will miss the mark on the obese side. Positive deviants may push themselves to the point of anorexia. Most young people's behavior will fall somewhere between these two extremes.

deviance behavior that departs from societal or group norms

negative deviance behavior that underconforms to accepted norms

positive deviance behavior that overconforms to social expectations

Connecting Sociology to Anthropology

MURDER IN CHEYENNE SOCIETY

Historically, the Cheyenne believed that when a member of the group committed murder, everyone in the group suffered the consequences. The punishment for this terrible crime was banishment. The ways in which the Cheyenne dealt with murder illustrate both deviance and social control.

PRIMARY SOURCE

"[The Cheyenne have] specific concepts related to the killing of a fellow tribesman and specific mechanisms for dealing with homicide when it does occur.

The first of these is purely mystical and relates to the major tribal fetish, the Four Sacred Arrows. A murderer becomes personally polluted, and specks of blood contaminate the features of the Arrows....

On the legal level, the ostracism takes the form of immediate exile imposed by the Tribal Council sitting as a judicial body. The sentence of exile is enforced, if need be, by the military societies. The rationalization of the banishment is that the murderer's stink is noisome to the buffalo. As long as an unatoned murderer is with the tribe, 'game shuns the territory; it makes the tribe lonesome.' Therefore, the murderer must leave.

Banishment is not itself enough, however. His act has disrupted the fabric of tribal life. Symbolically, this is expressed in the soiling of the Arrows, the allegorical identity of the tribe itself. As long as the Arrows remain polluted, bad luck is believed to dog the tribe. Not only does the spectre of starvation threaten, but there can be no success in war or any other enterprise. The earth is disjointed and the tribe out of harmony with it. The Arrow Renewal is the means of righting the situation. The oneness of the tribe is reasserted in the required presence at the ceremony of every family—save those of murderers."

—from E. Adamson Hoebel, *The Cheyennes: Indians of the Great Plains*, 1960

Group of three Cheyenne warriors on horseback

DBQ ▶ CRITICAL THINKING

1. **Summarizing** What are the two components of the Cheyenne response to a murder described in this excerpt?
2. **Constructing Arguments** Why do you think the Cheyenne would regard all members as somehow guilty and in need of atonement following a murder?

A Diverse America

VIOLENT CRIME
Although it has experienced a sharp and steady decline in recent years, the United States is still a leader among the major industrialized countries in rates of crimes such as murder. Crime rates in the United States differ greatly from state to state. This map indicates the number of violent crimes by state per 100,000 residents.

Geography Connection

1. **Places and Regions** Which states had the highest crime rates in 2010? Which states had the lowest rates?
2. **Places and Regions** What was the rate of violent crime in your state in 2010?
3. **Human Systems** What factors do you think play a role in producing higher or lower rates of violent crime in different states?

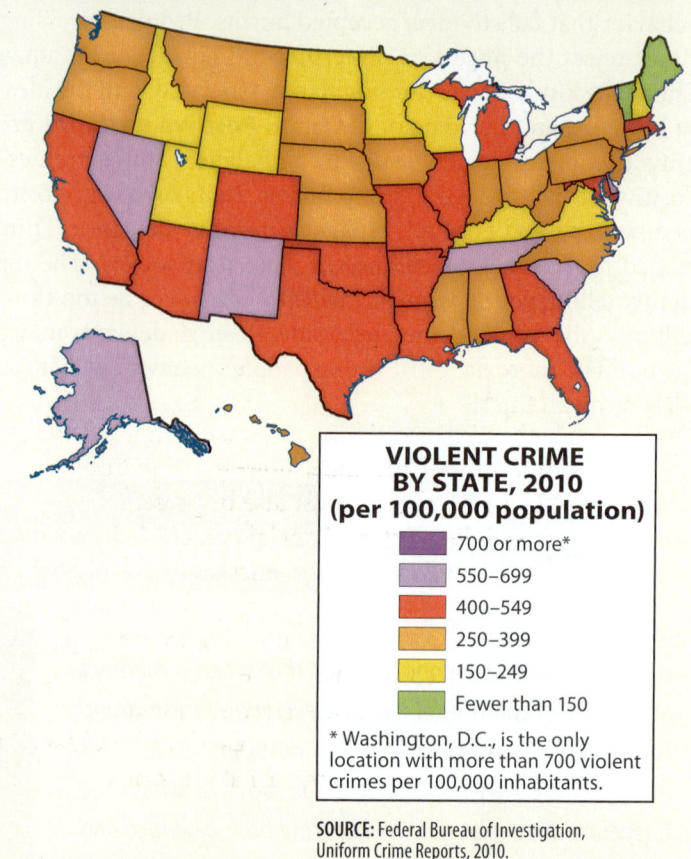

VIOLENT CRIME BY STATE, 2010 (per 100,000 population)
- 700 or more*
- 550–699
- 400–549
- 250–399
- 150–249
- Fewer than 150

* Washington, D.C., is the only location with more than 700 violent crimes per 100,000 inhabitants.

SOURCE: Federal Bureau of Investigation, Uniform Crime Reports, 2010.

---

violation the act of breaking or discarding

deviant a person who breaks significant societal or group norms

Minor instances of behavior that some might consider deviant occur frequently in modern societies. For that reason, sociologists generally reserve the term *deviance* for **violations** of significant social norms. Significant norms are those that are highly important either to most members of a society or to the members with the most power. For a sociologist, a **deviant** is a person who has acted in violation of one or more of society's most highly valued norms. Reactions to deviants are usually negative and usually involve attempts to change or control the deviant behavior.

✓ **READING PROGRESS CHECK**

Analyzing Why are ideas about what constitutes deviant behavior not the same everywhere and at all times?

Social Control

GUIDING QUESTION How do internal social control and external social control differ?

stability reliability; resistance to sudden change

social control ways to encourage conformity to society's norms

All societies have ways to promote order, **stability**, and predictability in social life. We feel confident that drivers will stop for red lights, waiters will not pour soup in our laps, and store clerks will give us the correct change. Without **social control**—ways to promote conformity to norms—social life would be unpredictable, even chaotic. Through social control, life has stability, which makes us more comfortable. There are two broad types of social control: *internal* and *external*.

Internal Social Control

Internal social control lies within the individual. It is developed during the socialization process. You are practicing internal social control when you do something because you know it is the right thing to do or when you don't do something because you know it would be wrong.

For example, most people most of the time do not steal. They act this way not just because they fear arrest or lack the opportunity to steal but because they consider theft to be wrong. The norm against stealing has become a part of them. This is known as the *internalization* of social norms.

External Social Control

The process of socialization does not ensure that all people will conform all the time, however. For this reason, external social control must also be present. It helps produce stability. External social control is based on **social sanctions**—rewards or punishments designed to encourage desired behavior.

Positive sanctions, such as awards, increases in allowances, promotions, and smiles of approval, are used to encourage conformity. Negative sanctions, such as criticism, fines, and imprisonment, are intended to stop socially unacceptable behavior by punishing violations of norms. Sanctions may be formal or informal. Ridicule, gossip, and smiles are examples of informal sanctions. Imprisonment, low grades, and official awards are formal sanctions.

Social Control and Power

Both internal and external social control, of course, are shaped heavily by those in power in a society. For instance, in a high school, administrators, who generally have more power than other individuals in the school, develop the rules, which are imposed through the use of formal sanctions. Similarly, the students who are seen as "popular," or having more power, often disproportionately influence the norms for social interaction, which are maintained through the use of informal sanctions.

✓ **READING PROGRESS CHECK**

Assessing When, in relation to internal social control, does external social control come into play?

"Did you hear? *Everybody's* talking about how you might actually wear that horrible mistake of a shirt today!"

∧ CARTOON
THE UNPOPULAR SHIRT
Conformity is encouraged through social sanctions such as ridicule, criticism, encouraging smiles, and positive rewards.

▶ **CRITICAL THINKING**
1. **Assessing** What type of social control is being exerted in the cartoon?
2. **Drawing Conclusions** Why are sanctions used as part of societal behavior?

social sanctions rewards or punishments that encourage conformity to social norms

---

LESSON 1 REVIEW

Reviewing Vocabulary
1. *Specifying* What is the term sociologists use for behavior that violates societal or group norms?
2. *Identifying* What is the purpose of a *social sanction*?

Using Your Notes
3. *Summarizing* Use your notes from your graphic organizer to write a statement summarizing why it may sometimes be difficult to identify deviance.

Answering the Guiding Questions
4. *Identifying* What do sociologists mean by *deviance*?

5. *Differentiating* How do internal social control and external social control differ?

Writing Activity
6. *Informative/Explanatory* At some point in growing up, nearly everyone engages in some minor deviant behaviors, such as cutting class or telling a lie. Getting caught in such behaviors often results in attempts at social control. Recall such an instance from your own life. How successful were the social controls at changing your behavior? Be specific about the type of social control used and its effect on you.

Deviance and Social Control 183

networks

There's More Online!

- ☑ **CHART** Two Types of Youth Deviance
- ☑ **GRAPHIC ORGANIZER** Functionalism and Deviance
- ☑ **IMAGE** Cashier in Grocery Store
- ☑ **SELF-CHECK QUIZ**

Reading HELPDESK

Academic Vocabulary
- concept
- appropriateness

Content Vocabulary
- anomie
- strain theory
- control theory

TAKING NOTES:
Key Ideas and Details

ANALYZING As you read about functionalism and deviance, use a graphic organizer like the one below to record information about the negative and positive effects of deviance.

Negatives	Positives

	2003	2005	2007
	17.1	18.5	18.0
	33.0	35.9	35.5

LESSON 2
Functionalism and Deviance

ESSENTIAL QUESTIONS • What is deviance? • Who defines deviance?

IT MATTERS BECAUSE
Understanding both the positive and negative effects of deviance can help us make better choices about how to respond to deviance.

Costs and Benefits of Deviance

GUIDING QUESTION What are the negative and beneficial effects of deviance?

As you probably remember from earlier chapters, the functionalist perspective emphasizes social stability and the way the different parts of society contribute to the whole. It may surprise you to know that functionalists believe that some deviance may benefit society. Deviance, therefore, has both positive and negative consequences.

Negative Effects of Deviance
Deviance erodes trust. If bus drivers do not follow planned routes or if parents are not consistent in their discipline, trust is undermined. A society with widespread distrust cannot function smoothly. If not punished or corrected, deviance can cause nonconforming behavior in others. If bus drivers regularly pass by students waiting for the bus, the students may begin to heave rocks at the bus. If parents neglect their children, more teenagers may turn to delinquency. Finally, deviant behavior is costly. It diverts human and monetary resources. Police may have to spend their time dealing with wayward bus drivers and angry students rather than performing more serious duties.

Beneficial Effects of Deviance
Society can sometimes benefit from deviance in spite of its negative effects. Émile Durkheim observed that deviance clarifies norms by causing society to exercise social control to defend its values; society defines, adjusts, and reaffirms norms. When parents are taken to court or lose their children because of neglect, for example, society shows other parents and children how it expects parents to act. Deviance can also be a temporary safety valve. Teens listen to music and wear clothes that adults may view as deviant. This relatively minor deviance may relieve some of the pressure teens feel from the many authority figures in their lives.

Deviance increases unity within a society or group. When deviance reminds people of something they value, it strengthens their commitment to that value. Consider spies who sell government secrets to an enemy. When they are caught, citizens who read about them experience stronger feelings of patriotism. Finally, deviance often promotes needed social change. Suffragists who took to the streets in the early 1900s scandalized the nation but helped gain women the right to vote.

✓ READING PROGRESS CHECK

Predicting What would society be like without deviance?

Strain Theory

GUIDING QUESTION *How do people respond to strain?*

According to Durkheim, **anomie** (A·nuh·mee) is a social condition in which norms are weak, conflicting, or absent. Without shared norms, individuals are uncertain about how they should think and act. Societies become disorganized. In 1968, sociologist Robert Merton adapted Durkheim's **concept** of anomie to deviant behavior and called his hypothesis the **strain theory**.

Strain and Deviance

Deviance, said Merton, is most likely to occur when there is a gap between culturally desirable goals, such as money and prestige, and a legitimate way of obtaining them. Every society establishes some goals and socially approved ways of reaching them. In the United States, an important goal is success and the material possessions that go with it. Education and hard work are two of the approved means for becoming successful. When people accept the goal and the means to achieve it, Merton calls this *conformity*.

Deviant Responses to Strain

By definition, conformity is not deviant behavior. Each of the remaining four responses to strain are considered deviant, however.

- In *innovation*, the individual accepts the goal (in this case, success) but uses illegal means to achieve it (for example, robbery or drug dealing). Innovation is the most widespread and obvious type of deviant response to strain.
- In *ritualism*, the individual rejects the goal (success) but continues to use the legitimate means. Here people go through the motions without believing in the process. An example is the teacher who works every day without any concern for students or the quality of his or her teaching.
- In *retreatism,* both the legitimate means and the approved goals are rejected. Skid-row alcoholics, drug addicts, and the homeless are retreatists; they have dropped out. They are not successful by either legitimate or illegitimate means, and they do not seek success. Of course, all addicts are not retreatists. The addict who participates actively in society and one who successfully attains goals such as money and prestige may not be considered deviant.

anomie a social condition in which norms are weak, conflicting, or absent

concept an idea

strain theory the theory that deviance is more likely to occur when a gap exists between cultural goals and the ability to achieve them

TWO TYPES OF YOUTH DEVIANCE	1995	1997	1999	2001	2003	2005	2007	2009	2011
Carried a weapon	20.0	18.3	17.3	17.4	17.1	18.5	18.0	17.5	16.6
Was in a physical fight	38.7	36.6	35.7	33.2	33.0	35.9	35.5	31.5	32.8

Source: "Trends in the Prevalence of Behaviors that Contribute to Violence," Centers for Disease Control and Prevention, 2012.

◂ CHART

YOUTH DEVIANCE
The government keeps statistics on many different kinds of criminal behaviors by youths and by adults.

▶ **CRITICAL THINKING**

1. **Analyzing Visuals** What trend can you see in both sets of data?
2. **Hypothesizing** Why do you think that more youths have engaged in fights than carry weapons?

- In *rebellion*, people also reject both the goal and the approved means for achieving it, but they substitute a new set of goals and means. Some militia group members in the United States illustrate this response. They may live in near isolation as they pursue the goal of changing society through deviant means: creating their own currency, deliberately violating gun laws, and acting violently.

☑ **READING PROGRESS CHECK**

Making Connections Describe a situation in which someone rebels in a positive way.

People engage in many social interactions every day that present them opportunities to conform or to show behavior that is deviant.

▶ **CRITICAL THINKING**

1. ***Analyzing*** Would Robert Merton say this shopper and cashier are conforming or not? Why?
2. ***Applying*** How does this situation show the presence of social trust?

control theory the theory that compliance with social norms requires strong bonds between individuals and society

appropriateness suitability; correctness

Control Theory

GUIDING QUESTION *What are the basic elements of social bonds?*

Sociologist Travis Hirschi's control theory is also based on Durkheim's views. According to **control theory**, conformity to social norms depends on the presence of strong bonds between individuals and society. Social bonds *control* behavior. If those bonds are weak—if anomie is present—deviance occurs. If they are strong, people conform because they do not want to lose face with others. According to Hirschi, social bonds have four basic components:

1. *Attachment*. The stronger your attachment to groups or individuals, the more likely you are to conform. In other words, the likelihood of conformity varies with the strength of ties with parents, friends, and institutions.
2. *Commitment*. The greater your commitment to social goals, the more likely you are to conform. People who strongly accept the American goal of success are more likely to conform to the social norms for achieving that success.
3. *Involvement*. Participation in approved social activities increases the probability of conformity. Besides positively focusing your time and energy, participation puts you in contact with people whose opinions you value.
4. *Belief*. Belief in society's norms and values promotes conformity. A belief in the **appropriateness** of social rules strengthens people's resolve not to deviate.

In short, when social bonds are weak, the chances for deviance increase. Individuals who lack attachment, commitment, involvement, and belief have little incentive to follow the rules of society.

☑ **READING PROGRESS CHECK**

Making Connections Which social bonds have a strong influence on you?

LESSON 2 REVIEW

Reviewing Vocabulary
1. ***Defining*** What did Durkheim mean by *anomie*?
2. ***Understanding Cause and Effect*** According to control theory, on what does conformity depend?

Using Your Notes
3. ***Identifying*** Use your notes to identify two positive and two negative effects of deviance.

Answering the Guiding Questions
4. ***Summarizing*** What are the negative and beneficial effects of deviance?

5. ***Analyzing*** How do people respond to strain?
6. ***Identifying*** What are the basic elements of social bonds?

Writing Activity
7. ***Argument*** According to strain theory, deviance occurs when there is a gap between culturally desirable goals and the ability to attain them. Do you agree with this theory? Why or why not? Make an argument either for or against the validity of strain theory. Support your argument with evidence from this textbook and from your own experience.

186

networks

There's More Online!

✓ **CARTOON** Labeling Theory
✓ **GRAPHIC ORGANIZER** Differential Association Theory and Labeling Theory
✓ **SELF-CHECK QUIZ**

LESSON 3
Symbolic Interactionism and Deviance

Reading HELPDESK

Academic Vocabulary
- label
- commit

Content Vocabulary
- differential association theory
- labeling theory
- primary deviance
- secondary deviance
- stigma

TAKING NOTES:
Integration of Knowledge and Ideas

DESCRIBING As you read about differential association theory and labeling theory, use a graphic organizer like the one below to record information and ideas.

Differential Association Theory	Labeling Theory

ESSENTIAL QUESTIONS • What is deviance? • Who defines deviance?

IT MATTERS BECAUSE
Just as culture is learned, sociologists think that deviance is learned and culturally transmitted. Understanding how and why this happens can help us deal with deviance more compassionately and effectively.

Differential Association Theory

GUIDING QUESTIONS *How is deviance learned?*

According to symbolic interactionism, deviance is transmitted through socialization in the same way that conformity is learned. *Differential association* and *labeling theory* both are based on symbolic interactionism. **Differential association theory** emphasizes the role of primary groups in transmitting deviance. Edwin Sutherland proposed this theory, in his 1939 book *Principles of Criminology*, which is an important proposition that human behavior was more affected by social and physical environments rather than genetic factors. Sutherland's emphasis on social context and environment led to an understanding of various types of delinquencies as related to factors such as income, family stability, and rental values of houses.

Just as people learn preferences in religion and politics from those they associate with closely, they can learn deviance by association. Three characteristics affect differential association:

- *The ratio of deviant to nondeviant individuals.* A person who knows mostly deviants is more likely to learn deviant behavior.
- *The significance of the person acting deviantly.* A person is more likely to copy deviant behavior from someone significant to him or her.
- *The age of exposure.* Younger children learn deviant behavior more quickly than older children.

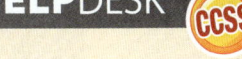 **READING PROGRESS CHECK**

Making Connections Have you ever made a decision not to spend time with someone due to his or her deviant behavior? Explain.

Deviance and Social Control **187**

Connecting Sociology to History

CRIME AND PUNISHMENT

For much of history, humans had a primitive understanding of themselves and their world. Primitive humans typically ascribed criminal behavior to supernatural forces. Someone who committed a crime might be deemed possessed by an evil spirit. This belief dictated harsh responses to crime. Often, it was considered necessary to kill the criminal or banish him or her to protect others from powerful supernatural forces.

As humans moved from superstition to reason, understanding of crime changed. Around 1700, European thinkers began to view deviant behavior as a rational choice based on a calculation of risks and benefits. In short, a person might conclude that crime does pay and so choose to do it. With this idea came a belief that punishment had to make the potential cost of crime exceed the benefit.

In time, this view gave way to an understanding that certain factors, such as a person's health or mental status, might affect judgment. In extreme cases, such factors might absolve a person of responsibility for behavior. Some thinkers even went so far as to theorize that criminal or deviant behavior was dictated by one's biology, subconscious thoughts, or environment. For others, the economic theories of Karl Marx, which explored the causes and effects of economic inequality, became an explanation for crime.

Understanding of the causes of deviance has changed through history.

▶ **CRITICAL THINKING**

1. **Making Connections** How does an understanding of the causes of criminal behavior affect decisions about punishing criminal behavior?
2. **Differentiating** How does a supernatural explanation for criminal and deviant behavior differ from a sociological explanation?

---

differential association theory the theory that individuals learn deviance in proportion to the number of deviant acts and norms to which they are exposed

labeling theory the theory that society creates deviance by identifying particular members as deviant

label to identify

Labeling Theory

GUIDING QUESTION *According to labeling theory, why is deviance relative?*

Strain theory, control theory, and differential association theory help us understand why deviance occurs. **Labeling theory** explains why deviance is *relative*, not only to the society or social group but also to the individual. In other words, it explains why we might **label,** or identify, one person engaging in a certain behavior as deviant but not so label another person engaging in exactly the same behavior.

According to labeling theory, deviant behaviors are always a matter of social definition. In this view, deviance exists when some members of a group or society label others as deviants. Howard Becker, a pioneer of labeling theory, explains:

> **PRIMARY SOURCE**
>
> "Social groups create deviance by making the rules whose infraction constitutes deviance, and by applying these rules to particular people and labeling them as outsiders. From this point of view, deviance is not a quality of the act the person commits, but rather a consequence of the application by others of rules and sanctions to an 'offender.' The deviant is one to whom that label has successfully been applied; deviant behavior is behavior that people so label."
>
> —*Outsiders: Studies in the Sociology of Deviance,* 1963, reprint 1991

Labeling theory allows us to understand the relativity of deviance. It explains, for example, why unmarried pregnant teenage girls are more negatively sanctioned than the teenage biological fathers. Pregnancy outside marriage requires two people, but usually only one is sanctioned. Traditionally, society expects females to set the boundaries—to be the ones to say no. When females become pregnant outside marriage, they have violated this norm and are labeled as deviant. On the other hand, males who father children outside marriage are not considered deviant because society's ideas about sexual responsibility are still different for males than for females. And, of course, it is easier to label women because advanced pregnancy is visible.

Edwin Lemert's distinction between primary and secondary deviance helps clarify the labeling process. In cases of **primary deviance**, a person engages only in isolated acts of deviance. For example, when college students are asked to respond to a checklist of unlawful activities, most admit to having violated one or more norms. Yet the vast majority of college students have never been arrested, convicted, or labeled as criminals. Certainly, those who break the law for the first time do not consider themselves criminals. If their deviance stops at this point, they have engaged in primary deviance; deviance is not a part of their lifestyles or self-concepts. Teens, likewise, may **commit** a few delinquent acts without necessarily embarking on a career of delinquency and without seeing themselves as delinquents.

Secondary deviance, in contrast, means deviance as a lifestyle and as part of one's personal identity. Individuals identify themselves as deviants and organize their behavior largely in terms of deviant roles. Other people also label them as deviant and respond to them accordingly. When this occurs, these individuals usually begin to spend most of their time committing acts of deviance. Deviance becomes a way of life, a career.

Labeling people as deviants can cause them pain and suffering, and it can determine the direction of their lives. Erving Goffman examined some of the negative effects of labeling when he wrote about **stigma**—an undesirable label used by others to deny the deviant full social acceptance. For example, an ex-convict is not accepted by many members of society. Why? Because a stigmatic label—*jailbird*—spoils the individual's entire social identity. One stigma, a prison record, is used to discredit the individual's entire worth.

✓ **READING PROGRESS CHECK**

Predicting What role might stigma play in turning a primary deviant into a secondary deviant?

"Yes, my client crashed his car through a house, burned down a restaurant, and shaved the mayor's cat. But what the prosecution failed to remind you is that he did all of this while being *famous*."

▲ **CARTOON**
LABELING THEORY
Labeling theory focuses on how people become branded as deviant.

▶ **CRITICAL THINKING**
1. ***Observing*** What is the defense lawyer saying is the cause of the deviant behavior in the cartoon?
2. ***Interpreting*** Why do you suppose the cartoonist depicted the celebrity smiling?

primary deviance only occasional breaking of norms

secondary deviance deviance that becomes a lifestyle and part of an individual's identity

commit to do or perform

stigma an undesirable label used to deny a deviant acceptance

---

LESSON 3 REVIEW

Reviewing Vocabulary
1. ***Specifying*** Which theory postulates that deviance is learned?
2. ***Identifying*** What is a *stigma*?

Using Your Notes
3. ***Summarizing*** Use your notes from the graphic organizer to summarize differential association theory and labeling theory.

Answering the Guiding Questions
4. ***Explaining*** How is deviance learned?
5. ***Explaining*** According to labeling theory, why is deviance relative?

Writing Activity
6. ***Narrative*** Think of someone you know or know of who has been labeled as deviant. Explain how this has affected the person labeled as deviant.

FOCUS on research

Case Study

CCSS

Saints and Roughnecks

In this classic study, William Chambliss observed the behavior of two white teenage gangs at "Hanibal High School" over a two-year period. In addition to gang activity, Chambliss documented the responses of parents, teachers, and police to the delinquent behavior he observed.

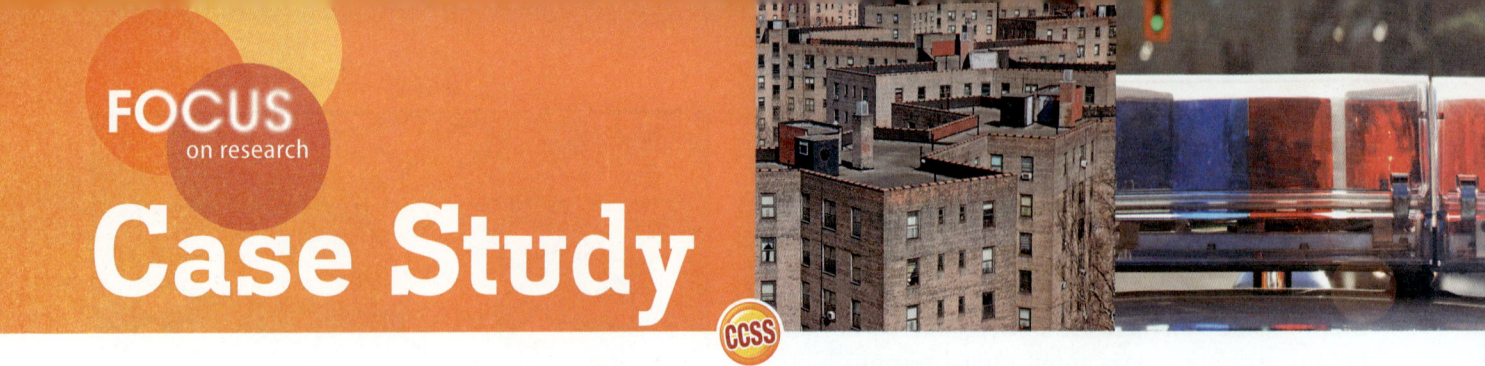

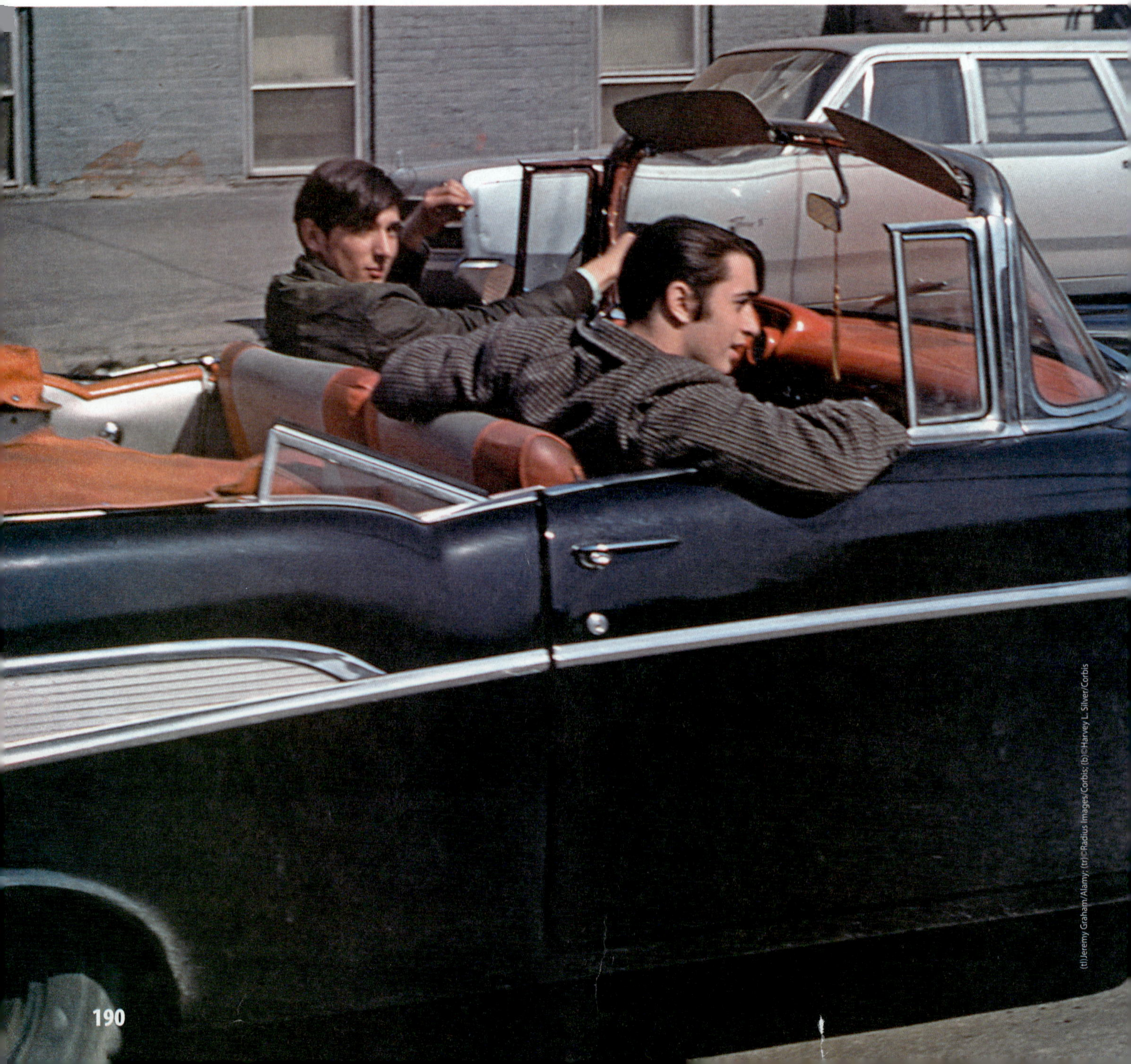

(tl)Jeremy Graham/Alamy; (tr)©Radius Images/Corbis; (b)©Harvey L. Silver/Corbis

PRIMARY SOURCE

The Saints Every Friday and Saturday night most of the Saints [a high school gang] would meet between 8:00 and 8:30 and would go into Big Town. Big Town activities included drinking heavily in taverns or nightclubs, driving drunkenly through the streets, and committing acts of vandalism and playing pranks....

Searching for 'fair game' for a prank was the boys' principal activity after they left the tavern. The boys would drive alongside a foot patrolman and ask directions to some street. If the policeman leaned on the car in the course of answering the question, the driver would speed away, causing him to lose his balance. The Saints were careful to play this prank only in an area where they were not going to spend much time and where they could quickly disappear around a corner to avoid having their license plate number taken.

Construction sites and road repair areas were the special province of the Saints' mischief. A soon-to-be-repaired hole in the road inevitably invited the Saints to remove lanterns and wooden barricades and put them in the car, leaving the hole unprotected. The boys would find a safe vantage point and wait for an unsuspecting motorist to drive into the hole. Often, though not always, the boys would go up to the motorist and commiserate [sympathize] with him about the dreadful way the city protected its citizenry.

Leaving the scene of the open hole and the motorist, the boys would then go searching for an appropriate place to erect the stolen barricade. An 'appropriate place' was often a spot on a highway near a curve in the road where the barricade would not be seen by an oncoming motorist. The boys would wait to watch an unsuspecting motorist attempt to stop and (usually) crash into the wooden barricade. With saintly bearing the boys might offer help and understanding....

The Roughnecks Townspeople never perceived the Saints' high level of delinquency. The Saints were good boys who just went in for an occasional prank. After all, they were well dressed, well mannered and had nice cars. The Roughnecks [another gang at the same high school] were a different story. Although the two gangs of boys were the same age, and both groups engaged in an equal amount of wild-oat sowing, everyone agreed that the not-so-well-dressed, not-so-well-mannered, not-so-rich boys were heading for trouble....

From the community's viewpoint, the real indication that these kids were in for trouble was that they were constantly involved with the police. Some of them had been picked up for stealing, mostly small stuff, of course, 'but still it's stealing small stuff that leads to big time crimes.' 'Too bad,' people said. 'Too bad that these boys couldn't behave like the other kids in town; stay out of trouble, be polite to adults, and look to their future.'...

The fighting activities of the group were fairly readily and accurately perceived by almost everyone. At least once a month, the boys would get into some sort of fight, although most fights were scraps between members of the group or involved only one member of the group and some peripheral hanger-on....

More serious than fighting, had the community been aware of it, was theft. Although almost everyone was aware that the boys occasionally stole things, they did not realize the extent of the activity. Petty stealing was a frequent event for the Roughnecks. Sometimes they stole as a group and coordinated their efforts; other times they stole in pairs. Rarely did they steal alone....

Roughnecks siphoned gasoline from cars as often as they had access to an automobile, which was not very often. Unlike the Saints, who owned their own cars, the Roughnecks would have to borrow their parents' cars, an event which occurred only eight or nine times a year. The boys claimed to have stolen cars for joy rides from time to time."

— William J. Chambliss, "The Saints and the Roughnecks," *Society* 11, November/December 1973

> "Townspeople never perceived the Saints' high level of delinquency. The Saints were good boys who just went in for an occasional prank. After all, they were well dressed, well mannered and had nice cars. The Roughnecks [a delinquent gang at the same high school] were a different story."

Working With the Research

1. **Explaining** From your understanding of Chambliss's study, is deviance socially created? Explain.
2. **Categorizing** Which one of the three major theoretical perspectives best explains Chambliss's findings? Explain.
3. **Making Connections** Do you think Chambliss's observations might help explain how rates of crime vary significantly from state to state and within states? Explain.

networks

There's More Online!

- ☑ **CHART** Theoretical Perspectives: Illustrating Sociological Concepts
- ☑ **GRAPHIC ORGANIZER** Conflict Theory
- ☑ **IMAGE** Bernie Madoff
- ☑ **SELF-CHECK QUIZ**

Reading HELPDESK

Academic Vocabulary
- cite
- minority

Content Vocabulary
- victim discounting
- white-collar crime

TAKING NOTES:
Key Ideas and Details

SUMMARIZING As you read about conflict theory, use a graphic organizer like the one below to record details.

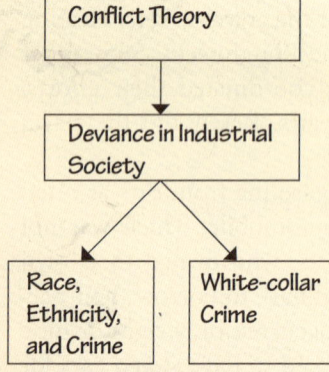

LESSON 4
Conflict Theory and Deviance

ESSENTIAL QUESTIONS • *What is deviance?* • *Who defines deviance?*

IT MATTERS BECAUSE
According to conflict theory, in an industrial society those in power define and punish deviance to maintain the status quo. This can create imbalances in the ways in which society deals with deviance.

Deviance in Industrial Society

GUIDING QUESTION *How does an industrial society defend itself against deviants?*

From the perspective of conflict theory, deviance in an industrial society is behavior that those in control of that society see as threatening to their interests. In this theoretical view, then, the rich and powerful use their positions to determine which acts are deviant and how deviants should be punished. In the process, they help protect their positions of power and their control of industrial society.

Sociologist Steven Spitzer has proposed some basic ways in which the culture of an industrial society defends itself against deviants.

1. Critics of industrial society are considered deviants because their beliefs challenge its economic, political, and social basis.
2. Because industrial society requires a willing workforce, those who will not work are considered deviants.
3. Those who threaten private property, especially that belonging to the rich, are defined as deviant and are prime targets for punishment.
4. Because of society's need for respect for authority, people who show a lack of respect for authority—for example, agitators on the job or people who stage nonviolent demonstrations against established practices—are treated as deviants.
5. Certain activities that might be considered deviant are nevertheless encouraged if they fit well within industrial society. For example, violent behavior in sports is accepted because it fosters competition, achievement, teamwork, and winning.

☑ **READING PROGRESS CHECK**

Making Connections According to the conflict perspective, industrial society defends itself by labeling people who criticize it as deviant. Can you think of any examples of this—either from your own experience or from the news?

Race, Ethnicity, and Crime

GUIDING QUESTION *How do race and ethnicity influence punishment for crime?*

There are other ways to apply conflict theory to the study of deviance in industrial society. The relationship between minorities and the judicial system is one.

Proponents of the conflict perspective argue that minorities receive unequal treatment in the American criminal justice system. They **cite** statistics showing that African Americans and Latinos are dealt with more harshly than whites throughout the criminal justice process—from arrest through indictment, conviction, sentencing, and parole. Even when the criminal offense is the same, African Americans and Latinos are more likely than whites to be convicted, and they serve more time in prison than whites.

Conflict theorists suggest several reasons for these differences. For one thing, minorities generally do not have the economic resources to buy good legal services. Thus, the outcomes of their trials are not likely to be as favorable to them. Another source of difference is that crimes against whites tend to be punished more severely than crimes against minorities. Conflict theorists believe this happens because society sees **minority** interests as less important than those of whites. **Victim discounting** reduces the seriousness of crimes directed at members of lower social classes. According to the logic behind victim discounting, if the victim is less valuable, the crime is less serious, and the penalty is less severe. Victim discounting seems to be exemplified by the fact that prosecutors are less likely to seek the death penalty when an African American has been killed, and juries and judges are less likely to impose the death penalty in cases involving African American victims.

cite to quote as an authoritative source

minority pertaining to a racial, religious, national, or other group regarded as different from the larger group of which it is a part

victim discounting the process of reducing the seriousness of the crimes that injure people of lower status

✓ **READING PROGRESS CHECK**

Making Inferences According to conflict theory, who is favored by our criminal justice system? Why do you think that is?

Theoretical Perspectives

ILLUSTRATING SOCIOLOGICAL CONCEPTS
This table illustrates approaches to understanding deviance using concepts associated with a particular theoretical perspective. Construct some examples of your own.

Theoretical Perspective	Sociological Concept	Example
Functionalism	Anomie	Delinquent gangs sell drugs because they want success without holding conventional jobs.
Conflict Theory	White-Collar Crime	A convicted Wall Street stockbroker (a more powerful member of society) may spend less time in prison than a factory worker (a less powerful member of society) found guilty of a less serious crime.
Symbolic Interactionism	Labeling	Some high-school students reject dating because they have been consistently treated and described as "not cool."

▶ **CRITICAL THINKING**

1. ***Identifying*** Which theoretical perspective would explain a group of lower-class youths being accused of a crime for behavior that higher-status teens have engaged in without punishment?

2. ***Connecting Ideas*** How do you think the conflict theory perspective might regard the concept of labeling? How would the symbolic interactionist perspective address white-collar crime? Provide examples for each of the above.

Deviance and Social Control

In 2009, financier Bernie Madoff pleaded guilty to multiple counts of fraud. He cost investors perhaps as much as $65 billion and was sentenced to 150 years in prison.

▶ **CRITICAL THINKING**

Interpreting Does Madoff's harsh sentence mean that conflict theorists are wrong in seeing bias in the American criminal justice system? Why or why not?

white-collar crime
job-related crimes committed by high-status people

White-Collar Crime

GUIDING QUESTION *What are the costs of white-collar crime?*

According to Edwin Sutherland, **white-collar crime** is any crime committed by respectable and high-status people in the course of their occupations. Officially, the term is used for economic crimes such as price fixing, insider trading, fraud, embezzlement, manufacture of hazardous products, and tax evasion.

According to the Department of Justice, it is impossible to know with certainty the annual costs of white-collar crime. Estimates suggest, however, that such crime is a serious problem. For example, U.S. businesses lose $10 billion a year to check fraud. Securities and commodities fraud totals $40 billion a year. Annual losses from health care fraud are thought to be $100 billion.

Punishment for White-Collar Criminals

Despite the fact that white-collar crime costs businesses and consumers such huge sums every year, the people who commit these crimes often are treated more leniently than other criminals. In federal court, where most white-collar cases are tried, probation is granted to 40 percent of antitrust law violators, 61 percent of fraud defendants, and 70 percent of embezzlers. If white-collar criminals are imprisoned, they receive shorter average sentences than other criminals and are more likely to be placed in prisons with extra amenities, such as tennis courts or private rooms. There are some recent exceptions, however. In 2005, for example, former WorldCom chief executive Bernard Ebbers was sentenced to 25 years in prison and forced to give up most of the money he made from the $11 billion fraud he orchestrated.

Punishment for Victimless Crime

White-collar crime is not victimless crime. Taxpayers pay the price for white-collar crime, as does anyone who pays an insurance premium inflated by fraud. Some crimes, however, are considered victimless. That is, they are illegal but do not infringe upon the rights of or victimize other people. For instance, taking illegal drugs and gambling are considered victimless crimes. Nonetheless, white-collar crime, which does have victims, is often punished less severely than victimless crime.

✓ **READING PROGRESS CHECK**

Generalizing What generalization can you make about how white-collar crime is dealt with in American society?

LESSON 4 REVIEW

Reviewing Vocabulary
1. *Defining* What is *victim discounting*?
2. *Identifying* What are some examples of white-collar crime?

Using Your Notes
3. *Describing* Use your notes to describe deviance according to conflict theory.

Answering the Guiding Questions
4. *Summarizing* How does an industrial society defend itself against deviants?

5. *Analyzing* How do race and ethnicity influence punishment for crime?

6. *Identifying* What are the costs of white-collar crime?

Writing Activity
7. *Informative/Explanatory* Read about recent examples of white-collar crime. Choose one example and research it. What was the crime, and who perpetrated it? What punishment did he or she receive? Write a short research paper about the case.

networks

There's More Online!

- ☑ **IMAGE** Modern Prisons
- ☑ **GRAPHIC ORGANIZER** Crime and Punishment
- ☑ **MAP** Death Penalty Policy
- ☑ **SELF-CHECK QUIZ**

Reading HELPDESK

Academic Vocabulary
- contrary
- occupation

Content Vocabulary
- crime
- criminal justice system
- deterrence
- retribution
- incarceration
- rehabilitation
- recidivism
- restitution

TAKING NOTES:
Key Ideas and Details

ORGANIZING As you read about crime and punishment, use a graphic organizer like the one below to record the types of consequences meted out for criminal behavior, both those that are retributive and those that are rehabilitative.

Retributive	Rehabilitative

LESSON 5
Crime and Punishment

ESSENTIAL QUESTIONS • What is deviance? • Who defines deviance?

IT MATTERS BECAUSE
Crime statistics in the United States come chiefly from the FBI. Four approaches to crime control are deterrence, retribution, incarceration, and rehabilitation. Crime and the measures used to control it are issues of concern to all Americans.

Measurement of Crime

GUIDING QUESTIONS *How is the crime rate measured?*

Most Americans think of **crime**—acts in violation of statute law—as including a narrow range of behavior. On the **contrary,** more than 4,000 acts are classified as federal crimes. Many more acts violate state and local statutes.

According to a national survey sponsored by the U.S. Department of Justice, approximately 18.7 million Americans aged 12 or over experienced one or more crimes in 2010. Although this figure may seem high, it actually represents a decrease of 6 percent from 2009. The majority of crimes included in the 2010 survey were property crimes, although more than 3 million people reported being the victims of violent crime. African Americans were slightly more likely than whites to experience violent crime, and households with lower incomes were more likely to experience property crime.

The major source of American crime statistics is the Federal Bureau of Investigation's *Uniform Crime Reports* (UCR). These official statistics are gathered from police departments across the country. Reports are submitted voluntarily by law-enforcement agencies. They track nine types of crimes (called crime index offenses): murder, forcible rape, robbery, aggravated assault, burglary, larceny-theft, motor vehicle theft, arson, and hate crimes.

A major strength of UCR statistics lies in the fact that experienced police officers, whose **occupation,** or job, requires them to be familiar with the law, decide if an incident should be reported as a crime. Some crimes (amateur thefts, minor assaults) are not as likely to be reported to the police as murder and auto thefts, though. Intoxicated persons are subject to arrest in public places but are fairly safe in private settings, for instance. It is estimated that about two-thirds of U.S. crimes are not reported at all.

☑ **READING PROGRESS CHECK**

Analyzing What factors contribute to the reliability of UCR statistics?

Deviance and Social Control **195**

A Global Perspective

DEATH PENALTY POLICY
Countries vary in their approaches to the control of crime. Some countries still utilize the most extreme form of social control—the death penalty, or capital punishment. At the same time, many countries have abolished capital punishment. This map shows variations in national policy regarding the death penalty.

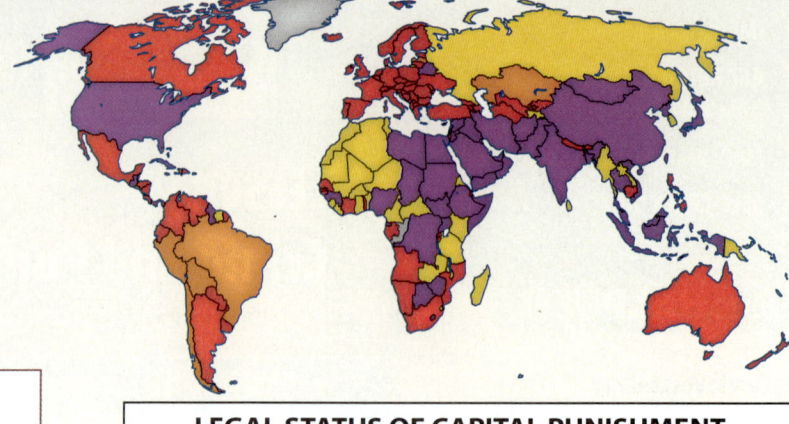

Geography Connection

1. **Places and Regions** What pattern or patterns, if any, in death penalty policies do you find?
2. **Making Connections** What connection, if any, do you think exists between the high crime rates in the United States and the use of the death penalty?

LEGAL STATUS OF CAPITAL PUNISHMENT
- Abolished for all crimes
- Abolished except for extraordinary crimes (such as crimes under military law or other unusual circumstances)
- Abolished in practice—retained but not used in last 10 years
- Retained
- No data

SOURCE: Amnesty International Publications, 2012.

---

crime an act committed in violation of the law

contrary the opposite of what was previously stated

occupation one's business or profession

Juvenile Crime

GUIDING QUESTION *What is the trend in juvenile crime?*

Juvenile crime refers to legal violations among those under 18 years of age. Juvenile offenders are the third-largest category of criminals in the United States. Teenage criminal activity includes theft, murder, rape, robbery, assault, and the sale of illegal substances. Juvenile delinquent behavior includes deviance that only the young can commit, such as failing to attend school, fighting in school, and underage drinking and smoking.

Violent juvenile crime reached its lowest level ever in 2009, a fall of 52.6 percent since 1994. Between 1994 and 2009, the juvenile murder arrest rate dropped by 29 percent. In that same period, juvenile arrests for weapons violations declined by 48.8 percent. The arrest rate for juvenile rape went down by 48 percent in those years.

There were also fewer juvenile victims of murder—down from about 2,840 in 1993 to 1,335 in 2009, a decline of 47 percent. Juvenile crime, in short, returned to the rates typical of the years prior to the crack epidemic of the late 1980s. (Crack is a highly addictive form of cocaine; use of crack surged in the 1980s, and juvenile crime rates rose along with crack use.) The victims of juvenile murder are disproportionately male and African American: In 2009, 68 percent were male and 47 percent were African American.

Several factors are thought to account for this decline in juvenile crime. For one, there has been a decline in the demand for crack cocaine. Remaining crack gangs that provided guns to juveniles have reached truces. Repeat juvenile offenders have been given stiffer sentences. Finally, police are cracking down on illegal guns on the street.

✓ **READING PROGRESS CHECK**

Analyzing Why has the juvenile crime rate declined?

Approaches to Crime Control

GUIDING QUESTION *What are the different approaches to controlling crime?*

The **criminal justice system** is made up of the institutions and processes responsible for enforcing criminal statutes. It includes the police, courts, and correctional system. A criminal justice system may draw on four approaches to control and punish lawbreakers—*deterrence, retribution, incarceration,* and *rehabilitation.*

The **deterrence** approach uses the threat of punishment to discourage criminal action. A basic idea of this approach is that punishment of convicted criminals will serve as an example to keep other people from committing crimes. While there is debate on the effectiveness of deterrence, some studies do suggest that the threat of deterrence reduces crime.

Capital punishment is a special case. Around 6,000 people have been executed in the United States since 1930, the year the federal government began gathering statistics on capital punishment. According to the Death Penalty Information Center, of those executed from 1976, the year the death penalty was reinstated, to 2012, the vast majority was male, and 77 percent were white, followed by 15 percent African American, and 7 percent Latino. Research indicates, however, that the murder rate remains constant, or even drops, following a decline in the use of the death penalty.

Only about 35 percent of Americans believe that the death penalty acts as a deterrent to murder. Of those Americans who favor the death penalty, approximately 69 percent indicate that they would continue to favor it even if new evidence showed that the death penalty does not deter murder and does not lower the murder rate. Feelings of revenge and a desire for retribution, then, appear to contribute more to support for capital punishment than do its deterrent effects. When asked to choose, a higher proportion of the American public supports the death penalty for murder (61 percent) than opposes it (35 percent).

Retribution is a type of punishment intended to make criminals pay compensation for their acts. It comes from the ancient principle of punishing a criminal to the same extent that his or her victim suffered injury. That principle is often expressed as "an eye for an eye and a tooth for a tooth." The law allows designated officials to demand retribution from criminals. It does not allow, however, individuals to take personal vengeance. On the contrary, if a mother takes the law into her own hands by shooting her son's killer, she is guilty of a crime and must also answer to society for her action.

The basic idea behind **incarceration**—keeping criminals in prisons—is that criminals who are not on the street cannot commit crimes. Recently, the United States has taken a tougher stance in favor of incarceration with such bills as the Three Strikes Law. As a result, the number of local, state, and federal prisoners increased from fewer than 1.6 million in 1995 to 2.2 million in 2010.

Rehabilitation is an approach to crime control that attempts to resocialize criminals. Most prisons have programs aimed at giving prisoners both social and work skills that will help them adjust to normal society after their release.

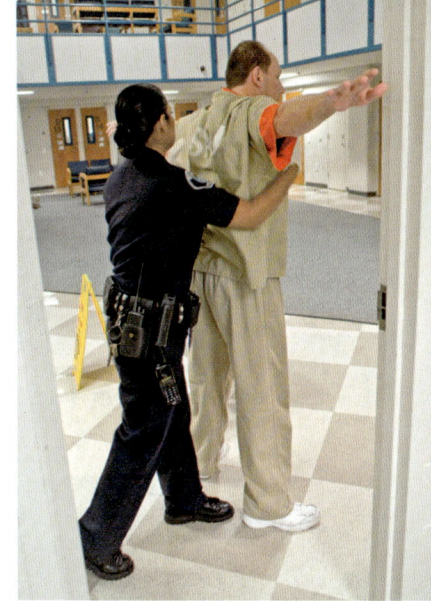

A prison guard pats down a prisoner to be sure he has no dangerous objects.

▶ **CRITICAL THINKING**
Summarizing Why has the number of Americans in prison increased in recent years?

criminal justice system a system comprising institutions and processes responsible for enforcing criminal statutes

deterrence discouraging criminal acts by threatening punishment

retribution punishment intended to make criminals pay compensation for their acts

Quick Case Study

DEVIANCE AND SOCIAL CONTROL

Everyone breaks the rules sometimes—and most of us follow them most of the time. What are the factors that influence this behavior?

Procedure

1. Interview five classmates about a time they each faced a decision about either obeying a rule or breaking it.
2. Ask your subjects what influenced their decisions to either follow the rule or break it.

Analysis

As you read, review the responses.

1. What reasons did subjects give for following rules?
2. How did subjects explain their choices to break a rule?
3. Do you think it was an internal force, such as an "inner voice," or an external one, such as fear of social condemnation, that drove your subjects' decisions?

incarceration a method of protecting society from criminals by keeping them in prison

rehabilitation the process of changing or reforming a criminal through socialization

recidivism a repetition of, or return to, criminal behavior

Unfortunately, more than half of those released from penal institutions are sent back to prison in three to five years. Their return to criminal behavior is called **recidivism**.

If prisons do not rehabilitate, what are some alternatives? Several are being considered, and some are currently in use.

- *A combination of prison and probation.* A mixed or split sentence, known as *shock probation*, is designed to shock offenders into recognizing the realities of prison life. Prisoners serve part of their sentences in an institution and the rest on probation.
- *Community-based programs.* By getting convicts out of prison for at least part of the day, community-based programs help break the inmate code. At the same time, prisoners have a chance to become part of society—participating in the community but under professional guidance and supervision.
- *Diversion strategy.* Diversion involves a referral to a community-based treatment program rather than a prison or a probationary program. Because offenders are handled outside the formal system of criminal law, authorities believe the offenders will not acquire stigmatizing labels and other liabilities.

Most of these alternative programs have not been sufficiently evaluated to determine how well they work. Continued use of these alternatives will depend on what American voters believe are the appropriate functions of prisons. These programs can exist only so long as rehabilitation has a high priority. Recently, in a contrary trend, Americans have taken a harsher view toward criminals, so support for alternatives may be eroding.

Other Methods of Dealing with Antisocial Behavior

Other alternatives to dealing with deviant behavior take two different approaches. They may focus on trying to find some other way of having a criminal pay a debt to society or to a victim. Some focus on attempts to change the person who committed the crime so he or she will not do so again.

1. *Restitution:* **Restitution** is a payment made by an offender to the victim.
2. *Community Service:* Instead of, or as part of, a jail sentence, judges sometimes order offenders to perform a certain number of hours of service beneficial to the community.
3. *Education:* Educational opportunities are available to many of the individuals incarcerated in the United States. Some studies suggest that these programs may help keep educationally disadvantaged convicts from committing future crimes.
4. *Therapy:* Another approach is to offer therapy programs, such as drug rehabilitation, to offenders, either during, or as an alternative to, incarceration.

restitution punishment intended to make criminals pay monetary compensation to make up for the financial damage caused by their acts

✓ **READING PROGRESS CHECK**

Analyzing How successful are our current approaches to controlling crime?

LESSON 5 REVIEW

Reviewing Vocabulary
1. *Specifying* What term describes the discouraging effect of punishment?
2. *Explaining* What is the purpose of rehabilitation?

Using Your Notes
3. *Summarizing* Use your notes to write a statement summarizing the use of retribution in our criminal justice system.

Answering the Guiding Questions
4. *Specifying* How is the crime rate measured?

5. *Summarizing* What is the trend in juvenile crime?
6. *Listing* What are the different approaches to controlling crime?

Writing Activity
7. *Argument* Under our current criminal justice system, the recidivism rate is still substantial. What do you think is the best way to reduce the rate of recidivism? Using information from the textbook and your own experience, describe the approach you think would be most effective.

CHAPTER 7 Assessment

Directions: On a separate sheet of paper, answer the questions below. Make sure you read carefully and answer all parts of the questions.

Lesson Review

Lesson 1

1. **Defending** Some might say that credit card fraud through computer use is not deviant but is just an example of utilizing an opportunity. Those who hold this position might say that it is the responsibility of a company or individual to set up protective measures that will guard against this theft—and that a failure to do so provides an opportunity that others are simply utilizing. Do you agree or disagree? Defend your position.

2. **Synthesizing** A teen stayed out past the curfew time set by the city where the teen lives. Identify one type of punishment that would be an example of a formal sanction against the teen and one that would be an example of an informal sanction.

Lesson 2

3. **Making Connections** What is the relationship between social bonds and deviance?

4. **Comparing and Contrasting** Create a graphic to compare and contrast four deviant ways of responding to strain.

Lesson 3

5. **Interpreting Significance** Which of the three characteristics affecting differential association do you believe is the most significant? Explain.

6. **Contrasting** What is the difference between primary deviance and secondary deviance?

Lesson 4

7. **Hypothesizing** Some say that law-enforcement officials do not work as vigorously to find kidnap victims from economically disadvantaged families as they do to find kidnap victims from wealthy families. Explain the practice that might be perceived as a cause.

8. **Analyzing** How does punishment for white-collar crimes differ from punishment for other types of crimes? Do you think this is fair? Explain.

Lesson 5

9. **Problem Solving** Select one of the limitations of the UCR statistics. What would you suggest as a method to help cure this limitation? Explain.

10. **Analyzing** Of the four approaches to crime control, which do you believe to be the most effective? Explain.

Analyzing Primary Sources

PRIMARY SOURCE

Use the cartoon to answer the following question.

"O.K.—let's review what you didn't know and when you didn't know it."

11. **Analyzing Visuals** Look at the setting and the appearance of the figures in the cartoon. What kind of crime do you think the cartoon is about? Why? What kind of attitude do you think the cartoonist has toward this crime? Why do you think so?

Need Extra Help?

If You've Missed Question	1	2	3	4	5	6	7	8	9	10	11
Go to page	180–183	183	186	185	187	189	193	194	195	197–198	194

CHAPTER 7 Assessment

Directions: On a separate sheet of paper, answer the questions below. Make sure you read carefully and answer all parts of the questions.

Critical Thinking

12 *Organizing* You are a sociologist who is developing a book proposal to send to a publisher. Your book is about deviance and social control, but it is written to provide interesting information to the general reading public, not to other sociologists. Provide a title for your book and develop a single sentence to open a letter about your book and "hook" the publisher into reading your book outline. Then create a book outline that includes chapter titles and very briefly states the overall idea for the content of each chapter.

21st Century Skills

CREATING AND USING GRAPHS, CHARTS, DIAGRAMS AND TABLES

13 *Creating Graphs and Charts* Consider the information you have learned about juvenile crime, white-collar crime, and violent crime. Then design a chart, diagram, or other visual to compare and contrast these types of crimes.

Exploring the Essential Questions

14 *Defending* You are debating abolition of the death penalty. Select a position—pro or con—and support your position by explaining, from a sociological viewpoint, how society has dealt with deviants in the past and how society currently deals with deviants. Write an essay and create a time line to show and explain how dealing with deviants has changed throughout history—and why. Your time line need not include exact dates but should chronologically depict the changing viewpoints regarding those who commit crimes.

College and Career Readiness Skills

15 *Exploring the Issues* Conduct online research to learn about careers in law enforcement. Write a brief essay to identify at least five law-enforcement careers. Determine which of these careers a graduate with a degree in sociology would most likely pursue. Explain why.

DBQ Analyzing Primary Sources

PRIMARY SOURCE

Use the document to answer the following question.

"Social groups create deviance by making the rules whose infraction constitutes deviance, and by applying these rules to particular people and labeling them as outsiders. From this point of view, deviance is *not* a quality of the act the person commits, but rather a consequence of the application by others of rules and sanctions to an 'offender.' The deviant is one to whom that label has successfully been applied; deviant behavior is behavior that people so label."

—Howard Becker, *Outsiders: Studies in the Sociology of Deviance*, 1973

16 *Analyzing Primary Sources* In this chapter, you read Howard Becker's view of deviance defined by the individual. Based on the quote above, discuss behaviors of gang members that others in a violent gang would likely consider deviant.

Research and Presentation

17 *Gathering Information* Consult the Bureau of Justice Statistics' National Crime Victimization Survey (NCVS) and compose a report that analyzes differences in crime and arrest rates by race and ethnicity, gender, socioeconomic status, and age.

18 *Comparing and Contrasting* On the computer, create a single graphic that shows how competency and insanity in a criminal case differ in definition—and how they are alike in their relationship to modern viewpoints regarding crime and deviant behavior. Write several paragraphs to share with the class to explain your graphic and your conclusions.

Need Extra Help?

If You've Missed Question	12	13	14	15	16	17	18
Go to page	180–199	195–197	180–199	180–199	188–189	195–198	187–189

Social Stratification

ESSENTIAL QUESTIONS • What is "equality"? • To what extent are societies unequal?

networks
There's More Online about social stratification.

CHAPTER 8

Technology & Society
Social Stratification and the Digital Divide

Lesson 1
Dimensions and Explanations of Stratification

Lesson 2
Social Class and Poverty in America

Lesson 3
Social Mobility

Lesson 4
Global Stratification

Sociology Matters...

Have you ever thought about what politicians and pundits mean when they talk about "middle-class America"? To hear people talk, you would think that most Americans share a similar, and very good, lifestyle. The truth is, however, that based on income most Americans are not middle class. Many lack the advantages of a middle-class lifestyle or live in poverty. On the other end of the scale, a small segment of American society is spectacularly wealthy. Why is wealth spread so unevenly? Sociology offers several explanations.

◀ As this street musician knows, American society is highly unequal.
B.O'Kane/Alamy

CHAPTER 8
Technology & Society

Social Stratification
and the Digital Divide

Use of the Internet seems universal, but some groups still remain unconnected.

Accessing the Internet has been made easier by the use of handheld devices. In 2007, the introduction of smartphones made it even more convenient, enabling access nearly everywhere through WiFi or mobile networks. But, while Internet use is a daily ritual for many, one out of every five American adults has no such access.

Even before the advent of smartphones, Internet use was on the rise. This new technology was bridging an originally large digital gap between younger and older Americans. Social networking decreased the gap even more. So who are the one in five Americans not using the Internet? A study by the Pew Internet and American Life Project found that most were senior citizens, adults in households earning less than $30,000 annually, adults with disabilities, Spanish speakers, and adults who have less than a high-school education.

Education and economics are not the only factors that affect non-Internet users. The majority of adult non-Internet users in the study said they chose not to use the Internet. Having little familiarity with the Internet and no household members to champion its use, they consider the Internet irrelevant in their lives. Many are simply not interested in sending and receiving e-mail or surfing the Web.

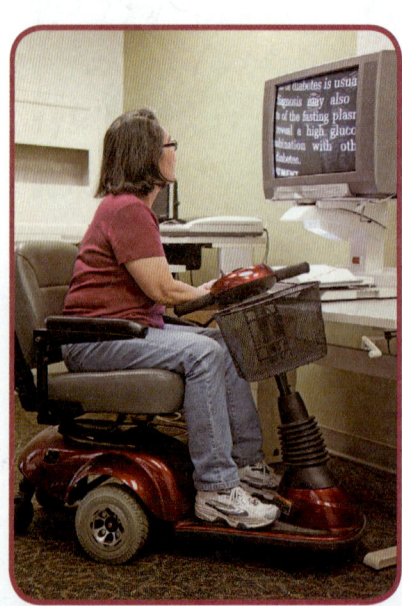

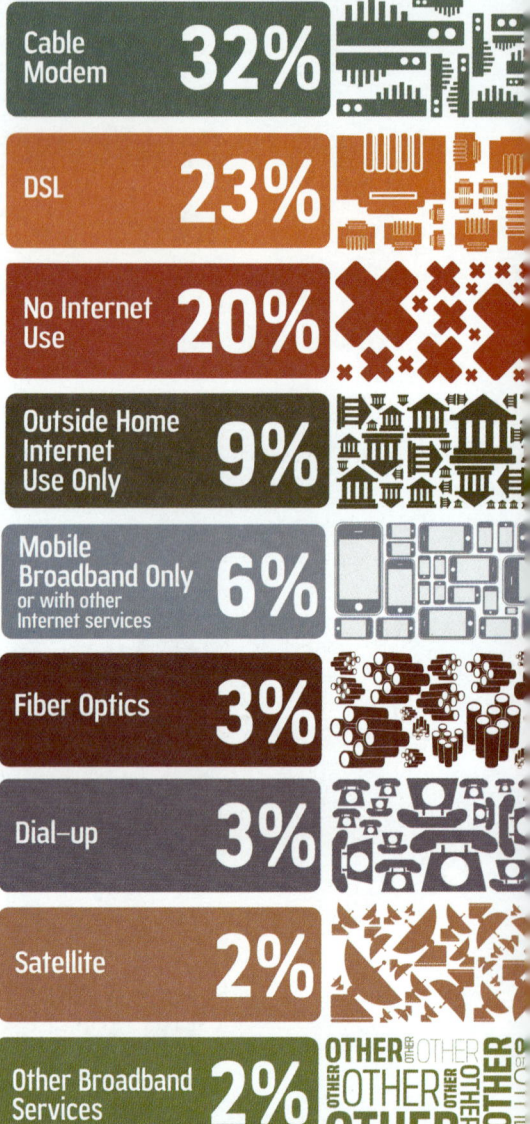

Cable Modem	32%
DSL	23%
No Internet Use	20%
Outside Home Internet Use Only	9%
Mobile Broadband Only or with other Internet services	6%
Fiber Optics	3%
Dial-up	3%
Satellite	2%
Other Broadband Services	2%

Source: U.S. Department of Commerce, *Exploring the Digital Nation: Computer and Internet Use at Home,* November 2011

▶ **CRITICAL THINKING**
Analyzing What factors do you think affect a physically challenged citizen's interest in using the Internet?

INTERNET ADOPTION BY TYPE OF TECHNOLOGY 2010

71% Have some type of Internet service at home

29% Use Internet service outside the home or do not use the Internet

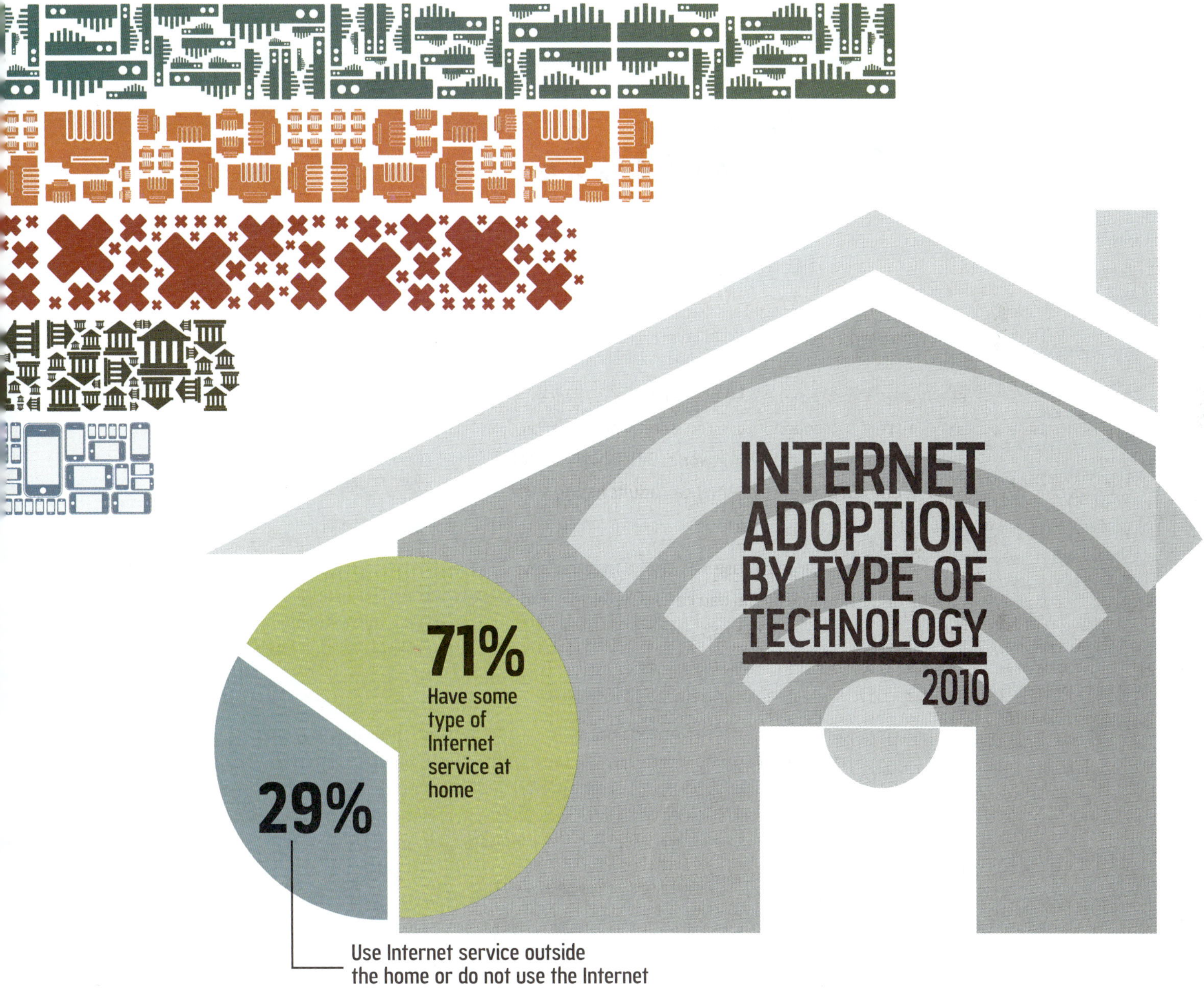

Thinking Like a Sociologist

1 Analyzing
Why do you think some Americans find the Internet irrelevant?

2 Contrasting
How does the data in the chart support or not support the information in the passage?

Social Stratification

networks

There's More Online!

- ☑ **CARTOON** Different Perspectives
- ☑ **CARTOON** Low Status
- ☑ **CHART** Prestige Rankings of Selected Occupations
- ☑ **GRAPHS** Measures of Stratification
- ☑ **SELF-CHECK QUIZ**

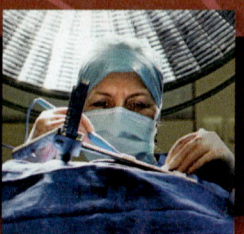

LESSON 1
Dimensions and Explanations of Stratification

Reading HELPDESK

Academic Vocabulary
- exploit
- income

Content Vocabulary
- social stratification
- social class
- bourgeoisie
- proletariat
- wealth
- power
- prestige
- false consciousness

TAKING NOTES:
Key Ideas and Details

ORGANIZING As you read about social stratification, use a graphic organizer like the one below to compare the three dimensions of stratification.

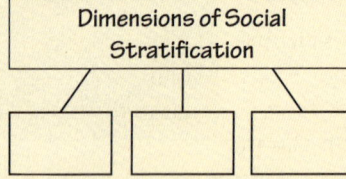

ESSENTIAL QUESTIONS • *What is "equality"?* • *To what extent are societies unequal?*

IT MATTERS BECAUSE
Society is divided into classes that have unequal levels of income, wealth, power, and prestige.

Social Stratification and Social Class

GUIDING QUESTION *How is social stratification related to social class?*

In one of his children's books, Dr. Seuss writes of the Sneetches, birds whose social status depends on whether they have a large star on their stomachs. Star-bellied Sneetches have high status, and plain-bellied Sneetches have low status. In *Animal Farm*, George Orwell creates a barnyard society where the pigs ultimately take over the previously classless animal society. The animals' motto changes from "All animals are equal" to "All animals are equal—but some animals are more equal than others." Both books mock the tendency of humans to arrange themselves by social class and how the people of each class do not enjoy the same privileges.

Sociologists call this social arrangement **social stratification**. It is the creation of layers (or strata) of people who possess unequal shares of scarce resources, particularly income, wealth, power, and prestige.

Each layer in a stratification system is a **social class**. Members of a social class have similar amounts of scarce resources. They share a lifestyle with common values, norms, and social status. The number of social classes in a society varies. Technologically developed countries generally have three broad classes—upper, middle, and lower—subdivided into smaller categories. In some less developed countries, there might be only an upper class and a lower class.

Two pioneers of sociology, Karl Marx and Max Weber, made the most significant early contributions to the study of social stratification. Marx explained the importance of the economic foundations of social classes, while Weber emphasized the prestige and power aspects.

☑ **READING PROGRESS CHECK**

Describing What are the elements of a social class?

Connecting Sociology to History

AN OUTSIDER'S VIEW OF AMERICAN SOCIETY

When French aristocrat Alexis de Tocqueville traveled to the United States in 1831, he was fascinated to see American democracy at work. More than three decades after both the American and French revolutions ended, de Tocqueville was eager to learn from America's democratic example and experience and to share the phenomenon with the French people. In this excerpt from his work Democracy in America, *de Tocqueville comments on equality and class at a time when America's agrarian society was shifting toward industrialization.*

PRIMARY SOURCE

"I am aware that among a great democratic people there will always be some members of the community in great poverty, and others in great opulence: but the poor, instead of forming the immense majority of the nation, as is always the case in aristocratic communities, are comparatively few in number, and the laws do not bind them together by the ties of irremediable and hereditary penury.

The wealthy, on their side, are scarce and powerless; they have no privileges which attract public observation; even their wealth, as it is no longer incorporated and bound up with the soil, is impalpable, and as it were invisible. As there is no longer a race of poor men, so there is no longer a race of rich men; the latter spring up daily from the multitude, and relapse into it again. Hence they do not form a distinct class, which may be easily marked out and plundered; and, moreover, as they are connected with the mass of their fellow-citizens by a thousand secret ties, the people cannot assail them without inflicting an injury upon itself.

Between these two extremes of democratic communities stand an innumerable multitude of men almost alike, who, without being exactly either rich or poor, are possessed of sufficient property to desire the maintenance of order, yet not enough to excite envy. . . .

If we attentively consider each of the classes of which society is composed, it is easy to see that the passions engendered by property are keenest and most tenacious among the middle classes. The poor often care but little for what they possess, because they suffer much more from the want of what they have not, than they enjoy the little they have. The rich have many other passions besides that of riches to satisfy; and, besides, the long and arduous enjoyment of a great fortune sometimes makes them in the end insensible to its charms. But the men who have a competency, alike removed from opulence and from penury, attach an enormous value to their possessions. As they are still almost within the reach of poverty, they see its

Alexis de Tocqueville originally came to America to study the U.S. penal system but was more captivated by Americans themselves.

privations near at hand, and dread them; between poverty and themselves there is nothing but a scanty fortune, upon which they immediately fix their apprehensions and their hopes. Every day increases the interest they take in it, by the constant cares which it occasions; and they are more attached to it by their continual exertions to increase the amount. The notion of surrendering the smallest part of it is insupportable to them, and they consider its total loss as the worst of misfortunes.

Now these eager and apprehensive men of small property constitute the class which is constantly increased by the equality of conditions. Hence, in democratic communities, the majority of the people do not clearly see what they have to gain by a revolution, but they continually and in a thousand ways feel that they might lose by one."

—from *Democracy in America*, 1847

DBQ ▶ CRITICAL THINKING

1. **Making Connections** How does the excerpt above illustrate the importance of historical perspective in interpreting the social world?
2. **Evaluating** How accurate was de Tocqueville's interpretation of America's social structure in the 1830s? Explain.

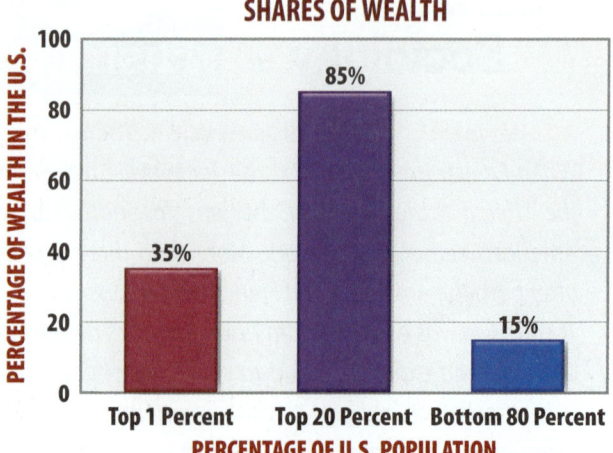

GRAPHS

MEASURES OF STRATIFICATION

The chart on the left shows income growth figures for four groups from the lowest-earning fifth of the population (1–20 percent) to the top 1 percent of earners. The chart on the right compares the share of national wealth owned by different segments of the population. In an unstratified society, the share of wealth would be proportionate to the group's share of the overall population.

▶ CRITICAL THINKING

1. **Drawing Conclusions** What generalizations can you make from the chart on the left about income growth in the United States in these years?

2. **Making Inferences** What does the chart on the right illustrate about social class and social stratification in the United States?

social stratification the ranking of people or groups according to their unequal access to scarce resources

social class a segment of society whose members have similar economic circumstances, norms, and status

bourgeoisie the class that owns the means of production

The Economic Dimension

GUIDING QUESTION *How is the distribution of economic resources related to social class?*

Marx identified several social classes in nineteenth-century industrial society. These included laborers, servants, factory workers, craftspeople, proprietors of small businesses, and moneyed capitalists. He predicted, however, that capitalist societies would ultimately be reduced to two social classes. He thought that those who owned the means of production would be the rulers. He called this class the **bourgeoisie**. Those who worked for wages—the **proletariat**—would be the ruled.

Marx further predicted that because the capitalists owned the means of production (factories, land, and so forth), they would both rule and **exploit**, or take advantage of, the working class. The working class would have nothing to sell but its labor. Marx believed that control of the economy gave the capitalists control over the legal, educational, and governmental systems as well. For Karl Marx, the economy determined the nature of society.

Income Versus Wealth

In his writings, Marx emphasized the unequal distribution of economic resources. How unequally are these resources distributed in the United States? When discussing this issue, economists often make a distinction between income and wealth. **Income** is the amount of money received within a given time period by an individual or group. **Wealth** refers to all the economic resources possessed by an individual or group. In brief, your income is your paycheck and your wealth is what you own.

Extremes of Income and Wealth in the United States

According to the 2010 U.S. Census, approximately 46.2 million Americans are living in poverty. (The federal government defines poverty as a family of four living on less than $22,314.) This is the largest number of people living in poverty since the government began publishing poverty statistics in 1959. At the other extreme, 3.1 million Americans are millionaires and around 400 are billionaires.

In 2010, the richest 20 percent of American households received over 50 percent of the nation's income. The poorest 20 percent received less than 3.5 percent. People with higher incomes found their incomes growing at a faster rate than people with lower incomes. The graph at the left shows the percentage changes in after-tax income in the United States over a 28-year period. After-tax income is annual income minus federal income taxes. During this time, the income of the top 1 percent of the population increased by 277 percent. Compare this to an 18 percent increase for the lowest fifth of the population.

Income distribution figures reveal economic inequality, but they do not show the full extent of inequality. For that, inequality in wealth must be considered. In the United States, wealth is concentrated in the hands of a small number of people. The top 1 percent alone has nearly 35 percent of the total wealth in the United States. The next 9 percent own 39 percent of the wealth. That leaves only about 27 percent of wealth for everyone else—90 percent of the population.

✅ **READING PROGRESS CHECK**

Analyzing How would you describe the distribution of wealth in the United States?

The Power Dimension

GUIDING QUESTION *How can power be exercised without wealth?*

Power is the ability to control the behavior of others, even against their will. Individuals or groups who possess power can use it to enhance their own interests, often at the expense of others.

According to Marx, those who own and control capital, or the means of production, have the power in a society. Weber argued that while wealth certainly helps, economic success and power are not the same. Money and ownership of the means of production are not the only resources that can be used as a basis for power. Expert knowledge can be a source of power, too. People can use their superior knowledge and skills to influence those around them. For example, lawmakers may place a high value on the expertise of certain professionals, such as scientists or economists. Experts can also use their superior knowledge to gain positions of power within an organization.

Power is also attached to the social positions we hold. For instance, elected officers in organizations have more power than rank-and-file members.

proletariat the class that labors without owning the means of production

exploit to take unfair advantage of

income amount of money received by an individual or group over a specific time period

wealth total economic resources held by a person or group

power the ability to control the behavior of others, even against their will

⌄ CARTOON

DIFFERENT PERSPECTIVES
Status is a social construct, dependent on how a person is perceived.

▶ **CRITICAL THINKING**

1. *Analyzing Visuals* What "complexities" is the man in the second frame ingesting?

2. *Drawing Inferences* What does the cartoon suggest about the way people see the actions of high-status individuals?

OCCUPATIONS	PRESTIGE SCORE	OCCUPATIONS	PRESTIGE SCORE	OCCUPATIONS	PRESTIGE SCORE
Surgeon	87	Police officer	61	Automobile dealer	43
Astronaut	80	Actor	60	Deep-sea diver	43
Lawyer	75	Journalist	60	Landlord	41
College professor	74	TV anchorman	60	Prison guard	40
Airline pilot	73	Businessperson	60	Auto mechanic	40
Dentist	72	Actress	59	Roofer	37
Priest	71	Nursery school teacher	55	Barber	36
Engineer	71	Fashion designer	55	Sales clerk in a store	36
TV anchorwoman	70	Firefighter	53	Bus driver	32
Secret Service agent	70	Airplane mechanic	53	Dry cleaner	32
School principal	69	Commercial artist	52	Waitress	29
Medical technician	68	Housewife	51	Taxicab driver	28
Optometrist	67	Funeral director	49	Used car salesperson	25
Registered nurse	66	Jazz musician	48	Bill collector	24
High school teacher	66	Mail carrier	47	Janitor	22
Air traffic controller	65	Insurance agent	46	Grocery bagger	18
Professional athlete	65	Mechanic	46	Street-corner drug dealer	13
Paramedic	64	Disc jockey	45	Fortune teller	13
Public grade school teacher	64	Photographer	45	Panhandler	11
Advertising executive	63	Plumber	45		
Veterinarian	62	Bank teller	43		

Source: General Social Survey, National Opinion Research Center, 1996

CHART
PRESTIGE RANKINGS OF SELECTED OCCUPATIONS IN THE UNITED STATES

▶ **CRITICAL THINKING**

1. **Analyzing** Which job listed holds the greatest prestige? The least? How would you explain the difference?
2. **Making Inferences** According to these responses, on what is occupational prestige based?

prestige recognition, respect, and admiration attached to social positions

People in top executive positions in the mass media are powerful even if they themselves do not have great wealth. They have this power because they can use their positions to influence people's opinions.

Individuals can wield great power without wealth if they have large numbers of people on their side or if they skillfully organize resources. Indian nationalist Mahatma Gandhi, for example, was able to bring about the end of centuries of British rule in India. He roused the support of millions of Indians to peacefully resist British colonial policies.

☑ **READING PROGRESS CHECK**

Applying What role does knowledge play in power?

The Prestige Dimension

GUIDING QUESTION *How is prestige awarded?*

People who are wealthy and powerful are often regarded as having characteristics they may not actually possess. Not all of these people are as intelligent and wise as is usually assumed. Still, these attributed characteristics help them gain **prestige**—recognition, respect, and admiration attached to social positions. Prestige is the third dimension of social stratification. It is defined by your culture and society. A Mafia leader, for example, may have the admiration and respect of the members of his criminal organization, but outside of their own circles, Mafia dons are usually held in low regard.

Prestige is given by others, not claimed by oneself. Scientists cannot proclaim themselves Nobel Prize winners, journalists cannot award themselves Pulitzer

Prizes, and corporate executives cannot grant themselves honorary doctorates. Recognition must come from others; it is socially constructed.

Because Americans place a high value on the acquisition of wealth and power, they tend to assign higher prestige to the wealthy and powerful. As the Mafia don example shows, however, wealth and power alone may not give high status. Other values also come into play. You may even enjoy high status without wealth or power. For example, nurses and priests have more prestige than actors and business executives. In America, prestige is often related to a person's occupation.

✓ READING PROGRESS CHECK

Identifying What factors besides wealth are related to prestige?

Theories of Stratification

GUIDING QUESTION *How do functionalism, conflict theory, and symbolic interactionism explain stratification?*

Why are societies stratified? Sociology's three major perspectives—functionalism, conflict theory, and symbolic interactionism—offer different explanations.

Functionalist Theory of Stratification

Functionalists look at stratification and see an ordered and stable society. They believe that every element of society serves a function that benefits the whole. According to the functionalists, stratification ensures that the most qualified people fill the most important positions, perform their tasks competently, and are rewarded for their efforts.

The functionalist theory holds that inequality exists because certain jobs are more important than others and that these jobs often require special talent and training. It is necessary to encourage people to make the sacrifices necessary to fill these jobs.

Each social class can be described in terms of its access to scarce resources and the shared lifestyle of its members.

▶ **CRITICAL THINKING**

Applying How would functionalists explain the different classes these people occupy in society? Do you agree?

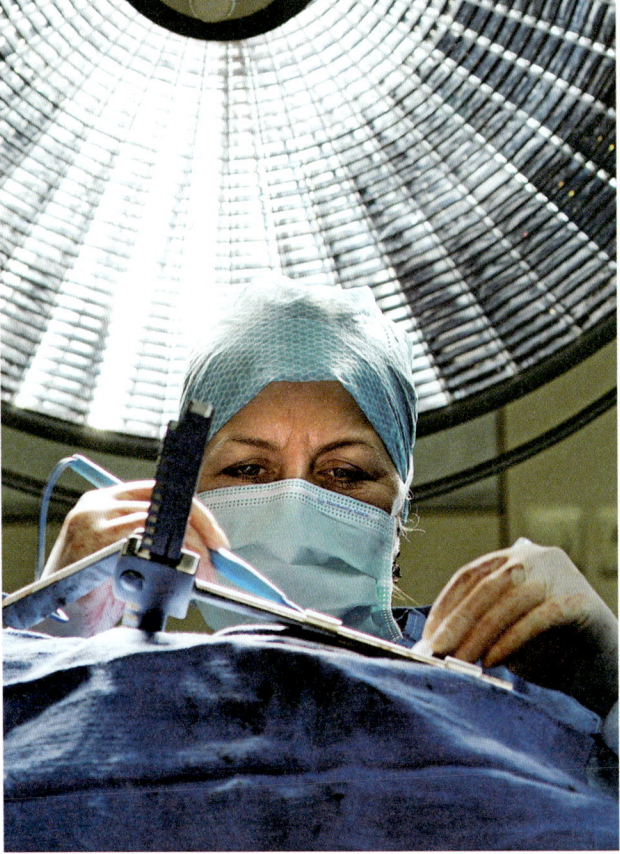

Social Stratification

> **CARTOON**
>
> **LOW STATUS**
> Lack of status can lead to painful isolation.
>
> ▶ **CRITICAL THINKING**
>
> 1. **Analyzing Visuals** How does the speaker try to console himself, and how effective is that effort? Why?
> 2. **Making Connections** Does the cartoon support Marx's or Weber's view of power? Why?

Society attaches special monetary rewards and prestige to positions that require advanced, specialized education. That is why doctors make more money and have more prestige than bus drivers. A higher level of skill is required in the medical profession, and our society's need for highly qualified doctors is great.

According to functionalist theory, society remains stable because everyone accepts the social order. Social institutions, such as family, religion, education, and government, help ensure that everyone adheres to the same norms and values.

Functionalism has been criticized because it seems to accept and even justify inequality. It also leaves no room to explain social change or social conflict. In addition, its view of different earnings for different professions cannot explain some features of the national income structure. Why do professional athletes or entertainers make far more money than physicians? Those individuals have special talents, but does society need entertainment more than it needs health care?

Conflict Theory of Stratification

For conflict theorists, stratification occurs as a result of the struggle for scarce resources. According to conflict theory, inequality exists because some people are willing to exploit others. Stratification, from this perspective, is based on force rather than agreement.

The conflict theory of stratification is based on Marx's ideas regarding class conflict. For Marx, all of history has been a class struggle between the powerful and the powerless, those who exploit and those who are exploited. Capitalist society is the final stage of the class struggle.

Although the capitalists are outnumbered, they are able to control the workers. This is because the capitalists have the power to promote a belief system that legitimizes the way things are. Those who own the means of production are able to spread their ideas, beliefs, and values through the schools, media, churches, and government. For example, the powerful spread the idea that income and wealth are based on ability, hard work, and individual effort. Marx used the term **false consciousness** to refer to working-class acceptance of capitalist ideas and values.

Later conflict sociologists proposed that stratification is based more on power than on property ownership. The United States's legal system, for example, is used by the wealthy for their benefit, and the political system is skewed toward the interests of the powerful.

Symbolic Interactionism and Stratification

Symbolic interactionism helps us understand how people are socialized to accept the existing stratification structure. According to this perspective, American children are taught that a person's social class is the result of talent and effort.

false consciousness according to Karl Marx, working-class acceptance of capitalist ideas and values

Theoretical Perspectives

SOCIAL STRATIFICATION

This table summarizes approaches of the major theoretical perspectives to issues of social stratification and makes predictions based on each perspective. The research topic could be analyzed from any of the three perspectives to produce different expected results.

Theoretical Perspective	Research Topic	Expected Result
Functionalism	Relationship between job performance and pay	Pay levels increase with job performance.
Conflict Theory	Relationship between social class and the likelihood of punishment for a crime	The chances for prosecution decrease as the level of social class increases.
Symbolic Interactionism	Link between social class and self-esteem	Self-esteem is higher among the upper class than the lower class.

▶ **CRITICAL THINKING**

1. *Identifying Central Ideas* Why would functionalists examine workers and how their job performance affects their pay?

2. *Contrasting* How are the three expected results different?

According to this view, those "on top" have worked hard and used their abilities, whereas those "on the bottom" lack the talent or the motivation to succeed. Hence, it is not fair to challenge the system. By being socialized in this way, people come to accept the existing system.

Symbolic interactionism's view of stratification says that social class has an impact on an individual's self-esteem, or feeling of personal worth. In the symbolic interactionist view, self-esteem is based on how we think others see us. Understandably, people in the lower social classes or social strata tend to suffer from lower self-esteem. How could it be otherwise when messages from all sides tell them they are inferior? Those at the top blame the people at the bottom for their low status; the people at the bottom blame themselves. The reverse is true for the higher classes. Those profiting most from the stratification structure tend to have higher self-esteem. This fuels their conviction that the present arrangement is just. In short, people's self-concepts also help preserve the status quo.

☑ **READING PROGRESS CHECK**

Applying Which theory is most likely to be supported by the upper classes? Why?

LESSON 1 REVIEW

Reviewing Vocabulary

1. *Explaining* What is *social stratification*?

2. *Describing* What is the difference between *income* and *wealth*?

Using Your Notes

3. *Summarizing* Use your notes to write a statement summarizing the three dimensions of social stratification.

Answering the Guiding Questions

4. *Explaining* How is social stratification related to social class?

5. *Finding the Main Idea* How is the distribution of economic resources related to social class?

6. *Analyzing* How can power be exercised without wealth?

7. *Specifying* How is prestige awarded?

8. *Comparing and Contrasting* How do functionalism, conflict theory, and symbolic interactionism explain stratification?

Writing Activity

9. *Narrative* Describe evidence of social stratification you see in the world around you. Identify examples of the three dimensions of social stratification.

networks

There's More Online!

- ☑ **CARTOON** An Unhealthy Situation
- ☑ **CHART** American Class Structure
- ☑ **GRAPH** Distribution of Poverty in the United States
- ☑ **GRAPH** The Federal Government Dollar—Where it Goes
- ☑ **MAP** Living in Poverty
- ☑ **SELF-CHECK QUIZ**

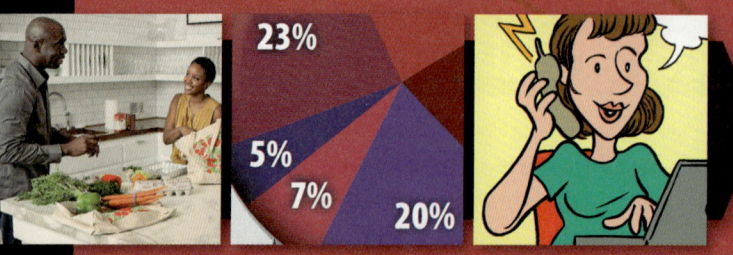

LESSON 2
Social Class and Poverty in America

ESSENTIAL QUESTIONS • What is "equality"? • To what extent are societies unequal?

Reading HELPDESK

Academic Vocabulary
- exclusive
- professional

Content Vocabulary
- class consciousness
- working poor
- underclass
- absolute poverty
- relative poverty
- feminization of poverty

TAKING NOTES:
Key Ideas and Details

ORGANIZING As you read about social class in the United States, use a graphic organizer like the one below to identify the characteristics of each class.

Social Classes in the U.S.	
Upper Class	
Middle Class	
Working Class	
Working Poor	
Underclass	

IT MATTERS BECAUSE
Sociologists have identified several social classes in the United States. They include the upper class, the middle class, the working class, the working poor, and the underclass.

Class Consciousness

GUIDING QUESTION *What is class consciousness, and does it exist in the United States?*

Americans have always been aware of inequality, but they have never developed a strong sense of **class consciousness**—a sense of identification with the goals and interests of the members of a particular social class. When the United States was founded, its leaders placed a particular emphasis on equality. You will recall that the Declaration of Independence states "that all men are created equal, that they are endowed by their Creator with certain unalienable Rights, that among these are Life, Liberty and the pursuit of Happiness."

In reality people were not equal and did not have equal opportunities to pursue happiness in the new nation. Americans, however, have long believed in individualism. Individualism stresses the economic and political independence of the individual in society. This belief puts greater attention on the individual rather than his or her social class.

In part because the American public has shown relatively little interest in social class, sociologists began to investigate inequality rather late. It was not until the 1920s that sociologists in the United States began systematically to identify social classes. Since that time, however, research on this subject has been plentiful. Early efforts to study stratification were mostly case studies of specific communities. Only relatively recently have attempts been made to describe the stratification of American society as a whole.

Since social classes are changeable and full of exceptions, any attempt to identify the social-class structure of American society is difficult. Nevertheless, sociologists have described some of the major classifications.

☑ **READING PROGRESS CHECK**

Explaining Why is it difficult to study class in the United States?

212

The Social Classes

GUIDING QUESTION What are the social classes in the United States, and what are their characteristics?

Sociologists recognize five main classes within the social structure of the United States. These classes are the upper class, the middle class, the working class, the working poor, and the underclass. Sociologists often discuss smaller divisions, or subclasses, within each class as well.

The Upper Class

The upper class includes only 1 percent of the population and may be divided into the upper-upper class and the lower-upper class. At the top is the aristocracy. Its members represent the old-money families whose names appear in high society—Ford, Rockefeller, Vanderbilt, and du Pont, among others. The basis for membership in this most elite of clubs is heritage rather than accomplishments. Parents in this class send their children to the best private schools and universities. People in this group seldom marry outside their class.

People are in the lower-upper class more often because of achievement and earned income than because of birth and inherited wealth. Some have made fortunes running large corporations or investing in the stock market. Members of this class may actually be better off financially than members of the upper-upper class. Despite that, they often are not accepted into the most **exclusive** social circles because they do not have the same family tradition of being in the upper-upper class.

The Middle Class

Most Americans think of themselves as middle class. In reality, though, only less than half of Americans fit this description. And most of these people are not in the upper-middle class.

The upper-middle class (14 percent of the population) is composed of those who have been successful in business, the professions, politics, and the military. Basically, this class is made up of individuals and families who benefited from the

class consciousness identification with the goals and interests of a social class

exclusive limited to possession, control, or use by a single individual or group

The upper class of the United States has access to the most exclusive luxuries.

▶ **CRITICAL THINKING**

Synthesizing To what else do you think the top 1 percent has access?

Social Stratification 213

CHART

AMERICAN CLASS STRUCTURE

This chart shows the five social classes sociologists identify in the United States along with their occupations and incomes. Although most Americans consider themselves middle class, the reality is far different.

▶ CRITICAL THINKING

1. **Analyzing** What percentage of Americans are living below the middle class? Above?

2. **Comparing and Contrasting** What is the income difference between the working poor and the middle class?

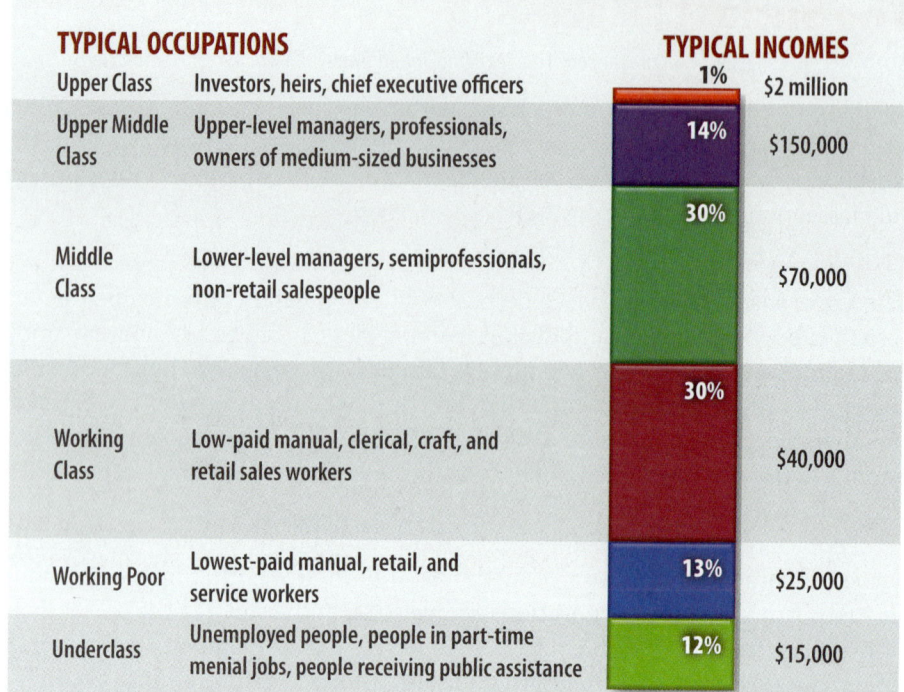

Typical Occupations		Percentage	Typical Incomes
Upper Class	Investors, heirs, chief executive officers	1%	$2 million
Upper Middle Class	Upper-level managers, professionals, owners of medium-sized businesses	14%	$150,000
Middle Class	Lower-level managers, semiprofessionals, non-retail salespeople	30%	$70,000
Working Class	Low-paid manual, clerical, craft, and retail sales workers	30%	$40,000
Working Poor	Lowest-paid manual, retail, and service workers	13%	$25,000
Underclass	Unemployed people, people in part-time menial jobs, people receiving public assistance	12%	$15,000

Source: Adapted from Dennis Gilbert, *The American Class Structure in an Age of Growing Inequality* (8th ed.), 2011.

professional relating to a job requiring specialized knowledge and academic preparation

tremendous corporate and **professional** expansion following World War II. Members of this class earn enough to live well and to save money. They are typically college educated. They have high educational and career goals for their children. Because of their advantages, those children have opportunities to reach those goals. They do not have national or international power, but they tend to be active in voluntary and political organizations in their communities.

The middle-middle class (30 percent of the population) is a very mixed bag. Its members include owners of small businesses and farms; independent professionals (small-town doctors and lawyers); other professionals (members of the clergy, teachers, nurses, firefighters, social workers, and police officers); lower-level managers; and some sales and clerical workers. Their household income level does not permit them to live as well as the upper-middle class. Many have only a high school education, although many have some college, and some have college degrees. Members of this class are interested in civic affairs. They participate in political activities less than the classes above them but more than either the working class or the lower class.

The Working Class

The working class (often referred to as the lower-middle class) comprises almost one-third of the population. Working-class people include roofers, delivery truck drivers, machine operators, and salespeople and clerical workers. Although some of these workers may earn more than some middle-class people, in general the economic resources of the working class are lower than those of the middle class.

Members of the working class have below-average income, and many have unstable employment. They generally lack health insurance and retirement benefits. The threat of unemployment or illness is real and haunting. Outside union activities, members of the working class have little opportunity to exercise power or participate in organizations. Members of the working class—even those with higher incomes—are not likely to enter the middle class.

The Working Poor

The **working poor** (13 percent of the population) consists of people employed in low-skill jobs with the lowest pay. Its members are typically the lowest-level clerical workers, manual workers (laborers), and service workers (fast-food servers).

Lacking steady employment and receiving only low wages, the working poor do not earn enough to rise above the poverty line ($22,314 for a family of four). The working poor tend not to belong to organizations or to participate in the political process. The struggle to survive consumes most of their time and energy, making such involvement impossible.

working poor people employed in low-skill jobs with the lowest pay who do not earn enough to rise out of poverty

The Underclass

The **underclass** (12 percent of the population) is composed of people who are usually unemployed and who come from families with a history of unemployment for generations. They either work in part-time menial jobs (unloading trucks, picking up litter) or are on public assistance. In addition to a lack of education and skills, many members of the underclass have other problems. Physical or mental disabilities are common among this group, and many are single mothers with little or no income.

The most common shared characteristic of the working poor and the underclass is a lack of skills to obtain jobs that pay enough to meet basic needs. There are many routes into these classes—birth, old age, loss of a marriage partner, lack of education or training, drug addiction or alcoholism, or physical or mental disability. There are, however, very few paths out.

underclass people typically unemployed who come from families that have been poor for generations

✓ READING PROGRESS CHECK

Identifying Central Issues How can a person have a job yet remain poor?

Social class affects where and how people live.

▶ **CRITICAL THINKING**

Analyzing Visuals To what social class do you think this man belongs? Why?

GRAPH >

DISTRIBUTION OF POVERTY IN THE UNITED STATES

Minority populations in the United States bear a disproportionate amount of the nation's poverty.

▶ **CRITICAL THINKING**

1. **Analyzing** Which population makes up the largest percentage of the poor in the United States?
2. **Explaining** How would you describe poverty among the groups in terms of each group's poverty rate and overall share of the population?

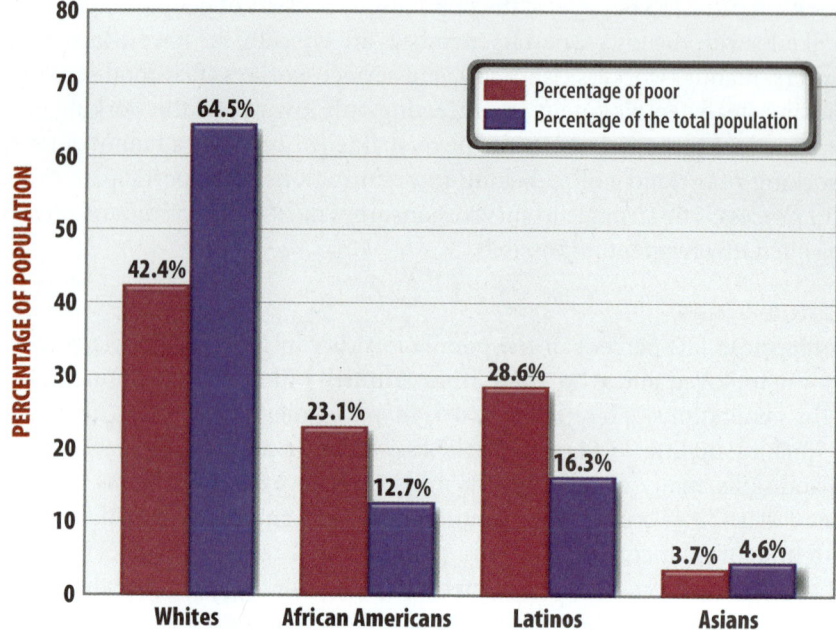

Source: U.S. Census Bureau, 2011.

Poverty in the United States

GUIDING QUESTION *Who are the poor in America?*

Before trying to understand poverty in America, we need to understand what poverty is. There are two different ways of looking at poverty. The term **absolute poverty** means the absence of enough money to secure life's necessities—having enough food and a safe place to live. It is possible, however, to have the things required to remain alive and still be poor. We measure **relative poverty** by comparing the economic condition of those at the bottom of a society with that of other members of that society. According to this measure, the definition of poverty can vary. It would not, for example, be the same in India as in the United States. That is because the average income in India is much lower than that in the United States.

absolute poverty the absence of enough money to secure life's necessities

relative poverty a measure of poverty based on the economic disparity between those at the bottom of a society and the rest of the society

Measuring Poverty in the United States

Poverty became a national political and social issue in the 1960s. More than fifty years later, poverty in the United States is still a problem. Historically, the United States government has measured poverty by setting an annual income level and considering people poor if their income is below that level. As noted earlier, in 2010 that figure was $22,314 for a family of four.

Poverty is widespread in the United States. According to 2010 U.S. Census Bureau reports, the poor make up 15 percent of the American population, or about 46 million people. Minorities, people who live in female-headed households, children under 18 years of age, and people with disabilities make up the most disadvantaged groups living in the United States today.

Nearly 43 percent of the poor in America today are non-Latino white. The poverty rate for African Americans and Latinos is much higher than that for whites, however. The poverty rate for all whites is 9.9 percent; for African Americans and Latinos it is more than 25 percent. African Americans and Latinos together account for only about one-fourth of the total population, but they make up more than half of the poor population.

Gender, Age, Disability, and Poverty

Beginning in the 1960s, changes in Americans' social lives brought about changes in their economic lives. Women and children began to make up a larger proportion of the poor. Sociologists refer to this trend as the **feminization of poverty**. There are several reasons women have a higher risk of being poor. In 2010, a woman earned only about $.81 for every dollar earned by a man. Women with children find it more difficult to find and keep regular, long-term employment. A lack of good child-care facilities adds to the likelihood that they will not be able to continue working. As a result, the poverty rate for female-headed households is about 32 percent. This rate is double the poverty rate for male-headed households.

More children under 18 years of age live in female-headed households than live in male-headed households. As a result, poverty rates for women are linked to poverty rates for children. Despite being only one quarter of the population, children make up more than a third of the poor. Children under 18 suffer a poverty rate of 22 percent. For related children living within a female-headed household the rate is more than double the rate for all children—47 percent.

People with disabilities also experience a high poverty rate. The poverty rate for people with disabilities between the ages of 18 and 64 is almost 28 percent. This group is more than twice as likely to live in poverty as are nondisabled people in the same age group. In addition, people with severe disabilities are more likely to live in poverty than are those with less severe disabilities.

> **feminization of poverty**
> a trend in U.S. society in which women and children make up an increasing proportion of the poor

A Diverse America

LIVING IN POVERTY

The United States government measures poverty using different thresholds each year, based on the income of individuals, the number of family members, and their ages. For example, in 2010, a family with two children was considered to be living in poverty if the annual household income was less than $22,113. This map of the United States shows the percentage of the population by state who were living in poverty in 2010.

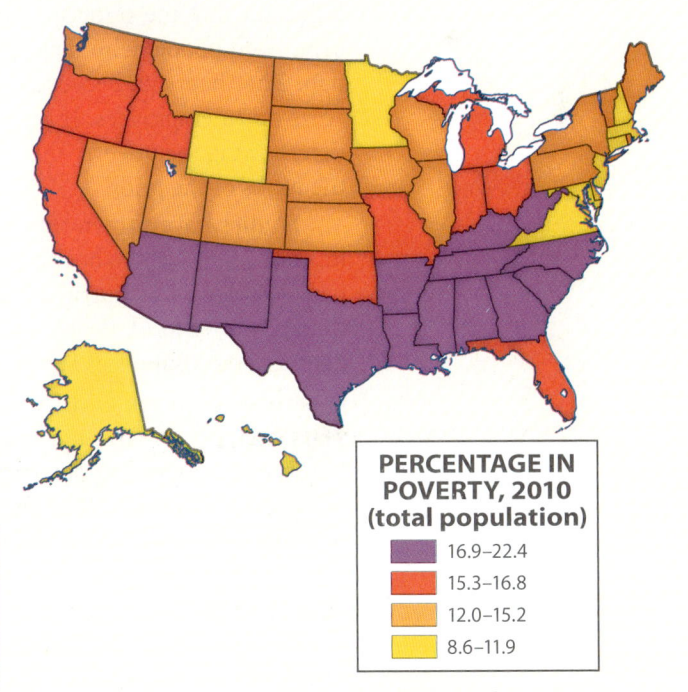

PERCENTAGE IN POVERTY, 2010
(total population)
- 16.9–22.4
- 15.3–16.8
- 12.0–15.2
- 8.6–11.9

SOURCE: U.S. Census Bureau, 2010.

Geography Connection

1. **Places and Regions** Which region has the lowest percentage of poverty? Which region has the highest percentage of poverty?
2. **The Uses of Geography** How might a sociologist make best use of the data in this chart? Explain.
3. **Environment and Society** What might be some reasons certain regions of the United States experience higher rates of poverty than others?

Social Stratification

CARTOON

AN UNHEALTHY SITUATION
People seeking employment often take job benefits into account as much as a job's wage or salary.

▶ **CRITICAL THINKING**

1. **Analyzing Visuals** Why does the woman joke that she might have a heart attack as a result of her job hunt?
2. **Making Connections** Why is health insurance so important to the woman?

People with disabilities often face barriers to education and employment. These barriers work to lower their income. They may also have very high medical expenses, which eat away at the income they do earn. The resulting loss of social and economic status leads to a poor quality of life.

The news is less grim for Americans over the age of 64. Our nation's elders experience poverty at a rate of about 9 percent.

Poverty and Health Care

Health care costs have been rising over the last few decades, and these rising costs cut into people's incomes. The poor and elderly are especially hard hit. One study estimates that the poor spend more than 20 percent of their income on health care. Even people who have health insurance through an employer feel the burden. That happens because, as health care costs rise, employers pass the rising costs on to employees. If the impact of health care costs were considered when determining the poverty threshold, another 10 million people would be added to the ranks of the poor.

Studies have shown that health and poverty are connected: Poor people are less healthy. Access to health care is not the only issue. People with fewer resources have less access to nutritious foods. Junk food tends to be much less expensive than healthful food. People with low incomes tend to suffer more chronic illness, disease, and disabilities and die younger than more affluent Americans.

The War on Poverty

Before the mid-1960s, fighting poverty was not a major goal of the federal government. Some programs, such as Social Security and the precursor to Aid to Families with Dependent Children (AFDC), had been enacted during the Great Depression. AFDC was a welfare program—a program to provide money or equivalent aid to eligible citizens. These measures did not usually reach the neediest citizens, however. Then in 1964, President Lyndon Johnson declared a so-called War on Poverty.

The philosophy behind the War on Poverty was to help poor people help themselves. President Johnson's predecessor, President John Kennedy, believed that poverty could be eliminated through self-improvement as opposed to temporary relief. Accordingly, almost 60 percent of the first poverty budget was earmarked for youth opportunity programs and work experience programs (work and job-training programs designed for welfare recipients and unemployed fathers).

Not all the programs were as successful as predicted. Indeed, some came under severe criticism. Some critics charged that these programs actually encouraged people to become dependent on government assistance or to take unfair advantage of it instead of using the help for temporary relief.

Welfare Reform

A push for welfare reform ended Aid to Families with Dependent Children (AFDC). Legislation enacted in 1996 replaced AFDC with a program known as Temporary Assistance for Needy Families (TANF). The TANF program limits the amount of time that those who are able to work can receive welfare payments. The law has three major elements: It reduces welfare spending, it increases state and local powers to oversee welfare rules, and it adds new restrictions on welfare eligibility. For example, benefits to children of unmarried teenage mothers are denied unless the mothers remain in school and live with an adult. Able-bodied adults must find work within two years or lose cash aid.

The success of TANF is a subject of debate. According to the Administration of Children and Families, the government agency that administers TANF, welfare rolls have decreased substantially since the program went into effect. Critics argue, however, that the rolls have decreased but not the ranks of the poor. In addition, most of the people who left the welfare rolls could find only low-wage jobs in industries such as food service, home health care, and retail sales. In the early 2000s, an economic downturn caused many such jobs to disappear. At the same time, wages grew more slowly or actually fell. As a result, many of those who left the welfare rolls continue to live in or near poverty. Research suggests that the current emphasis of welfare reform on reducing the welfare rolls rather than on reducing poverty hampers the long-term economic well-being of the needy.

✓ **READING PROGRESS CHECK**

Identifying Central Issues How are age and gender linked to poverty?

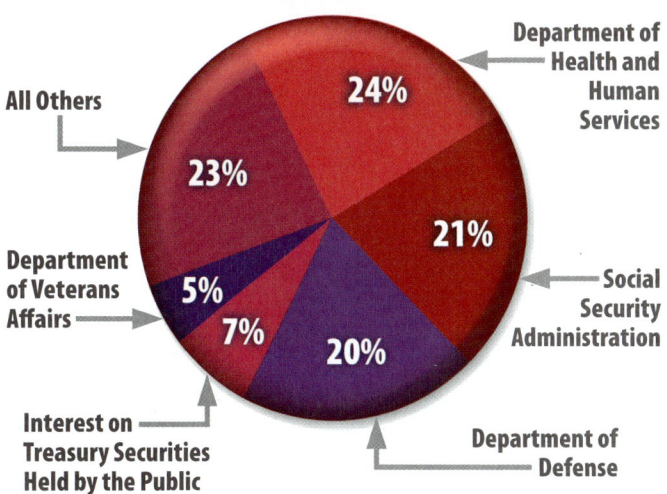

THE FEDERAL GOVERNMENT DOLLAR—WHERE IT GOES

- Department of Health and Human Services: 24%
- Social Security Administration: 21%
- Department of Defense: 20%
- Interest on Treasury Securities Held by the Public: 7%
- Department of Veterans Affairs: 5%
- All Others: 23%

Source: Citizen's Guide to the 2011 Financial Report of the United States Government

△ **GRAPH**

THE FEDERAL GOVERNMENT DOLLAR— WHERE IT GOES

This chart shows the major categories for federal spending.

▶ **CRITICAL THINKING**

1. *Analyzing* Where do most federal dollars go?
2. *Speculating* What does this spending tell you about the government's approach to poverty?

LESSON 2 REVIEW

Reviewing Vocabulary

1. *Defining* What is *absolute poverty*?
2. *Explaining* How does *relative poverty* differ from *absolute poverty*?

Using Your Notes

3. *Summarizing* Use your graphic organizer to summarize the class structure of the United States.

Answering the Guiding Questions

4. *Identifying* What is class consciousness, and does it exist in the United States?

5. *Differentiating* What are the social classes in the United States, and what are their characteristics?

6. *Analyzing* Who are the poor in America?

Writing Activity

7. *Argument* How do you think the development of class consciousness would affect the social stratification of the United States? Support your position by citing facts about social class in America.

Social Stratification

FOCUS on research
Field Research

Nickel and Dimed

Barbara Ehrenreich grew up in a middle-class family in Montana and became a writer and journalist. To find out if it was possible to make ends meet working for around minimum wage, she did just that—she tried to survive living in poverty by taking very low-paying jobs in several states and living within her means. In her book Nickel and Dimed: On (Not) Getting By in America, *she exposed the inequality and prejudice that a large number of Americans face each day just working to survive.*

Ehrenreich investigated the many "hidden" costs faced by low-wage workers. Many low-wage workers pay a high cost for hotel or motel rooms since they cannot afford the security deposits on an apartment rental. Food was also expensive and not terribly healthful as these workers lacked kitchens and adequate refrigeration.

One of the cities Ehrenreich worked in was Portland, Maine. In the course of her experiment on living on or just above the minimum wage, she was asked to take several preemployment tests as part of the job application process.

PRIMARY SOURCE

"What these tests tell employers about potential employees is hard to imagine, since the 'right' answers should be obvious to anyone who has ever encountered the principle of hierarchy and subordination. Do I work well with others? You bet, but never to the point where I would hesitate to inform on them for the slightest infraction. Am I capable of independent decision making? Oh yes, but I know better than to let this capacity interfere with a slavish obedience to orders. At The Maids, a housecleaning service, I am given something called the 'Accutrac personality test,' which warns at the beginning that 'Accutrac has multiple measures which detect attempts to distort or 'psych out' the questionnaire.' Naturally I 'never' find it hard 'to stop moods of self-pity,' nor do I imagine that others are talking about me behind my back or believe that 'management and employees will always be in conflict because they have totally different sets of goals.' The real function of these tests, I decide, is to convey information not to the employer but to the potential employee, and the information being conveyed is always: You will have no secrets from us. We don't just want your muscles and that portion of your brain that is directly connected to them, we want your innermost self.

The main thing I learn from the job-hunting process is that, despite all the help-wanted ads and job fairs, Portland is just another $6–$7-an-hour town. This should be as startling to economists as a burst of exotic radiation is to astronomers. If the supply (of labor) is low relative to demand, the price should rise, right? That is the 'law.' At one of the maid services I apply at—Merry Maids—my potential boss keeps me

> "The main thing I learn from the job-hunting process is that, despite all the help-wanted ads and job fairs, Portland is just another $6–$7-an-hour town. This should be as startling to economists as a burst of exotic radiation is to astronomers. If the supply (of labor) is low relative to demand, the price should rise, right? That is the 'law.'"

for an hour and fifteen minutes, most of which is spent listening to her complain about the difficulty of finding reliable help. It's easy enough to think of a solution, because she's offering '$200 to $250' a week for an average of forty hours' work. 'Don't try to put that into dollars per hour,' she warns, seeing my brow furrow as I tackle the not-very-long division. 'We don't calculate it that way.' I do, however, and $5 to $6 an hour for what this lady freely admits is heavy labor with a high risk of repetitive-stress injuries seems guaranteed to repel all mathematically able job seekers. But I am realizing that, just as in Key West, one job will never be enough. In the new version of the law of supply and demand, jobs are so cheap—as measured by the pay—that a worker is encouraged to take on as many of them as she possibly can."

— from *Nickel and Dimed: On (Not) Getting By in America*

Working with the Research

1. **Making Connections** How did Ehrenreich's personal experience working at low-paying jobs affect her understanding of the challenges that many Americans face?
2. **Identifying Cause and Effect** What effect do you think Ehrenreich's book had on the public perception of poverty in America?
3. **Drawing Inferences** How do you think society could improve conditions so that people with low-paying jobs would be able to survive financially?

There's More Online!

- ☑ **CHART** Intergenerational Mobility in the United States
- ☑ **GRAPHIC ORGANIZER** Social Mobility
- ☑ **IMAGE** Indian Social Order
- ☑ **SELF-CHECK QUIZ**

Reading HELPDESK

Academic Vocabulary
- occupation
- category

Content Vocabulary
- social mobility
- horizontal mobility
- vertical mobility
- intergenerational mobility
- caste system
- open-class system

TAKING NOTES:
Key Ideas and Details

ORGANIZING As you read, use a graphic organizer like the one below to diagram social mobility. Add a definition to each arrow.

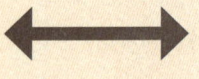

LESSON 3
Social Mobility

ESSENTIAL QUESTIONS • *What is "equality"?* • *To what extent are societies unequal?*

IT MATTERS BECAUSE
Social mobility, the movement of individuals or groups within the stratification structure, is usually measured by changes in occupational status. Sociologists are most interested in upward or downward (vertical) mobility. Closed-class systems permit little vertical mobility; open-class systems, such as those in industrialized countries, allow considerable vertical mobility.

Types of Social Mobility

GUIDING QUESTION *What are the types of social mobility?*

Mobility is, quite simply, the ability to move. People move in many ways. They may change jobs or move from a city to a suburb or one neighborhood to another.

In a social science context, mobility is most often used to refer to the movement of individuals, families, or groups within the layers of a stratified social structure. In other words, **social mobility** is the movement of people or groups between social classes. Social mobility can be *horizontal* or *vertical*.

Horizontal mobility involves changing from one **occupation** to another at the same social class level, as when an army captain becomes a public school teacher, a minister becomes a psychologist, or a restaurant server becomes a taxi driver. Because horizontal mobility involves no real change in occupational status or social class, sociologists are not generally interested in investigating it.

Vertical mobility, however, is another story. With **vertical mobility**, a person's occupational status or social class moves upward or downward. The change can be viewed in terms of just the individual or in the context of his or her family. When the change takes place over a generation, it is called **intergenerational mobility**. A plumber's daughter becoming a physician is a case of upward intergenerational mobility. If a lawyer's son becomes a carpenter, downward intergenerational mobility has occurred.

☑ **READING PROGRESS CHECK**

Finding the Main Idea What role does class play in vertical mobility?

Caste and Open-Class Systems

GUIDING QUESTION *How is a caste system different from an open-class system?*

The extent of vertical mobility varies from society to society. Some societies have considerable mobility. Others have little or none. This is the major difference between caste (or closed-class) systems and open-class systems.

In a **caste system** there is no social mobility because social status is inherited and cannot be changed. In a caste system, statuses (including occupations) are ascribed, or assigned, at birth. Individuals cannot change their status through any efforts of their own. Those in one caste are allowed to marry only within their own caste. They must limit relationships of all types with those below and above them in the stratification structure. Apartheid, as practiced in South Africa before the election of Nelson Mandela, was a caste system based on race.

social mobility the movement of individuals or groups between social classes

horizontal mobility a change in occupation within the same social class

occupation one's business or profession

Connecting Sociology to Anthropology

INDIA'S TRADITIONAL SOCIAL SYSTEM

Anthropologists study how people and cultures are distinct from other people and cultures. One way to illustrate a distinction is to study the class system. It became an important part of Indian life and culture and is still practiced today, although not officially. In this excerpt from an introduction to anthropology, John Monaghan and Peter Just describe the traditional Indian social order.

PRIMARY SOURCE

"Classic Hindu cosmology provides a coherent model of a fixed social order that combines marriage within the group (and therefore shared blood), occupational specialization (and therefore the division of labor in society), and relative degrees of spiritual purity (and therefore hierarchical ranking). In theory every person is born into a *jati*, a group which has a local monopoly on a particular occupation (such as blacksmiths, weavers, and so on). A person takes a spouse from within the *jati*, as do all of the person's descendants. The various *jatis* are hierarchically ranked with respect to one another, a ranking that is reinforced in daily behavior by prohibitions against higher-caste individuals taking food and drink from those of a lower caste. All of this is supported by an elaborate system of meaning and belief, much of it given spectacular ritual expression, that lies at the heart of Hinduism. In reality, of course, things are more fluid and complex, especially in contemporary India: *jatis* are actually far from endogamous, individuals are free to pursue occupations not reserved to a specific *jati* in a particular place, and the relative rankings of *jatis* turn out to shift over time and space in subtle ways."

—from *Social and Cultural Anthropology*, 2010

In India's traditional social system, *Dalits* were below the lowest class.

DBQ ▶ CRITICAL THINKING

1. **Contrasting** How do sociologists and anthropologists analyze India's class system differently?

2. **Identifying Central Issues** How have *jatis* "modernized" in contemporary India?

Social Stratification

vertical mobility a change upward or downward in occupational status or social class

intergenerational mobility a change in status or class from one generation to the next

caste system a stratification structure that does not allow for social mobility

category a defined group

Sociologists consider India's traditional social system to be a caste system as well. Historically, the class system in India, known as the *varna* system, was based on ideas about religious purity. People did traditional occupations based on *varna*, or class into which they were born. There were four *varnas*. The Brahmins served as priests and scholars. *Kshatriyas* served in professional, governing, and military occupations. *Vaisyas* were merchants and other businesspeople. *Sudras* were farmers, craft workers, and laborers. Outside of the *varna* system was a fifth **category**, the *Dalits*, who have also been referred to as the "Untouchables." Traditionally, this group has been seen as the most impure and polluted group. Their occupations included jobs that were seen as unclean, such as leatherworking, handling dead bodies, and collecting trash. The *varna* system is not legally enforced and is not officially recognized by the Indian government, which has worked for decades to eliminate the system from Indian life.

People in urban India have become less rigid about following the class system than people in rural areas. Where traditional rules are followed, not everyone understands the religion the same way, and movement into a higher class is difficult. It is also difficult to date or marry someone from a higher class.

Open-Class System

open-class system a system in which social class is based on merit and individual effort; movement is allowed between classes

In an **open-class system**, an individual's social class is based on merit and individual effort. Individuals move up and down the stratification structure as their abilities, education, and resources permit. Most people in the United States believe they live in an open-class system. In reality, the opportunity for upward mobility can be limited for individuals or groups in the United States. For example, because of discrimination or lack of resources, some members of minority groups have been denied opportunities for social mobility. Therefore, because it imposes some limitations on upward mobility, American society cannot be considered truly and completely open. It is, however, a relatively open-class system.

✓ **READING PROGRESS CHECK**

Explaining How does ascribed status affect social mobility?

> **CHART >**
>
> **INTERGENERATIONAL MOBILITY IN THE UNITED STATES**
> This chart shows the movement between classes from one generation to the next. Each bar represents the income class of a child's parent. The colors represent the income class of the child. For example, the last bar shows that 11 percent of children who came from the top income class fell to the bottom class.
>
> ▶ **CRITICAL THINKING**
> 1. ***Classifying*** Which income class shows the least intergenerational upward mobility?
> 2. ***Analyzing*** What percentage of children from middle-income families experienced downward mobility?

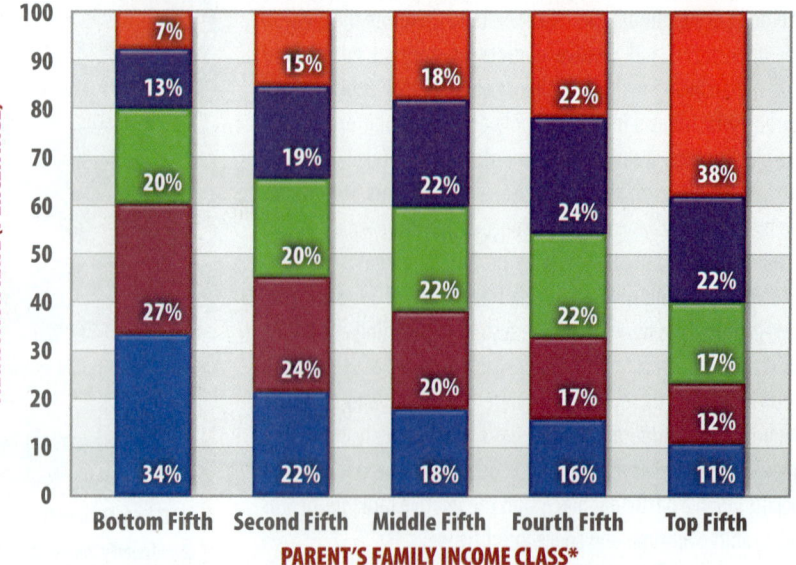

PERCENTAGE OF CHILDREN REACHING EACH INCOME CLASS

*Totals may not equal 100% due to rounding.

Source: Bhashkar Mazumder, *Upward Intergenerational Economic Mobility in the United States*, 2008.

Upward and Downward Mobility

GUIDING QUESTION *What does it mean to be upwardly or downwardly mobile?*

Few countries provide the opportunities for advancement available in the United States. Nevertheless, countless Americans fail to be upwardly mobile despite talent and hard work. Many people find this hard to accept because American tradition—historical and fictional—has many examples of upward mobility.

Earlier generations of Americans were raised on the "rags to riches" stories of Horatio Alger. The books taught that the only things standing between any American and success were talent, a willingness to work, and perseverance. People also point to political leaders like Abraham Lincoln and business leaders like Henry Ford to support the idea of unlimited mobility in American society. In truth, these men are exceptions. Great leaps in social class are rare. Upward mobility typically involves only a small improvement over the social class situation of one's parents.

After World War II, an explosion in the availability of high-paying manufacturing jobs made it relatively easy for people to move upward. Americans came to expect that their children would have more than they had, but this may not be the case today. This change is the result of new technology and the globalization of business. Computer-driven production and faster means of communication and transportation allow American companies to lower their costs by moving manufacturing operations overseas, eliminating many high-paying manufacturing jobs at home. American workers who lack the education needed to perform more technologically sophisticated jobs are being forced to take lower-paying jobs.

An economic recession beginning in late 2007 cost many Americans their jobs. Circumstances forced some people into lower-paying jobs while others took cuts in pay and benefits. Millions of families lost their homes to foreclosure. Compared to their parents, more U.S. workers are experiencing downward mobility.

In *Falling from Grace*, sociologist Katherine Newman describes America's enduring belief in the rewards of hard work. This belief, she writes, prevents recognition of the downward mobility experienced by many middle-class people. She argues that the consequences are enormous for people in a society that measures worth by occupational status. Downwardly mobile people experience lowered self-esteem, despair, depression, feelings of powerlessness, and a loss of sense of honor.

✅ **READING PROGRESS CHECK**

Identifying What are some of the signs of downward mobility in the United States?

British author J.K. Rowling is an example of extreme upward mobility as she rose from extreme poverty to great wealth as a result of the success of her Harry Potter books.

▶ **CRITICAL THINKING**

Synthesizing Why is J.K. Rowling an exception to the rule in terms of social mobility?

LESSON 3 REVIEW

Reviewing Vocabulary
1. *Defining* What is a caste system?
2. *Describing* What is the key element of intergenerational mobility?

Using Your Notes
3. *Explaining* Use the notes in your graphic organizer to describe social mobility.

Answering the Guiding Questions
4. *Identifying* What are the types of social mobility?

5. *Contrasting* How is a caste system different from an open-class system?
6. *Explaining* What does it mean to be upwardly or downwardly mobile?

Writing Activity
7. *Argument* How do you think the myth of upward mobility affects actual upward mobility in the United States?

Social Stratification

networks

There's More Online!

- ☑ **GRAPH** Global Stratification
- ☑ **GRAPHIC ORGANIZER** Layers of American Class Structure Global Stratification
- ☑ **IMAGE** Developing World
- ☑ **MAP** Chronic Poverty
- ☑ **SELF-CHECK QUIZ**

LESSON 4
Global Stratification

ESSENTIAL QUESTIONS • What is "equality"? • To what extent are societies unequal?

Reading HELPDESK

Academic Vocabulary
- industry
- indicator

Content Vocabulary
- global stratification
- standard of living
- industrialization
- globalization

TAKING NOTES:
Key Ideas and Details

ORGANIZING As you read, use a graphic organizer like the one below to identify the layers of global stratification.

Global Stratification			
	Income	Example	Brief Description
High-income countries			
Middle-income countries			
Low-income countries			

IT MATTERS BECAUSE
Thinking on a global scale, inequality seems less about what social class you occupy than about what place on the globe you occupy. According to various measures, the top 20 percent of nations has more than 60 percent of the world's wealth. The bottom 20 percent has only 3 percent of the world's wealth.

High-Income Countries

GUIDING QUESTION What are the characteristics of high-income countries?

Global stratification is the unequal distribution of wealth, power, and resources among the countries of the world. World systems theory holds that relationships among nations is based on inequality. The earliest nations to develop capitalist economies came to dominate other countries and in the process impeded their economic development.

People have used various terms to classify nations. Terms like "first world" and "third world" or "developed nations" and "developing nations" have fallen out of favor. Instead, experts classify nations first and foremost according to income. The World Bank, for example, uses the categories high-income, upper-middle income, lower-middle income, and lower income. One approximate measure of income is Gross National Income (GNI) per capita. GNI per capita is the total annual income earned by the people of a country divided by the number of people. This measure provides a snapshot of a society's economic well-being.

High-income nations have a GNI per capita of $12,276 or higher. Such wealth gives a population access to resources that help define a high standard of living. **Standard of living** refers to the necessities, comforts, and luxuries people in a society enjoy. It includes not only material wealth but factors such as education, health, life expectancy, and gender equality.

The United States is a high-income nation. Its 2010 GNI per capita was $47,310. Other high-income nations include countries such as Australia, Bahrain, Canada, the Czech Republic, Germany, Japan, Norway, the United Arab Emirates, and the United Kingdom. Stratification may and does occur within these nations, but compared to other nations, they enjoy a high standard of living.

High-income nations are modern, urban, and industrialized. **Industrialization** is the movement from an economy based on agriculture to one based on manufacturing. The process of industrialization modernizes society. It moves people into cities. Industrialization goes hand in hand with the development of science and technology.

Industrialization first began in Britain in the eighteenth century, launching what historians call the Industrial Revolution. The growth of **industry** created a need for increased amounts of materials, such as iron and steel, and for new energy sources, such as coal, steam, electricity, and petroleum. Energy was needed not only to produce goods but to move them from place to place. The development of industry led to the invention of new technologies and the growth of communication and transportation networks.

Industrialization brought about big changes to society. A working class of laborers developed along with a middle class of business owners. This created a need for greater literacy and formal education in areas such as science. Compared to agrarian societies, industrialized societies have a lower level of social inequality despite extremes of wealth and poverty. Industrialization also affects inequality across the globe, as you will learn later in this lesson.

global stratification the unequal distribution of wealth, power, and resources among the countries of the world

standard of living the necessities, comforts, and luxuries enjoyed by an individual or group

industrialization the movement from an economy based on agriculture to one based on manufacturing

industry a group of productive enterprises or organizations that produce or supply goods or services

✓ **READING PROGRESS CHECK**

Identifying What are the traits of high-income countries?

Applying Sociology

NONGOVERNMENTAL ORGANIZATIONS

Nongovernmental organizations (NGOs) are nonprofit groups that work to solve public issues. NGOs work:

- at the local, national, or international level.
- to raise government awareness of public concerns.
- with other groups that share common concerns.
- to follow the progress of programs that they have initiated.
- to support humanitarian needs.
- to help guide government reform and policy at all levels.
- to engage community support and involvement.

NGOs employ sociologists to research and analyze issues. Sociologists conduct field studies and research and then present their findings and reports. In turn, the results of their work can be used to help support ideas for reform and guide government policy. Oxfam International, for example, is an NGO confederation of more than a dozen organizations that work together to end global poverty and injustice. Oxfam aims to empower people who live in poverty so that they will be able to improve their lives. Oxfam also provides emergency relief.

▶ **CRITICAL THINKING**

1. **Evaluating** Evaluate the importance of sociological work for NGOs.
2. **Researching** Research a sociology position at an NGO. Make a list of the qualifications and skills that the job requires and compare them to the skills and work described in the passage above.

Many NGOs do humanitarian work.

A Global Perspective

CHRONIC POVERTY

A cartogram is a type of map and chart combined. It expresses data by relative size. For example, on this cartogram, India's size is at a larger proportion than it actually is geographically because so much of its total population lives in poverty compared to other nations. Iraq, which is a relatively small nation in terms of geographic size and population, also appears larger here than it is because a vast majority of its population is chronically deprived.

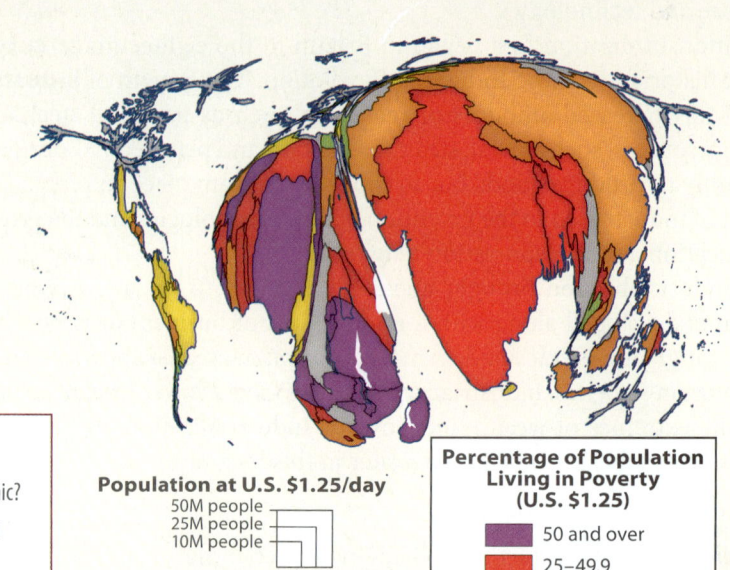

Population at U.S. $1.25/day
- 50M people
- 25M people
- 10M people

Percentage of Population Living in Poverty (U.S. $1.25)
- 50 and over
- 25–49.9
- 10–24.9
- 2–9.9
- Less than 2
- No data

SOURCE: PovcalNet: the on-line tool for poverty measurement developed by the Development Research Group of the World Bank.

Geography Connection

1. **Places and Regions** In what world regions is poverty chronic?
2. **The World in Spatial Terms** About how much of the world suffers from chronic poverty? Which hemispheres are most affected by poverty?

Middle-Income Countries

GUIDING QUESTION *What are the characteristics of middle-income countries?*

Slightly more than half of the countries in the world (51 percent) are middle income. Middle-income countries are divided into upper-middle income countries and lower-middle income countries. Upper-middle-income countries have a GNI per capita between $12,275 and $3,976. They include countries such as Albania, Algeria, Belarus, Botswana, Brazil, Cuba, the Dominican Republic, Gabon, Jamaica, Libya, Mexico, Romania, the Russian Federation, South Africa, Turkey, and Venezuela. Lower-middle-income countries have a GNI per capita between $3,975 and $1,006. They include countries such as Armenia, Belize, Cameroon, Djibouti, El Salvador, Georgia, India, Iraq, Mongolia, Pakistan, Nigeria, Ukraine, Vietnam, and Yemen.

The income and living standards of the middle class of the United States vary greatly. The same can be said about the income and living standards of middle-income countries. (Note that the upper income limit for middle-income countries is nearly 12 times greater than the lower income limit.) As more nations are elevated from low-income to middle-income status, middle-income countries are seeing a larger share of the world's poor. In fact, nearly three-quarters of the world's poor live in middle-income countries. (The global poverty line is defined as living on less than $1.25 per day.)

Nations such as India, Pakistan, Indonesia, and Nigeria have seen a rise in GNI per capita in recent years, moving them into the middle-income category.

Large wealth gaps in these countries mean that millions of the poor have become part of the middle-income group of nations, however. India, with a population of 1.2 billion, accounts for one-third of the world's poor.

It is exceedingly difficult to talk about the average standard of living in middle-income countries. Take India as an example again. Since the mid-to-late 1990s, India's economy has grown very rapidly. Most of this growth has been in the service industries, and India is now a major exporter of information technology and software services. These changes have largely taken place in India's cities, however. Despite this modernizing success, around 70 percent of Indians live in villages and follow more traditional lifestyles. More than half the population depends on agriculture for its livelihood. The caste system still plays a major role in determining people's lifestyles, too. There are 1.6 million Indian millionaires, but 700 million Indians live on $2 per day or less.

✓ **READING PROGRESS CHECK**

Explaining Why is it difficult to generalize about middle-income countries?

Low-Income Countries

GUIDING QUESTION *What are the characteristics of low-income countries?*

Low-income countries have a GNI per capita of $1,005 or less. As of 2012, 35 countries fell into this category. They included countries such as Afghanistan, Bangladesh, Cambodia, Chad, Ethiopia, Haiti, Kenya, North Korea, Malawi, Myanmar (Burma), Nepal, Somalia, Tajikistan, Tanzania, and Uganda.

As mentioned earlier, income alone does not give the full picture of standard of living. When measuring poverty, experts turn to other **indicators**, or gauges. The most useful are those called human-development indicators. These indicators relate to the quality of life, such as infant mortality rate, percentage of children who are underweight, life expectancy, access to contraception, literacy, gender equality, public dollars spent on health per person, and access to clean drinking water.

As you can imagine, these poorest nations rank low in human-development indicators. In Afghanistan, for example, one-third of children are underweight, and life expectancy is only 44 years. Compare that to the United States, where 1 percent of children are underweight and life expectancy is 78.

Sociologists have come up with several explanations as to why some countries are mired in poverty. Structural functionalists maintain that some countries are poverty-stricken because they failed to modernize. So-called modernization theory holds that values of traditional societies prevent the nations from developing economically.

Other sociologists put forth the notion that many poor nations are poor because they are economically dominated by the industrialized countries. This relationship began in the colonial era when wealthy and powerful nations took control of undeveloped countries to extract their natural resources.

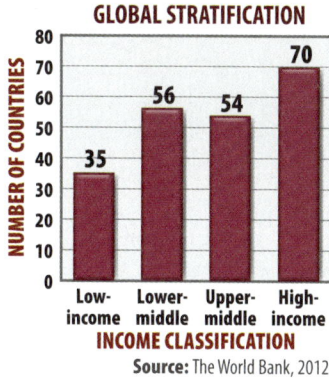

GLOBAL STRATIFICATION

Low-income: 35
Lower-middle: 56
Upper-middle: 54
High-income: 70

INCOME CLASSIFICATION

Source: The World Bank, 2012

▲ **GRAPH**

▶ **CRITICAL THINKING**

1. *Comparing* How does the number of low-income countries compare to the number of high-income countries?

2. *Analyzing Visuals* How many countries have a high income?

indicator a measurement, based on some standard or system, taken to gauge the status of the whole

Low-income nations have fewer resources to help them modernize as industrialized nations. Below, children making clothes in modern-day Saigon, Vietnam.

▶ **CRITICAL THINKING**

Describing What characteristics of high-income nations make them better equipped to be economically successful?

Social Stratification 229

Quick Case Study

WHAT MAKES A NATION LOW INCOME OR HIGH INCOME?
Inequality exists globally. How can you identify low-income and high-income nations?

Procedure
1. Have students choose five nations from a world map or globe.
2. Ask students to find the gross domestic product (GDP) of each nation.

Analysis
As you locate the GDP of each nation, consider these questions:
1. Does the nation's GDP make it a low-income or high-income nation?
2. What generalizations can you make about low-income and high-income nations and poverty?
3. What conclusions can you draw about a nation's GDP and global inequality?

Many former colonies, though technically independent, remain politically and economically dependent on their former colonizers. In addition, some countries have become dependent on economically powerful nations, such as Japan and the United States. This dependency is referred to as *neocolonialism*. Dependency theory also maintains that rich countries use economic aid and other assistance to maintain control over weaker, poorer countries.

Some people argue that globalization causes or contributes to global stratification. **Globalization** is the development of an increasingly integrated global economy. It is closely tied to the integration of cultures and government policies. Globalization is based upon free trade, the free flow of investment dollars, and the use of cheaper foreign labor. Large corporations now conduct their operations on a global scale. To produce their goods, they use the materials, labor force, and markets in whatever country gives them the greatest advantage. The problem with this, critics of globalization argue, is that the economic power of multinational corporations and global markets begins to eclipse the ability of poor countries to manage their economies. Globalization, while it may benefit rich nations, exploits the conditions of poor nations and limits their economic development.

globalization the development of an increasingly integrated global economy

☑ **READING PROGRESS CHECK**

Analyzing What do human-development indicators tell us about low-income countries?

LESSON 4 REVIEW

Reviewing Vocabulary
1. *Defining* What is global stratification?
2. *Making Connections* How did industrialization lead to modernization?

Using Your Notes
3. *Explaining* Use the notes in your graphic organizer to describe the ways in which the globe is stratified.

Answering the Guiding Questions
4. *Identifying* What are the characteristics of high-income countries?

5. *Identifying* What are the characteristics of middle-income countries?

6. *Identifying* What are the characteristics of low-income countries?

Writing Activity
7. *Informative/Explanatory* Describe, in your own words, the strengths and weaknesses of using GNI per capita to characterize global stratification.

CHAPTER 8 Assessment

Directions: On a separate sheet of paper, answer the questions below. Make sure you read carefully and answer all parts of the questions.

Lesson Review

Lesson 1

1 *Assessing* Why does the number of social classes in a society vary? Do you think it is beneficial to a society to have more or fewer social classes? Explain.

2 *Diagramming* Create a diagram to contrast reasons for inequality, as viewed through perspectives of functionalism, conflict theory, and symbolic interactionism.

Lesson 2

3 *Explaining* Would it be accurate to state that most Americans are middle class? Would it be accurate to state that most Americans think of themselves as middle class? Explain.

4 *Predicting* The text explains that the poverty rate of female-headed households is double that of male-headed households. What do you think caused this to be the case? Do you predict this will change in the future? Explain.

Lesson 3

5 *Comparing and Contrasting* Is it possible for horizontal mobility or vertical mobility to occur during intergenerational mobility? Explain your answer by defining each of these types of mobility.

6 *Identifying Central Issues* Is the role of ascribed status important in a caste system? Explain.

Lesson 4

7 *Interpreting Significance* What is the connection between the Industrial Revolution and social classes?

8 *Making Connections* Income alone does not give the full picture of standard of living. Why not?

DBQ Analyzing Primary Sources

Use the document to answer the following questions.

PRIMARY SOURCE

Average Annual Expenditures of All Consumer Units by Race, Latino Origin, and Age of Householder: 2009

Type	All consumer units	White and all other races	Asian	African American	Latino	Age of Householder Under 25 years	Age of Householder 65 years old and over
Food	6,372	6,585	7,565	4,524	6,094	4,179	4,901
Housing	16,895	17,224	20,395	13,503	15,983	9,735	13,196
Apparel and services	1,725	1,704	2,150	1,755	2,002	1,396	1,068
Transportation	7,658	7,950	8,784	5,302	7,156	5,334	5,409
Health care	3,126	3,351	2,498	1,763	1,568	676	4,846
Education	1,068	1,080	2,327	591	707	1,910	162
Personal insurance and pensions	5,471	5,674	7,117	3,550	4,230	1,988	1,856

U.S. Census Bureau, *Statistical Abstract of the United States: 2012*

The table presents data related to expenditures of American households. Studying the table should lead you to inferences regarding income levels and budgets.

9 *Analyzing Primary Sources* Based on the information in the chapter and this document, what conclusions could reasonably be drawn regarding the availability of health care to African Americans and Latinos as compared to availability of health care to all groups? Explain.

10 *Synthesizing* Based on the document and the information in the chapter, what overall conclusion would you draw regarding the distribution of economic resources related to social class and ethnicity? Write a short essay to explain.

Need Extra Help?

If You've Missed Question	1	2	3	4	5	6	7	8	9	10
Go to page	204	209–211	212–215	217	222	223–224	227	226–230	204–219	204–219

Social Stratification

CHAPTER 8 Assessment

Directions: On a separate sheet of paper, answer the questions below. Make sure you read carefully and answer all parts of the questions.

Exploring the Essential Questions

11 *Drawing Conclusions* Survival rates and loss of life pursuant to the famous *Titanic* sinking can be said to provide insight into social classes. Among first-class passengers, only 3 percent of women died and no children lost their lives. Among third-class passengers, 45 percent of the women died and 70 percent of children lost their lives. In total, 76 percent of the third-class passengers died and 40 percent of first-class passengers died. Based on these percentages, what implications would you draw regarding the impact of social classes? Is it a relevant factor that third-class passengers were restricted to lower decks so they were farther away from the lifeboats than first-class passengers were? Explain. Support your responses with information from the chapter.

21st Century Skills

CREATING AND USING GRAPHS, CHARTS, DIAGRAMS AND TABLES

12 *Creating Graphs and Charts* Consider the information you have learned about social stratification and social class, social classes in the United States, and types of social mobility. Then design a chart, diagram, or other visual to explain how each of these helps you understand the others.

College and Career Readiness Skills

13 *Exploring the Issues* You are the assistant manager of a clothing store. There is a position open for a salesperson. The store manager has narrowed the decision to two candidates. One is trying to supplement her family's income through working. The other is clearly from a middle-class background and wants extra income to buy more clothes for herself. The store manager, who has a class bias, thinks the middle-class candidate should be hired. You disagree. Based on information in the chapter, brainstorm a list of your ideas regarding this situation, knowing that you will edit these thoughts before you present them to your manager. Additionally, conduct online research to find information regarding benefits that can come of hiring people from economically disadvantaged backgrounds. Write a summary of the information you discover and include sources with your summary.

Critical Thinking

14 *Making Inferences* Social stratification and social class arise from historical events—and people's current perceptions and misperceptions. You read about Dr. Seuss's book featuring Sneetch characters. Write a children's story or picture book of your own to show the tendency of humans to arrange themselves according to social class. Then write a short essay, based on information in the chapter, to explain how your book or story accomplishes this task.

Research and Presentation

15 *Gathering Information* The National Center for Children in Poverty measures poverty rates for children in the United States. Visit its web site and research information for your state. In a couple of paragraphs, summarize the information you learn about poverty related to early childhood and adolescents in your state.

16 *Organizing* At the same web site you used in the previous activity, research projects that would be feasible to complete in your town. If it is not feasible to complete any of the projects based on time or other limitations for your class, you may create a presentation to explain how a project would benefit children or adolescents. If it is feasible to complete the project, as a class, select a project to complete and work together to carry it out. Then provide a presentation to your class or the school regarding the project, your role in the project, and what you learned from working on the project.

Need Extra Help?

If You've Missed Question	11	12	13	14	15	16
Go to page	204–219	212–219	204–225	204–215	212–219	212–219

Inequalities of Race and Ethnicity

ESSENTIAL QUESTIONS • What challenges do minority groups face? • What are the causes and effects of racial and ethnic discrimination in society?

networks

There's More Online about inequalities of race and ethnicity.

CHAPTER 9

Technology & Society
High-Tech Hate

Lesson 1
Minority, Race, and Ethnicity

Lesson 2
Racial and Ethnic Relations

Lesson 3
Theories of Prejudice and Discrimination

Lesson 4
Minority Groups in the United States

Sociology Matters...

News stories and statistics suggest that African Americans and white Americans live in two different worlds. A survey conducted by the Pew Research Center showed that they see the world differently, too. More than two out of five African Americans thought there was a great deal of discrimination against members of their group. Only one in eight whites thought there was a lot of discrimination against African Americans. Why are there racial and ethnic inequalities?

◄ Many Americans see the world differently depending on their race or ethnicity.

Jose Luis Pelaez/age fotostock

CHAPTER 9
Technology & Society

High-Tech Hate

The Internet has created an all-too-handy platform for hate groups to reach out to others and spread their messages.

Hatred toward minority groups—for example, Jews, African Americans, or homosexuals—is not new. But the tools used by groups devoted to racism, discrimination, and violence to spread their messages and find like-minded followers have changed. The Internet has emerged as a favored medium of white supremacists, neo-Nazis, and many other hate-inspired groups.

The Internet is a potent tool. One of its features is speed. False, malicious rumors about individuals or groups can spread rapidly, reaching millions before responsible people can refute them. The Internet is also a multimedia venue—games, music, and videos spread quickly over time and space via computers and phones. Hate-filled music, images, and experiences present a seemingly friendly and accessible aspect that can draw in the uninformed or unsuspecting. Another aspect of the Internet that makes it open to abuse by hate groups is the relative lack of filters—it is hard to keep those who spread false information from enjoying access equal to those who tell the truth.

Of course, using the Internet to spread messages of hate is a double-edged sword. Critics who watch the activities of hate groups also have a lot more information with which to work. The same power that allows hate groups to reach more people also makes it possible to monitor and combat them.

▶ **CRITICAL THINKING**
Speculating How do you suppose groups that monitor hate groups use the Internet to achieve their goals?

GROUPS THAT MONITOR HATE AND DISCRIMINATORY GROUPS

THE ANTI-DEFAMATION LEAGUE (ADL)
Although the ADL began as a group "to stop the defamation of the Jewish people and to secure justice and fair treatment to all," the organization has extended its scope to include protecting democratic ideals and civil rights for all people.

CENTER FOR NEW COMMUNITY
The Center for New Community, an organization grounded in many faith traditions, works to build a democratic and inclusive community "on the ground" nationwide.

CENTER FOR THE STUDY OF HATE AND EXTREMISM
The Center for the Study of Hate and Extremism at California State University, San Bernardino, is a nonpartisan group opposed to censorship, violence, attacks on pluralistic democracy, and falsehoods.

PENNSYLVANIA HUMAN RELATIONS COMMISSION
The Pennsylvania Human Relations Commission is dedicated to enforcing the state's anti-discrimination laws and promoting equal opportunity.

SOUTHERN POVERTY LAW CENTER (SPLC)
The SPLC is based in Montgomery, Alabama. The organization tracks hate groups, defends victims of discrimination, and provides materials to help educate students on equality and promote tolerance.

networks
There's More Online!

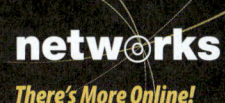

INFOGRAPHIC Explore the interactive version of the infographic on Networks.

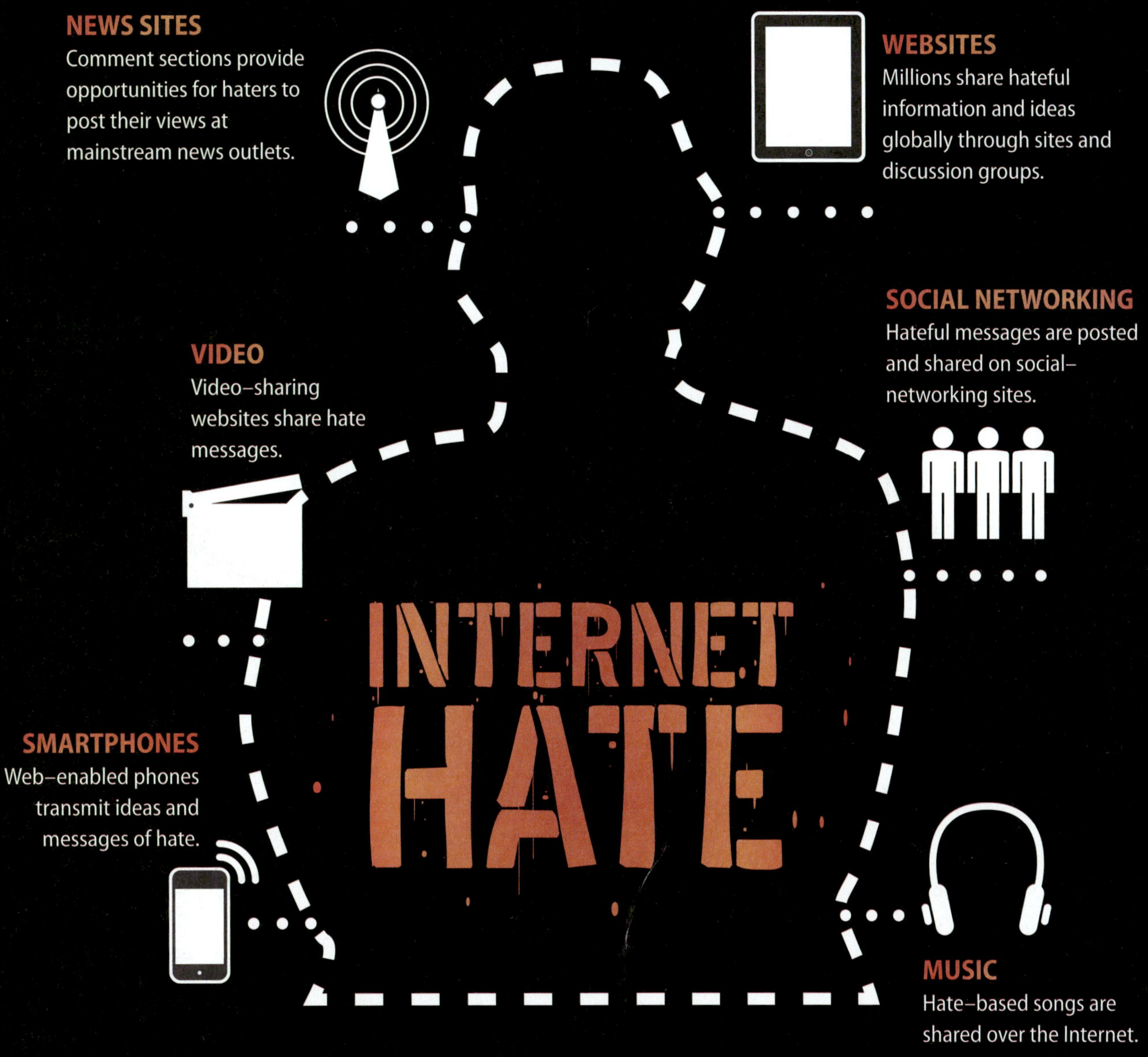

INTERNET HATE
NEWS SITES
Comment sections provide opportunities for haters to post their views at mainstream news outlets.
WEBSITES
Millions share hateful information and ideas globally through sites and discussion groups.
SOCIAL NETWORKING
Hateful messages are posted and shared on social-networking sites.
VIDEO
Video-sharing websites share hate messages.
SMARTPHONES
Web-enabled phones transmit ideas and messages of hate.
MUSIC
Hate-based songs are shared over the Internet.

Thinking Like a Sociologist

1. **Compare and Contrast**
Do you think the Internet makes it harder or easier for people to share hateful information and messages? Explain.

2. **Draw Conclusions**
Do you think the proliferation of electronic communications will help hate groups succeed or will it lead to their downfall? Explain.

networks

There's More Online!

- ☑ **GRAPH** Attitudes Toward Minorities
- ☑ **GRAPHIC ORGANIZER** Minorities, Race, and Ethnicity
- ☑ **IMAGE** Diverse Friends
- ☑ **MAP** The African Diaspora
- ☑ **SELF-CHECK QUIZ**

LESSON 1
Minority, Race, and Ethnicity

ESSENTIAL QUESTIONS • What challenges do minority groups face? • What are the causes and effects of racial and ethnic discrimination in society?

Reading HELPDESK

Academic Vocabulary
- conception

Content Vocabulary
- minority
- race
- ethnic minority

TAKING NOTES:
Key Ideas and Details

DESCRIBING As you read about minorities, race, and ethnicity, use a graphic organizer like the one below to record the characteristics of key lesson concepts.

Category	Characteristic
Minority	
Race	
Ethnicity	

IT MATTERS BECAUSE
Sociologists have specific definitions particular to their field of study for minority, race, and ethnicity. Ethnic minorities have historically been subjected to prejudice and discrimination.

Minorities

GUIDING QUESTION *What are the characteristics of a minority?*

Suppose that you and eight friends are deciding whether to go bowling or to the movies. You decide to put the question to a vote. If only three of you want to see a movie, you three are a **minority**.

But numbers alone are not the basis of the sociological definition of minority. Women in the United States outnumber males, and yet they are still referred to as a minority. African Americans in many large American cities outnumber whites. Nevertheless, they are considered minorities. For sociologists, a minority population is defined by something more than size or number. In 1945, sociologist Louis Wirth offered this sociological definition of minority:

PRIMARY SOURCE

"We may define a minority as a group of people who, because of their physical or cultural characteristics, are singled out from the others in the society in which they live for differential and unequal treatment, and who therefore regard themselves as objects of collective discrimination. The existence of a minority in a society implies the existence of a corresponding dominant group with higher social status and greater privileges."

—"The Problem of Minority Groups"

Based on Wirth's definition, a minority has several key features:
1. *A minority has distinctive physical or cultural characteristics that can be used to separate members of the minority from the majority.* Physical characteristics may include skin color, facial features, and disabilities. Cultural characteristics may include accent, religion, language, and parentage. In the past, some people have been forced to carry papers or wear badges that marked them as members of a minority. For example,

236

in Nazi-controlled Germany, Jews in German-occupied areas were forced to wear yellow stars to separate them from non-Jewish citizens.

2. *The minority is dominated by the majority.* The majority holds an unequal share of the society's desired goods, services, and privileges. The minority has fewer opportunities to attain these socially desirable goals. The best jobs are hard for minorities to get because of a lack of education or unfair hiring practices.

3. *Members of the majority often consider minority traits to be inferior.* This presumed inferiority can be used to justify unequal treatment. For example, a majority may justify job discrimination by depicting members of a minority as shiftless or lazy.

4. *Members of a minority have a common sense of identity and strong group loyalty.* The majority's efforts to keep a minority isolated create empathy among members of a minority group. Within both a minority and a majority, there is a "consciousness of kind." Members of both groups employ a "we" and "they" vocabulary.

5. *Membership in the minority group is an ascribed status applied at birth by the majority.* The difficulty of escaping this ascribed status is especially true when it is based on physical characteristics such as race.

minority a group of people who, because of physical or cultural traits, are differentiated from the dominant group in a society and treated unequally

✓ READING PROGRESS CHECK

Interpreting What is significant about minority being an ascribed status?

Defining Race

GUIDING QUESTION *Is there a scientific basis for race?*

Members of a **race** share certain biologically inherited physical characteristics that are considered important within a society. People use characteristics such as skin color, hair texture, facial features, head form, and height to determine race.

race people sharing certain inherited physical characteristics that are considered important within a society

A Global Perspective

THE AFRICAN DIASPORA

Between the 1400s and 1800s, perhaps as many as 12 million Africans were taken forcibly from their homelands and shipped to the Americas and elsewhere as part of the Atlantic slave trade. Well over 90 percent of these enslaved people were taken to the West Indies and South America.

The slave trade was a horrific assault on African cultures. But this enormous migration, also called the "African Diaspora," changed and enriched life in the Americas as the various African cultures mixed with European and Native American cultures to produce a new, African American identity.

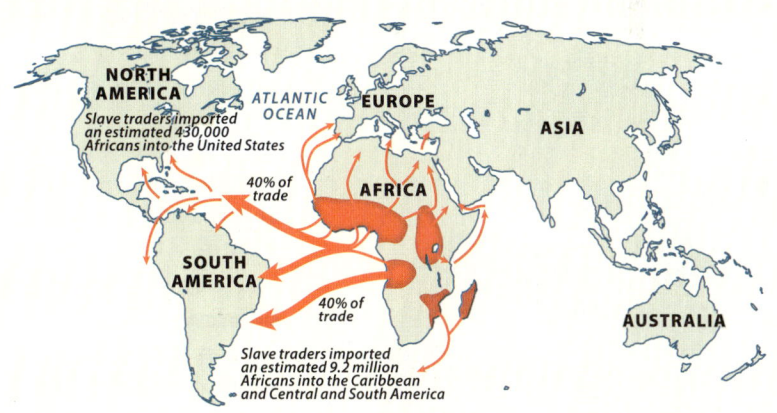

Geography Connection

1. **Places and Regions** From what part of Africa were most of the enslaved people taken?
2. **Human Systems** How do you think the circumstances of this African diaspora have affected the development of African American culture? Explain.

Traditionally anthropologists maintained that there were three races—Negroid, Mongoloid, and Caucasoid—but today there is a much more complex understanding of race.

Certain physical features were long associated with particular races. Scientists, however, have long known that there is no such thing as distinct biological races among humans. According to racial formation theory, racial categories are socially constructed and have changed over time to exclude or include different ethnic groups. In sociology, the social, political, and economic processes through which a population is classified a "race" is known as "racialization." Most scientists today consider racial classifications to be arbitrary and misleading.

Along with attempting to identify races on the basis of physical features, some writers in the past argued that certain of these characteristics were superior and others inferior. In fact, physical characteristics are superior only in the sense that they provide advantages for living in particular environments. For example, a narrower opening between eyelids protects against bright light and extreme cold, conditions in areas such as Siberia and Alaska. A darker skin is better able to withstand sun damage. But these physical differences are controlled by a very few genes. In fact, geneticists say that there may be more genetic differences between a tall person and a short person than between two people of different so-called races who are the same height. Only about six genes in the human cell control skin color; dozens of them are needed to determine a person's height.

There is no scientific evidence for distinct human races. And there is no scientific evidence connecting any "racial" characteristic with innate superiority or inferiority. There is, for example, no evidence of innate differences in athleticism or intelligence among the various races. For sociologists, social attitudes and characteristics that relate to race are more important than physical differences.

☑ **READING PROGRESS CHECK**

Paraphrasing Why have scientists rejected the idea of biological races?

Ethnicity

GUIDING QUESTION *What is an ethnic minority?*

The term *ethnicity* comes from the Greek word *ethnos*, originally meaning "people" or "nation." Thus, the Greek root refers to cultural and national identity. Today, an  is socially identified by unique characteristics related to culture or nationality. Just as physical characteristics define racial minorities, cultural differences define ethnic minorities.

An ethnic minority is a subculture defined by its own language, religion, values, beliefs, norms, and customs. Like any subculture, it is part of the larger culture—its members work in the majority, or host, economy. They send their children through the host educational system and are subject to the laws of the land.

Ethnic minorities are also separate from the larger culture. The separation may be maintained by the ethnic minority because its members wish to preserve their cultural and national origins. The separation could also result from the majority erecting barriers that prevent the ethnic group from blending in with the larger culture.

Negative attitudes toward ethnic minorities exist in part because of ethnocentrism. *Ethnocentrism* involves judging others in terms of one's own cultural standards. Ethnocentrism results

---

ethnic minority group identified by cultural, national, or religious characteristics

Most of the American population identifies itself as white (72 percent). Thirteen percent identify themselves as African American, 5 percent as Asian, and less than 1 percent as Native American or Native Alaskan. A growing number consider themselves members of more than one race (about 3 percent of the population).

▶ **CRITICAL THINKING**

Making Connections According to scientists and sociologists, what is problematic about identifying someone's race?

Connecting Sociology to Economics

ATTITUDES TOWARD MINORITIES

Negative attitudes about minorities are not uncommon. But research suggests that attitudes toward minorities change as overall levels of wealth rise or fall.

This graph measures responses to the question "Is the city or area where you live a good place or not a good place for racial or ethnic minorities?"

The part of the graph in red shows how, for countries with average annual incomes below $8,000 (below 4.0 on the Log GDP scale), the percentage of people answering "yes" to that question goes down as incomes rise. But in countries where the average income is $8,000 or above, the opposite is true: As incomes go up, the percentage of people answering "yes" to that question goes up.

There are some theories behind this pattern. For example, some experts think that income inequality often grows in poor countries that are just beginning to achieve growth. But once societies achieve a certain level of wealth, they begin to develop a greater commitment to equality. The push to include all members of society increases.

The theories may be complex. But the basic message is clear: Acceptance of minority groups varies based on economic factors.

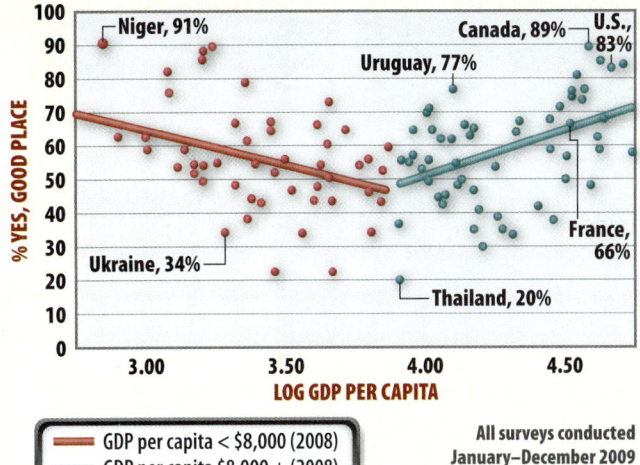

This graph shows how acceptance of minority groups varies in countries around the world depending on Gross Domestic Product.

▶ CRITICAL THINKING
1. **Synthesizing** In which type of country are people most likely to believe that their communities are good places for minorities to live?
2. **Identifying Central Issues** What does this graph suggest about the relationship between tolerance and economics?

---

from the feeling of "us," one's own group, versus "them," other groups. People in the majority may consider the cultural standards of other groups to be inferior. Because members of ethnic minorities do not measure up to the majority's **conception**, or idea, of appropriate ways of behaving, that majority may assume that something is wrong with them. The result is prejudice and discrimination.

conception idea

✓ READING PROGRESS CHECK

Making Connections How is ethnocentrism connected to a sense of shared identity in the majority?

LESSON 1 REVIEW

Reviewing Vocabulary
1. **Contrasting** How are the ideas of race and ethnicity different?
2. **Synthesizing** If race and ethnicity are different, why can both races and ethnic groups be minorities?

Using Your Notes
3. **Summarizing** Based on the notes you took in your graphic organizer, identify an example of a racial and an ethnic minority in the United States.

Answering the Guiding Questions
4. **Evaluating** What are the characteristics of a minority?
5. **Analyzing** Is there a scientific basis for race?
6. **Drawing Conclusions** What is an ethnic minority?

Writing Activity
7. **Informative/Explanatory** Using the text's explanation of Wirth's definition of *minority*, write a description of *majority*.

Inequalities of Race and Ethnicity 239

networks

There's More Online!

- ☑ **CARTOON** Salad Bowl and Melting Pot
- ☑ **GRAPHIC ORGANIZER** Assimilation and Conflict
- ☑ **IMAGE** Tejano Culture
- ☑ **SELF-CHECK QUIZ**

LESSON 2
Racial and Ethnic Relations

ESSENTIAL QUESTIONS • What challenges do minority groups face? • What are the causes and effects of racial and ethnic discrimination in society?

Reading HELPDESK

Academic Vocabulary
- accommodation

Content Vocabulary
- assimilation
- cultural pluralism
- subjugation
- de jure segregation
- de facto segregation
- genocide

TAKING NOTES:
Key Ideas and Details

DEFINING As you read about racial and ethnic relations, use a graphic organizer like the one below to define patterns of assimilation and conflict.

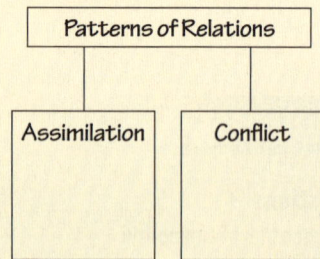

IT MATTERS BECAUSE
Patterns of racial and ethnic relations take two forms: assimilation and conflict. Patterns of assimilation include Anglo-conformity, the melting pot, cultural pluralism, and accommodation. Conflict patterns include genocide, population transfer, and subjugation.

Patterns of Assimilation

GUIDING QUESTION *How do assimilation and accommodation differ?*

Generally, minority groups are either accepted—which leads to assimilation—or rejected—which leads to conflict. Within these two broad approaches is a range of outcomes.

Assimilation refers to the blending of a minority group into the dominant society. When a racial or ethnic minority is integrated into a society, its members fully participate in all aspects of the society. Assimilation differs from acculturation. Acculturation is the process by which a culture is passed on to a new generation. Assimilation, the result of cultural mixing, follows one of four patterns.

Anglo-conformity has been the most prevalent pattern of assimilation in the United States. *Anglo* indicates an American of English descent. In Anglo-conformity, immigrants are accepted as long as they conform to dominant Anglo standards. In this way, Anglo-American institutions are maintained—and remain dominant. Anglo-conformity is the least egalitarian type of assimilation because the immigrant minority is required to conform. By implication, it must either give up or suppress its own values.

The metaphor for a second pattern of assimilation is the melting pot. In this pattern of assimilation all ethnic and racial minorities voluntarily blend together. Older history textbooks, in describing the immigrant experience in the United States, often referred to a melting pot of cultures. There is some question about how much fusing of cultures has really taken place, however.

240

Instead of a melting pot, many sociologists now use the metaphor of a tossed salad, in which different traditions and cultures exist side by side. The cultures of the Tejanos in Texas and the Creoles of New Orleans are examples of distinct cultures. This pattern of assimilation is called **cultural pluralism**. Ethnic and immigrant groups maintain some of their uniqueness while they have an influence on the society at large. Because of the large number of Latino immigrants in the United States, for example, many public school systems have instituted bilingual education programs. The government routinely makes official forms available in both English and Spanish, many churches conduct services in both languages, and cable television stations offer English and Spanish audio tracks. The popularity of different ethnic foods also shows the impact of cultural pluralism on American society.

Accommodation is an extreme form of cultural pluralism. It occurs when a minority maintains its own culturally unique way of life. The minority learns to deal with, or accommodate, the dominant culture when necessary but remains independent in language and culture. The Cubans in Miami and the Amish in Pennsylvania are examples of distinct groups within larger communities that have maintained separate identities. Children in these groups are socialized to adopt the traditions and values of the group. That helps maintain the group's culture.

assimilation the blending or fusing of a minority group into the dominant society

cultural pluralism the desire of a group to maintain some sense of identity separate from the dominant group

accommodation a choice by a minority group to maintain its own culturally unique way of life independent of the dominant culture

✓ **READING PROGRESS CHECK**

Contrasting What is the difference between cultural pluralism and accommodation?

Connecting Sociology to Human Geography

TEJANO CULTURE

The border between the United States and Mexico is a political creation established by diplomats long ago. But it is also a unique cultural epicenter where different peoples come together, each in close proximity to places where their original cultures hold sway. On the United States side of the border, many Mexican Americans—not to mention immigrants from other Latin American nations—retain close connections to their homeland. In this area, the presence of their Latino cultures clearly demonstrates the concept of cultural pluralism.

In Texas, Tejanos—residents of Hispanic or Latin American descent—actively celebrate the many strands of their cultural history. It is common in this region to see Mexican flags flying alongside American flags, an expression of the desire of Tejanos to maintain links to their country of origin while simultaneously honoring their homeland. Tejanos have also been successful in getting the state of Texas to share in their celebrations. The Texas Historical Commission holds events and shares information designed to promote and celebrate Tejano culture in the state. Less formally, in communities and cities throughout the borderland region, music, food, architecture, and many other cultural expressions reflect the influence of Mexico or Spain.

Cultural pluralism also places some burdens on the dominant culture. In California, pressure to help students preserve their original languages places significant demands on the educational system. These demands help create pressure on cultural groups to assimilate more fully into the larger culture.

Music is an important and thriving part of Tejano culture.

▶ **CRITICAL THINKING**

1. **Defending** Why might a member of a minority group want to maintain parts of his or her culture?
2. **Differentiating** In many parts of the borderlands, Latinos are a majority of the local population. Why are they still considered a minority group?

Inequalities of Race and Ethnicity

Connecting Sociology to Political Science

MINORITY VOTING BEHAVIOR

Consider the position of minority groups in a democratic society such as the United States. Here is a situation in which minorities, in spite of their weakness relative to the larger society, have a real voice. How do such groups behave?

You might be surprised to know that minority groups typically have a low level of voter registration and voter turnout compared to the majority white population in the United States. In 2010, for example, minority groups such as African Americans and Latinos registered and voted in relatively low numbers compared to white Americans.

Of course, these numbers change somewhat from election to election. In 2008, African American women turned out to vote at a higher rate than any other demographic group. One explanation is that the race for the main office at stake in this election—president of the United States—featured African American Barack Obama.

The voting preferences of minority groups are also distinctive. In 2008, 95 percent of African American voters voted for Obama, as did 67 percent of Latinos and 62 percent of Asian Americans. (Just 43 percent of white voters did so.) Similar patterns held in the 2010 congressional elections. Among African American voters, 89 percent voted Democratic. Latinos and Asian Americans voted Democratic at 60 and 58 percent, respectively. Of white voters, though, 60 percent cast their ballots for Republicans.

Minority groups typically participate less fully in the electoral process compared to white voters.

▶ **CRITICAL THINKING**

1. **Defending** Why might members of minority groups be less likely to register and vote compared to members of the majority group?
2. **Differentiating** How would you characterize the voting behaviors of the three main minority groups—African Americans, Latinos, and Asian Americans?

Patterns of Conflict

GUIDING QUESTION *What are the three patterns of racial and ethnic conflict?*

In looking for patterns of conflict, sociologists examine historical records and current events. They have identified three basic patterns that dominant cultures take when they reject minorities: *subjugation, population transfer,* and *genocide.*

Subjugation is the most common pattern of conflict. A subjugated minority is denied equal access to the larger society's culture and lifestyle. Subjugation takes two forms.

De jure segregation is based on the law. *De jure* segregation ruled many aspects of daily life in the United States during the latter part of the nineteenth century and the first half of the twentieth century. In *Brown v. Board of Education of Topeka* (1954), the Supreme Court made segregation illegal in public education. That decision was one of several court decisions and laws in the 1950s and 1960s that dismantled *de jure* segregation. Another example is the *apartheid* policy of racial segregation practiced in South Africa from 1948 to 1994. That policy—instituted by the dominant white minority—put severe legal limitations on the black majority and other nonwhites.

Subjugation may also arise from everyday practices rather than by law. The term *de facto* describes an effect that is real although not based in law. **De facto segregation** operates when, for example, neighboring homeowners agree among themselves not to sell to members of certain ethnic groups or races. *De facto*

---

subjugation the process by which a minority group is denied equal access to the benefits of a society

***de jure* segregation** the denial of equal access based on the law

***de facto* segregation** the denial of equal access based on common prejudice

discrimination exists when people of certain backgrounds are denied promotions because of widely held stereotypes.

In the United States, both *de facto* and *de jure* discrimination have been made illegal by civil rights laws and rulings in federal court. Under these protections, discrimination based on race, color, sex, disability, religion, familial status, or national origin is illegal. The system of *de jure* segregation has been dismantled. The difficulty of proving bias, however, means that *de facto* segregation persists.

In population transfer, a minority is forced either to move to a remote location or to leave entirely the territory controlled by the majority. This policy is exemplified by the movement of Native Americans from their traditional lands to reservations. In a dramatic example, in the 1830s some 16,000 Cherokee were forced to march from the southeastern United States to what is now Oklahoma. An estimated 4,000 Cherokee died along the route, known as the "Trail of Tears."

More recent examples arose in the 1990s, when the nation of Yugoslavia broke into several separate ethnic states. While some ethnic groups hoped to establish their own homelands, other groups also lived in those areas. The desire for ethnically "pure" states produced several instances of forced removal of one ethnic group from the territory another group wanted as its own. Serbians—who coined the term *ethnic cleansing* for their actions—began this practice by forcing the removal of Muslims in Bosnia and Kosovo. The Serbians were not the only perpetrators, however. Croatians expelled Serbians in their own attempt at ethnic cleansing, as did Albanians living in Kosovo.

At the extreme, conflict takes the form of **genocide**, the systematic effort to destroy an entire population. One of the best-known examples is the Holocaust, Adolf Hitler's attempt to destroy all European Jews during the 1930s and 1940s. Nearly two out of every three European Jews were killed during the Holocaust. Less well known is the "Rape of Nanking," begun in 1937, during which the Japanese massacred an estimated 260,000 to 350,000 Chinese men, women, and children.

Tragically, genocide campaigns are more common in world history than might be supposed. Even in recent times the world has witnessed horrible acts of genocide. For example, in 1994 the Hutu ethnic group of Rwanda slaughtered 500,000 to 800,000 of the minority Tutsis.

✓ **READING PROGRESS CHECK**

Explaining Whose perspective is reflected in use of the term *ethnic cleansing* for population transfer? Why?

CARTOON

SALAD BOWL AND MELTING POT
Two patterns of assimilation have been described by the metaphors of a "melting pot" and a "tossed salad."

▶ **CRITICAL THINKING**

1. *Analyzing Visuals* Explain the two patterns of assimilation represented by the illustrations of the tossed salad and the melting pot.

2. *Drawing Inferences* What in your opinion are the pros and cons of the two patterns of assimilation?

genocide the systematic effort to destroy an entire population

---

LESSON 2 REVIEW

Reviewing Vocabulary

1. *Sequencing* Rank the four patterns of assimilation from most accepting of minority culture to least accepting. Explain your rankings.

2. *Comparing and Contrasting* How are *de jure* and *de facto* segregation similar? How are they different?

Using Your Notes

3. *Analyzing* Based on your notes, what is the difference between cultural assimilation and conflict?

Answering the Guiding Questions

4. *Analyzing* How do assimilation and accommodation differ?

5. *Making Connections* What are the three patterns of racial and ethnic conflict?

Writing Activity

6. *Argument* International legal bodies have been working to define ethnic cleansing and make it a crime. Write a paragraph for or against these efforts, explaining your reasoning.

Inequalities of Race and Ethnicity **243**

FOCUS on research

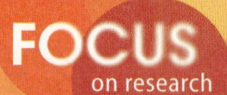

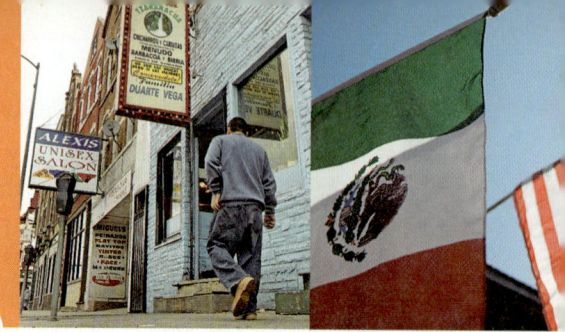

Survey Research

CCSS

Narratives of Mexican American Women

In this study, Alma García summarizes the conflicted views of three Mexican American women. The narrative here describes the tensions of a life that includes aspects of two cultures. García describes the forces pulling on the women from opposite directions as they seek to fit into one world while maintaining links to another.

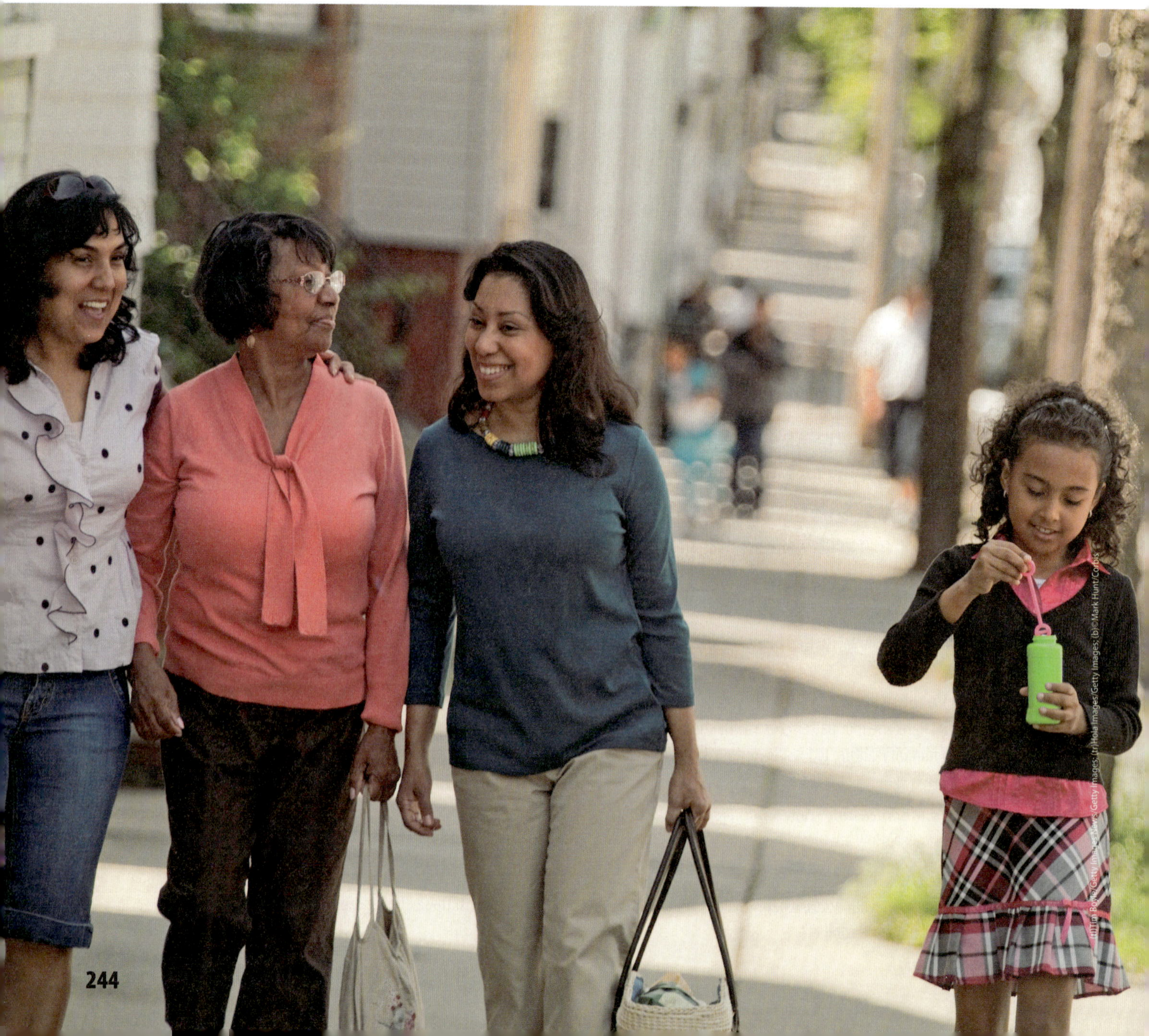

PRIMARY SOURCE

"The life history sketches of María, Sonia, and Carmen reveal the tensions and contradictions present in the lives of the Mexican American women in this study. Their parents came to the United States in search of the American Dream: the opportunity for better lives than the ones their families had in Mexico. They struggled to provide their children with the means to achieve upward mobility, such as obtaining a university degree. . . .

Respondents described themselves in ways that capture the meaning of emergent ethnicity. They have Mexican surnames but are Americans, speak English and Spanish, prefer life in the United States, and only occasionally visit Mexico, where their relatives often criticize them for being Americanized. They live in predominantly Mexican immigrant and Mexican American neighborhoods where, as one student said, Mexico 'was all around them.' . . . These women's narratives reveal the shifting nature of ethnic identity by using various ethnic labels interchangeably. They call themselves Mexicans, Mexicanas, Mexican Americans, Americans, and Latinas in specific situations and interchangeably. They use 'Latina' when they find themselves in a group of women from other countries in Latin America. They use 'American' when they describe instances of ethnic profiling by school administrators and law enforcement officers. They adopt the ethnic label of 'Mexican American' to distinguish themselves from Mexican immigrants. Sometimes they use a combination of all these ethnic labels. The women recalled that as 'Mexican Americans,' they wanted to fight for their civil rights as 'Americans,' but know that they are 'Mexicanas' living in an American world, one that sees them and their parents as 'Mexicans' and 'foreigners' or 'illegal aliens.' . . .

Their university experiences mirror the ethnic prejudices and discrimination prevalent in the United States. The students recalled painful ethnic episodes that increased their feelings of alienation. They (re)constructed their identities as a coping mechanism. They created a Mexican American student community of shared identity. They adopted visible signs of imagined ethnicity: language, dress, lifestyle, music, art, and other aspects of Mexican material culture. Their attempts to cope with a hostile university environment led to confrontations with their parents, who did not understand their daughters' emergent identities. . . .

The students did not resolve the tensions and contradictions of second-generation Mexican American women. They saw themselves as Americans when others stereotyped them as foreigners. They saw themselves as foreigners when with Mexican-born family and friends who, in turn, saw them as Americanized Mexicans. As women, they defined themselves as independent and equal when their fathers exerted patriarchal authority over them. In sum, an unfolding process of constructing emergent identities and negotiated spaces shaped their lives."

—from *Narratives of Mexican American Women*, 2004

> "They call themselves Mexicans, Mexicanas, Mexican Americans, Americans, and Latinas in specific situations and interchangeably. They use 'Latina' when they find themselves in a group of women from other countries in Latin America. They use 'American' when they describe instances of ethnic profiling by school administrators and law enforcement officers."

Working With the Research

1. **Explaining** The author writes of "tensions and contradictions" in the stories of María, Sonia, and Carmen. To what do you think this refers?
2. **Describing** What does the author mean by "emergent identities"?
3. **Making Connections** What does it mean that the women regularly chose different terminology to describe themselves and their ethnic identities?

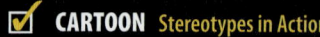

There's More Online!

- ☑ **CARTOON** Stereotypes in Action
- ☑ **CHART** Theoretical Perspectives: Prejudice and Discrimination
- ☑ **GRAPHIC ORGANIZER** Prejudice and Discrimination
- ☑ **IMAGE** Organized Hate
- ☑ **MAP** Hate Groups in the United States
- ☑ **SELF-CHECK QUIZ**

LESSON 3
Theories of Prejudice and Discrimination

ESSENTIAL QUESTIONS • What challenges do minority groups face? • What are the causes and effects of racial and ethnic discrimination in society?

Reading HELPDESK

Academic Vocabulary
- bias
- discrimination

Content Vocabulary
- prejudice
- racism
- stereotyping
- hate crime
- self-fulfilling prophecy

TAKING NOTES:
Key Ideas and Details

MAKING CONNECTIONS As you read about prejudice and discrimination, use a graphic organizer like the one below to record key concepts.

Bias:
Prejudice:
Racism:
Discrimination:
Stereotype:
Hate crime:

IT MATTERS BECAUSE

Prejudice involves attitudes, while discrimination is about behavior. Prejudice often leads to discrimination. In some instances, discrimination creates prejudiced attitudes through stereotyping. The three major sociological perspectives offer different explanations of prejudice and discrimination.

Prejudice, Racism, and Discrimination

GUIDING QUESTION *How is discrimination different from prejudice?*

Individuals have many preferences for or against one thing or another. Some are the result of taste—you may prefer strawberries to blueberries or long sleeves to short sleeves. Some of these preferences are the result of **bias**—positive or negative preconceptions about something. Bias is more significant than mere taste because it shapes how we view the world. As a result, bias may have an effect on how we interact with others.

The word *prejudice* is sometimes used in ordinary conversation to mean the same thing as *bias*. To a sociologist, however, prejudice has a very particular meaning. In sociology, **prejudice** refers to widely held negative attitudes toward a group (minority or majority) and its individual members. Prejudice inclines members of a majority or minority group against people in other groups. The key to prejudice is that it is directed against *all* members of another group. Prejudice is not dislike for a particular person because of his or her actions; it is dislike of that person because of his or her membership in a disliked group. Prejudice arises from "us" and "them" group identities. It involves a generalization based on bias or on incomplete or slanted information.

Prejudice has great power because it is typically based on strong emotions, which can be deeply held and, therefore, often difficult to change, even in the face of overwhelming evidence. Prejudice can take many forms. **Racism** is an extreme form of prejudice based on race. It not only involves judging people unfairly, but it assumes that a person's own race or ethnic group is superior to another racial group—or to *all* other racial groups. *Sexism*—the belief that one gender is superior to another—is another extreme form of prejudice.

While prejudice involves holding biased opinions, **discrimination** is acting upon those opinions by treating people unfairly. Discrimination takes many forms, including avoiding social contact with members of minority groups, denying them positions of authority, and blocking their access to socially desirable goods, such as advanced education, well-paying jobs, expensive goods and services, or desirable neighborhoods. It can even involve such extremes as attacking or killing members of a minority group.

✓ **READING PROGRESS CHECK**

Contrasting How is prejudice different from bias?

Stereotypes and Hate Crimes

GUIDING QUESTIONS What is a stereotype? How does sociology interpret hate crimes?

In 1998, James Byrd, Jr., an African American from Texas, was chained by two white supremacists to a pickup truck and then dragged to death. That same year, college student Matthew Shepard was tied to a fence and beaten to death by two men who thought he was a homosexual.

What causes individuals to carry out such brutal crimes? Clearly extreme prejudice is involved. From where does that prejudice come? Remember that prejudice is aimed not at individuals but at all members of a group. At the base of prejudice, then, is the distorted kind of group labeling called **stereotyping**.

Stereotyping

A *stereotype* is a set of ideas—based on distortion, exaggeration, and oversimplification—applied to all members of a group. Stereotypes appear in any society. To identify some common American stereotypes, think of stock characters portrayed in movie and television comedies. The dumb blonde, the absentminded scientist, and the socially inept computer whiz are all common stereotypes.

bias negative or positive preconceptions

prejudice deeply held negative attitudes toward a group (minority or majority) and its individual members

racism an extreme form of prejudice that assumes superiority of one racial group over others

discrimination unfair treatment of a minority by the dominant group

stereotyping a labeling of a group based on distorted, exaggerated, or oversimplified images of that group

An African American minister stands outside the remains of his church, one of many African American churches deliberately destroyed in the 1990s.

▶ **CRITICAL THINKING**

Finding the Main Idea Would you classify this act of violence a hate crime? Explain.

Inequalities of Race and Ethnicity **247**

A Diverse America

HATE GROUPS IN THE UNITED STATES

Hate groups are groups with beliefs or practices that target an entire group of people for hatred or mistreatment. Each year, the Southern Poverty Law Center tracks the number of active hate groups operating in the United States. These groups include black separatists, white supremacists, neo-Nazis, and others. In 2011, there were more than 1,000 such groups active in the United States.

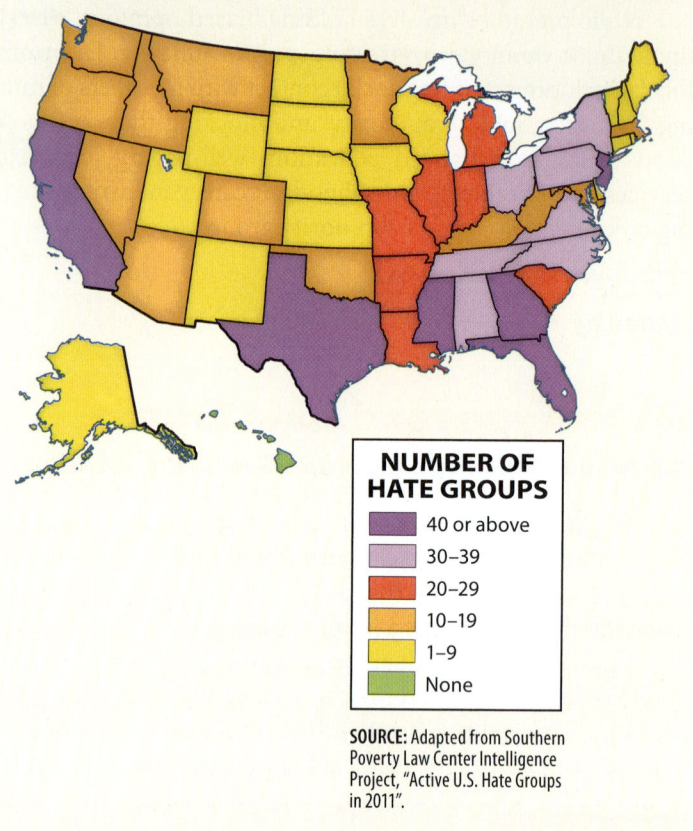

NUMBER OF HATE GROUPS
- 40 or above
- 30–39
- 20–29
- 10–19
- 1–9
- None

SOURCE: Adapted from Southern Poverty Law Center Intelligence Project, "Active U.S. Hate Groups in 2011".

Geography Connection

1. **Places and Regions** Which states had the highest number of hate groups in 2011? Which states had the lowest number?
2. **Places and Regions** How many hate groups are active in your state? Does this surprise you? Explain.
3. **Human Systems** Do you think it is important to track the numbers of such groups? Why or why not?

Comedy writers include them because they know that these characters will be widely recognized, which is true because the stereotypes are so common in American society.

How widespread is stereotyping? Various studies have shown that many different groups hold prejudiced views of other groups. Two sociologists who conducted a survey in Detroit found that Latinos were seen in negative ways by both whites and African Americans. Other studies have shown that almost half the Latinos surveyed agreed with negative statements about Asian Americans, while two-thirds of Asian Americans agreed with a negative statement about Latinos.

Once they take hold, stereotypes are difficult to shake. Even if we meet someone who does not fit the stereotype, it is easier to explain him or her as an exception than it is to reexamine—and possibly reject—the whole set of established beliefs. For example, many people believe that Asian students have a particular gift for mathematics. Suppose that Susie is one of these people. In algebra class, she sits next to an Asian student who is not doing well. Will Susie change her idea about the mathematical abilities of all Asian students as a result of this? Probably not. It will be less trouble for her to think that this one Asian student is the exception to the rule.

As the example of Asian talent at math shows, stereotypes are not always negative. Often, though, these examples of distorted thinking are negative—and very damaging to the target group. Stereotypes are sometimes created to justify unethical behavior toward minority groups. For example, the relations between the European colonists and Native Americans in very early colonial times were relatively peaceful and cooperative. As the white population of the colonies grew, however, conflicts over land and resources became more frequent and intense. To justify expansion into their territory, the colonists began conceiving of Native Americans in negative ways, viewing them as "lying, thieving, un-Christian savages" who did not deserve the rights that white settlers—who saw themselves as representing a superior civilization—deserved. This image helped the colonists defend their otherwise unjustifiable treatment of Native Americans, which included taking their land, waging war on them, and persecuting them in other ways.

Stereotypes can change over time. From colonial times until the late 1900s, white Americans sometimes stereotyped African Americans as lazy. The Black Power movement of the 1960s and urban riots that occurred in that decade created a different stereotype. Suddenly a high percentage of whites responded to one survey by saying that African Americans were too pushy, asking for too many changes too fast. In just a short time, whites came to view African Americans as overly aggressive.

Hate Crimes

A **hate crime** is a criminal act motivated by extreme prejudice. Such crimes are often crimes of violence motivated by bias related to race, religion, sexual orientation, ethnicity, or disability. Victims include, but are not limited to, African Americans, Latinos, Asian Americans, Jews, gays and lesbians, and people with disabilities. The first federal antihate-crime law was passed in 1969. It came in the wake of violence committed against African Americans during the civil rights movement and was aimed at racially motivated crimes committed against people trying to exercise their civil rights, including voting and going to school. A tougher law was passed in 2009 and named for Matthew Shepard and James Byrd. The new law extended hate crime protection to individuals regardless of what they were doing when victimized.

Data on hate crimes were not formally collected until 1990, when Congress passed the Hate Crimes Statistics Act. Since then, these statistics have been a standard part of the FBI's crime reports. In 2010, more than 6,600 hate crimes took place. Just under half were racially motivated. Religious prejudice and bias against particular sexual orientations were both at the root of nearly 20 percent of these crimes; ethnicity was the cause in nearly 13 percent. Most of the individuals committing these crimes—almost 6 out of 10—were white. Just over 18 percent were African Americans.

Each of the three chief sociological theoretical perspectives can help us understand hate crimes. The functionalist might note that members of a group are bolstering their sense of unity against a common enemy. Some hate crimes, consistent with conflict theory, are based on the belief that the victim is somehow threatening the perpetrator's livelihood or self-interest. This is the case when immigrants are attacked out of fear that they will take the jobs of the white majority. Finally, as symbolic interactionists point out, hate crimes always involve labeling. People who commit hate crimes have vocabularies filled with demeaning stereotypes that attempt to justify violence directed against the victims.

✓ **READING PROGRESS CHECK**

Explaining From a sociological point of view, why do whites commit the majority of hate crimes?

hate crime a criminal act motivated by extreme prejudice

Neo-Nazis demonstrated at the 2009 opening of the Illinois Holocaust Museum and Education Center in Skokie, Illinois. A neo-Nazi is a member of a group that shares the racist ideologies of Hitler's Nazis.

▶ **CRITICAL THINKING**

Analyzing How would a symbolic interactionist explain the gesture of this neo-Nazi?

Theoretical Perspectives on Discrimination

GUIDING QUESTION How do functionalism, conflict theory, and symbolic interactionism explain prejudice and discrimination?

Psychologists try to explain prejudice and discrimination by looking at the mental states of individuals. Sociologists, though, are more interested in how societies foster development of these attitudes and practices. Each of the three main theoretical perspectives of sociology helps shed some light on the issues of prejudice and discrimination.

The Functionalist Perspective

Functionalists focus on the functional and dysfunctional aspects of prejudice and discrimination. The chief functional benefit of fostering prejudice is that a dominant group can create a feeling of superiority over minority groups. This feeling can strengthen its members' own self-concepts.

This kind of impact became clear in an interesting study conducted by two researchers. The researchers organized boys at a summer camp into two different groups. The researchers took steps to foster competition between the two groups. Within days, the groups had developed a strong sense of group identity, complete with strongly positive views of members of their group and strongly negative attitudes toward members of the other group. The adoption of these negative views even overcame positive feelings that boys had felt for members of the other group beforehand. For instance, friends placed in different groups abandoned their friendships and called each other by the pejorative names their groupmates applied to all members of the other group.

Of course, prejudice and discrimination have dysfunctional aspects as well. When minorities are exploited or oppressed, the social, political, educational, and economic costs to society are extremely high. Denying members of a minority group educational opportunities means a society cannot benefit fully from their abilities. Furthermore, the safety and stability of the larger society are at risk because violence periodically erupts between the groups.

Theoretical Perspectives

PREJUDICE AND DISCRIMINATION

This table illustrates approaches to understanding prejudice and discrimination using concepts associated with a particular theoretical perspective. Construct some examples of your own.

Theoretical Perspective	Sociological Concept	Example
Functionalism	Ethnocentrism	White colonists used negative stereotypes as a justification for taking Native American land.
Conflict Theory	Competition for power	African Americans accuse Latinos of using their political clout to win advantages for themselves.
Symbolic Interactionism	Self-fulfilling prophecy	Members of a minority fail because of the low expectations they have for their own success based on stereotyping by the majority.

▶ **CRITICAL THINKING**

1. **Identifying** Which theoretical perspective would best explain and defend the use of affirmative action—the preference in the hiring, admission, or promotion of minorities to make up for past discrimination?

2. **Connecting Ideas** Explain how the idea of affirmative action might become a self-fulfilling prophecy for a particular minority group.

CARTOON
STEREOTYPES IN ACTION
Stereotypes can have a powerful effect on how people perceive the world.

▶ **CRITICAL THINKING**
1. *Analyzing Visuals* Why is this statement an example of a stereotype in action?
2. *Identifying Bias* How useful would be the results of surveys issued by this pollster's organization? Why?

"Thanks for taking the survey, but could you take it again? Your answers weren't very 'black.'"

The Conflict Perspective
According to conflict theory, a majority uses prejudice and discrimination as weapons of power to control a minority. The majority does this to increase its control over property, goods, and other resources. The example of stereotypes used by colonists to portray Native Americans is based on the conflict perspective.

From the conflict perspective, despite being common targets for unfair treatment by the majority group, different minorities tend to view one another as competitors rather than as allies in their struggle against the majority. Conflict among minorities, particularly African Americans and Latinos, increased in the United States as whites left cities and African Americans assumed political power. To many urban African Americans, Latinos appeared to be benefiting from the civil rights movement waged by African Americans without having taken part in that movement. Many Latinos, on the other hand, believed that African Americans used their newfound political clout to push an agenda that favored their own community at the expense of others. It remains to be seen if urban African Americans and Latinos will become allies for their mutual welfare or if they will engage in conflict over the scarce resources available to them.

The Symbolic Interactionist Perspective
According to the symbolic interactionist perspective, members of a society learn to be prejudiced in much the same way that they learn to be patriotic. Sociologist Gordon Allport described two stages in the learning of prejudice. In what he called the pregeneralized learning period, children may overhear parents make racist or prejudiced statements, but they have not yet learned to separate people by race or ethnic group. As a result, in this stage, they cannot apply those prejudiced statements to other people. By the time children reach the total rejection stage, however, they are able to use physical clues to sort people into groups. If children repeatedly hear parents malign a minority, they will reject all members of the group on all counts and in all situations.

Symbolic interactionists also point out that language itself can reflect prejudices. For example, in English, many terms that include the word *black* are negative. Such terms as *blackball, blacklist, black mark,* and *black eye* illustrate the negative slant associated with the word *black*.

These are the children whose educational opportunities were at stake in the 1954 Supreme Court case *Brown* v. *Board of Education of Topeka, Kansas,* that ruled segregation in public schools unconstitutional. In his ruling, Chief Justice Earl Warren declared: "To separate them from others of similar age and qualifications solely because of their race generates a feeling of inferiority as to their status in the community that may affect their hearts and minds in a way unlikely ever to be undone."

▶ **CRITICAL THINKING**

1. **Distinguishing** Which theoretical perspective emphasizes how people learn prejudice?
2. **Drawing Inferences** How can adults foster development of tolerance rather than prejudice?

self-fulfilling prophecy
an expectation that leads to behavior that causes the expectation to become a reality

Symbolic interactionism underlies the concept of the **self-fulfilling prophecy**—an expectation that becomes true because it leads to behavior that then causes the expectation to become a reality. For example, if a student is continually encouraged and told that she is capable of succeeding at a task, she will likely believe the message and act as if she can succeed. If, however, she is discouraged from trying and told she will probably fail, that same student will likely believe the message and act in a manner that will cause her to fail. Similarly, if members of any minority group are continually treated as if they are less intelligent or less competent than the majority group, they may eventually accept this limitation. This acceptance, in turn, may lead them to place less emphasis on education as a path to future success. Given this negative interaction, and the lack of opportunity to develop their abilities, members of minority groups may become locked in poverty and low-level jobs.

☑ **READING PROGRESS CHECK**

Explaining If discrimination is dysfunctional, why do societies practice it?

LESSON 3 REVIEW

Reviewing Vocabulary
1. ***Distinguishing*** What is an example of a self-fulfilling prophecy?
2. ***Defining*** Using your own words, define *stereotyping*.

Using Your Notes
3. ***Making Connections*** Based on the notes you took, explain the connection between prejudice and stereotyping.

Answering the Guiding Questions
4. ***Differentiating*** How is discrimination different from prejudice?

5. ***Assessing*** What is a stereotype? How does sociology interpret hate crimes?
6. ***Comparing*** How do functionalism, conflict theory, and symbolic interactionism explain prejudice and discrimination?

Writing Activity
7. ***Argument*** Which of the three sociological theoretical perspectives do you think best explains prejudice and discrimination? Why?

networks

There's More Online!

- ☑ **CHART** Median Family Income for Majority and Minority Groups
- ☑ **CHART** Minority Population Growth
- ☑ **CHART** Racial and Ethnic Minority Groups in the United States
- ☑ **CHART** Socioeconomic Indicators for Racial and Ethnic Groups
- ☑ **IMAGE** Obama as a Symbol
- ☑ **SELF-CHECK QUIZ**

Reading HELPDESK

Academic Vocabulary
- virtually
- considerably

Content Vocabulary
- institutionalized discrimination
- hidden unemployment
- underclass

TAKING NOTES:
Key Ideas and Details

IDENTIFYING As you read about minority groups in the United States, use a graphic organizer like the one below to record key facts.

Group	Key Facts
African Americans	
Latinos	
Asian Americans	
Native Americans	
Other Ethnic Groups	

LESSON 4
Minority Groups in the United States

ESSENTIAL QUESTIONS • *What challenges do minority groups face?* • *What are the causes and effects of racial and ethnic discrimination in society?*

IT MATTERS BECAUSE
Discrimination in the United States has caused some ethnic and racial groups to lag behind the white majority in jobs, income, and education. Progress is being made, but gains remain fragile. African Americans and Latinos are the two largest minority groups in the United States.

Institutionalized Discrimination

GUIDING QUESTION *What is institutionalized discrimination?*

Many people believe that discrimination in the United States ended when civil rights legislation was passed in the 1960s. These laws did stop many discriminatory practices. Nevertheless, some minorities in this country still suffer from **institutionalized discrimination**. This type of discrimination results from unfair practices that are part of the structure of society and that have grown out of traditional, accepted behaviors. For several minority groups, the costs of institutional discrimination have been enormous.

For years, seniority systems, in which promotion and pay increased with years of service, discriminated against minority workers. Because they had been shut out of jobs in the past, minorities entered these systems later. Because they had fewer years of service than majority members, their chances for promotion were diminished and their incomes lagged.

Another example of institutionalized discrimination exists in public education. Schools with large numbers of minority students are more likely to be located in large urban areas than in wealthier suburbs. As a result, minority children in many states are more concentrated in school districts with a tax base too low to provide resources equal to those in the suburbs. This lack of funding means that teachers in minority schools receive fewer opportunities for training. Textbooks are often outdated. Parental and community support is generally not as strong. There is little, if any, money for new technology, and many buildings are badly in need of repair.

☑ **READING PROGRESS CHECK**

Making Connections Is institutional discrimination more similar to *de facto* or *de jure* segregation? Why?

Inequalities of Race and Ethnicity 253

Applying Sociology

STUDIES OF DISCRIMINATION AND FORMATION OF POLICY

Ongoing inequality in many areas, such as in employment or educational achievement, strongly suggests that discrimination continues to plague our society. Yet with many of the more overt forms of discrimination effectively outlawed, researchers today are looking for behaviors and attitudes that are subtler and harder to measure. In this search, they have many tools at their disposal.

Analyzing data about the actual effects of discrimination—lower incomes or test sores, for instance—can provide clues about discrimination. Carefully constructed statistical analysis can control for factors other than race or other features that might confound the results.

Another type of study relies on the perception of discrimination by its victims or reports of discriminatory attitudes by those who engage in it. As with statistical analysis, careful construction of surveys can minimize the obvious pitfalls of relying on the recollections or stated views of survey subjects.

Researchers also construct experiments on discrimination in laboratory settings. Such studies allow for a careful controlling of factors and a more precise identification of cause and effect.

Discrimination today is often subtle in its execution and impact. Careful studies that produce solid evidence of its effects can help shape legal and other responses to it.

Although illegal, studies show that racial discrimination in lending still occurs today.

▶ **CRITICAL THINKING**

1. **Exploring Issues** Why is discrimination difficult to study today?
2. **Finding the Main Idea** How can sociological studies help inform legal or other responses to discrimination today?

African Americans

GUIDING QUESTION What challenges do African Americans face as a minority group?

African Americans make up the largest racial minority group in the United States, numbering more than 39 million people in 2010, or about 12.2 percent of the total population. (Latinos—who can be of any race—are now the largest minority group.) This number includes people who identified themselves as African American only or as African American and one or more other races.

Barriers to Assimilation

There are many reasons that African Americans have historically faced barriers to full acceptance into mainstream society. First, skin color and physical features make it easy to identify many people of African American lineage. This makes it easy for the majority white population to attach negative stereotypes to them.

A second reason for the continuing minority status of African Americans has its roots in hundreds of years of American history. Brought to the country involuntarily, African Americans were enslaved and assigned to the lowest possible class status. Even those who were born free or who bought their freedom were rarely accepted as equal to free whites. Upward social mobility for African Americans—enslaved or free—was **virtually**, or almost, impossible.

While slavery was legally abolished by the Thirteenth Amendment in 1865, the legacy of prejudice and discrimination that grew out of it affects African Americans to this day. After slavery ended, practices and laws that segregated the

---

institutionalized discrimination unfair practices that grow out of common behaviors and attitudes and that are a part of the structure of a society

virtually almost; for all practical purposes

Minority Group	Population in 2000 (in thousands)	Population in 2010 (in thousands)	Percentage change, 2000–2010
African American only	34,658	38,929	12.3%
Asian American only	10,243	14,674	43.3%
American Indian and Alaska Native only	2,476	2,932	18.4%
Native Hawaiian and Pacific Islander only	399	540	35.4%
Some other race*	15,359	19,107	24.4%
More than one race	6,826	9,009	32.0%
Latino**	35,306	50,478	43.0%

* Any response that did not name one of the other categories or that named a particular Latino group.
** Latino is an ethnic, not a racial, category; Latinos can identify themselves as being of any race.

Source: U.S. Census Bureau, *Overview of Race and Hispanic Origin: 2010* (Washington, D.C.: Census Bureau, March 2010), Table 1

> **CHART**
>
> **RACIAL AND ETHNIC MINORITY GROUPS IN THE UNITED STATES, 2000 AND 2010**
>
> Asian Americans and Latinos are the fastest-growing minority groups.
>
> ▶ **CRITICAL THINKING**
>
> 1. **Summarizing** How do Latinos overlap with some of the other groups listed in the chart?
> 2. **Hypothesizing** What can explain why Asian American and Latino populations are growing at a faster rate than African American and Native American populations?

races became institutionalized throughout the country, especially in the South. Only in the 1950s and 1960s was this segregation made illegal by the passage of civil rights legislation and by court decisions. In a very real sense, then, African Americans have experienced barely 50 years of constitutional equality. The gap between African Americans and whites in education, income, wealth, and employment represents the legacy of centuries of racial prejudice and discrimination.

Income

Average income for African Americans in the United States is far less than average income for whites. Median family income for African Americans is 61 percent that of the median family income for whites. This means that for every $100 an average white family earns, an average African American family earns only $61. While that represents an increase over the situation in 1990, the increase is only 3 percent, virtually meaningless over a 20-year period.

Not surprisingly, African Americans and whites also differ in wealth, which means ownership of a home and car, business assets, and the like. Even if home equity is excluded, the average African American household holds only about $5,000 in wealth—far less than the $100,000 owned by the average white family. This gap increased nearly four and a half times from 1984 to 2009. Further, more than one in four African Americans lives below the government-defined poverty threshold—twice the rate for whites.

Employment

Part of the reason for these economic differences can be traced to employment patterns. Only 31.4 percent of employed African American men and women have managerial, professional, and related jobs, compared to 40.9 percent of white men and women. African Americans are nearly twice as likely as whites to work in low-paying service jobs (24 percent to 14 percent).

Patterns of unemployment severely affect the economic status of African Americans. In 2010, the jobless rate among African Americans (16 percent) was nearly double that of whites (8.7 percent). Moreover, official jobless rates actually undercount all unemployed persons. The traditional unemployment rate is based on the number of unemployed people who are actively looking for work.

With a white mother and an African father, President Barack Obama is part of the growing number of Americans who belong to more than one racial group.

▶ **CRITICAL THINKING**

Interpreting Significance Does Obama's election mean that racial discrimination in the United States has ended? Why or why not?

hidden unemployment unemployment that includes people not counted in the traditional unemployment rate

considerably substantially; to a significant degree

underclass people typically unemployed, who come from families that have been poor for generations

It does not include so-called **hidden unemployment**—discouraged workers who have stopped looking, the self-employed, or part-time workers who would prefer to have full-time jobs. When hidden unemployment is considered, the jobless rate for the nation is **considerably**, or substantially, higher than official numbers indicate. This is particularly true for African Americans.

Differences in unemployment rates between white and African American workers exist even for college-educated people. These differences, however, are not as large as for the nation as a whole. The greatest unemployment discrepancy is among teenagers. According to official statistics, more than 40 percent of African American teenagers were unemployed in early 2010, compared to just over 25 percent of all teenagers.

Assessing Progress

Education is the traditional path to economic gain and occupational prestige. The story for African Americans is mixed. As of 2009, nearly 89 percent of whites had finished high school, compared with just over 81 percent of African Americans. Similarly, whereas more than 29 percent of whites had completed college, less than 18 percent of African Americans had done so.

Moreover, higher educational attainment often does not pay off for African American men as it does for white men. Although income tends to rise with educational level for all races, the income of African American men lags behind that of white men at all educational levels. White male high-school graduates, on the average, earn nearly as much a year ($40,000 in 2007) as African American men with an associate degree ($41,000). African American men with a bachelor's degree earn only $50,000; white men with that degree earn $65,000. Interestingly, the income gap between African American women and white women is smaller—though both groups earn less than their male counterparts.

Although these figures may seem discouraging, real gains have been made. Nearly a third of African Americans now work in professional and managerial occupations. These occupations include chief executives, lawyers, accountants, computer scientists, and teachers. Also, business ownership by African Americans has been increasing dramatically. Between 2002 and 2007, the number of African American-owned businesses rose more than 60 percent, to 1.9 million. These businesses earned nearly $140 billion. As a result of the recent upward mobility of educated African Americans, some scholars see the emergence of two black Americas—a growing African American middle class and an African American **underclass**, composed of unemployed people whose families have been poor for generations.

African Americans have also increased their political presence. In 2008, voters elected the first African American president, Barack Obama. Forty-four African Americans served in the House of Representatives in the 112th Congress, although there were none in the U.S. Senate. African Americans have held cabinet posts, chaired the Joint Chiefs of Staff, and served as state governors. In 2012, more than 10,500 African Americans served as elected officials in the United States, a huge increase over the 1,469 who held elective office in 1970. The election of African Americans in predominantly white areas is a hopeful sign, too. African Americans, though still vastly underrepresented, have entered the "power elite" of America.

✓ **READING PROGRESS CHECK**

Synthesizing What are two examples of the results of continued discrimination against African Americans?

Latinos

GUIDING QUESTION *What challenges do Latinos face as a minority group?*

Latino is a term that refers to minorities who trace their heritage to Latin America, a region that includes Mexico, Central America, South America, and the islands of the Caribbean. Latinos are on average younger than non-Latino white Americans. This means that more Latino women (*Latinas*) are of child-bearing age, which results in a higher birthrate among Latinos. This, combined with high immigration rates, makes Latinos (along with Asian Americans) one of the fastest-growing minorities in the United States. In fact, early in the twenty-first century, Latinos overtook African Americans as America's largest minority group. If current trends continue, nearly one out of every three Americans will be Latino by the year 2050.

Latino Groups

Nearly 63 percent of Latinos in 2010 were of Mexican descent. More than half of them lived in California and Texas. Arizona and Illinois also have large numbers of Mexican Americans. Puerto Ricans are the next largest group, at just over 9 percent of the total Latino population. Most Puerto Ricans are concentrated in New York City and New Jersey, although there are substantial numbers also in Florida and, to a lesser degree, in Pennsylvania and Massachusetts. Cubans are the third most populous group of Latinos, with nearly 1.8 million people, or 3.5 percent of all Latinos. Most Cuban Americans are located in southeastern Florida, in and around Miami, although there is also a sizable number in New York and New Jersey.

Like European Americans, African Americans, Asian Americans, and Native Americans, Latino peoples are diverse. First, it must be remembered that Florida and the southwestern states from Texas to California were originally Spanish colonies and (except for Florida) then were Mexican territory. Some Latinos in these areas trace their families' histories back hundreds of years.

Even those who immigrated to the United States or are descended from immigrants came from nearly two dozen countries. Each group came to the United States from a unique national culture, and each retains a sense of its own identity and separateness. In addition, there are significant internal differences within individual Latino groups. For example, the first large group of Cuban immigrants was made up of successful middle- and upper-class people who fled from Cuba when Fidel Castro instituted a communist dictatorship there in the late 1950s. Later arrivals include a mix of educated, skilled workers and less educated people.

Fewer than two out of every five Latinos are foreign born. That is even true among Mexicans. Of the ten largest Latino groups, those with the highest percentage of foreign-born individuals are Hondurans, Guatemalans, Peruvians, and Colombians. All have come in recent years, fleeing poverty or civil unrest in their homelands.

GRAPHS

MINORITY POPULATION GROWTH, 2010–2050 (PROJECTED)

By 2050, Latinos will almost double their population in the United States and Asian Americans will see a marked increase.

▶ **CRITICAL THINKING**

1. **Identifying** Which racial or ethnic group is expected to see a large population decrease by 2050?
2. **Explaining** What is likely to be the cause of the increased proportion of people of more than one race?

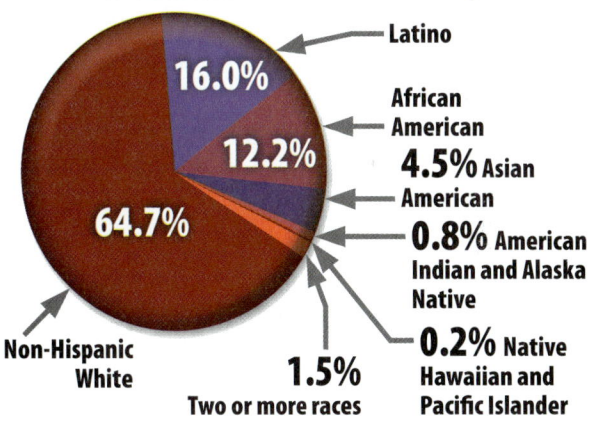

POPULATION BY RACE AND ETHNICITY, 2010

- Non-Hispanic White: 64.7%
- Latino: 16.0%
- African American: 12.2%
- Asian American: 4.5%
- American Indian and Alaska Native: 0.8%
- Native Hawaiian and Pacific Islander: 0.2%
- Two or more races: 1.5%

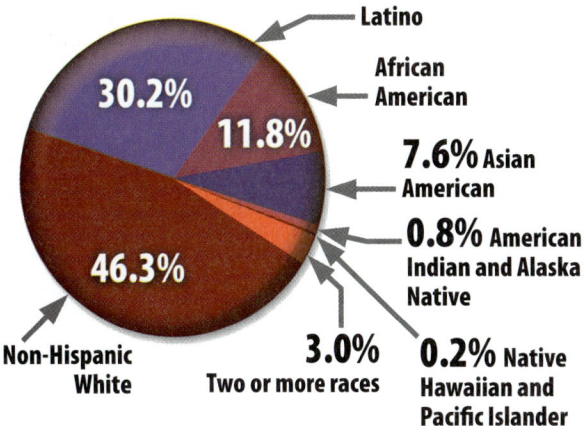

POPULATION BY RACE AND ETHNICITY, 2050

- Non-Hispanic White: 46.3%
- Latino: 30.2%
- African American: 11.8%
- Asian American: 7.6%
- American Indian and Alaska Native: 0.8%
- Native Hawaiian and Pacific Islander: 0.2%
- Two or more races: 3.0%

Source: U.S. Census Bureau, *Projections of the Population by Sex, Race, and Hispanic Origin for the United States: 2010 to 2050*

Just as American cities in the past adopted St. Patrick's Day and Columbus Day festivities in response to large numbers of Irish and Italian Americans, many now are holding Cinco de Mayo events as a result of large Mexican American populations.

▶ **CRITICAL THINKING**

Making Connections Why are Cinco de Mayo parades most likely to be held in the southwestern states?

Puerto Ricans report the highest English-language skills. About eight in ten say they can speak English with proficiency. Mexicans and Cubans, at about three out of five each, are not far behind. More recent arrivals, of course, are more likely to speak Spanish. As many immigrants settle in Latino-dominated communities, they can use Spanish outside the home.

Education

Latinos trail white Americans in formal education. Just about 61 percent of adult Latinos have completed high school, compared with 90 percent of non-Latino whites. Of the three main groups, Mexican Americans have the lowest educational attainment and Cuban Americans the highest.

Income

Median income for Latino families ($39,730 in 2009) is slightly greater than that of African American families ($38,409) but well behind that of whites overall ($62,545). There is great variation among Latinos, however. Of the ten largest Latino groups, Ecuadorians, Colombians, and Peruvians are considerably better off than other groups. Their median household income is comparable to the figure for all white households. The poorest among the ten large Latino groups are Dominicans, whose median household income is only about two-thirds that for white households. A quarter of Latinos live below the poverty level, about the same as African Americans and twice the rate for non-Latino whites.

From the data above, it should come as no surprise that many Latinos work in low-paying and low-status jobs as semiskilled workers and unskilled laborers. Mexican Americans make up the majority of migrant workers in the country. At the

GRAPH ▶

MEDIAN FAMILY INCOME FOR MAJORITY AND MINORITY GROUPS, 1990 AND 2009

These statistics show the 1990 income figure in terms of 2009 dollars rather than the value of the dollar in 1990.

▶ **CRITICAL THINKING**

1. ***Comparing*** Which group saw the biggest dollar increase from 1990 to 2009?
2. ***Interpreting*** What is the purpose of showing 1990 income in terms of 2009 dollars?

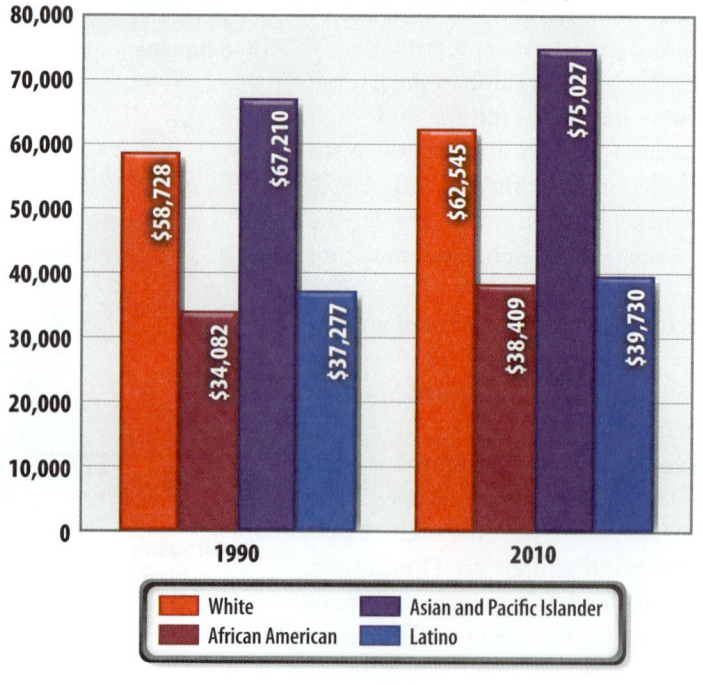

MEDIAN FAMILY INCOME FOR MAJORITY AND MINORITY GROUPS, 1990 AND 2009 (CONSTANT 2009 DOLLARS)

1990: White $58,728; African American $34,082; Asian and Pacific Islander $67,210; Latino $37,277
2010: White $62,545; African American $38,409; Asian and Pacific Islander $75,027; Latino $39,730

Group	Education (percentage with bachelor's degree, 2009)	Education (percentage with master's degree or above, 2009)	Median Male Income (2009)	Managerial or Professional Occupation (2010)	Unemployment Rate (2010)	Persons Below Poverty Level (2009)
Asian American*	29.4%	20.2%	$37,330	48.6%	7.5%	12.5%
Non-Latino White*	19.5%	11.6%	$36,785	40.9%	8.7%	12.3%**
African American*	11.5%	6.0%	$23,738	31.5%	16.0%	25.8%
Latino	8.7%	4.0%	$22,256	20.4%	12.5%	25.3%

*Data is for those who identified themselves in the census as Asian American, African American, or non-Latino white *only*, not in combination with another race.
**Data is for all whites, which includes Latino whites.
Sources: U.S. Census Bureau, *Educational Attainment in the United States: 2009* (Washington, D.C.: Census Bureau, 2012), Table 1; *Statistical Abstract of the United States* (Washington, D.C.: Census Bureau, 2012), Tables 701, 711, 622, 619

same time, Mexican Americans have made substantial progress in recent decades. Fifty percent of Mexican households are resident owned; for Cuban Americans, the rate is 59 percent. The number of Latino-owned businesses also boomed from 2002 to 2007, surpassing 2.3 million. These firms generated just under $350 million in sales, more than double the total for African American-owned firms.

Latinos and Politics

Politically, Latinos are becoming a force. In 2012, there were 32 Latinos serving in the U.S. Congress—30 in the House of Representatives and 2 in the Senate. In total, there were more than 5,000 Latino elected officials in the United States, although that represents but a fraction of all elected offices.

The intense debate over immigration in recent decades has galvanized political involvement among Latinos, many of whom see the push to curb immigration as directed at them. Latino turnout in both the 2004 and 2008 presidential elections increased from prior elections. Latino voters also played a more decisive role in those elections, providing margins of victory for the winning candidates in key battleground states. As Latinos become a significant share of the population in more states, they are likely to be courted by candidates from both major political parties.

✔ READING PROGRESS CHECK

Analyzing Why is it difficult to generalize about the socioeconomic position of Latinos?

Asian Americans

GUIDING QUESTION *What challenges do Asian Americans face as a minority group?*

In 2010, about 15 million people living in the United States reported themselves as being exclusively Asian or Asian in combination with another race. That means about 4.5 percent of the population is all or partly Asian. Like Latinos, Asians have been here for varying lengths of time. Many Chinese, Japanese, and Filipinos immigrated to the United States in the 1800s. Koreans, Vietnamese, and South Asians tend to be more recent arrivals. Also like Latinos, Asian Americans are a diverse group with many different national and ethnic backgrounds.

▲ CHART

SOCIOECONOMIC INDICATORS FOR RACIAL AND ETHNIC GROUPS

Asian Americans rank higher than other minority groups across several indicators of socioeconomic status.

▶ CRITICAL THINKING

1. ***Comparing*** In which area do Asian Americans show the greatest achievement?

2. ***Making Connections*** What is the connection between rates of holding managerial and professional jobs and median income?

During World War II, more than 100,000 Japanese Americans—many of whom were native-born American citizens—were forced to leave their homes on the West Coast and live in internment camps guarded by American soldiers. Though the United States also fought Germany and Italy in the war, large numbers of German and Italian Americans were not treated the same way.

▶ **CRITICAL THINKING**

Identifying Cause and Effect What best explains why Japanese Americans and not German or Italian Americans were treated in this way?

The largest groups are from China, the Philippines, India, Vietnam, Korea, and Japan.

Two of the most successful minority groups in the United States are Chinese Americans and Japanese Americans. That success has chiefly resulted from using education for upward mobility, as shown by their high levels of schooling. Even for them, however, the road has not been smooth. Remember, too, that all Asian Americans have not enjoyed the same success as these groups—nor has that success been uniform within those two groups.

Chinese Americans

Attracted by the California gold rush, Chinese immigrants first arrived in large numbers in the 1850s. In addition to mining, they worked as agricultural laborers and on railroad crews. When hard times hit in the 1870s, unemployed white Americans began to compete with the Chinese for jobs. Race riots erupted. Unrest led to passage of the Chinese Exclusion Act of 1882, which virtually ended Chinese immigration until limits were lifted after World War II. Chinese Americans lived mainly in California and other western states, often clustered in Chinatowns.

Although Chinese Americans were historically isolated from mainstream American society, their situation began to improve after 1940. American-born Chinese college graduates entered professions, and Chinese American scholars and scientists began to make publicly recognized contributions to science and the arts.

Immigration from China has seen a new surge in recent years, and about 1.6 million foreign-born Chinese lived in the United States in 2008. These immigrants have been of two groups. About half have been college-educated professionals. The other half have been from the working class. To gain social mobility, they will probably have to learn English. Three out of five of these immigrants have limited English proficiency.

Japanese Americans

Beginning in 1885, large numbers of Japanese men immigrated to the West Coast of the United States. Their arrival coincided with the movement to exclude Chinese immigrants. The Japanese suffered prejudice and discrimination during these early years. Nevertheless, they moved from being laborers in certain industries (railroads, canning, logging, mining, and meatpacking) to being successful farmers. When the Japanese began to compete with white farmers, however, anti-Japanese legislation was passed. California's Alien Land Bill of 1913, for example, permitted Japanese to lease farmland for a maximum of three years; it did not allow land they owned to be inherited by their families. In 1924, Congress halted all Japanese immigration, and the 126,000 Japanese already in the United States became targets for still more prejudice and discrimination.

Worse events followed. In 1941, Japan attacked the Pearl Harbor naval base in Hawaii, bringing the United States into World War II. Wartime hysteria generated fear of a possible Japanese invasion that led President Franklin Roosevelt to issue Executive Order 9066. This emergency law moved more than 110,000 Japanese people on the West Coast into internment camps in the interior. They were forced to sell their homes and businesses on short notice, incurring considerable losses. Historians agree that these Japanese Americans had posed no security threat. No Japanese Americans on Hawaii—home to the navy's largest Pacific base—were interned. They were too numerous and too vital to the islands' economy. Only in late 1944—near the war's end—did the Supreme Court rule that holding Japanese Americans without cause was illegal. In 1945, the remaining internees were finally allowed to leave the camps. Eventually, in the 1980s, the U.S. government formally apologized to Japanese American internees and paid them $20,000 each in compensation.

Japanese Americans have not had to deal with the centuries of discrimination endured by African Americans and Native Americans. Nevertheless, they have overcome great hardship.

✓ **READING PROGRESS CHECK**

Summarizing What is one example of hostility toward Asian Americans from American history?

Quick Case Study

RACE IN THE MEDIA

Attitudes about racial and ethnic groups are not always easy to identify and isolate. Discriminatory and prejudiced attitudes can be subtle and obscure even to those who hold them. One way to get a view of prevalent attitudes is to examine portrayals of ethnic groups in the media, such as advertising.

Procedure

1. Choose a mass-circulation print magazine, such as a major news or celebrity magazine to examine.
2. Record the representation of different racial and ethnic groups in the advertisements.
3. Note whether the presentation is largely positive or negative.

Analysis

Review your findings and answer the following questions:

1. Was there adequate representation of different ethnic groups in the advertisements? Explain.
2. Was the portrayal of different racial or ethnic groups positive or negative? Were there any potential stereotypes you noticed?
3. What do you think the advertisements in the magazine you examined suggest about attitudes toward race?

Native Americans

GUIDING QUESTION *What challenges do Native Americans face as a minority group?*

In 2010, the number of Americans who identified themselves solely as Native Americans or Alaska Natives numbered 2.9 million. More than 500 separate native groups have been identified in the United States. This great diversity is generally unrecognized because of stereotyped images of Native Americans based on dated Hollywood films.

Native Americans Today

Native Americans, perhaps more than any other minority, are suffering today from the effects of hundreds of years of discrimination. Abject poverty remains prevalent among Native Americans, especially those living on reservations. About a quarter of Native Americans live below the poverty line. On reservations, that number can exceed 50 percent. Native Americans have the lowest median household income of any minority group in the United States ($31,600). In addition, Native Americans have a lower life expectancy than the national average.

The Impact of Gaming

A relatively recent development on Native American reservations is the introduction of casino-type gaming establishments. Native American gaming has grown into a major industry. In a recent year, more than 200 native groups were operating over 350 gaming facilities in the United States. Gaming revenues in 2002 exceeded $14.5 billion. The casinos generated 400,000 jobs—though only a quarter were held by Native Americans. Most governments on reservations use the proceeds from gaming to provide services and promote economic growth.

A study by two scholars evaluated the extent to which gaming has affected Native Americans living on reservations. According to this study, between 1990 and 2000 the growth in median household income for Native American-held areas was six times that of the overall U.S. growth rate.

During World War II, Navajo men served in the U.S. Marines as "code talkers," communicating between fighting units during battles. By using their native language, the Navajo prevented their messages from being intercepted and understood by enemy fighters.

▶ **CRITICAL THINKING**

Hypothesizing Would the Navajo language, so valued during the war, be as valued in peacetime? Why or why not?

Brighton Beach, a neighborhood in Brooklyn, New York, is now an ethnic enclave for recent Russian immigrants.

▶ CRITICAL THINKING

Assessing What are the benefits of ethnic groups maintaining their heritage?

Moreover, during that same time period, unemployment decreased by twice as much on reservations with gaming compared to those without gaming. While the findings are promising, life on Native American reservations still presents huge challenges that need to be overcome.

☑ READING PROGRESS CHECK

Drawing Inferences How do you think the policy of placing Native Americans on reservations contributed to discrimination against them?

Other Ethnic Groups

GUIDING QUESTION *What other ethnic groups maintain ties based on their heritage?*

People of European ancestry can also be members of an ethnic group and many maintain bonds based on their heritage. European ethnics include the descendants of immigrants from Eastern and Southern European nations, particularly Italy and Poland. They also include Greek, Irish, and Slavic peoples. Europeans were the largest group of immigrants in the 1800s and into the early 1900s. Chiefly poor laborers, immigrants often faced occupational discrimination and hostility. Irish immigrants, for instance, encountered signs announcing job openings that included the admonition "No Irish need apply." Italians, Poles, and others faced discrimination and ethnic slurs.

In the late 1900s, many European ethnic groups became very conscious of their cultural and national origins, giving birth to an ethnic "roots" movement. This trend began in the wake of the black power movement of the 1960s. Just as many African Americans decided that they wanted to preserve their cultural identities, many of these ethnic groups concluded that the price of completely abandoning one's cultural and national roots was simply too high.

In the past 30 years, immigration from Eastern Europe—particularly Poland and areas of the former Soviet Union—has surged. More than a million immigrants have arrived from these lands since 1981. These groups tend to be well educated and have high incomes. Nearly half of European immigrants have a bachelor's degree, and the median household income for European immigrant households was more than $64,000 in 2009.

☑ READING PROGRESS CHECK

Contrasting How do the European immigrants of the 1800s compare to the European immigrants of the past three decades?

LESSON 4 REVIEW

Reviewing Vocabulary
1. **Making Connections** How does institutional discrimination contribute to the creation of an African American underclass?
2. **Explaining** Why is hidden unemployment important to consider along with the traditional unemployment rate?

Using Your Notes
3. **Comparing** Based on the notes you took from the lesson, which groups are the most and least successful? Why?

Answering the Guiding Questions
4. **Explaining** What is institutionalized discrimination?
5. **Evaluating** What challenges do African Americans face as a minority group?
6. **Evaluating** What challenges do Latinos face as a minority group?
7. **Evaluating** What challenges do Asian Americans face as a minority group?
8. **Evaluating** What challenges do Native Americans face as a minority group?
9. **Assessing** What other ethnic groups maintain ties based on their heritage?

Writing Activity
10. **Argument** Do you think it is fair or unfair to discuss white ethnic groups in the same context as other minority groups? Why or why not?

CHAPTER 9 Assessment

Directions: On a separate sheet of paper, answer the questions below. Make sure you read carefully and answer all parts of the questions.

Lesson Review

Lesson 1

1. **Understanding Historical Interpretation** Is today's understanding of specific races more or less complex than it has traditionally been in the past? Explain.

2. **Drawing Conclusions** Why might the members of an ethnic group choose to maintain their cultural characteristics even if doing so means they are treated as a minority?

Lesson 2

3. **Making Connections** What is the relationship of cultural pluralism to the metaphors *melting pot* and *tossed salad*?

4. **Assessing** What is the origin of the term *Trail of Tears*? Explain whether the Trail of Tears is a good example of population transfer.

Lesson 3

5. **Analyzing** Why are stereotypes difficult to break?

6. **Explaining** Define the concept of *self-fulfilling prophecy* and provide an example. Explain whether this concept is supported by symbolic interactionism.

Lesson 4

7. **Identifying Central Issues** Why did the civil rights legislation of the 1950s and 1960s in the United States fail to stop discrimination when the laws were designed and passed specifically for this purpose?

8. **Comparing Advantages and Disadvantages** Discuss the advantages and disadvantages of allowing gaming on Native American reservations.

DBQ Analyzing Primary Sources

PRIMARY SOURCE

Use the document to answer the following question.

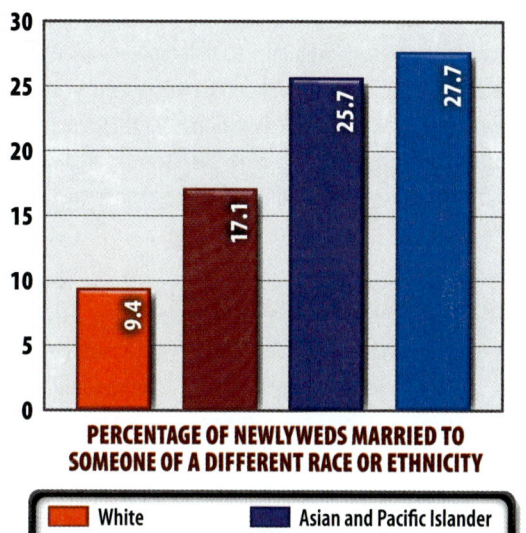

RATES OF INTERMARRIAGE BY RACE AND ETHNICITY

White: 9.4
African American: 17.1
Asian and Pacific Islander: 25.7
Latino: 27.7

PERCENTAGE OF NEWLYWEDS MARRIED TO SOMEONE OF A DIFFERENT RACE OR ETHNICITY

Source: *The Rise of Intermarriage*, Pew Research Center, 2012

9. **Drawing Conclusions** In the United States in 1980, only 3.2 percent of people were married to someone of a different race or ethnicity. By 2008, that figure had risen to 8 percent. At that time, 63 percent of people surveyed stated they would be fine with a family member marrying someone of a different race—any race. Attitudes toward interracial marriage have clearly been changing throughout the decades. Discuss the disparity among the rates for the different groups represented in the graph. What conclusions can you draw? What generalizations could you make to explain the disparities? Support your conclusions with chapter content.

Need Extra Help?

If You've Missed Question	1	2	3	4	5	6	7	8	9
Go to page	237–238	238–239	240–241	242–243	247–249	252	254–256	261	236–242

CHAPTER 9 Assessment

Directions: On a separate sheet of paper, answer the questions below. Make sure you read carefully and answer all parts of the questions.

Critical Thinking

10 *Drawing Inferences* A documentary analyzed events in a Midwestern suburb where the racial balance had gradually changed from primarily white to primarily African American. Even though statistics proved that school scores had not dropped and government services remained the same, the general perception was that property values had declined. Using information from the chapter and your own experience, explain likely reasons for this perception. Also explain whether you believe these reasons are fair or unfair. Support your position with information from the chapter.

College and Career Readiness Skills

11 *Decision Making* In this chapter, you read about the impact of a variety of ethnic groups on American culture. Imagine you and some business partners want to open a new restaurant in your town, one that features ethnic food. You are considering which ethnicity's food to feature. You know, for example, that Mexican restaurants were initially established in the Southwest due to the large Mexican community there and that sushi restaurants first became popular in California because of Japanese immigration there. Conduct online research to determine strong ethnic populations in your town, and decide whether you will focus on a food tied to an ethnicity with a strong presence in your area or on a type of cuisine tied to another ethnicity. Write a summary for your business partners to explain your decision.

21st Century Skills
CREATING AND USING GRAPHS, CHARTS, DIAGRAMS AND TABLES

12 *Creating Diagrams* Create a diagram to show the cause-and-effect relationship between discrimination and poverty. At a minimum, incorporate in your diagram the elements of educational opportunity, hiring practices, and low-level jobs.

Exploring the Essential Questions

13 *Comparing and Contrasting* Imagine you have been appointed to a supervisory position for the Southern Poverty Law Center, an organization whose mission is to fight hatred and bigotry and to seek justice. You have been asked to develop a new program that will be published online, a program designed to educate others regarding the inequalities of race and ethnicity. In preparation for development of the program, you have selected what you consider to be the three most important major points from each lesson in this chapter. State these major points—by lesson—and explain your reasons for selecting them.

Research and Presentation

14 *Gathering Information* This chapter provides information regarding stereotypes, explaining that a stereotype is a set of ideas based on distortion, exaggeration, and oversimplification and applied to all members of a social category. Popular media forms often play into stereotypes to convey assumed meanings about characters and situations. Search the Internet for information about racial and ethnic stereotypes in movies. Choose a particular ethnic or racial group and investigate how it has been portrayed since the early days of film. Have the same clichés been repeated through the decades? Have portrayals become more positive and varied? Take notes on what you find and create a multimedia presentation in which you show images of the characters and provide captions describing how they represent an ethnic stereotype. Conclude your presentation with an analysis of how movies portray persons who are ethnic or racial minorities today.

15 *Evaluating* Create a presentation for the class to explain why each of the images provides a stereotype; explain how each could be cured to present a character or situation that would not be stereotypical.

Need Extra Help?

If You've Missed Question	10	11	12	13	14	15
Go to page	236–262	236–242	246–262	236–262	246–252	246–249

Inequalities of Gender and Age

ESSENTIAL QUESTIONS • What are the causes and effects of discrimination in society? • How is gender discrimination reflected in the legal and economic systems? • What are the effects of age discrimination?

networks

There's More Online about inequalities related to gender and age.

CHAPTER 10

Technology & Society
Technology Use Varies by Gender and Age

Lesson 1
Sex and Gender Identity

Lesson 2
Theoretical Perspectives on Gender

Lesson 3
Gender Inequality

Lesson 4
Ageism

Lesson 5
Inequality in America's Elderly Population

Sociology Matters...

Throughout history, men have dominated the social, political, and economic realms, while women have been relegated to managing the home. For a variety of reasons, women today have opportunities that few men or women could envision just a few generations ago.

◄ Women have shown that they have the physical, mental, and emotional skills to succeed at nearly every type of job.

©Hill Street Studios/Corbis

CHAPTER 10
Technology & Society

Technology Use Varies by Gender and Age

Use of texting and cell phones depends on gender and age.

People use technology at home, at work, at school, and just about anywhere they can connect—technologically speaking. About 80 percent of Americans use the Internet in their homes. The remaining 20 percent choose not to use the Internet in their homes or anywhere, and a large proportion of these nonusers is composed of senior citizens. Texting is another technological tool that Americans use, but the demographics are narrower.

Texting, on a cell phone or smartphone, by the 18-to-24 age group is more than double the mean average of texting by the next age group, ages 25 to 34. In the highest age group, those over 65, the mean average is less than five text messages sent or received daily. Among males and females, females have the higher mean average across all age groups. In fact, teenage girls, ages 14 to 17, send more than three times as many text messages as teenage boys.

The majority of Americans who were studied indicated that they preferred texting to having a conversation on their cell phones. Texting aside, cell phone usage has risen dramatically in the 65+ age group. More than 50 percent of the people who fall within this age group owned a cell phone in 2010. However, only 5 percent use their cell phones to make or receive most or all of their calls.

median # of text messages sent / received per day by different groups

based on cell owners who use text messaging

Source: *Americans and Text Messaging*, Pew Research Center, 2011

CRITICAL THINKING
Drawing Conclusions How do people of different ages use texting as a tool for fast communication?

INFOGRAPHIC Explore the interactive version of the infographic on Networks.

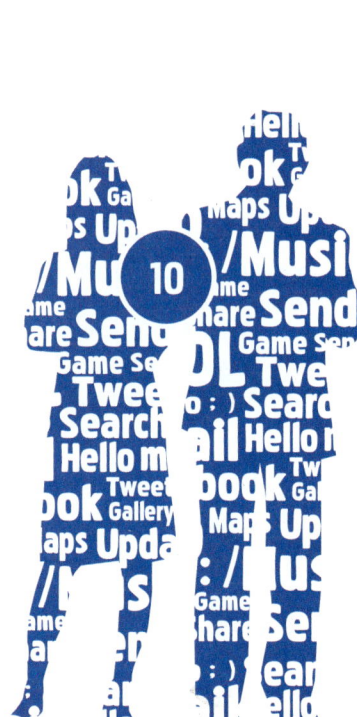

15 WOMEN **10 MEN**

40 AGES: 18 - 29
10 AGES: 30 - 49
3 AGES: 50 - 64
2 AGES: 65 +

Thinking Like a Sociologist

1 Analyzing
Why do you think some teenagers prefer to use texting over calling for communication?

2 Explaining
Why do you think that, while 50 percent of senior citizens own cell phones, only 5 percent use them for most of their calls?

Inequalities of Gender and Age

networks

There's More Online!

- ☑ **CARTOON** Gender Identity
- ☑ **GRAPHIC ORGANIZER** Sex and Gender
- ☑ **IMAGE** Female Construction Worker
- ☑ **IMAGE** Margaret Mead
- ☑ **IMAGE** Toddler Boy
- ☑ **IMAGE** Toddler Girl
- ☑ **SELF-CHECK QUIZ**

LESSON 1
Sex and Gender Identity

ESSENTIAL QUESTIONS • What are the causes and effects of discrimination in society? • How is gender discrimination reflected in the legal and economic systems? • What are the effects of age discrimination?

Reading HELPDESK

Academic Vocabulary
- passive
- adaptive

Content Vocabulary
- sex
- biological determinism
- gender identity

TAKING NOTES:
Key Ideas and Details

SUMMARIZING As you read about sex and gender, use a graphic organizer like the one below to record details.

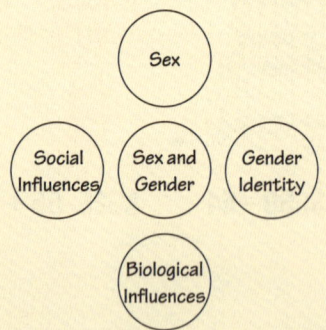

IT MATTERS BECAUSE

All societies expect people to behave in certain ways based on their sex. Through socialization, members of a society acquire an awareness of themselves as masculine or feminine. Behavioral differences between men and women are culturally conditioned.

Defining Male and Female

GUIDING QUESTION *What is gender identity?*

> *What are little girls made of?*
> *Sugar and spice*
> *And everything nice*
> *That's what little girls are made of.*
>
> *What are little boys made of?*
> *Snips and snails*
> *And puppy dog tails*
> *That's what little boys are made of.*

As this well-known nursery rhyme indicates, when it comes to males and females, most Americans believe that anatomy is destiny. If men and women behave differently, it is assumed to be because of their **sex**—the biological distinction between male and female. Males are assumed to be naturally more aggressive than females and to be built for providing and protecting. Females are believed to be naturally more **passive** than males and in greater need of protection. If these common conceptions were true, men and women in all societies would behave uniformly because of inborn biological forces beyond their control. This way of thinking is called **biological determinism**—the belief that behavioral differences are the result of inherited physical characteristics.

The theory of biological determinism lacks scientific proof. Significant behavioral differences between men and women have not been causally linked to biological characteristics. Although biology may create some behavioral tendencies in the sexes, such tendencies are so weak that they are easily overridden by cultural and social influences.

268

From the moment of birth—on the basis of obvious external biological characteristics—males and females are treated differently. Few parents in American society point with pride to the muscular legs and broad shoulders of their baby girls or to the long eyelashes, rosebud mouth, and delicate curly hair of their baby boys. Rather, parents stress the characteristics and behaviors that fit the society's image of the male or female ideal, including modes of dress, ways of walking, manner of talking, play activities, and life aspirations.

Girls and boys gradually learn to behave as their parents expect. From this process comes **gender identity**—an awareness of being masculine or feminine, based on culture. Sociologist Margaret Andersen succinctly captured the difference between sex and gender:

PRIMARY SOURCE

"Sociologists use the term **gender** to refer specifically to the social and cultural patterns that we associate with women in society. **Sex** refers to the biological identity of the person and is meant to signify the fact that one is either male or female. One's biological sex usually establishes a pattern of gendered expectations, although … biological sex identity is not always the same as gender identity, nor is biological identity always as clear as this definition implies. *Gender* is a social, not a biological concept. Simply put, being 'female' and 'male' are biological facts; being a woman or a man is a social and cultural process--one that is constructed through the whole array of social, political, economic, and cultural experiences in a given society."

—from *Thinking About Women: Sociological Perspectives on Sex and Gender*, 2009

Sociologists are part of an ongoing debate concerning the reasons for gender differences. At the heart of the debate is the so-called nature-versus-nurture issue: Does biology or does socialization play a greater role in gender differences? Today, research by sociologists and other investigators is aimed at answering these questions scientifically. Definitions of masculinity and femininity are now based on research rather than just on tradition and "common knowledge."

✓ **READING PROGRESS CHECK**

Analyzing Identify at least two of your behaviors that you believe are affected by your gender identity.

sex the classification of people as male or female based on biological characteristics

passive accepting what happens without active response or resistance

biological determinism the principle that behavior differences are the result of inherited physical characteristics

gender identity a sense of being male or female based on learned cultural values

Many people believe that behavioral differences in males and females begin immediately at birth because of physical differences.

▶ **CRITICAL THINKING**

Hypothesizing Do you think male children are naturally more physically active than female children? Why or why not?

Connecting Sociology to Anthropology

GENDER BEHAVIOR

Cultural anthropologist Margaret Mead was influenced at a young age by the work of her sociologist mother. Later, she went with her husband to Papua New Guinea to study the native people there and the differences in their gender behavior as compared to that of Americans. This excerpt from her book describes some of her ideas.

PRIMARY SOURCE

"There are at least three courses open to a society that has realised the extent to which male and female personality are socially produced. Two of these courses have been tried before, over and over again, at different times in the long, irregular, repetitious history of the race. The first is to standardize the personality of men and women as clearly contrasting, complementary, and antithetical, and to make every institution in the society congruent with this standardisation. If the society declared that woman's sole function was motherhood and the teaching and care of young children, it could so arrange matters that every woman who was not physiologically debarred should become a mother and be supported in the exercise of this function. It could abolish the discrepancy between the doctrine that women's place is the home and the number of homes that were offered to them. It could abolish the discrepancy between training women for marriage and then forcing them to become the spinster supports of their parents.

Such a system would be wasteful of the gifts of many women who could exercise other functions far better than their ability to bear children in an already overpopulated world. It would be wasteful of the gifts of many men who could exercise their special personality gifts far better in the home than in the market-place. It would be wasteful, but it would be clear. It could attempt to guarantee to each individual the role for which society insisted upon training him or her, and such a system would penalise only those individuals who, in spite of all the training, did not display the approved personalities."

—Margaret Mead, *Sex and Temperament in Three Primitive Societies*, 1935

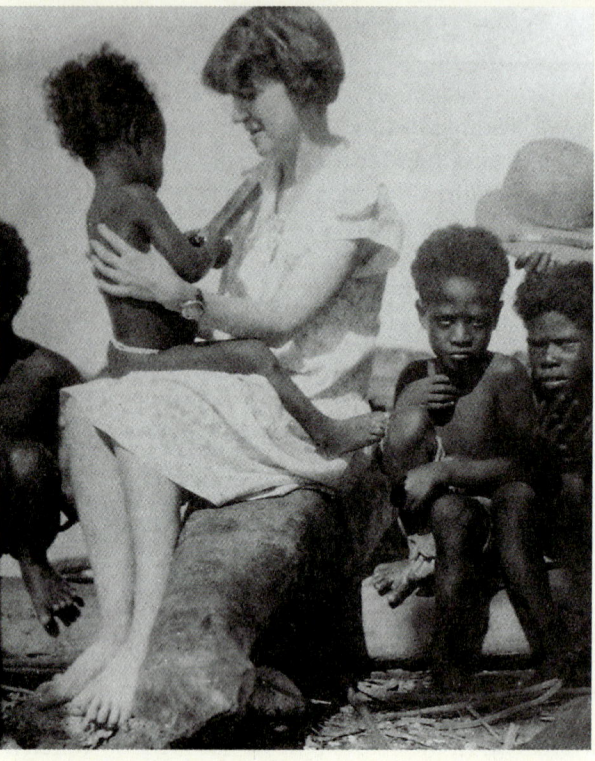

Margaret Mead grew up during the Progressive Era, a time when social and educational reforms were major issues.

DBQ ▶ CRITICAL THINKING

1. **Making Connections** How does the excerpt illustrate the importance of studying other cultures in understanding gender identity?
2. **Analyzing** Do you agree with Mead's conclusion about society's influence on the roles of men and women? Explain.

Biology, Culture, and Behavior

GUIDING QUESTIONS *Are male and female brains different? If so, in what ways?*

As noted earlier, there are obvious biological differences between males and females. Biological differences between the sexes include distinctive muscle-to-bone ratios and how fat is stored. The differences in reproductive organs, however, are much more important, because they result in certain facts of life. Only men can impregnate; only women are able to produce eggs, give birth, and nurse infants. Throughout life, reproductive hormones influence development in both males and females.

Differences in Male and Female Brains

Recent research indicates that the brains of men and women are slightly different in structure. For example, men show more activity in a region of the brain thought to be tied to **adaptive** evolutionary responses, such as fighting. Women have more activity in a newer, more highly developed region of the brain thought to be linked to emotional expression. The female brain is less specialized than the male brain. Women tend to use both sides of the brain simultaneously when performing a task. Men tend to process verbal tasks on the left side of the brain only while women are more likely to use both sides.

"I broncobust <u>and</u> I Dust–Bust. You got a problem with that?"

Biological Differences and Social Behavior

For many years, biological determinists assumed, without evidence, that physical differences result in biologically programmed differences in social behavior. It is true that female babies are more sensitive to sound, probably because they listen with both ears rather than one. And male infants and children are more active in play—shouting, yelling, hitting—than females.

Biological determinists point to research that indicates that men and women in dozens of different cultures (at varying stages of economic development) are associated with some distinctly different ways of behaving. For example, men and women differ in what they look for in romantic and sexual partners. Men value physical appearance more than women do. Women place more emphasis on social class and income. Men tend to prefer slightly younger mates while women favor slightly older ones. In addition, males in general tend more toward physical aggressiveness in conflict situations.

The fact that such differences appear in many cultures suggests to some people that they have a biological cause. We do not yet know for sure to what extent these differences result from biology or culture, and the debate on this issue can be furious.

Biological determinism is not supported by continuing research on transsexualism, which occurs when people have physical characteristics of one sex but believe they should be a member of the other. Some children show this belief and corresponding gender-related behavior very early. Some people also exhibit physical intersexuality, where biological characteristics of both sexes are present.

Sociologists and Gender-Related Behavior

The majority of sociologists argue that gender-related behavior is not primarily the result of biology. They look to culture for clues. In her classic study of the indigenous peoples of New Guinea, anthropologist Margaret Mead demonstrated the influence of culture and socialization on gender-role behavior.

Among the Arapesh, Mead found that both males and females were conditioned to be cooperative, unaggressive, and empathetic. Men and women behaved in a way consistent with the more traditional concept of the female gender role.

⌃ CARTOON
GENDER IDENTITY
This cartoon suggests that gender identity is more flexible than is commonly believed.

▶ **CRITICAL THINKING**
1. **Analyzing Visuals** What does the speaker mean when he says he "Dust-Busts"?
2. **Identifying Perspectives** Why does the cartoonist's choice for a speaker help make the point of the cartoon?

adaptive being able to change behavior as necessary

Although gender stereotypes keep some people from pursuing certain activities, there are actually very few behaviors that cannot be performed by either sex.

▶ CRITICAL THINKING

Explaining In the past, what reasons were given to explain why women were not allowed to perform certain jobs, such as serving as a firefighter or a police officer?

By contrast, in Mundugumor society, both men and women were trained to be "masculine"—they were aggressive, ruthless, and unresponsive to the needs of others. In yet another example, the Tchambuli, the gender roles were the opposite of those found in Western society. Women were dominant, impersonal, and aggressive, and men were dependent and submissive.

On the basis of this evidence, Mead concluded that human nature is sufficiently flexible to rule out biological determinism. Cross-cultural research since Mead's landmark work has clearly supported her findings: Gender roles are not fixed at birth.

Case studies have also examined infants whose parents intentionally treated their children as if they belonged to the opposite sex. Children can fairly easily be socialized into the gender of the opposite sex. What is more, after a few years, these children resist switching back. In general, research on gender identity indicates that biological tendencies can be greatly influenced by culture and society.

Conclusions About Male and Female Behaviors

In general, researchers investigating behavioral differences between the sexes have not been able to prove that any particular behavior has a biological cause. One researcher's findings tend to contradict another's.

Any conclusions we reach should also take into account several difficulties with the research. Many studies seek to find differences but ignore the overriding similarities between males and females. To make matters worse, researchers often fail to note the substantial variation that exists *within* each sex, which is often greater than the variation *between* sexes. Some men, for example, tend to be submissive and noncompetitive, and some women are aggressive and competitive.

Sociologists believe that biological characteristics exist, but they can be modified through social influences. In other words, men and women can learn to be submissive or aggressive by mirroring the behaviors of influential role models, such as parents or siblings. It is also clear that human behavior is the result of multiple causes.

☑ **READING PROGRESS CHECK**

Interpreting Why is the debate on gender called "nature versus nurture"?

LESSON 1 REVIEW

Reviewing Vocabulary
1. ***Contrasting*** How are sex and gender identity different?
2. ***Comparing*** What is the main idea of biological determinism?

Using Your Notes
3. ***Identifying*** Use your notes to write a sentence or two describing the two basic sociological approaches to sex and gender identity.

Answering the Guiding Questions
4. ***Defining*** What is gender identity?

5. ***Contrasting*** Are male and female brains different? If so, in what ways?

Writing Activity
6. ***Narrative*** Identify a time when you or someone you know or observed was directly told or pressured to act in a certain way because of the social expectations for gender. Describe the situation, how the pressure was applied, and if the person's actions changed.

networks

There's More Online!

- ☑ **CARTOON** Gender Roles
- ☑ **CHART** Gender Inequalities
- ☑ **GRAPHIC ORGANIZER** Theoretical Perspectives on Gender
- ☑ **IMAGE** Female Soldier
- ☑ **IMAGE** Powerful Women
- ☑ **SELF-CHECK QUIZ**

LESSON 2
Theoretical Perspectives on Gender

ESSENTIAL QUESTIONS • What are the causes and effects of discrimination in society? • How is gender discrimination reflected in the legal and economic systems? • What are the effects of age discrimination?

Reading HELPDESK

Academic Vocabulary
- prohibit
- reinforce

Content Vocabulary
- gender socialization

TAKING NOTES:
Key Ideas and Details

SUMMARIZING As you read about theoretical perspectives on gender, use a graphic organizer like the one below to summarize key ideas.

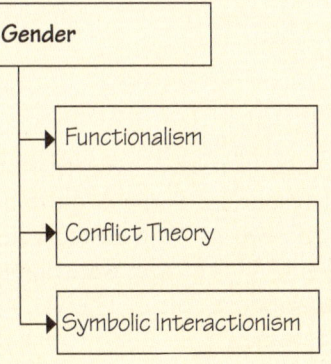

IT MATTERS BECAUSE
All societies expect people to behave in certain ways based on their sex. Through socialization, members of a society acquire an awareness of themselves as masculine or feminine. Behavioral differences between men and women are culturally conditioned.

Functionalism and Gender

GUIDING QUESTION *How does functionalism explain gender differences?*

Functionalists argue that any pattern of behavior that does not benefit society will become unimportant. According to functionalism, the division of responsibilities between males and females survived because it benefited human survival. Early humans found that the division of labor based on sex was efficient. In part because of their size and muscular strength, men hunted and protected. In addition, men took on these dangerous tasks because they were more expendable than women. One man was enough to ensure the group's chances of surviving through reproduction; one woman was not. Thus, it hurt the group's chances of survival more to lose a woman.

Today, as most societies have become industrial or postindustrial, these divisions of labor are no longer necessary or beneficial. Although men are still generally larger and stronger, many women have shown that they are capable of excelling at extremely physical jobs, such as those in construction. Certainly, survival as a group or species does not currently rely on the survival of females any more than males.

Any mental or emotional limitations implied by early divisions of labor have been disproven by the large number of successful women in leadership positions in every facet of public life: business and finance, law, medicine, law enforcement, public policy and government, the military, space exploration, and more. Functionalists recognize that the traditional division of labor has created problems, or dysfunctions, for modern society. These dysfunctions are examined in Lesson 3.

☑ **READING PROGRESS CHECK**

Paraphrasing Why are traditional divisions of labor no longer functional?

Inequalities of Gender and Age **273**

Applying Sociology

WOMEN IN THE MILITARY

Women in the United States have helped behind the front lines since the American Revolution, when wives often accompanied their husbands on the march and did cooking and laundry work in camp. During the Civil War, Clara Barton and others took the initiative to recruit and train women to nurse wounded soldiers. Over time, the role of women in the U.S. military expanded to include support roles on the front lines. Yet there were always restrictions on the types of roles they could take; women were never assigned to combat units. Today, women in active duty are represented in the vast majority of U.S. military occupations, but the issue of whether women should serve in combat is still debated.

The U.S. military and government used data from research and public opinion polls to help guide its policy on women and combat roles. Much of what they learned was that less than half of the American public would support women volunteering for combat. In 1999, the U.S. government established that women were not allowed to engage in combat. Yet researchers at the Army War College determined that women on or near a battlefield would be at risk for engaging in combat despite restrictions.

Military sociologist Brenda Moore interviewed female soldiers after they returned from the Iraq War to find out if women were taking part in combat despite U.S. policy against it. What she discovered was that women who were put in support roles found themselves in combat situations. The battleground moves, especially in a conflict with insurgents, and female soldiers were often placed right there in the action. Even though Congress passed legislation that allows women to fly combat aircraft and be assigned to combat ships, it was the military conflicts themselves that drew women into combat rather than government policy.

U.S. Navy Aviation Warfare Systems Operator

▶ **CRITICAL THINKING**

1. **Identifying Bias** Why do you think many Americans do not support women taking on combat roles in the military?
2. **Identifying Cause and Effect** How have sociological work and studies affected U.S. policy toward women in the military?

Conflict Theory and Gender

GUIDING QUESTION *How does conflict theory explain gender differences?*

According to conflict theory, it is to men's advantage to prevent women from gaining access to political, economic, and social resources. Perhaps the most recent example of maintaining the gender status quo was in Afghanistan when the ruling Taliban militia practiced "gender apartheid." This gender war trapped women in a way of life unknown elsewhere in the modern world. The Taliban **prohibited** girls from attending school and banned women from all work outside the home. Women who left home without the protection of a male relative were punished, and the windows of houses were painted black to prevent anyone from catching a glimpse of the women inside. In public, women had to wear shoes with soft soles to prevent them from drawing attention to themselves.

Like functionalists, conflict theorists see traditional gender roles as outdated. They believe that men have maintained their controlling role in government, the workplace, social settings, and at home not because it helps society function

prohibit to prevent by rule or law

better but because they want to keep their own power and advantage. Men have continued their dominance, which began in agrarian societies, because it allows them access to a disproportionate share of the available resources and power. Conflict theorists say that such a social order amounts to unfair exploitation of women.

Although women have made great strides in gaining a larger share of power and resources in recent years, conflict theorists can point to numerous statistics that indicate that men have maintained a significant advantage in power and resources. It is this continued dominance at the very top levels of business and political organizations that has inspired terms like "the glass ceiling," the idea that women can rise in power and importance in business and society but can never reach the very highest levels because they are restricted by an invisible barrier erected by men intent on maintaining dominance.

Both functionalists and conflict theorists believe that these conventional roles may have been appropriate in hunting and gathering, horticultural, and agricultural societies but are inappropriate for the industrial and postindustrial era. In addition, demographic characteristics make women today more available for work outside the home. Women are marrying later, having fewer children, younger when their last child leaves home, remaining single in greater numbers, and increasingly choosing to be single parents.

According to conflict theorists, women who prefer careers in fields formerly reserved for men have every right to make that choice. Not only is it a more equitable allocation of resources and power, it also addresses the dysfunctions created by traditional gender roles. Indeed, these choices are more functional for society because as a result of these choices society can benefit from the talents of these women, which would otherwise be lost.

✓ READING PROGRESS CHECK

Making Generalizations In what ways would a more equitable allocation of power and resources affect the role of men in society?

Symbolic Interactionism and Gender

GUIDING QUESTION *How does symbolic interactionism explain gender differences?*

Symbolic interactionists focus on how boys and girls learn to act the way they are "supposed to act." This process is called **gender socialization**. Gender is acquired in large part from interaction with parents, teachers, and peers. In addition, gender concepts are taught through the mass media. Indeed, the effect of the media is very powerful.

Parents and Gender Socialization

Parents are vitally important in gender socialization because they transfer values and attitudes regarding how boys and girls should behave. The learning of gender begins at birth and is well established by the time the child is two-and-a-half years old. Immediately after birth, friends and relatives give gifts seen as appropriate to the child's sex, such as blue or pink blankets, baseball playsuits, or frilly dresses.

gender socialization the social process of learning how to act as a boy or girl

In recent decades, women have increasingly assumed leadership positions in business, government, and other areas of public life.

▶ CRITICAL THINKING

Analyzing What skills do some women share with some men to enable them to become leaders in business and government?

Theoretical Perspectives

GENDER INEQUALITIES

Each of the major theoretical perspectives suggests that most societies show significant gender inequalities and explains and illustrates them in a unique way.

Theoretical Perspective	Social Arrangement	Example
Functionalism	Gender-based division of labor	Women are expected to perform household tasks because this division of labor benefits society.
Conflict Theory	Patriarchy (male domination)	Women are denied high-status occupations because men want to maintain their power and control of resources.
Symbolic Interactionism	Favoring males over females in the classroom	Few females believe they can become scientists or mathematicians; few males believe they can excel in fields like nursing or the arts.

▶ **CRITICAL THINKING**

1. **Hypothesizing** How might a more equitable division of household tasks benefit society overall?

2. **Differentiating** In what areas or situations have you observed males being favored over females or vice versa?

Boys may be given building blocks and trucks, while girls receive cooking-related toys or dolls. (In fact, when boys do play with dolls, they are called action figures to distinguish them from "girl" toys.)

Studies of infant care have found that girls are cuddled more, talked to more, and handled more gently than are boys. Parents expect boys to be more assertive than girls are, and they discourage them from clinging. Gender is also taught and **reinforced** in the assignment of family chores. In an investigation of almost 700 children between the ages of 2 and 17, sociologists Lynn White and David Brinkerhoff found that boys were often given "masculine" jobs, such as cutting grass and shoveling snow. Girls were more often assigned "feminine" chores, such as washing dishes and cleaning up the house. Another study, by Sara Raley and Suzanne Bianchi, indicates that girls do more housework than boys, which mirrors the division of labor generally found in adults.

reinforce to strengthen an existing structure, belief, or behavior

Schools and Gender Socialization

Although the most critical period of gender socialization is early childhood, gender socialization occurs in school as well. Observation of preschool teachers reveals that many of them encourage different behaviors from boys and girls.

This pattern continues in the elementary-school years. Myra Sadker and David Sadker, in an extensive study of fourth-, sixth-, and eighth-grade students, found boys to be more assertive in class. Boys were eight times more likely than girls to call out answers, whereas girls sat patiently with their hands raised. The researchers linked the students' behavior to the differential treatment given boys and girls by teachers. Teachers were more likely to accept the answers given by boys who called out answers. Girls who called out in class, on the other hand, were given such messages as "In this class we don't shout out answers; we raise our hands." According to Sadker and Sadker, the message is subtle and powerful: "Boys should be academically assertive and grab teacher attention; girls should act like ladies and keep quiet."

There are other areas in junior high school and high school where gender socialization is concentrated. These include clothing styles, school elections, social functions, and after-school activities. In their book *Failing at Fairness: How*

CARTOON
GENDER ROLES
Athletics is one area in which females have made considerable strides in breaking gender role limits in recent years.

▶ **CRITICAL THINKING**

1. Analyzing Visuals Which of the two main figures in the cartoon do you think is more unusual? Why?

2. Making Connections What position does this cartoon take on the "nature versus nurture" debate over gender roles? Why do you think so?

Our Schools Cheat Girls, the Sadkers examined sexism from elementary school through college. They concluded that, through differential treatment, America's schools often shortchange females. Academically, girls typically outperform boys in the early years of school. Through the transmission of gender role values, well-intentioned teachers often dampen female competitiveness. Girls, the study concludes, are subtly but systematically taught to be passive, to dislike math and science, and to defer to boys. Females tend to carry these attitudes into adult life and into the working world.

Peers and Gender Socialization

Adolescents want to be liked, so acceptance or rejection by peers greatly influences their self-concepts. Teens who most closely mirror traditional gender roles, such as male football players and female cheerleaders, are generally given the greatest respect, whereas "feminine" boys and "masculine" girls are assigned low status.

This peer group pressure encourages teenagers to try to conform to idealized role models. For adolescents to behave otherwise is to risk rejection and a significant loss of self-esteem.

✓ **READING PROGRESS CHECK**

Evaluating Which influence do you think is the most powerful in gender socialization: parents, schools, or peers?

LESSON 2 REVIEW

Reviewing Vocabulary
1. Interpreting Why is gender socialization primarily connected to symbolic interactionism?

Using Your Notes
2. Describing Use your notes to describe the reasons functionalists and conflict theorists believe a traditional division of labor is not applicable to modern society.

Answering the Guiding Questions
3. Explaining How does functionalism explain gender differences?

4. Explaining How does conflict theory explain gender differences?

5. Explaining How does symbolic interactionism explain gender differences?

Writing Activity
6. Argument Consider the idea that more women should enter the workforce and compete for the best jobs. Decide if you agree or disagree with this idea, and write a persuasive paragraph that explains your position.

Inequalities of Gender and Age **277**

networks

There's More Online!

- ☑ **CARTOON** Gender Inequality
- ☑ **GRAPH** - Composition of the U.S. Labor Force by Sex
- ☑ **GRAPH** Women's Earnings Compared to Men's
- ☑ **GRAPH** Women's Wages Compared to Men's Wages by Race and Ethnicity
- ☑ **GRAPH** Percentage of Women in Elective Offices
- ☑ **MAP** Women in National Parliaments
- ☑ **SELF-CHECK QUIZ**

Reading HELPDESK

Academic Vocabulary
- sphere
- somewhat

Content Vocabulary
- sexism
- occupational sex segregation

TAKING NOTES:
Key Ideas and Details

SUMMARIZING As you read about gender inequalities, use a graphic organizer like the one below to summarize key ideas.

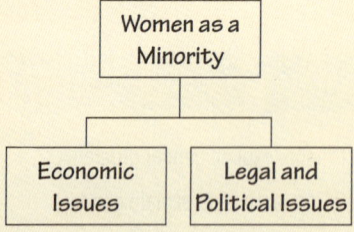

LESSON 3
Gender Inequality

ESSENTIAL QUESTIONS • *What are the causes and effects of discrimination in society?* • *How is gender discrimination reflected in the legal and economic systems?* • *What are the effects of age discrimination?*

IT MATTERS BECAUSE
Although great progress has been made, women today are still subject to prejudice and discrimination. This imbalance of power is seen most clearly in the areas of economics, law, and politics.

Women as a Minority Group

GUIDING QUESTIONS *Is discrimination against women disappearing? Why or why not?*

Most sociologists consider biological determinism to be a moral threat because, historically, it has been used to rationalize the treatment of some people as inferior. This view, in short, has led to racism and sexism. **Sexism** is defined as a set of beliefs, attitudes, norms, and values used to justify gender inequality. Just as minorities suffer from the effects of racism, women are hurt by sexism. Sexist ideology—the belief that men are naturally superior to women—has been used, and is still being used, to justify men's leadership and power positions in the economic, social, and political **spheres** of society.

Some people believe that sex discrimination is disappearing. Indeed, it is fair to say that there has been considerable progress in recent decades. Some segments of American society now have more positive attitudes about women. More women now hold key positions in jobs traditionally reserved for men. In 1999, for example, Carly Fiorina became the first female CEO (chief executive officer) of one of the 30 companies that make up the Dow Jones Industrial Average. In that same year, Eileen Collins became the first female NASA shuttle commander. Women's work has gained increasing recognition in other ways as well. In 2010, Kathryn Bigelow became the first woman to win an Oscar for best director.

In addition to these successful individuals, large numbers of women have made impressive gains in their own lives. Some of the most impressive gains women have made have come in education. In 1970, 13.5 percent of all American males were college graduates but only 8.1 percent of women were. In 2010, while the share of male college graduates had more than doubled to 30.3 percent, the percentage of female college graduates had more than tripled to 29.6, nearly equaling that of men.

In a few years, in fact, women are likely to exceed men in educational attainment. According to *Statistical Abstract of the United States: 2012*, a higher share of recent female high school graduates (nearly 74 percent) than recent male high school graduates (about 66 percent) were in college in 2009. In fact, women outnumbered men in college with some 11.7 million women enrolled compared to not quite 8.8 million men. Since 1990, more women than men have been enrolled in graduate school, and nearly as many women as men now attend professional school.

Despite these advances, a careful examination reveals many gaps in social rights, privileges, and rewards for women in the United States. These gaps, although they have closed **somewhat** in recent years, are reflected in the continuing inequality experienced by American women.

sexism a set of beliefs, attitudes, norms, and values used to justify sexual inequality

sphere a defined area or subject

somewhat partially; in a limited way

✓ **READING PROGRESS CHECK**

Making Connections Do you think there is discrimination against girls in schools?

Occupational and Economic Inequality

GUIDING QUESTION *What is occupational sex segregation, and how does it affect earnings?*

By far the most important labor development in the United States in recent decades has been the dramatic increase in the number and proportion of women in the workforce. In 2010, nearly 59 percent of women worked outside the home, compared with more than 71 percent of men. That year, women represented just over 47 percent of the overall American labor force. That is a significantly greater share of women working outside the home than at any time in the past. As the charts show, nearly a hundred years ago, only a fifth of women worked outside the home. Three decades later, the proportion had increased only to a quarter. Today, it is nearly half.

The greatest change in patterns of work involves married women with children under six years of age. According to the U.S. Bureau of Labor Statistics, the proportion of women in this group who work outside the home soared from 19 percent in 1960 to 37 percent in 1975 to 64 percent in 2008.

▽ **GRAPHS**

COMPOSITION OF THE U.S. LABOR FORCE BY SEX, 1890–2010

The number and percentage of women in the U.S. labor force have been growing steadily for more than 100 years.

▶ **CRITICAL THINKING**

1. *Analyzing* What do you think is the most important societal consequence of this change?
2. *Hypothesizing* Do you think the percentage of female workers will continue to grow? Why or why not?

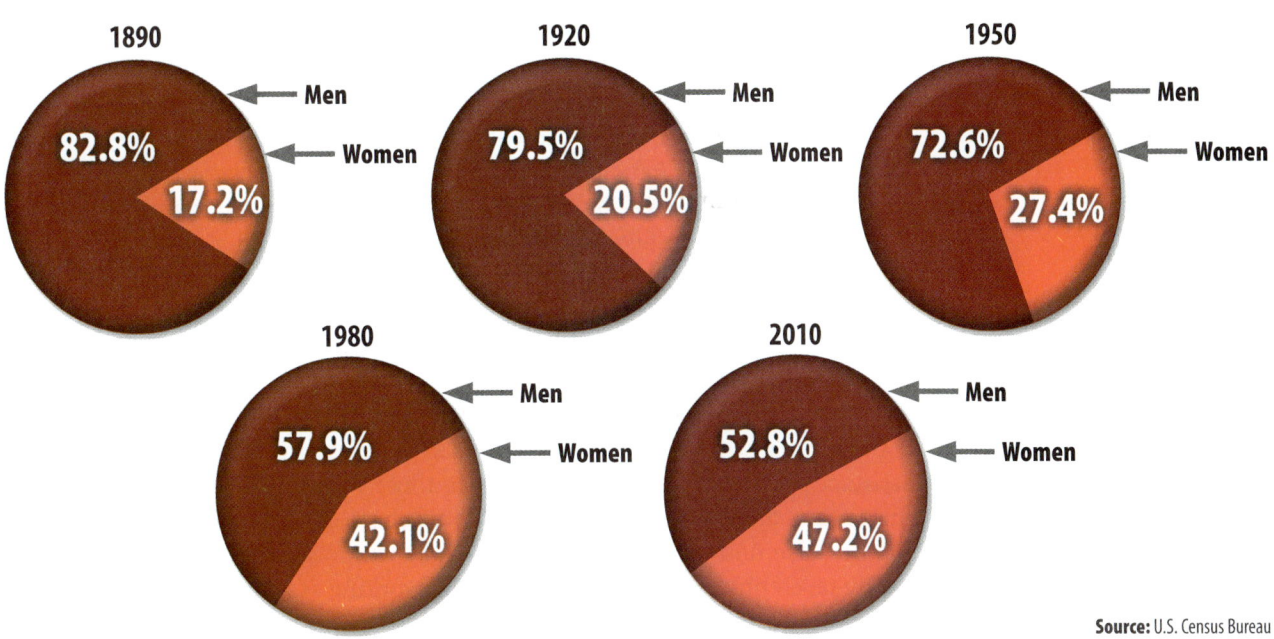

COMPOSITION OF THE U.S. LABOR FORCE BY SEX: 1890–2010

1890 — Men 82.8%, Women 17.2%
1920 — Men 79.5%, Women 20.5%
1950 — Men 72.6%, Women 27.4%
1980 — Men 57.9%, Women 42.1%
2010 — Men 52.8%, Women 47.2%

Source: U.S. Census Bureau

GRAPHS ▶
WOMEN'S EARNINGS COMPARED TO MEN'S
The top graph traces the change in the percentage of women's earnings compared to men's earnings. The bottom graph shows how much women in certain occupations earn compared to men in those occupations.
▶ **CRITICAL THINKING**
1. Summarizing Write a sentence that summarizes the information in the top graph.
2. Analyzing Visuals In which of the occupations shown in the bottom graph do females earn the least compared to males? In which do they earn the most?

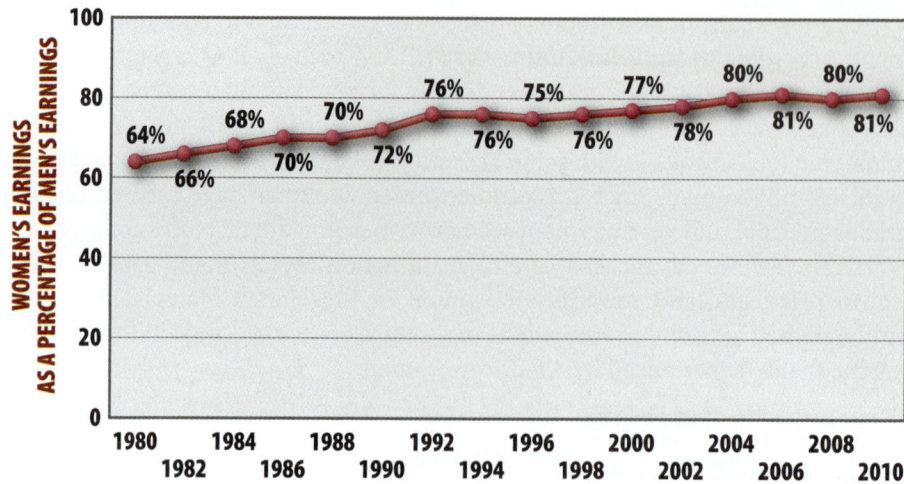

Source: U.S. Department of Labor, Bureau of Labor Statistics, 2011

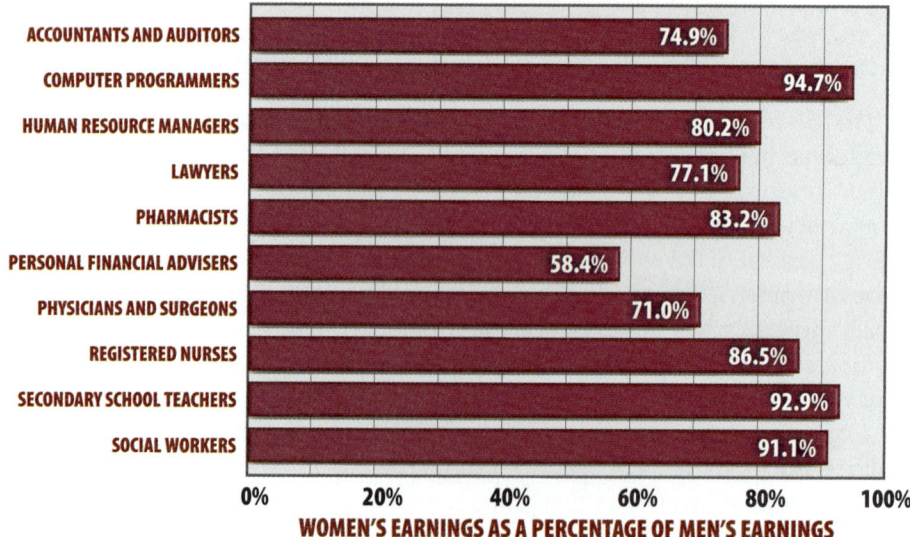

Source: "Highlights of Women's Earnings in 2010," U.S. Department of Labor, U.S. Bureau of Labor Statistics, July 2011

Types of Women's Jobs

Although women are participating in the labor force at increasing levels, they are concentrated in lower-status occupations. This is known as **occupational sex segregation**. In 2010, less than 10 percent of civil engineer positions were held by women, and only about 31 percent of attorney jobs were. By contrast, a report by the U.S. Bureau of Labor Statistics shows that women occupy a large majority of the "pink-collar" jobs—office and administrative support occupations whose purpose is to support those higher up the occupational ladder.

Moreover, when women do reach high-status occupations, such as physicians, they are concentrated in lower-prestige, lower-paid jobs, such as pediatrics. Female lawyers in firms seldom occupy the higher-level administrative positions. Even within female-dominated occupations, such as education, their hold on the most powerful positions is less than their overall participation in the field. In 2008, women who worked as top school system administrators, principals, and assistant principals outnumbered men in those jobs by 145,000 to 122,000. Yet there were three times as many female teachers as there were male teachers. Women also dominated the lower-level jobs within public schools. There were nearly seven times as many women as men working as teacher's aides and nearly thirty times as many working in clerical jobs.

occupational sex segregation the concentration of women in lower-status positions

Women's Earnings

There is a wide discrepancy between the earnings of American women and men. In 2010, women who worked full-time earned only 81 cents for every dollar earned by men. To put it another way, women now work more than six days to earn as much as men earn in five days. The good news is that this salary gap has decreased since 1980, when women were earning 64 percent as much as men, as shown in the top graph on the opposite page. The bad news is that women are closing this gap at less than 1 percent a year. At this rate, it will take another 30 years before women's earnings reach those of men.

In virtually every occupational category, men's earning power outstrips that of women. Women in the same professions as men earn less than their male counterparts, as illustrated in the bottom graph on the opposite page. The earnings gap persists, regardless of educational attainment. All of the occupations shown in that graph require at least a bachelor's degree and some, like attorney and physician, require advanced degrees. Yet it is these very professions where women's share of men's earnings is smallest.

The earnings gap is true even for women who have pursued careers on a full-time basis for all of their adult lives. Furthermore, males in female-dominated occupations typically earn more than women. This persistent gap causes many women's groups to demand what they call "equal pay for equal work." They buttress their argument by pointing out that Congress passed a law requiring that standard in 1963 and that employment discrimination based on sex was outlawed by the Civil Rights Act of 1964.

The Effects of Race and Ethnicity on Earnings

As mentioned earlier, women in the United States earn about 81 percent of what American men earn. Comparing groups of women by race and ethnicity, however, presents another picture. The graph on the bottom of this page compares the earnings of women of different racial or ethnic groups to the average earnings for men of the same racial or ethnic group. As you can see, the results vary dramatically from group to group. African American and Latino women tend to do the best, earning the closest to what men in their group earn. White women do the worst compared to white men, and there are so many white women in the labor force that they drag down the overall earnings of women.

✓ READING PROGRESS CHECK

Summarizing In general, how do women's earnings compare with men's earnings?

◁ GRAPH

WOMEN'S WAGES COMPARED TO MEN'S WAGES BY RACE AND ETHNICITY, 2010

Although women of all racial and ethnic groups earn less than the men from their groups, there are startling differences.

▶ **CRITICAL THINKING**

1. **Analyzing Visuals** Which group has the highest percentage of earnings compared to men's wages? Which has the lowest percentage?

2. **Hypothesizing** What explanation can you offer for these racial and ethnic differences?

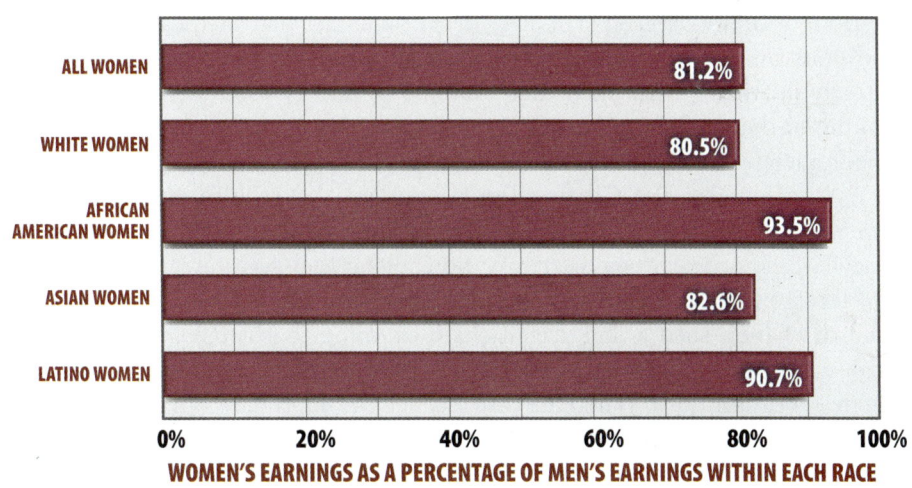

Source: "Highlights of Women's Earnings in 2010," U.S. Department of Labor, U.S. Bureau of Labor Statistics, July 2011, Table 1, p. 9

Inequalities of Gender and Age

Connecting Sociology to Economics

THE GLASS CEILING

Women have long experienced inequality in pay. After 1950, when women joined the workforce in large numbers, women performing the same jobs as men were earning about 60 percent of what men made. At first, less education, lack of skills, and inexperience were the reported reasons women received lower pay. Times have changed; however, women still earn about 20 percent less than men who hold the same jobs. Why is there still a gap? A 2000 study conducted by economists Francine Blau and Lawrence Kahn showed that women have attained higher education, improved skills, and proficiency. Blau and Kahn concluded that the remaining difference is "unattributable."

The gap in pay is one example of discrimination in the workplace; another is the glass ceiling. The term itself was first used in the *Wall Street Journal* in 1986. Like the "iron curtain" during the Cold War, it is invisible but real. It refers to the barriers that women face climbing the corporate ladder. These barriers range from corporate policy to a lack of mentoring to behavioral and cultural issues.

Even though the percentage of the U.S. workforce by gender is approaching equal representation, only about 20 percent of Fortune 500 companies employ women in high leadership positions such as chief executive officer, chief financial officer, or chief operating officer. The numbers do not lie. Economists have seen that women in top management positions have produced financial gains for the companies that employ them versus companies with low female business leadership. In fact, a recent study showed that Fortune 500 companies with a higher percentage of female managers had higher financial returns.

▶ **CRITICAL THINKING**

1. **Making Connections** How does the text illustrate how gender inequality in the workplace affects economic performance?
2. **Analyzing** Do you agree with Blau and Kahn's conclusion about why a wage gap based on gender still exists? What societal factors do you think contribute to the part of the gap that is described as "unattributable"?

Legal and Political Inequality

GUIDING QUESTION *How is gender inequality embedded in the law and the political system?*

Supporters of women's rights point to laws that show a bias against women. National, state, and local legal codes, they claim, reflect a sexual bias that results in important differences between the levels of political power that women and men can attain.

Some Biases in Law

One notable example of legal bias is the U.S. Supreme Court decision that refused to grant women the legal guarantee of health insurance benefits for pregnancy-related medical costs. This included costs related to both contraception and lactation, or breast-feeding. This was despite the fact that medical coverage for conditions unique to men—such as prostate problems and vasectomies—was routinely provided. This particular example of bias is scheduled to change in 2014 under the Affordable Health Care Act, which was passed by Congress and signed into law in 2010.

As mentioned earlier, Congress has passed laws that require employers to pay women equally to men and that ban sex discrimination in employment. Under the law, women can file sex discrimination suits if they feel they have been paid or otherwise treated unfairly by their employers on the basis of sex. In 2011, a group of women sued a large retail chain claiming that it paid its 1.5 million female employees far less than it paid male employees for the same work and gave them fewer promotions. When the case reached the Supreme Court, however, the majority of justices ruled against the female employees. The Court said they had to prove that company management undertook a conscious policy to pay women less. Proving that type of policy is very hard to do without specific written documents establishing the policy.

"The subject of tonight's discussion is: Why are there no women on this panel?"

CARTOON

GENDER INEQUALITY
This cartoon suggests that gender inequality is commonly understood to be the norm.

▶ **CRITICAL THINKING**

1. **Analyzing Visuals** What is humorous about the speaker's question?
2. **Making Connections** What points about gender inequality might the panel make?

Historically, state laws have limited women's rights as well and traditionally refused women the right to keep their own surnames after marriage. Some states had legislation restricting women's workplace rights. Others enacted laws to limit the number of hours women could work and limited the conditions under which they could work, with actions such as barring women from toxic areas because of potential birth defects in their children. Some of these laws limited the kinds of work women could do by regulating such matters as the amount of weight a woman could be permitted to lift (thirty pounds). Supporters of these workplace laws viewed them as safeguards against abuse and exploitation of women. In fact, many advocates for women's rights in the early 1900s supported the passage of these laws in the hopes of protecting women in the workplace.

The result of these laws, however, was that women were denied certain jobs, many of which paid better than more traditional occupations for women. Passage of the Civil Rights Act of 1964 nullified such laws. Unfortunately, just as *de facto* segregation has continued to result in discrimination against African Americans despite the banning of *de jure* segregation, some of these practices that limit women's rights still linger.

Laws can also have unintended negative consequences for women. For example, the Family and Medical Leave Act (1993), which requires that employees be given up to 12 weeks without pay for childbirth, adoption, personal illness, or caring for a family member with a serious illness, can negatively affect women. Since women are more likely to take maternity leave than men are to take paternity leave, the law can lead some employers to give hiring preference to men.

There are differences by gender in criminal law as well. Certain crimes are typically associated with one sex rather than the other, and sometimes those laws result in discriminatory treatment of women. For example, laws against prostitution are generally prosecuted and enforced against only the female prostitutes, while their male customers often go free.

A Global Perspective

WOMEN IN NATIONAL PARLIAMENTS

The percentage of women serving in national parliaments has risen globally from 9 percent in 1987 to 19 percent in 2009. The highest percentage of women in parliaments is in Northern Europe, with more than 40 percent, while the lowest percentage is found in Southwest Asia, with not a single female serving in some countries. Gender inequality in parliament results in a weaker female voice and influence within a nation.

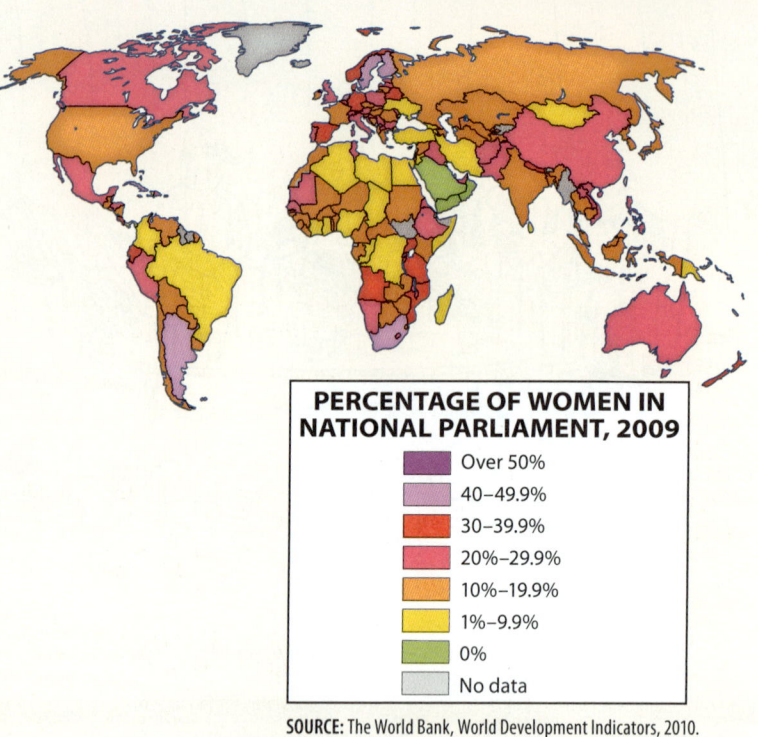

PERCENTAGE OF WOMEN IN NATIONAL PARLIAMENT, 2009
- Over 50%
- 40–49.9%
- 30–39.9%
- 20%–29.9%
- 10%–19.9%
- 1%–9.9%
- 0%
- No data

SOURCE: The World Bank, World Development Indicators, 2010.

Geography Connection

1. **Places and Regions** Why do you think there is more female representation in parliaments in Northern Europe?
2. **Environment and Society** How do gender inequalities in society affect female representation in government?

Women in Politics

Women appear to be participating in elective politics at an increasing rate. Recently, the numbers of female governors, lieutenant governors, attorneys general, and mayors have been growing. Some increases have occurred at the national level as well. In 1984, Geraldine Ferraro became the first female vice-presidential candidate in American history, and she was followed by Sarah Palin in 2008. Madeleine Albright was named the first female secretary of state in 1996, and two more women have held that post—traditionally seen as the highest cabinet post—since then. Elizabeth Dole campaigned for her party's nomination for president before the election of 2000, and Hillary Clinton ran a nearly successful campaign for her party's nomination in 2008. Still, although women constitute more than half the population, they hold a relatively small proportion of important political positions.

Women occupied only 16.8 percent of the seats in the U.S. House of Representatives in 2012. And although the number of female U.S. senators increased from 2 to 17 over the 1990s, women still represented just 17 percent of the Senate in 2012. Although Nancy Pelosi became the first woman Speaker of the House in 2007 and became minority leader in 2011, women in Congress have seldom risen to positions of power. Only 16 women hold House or Senate leadership roles. Women have also been historically underrepresented in appointed political positions. Although there have been recent increases in the number of appointments, the total is extremely small.

When President Jimmy Carter appointed two women to his cabinet in 1977, it was the first time two women had sat in the cabinet at one time. President Bill Clinton, almost 20 years later, appointed three women to cabinet posts. In 2009, President Barack Obama named Hillary Clinton as secretary of state, and four

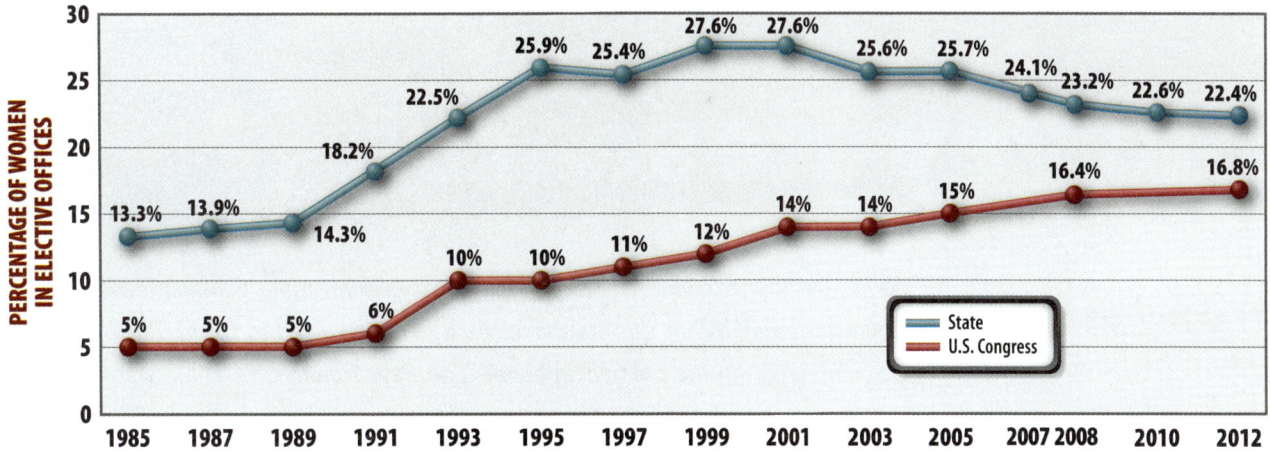

other women were appointed to head his cabinet departments. Still, the total number of women who have ever served as cabinet officers is very small.

The representation of women on the United States Supreme Court has grown in recent decades. President Ronald Reagan appointed the first female Supreme Court justice, Sandra Day O'Connor, in 1981, and President Clinton elevated Ruth Bader Ginsburg to the high court in 1993. Since 2009, President Obama has named two other women, Sonia Sotomayor and Elena Kagan, to the high court. Only a small percentage of federal judges is women, however.

The number of women holding public office in the United States is among the lowest in the Western world. With some notable exceptions, Western European nations have much greater female political leadership. In the Scandinavian countries, for example, up to 20 percent of members of parliament are women.

Sociologists Richard Zweigenhaft and William Domhoff do point out that women are now part of the power elite. The power elite is no longer the exclusively male group it used to be. Still, women are seriously underrepresented, and most of those women who do join the power elite come from upper-class backgrounds.

✓ READING PROGRESS CHECK

Making Predictions Do you think the percentage of women in elected offices will continue to increase in the future? Why?

▲ GRAPH

PERCENTAGE OF WOMEN IN ELECTIVE OFFICES
This graph illustrates the percentage of women elected to state and national government positions over a nearly 30-year period.

▶ CRITICAL THINKING

1. **Analyzing Visuals** How would you compare the rate of change in women elected to state elective offices with that of women elected to U.S. Congress?

2. **Analyzing** How has sexism affected the totals and the trend in women's elections?

LESSON 3 REVIEW

Reviewing Vocabulary
1. **Defining** What is the intent of sexist beliefs?
2. **Explaining** How does occupational sex segregation affect the jobs women perform?

Using Your Notes
3. **Describing** Use your notes to list an example of sexism in economic, legal, and political spheres.

Answering the Guiding Questions
4. **Assessing** Is discrimination against women disappearing? Why or why not?

5. **Making Connections** What is occupational sex segregation, and how does it affect earnings?
6. **Explaining** How is gender inequality embedded in the law and the political system?

Writing Activity
7. **Narrative** Identify a time when you felt or noticed sexism. Describe the situation and how you think it affected you or the people involved.

Inequalities of Gender and Age **285**

FOCUS on research

Survey Research

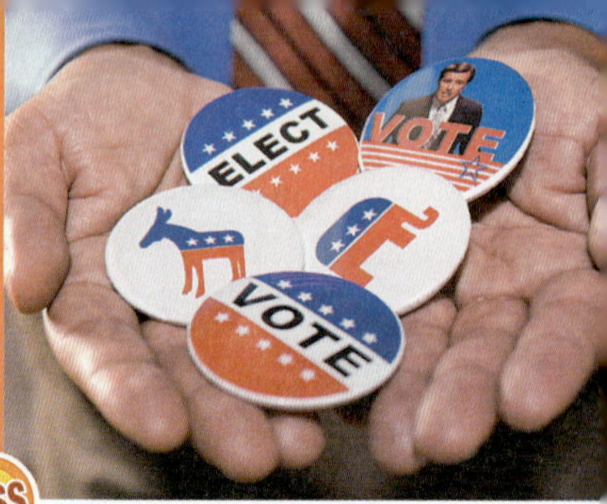

CCSS

Obstacles to Female Political Leadership

Why are there fewer female political leaders than male political leaders in the United States? What societal barriers do women need to break through to end discrimination in the political sphere? The Pew Research Center wanted to find out and in 2008 conducted a survey. The center found that only 21 percent of those who were polled think that men make better leaders. But more than two-thirds responded that men and women both made good candidates for elective office. So what accounts for women's underrepresentation in political office?

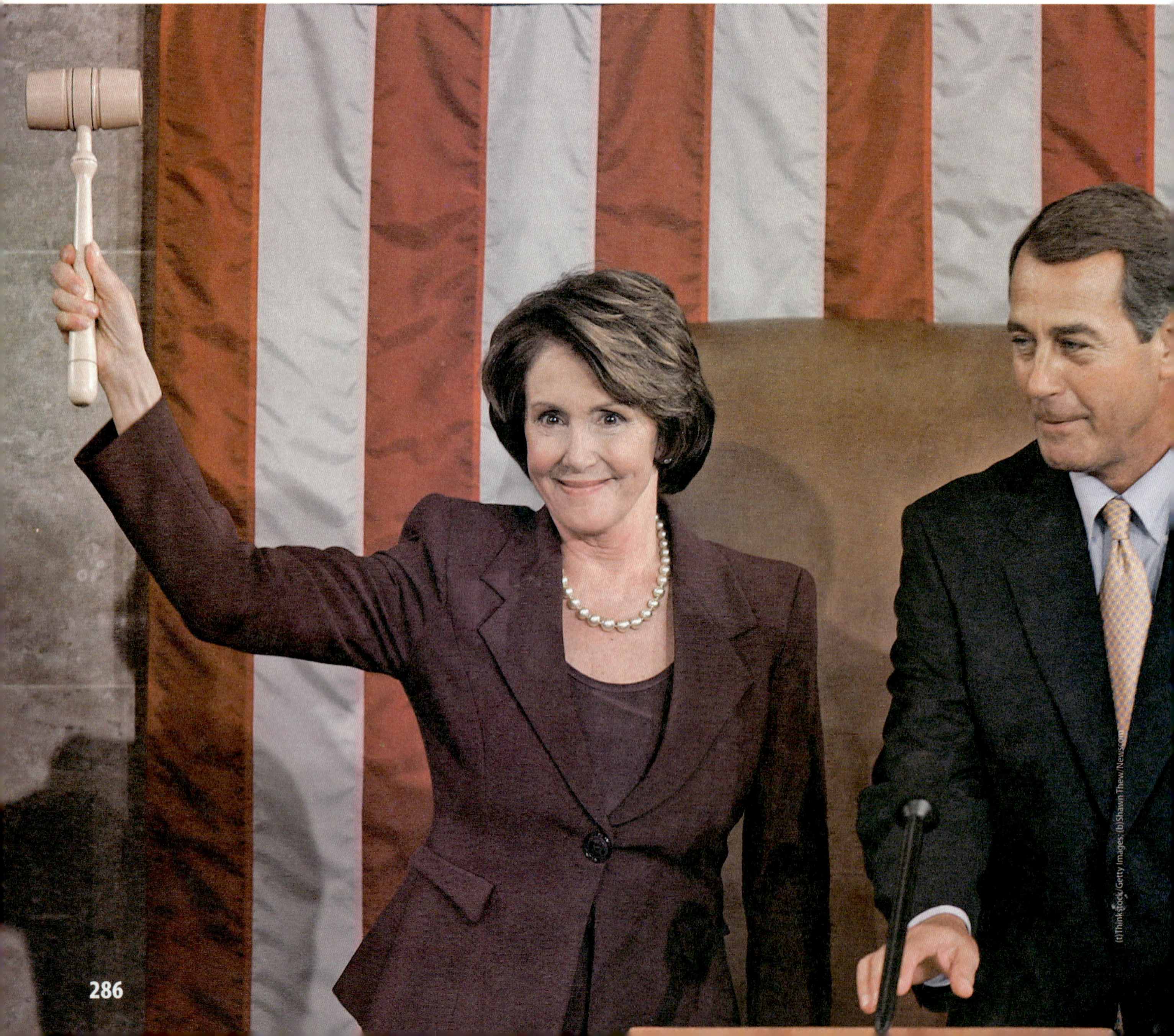

(t)Thinkstock/Getty Images; (b)Shawn Thew/News.com

PRIMARY SOURCE

"Why are there not more women in the nation's top political offices? ... [Our survey shows that] the public does not believe women lack the character traits to be elected senator or governor. Instead, Americans are more likely to cite obstacles: Voters aren't ready to elect them. Discrimination or male resistance holds them back. Family responsibilities take precedence.

Men and women equally reject the explanation that women are not tough enough or lack the leadership skills needed for high office. But there is a gender gap on attitudes about other possible explanations. Women are more likely than men to believe that gender discrimination, male resistance, and voters' unreadiness for change are major reasons there are more men than women in top jobs. Men are more likely than women to say those are minor reasons or not reasons.

Among major demographic groups, black and Hispanic respondents are more inclined than whites to cite discrimination and male resistance as major forces. So are Democrats and Independents, compared with Republicans. Older Americans, and those with the lowest income and education levels, are more likely than others to see family responsibilities as a key driver.

Major Reasons for Lack of Female Political Leaders

The nation has eight female governors out of 50, and 16 female U.S. senators out of 100—a 16% proportion of each group [as of 2008]. The survey presents these statistics, offers seven possible explanations for the gender disparity in top political leadership and asks respondents whether they believe each is a major reason, a minor reason or not a reason.

Of the choices offered, the most popular explanation is that many voters are not ready to elect female politicians. About half (51%) say that is a major reason and another 28% say it is a minor reason. Only 18% say it is not a reason.

The next two most widely chosen reasons have to do with prejudice and bias. Four-in-ten Americans (43%) say a major reason for women's lower share of political jobs is that women who are active in party politics are held back by men. A third (32%) say that is a minor reason, and 21% say it is not a reason.

Are politics no exception to a general pattern of discrimination against women? This is deemed a major reason for the male-female disparity in holding office by 38% of respondents and a minor one by 33%. About a quarter—27%—say that is not a reason.

Perhaps women are unable to attain high office because their family responsibilities do not leave time for politics. This explanation is not as widely embraced as is discrimination or lack of voter readiness, but 27% of Americans say it is a major reason there are not more female leaders. Four-in-ten (40%) say it is a minor reason, and 31% say it is not a reason.

Or could the explanation be that, compared with men, women lack the right kind of experience for political leadership? About one-in-four respondents (26%) say lack of experience is a major reason, and 37% say it is a minor reason. About a third—34%—say that is not a reason there are not more females elected to high office.

Americans are much less inclined to say that women do not have the leadership qualities or toughness needed to propel them into high office. Most people say that a deficit of leadership skills (53%) or toughness (54%) are not reasons for the gender gap in political job-holding. A lack of leadership skills is deemed a major reason by just 16% of respondents and a minor reason by 29%. A lack of toughness is called a major reason by only 14% of respondents and a minor reason by 31%."

—Pew Research Center, "Men or Women: Who's the Better Leader? A Paradox in Public Attitudes," 2008

> "The public does not believe women lack the character traits to be elected senator or governor. Instead, Americans are more likely to cite obstacles: Voters aren't ready to elect them. Discrimination or male resistance holds them back. Family responsibilities take precedence."

Working With the Research

1. **Making Connections** How are discrimination and prejudice related to the proportion of female political leaders in the United States?
2. **Identifying Cause and Effect** What effect did gender bias have on individual respondents in the survey?
3. **Evaluating Counter Arguments** Do you agree with the respondents who said that women in politics are held back by men? What argument could you make to refute that perception?

networks

There's More Online!

- ☑ **GRAPH** Suicide Rates by Age, Gender, and Racial Group
- ☑ **GRAPHIC ORGANIZER** Ageism
- ☑ **IMAGE** Older Woman Using Smartphone
- ☑ **SELF-CHECK QUIZ**

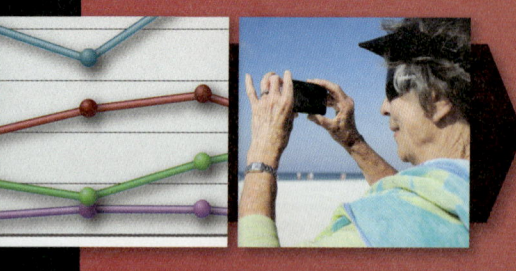

LESSON 4
Ageism

ESSENTIAL QUESTIONS • What are the causes and effects of discrimination in society? • How is gender discrimination reflected in the legal and economic systems? • What are the effects of age discrimination?

Reading HELPDESK

Academic Vocabulary
- utilize
- aspect

Content Vocabulary
- age stratification
- ageism

TAKING NOTES:
Key Ideas and Details

TAKING NOTES As you read about ageism, use a graphic organizer like the one below to help you take notes.

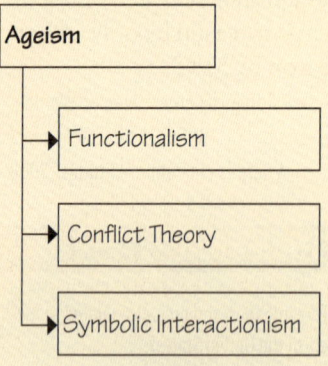

IT MATTERS BECAUSE
The relatively low social standing of older people is based on ageism. Each of the theoretical perspectives has a unique slant on ageism. Stereotypes are often used to justify prejudice and discrimination, which can harm the self-concepts of older people.

Functionalism and Ageism

GUIDING QUESTION *How does functionalism explain ageism?*

Chronological age is another basis for social ranking. For this reason, sociologists are interested in **age stratification**—when the unequal distribution of scarce resources (power, wealth, prestige) in a society is based on age. Like inequality based on race, ethnicity, or gender, age stratification must be socially justified. The rationale for age-based inequality comes in the form of **ageism**—a set of beliefs, attitudes, norms, and values used to justify prejudice and discrimination against a particular age group.

Age can be an advantage or a disadvantage for any group. For example, children and teenagers under 18 in the United States are almost twice as likely to be living in poverty as the groups aged 18 to 64 and 65 and older. Currently, sociologists are especially interested in inequality among older people. As the median age of the U.S. population moves up, this form of ageism affects more and more people.

According to functionalists, elderly people in a given society are treated according to the role the aged play in that society. In many societies, ageism is not an issue. In fact, elderly people in many cultures are treated with respect and honor. In agricultural societies, elderly males usually play important roles, such as the role of priest or elder. Donald Cowgill and Lowell Holmes give examples of societies in which the elderly are highly valued:

PRIMARY SOURCE

"In all of the African societies, growing old is equated with rising status and increased respect. Among the Igbo, the older person is assumed to be wise; this not only brings him respect, since he is consulted for his wisdom, it also provides him with a valued role in his society. The Bantu elder is 'The Father of his People' and revered as such. In Samoa too, old age is 'the best time of life' and older persons are accorded great respect. Likewise, in Thailand, older persons are honored and deferred to and Adams reports respect and affection for older people in rural Mexico."

—from *Aging and Modernization*, 1972

Similarly, in colonial America, to be elderly brought respect along with the opportunity to fill the most prestigious positions in the community. It was believed that God looked with favor on those who reached old age. The longer one lived, the more likely he or she was to have been chosen to go to heaven. The Bible linked age with living a moral life: "Keep my commandments, for length of days and long life and peace shall they add unto thee." During the 1600s and 1700s, Americans even tried to appear older than they actually were, using clothing and wigs. During the 1700s, people often inflated their age when reporting to census takers.

Attitudes about aging changed greatly as industrialization changed the nature of work. In a technical society, an adult's value lessens when he or she no longer contributes fully to the common good. Thus, aging tends to lead to lower status. Because modern societies change rapidly, younger workers are more likely to possess the current skills needed in the workplace, while older workers' skills are more likely to be out of date. Thus, they lack the "wisdom" that is most highly valued. This loss of status with older age might help explain the increase in the suicide rate for men beginning at about retirement age illustrated in the graph. Men may have greater difficulty in older age than women because they have been socialized in a culture that encourages men to identify strongly with work while they are younger but denies them a sense of value after retirement.

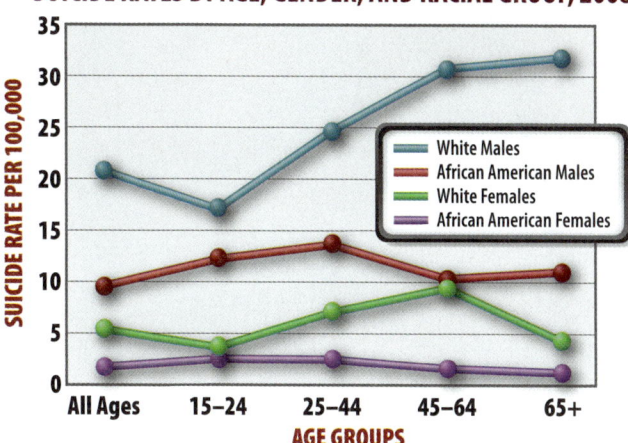

GRAPH

SUICIDE RATES BY AGE, GENDER, AND RACIAL GROUP, 2008
Suicide rates vary greatly according to age and racial group.

▶ **CRITICAL THINKING**

1. **Analyzing Visuals** Which group consistently has the lowest rate of suicide? Which group has the highest?
2. **Making Connections** How does functionalism explain the increased rate of suicide for white males after the age of 65?

☑ **READING PROGRESS CHECK**

Drawing Inferences Why do many modern men and women use clothing and other methods to try to look younger?

Conflict Theory and Ageism

GUIDING QUESTION *How does conflict theory explain ageism?*

Competition over scarce resources lies at the heart of ageism from the conflict perspective. Elderly people compete with other age groups for economic resources, power, and prestige. In pre-industrial societies, older people often get a fair share of the scarce resources. This is because work in such a society is labor intensive and all available hands must be **utilized**. Also, the elderly are sources of valuable knowledge about practices and history.

Quick Case Study

HOW IS AGEISM A FORM OF SOCIAL INEQUALITY?

As people age, they may lose feelings of importance and self-worth due to ageism. How can you identify ageism?

Procedure

1. Interview five people of varying age groups, including at least one senior citizen.
2. Ask them to whom a job should be given—a person who has just graduated from college with no work experience or a person in his or her early sixties with a lot of work experience—and why they think as they do. Record their responses.

Analysis

As you read through their responses, consider these questions:

1. In what ways did the responses of the people show ageism?
2. How did the people's reasoning justify their choice?
3. What conclusions can you draw about ageism and how it relates to social inequality?

Inequalities of Gender and Age **289**

Industrial society, in contrast, usually has more workers than it needs and saves scarce resources by replacing high-priced older workers with less costly younger ones. Forced retirement is one way the more powerful age groups remove elderly competitors.

According to conflict theory, prejudice and discrimination are used by the dominant group as weapons in the control of minority groups. If older people can be stereotyped as intellectually dull, closed minded, inflexible, and unproductive, forcing their retirement from the labor market becomes relatively easy. This leaves more jobs available for younger and less expensive workers.

✓ **READING PROGRESS CHECK**

Analyzing According to conflict theory, which group is most responsible for ageism? Why?

False, negative stereotypes often suggest that older people have a hard time learning new things.

▶ **CRITICAL THINKING**

Making Generalizations What can older people do to combat negative stereotypes?

age stratification the unequal distribution of scarce resources based on age

ageism a set of beliefs, attitudes, norms, and values used to justify age-based prejudice and discrimination

utilize to use

aspect a particular trait or feature of something

Symbolic Interactionism and Ageism

GUIDING QUESTION *How do symbolic interactionists explain ageism?*

Like racism, ageism involves creating negative stereotypes. According to symbolic interactionists, children learn negative images of older people just as they learn other **aspects** of culture. Through the process of socialization, stereotypes of elderly people are often firmly implanted into a child's view of the world. A 1999 study by Susan Hiller and Georgia M. Barrow observed negative images of older people in children as young as three years old.

By definition, stereotypes are inaccurate because they do not apply to all members of a group. Stereotypes of older people are no exception. Most elderly people are not senile, forgetful, or "daft." Old age is not a sexless period for the majority of those over 65. There are few age differences on job-related factors either. Most elderly people are able to learn new things and adapt to change.

In summary, there is enough evidence to challenge the truth of popular stereotypes of elderly people. Of course, some older people do fit one or more of these stereotypes (as some young people fit societal stereotypes), and many individuals are likely to fit one or more of them as they reach age 70. This fact, however, does not justify applying the stereotypes to all older people at any age or mindlessly applying them to individuals in their fifties and sixties.

✓ **READING PROGRESS CHECK**

Summarizing What are some common negative stereotypes of older people?

LESSON 4 REVIEW

Reviewing Vocabulary
1. *Defining* What is age stratification?
2. *Explaining* Is ageism common in all cultures? Explain.

Using Your Notes
3. *Evaluating* Use your notes to write a sentence or two describing which explanation of ageism you find most convincing and why.

Answering the Guiding Questions
4. *Explaining* How does functionalism explain ageism?
5. *Explaining* How does conflict theory explain ageism?
6. *Explaining* How does symbolic interactionism explain ageism?

Writing Activity
7. *Informative/Explanatory* Identify an older person you are close to and explain how that person fits or does not fit negative stereotypes of elderly people.

networks

There's More Online!

- ☑ **CARTOON** Income and the Elderly
- ☑ **CHART** Poverty Rates Among Americans 65 and Over
- ☑ **GRAPHIC ORGANIZER** Inequality Among Elders
- ☑ **IMAGE** Elderly Activism
- ☑ **MAP** An Aging Population
- **SELF-CHECK QUIZ**

LESSON 5
Inequality in America's Elderly Population

ESSENTIAL QUESTIONS • What are the causes and effects of discrimination in society? • How is gender discrimination reflected in the legal and economic systems? • What are the effects of age discrimination?

Reading HELPDESK

Academic Vocabulary
- diminished
- underlying

Content Vocabulary
- interest group

TAKING NOTES:
Key Ideas and Details

ORGANIZING As you read about inequality in America's elderly population, use a graphic organizer like the one below to summarize key ideas.

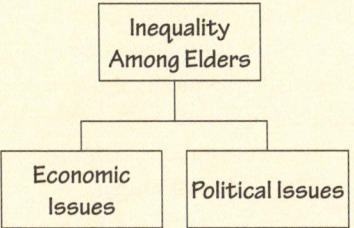

It Matters Because

The poverty rate for America's elderly population is just below 10 percent. Members of racial and ethnic minorities are in the poorest ranks. The political process offers the major source of power for elderly Americans. Older people exert political influence through their high voting rate and their support of special-interest groups.

Economics of the Elderly

GUIDING QUESTION What factors contribute to poverty among older Americans?

Because early research on older people tended to study those who had been placed in institutions, studies focused on people with **diminished** mental and physical capacities. This perspective coincided with the American public's negative view of elderly people.

Sociologists believe that the best way to expose this blaming of older people for their situation is to view them as a minority. Racial, ethnic, and religious groups have long been considered as minorities. Women have recently been recognized as a minority group and so have people with mental and physical disabilities. Not until recently have researchers viewed older people as a distinct segment of society subject to the same discrimination and stereotyping as other minority groups.

Measuring Poverty for Older People

The economic situation among America's older people has improved greatly since about 1960, but as a group, older Americans are far from being well off. Several **underlying** causes make it hard to determine exactly how elderly people compare economically with other groups, however. For one thing, the way poverty among older people is measured distorts the real picture.

The official measures of poverty for all people are badly out of date, relying on formulas developed more than 50 years ago. In 1995, the National Academy of Sciences (NAS) created a new measure for poverty, which was first used along with the previous measures, beginning in 2011.

Inequalities of Gender and Age **291**

"Have you given much thought to what kind of job you want after you retire?"

> **CARTOON**
>
> **INCOME AND THE ELDERLY**
> Retirement income from Social Security and other sources often does not cover basic needs for elderly people.
>
> ▶ **CRITICAL THINKING**
>
> 1. **Analyzing Visuals** Why is the use of the word *retire* funny in this instance?
> 2. **Making Connections** What changes in the cost of living have made elders less able to live on a fixed income?

diminished reduced; limited

underlying important but not obvious

Using the new NAS measure of poverty for incomes in 2008, the elderly poverty level is nearly double that of the level using the previous measure, rising from 9.7 percent to 18.7 percent, greater than for any other age group, including children. The graph on the opposite page shows the changes in the poverty level for older Americans over four decades using the older poverty measures. These percentages also do not show the number of elderly people considered "near poor." Adding those figures to those below the poverty level raises the level of elderly people with low income to more than 36 percent.

The income gap among elderly people also distorts the economic picture. The existence of a small percentage of high-income older people gives the false impression that most older people are economically well off. Some older people have moderate to high incomes based on dividends from assets, cash savings, and private retirement programs. On the other end, about 40 percent of elderly Americans rely on Social Security benefits for more than 90 percent of their income. Social Security payments replace only about 55 percent of income for low-wage earners and about half of the income earned by high-wage earners. Barely half of an already low income means those low-income earners have little to live on in retirement.

Other Factors Affecting Elderly Americans

Older people who are members of racial or ethnic minority groups are generally in worse economic condition than older white Americans. The poverty rate among older African Americans is almost three times that for whites. For older Latinos, the poverty rate is more than two-and-one-half times that of non-Latino white Americans. Problems that racial and ethnic minorities face because of discrimination become magnified in old age.

Elderly women constitute one of the poorest segments of American society. According to a 2008 report by the Congressional Research Service, women over age 65 are nearly twice as likely to live in poverty as their male counterparts. Elderly women most likely to be poor are single women who have never married or are divorced, separated, or widowed. This is not surprising because the roots of poverty among older women lie in their work-related experiences. Because older women were discouraged or blocked from better jobs throughout their working lives, they are unable to support themselves in their later years.

Surprisingly, the recession that began in late 2007 did not harm the incomes of elderly people as much as it did the incomes of younger people. This is because much of most elders' incomes is fixed, in the form of Social Security payments and in some cases pensions. As a result, income levels were not affected by issues such as job loss or losses from shorter-term investments. As life expectancy continues to climb, however, the savings and other income of elderly people will need to last longer.

The Economic Position of Older People in the United States

In summary, then, elderly people today are economically better off than they were four decades ago. Despite this improvement, large segments of Americans over 65 years of age live in poverty or near poverty. This is especially true for elderly members of racial and ethnic minorities and for elderly women.

✓ **READING PROGRESS CHECK**

Making Generalizations How does the job experience of women during their working years affect their incomes when they become elderly?

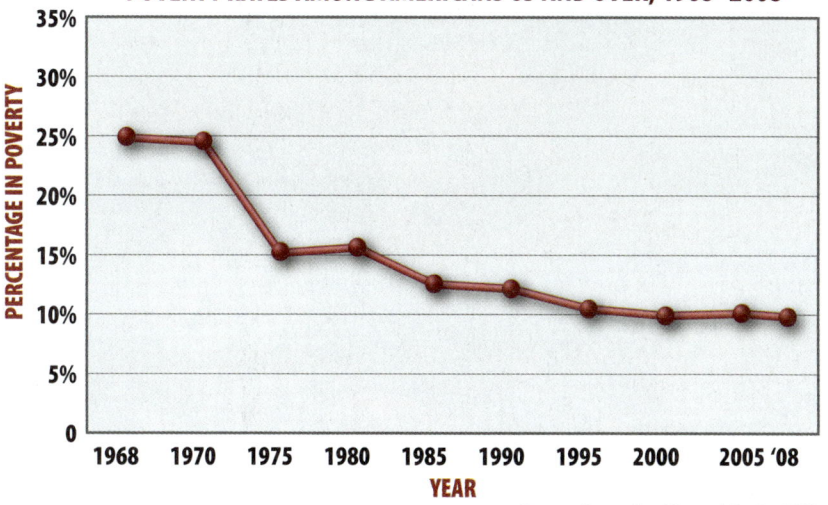

GRAPH

POVERTY RATES AMONG AMERICANS 65 AND OVER, 1968–2008

This graph uses the poverty definition established about 50 years ago.

▶ **CRITICAL THINKING**

1. **Hypothesizing** Why do you think elderly poverty rates have dropped so dramatically since 1968?

2. **Identifying** Which groups of elderly people are not reflected in this graph?

Political Power and the Elderly

GUIDING QUESTION *How have the elderly exerted political power?*

Given the limited economic resources of older people, it is clear that any power they hold is gained through the political process. Especially important are the voting booth and political-interest groups.

Voter Turnout Among Elderly Americans

Voter turnout in the United States increases with age. Americans aged 65 and over have become the most active voters in presidential and congressional elections. In the 2008 presidential election, for example, over 70 percent of this group voted.

A Diverse America

AN AGING POPULATION

The 2010 U.S. Census showed that the aging population, defined as 65 and older, in the United States is the largest of any previous census. The same age group also grew more quickly between 2000 and 2010 than did the total U.S. population, at a rate of nearly 6 percent faster. This map shows the percentage of the population who are age 65 and over, by state, in 2010.

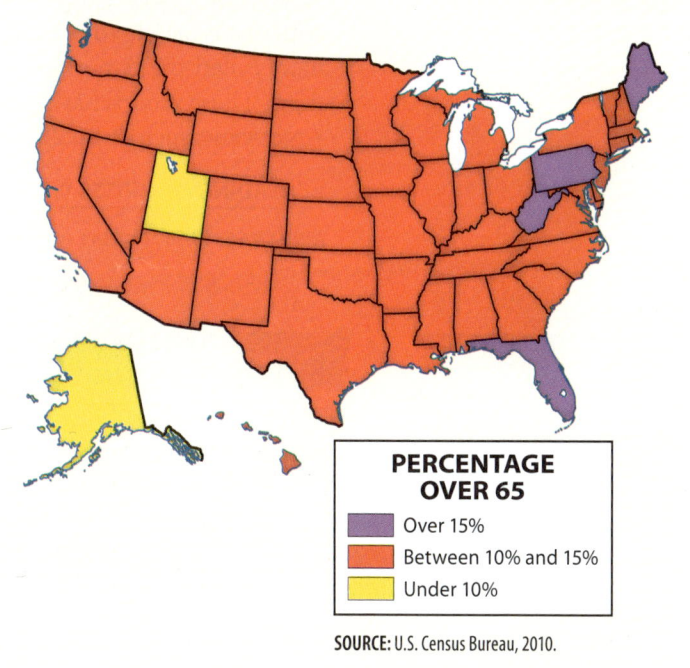

PERCENTAGE OVER 65
- Over 15%
- Between 10% and 15%
- Under 10%

SOURCE: U.S. Census Bureau, 2010.

Geography Connection

1. **Places and Regions** Where is the population over the age of 65 particularly high, as compared to the rest of the nation?

2. **Human Systems** What impact would these figures be likely to have on the governments of those states?

3. **Human Systems** What generalizations about employment can you make about America's population based on this map?

Inequalities of Gender and Age

Older people have shown that they can be a powerful political force.

▶ CRITICAL THINKING

Analyzing Why do some politicians regularly try to please the elderly population?

In contrast, about 49 percent of 18-to-24-year-olds and about 57 percent of 25-to-34-year-olds turned out to vote in that election.

Most analysts believe that the potential political power of elderly Americans as a group is not fully realized because of the diversity of the older population. Because older people cut across many important divisions in American society—social class, ethnicity, race, geographic area, religion—they do not speak with a unified political voice. In fact, they do not vote as a bloc on any political question, even on issues related directly to their interests. This lack of unity weakens their political clout. As the population of the United States ages, however, and the number of elderly voters increases, it is likely that "gray power" will become a significant political force.

Interest Groups

Interest groups are organized to influence political decision making. Millions of Americans belong to interest groups that target ageism, such as the AARP—originally called the American Association of Retired Persons—and the Gray Panthers. These groups have been effective in protecting programs that benefit older Americans, such as Medicare and Social Security.

interest group a group organized to influence political decision making

✓ READING PROGRESS CHECK

Analyzing What factors limit the political power of the elderly?

LESSON 5 REVIEW

Reviewing Vocabulary
1. *Defining* What is the purpose of an interest group?

Using Your Notes
2. *Summarizing* Use your notes to write a sentence or two characterizing the economic status of the elderly.

Answering the Guiding Questions
3. *Identifying* What factors contribute to poverty among older Americans?
4. *Explaining* How have the elderly exerted political power?

Writing Activity
5. *Informative/Explanatory* Think of one elderly person you know and describe his or her economic situation and the reasons for it. (You do not have to use a real name.)

CHAPTER 10 Assessment

Directions: On a separate sheet of paper, answer the questions below. Make sure you read carefully and answer all parts of the questions.

Lesson Review

Lesson 1

1 **Exploring the Issues** Why and how was the theory of biological determinism used in the past? Explain whether this is a scientifically based theory.

2 **Identifying Central Issues** What is the connection between the nature-versus-nurture argument and gender differences?

Lesson 2

3 **Simulating** Discuss steps you could take as a preschool teacher to promote gender equality in your school. Explain why such steps are important for students of this age.

4 **Comparing and Contrasting** Create a Venn diagram to compare and contrast explanations of gender differences based on functionalism, conflict theory, and symbolic interactionism.

Lesson 3

5 **Analyzing** Do women's educational gains mean that gender inequality will end? Why or why not?

6 **Analyzing** Do recent stellar accomplishments by women, such as Hillary Clinton serving as U.S. secretary of state, reflect an end to gender inequality? Why or why not?

Lesson 4

7 **Making Generalizations** Provide a generalization regarding the impact of changes in technology on an older adult's status as he or she ages.

8 **Discussing** Would it be correct to state that all stereotypes are inaccurate? Explain, providing an example in your explanation.

Lesson 5

9 **Making Predictions** Discuss the economic situation among America's elderly, explaining whether it has improved and whether they are currently doing well economically in general. Predict whether this will change or remain the same, and explain why you think so.

10 **Drawing Conclusions** Why do you think voter turnout in the United States increases with age? Do you think this bears any relationship to the economic situation of older Americans?

DBQ Analyzing Primary Sources

Use the table to answer the question below.

PRIMARY SOURCE

Ratio of Female to Male Earnings in Manufacturing		
	1990–1992	2006–2008
Australia	82	90
Egypt	68	66
Japan	41	61
Mexico	50	72
Paraguay	66	86
South Korea	50	57
Singapore	55	65
Sri Lanka	88	77
Sweden	89	91
United Kingdom	61	75

Source: UN Statistics Division, *The World's Women 2010: Trends and Statistics*

11 **Hypothesizing** In this chapter, you read about inequity in pay for men and women. In the table, data for the ratio of female to male earnings is provided for a variety of countries. Study the table, and then develop three hypotheses based on the data. Your hypotheses might compare earnings for the two periods reported or earnings for nations and regions, or you might try to explain the reasons for similarities or disparities among nations and regions.

Need Extra Help?

If You've Missed Question	1	2	3	4	5	6	7	8	9	10	11
Go to page	268–269	269–272	275–277	273–277	278–285	273–275	288–289	290	291–292	293–294	278–281

CHAPTER 10 Assessment

Directions: On a separate sheet of paper, answer the questions below. Make sure you read carefully and answer all parts of the questions.

College and Career Readiness Skills

12 *Change and Continuity of Groups* While many jobs no longer require physical strength and stamina as they once did, some—such as firefighting and construction—still do. It has been argued that due to biology, men are better suited for these positions than women, though this argument has been strongly refuted and a variety of laws have been passed in an effort to eliminate discrimination. Some cities and townships have followed anti-discrimination laws and guidelines, and others have tried to fight them. Imagine you are a mayor. Write a memo to your city council to explain your position on this issue. Support your position with content from the chapter and your personal knowledge and experience.

Critical Thinking

13 *Identifying Perspectives* A variety of stereotypes have arisen in relation to gender and age. Utilizing historical and current perspectives regarding gender and age, develop at least four potential solutions to guard against—as much as possible—continued stereotyping. Utilize information from each lesson to explain conditions that have given rise to issues you are addressing in your solutions.

21st Century Skills

CREATING AND USING GRAPHS, CHARTS, DIAGRAMS AND TABLES

14 *Compare and Contrast* Imagine the experiences you might have within a week if you awoke to find that your gender had changed. Create a diagram to compare and contrast the experiences you generally have within a week with those you might experience due to such a change. When your diagram is complete, write conclusions you have drawn regarding the ways a person's life might be different if his or her gender were to change.

Exploring the Essential Questions

15 *Comparing and Contrasting* There are many similarities and differences among causes and effects of gender discrimination and of ageism. Write a short essay to discuss these similarities and differences. Then conduct online research to locate university sites and other reliable sites that address gender discrimination and ageism. Develop a list of resources, with a short summary of the mission statement for each.

Research and Presentation

16 *Gathering Information* The Center for American Women and Politics provides information regarding women in public office in the United States. Search for information about your state. Locate the answers to these questions: How many women from your state are currently serving in the U.S. Senate and the U.S. House of Representatives? How many women are currently serving in your state's legislature? What is the percentage of women currently serving in your state's legislature? What is your state's ranking among state legislatures across the nation for the percentage of women? After you have answered these questions for your state, select one other state and respond to the same questions for that state.

17 *Making Predictions* Take the following steps to prepare a presentation for the class: On the computer, develop a visual to show how your state compares to the additional state you selected—and how each state compares with the national figures. Discuss your conclusions regarding the reasons for your state's ranking. Based on the knowledge you have gleaned through studying the chapter, through your research for this project, and through your own experience, predict the likely future for women aspiring to be legislators in your state. Present your visual, conclusions, and predictions to the class.

Need Extra Help?

If You've Missed Question	12	13	14	15	16	17
Go to page	268–285	268–294	268–285	268–294	284–287	284–287

The Family

ESSENTIAL QUESTION • *What makes a family?*

networks
There's More Online about the family.

CHAPTER 11

Technology & Society
Families and Technology

Lesson 1
Family and Marriage Across Cultures

Lesson 2
Theoretical Perspectives and the Family

Lesson 3
Family and Marriage in the United States

Lesson 4
Changes in Marriage and Family

Sociology Matters...

Throughout history and around the world, the family has been the basic unit of social organization. Definitions of *family* vary somewhat from culture to culture, as do family roles and practices for forming and dissolving families. But people everywhere form and live in intimate groups that produce offspring, share basic values and traditions, and fulfill long-term commitments to one another. The experience of family is one that unites all human beings.

◄ The formation of family units through marriage is a ritual practiced in many societies.

imagebroker.net/SuperStock

CHAPTER 11
Technology & Society

Families and Technology

Families can stay better connected than ever before.

For many American families, staying in touch is easier than it was a decade ago. The myriad of technological options makes it difficult to decide which one to use—and when. Cell phones allow parents and children to stay in contact via texting, e-mail, and calling. Smartphones offer even more possibilities. Many include video features or, through applications called "apps," the ability to chat face-to-face. For working parents with small children in day care, video monitors present another constant-contact function. From their computers or smartphones, they can "visit" their children with or without having a conversation. They can watch their children napping, eating, and playing from their offices or even during an out-of-town trip.

Think about the uses of communication technology for military families. In World War II, GIs wrote letters to their loved ones who were anxiously awaiting them. Today, a family whose child is in the military and stationed overseas or a parent in the military who has been stationed on another continent can stay in touch by making Internet calls from a personal computer.

For some, the ease of communication today may not be as welcome. Adolescents who carry a device such as a smartphone with global positioning system (GPS) technology enabled can be tracked by their parents. These teens can choose to ignore text messages, e-mails, and phone calls, but they cannot necessarily escape GPS. Their parents have the ability to know where they are at all times. Today, sometimes it is more difficult to be unreachable because of the endless high-tech communication options that are available.

Internet video call
Mother deployed by the military in a foreign country talks regularly to her children thousands of miles away every week via free video calls over the Internet.

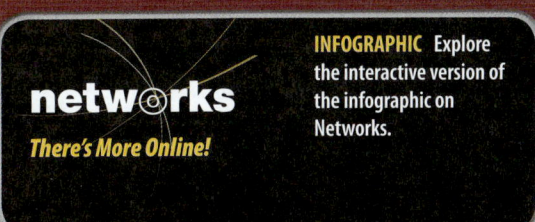

INFOGRAPHIC Explore the interactive version of the infographic on Networks.

FAMILIES STAYING CONNECTED

e-mails and texting
High schooler son is e-mailing his teacher about questions on his homework as well as texting his friend about weekend plans.

GPS technology
Older sister checks smartphone GPS to make sure that her younger sister is on her way home from band practice.

Smartphones and cell phones
Father calls daughter on his way home from work to see what kind of pizza she wants for dinner.

Thinking Like a Sociologist

1 Analyzing
How has communication technology and the use of it by families changed over time?

2 Contrasting
How is the way you personally communicate with your family different from how it was five years ago?

The Family 299

There's More Online!

- ☑ **CHART** Families and Marriages
- ☑ **GRAPHIC ORGANIZER** Family and Marriage
- ☑ **IMAGE** Mixed Matches
- ☑ **MAP** Minimum Legal Age at Marriage for Women
- ☑ **SELF-CHECK QUIZ**

Reading HELPDESK

Academic Vocabulary
- orientation
- mutual

Content Vocabulary
- nuclear family
- extended family
- patriarchy
- matriarchy
- egalitarian
- monogamy
- polygamy
- polygyny
- polyandry
- incest taboo

TAKING NOTES:

KEY IDEAS AND DETAILS As you read about families and marriage, use an outline like the one below to record key ideas and details about marriage and family.

    Family and Marriage
  I. Family
     A. Definition
     B. Types
     C. Structures
  II. Marriage
     A. Arrangements
     B. Spouse selection

LESSON 1
Family and Marriage Across Cultures

ESSENTIAL QUESTION • *What makes a family?*

It Matters Because

In all societies, the family has been the most important of all social institutions. It is responsible for producing new generations; socializing and caring for the young; regulating sexual behavior; transmitting social status and property; and providing care, protection, and economic support for all people.

Defining the Family

GUIDING QUESTION *How do sociologists define family?*

When we hear the word *family*, we all have some idea of what it means. Most of us live in what we would call a "family setting." In fact, families come in many different forms, and coming up with a single definition of the word is surprisingly difficult. In a legal sense, the word describes many relationships; for example, between parents and children; among people related by blood, marriage or adoption; or among any group of people living together in a single household.

Because the word *family* does not have a single meaning, laws often specify a definition. A zoning law, which seeks to set aside certain areas for single-family homes, may define family one way. Laws regulating insurance or government benefits may define it in some other way. Sociologists have their own definition: a *family* is a group of people related by marriage, blood, or adoption.

While the concept of family may seem simple and familiar to us, the family is actually a complex social unit with many facets. And no other social institution has a greater impact on the life and behavior of the individual.

Sociologists make further distinctions about family. A person's *family of orientation* is the one into which a person is born. It provides a person with his or her name, an identity, and a heritage. It gives the person an ascribed status in the community. The family of **orientation** "orients" children to their community and society and locates them in their world.

People also often have a *family of procreation*. These are formed when people marry. Marriage is a legal union between people based on **mutual** rights and obligations. Most marriages in the United States are

300

between a man and a woman, although recently several states have begun to recognize same-sex marriage. In either case, a family of procreation becomes a family of orientation for any children born or adopted into it.

✓ READING PROGRESS CHECK

Differentiating How is a family of orientation different from a family of procreation?

Two Basic Types of Families

GUIDING QUESTION *What are the two basic types of families, and how did they develop?*

When people speak of their families, they may be speaking of one of two different groups. They may be referring to their nuclear families or to their extended families.

Nuclear and Extended Families

The **nuclear family**, the smallest grouping of individuals that can be called a family, is made up of a parent or parents and any children. The **extended family** consists of two or more adult generations of the same family whose members share economic resources and live in the same household. Extended family may also contain close relatives, such as grandparents, grandchildren, aunts, uncles, and cousins.

How Family Structures Developed

The development of agriculture and industry shaped society. These developments also shaped family structure.

In the first human societies, family activity revolved around the hunting and gathering of food. Small bands of nuclear families followed herds of animals during the changing seasons, moving constantly.

About 10,000 years ago, human beings developed the capacity to cultivate crops and domesticate animals. With the ability to grow food in a single location came a change in family structure. Families began to settle down in a single place. Family life focused on farming, which required large numbers of workers; parents then tended to have more children. Extended families grew, and a division of labor began to appear, with different family members performing different specialized tasks.

As technology developed and societies eventually moved from agricultural economies to industrialization, the extended family was slowly replaced by the nuclear family. Industrial life did not require large families for agricultural work. In fact, industrial economies tended to favor smaller family units with fewer mouths to feed and greater mobility. Postindustrial economies, such as our own, favor similar types of families.

✓ READING PROGRESS CHECK

Analyzing Why did farming favor larger, extended families?

orientation direction, place, or relative location

mutual shared

nuclear family a group that includes a parent or parents and any children

extended family two or more adult generations of the same family whose members share economic resources and live in the same household—and sometimes close relatives such as grandparents, grandchildren, aunts, uncles, and cousins

Extended families, which include larger numbers of people compared to nuclear families, became common after the agricultural revolution.

▶ **CRITICAL THINKING**

Explaining Why might a large group like this be problematic if the primary economic activity was hunting and gathering?

Connecting Sociology to Human Geography

FAMILY STRUCTURES AROUND THE WORLD

Family structures vary around the globe and are influenced by culture, tradition, environment, and physical geography. In the United States, the family structure has changed over time. Divorce, the adoption of a child, the death of a parent, and other factors have produced families that do not conform to one family structure. A child's descent is usually traced not solely according to patrilineal or matrilineal descent but through both the mother and the father. This, however, is not the case globally. Many cultures trace their descent based on traditions they have followed for centuries.

The Pueblo peoples primarily live in the southwestern United States. They, like the Cherokee, practice the tradition of matrilineal descent. They honor women in their culture and women generally lead the family, whereas, traditionally, only men have held this position in most other Native American groups.

In Asia, countries such as Iraq and China have traditionally followed a patriarchal pattern of authority. This patriarchal tradition has existed in their cultures for centuries, and it has strengthened and fortified the family structure. Although there have been changes in recent decades, women still often have little power in the family. They follow the lead of the male who heads the household.

Polygyny is another traditional practice common in some cultures but not in the United States. Polygyny is when a man has more than one spouse at the same time. In Kenya, Senegal, South Africa, and the Sudan, polygyny is widely practiced. In India, Hindus are not allowed to take part in polygyny, but many Muslim men do have multiple wives, a tradition in the religion of Islam.

These women and girls are Zunis, one of the Pueblo peoples who trace their lineage matrilineally.

▶ CRITICAL THINKING

1. **Identifying Perspectives** Why do you think some cultures choose to follow matrilineal or patrilineal descent or both?
2. **Researching** How could you verify and compare the information in this passage about family structures?

Patterns of Family Structure

GUIDING QUESTION *How do different types of families determine who inherits, who is in authority, and where couples live?*

Families of all types and sizes tend to behave in similar ways across cultures. These patterns of behavior relate to common family questions—inheritance, authority, and place of residence.

Inheritance

Families need to answer the question of inheritance. From which parent do children receive their name, family property, or membership in an ethnic group?

- In a *patrilineal* arrangement, descent and inheritance are passed from the father to his male descendants. Iraq is an example of a patrilineal society.
- In a *matrilineal* arrangement, descent and inheritance pass from the mother to her female descendants. Some Native American groups have been matrilineal.
- In some societies, descent and inheritance are *bilineal*—they are passed equally through both parents. Thus both the father's and mother's relatives

are accepted equally as part of the kinship structure. Most families in the United States are bilineal.

Authority

The question of authority in families works similarly to the question of inheritance.

- In a **patriarchy**, the oldest man living in the household has authority over the rest of the family members. Patriarchy is common in many countries around the world, such as in China. In fact, the patriarchal family pattern is nearly universal. In its purest form the father is the absolute ruler of the family.
- In a **matriarchy**, the oldest woman living in the household holds the authority. This arrangement is uncommon, and in fact there is controversy over whether any society has ever featured a genuine and pervasive matriarchal family structure.
- In an **egalitarian** system, authority is split evenly between a husband and wife. Many families in Scandinavian countries and the United States follow an egalitarian arrangement. This pattern has become more prominent in recent decades than it was in the past.

Where Couples Live

Typically, when a couple marries, they set up a new home together. There is a cultural pattern to how and where this happens.

- The *patrilocal* pattern, such as in premodern China, calls for the couple to live with or near the husband's parents.
- If living with or near the family of the woman is expected, a *matrilocal* pattern exists.
- In the *neolocal* pattern, new couples are expected to establish new residences of their own. This is the model practiced in Europe and the United States today.

Marriage Arrangements

In the United States, marriage rituals are widely recognized. It is common for a bride to wear a white gown. The couple makes vows that involve promises to love and honor each other. There is music as the couple marches out from the house of worship. In other cultures, however, wedding ceremonies can look very different. This is part of the ceremony among the Reindeer Tungus, a reindeer-herding people who live in Siberia:

PRIMARY SOURCE

"After the groom's gifts have been presented, the bride's dowry is loaded onto the reindeer and carried to the groom's lodge. There, the rest of the ceremony takes place. The bride takes the wife's place—that is, at the right side of the entrance of the lodge—and members of both families sit around in a circle. The groom enters and follows the bride around the circle, greeting each guest, while the guests, in their turn, kiss the bride on the mouth and hands. Finally, the go-betweens spit three times on the bride's hands, and the couple is formally 'husband and wife.' More feasting and revelry bring the day to a close."

—Carol Ember and Melvin Ember, *Countries and Their Cultures*, 2001

Families and Marriages

Nuclear Family Composition	Parents and children
Extended Family Composition	Parents, children, and other relatives
Inheritance	Patrilineal (inherit through the father) Matrilineal (inherit through the mother) Bilineal (inherit through both)
Authority	Patriarchal (father rules the family) Matriarchal (mother rules the family) Egalitarian (parents share authority)
Residence	Patrilocal (couple lives with or near husband's parents) Matrilocal (couple lives with or near wife's parents) Neolocal (couple lives apart from both sets of parents)
Marriage Composition	Polygyny (one husband, many wives) Polyandry (one wife, many husbands) Monogamy (one husband, one wife)

^ CHART

FAMILIES AND MARRIAGES

This chart summarizes possible variations in family and marriage forms.

▶ **CRITICAL THINKING**

1. **Describing** Describe the general pattern of the American family using terms from this table.
2. **Analyzing** What do you think the pattern of marriage and family in the United States says about prevailing views about gender roles?

patriarchy when authority in a family is assigned to the oldest man

matriarchy when authority in a family is assigned to the oldest woman

egalitarian when authority is split evenly between a man and a woman

The Family 303

A Global Perspective

MINIMUM LEGAL AGE AT MARRIAGE FOR WOMEN

The age at which Americans marry has been rising for decades. Consequently, only a very small percentage of American adolescents are married. That is not the case in all countries, however. This map shows how the laws of various nations define the legality of marriage for young women aged 18 or under.

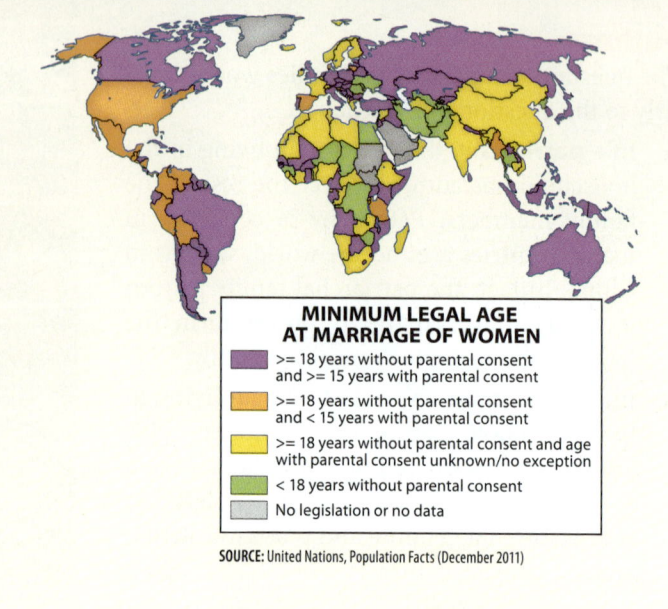

Geography Connection

1. **Places and Regions** What two general statements can you make about the data shown on the map, in terms of regions?
2. **Environment and Society** How might allowing adolescent marriages affect a country's population growth?

This ceremony may seem different from any you may have witnessed, but the purpose is the same as it is with any marriage in the United States. It is a ritual announcing that a new family has been formed and that any children of the couple can legitimately inherit the family name and property.

What Forms Do Marriages Take?

The marriage of one person to one person—**monogamy**—is the most widely practiced form of marriage in the world today. In fact, it is the only form of marriage that is legally acceptable in the United States and in most other Western societies. Serial monogamy—having several marriage partners—is not uncommon, but in order to be legal, a person can only have one marriage at a time. A marriage must end, by divorce or the death of the spouse, before a person can marry another person.

In contrast to monogamy, **polygamy** means the marriage of one person to multiple people at a time. Polygamy is also referred to as plural marriage. It generally takes one of two forms:

- **Polygyny** means marriage of one man to two or more women at the same time. Though still legal in parts of Africa and Asia, it is not widely practiced in any society today.
- **Polyandry**—marriage of one woman to two or more men at the same time—is an even rarer form of marriage. It is known to have been common in only three societies: in Tibet, in parts of Polynesia, and among the Todas and other hill peoples of India.

monogamy marriage between one person and one other person

polygamy marriage of one person to multiple partners at the same time

polygyny marriage of one man to more than one woman at a time

polyandry marriage of one woman to more than one man at a time

✓ **READING PROGRESS CHECK**

Summarizing What are the key questions that marriage forms and practices seek to answer?

Choosing a Spouse

GUIDING QUESTION *What factors influence the choice of a spouse?*

For many young people raised in the United States, the idea that your choice of a future partner may be made for you by your parents when you are young may seem odd and even unfair. The notion that the family of one young person may have to pay a large dowry to the family of another young person in order to make a wedding possible may seem unusual as well. These are not customary practices in the United States. If, however, you think that young people growing up in this culture have complete freedom in selecting a marriage partner, you would be wrong. All societies, including the United States, have norms and laws about who can marry whom.

Exogamy is a word that refers to mate-selection norms that require a person to marry outside their kind or group. (*Exo* is a prefix meaning "outside.") The most important exogamy norms are called **incest taboos**, which forbid marriage between certain relatives. In traditional Chinese culture, for example, two people with the same family name cannot marry unless their family lines split at least five generations earlier. In the United States, you are not legally allowed to marry a son or daughter, brother or sister, mother or father, niece or nephew, or aunt or uncle. Many states have laws against marrying a first cousin.

incest taboo a rule against marriage between certain kinds and degrees of relatives

Applying Sociology

FINDING A MATE

This activity will give you some ideas for finding a mate for a successful long-term relationship. It also may help you decide if your current boyfriend or girlfriend makes the cut.

From the list below (and on a separate sheet of paper), list the ten qualities that are most important to you in a partner. (Number 1 is the most important, number 2 the next most important, and so forth.) Then fold your paper in half. In the right-hand column, either have your partner fill out the questionnaire or rank the characteristics yourself according to how you think your partner would.

EVALUATING YOUR RESPONSES

Which of the items listed do you think are the most important in predicting marital success? According to research, the last seven items (17–23) are the most important.

High compatibility between you and your mate on these seven characteristics would probably increase your chances of marital success. A low degree of matching does not, of course, ensure an unhappy marriage or a divorce, but it does suggest areas that may cause problems in the future.

I am looking for a partner who . . .

#	Partner	ME	
1.			is honest and truthful.
2.			is fun to be with.
3.			is of the same educational background.
4.			will take care of me.
5.			wants to have children.
6.			communicates well with me.
7.			will share household jobs and tasks.
8.			is a good friend with whom I can talk.
9.			is of the same religious background.
10.			makes good decisions.
11.			earns good money or has a good job.
12.			is physically attractive.
13.			is in love with me and I with him/her.
14.			encourages me to be my own person.
15.			has interests like mine in making money and having fun.
16.			makes me feel important.
17.			is faithful.
18.			shares mutual interests in home, children, romantic love, and faith.
19.			has had a happy childhood with happily married parents.
20.			is emotionally mature.
21.			is prepared to support a family.
22.			is interested in waiting to marry until age twenty-two or older.
23.			wants a six-month to two-year engagement.

▶ **CRITICAL THINKING**

1. **Evaluating** Were you surprised by your answers? Your partner's answers? Why or why not?
2. **Assessing** How effective do you think it is to ask these questions when you are considering a long-term relationship?
3. **Drawing Conclusions** How will these questions help you find the most compatible long-term mate?

Marriage between people of different racial, ethnic, or religious backgrounds is more common in the United States today than in the past.

▶ **CRITICAL THINKING**

Drawing Conclusions How do you think the media has contributed to rising heterogamy?

Incest is almost universally prohibited, though exceptions were once common among royalty in ancient Egypt and elsewhere. Yet even in these cases, royals who married family members often chose partners to whom they were not related by blood.

Endogamy involves mate-selection norms that require individuals to marry persons of a similar background. (*Endo* is a prefix that means "inside.") In the United States, for example, norms of the past have required that marriage partners be of the same race or even the same religion. These norms have weakened significantly. One recent study found that about 15 percent of new marriages in the United States were between members of different racial or ethnic groups. Of course, same-sex marriage is also growing in acceptance. Class lines are also broken with increasing frequency because more Americans of all social classes are attending college together and meeting future spouses there.

Norms encouraging but not requiring marriage within a group are common. And people are most likely to know and prefer to marry others like themselves. For these reasons, people tend to marry partners with social characteristics like their own. This tendency, which is the result of choice, is called *homogamy*. For example, it is rare for a child of a multimillionaire to marry someone from a lower class.

In the United States, most marriages occur between people of about the same age. Most people marrying for the first time marry others who have not been married. Most divorced people marry others who have been married before. People tend to choose partners from their own community as well.

Though less common, *heterogamy*—marriage between partners who are dissimilar in some key characteristic—is rising in the United States. More American marriages are crossing traditional barriers of age, race, social class, and ethnicity. The United States, after all, is more racially and ethnically integrated than many other nations. The media has helped create a mass culture that is increasingly sympathetic to portrayals of heterogamy.

✓ **READING PROGRESS CHECK**

Identifying Trends Identify one trend in the selection of spouses seen in the United States in recent times.

LESSON 1 REVIEW

Reviewing Vocabulary
1. **Explaining** What is the difference between a nuclear family and an extended family?
2. **Contrasting** What is the difference between patriarchal, matriarchal, and egalitarian family structures?

Using Your Notes
3. **Identifying** Based on your notes from the lesson, what three questions help shape family structure?

Answering the Guiding Questions
4. **Finding the Main Idea** How do sociologists define family?

5. **Identifying Cause and Effect** What are the two basic types of families, and how did they develop?
6. **Comparing and Contrasting** How do different types of families determine who inherits, who is in authority, and where couples live?
7. **Identifying Central Issues** What factors influence the choice of a spouse?

Writing Activity
8. **Argument** Using information from your reading, make an argument for or against patriarchy or matriarchy as an effective family structure.

networks

There's More Online!

- ☑ **CHART** Theoretical Perspectives: Perspectives on the Family
- ☑ **CHART** Youths Grade Their Parents
- ☑ **IMAGE** Stay-at-Home Dad
- ☑ **SELF-CHECK QUIZ**

Reading HELPDESK

Academic Vocabulary
- integrate
- dominant

Content Vocabulary
- **socio-emotional maintenance**

TAKING NOTES:
Key Ideas and Details

LISTING As you read about the three theoretical perspectives and the family, use a graphic organizer like the one below to list the main observations of each.

Functionalism	Conflict	Symbolic Interactionism
•	•	•
•	•	•
•	•	•
•	•	•
•	•	•

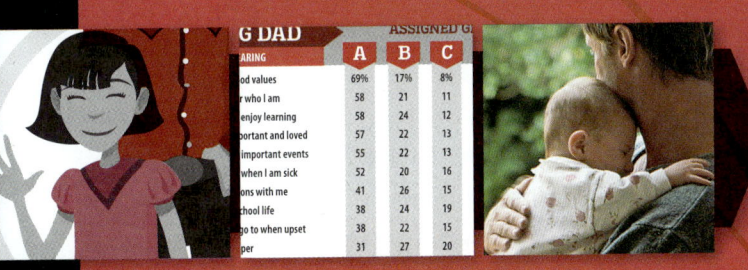

LESSON 2
Theoretical Perspectives and the Family

ESSENTIAL QUESTION • *What makes a family?*

IT MATTERS BECAUSE
Functionalism focuses on the origins of gender differences. Conflict theory looks at the reasons gender differences continue to exist. Symbolic interactionism attempts to explain the ways in which gender is acquired.

Functionalism

GUIDING QUESTION *How does functionalism explain the roles and functions of families?*

Functionalists see the family as filling many key social roles. Family socializes the young and provides them with the social and emotional support they need to grow securely. It manages reproduction and regulates sexual activity. Family transmits social status and serves as an economic center as well.

Socializing Children

Parents of course do much more than care for a child's physical needs. From the very start of life, parents begin teaching children what they need to know to take part in society. At first, this socialization includes language, which the child begins to mimic in the first year or so. As the baby becomes a toddler and begins to move and become more interactive, parents teach norms of behavior and values.

At each new stage of development, parents and other family members serve as role models and teachers to children. In this way, the process of socialization continues throughout childhood and adolescence, as young people learn more and more about their society and how they are supposed to interact with others.

The Socio-Emotional Function

Family provides **socio-emotional maintenance**—it provides acceptance and support for its members. In theory, family is the one place in society in which an individual is unconditionally accepted and loved. Family members typically accept one another as they are, and they recognize and value each person's unique qualities. Without this care and affection, research shows that children will not grow and develop normally.

The Family **307**

GRADING DAD

ASPECT OF CHILD REARING	ASSIGNED GRADE				
	A	B	C	D	F
Raising me with good values	69%	17%	8%	4%	2%
Appreciating me for who I am	58	21	11	8	2
Encouraging me to enjoy learning	58	24	12	4	2
Making me feel important and loved	57	22	13	6	2
Being able to go to important events	55	22	13	5	5
Being there for me when I am sick	52	20	16	8	4
Establishing traditions with me	41	26	15	11	7
Being involved in school life	38	24	19	12	7
Being someone to go to when upset	38	22	15	12	13
Controlling his temper	31	27	20	10	12
Knowing what goes on with me	31	30	17	12	10

GRADING MOM

ASPECT OF CHILD REARING	ASSIGNED GRADE				
	A	B	C	D	F
Being there for me when I am sick	81%	11%	5%	2%	1%
Raising me with good values	74	15	6	3	2
Making me feel important and loved	64	20	10	5	1
Being able to go to important events	64	20	10	3	3
Appreciating me for who I am	63	18	8	6	5
Encouraging me to enjoy learning	59	23	12	3	3
Being involved in school life	46	25	13	10	6
Being someone to go to when upset	46	22	13	8	9
Spending time talking with me	43	33	14	6	4
Establishing traditions with me	38	29	17	10	6
Knowing what goes on with me	35	31	15	10	9
Controlling her temper	29	28	19	12	11

Sources: Ellen Galinsky, *Ask the Children*

CHART
YOUTHS GRADE THEIR PARENTS

▶ **CRITICAL THINKING**

1. **Comparing** How do the results for fathers and mothers compare?
2. **Evaluating** Which three aspects of child rearing do you think are the most important? Why?

Without socio-emotional maintenance, children may have low self-esteem or a feeling that they have little worth. They may also fear rejection and feel insecure. These feelings may make it difficult for them later to adjust to marriage or express affection to their own children. The need for socio-emotional maintenance is ongoing. Even individuals who are well **integrated** into society require support when adjusting to changing norms and in developing and continuing healthy relationships. Here again, the family can provide socio-emotional support.

The Reproductive Function

Family provides an orderly and regulated system for producing the new members that every society needs to survive. So important is the function of reproduction that in many cultures and religions, it is the primary purpose for sexual relations. In some societies, failure of a wife to bear children can be a cause for divorce. Residents of places such as the Punjab region of northern India, for example, view children as an economic necessity. New members help produce food and income that the family needs to survive. Recall what you read earlier about the effects of the agricultural revolution on the development of extended families.

The significance of having children is also seen in the hundreds of rituals, customs, and traditions that are associated with pregnancy and birth in virtually all cultures around the world. (Later in the chapter, we look at a trend that contradicts this long-standing function of the family, the rise of marriages without children in the United States.)

Regulating Sexual Activity

People are not given total sexual freedom in any known society. Even in societies noted for a high degree of sexual permissiveness, such as the Hopi culture of the southwestern United States, there are rules about mating and marrying.

Norms regarding sexual activities vary from place to place. Families in a few cultures, such as in the Trobriand Islands, encourage the practice of premarital sex. Other societies, such as those in Iran and Afghanistan, go to great lengths to limit even casual contact between unrelated single males and females. Violations of rules may lead to violent retribution, including, in extreme cases, a so-called honor killing, in which a person whose behavior is thought to bring disgrace on the family is murdered by family members.

The United States has traditionally fallen somewhere in between the extremes in its sexual norms. In the ideal culture in the United States, adolescents would abstain from sexual activity. In real culture, however, the abundance of sexual references directed at teens by the advertising and entertainment industries makes abstinence seem very difficult and even undesirable. Clearly American society is sending a mixed message to young people today. One of the consequences of this cultural confusion is the large number of teenage pregnancies and teenagers having abortions. The numbers have been dropping in recent decades but remain high compared to other industrialized countries. Today, around 7 percent of American females aged 15 to 19 become pregnant each year. The rate is even higher among some subgroups.

The important thing to note is that norms vary widely and may be confusing. In any case, it is the family that enforces them.

Transmitting Social Status

Families provide economic resources that open and close occupational doors. The children of high-income professionals, for example, are more likely to be able financially to attend college and graduate school than are the children of working-class parents. As a result of greater access to higher education, including postgraduate studies, the children of professionals are more likely, as adults, to enter professional occupations.

The family also passes on values that affect social status. The children of professionals, for example, tend to feel a greater need to pursue a college degree than their counterparts from working-class families. In these and many other ways, the family affects the placement of children in the social stratification structure.

The Economic Function

At one time families were self-sufficient economic units whose members all contributed to the production of needed goods. Every family member would join in such tasks as growing food, making cloth, and caring for livestock. Technological change has altered these relationships. The modern family is a unit of consumption, not production. Adult members—increasingly including working mothers—are employed outside the home and pool their resources to buy what they need. The end result, though, is the same: The family provides what is needed to survive.

socio-emotional maintenance the provision of acceptance and emotional support

integrate to mix; to blend

✓ **READING PROGRESS CHECK**

Listing What are the key functions of the family?

Conflict Theory

GUIDING QUESTION *How does conflict theory explain the roles and functions of families?*

Conflict theorists focus on the way family members compete and cooperate with one another. Most family systems have a built-in gender inequality. That is because most familial structures throughout history has been patriarchal and patrilineal. Women have historically and traditionally been considered the property of men, and the control of family members has typically passed through male bloodlines. This male dominance has been considered "natural" and "legitimate."

Conflict Theory and Gender Relationships

According to conflict theorists, since males are **dominant** and in control, females have typically been expected to be submissive and accept the role of helpers.

In the traditional division of labor, males work outside the home for money to provide economic support for the family. Women remain at home to prepare meals, keep house, and care for the children. As a result of this arrangement, women are effectively unpaid laborers who make it possible for men to earn wages. Conflict theorists point out that women's power was further reduced by limits on their rights to own or inherit property. With men having control over the money, wives and mothers are kept in a dependent and powerless role. They are literally without any means to provide for themselves. According to the conflict perspective, families in the past fostered social inequality.

Feminist Writers and Conflict Theory

Writers and activists who organize on behalf of women's rights and interests have come to be called *feminists*. Many feminists today view the family from the conflict perspective. They believe that family structure is the source of the inequality between men and women in society. They point out that men have had control over women since before private property and capitalism existed. Women's contributions in the home (mother and homemaker) are not paid and are therefore undervalued in a capitalist society. Attempts by women to gain more power within the family structure can result in conflict.

✓ **READING PROGRESS CHECK**

Explaining What do conflict theorists say has been the result of men's historical economic dominance in the family?

Symbolic Interactionism

GUIDING QUESTION *How does symbolic interactionism explain the roles and functions of families?*

Symbolic interactionists take a different approach to understanding families. To them, the key to understanding behavior within the family lies in the interactions among family members and the meanings they assign to those interactions.

Today, both partners work in about two of three marriages. In about a third of those cases, the wife earns more than the husband.

▶ **CRITICAL THINKING**
Assessing What impact do you think wives earning more than husbands will have on the family? Why?

dominant having power over others

Theoretical Perspectives

PERSPECTIVES ON THE FAMILY
Both functionalism and conflict theory are concerned with how social norms affect the nature of the family. Symbolic interactionism tends to examine the relationship of the self to the family. How might functionalism and conflict theory focus on the self?

Theoretical Perspective	Social Arrangement	Example
Functionalism	Sex norms	Children are taught that sexual activity should be reserved for married couples.
Conflict Theory	Male dominance	Husbands use their economic power to control the ways money is spent.
Symbolic Interactionism	Developing self-esteem	A child abused by his or her parents learns to dislike himself or herself.

▶ **CRITICAL THINKING**
1. **Hypothesizing** How might symbolic interactionism focus on male dominance?
2. **Formulating Questions** What questions about family might you ask a person who is trying to develop his or her self-esteem?

As you have read, socialization begins within the family. As family members share meanings and feelings, children develop their own self-concepts and learn to put themselves mentally in the place of others. Interactions with adults help children acquire human personality and social characteristics. This process continues as children meet others outside the home.

According to symbolic interactionists, relationships within the family are constantly changing. A newly married couple will spend many months or even longer testing out their new relationship. As time passes, the early relationship changes, along with parts of each person's personality and self-concepts.

The arrival of children brings new adjustments. Parents or other family members may have different ideas about child rearing, family size, or many other issues. The addition of a child also changes the way people interact with one another. Married couples find they do not have as much time for each other after having children as they did before. More adjustments are needed when two single parents with children marry and combine their families.

☑ **READING PROGRESS CHECK**

Explaining Why do symbolic interactionists think family relationships are constantly changing?

LESSON 2 REVIEW

Reviewing Vocabulary
1. *Explaining* What is socio-emotional maintenance, and what is its relationship to the family?

Using Your Notes
2. *Listing* Use your notes to explain how the different theoretical perspectives regard the family?

Answering the Guiding Questions
3. *Finding the Main Idea* How does functionalism explain the roles and functions of families?

4. *Identifying Cause and Effect* How does conflict theory explain the roles and functions of families?

5. *Identifying Central Issues* How does symbolic interactionism explain the roles and functions of families?

Writing Activity
6. *Argument* Using information from your reading, make an argument for or against greater gender equality in families and in society generally.

networks

There's More Online!

- ☑ **CARTOON** Families and Marriages
- ☑ **CHART** Family Violence
- ☑ **GRAPH** Marriage and Divorce Rates
- ☑ **IMAGE** Bobo the Doll
- ☑ **MAP** Marriage Rates
- ☑ **SELF-CHECK QUIZ**

LESSON 3
Family and Marriage in the United States

ESSENTIAL QUESTION • What makes a family?

Reading HELPDESK

Academic Vocabulary
- motivation
- widespread

Content Vocabulary
- marriage rate
- divorce rate

TAKING NOTES:
Key Ideas and Details

ORGANIZING As you read about families and marriage in the United States, use a graphic organizer like the one below to record key ideas and details about marriage and family.

Romantic Love	Divorce	Violence
•	•	•
•	•	•
•	•	•
•	•	•

It Matters Because

Family and marriage in the United States take many forms but overall reflect certain social and cultural norms and stresses. These can be seen in the divorce rate and the rates of family violence.

The Nature of the American Family

GUIDING QUESTION What characteristics typify an American family?

The United States is a large and diverse society, with influences from cultures and societies from around the world. Nearly 13 percent of the population was born in another country, with significant numbers coming from Latin America but also Africa, Asia, Europe, and even Oceania. Americans speak over 380 languages. The largest segment describes themselves as Christian, but there are many people of the Jewish, Muslim, Buddhist, and Hindu faiths, to name just a few. Because of this diversity, describing the "typical" American family might seem impossible.

In spite of this great diversity, however, there are more similarities than there are differences among American families. And while there is still a steady influx of people and ideas, as various ethnic groups blend into life in the United States, families tend to follow a set pattern:

- Families are *nuclear*—that is, each household contains only one set of parents and their children.
- Families are *bilineal*—tracing their lineage and passing inheritance equally through both parents.
- Families are *egalitarian*—both partners share in decision making.
- Families are *neolocal*—meaning that they locate their homes apart from one or another of the partners' families.
- Families are *monogamous*—each includes two people, each married to only one other person at a time.

☑ **READING PROGRESS CHECK**

Explaining Would you say American families are more similar or more different? Why?

312

Romantic Love and Marriage

GUIDING QUESTION *How does the relationship between love and marriage vary among cultures?*

To Americans, it's like the old song says—"Love and marriage go together like a horse and carriage." In a recent poll of the American public, 84 percent of unmarried people and 93 percent of those already married answered "love" when identifying the most important reason for getting married.

The relationship between love and marriage has not always been viewed in this way. Among the British feudal aristocracy, romantic love was pursued outside marriage. Marriage was not thought to be compatible with deeply romantic feelings but was instead a matter of securing property and maintaining the family's social position. In ancient Japan, love was considered a barrier to the serious business of arrangement of marriages by parents. Among fundamentalist Hindus in India today, parents or other relatives are expected to find suitable mates for the young. Criteria for mate selection include class, wealth, family reputation, and appearance. Love is not necessarily absent in marriage in these other cultures or historical periods, but love followed marriage rather than the other way around. Couples could develop love over time. And even in this country, love is not the only reason people marry. In the same poll referred to earlier, 31 percent of married people and 30 percent of single people identified financial stability as an important reason for marrying.

Indeed, while romantic love is almost always stated as a condition for marriage in modern societies, it is seldom the only condition. In addition to romantic love, a person may also marry to enter a powerful family or to advance a career. One of the strongest **motivations** for marriage is conformity. Marriage rates in the United States are going down. In 2010, barely half of all adults were married.

motivation a factor that causes movement, change, or action

A Diverse America

MARRIAGE RATES

The U.S. marriage rate overall has declined dramatically since the mid-1940s. Variation in the marriage rate among individual states is interesting. In 2009, the highest marriage rate occurred in Nevada (40.9 per 1,000 people). Washington, D.C., had the absolute lowest rate (4.7 per 1,000 people), but many states had a marriage rate of less than 6 per 1,000 people.

Geography Connection

1. **Places and Regions** What generalizations can you make about regions with a low or high marriage rate?
2. **Human Systems** Does this map tell you what share of a state's population is married? Why or why not?
3. **Human Systems** How might the age of a state's population affect its marriage rate?

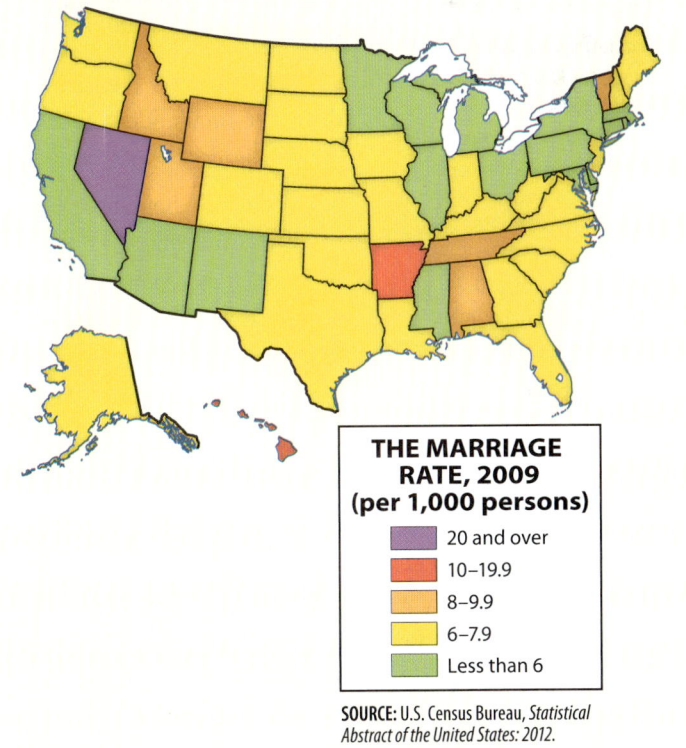

THE MARRIAGE RATE, 2009 (per 1,000 persons)
- 20 and over
- 10–19.9
- 8–9.9
- 6–7.9
- Less than 6

SOURCE: U.S. Census Bureau, *Statistical Abstract of the United States: 2012.*

The Family 313

"Heads, you live happily ever after blah blah blah; tails, we call this charade off and all go our separate ways."

CARTOON

FAMILIES AND MARRIAGES

The concept of families and the process by which they are created has undergone enormous changes in the last 60 years in the United States.

▶ **CRITICAL THINKING**

1. **Analyzing Visuals** What is the attitude of the priest in the cartoon? Would the statistics on divorce support his claim?
2. **Evaluating** The increase in the divorce rate since the 1940s can be attributed to a number of factors. What is one of those factors to which the cartoon is referring?

marriage rate the number of marriages per year for every thousand members of the population

divorce rate the number of divorces per year for every thousand members of the population

Still, parents often expect their children to marry after a certain age and worry about them—perhaps even pressure them—if they remain single very long. Peers are another source of pressure.

Americans typically believe that a marriage that is not based on romantic love cannot last. It is more accurate to say that a marriage based only on romantic love is almost sure to fail. While love may be a good start, it is just that—a start. Research suggests that for a marriage to last, a couple must build a relationship that goes beyond romantic love.

The **marriage rate**—the number of marriages per year for every thousand members of the population—has fluctuated in the United States since 1940. As you can see in the graph on the next page, the marriage rate peaked at over 16.0 immediately following World War II. Since then, the marriage rate, with ups and downs, has fallen by more than 50 percent.

✓ **READING PROGRESS CHECK**

Describing What is the role of romantic love in marriage in the United States?

Divorce

GUIDING QUESTION What are the causes of divorce?

The **divorce rate**, then, is the number of divorces per year for every one thousand members of the population. Except for a peak and decline after World War II, the divorce rate in the United States increased slowly between 1860 and 1960. This was followed over the next 20 years by a dramatic increase when the divorce rate more than doubled (from 2.2 in 1960 to 5.3 in 1981). Since then, the divorce rate has been in a slow but steady decline, decreasing to 3.5 in 2009.

The Causes of Divorce

Both personal and societal factors influence why people divorce. At the individual level, these factors include:

- the age of the people when they married. The later the age upon marriage, the lower the chance of divorce.
- how many years the partners have been married. The longer the marriage, the lower the chance of divorce.
- the nature and quality of the relationship. The more respect and flexibility exist between the partners, the lower the chance of divorce.

There are many social problems that can place strain on an individual marriage. Abuse in the family, addiction, and strains from unemployment or other economic troubles are examples of things that challenge relationships.

Sociologists, however, are most concerned with how larger forces in society affect marriages. There are four main factors. First, the divorce rate rises during times of economic prosperity and goes down when times are hard. This is probably because people are more likely to make changes and take chances—such as leaving a marriage—when they are not worried about basic survival.

Second, the rise of the divorce rate after 1960 followed the maturation of the baby boom generation. Baby boomers did not attach a stigma to divorce the way earlier generations did and so were more likely to leave unhappy marriages.

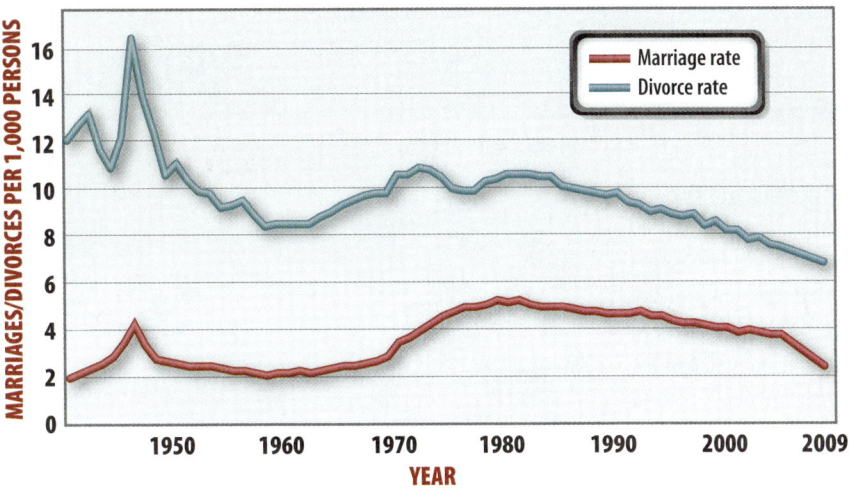

GRAPH

MARRIAGE AND DIVORCE RATES
This line graph shows changes in the marriage rate and divorce rate in the United States from 1940 to 2009.

▶ **CRITICAL THINKING**

1. **Hypothesizing** How do you think the peak in the marriage rate after 1945 related to the peak in the divorce rate around the same time?

2. **Observing** What general relationship do you see between marriage and divorce rates over this time period?

Third, more women are working now than did in the past. They are not as financially dependent on men and so are more willing to end a bad marriage.

Finally, American values and attitudes about marriage and divorce are changing. Society is much more forgiving of divorce and remarriage. Women, especially, are no longer punished socially for leaving a marriage, as they used to be.

The Future of Marriage

For several reasons, there is a good chance the recent decline in the divorce rate will continue. For one thing, the average age of first marriage is rising. We know the later people marry, the less likely they are to divorce. This may be the result of greater maturity and more realistic expectations.

Another factor is that the average age of the population in the United States is increasing as baby boomers grow older. This exceptionally large generation set records for divorce in the late 1960s and 1970s. Baby boomers now range in age from about 50 to almost 70. This removes them from the age bracket that produces the highest divorce rates.

Finally, couples are having fewer children, and children are spaced further apart. This reduces pressures in a marriage.

☑ **READING PROGRESS CHECK**

Describing What is the likely future of divorce in the United States?

Family Violence

GUIDING QUESTION *What forms does family violence take?*

Americans have traditionally denied the existence of **widespread** violence in the family setting. In the past violent behavior was mistakenly associated mostly with lower-class families. Part of the reason for this attitude was the fact that the first research in this area used law enforcement and medical records. Because the police and hospitals dealt mostly with the lower classes—middle and upper classes had lawyers and private doctors—the statistics were skewed toward the lower class. We have since learned that domestic violence occurs at all social class levels.

The Frequency of Family Violence

Although the family can provide a safe and warm emotional haven, it can in some cases create a hostile environment. Family, or domestic, violence can affect all members of the family—children, spouses, and older people.

widespread commonly found; frequently occurring

Connecting Sociology to Psychology

THE BOBO DOLL EXPERIMENT

In 1961 psychologist Albert Bandura began to study the effect of children's social environment on their behavior. He conducted an experiment, called the Bobo doll experiment, in which researchers who were in a room with preschool-age children repeatedly hit and verbally abused the plastic, inflatable Bobo dolls that had been painted to resemble clowns. The result of the experiment led to the children mimicking the behavior of the researchers. About 90 percent of the children modeled the same behavior, showing the same aggressiveness as the researchers. Interestingly, Bandura found that boys were more likely than girls to show their aggression physically. Girls were more likely to be verbally aggressive.

From this experiment, Bandura developed the social learning theory that children learn behavior through modeling and observation. Essentially, he explained that through social modeling, children learn social behavior.

Bandura used the same experiment months later to test long-term effects of social modeling. He found that eight months after the initial experiment was conducted, some 40 percent of the children still showed the same type of aggressive behavior.

Criminologists and sociologists have used Bandura's study to draw conclusions about the origins of criminal and violent behavior. Some have asserted that criminal and violent acts by children and adults can be traced back to the family. From this perspective, children who observe violent behavior from members of their own families are the children most likely to show aggressive behavior themselves. They may be difficult to control at school and may be more likely to respond aggressively to challenges from other children. When they grow up, these children are also likely to model violent behavior as adults.

Bandura's study has been criticized. One criticism points to the rounded bottom of the Bobo doll, which causes it to rock upright after being hit, putting it in position to be struck again. Children, the critics say, are likely to perceive the doll as part of a game.

Children exhibited aggressive behavior during the Bobo doll experiment, modeling the behavior they had observed in the adults.

▶ **CRITICAL THINKING**

1. **Making Connections** How did the Bobo doll experiment help sociologists?
2. **Making Predictions** How might a psychologist who is working to help defend a person on trial for a violent crime use the social learning theory in the defense?
3. **Analyzing Visuals** How does this child's behavior illustrate Bandura's social learning theory?

The statistics and studies about family violence and its prevalence are shocking. For example, there are 3.3 million reports of child abuse every year, and as many as 6 million children are involved in these incidents every year. One recent survey found that more than a third of women and a quarter of all men have experienced rape or physical violence at the hands of an intimate partner. Experts also believe that over 2 million older Americans suffer some form of physical or psychological abuse or neglect each year. Experts also fear that this type of abuse will rise as the population ages. Perhaps the most disturbing fact is that, however large the number of reported cases of child, spouse, and elder abuse, many cases go unreported. That is, we do not really know the full extent of the problem.

Abuse takes many forms. Physical violence may range from pushing, slapping, shoving, kicking, or striking. Family members may be threatened with weapons. Of course, these sorts of acts harm those who experience them directly, but they have other victims as well. They also cause trauma to those who witness them.

As many as 2,000 children die each year from abuse or neglect. Most recent statistics list 1,500 annual cases of homicide involving intimate relationships. (These include married and unmarried intimate partners.) About 80 percent of these victims were female. There are also cases of children killing parents and one another.

Sexual violence against family members is also shockingly prevalent. There are up to 80,000 cases of child sexual abuse reported each year. Most experts believe that this number is only a small fraction of the real number of incidents that occur. Abuse ranges from rape to unwelcome touching to exposure to pornography.

Spousal Abuse

Contrary to popular myth, women are not the only victims of abuse. Husband abuse is frequently overlooked in studies of physical abuse. Although marriages in the United States are generally male dominated, it seems wives do abuse husbands with great regularity. Abuse is also a common problem in same-sex relationships.

Verbal and Psychological Abuse

Family violence is not limited to physical abuse. Verbal and psychological abuse are also part of many families. Psychologists report that the feelings of self-hate and worthlessness that are often the effects of these types of abuse can be as damaging as physical wounds. Neglect is another type of abuse that affects millions of children. It can leave its mark in such problems as poor nutrition, illness, and mental and emotional difficulties.

Sibling Violence

A frequent—and frequently tolerated—form of violence in the family occurs among children. This *sibling violence* appears to be prevalent and on the rise. Abuse among siblings may be based on rivalry, jealousy, disagreement over personal possessions, or incest.

✓ READING PROGRESS CHECK

Identifying At which class levels is family violence present?

FAMILY VIOLENCE STATISTICS

SPOUSE ABUSE:
Experienced rape, physical violence, and/or stalking by an intimate partner at some time.

Women	35.6%
Men	28.5%

CHILDREN AND ABUSE:

Suffered some form of mistreatment	10.2%
Witnessed a family assault	9.8%
Reported some form of sexual victimization	6.1%

ELDER ABUSE:

Suffered physical, sexual, psychological or financial abuse or neglect	4–6%

Sources: National Criminal Justice Reference Service; National Committee for the Prevention of Elder Abuse.

△ CHART

FAMILY VIOLENCE
The problem of family violence affects all members of the family—as victims and as perpetrators.

▶ CRITICAL THINKING

1. *Categorizing* Which of the three types of child abuse would include neglect?
2. *Analyzing* Why do states have laws that require people like doctors and teachers to report suspicions of child abuse?

LESSON 3 REVIEW

Reviewing Vocabulary
1. *Defining* What is the *marriage rate*, and what is the *divorce rate*?

Using Your Notes
2. *Identifying* What are the impacts of romantic love, divorce, and the violence on the American family?

Answering the Guiding Questions
3. *Defining* What characteristics typify an American family?

4. *Differentiating* How does the relationship between love and marriage vary among cultures?
5. *Describing* What are the causes of divorce?
6. *Examining* What forms does family violence take?

Writing Activity
7. *Narrative* Suppose that you are trying to describe the institutions of marriage and family in the United States to someone from another culture. How would you explain it?

The Family 317

FOCUS on research
Case Study

Family Violence

Annette Lareau is a sociologist who studies social stratification and its effects on shaping daily life. In her book Unequal Childhoods: Class, Race, and Family Life, *she shares the results of her study of how social class affects parenting. Her case studies include both white and African American families as well as working-class and middle-class families. The excerpt below is from one of her case studies, the Yanelli family, a white working-class family with a ten-year-old child named Billy.*

PRIMARY SOURCE

"While we were visiting, it would come up from time to time depending on how the day was going, but we observed [Ms. Yanelli, the mother] hit [Little Billy] with a belt or threaten to hit with a belt once a week. In some working-class families, the lines were clearer. It is also important to stress that some working-class families in the study did not use hitting or belts. Thus, there was important variation within the class. But this form of discipline was not observed in middle-class families.

. . . The school selectively validated certain cultural practices as legitimate. Other practices, such as hitting children, while virtually universal in other historical periods, were deemed unacceptable. Adherence to the practices of the accomplishment of natural growth, rather than concerted cultivation, had important consequences when the families interacted with the school. The Yanelli family keenly felt the school to be a threatening force. In other words, their failure to use elaborate reasoning (a cultural practice) was transformed into a lack of resources when they confronted school authorities. They felt worried, powerless, and scared.

For example, Little Billy's mother was worried that the school might turn her in to the state. Because of behavior problems at school, the educators stridently insisted that the school therapist who regularly visited the school see Little Billy. Once Billy's mother met with the school counselor, however, he warned her . . . that he was legally required to turn her in to government officials if he found that she was engaging in child abuse. Ms. Yanelli felt rightfully threatened, since she felt that . . . 'Billy gets so out of control that maybe he does need it once in a while.'

'I said to the therapist, you know, we'll be in [the grocery store] once in a while and Billy will slide down the aisle on his stomach and I'll take him by the hair and I'll pull him down the aisle. Is that child abuse? . . . So, am I going to have people over here saying I abuse my child if Billy sits in a class with him and says my mom pulled my hair? . . . I don't know. I guess I'll just have to take it as it comes. But there are times when I chase him up the stairs with a belt in my hand. I do.'

This clash, between the parents' ideas of what Billy needs and the school standards for child rearing, created small crises in the home. One day in May, for example, I stopped by for a visit . . . to find Ms. Yanelli deeply upset. She had been disciplining him, and Billy had raised his arm to block the impact of his mother's belt, ending up with three very distinct red marks on his forearm from where it had landed. His mother was

> "Little Billy's mother was worried that the school might turn her in to the state. . . . The school counselor . . . warned her . . . that he was legally required to turn her in to government officials if he found that she was engaging in child abuse."

frantic that 'he had to go to school that way.' . . .

In short, Ms. Yanelli's failure to use reasoning and her adoption of a belt made her vulnerable, since she moved in a 'field' (the school) that privileged reasoning. If she had lived a century earlier, the use of a belt would not have been so problematic. Today, however, it carries a potentially catastrophic risk: that her son could show the teacher his marks on his arm, she could be arrested for child abuse, and her son could be put in foster care temporarily or permanently. Regardless of the likelihood of this sequence occurring, Ms. Yanelli was worried about the actions of the school.

Thus, different family backgrounds engender different levels of benefit in educational fields. In this instance, the cost to working-class families for their lack of capital takes the form of an ongoing feeling of the threat of a looming catastrophe. This gap in the connections between working-class and poor families and schools is important. It undermines their feeling of trust or comfort at school, a feeling that other researchers have argued is pivotal in the formation of effective and productive family-school relationships."

—from *Unequal Childhoods: Class, Race, and Family Life*, 2011

Working With the Research

1. **Making Connections** What social problems and issues does Lareau's case study reveal about social class and parenting?
2. **Identifying Cause and Effect** What effects do trust and economic security have on parenting in working-class families?
3. **Analyzing** How important are the last two paragraphs of this excerpt in understanding parenting and its effects on family-school relationships? Explain.

networks

There's More Online!

- ☑ **CARTOON** Boomerang Children
- ☑ **CARTOON** A Working Mother
- ☑ **GRAPH** Single-Parent Families
- ☑ **IMAGE** Blended Families
- ☑ **SELF-CHECK QUIZ**

Reading HELPDESK

Academic Vocabulary
- ambiguous
- abandon

Content Vocabulary
- blended family
- adolescent
- two-income marriage
- cohabitation
- boomerang kid

TAKING NOTES:
Key Ideas and Details

LISTING As you read about changes in the types and varieties of families, use a graphic organizer like the one below to record key ideas and details.

Varieties of Families
•
•
•
•
•

LESSON 4
Changes in Marriage and Family

ESSENTIAL QUESTION • *What makes a family?*

IT MATTERS BECAUSE
Life in the United States is constantly changing, and marriage and family living patterns have undergone substantial shifts in recent years.

Varieties of Families

GUIDING QUESTION *What are the common varieties of families and what are their characteristics?*

Just a generation or two ago, few if any Americans used terms such as *blended family, cohabitation,* or *same-sex partners*. There were single-parent families and some couples never had children, but people in these situations were typically seen as objects of pity. Today, the patterns and norms of family have changed substantially.

Blended Families

The relatively high divorce rate in the United States has created the **blended family**—a family formed when at least one of the partners has a child or children from a previous marriage or relationship.

This type of family can become extremely complicated. Here's an example: A former husband (with two children in the custody of their biological mother) marries a new wife with two children in her custody. The new couple has two children of their own. The former wife of the husband also remarries a man with two children, one in his custody and one in the custody of his former wife. That former wife has remarried and has had a child with her second husband, who has custody of one child from his previous marriage. The former husband's parents are divorced, and both have remarried. Thus, when he remarries, his children have two complete sets of grandparents on his side, plus one set on the mother's side, plus perhaps more on the stepfather's side.

Blended families create a new type of extended family, a family that is not based strictly on blood relationships. As the example above shows, it is possible for a child in a blended family to have eight grandparents. Of course, not all blended families are that complicated. But 9 percent of all children living in a two-parent household are living with a nonbiological or adoptive parent.

320

Many blended families are successful, especially if they make adjustments during the first few years. Children from previous marriages, however, are one cited factor in the higher divorce rate for second marriages.

Sociologists do point to three major challenges facing blended families: a lack of money, stepchildren's dislike of a new spouse, and uncertainty about the new roles played by stepparents.

- **Money difficulties** Financial demands from both the former and present families generally result in stepfamilies having lower incomes. One partner may well be legally obligated to support children from their previous marriages. This can cause strain with the new partner.
- **Stepchild unhappiness** Children of divorce may wish for the reunion of their original parents. For this reason, stepchildren may seek to derail the new relationship. Even five years after divorce, about one-third of stepchildren continue to strongly disapprove of their original parents' decision to break up. This is especially true for teenagers, who can be very critical of their parents' values and personalities even if divorce is not involved.
- **Unclear roles** The roles of stepparents in a blended family are often **ambiguous** and conflicting. It may not be clear to stepparents or stepchildren how much authority a new spouse really has. Again, the presence of teenaged children especially can lead to frequent power struggles in such situations.

Single-Parent Families

The share of American households headed by a single parent is about 9 percent. More than 80 percent of these households are headed by a woman.

Why are so many single-parent households headed by women? Although courts today are more sensitive to fathers' claims, women in all social classes are still more likely to win custody of their children in cases of separation and divorce. Single mothers or women **abandoned** by their husbands or the fathers of their children make up a large part of poor single-parent households. Finally, poor women marry (or remarry) at a very low rate.

blended family type of family in which at least one of the partners has a child or children from a previous marriage

ambiguous unclear

abandon to suddenly leave a person or activity

Blended families bring a lot of history together under one roof.

▶ **CRITICAL THINKING**

Explaining Why do blended families pose challenges to the children living in them?

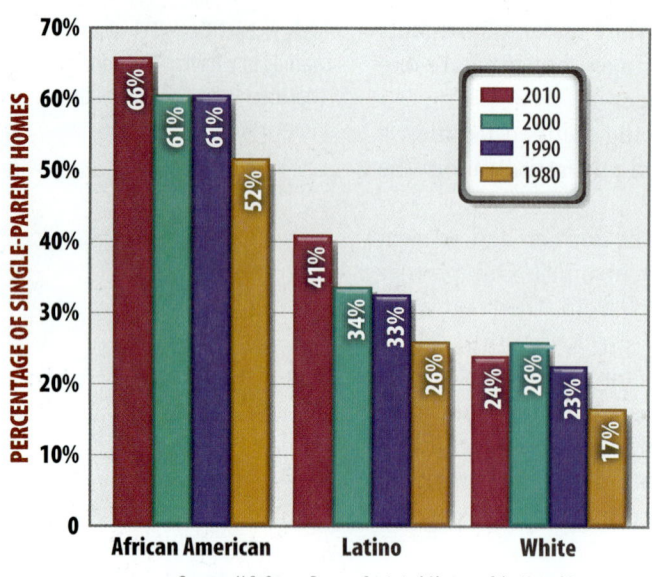

GRAPH

SINGLE-PARENT FAMILIES

This graph shows the change in the percentage of single-parent families from 1980 to 2010.

▶ **CRITICAL THINKING**

1. **Summarizing** How would you describe the trend in the percentage of single-parent families, including the trend in different racial groups?

2. **Speculating** What might be the possible explanation for differences in the rates between different groups?

adolescent person between the ages of 12 and 17

There are a number of well-educated, professional women who head single-parent households. With the stigma of single motherhood declining, more affluent women are choosing to have children or adopt children and to care for them alone. These women have the economic resources to support an independent family. On the other hand, since they are single parents, they also have no help from a partner in handling the responsibilities of parenting, which can cause stress.

Some 30 percent of America's children under the age of 18 live in households with one parent. African American and Latino children are statistically more likely than white children to live with only their mothers. This disparity increases for low-income children. Data show that the percentage of single parents of all races has increased in recent years. In general, the chances are increasing that an American child will live at least part of his or her youth in a single-parent—usually fatherless—home.

Adolescents—persons between the ages of 12 and 17—who live with one parent or with a stepparent have much higher rates of deviant behavior, including delinquency, drug and alcohol abuse, and teenage pregnancy, than adolescents living with both natural parents. A national sample of 12-to-17-year-olds indicates that arrests, school discipline, truancy and dropping out of school, running away, and smoking occur more often in single-parent and stepparent families, regardless of income, race, or ethnic background.

These figures do not point to a lack of concern in single parents as much as they show the built-in problems of single parenting. Single working parents must struggle alone to provide their children with the time, attention, and guidance that two parents can give. In addition, many single mothers earn little money, so they have added financial problems. Finding good child care and adequate housing in a suitable neighborhood can be difficult for single mothers.

Childless Marriages

In the past, married women without children were seen as failing to fulfill their "duty" as wives. In fact, in some religions, the inability of a woman to have children is still grounds for divorcing her. Historically, married childless women were pitied and looked down upon, and single women rarely achieved respectability outside the role of "spinster aunt."

Today, the likelihood of a woman remaining childless is much higher than in the past. Even among married women, the trend is sharply up, going from one in ten in 1976 to nearly two in ten today. This is true for all racial and ethnic groups. It is also true for unmarried women. The number of childless women aged 40 to 44 who have never been married rose from 11 to 13 percent between 1994 and 2008.

It is unclear if this trend will continue. Today, the reasons married women give for choosing not to have children are varied. Social stigmas against childless married women are disappearing. It is no longer automatically accepted that having children is the primary reason for marriage. Some women have elected to pursue personal or career goals instead—though it is worth noting that one of the few groups of women who are having more children today than in the past are the most educated women. Other people have moral issues about raising children in what they consider to be an immoral world. Increasingly, marriage

Quick Case Study

HOW ARE FAMILY ARRANGEMENTS ALIKE AND DIFFERENT?
Families are not as traditionally arranged today as they were in past. What kinds of family arrangements can you identify?

Procedure
1. Ask five classmates to name the members of their families who live at home with them.
2. Ask each person to indicate if they live in a traditional nuclear family or a blended, extended, or single-parent family. Record their responses.

Analysis
As you read through the responses, consider these questions:
1. In what ways did the responses show a variety of family arrangements? How many and what types?
2. How were the family arrangements alike and different?
3. What trends can you identify in family arrangements today?

two-income marriage a marriage in which both spouses work outside the home

CARTOON
A WORKING MOTHER
Working mothers have huge demands placed on them both at home and at work.

▶ CRITICAL THINKING
1. **Analyzing Visuals** How does the cartoonist portray those conflicting demands?
2. **Identifying Cause and Effect** How do husbands contribute to this problem?

or having children is put off, which may make it difficult for couples to make the adjustment to raising a family. It also increases the risk of physical problems preventing pregnancy.

Are childless marriages happy marriages? The answer to that question generally depends on the couple's decision about having children. Among childless couples who want children, marital happiness is generally lower than for married couples with children. Research, however, shows that couples who by choice have no children appear to be happier and more satisfied with their marriages and lives than do couples with children.

Two-Income Marriages
In families where both spouses are working outside the home, the marriage faces special strains. Women in these **two-income marriages** are often expected to handle most of the household and child-care responsibilities in addition to their full-time jobs. Because they must combine employment with child care and household tasks, married working women work about 15 hours more a week than men. Sociologist Arlie Hochschild calls this home- and child-based work "the second shift." In contrast, men spend an average of four to six hours per week in household and child-care duties.

Women in two-income marriages may also face role conflict. They can feel torn between the time requirements of their jobs and their desire to spend more time with their families. Feelings of guilt arise from not meeting all the expectations of being a wife, mother, and breadwinner.

Men in two-income marriages are often unwilling to assume household responsibilities equally with their wives. Even so, they feel the effects of role conflict and heavy time demands. Having an employed wife, particularly if she earns more than he does, may not fit with a man's image of himself as a provider.

Two-income marriages do enjoy some advantages. On balance, the effects of employment on the psychological well-being of women have been beneficial. Working outside the home provides a wider set of social relationships and greater feelings of control, independence, and self-esteem. Employment also provides a social and emotional cushion for mothers when their children leave home. Compared to women who do not work outside the home, employed women tend to have more outlets for self-expression.

Other family members also benefit from a mother's employment. Two incomes can mean more money. Sons and daughters of working mothers also benefit in noneconomic ways. Daughters are more likely to see themselves as potential working adults capable of being economically independent and as benefitting from further education. Sons are more likely to choose wives with similar attitudes toward education and employment.

For men, the benefits of two-income marriage include freedom from responsibility of being the sole provider and increased opportunity for job change or continued education. Men with employed wives can share the triumphs and defeats of the day with someone who is in a similar situation. If their wives are happy in their jobs, both partners can enjoy a happier relationship. Fathers who choose to can enjoy benefits of being a more involved parent.

A growing number of Americans are choosing to remain single, preferring independence to marriage.

▶ **CRITICAL THINKING**

Assessing What are the advantages and disadvantages of being single?

cohabitation a marriage-like living arrangement without the legal obligations and responsibilities of formal marriage

Cohabitation

Cohabitation—living with someone in a marriage-like arrangement without the legal obligations and responsibilities of formal marriage—has become an increasingly common alternative to traditional marriage. The percentage of cohabiting unmarried partners has nearly doubled since 1990. The U.S. Census reports that there were 7.5 million cohabiting opposite-sex couples in 2010—up 13 percent from just the year before. Cohabitation has risen among people of all ages and marital statuses.

Research on cohabitation is not encouraging. Cohabitations generally do not last as long as marriages. Some do transition to marriage, but those marriages are more likely to dissolve than marriages not preceded by cohabitation. Studies also show lower levels of relationship quality and lower incomes for cohabiting couples compared to married couples. There is also evidence that cohabiting may have a negative impact on children, perhaps because of lower incomes or family instability.

Single Life

A growing number of Americans are choosing to remain single rather than to marry. Almost half of all adults in the United States were unmarried in 2010. This reflects the increasing number of Americans who have never been married. According to the U.S. Census, 27 percent of all households in 2010 consisted of a single person living alone. Although many of these people will eventually marry, an increasing percentage will remain single all their lives.

Remaining single has traditionally been a choice that carried a stigma. Not marrying was seen as a form of deviance. Missouri actually taxed bachelors, starting in 1820. This stigma has faded over the past several decades as more people have chosen not to marry.

Same-Sex Domestic Partners

Because of the social stigma that continues to surround homosexuality, it is impossible to know exactly how many Americans are gay. The Kinsey Institute, a leader in research on human sexuality, estimates that homosexuals make up about 10 percent of the U.S. population. The Census Bureau reports that there were about 600,000 same-sex-couple households in the United States in 2010.

In recent years, gay activists and their supporters have fought to achieve the same rights for gay couples as married couples have, including tax and insurance benefits. Several states have made same-sex marriage legal, and others recognize "civil unions" that confer the same legal benefits as marriage. Yet some states have explicitly forbidden gay marriage by amending their constitutions.

This subject is certain to remain controversial for some time. Some lawsuits have been brought challenging laws that ban gay marriage on constitutional grounds. Federal courts have issued conflicting rulings in these cases. In the coming years, the U.S. Supreme Court may agree to hear appeals on these decisions. If so, the Court could issue a ruling that would settle the issue.

boomerang kid a young adult who stays at home or returns home to live with parents

Boomerang Kids

A boomerang is a weapon that, when thrown, returns to the thrower. The term **boomerang kid** is applied to a young adult who stays at or returns home to live with his or her parents. According to a study published by the Pew Research Center in 2012, 39 percent of people aged 18 to 34 lived with their parents or had lived with them on a temporary basis in recent years—sharply up from three decades ago.

There are many reasons for this trend. Young adults are marrying later and so staying home longer. More are continuing their education and find living at home a cost-effective solution to this financial challenge of paying for college. Many, however, return home after finishing school because the cost of living outstrips their earning capacity. Parents often shelter a young adult after the breakup of a marriage or cohabitation arrangement.

"Sure, I can make the 2:30 at the branch office. I just need to wait for my mom to finish drying my socks."

Boomerang children impose a financial strain on older parents. Many parents complain that children do not share in expenses or contribute to household work. Parents also lose privacy and the chance to develop their relationships with each other and with friends. It is not surprising that marital dissatisfaction among middle-aged parents is associated with adult children living at home.

Being a boomerang kid is not easy, either. Most have returned home for lack of better options. They know the burden that they represent. They also understand that living at home means giving up some freedom.

In spite of these challenges, most families appear to adjust well to the return of older children. This is most true when the child is able to help with expenses and duties.

✓ READING PROGRESS CHECK

Identifying Trends Are families getting more or less diverse in type and structure? Explain.

⌃ CARTOON

BOOMERANG CHILDREN
Adult children returning home to live are doing so because they lack other options.

▶ **CRITICAL THINKING**

1. ***Analyzing Visual*** How does the cartoon show that unemployed young adults living with parents is a growing trend?

2. ***Exploring Issues*** What adjustments can young adults living with their parents make to not be a burden?

Looking Forward

GUIDING QUESTION *What is the future of the American family?*

Marriage and family have always been subjects of intense interest for people in the United States. In recent years, however, they seem to have become something of a sideshow. Reality television has turned the routines of courtship, marriage, and family into a spectacle conjured up—and spiced with made-for-TV drama—for the entertainment of the viewers. In "real life," however, the American family remains in many respects what it has always been.

If the frequency of marriage and remarriage is any indication, the nuclear family is not disappearing. A very high percentage of Americans marry at some point in their lives, and although Americans have been experimenting with alternative living arrangements, the nuclear family still remains a popular choice for millions of Americans. Well over 60 percent of children are raised in two-parent households—though that number is declining. Contrary to long-standing fears, many Americans are not avoiding marriage permanently. They are simply postponing it or sampling it more often.

The American family is changing, however. You just read, for example, that the percentage of children being raised by two parents is dropping. Even in those two-parent households, the pattern in which the wage-earning father supports a work-at-home mother has decreased substantially over the years and is expected to keep decreasing. The trend toward more working parents is likely to continue. This will produce its own strains for parents, children, and society—as well as rewards. Adjusting to the challenges and maximizing the benefits of these changes will remain a challenge for the future. Continued increases are expected for other family types, such as the single-parent family. If divorce rates continue to fall, the number of blended families may not increase, but the variety of American families is unlikely to change significantly in the coming years. The question, then, is not whether the family will survive, but what form it will take.

Concerns include the impact of poverty on the family. In recent times, one in five American children has lived in a family whose income was below the poverty line. Poverty harms children and families in many ways, as previously discussed.

The aging of the American population is also a possible strain on families. As the baby boom generation ages, more American families are likely to face the challenge of caring for an aging parent or parents. The already serious problem of elder abuse may grow. Additionally, some married people will find themselves in the "sandwich generation"—caught between caring for both their own children and their aged parents.

✓ **READING PROGRESS CHECK**

Explaining What changes are expected in the years ahead for the American family?

LESSON 4 REVIEW

Reviewing Vocabulary

1. *Explaining* How are blended families formed?
2. *Contrasting* How do two-income marriages differ from more traditional arrangements?

Using Your Notes

3. *Listing* What are the different varieties of family now found in American society?

Answering the Guiding Questions

4. *Differentiating* What are the common varieties of families and what are their characteristics?
5. *Speculating* What is the future of the American family?

Writing Activity

6. *Informative/Explanatory* Summarize the broad changes that have taken place in the American family in recent decades, including possible causes of these changes.

CHAPTER 11 Assessment

Directions: On a separate sheet of paper, answer the questions below. Make sure you read carefully and answer all parts of the questions.

Lesson Review

Lesson 1

1. **Identifying Central Issues** Why is defining the term *family* so difficult?
2. **Making Connections** What is the role of gender in defining the patterns of family structure?

Lesson 2

3. **Explaining** Explain how marriage serves to regulate human reproductive and sexual activity.
4. **Synthesizing** How might the conflict perspective on gender relations explain the strain experienced by many married mothers who hold a job outside the home?

Lesson 3

5. **Assessing** Discuss the role of romantic love in the institution of marriage in the United States.
6. **Analyzing** What factors lead to a logical prediction that the divorce rate in the United States will continue to decline?

Lesson 4

7. **Categorizing** Suppose two people divorce their spouses. Then they meet and begin to spend time together. The two decide to become a family. Both people have children from prior relationships, and both bring their children into their new home. What is the correct term for this new family? Explain.
8. **Making Connections** Explain the relationship between the nuclear family and the frequency of marriage in today's society.

21st Century Skills

USING TABLES

Use the table to answer the following questions.

Married Couples by Labor Force Status of Spouses (in thousands)				
Year	All Married Couples	In Labor Force		
		Wife and Husband	Husband Only	Wife Only
TOTAL				
1990	52,317	28,056	13,013	2,453
2000	55,311	31,095	11,815	3,301
2010	60,384	32,731	13,074	4,526
WITH CHILDREN YOUNGER THAN 18				
1990	24,537	15,768	7,667	558
2000	25,248	17,116	6,950	795
2010	25,317	16,710	7,220	962
WITH CHILDREN YOUNGER THAN 6				
1990	12,051	6,932	4,692	192
2000	11,393	6,984	4,077	211
2010	11,599	6,924	4,181	335

Source: U.S. Census Bureau, *Statistical Abstract of the United States: 2012*

9. **Identifying Change** Discuss at least two specific changes in the labor force as depicted in the table. In your discussion, include details from each of the three decades shown.
10. **Understanding Relationships Among Events** Discuss at least one aspect of history leading up to the year 2000 that likely led to the data shown in the table.

Need Extra Help?

If You've Missed Question	1	2	3	4	5	6	7	8	9	10
Go to page	300–301	302–304	308–309	310	313–314	314–315	320–321	320–326	312–326	312–326

CHAPTER 11 Assessment

Directions: On a separate sheet of paper, answer the questions below. Make sure you read carefully and answer all parts of the questions.

Exploring the Essential Question

11 *Understanding Historical Interpretations* Consider what you have learned about the purposes and functions of the family in history. Considering each of these functions, examine whether, in your opinion, society has developed alternative means of accomplishing these goals. Based on your critical examination of society and the family's role in it, offer your own definition of *family*.

DBQ Analyzing Primary Sources

PRIMARY SOURCE

Use the document to answer the following questions.

> "Home is the place where, when you have to go there, They have to take you in."
>
> —Robert Frost
> "Death of a Hired Man"

12 *Interpreting* Discuss this quote about family from the functionalist perspective.

13 *Interpreting* Discuss this quote about family from the perspective of the conflict theorist.

Critical Thinking

14 *Making Connections* Cite examples from prehistory and modern times to support this statement: "Economic factors have always played a role in the formation and development of families."

15 *Exploring Issues* Changes in social norms and expectations influence people's behavior in many ways. Provide examples to explain how such changes are currently affecting the American family.

College and Career Readiness Skills

16 *Decision Making* Imagine you are developing the curriculum for a college. There has been debate at the school regarding whether taking a course in Family and Marriage in the United States should be required of all students for graduation. Take a pro or con position; then write a brief course description and complete a recommendation report to the college's dean and board of directors to defend your position. Incorporate information from the chapter into your course description that supports your position.

Research and Presentation

17 *Identifying Perspectives* Some believe that marriages are failing at the current rate because the institution of marriage has received such negative media attention recently. For this project, your task is to create a print advertisement to promote marriage and family. Using what you have learned in this chapter about the roles and purposes of marriage and family, create an ad that helps encourage people to see the benefits of marriage and family. The ad should be designed to induce them to make the choice to pursue marriage.

18 *Gathering Information* Conduct Internet research to learn more about the recent trend of Americans' choice to delay marriage. Write an essay that explores the causes and effects of this practice on individuals and the country. Create a class presentation to discuss your ad and a summary of your essay. Explain how the two address a divergence of purpose—and how they also address common ground.

Need Extra Help?

If You've Missed Question	11	12	13	14	15	16	17	18
Go to page	300–326	307–309	310	312–326	312–326	300–326	300–326	300–326

Education

ESSENTIAL QUESTION • *What purposes does education serve?*

networks
There's More Online about education.

CHAPTER 12

Technology & Society
Education and Technology

Lesson 1
Development and Structure of Education

Lesson 2
Functionalist Perspective

Lesson 3
Conflict Perspective

Lesson 4
Symbolic Interactionism

Sociology Matters...

"Do I need to know this for the test?" Sometimes it is easy to forget why you are sitting in a classroom. School will prepare you to enter the adult world of work and teach you the skills you need to be a good citizen. Theories abound about the best way to teach you the curriculum. But did you know you are also being taught a hidden curriculum? Hidden lessons can teach you good values, but they can also enhance or limit your success in the world.

◄ While new technology has changed some aspects of education, its purposes remain the same.

Paul Bradbury/OJO Images/Getty Images

CHAPTER 12
Technology & Society

Education and Technology

All children do not have equal access to the technology necessary to succeed in school.

It might seem that, in the United States, nearly everyone has a computer or has access to one at home, but statistics show that whether a family owns a computer that has Internet access is based primarily on socioeconomic and demographic factors. For example, a middle-class white family is highly likely to have at least one computer with Internet access at home. African American and Latino families are less likely to own a computer, less likely to have Internet access at home, and less likely to have high-speed or wireless Internet access.

One key problem created by this digital divide is homework. What happens when a teacher makes using a computer and the Internet mandatory to read and complete assignments? How do children of working-class and impoverished families handle this challenge? Certainly, many schools and libraries have computer labs or public access to computers and the Internet, but there are some obstacles even to using this equipment. Scheduling time to use public or school computers may not be easy due to transportation needs, limited hours of access, and competition among students. The time saved by students who have computers and Internet access at home gives them an obvious advantage in completing their work. They do not have to schedule time and a ride to the library to use a computer to read and possibly complete an assignment.

Students from lower-income families who may not have a computer and Internet access at home face another difficulty: They may also be required to go home immediately after school to care for their sisters or brothers while their parents work. When it comes down to making the grade, students without a home computer and Internet access are at an extreme disadvantage in today's world.

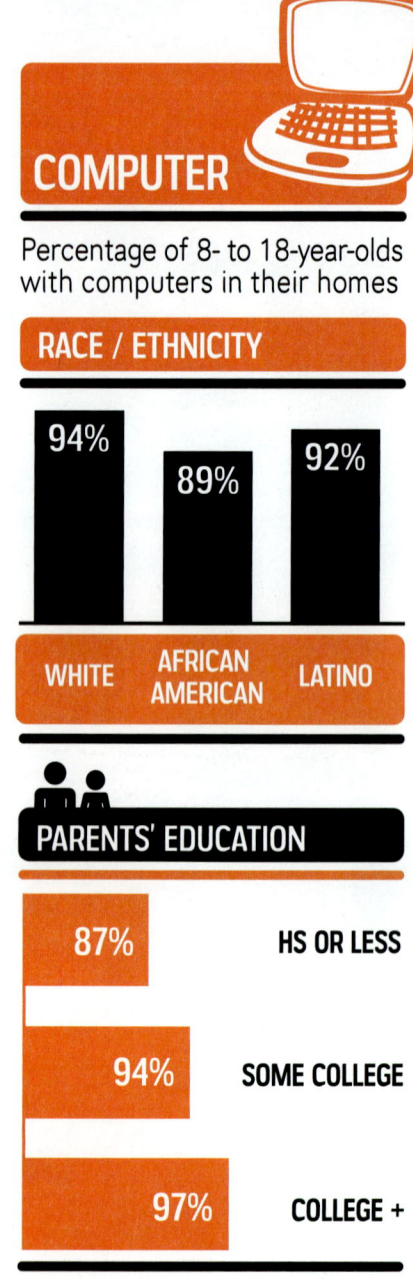

COMPUTER

Percentage of 8- to 18-year-olds with computers in their homes

RACE / ETHNICITY

- WHITE: 94%
- AFRICAN AMERICAN: 89%
- LATINO: 92%

PARENTS' EDUCATION

- HS OR LESS: 87%
- SOME COLLEGE: 94%
- COLLEGE +: 97%

Source: Victoria J. Rideout, Ulla G. Foehr, and Donald F. Roberts, *Generation M^2: Media in the Lives of 8- to 18-Year-Olds* (Kaiser Family Foundation, 2010)

THE DIGITAL DIVIDE

INTERNET ACCESS
Percentage of 8- to 18-year-olds with the Internet in their homes

RACE / ETHNICITY

- WHITE: 88%
- AFRICAN AMERICAN: 78%
- LATINO: 74%

PARENTS' EDUCATION

- HS OR LESS: 74%
- SOME COLLEGE: 84%
- COLLEGE +: 91%

HIGH-SPEED/WIRELESS ACCESS
Percentage of 8- to 18-year-olds with high-speed / wireless access in their homes

RACE / ETHNICITY

- WHITE: 61%
- AFRICAN AMERICAN: 55%
- LATINO: 52%

PARENTS' EDUCATION

- HS OR LESS: 49%
- SOME COLLEGE: 64%
- COLLEGE +: 65%

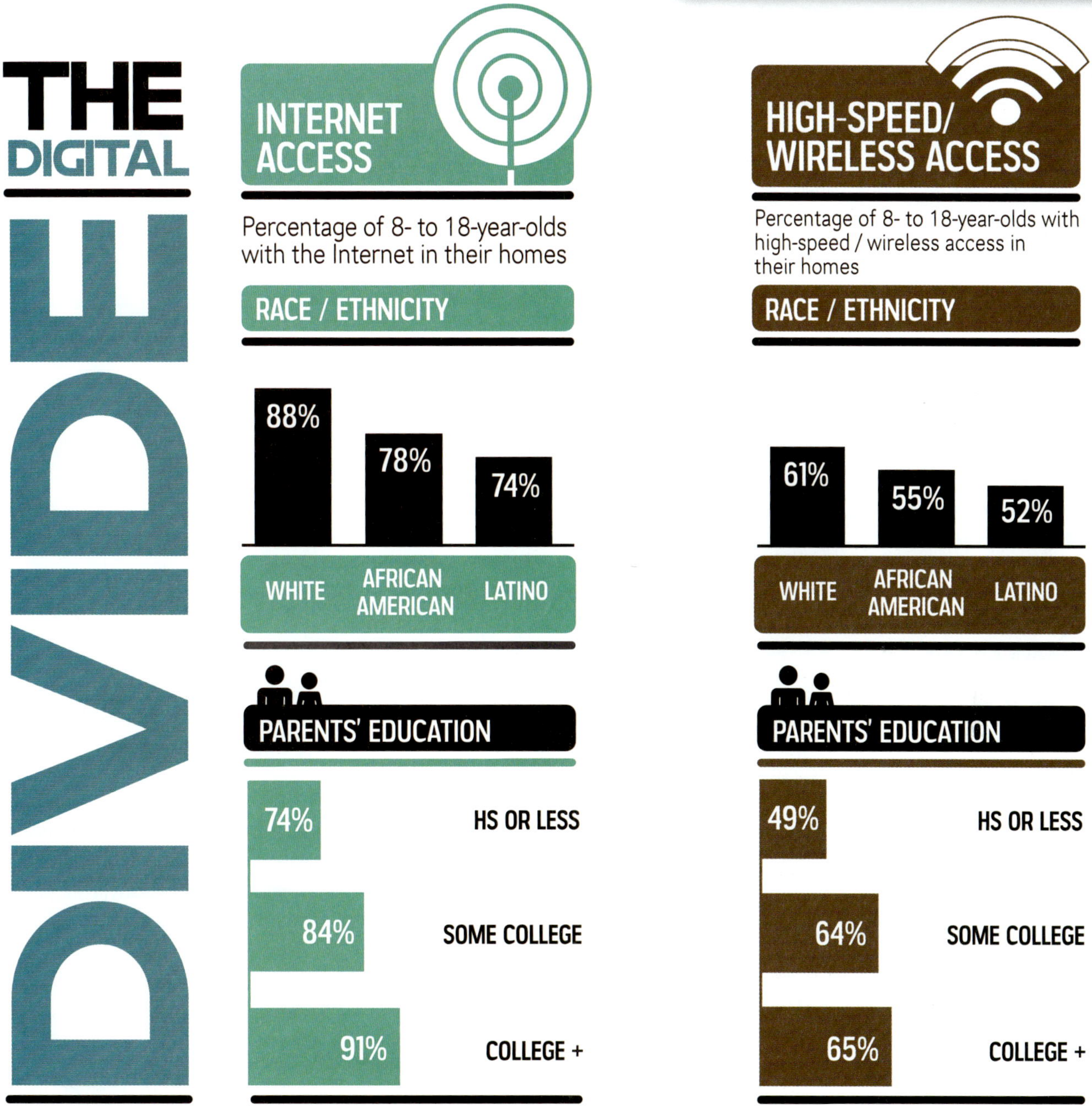

Thinking Like a Sociologist

1 Analyzing
Why do you think that some teachers and schools make assignments that require the use of a computer and the Internet?

2 Defending
How could you defend a student who has not completed an assignment because he or she does not have a computer or Internet access at home?

networks

There's More Online!

- ☑ **CARTOON** School Vouchers
- ☑ **GRAPH** High School Graduates
- ☑ **IMAGE** Magnet Schools
- ☑ **MAP** School Expenditures
- ☑ **SELF-CHECK QUIZ**

Reading HELPDESK

Academic Vocabulary
- ideology
- intelligence

Content Vocabulary
- formal schooling
- open classroom
- cooperative learning
- integrative curriculum
- voucher system
- charter schools
- magnet schools
- for-profit schools

TAKING NOTES:
Key Ideas and Details

ORGANIZING As you read, complete a time line like the one below illustrating changing theories about education.

LESSON 1
Development and Structure of Education

ESSENTIAL QUESTION • *What purposes does education serve?*

It Matters Because
Schools today are very bureaucratic in nature. Advocates of open classrooms and cooperative learning contend that bureaucratically run schools fail to take into account the emotional and creative needs of individual children.

Bureaucracy in Education

GUIDING QUESTION *Should schools be standardized?*

School administration in the early 1900s was based on a factory model of education. Educators believed that children could be and should be educated in much the same way that cars were mass-produced:

PRIMARY SOURCE

"Schooling came to be seen as work or the preparation for work; schools were pictured as factories, educators as industrial managers, and students as the raw materials to be inducted into the production process. The **ideology** of school management was recast in the mold of the business corporation, and the character of education was shaped after the image of industrial production."

—David Cohen and Marvin Lazerson, "Education and the Corporate Order," 1972

Although teachers and administrators work hard today to personalize the time you spend in school, public education in this country remains very much an impersonal bureaucratic process. Most schools today are still based on specialization, rules and procedures, and impersonality.

The Purpose of Standardization
For administrators, there are many advantages to following a bureaucratic model. For instance, one of the characteristics of a bureaucracy is the tendency to specialize. Professional educators are specialists—administrators, classroom teachers, librarians, and curriculum specialists decide on courses, content, teaching methods, and so on.

In the bureaucratic model, education can be accomplished most efficiently for large numbers of students when they are at similar stages in their ability and development. There are approximately 65 million students in the public school system. By placing students of similar ability levels in the same classroom, education can be carried out in a rational, straightforward way. A teacher can develop one lesson plan that works for a large number of students, which is an efficient use of the teacher's planning and instructional time. Age-based classrooms, in which all students receive the same instruction, reflect the impersonal, bureaucratic nature of schools.

Efficiency, the ultimate goal of a bureaucracy, is also increased when teachers teach the same, or at least similar, content. Materials can be approved and purchased in bulk, and testing can be standardized. This practice also allows students to transfer from one school to another and continue studying approximately the same content. Rules and procedures exist to ensure that all of this happens.

Schools are also part of a much larger bureaucratic system. This system begins with the federal government and progresses, layer by layer, down through state and local governments.

Criticisms of the Bureaucratic Model

Critics claim that the old factory, or bureaucratic, model is not appropriate for schooling. Children, they point out, are not materials to be processed on an assembly line. Children are human beings who come into school with previous knowledge and who interact socially and emotionally with other students. According to critics of **formal schooling**, education that is provided and regulated by society, the schools' bureaucratic nature is unable to respond to the expressive, creative, and emotional needs of all children. These critics prefer several less rigid, more democratic alternatives.

✓ **READING PROGRESS CHECK**

Finding the Main Idea What is the ultimate goal of bureaucracy?

ideology ideas characteristic of a person, group, or political party

formal schooling education that is provided and regulated by society

The 1950s-era classroom on the left reflects the traditional mass-production approach to education. More recently, as seen in the photo at the right, classrooms have become more personalized.

▶ **CRITICAL THINKING**

Contrasting How do these photographs demonstrate the different ideologies of bureaucratic and more personalized approaches to education?

Democratic Reforms in the Classroom

GUIDING QUESTION *What are the alternatives to the bureaucratic model of education?*

Since colonial times, providing citizens with a good education has been an important value in the United States. The Puritans in Massachusetts in 1647 required towns with more than 50 families to hire a schoolmaster. The Land Ordinance of 1785 required that some of the income from the sale of public land north of the Ohio River be used to support public schools.

The first public schools were quite authoritarian, with firm rules and sharp lines drawn between students and teachers. The American progressive education movement of the 1920s and 1930s was a reaction to the strict Victorian authoritarianism of early nineteenth-century schools. Educational philosopher John Dewey (1859–1952) led the progressive education movement, which emphasized knowledge related to work and to individual student interests. The progressive movement, with its child-centered focus, almost disappeared in the 1950s. In the 1960s, it reappeared as the humanistic movement. The humanistic movement supported the elimination of restrictive rules and codes and promoted the involvement of students in the educational process. The aim of the humanistic movement was to create a more democratic, student-focused learning environment very different from that created under the bureaucratic model.

The humanistic movement in education has proven to be an influential forerunner of classroom reform. Three ways to express the humanistic educational impulse are the *open classroom, cooperative learning,* and the *integrative curriculum.*

The Open Classroom

The **open classroom** is a non-bureaucratic approach to education based on democratic relationships, flexibility, and non-competitiveness. In this type of setting, educators avoid the sharp authoritarian line traditionally drawn between teachers and students. The open classroom drops the idea that all children of a given age should follow a standardized curriculum. On the belief that competition is not a good motivator for children, the open classroom abandons the use of graded report cards based on comparison of student performance.

The open classroom was introduced in the 1960s and then faded from use. It resurfaced in the 1990s, however. Cooperative learning and the integrative curriculum are two important extensions of the open-classroom approach.

Cooperative Learning

Cooperative learning takes place in a non-bureaucratic classroom structure in which students study in groups with teachers as guides rather than as the controlling agents. According to this learning method, students learn more if they are actively involved with others in the classroom. The traditional teacher-centered approach rewards students for being passive recipients of information and requires them to compete with others for grades and teacher recognition. Cooperative learning, with its accent on teamwork rather than individual performance, is designed to encourage students to

---

open classroom a non-bureaucratic approach to education based on democracy, flexibility, and non-competitiveness

cooperative learning an instructional method that relies on cooperation among students

GRAPH

HIGH SCHOOL GRADUATES, 1970 AND 2010

The graph shows percentages, by racial and ethnic category, of persons 25 years old and older who completed high school in 1970 and in 2010.

▶ **CRITICAL THINKING**

1. **Making Generalizations** What is the overall trend shown on the graph?
2. **Analyzing Visuals** Which group experienced the greatest change?

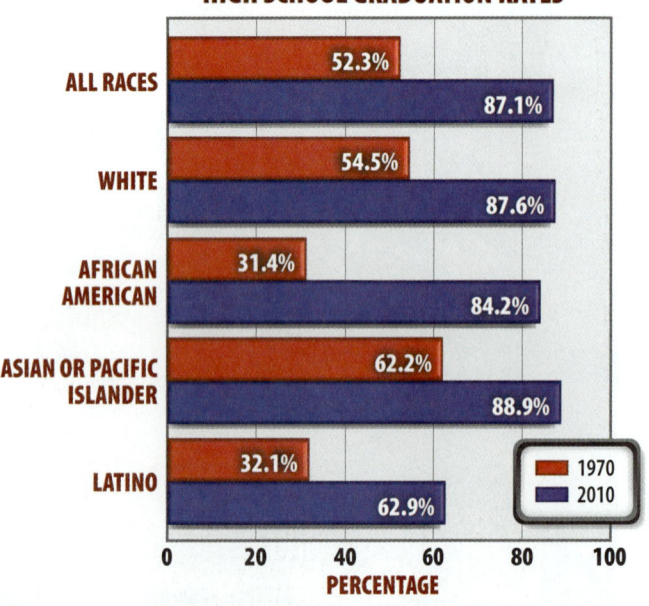

HIGH SCHOOL GRADUATION RATES

- ALL RACES: 52.3% (1970), 87.1% (2010)
- WHITE: 54.5% (1970), 87.6% (2010)
- AFRICAN AMERICAN: 31.4% (1970), 84.2% (2010)
- ASIAN OR PACIFIC ISLANDER: 62.2% (1970), 88.9% (2010)
- LATINO: 32.1% (1970), 62.9% (2010)

Source: U.S. Census Bureau, *Statistical Abstract of the United States: 2012*

concentrate more on the process of getting results than on how their answers compare to those of other students. Cooperation replaces competition. Students typically work in small groups on specific tasks. Credit for completion of a task is given only if all group members do their parts.

Using this approach successfully requires some expertise on the part of the teacher and can initially discourage students who are motivated by letter grades based on individual work. Nevertheless, some benefits of the cooperative learning approach have been documented. For example:

- Uncooperativeness and stress among students is reduced
- Academic performance increases
- Students have more positive attitudes toward school
- Racial and ethnic antagonism decreases
- Self-esteem increases

Integrative Curriculum

In the traditional classroom, the curriculum is predetermined for students. In the **integrative curriculum**, however, students and teachers collaborate to create the curriculum. Since students are asked to participate in curriculum design and content, the integrative curriculum is democratic in nature.

In an integrative curriculum, subject matter is selected and organized around certain real-world themes or concepts. It emphasizes hands-on experience and takes advantage of the various ways students express their **intelligence**. Different units of study will engage students in varying ways.

☑ READING PROGRESS CHECK

Making Connections How does a cooperative classroom differ from a formal classroom?

The Back-to-Basics Movement

GUIDING QUESTION *What started the back-to-basics movement?*

In the 1990s, the "back-to-basics" movement emerged alongside cooperative learning and the integrative curriculum. Worried by low scores on achievement tests, supporters of this movement pushed for a return to a traditional curriculum ("reading, writing, and arithmetic") based on more bureaucratic methods.

The back-to-basics movement can be traced back to the publication of a study in 1983 that alarmed many Americans. The National Commission on Excellence in Education issued a report titled *A Nation at Risk*. It warned of a "rising tide of mediocrity" in America's schools. Because of deficiencies in its educational system, the report claimed, America was at risk of being overtaken by some of its global economic competitors.

Unlike the recommendations of the progressive and humanistic reform movements, most of the solutions offered by the commission were bureaucratic in nature. The report urged a return to more teaching of basic skills, such as reading and mathematics. High school graduation requirements, it said, should be strengthened to include four years of English, three years of mathematics, three years of science, three years of social studies, and a half year of computer science.

integrative curriculum an approach to education based on student-teacher collaboration

intelligence the ability to learn or understand or to deal with new or difficult situations; the ability to apply knowledge

Science teachers sometimes take students on field trips so they can apply what they have learned in the classroom.

▶ **CRITICAL THINKING**
Categorizing What type of educational model do you think this practice reflects? Why?

School days, the school year, or both should be lengthened. Standardized achievement tests should be administered as students move from one level of schooling to another. High school students should be given significantly more homework. Discipline should be tightened through the development and enforcement of codes for student conduct.

✓ READING PROGRESS CHECK

Making Connections What did the back-to-basics movement emphasize?

Alternatives to the Public School System

GUIDING QUESTION *What is the school choice movement?*

The debate over the most effective classroom methods continues. Meanwhile, educators and politicians are looking beyond the classroom to how schools are organized, funded, and administered. A new debate has arisen over school choice. The school choice movement promotes the idea that the best way to improve schools is by using the free enterprise model to create some competition for the public school system. Supporters of school choice believe that parents and students should be able to select the school that best fits their needs and provides the greatest educational benefit. School choice includes the *voucher system, charter schools, magnet schools,* and *for-profit schools.*

The Voucher System

People in favor of a **voucher system** say that the government should make the money spent per child on public education available to families to use as they wish, choosing public, private, or religious schools for their children. Families who chose a public school would pay nothing, just as in the current system. Parents who chose a religious or other private school would receive a government voucher to be used to pay a portion of the tuition equal to the amount the government spends per child in the public school system. Any additional tuition would be paid by the parents.

Proponents argue that public schools will have to compete for students and thus will improve their services. If parents are not happy with a school, they have the freedom to remove their children and place them elsewhere.

voucher system a system in which public school funds may be used to support public, private, or religious schools

Some critics of the back-to-basics movement say that emphasis on standardized tests ignores the importance of developing writing skills.

▶ **CRITICAL THINKING**
Constructing Arguments How do you think proponents of the back-to-basics movement would respond to that criticism?

CARTOON
SCHOOL VOUCHERS
School vouchers are an attractive approach to reforming education to some critics of public education.

▶ **CRITICAL THINKING**

1. **Analyzing Visuals** How does the cartoonist portray vouchers?
2. **Analyzing** Why has adoption of school vouchers been rather slow?

Reaction to the school-voucher approach has been mixed. So far only eight states and the District of Columbia have adopted school voucher programs. One reason for the slow spread of voucher programs among the states is that 36 state constitutions contain various restrictions on aid to private and religious institutions. Amendments to an additional 11 state constitutions restrict the public funding of education to public schools only. Thus, the introduction of voucher systems in these states must first be tested in the courts. A number of state courts, including those in Florida, Vermont, Maine, and Pennsylvania, have already declared vouchers unconstitutional. Legal challenges continue in some states. In 2012, an Arizona superior court judge upheld the constitutionality of a new voucher program for students with disabilities. The program had been challenged for providing public money to fund religious schools. On the other hand, in the same year a similar voucher program was struck down in Oklahoma.

A Diverse America

SCHOOL EXPENDITURES
Everyone has heard the expression "You get what you pay for." Because of this idea, many people use the amount of money spent on public schools as a measure of the quality of that education. The accompanying map shows that some states spend more than twice as much per student as other states.

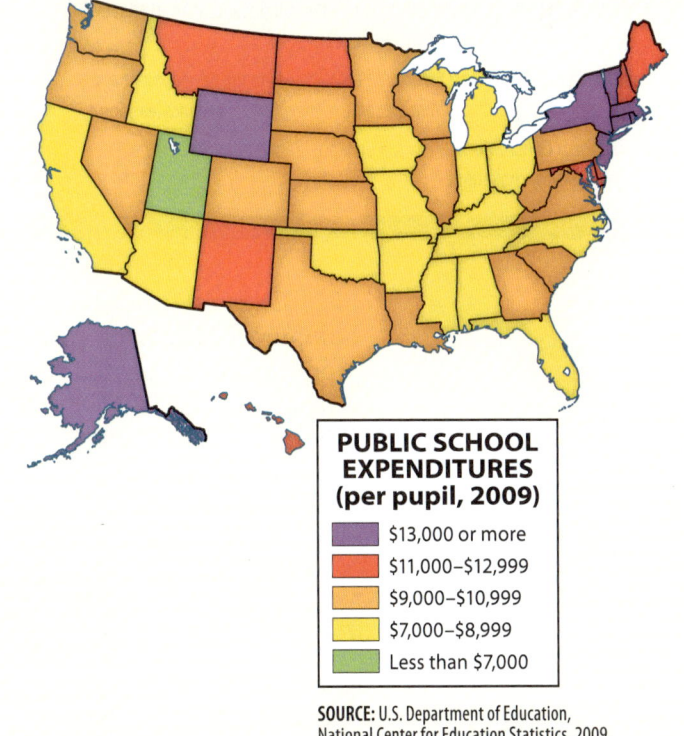

PUBLIC SCHOOL EXPENDITURES (per pupil, 2009)

- $13,000 or more
- $11,000–$12,999
- $9,000–$10,999
- $7,000–$8,999
- Less than $7,000

SOURCE: U.S. Department of Education, National Center for Education Statistics, 2009.

Geography Connection
1. **Places and Regions** What generalizations might you make about regions with higher expenditures per student than those with lower expenditures?
2. **Places and Regions** How does your state compare to other states in your region?
3. **The Uses of Geography** How might this information be useful to families with students enrolled in school?

Applying Sociology

DISTANCE LEARNING

Distance learning, or distance education, has grown in popularity over the last decade. Colleges and universities around the world offer courses via distance learning. At the beginning of the twenty-first century, about half of higher-education institutions offered distance learning. Offering distance-learning courses provides an economic incentive to both students and educational institutions because classrooms are not needed. Colleges and universities can increase enrollment because students can take a course from anywhere without having to live near or on campus.

More secondary schools also have begun to expand their course offerings through distance education. Many homeschooled students benefit from this technology, as do teenage parents. Virtual high schools offer courses to students who may have to retake a class to graduate but cannot do so because of scheduling issues. Taking a virtual high-school course allows the student to earn the needed credit to graduate. Some critics assert that a distance-learning course does not offer the same experience or cover the same content as a course would in a real-life classroom setting. In a 2011 Pew Research survey, about 50 percent of the college presidents surveyed said that they thought online courses provided the same value as courses that were taken in the classroom. Public opinion was much more negative, however. Only about 30 percent of the people surveyed thought that online courses offered the same value as courses that students take in the classroom.

▶ **CRITICAL THINKING**

1. **Evaluating** What additional drawbacks might distance learning have that were not mentioned in the passage?
2. **Identifying Cause and Effect** What factors led to the development and use of distance learning? What are some of the effects of distance learning?
3. **Drawing Conclusions** How can distance learning benefit those who are physically challenged?

Critics of vouchers argue that no clear evidence suggests that vouchers have improved educational performance. Studies have shown that children who attend private schools on vouchers do not achieve higher test scores than those who remain in public schools. Cleveland's voucher system, for example, began in 1995. In the 2009–2010 school year, voucher students were required to take the state's proficiency exams for the first time. According to Ohio's Department of Education, Cleveland public school students often scored better than their voucher program counterparts.

School voucher programs have proved to be one of the most controversial educational issues of the twenty-first century. Supporters of school vouchers believe they will help children in failing schools achieve a better education and force public schools to improve to stay competitive. Opponents of voucher systems fear that they will drain needed funds from the public school system and result in racial and class segregation in American schools. Some states now are considering alternatives to vouchers that still provide parents with options, such as tax credits for private and religious school payments. The important role that education plays in the lives of Americans suggests that the issue of school vouchers will be debated for years to come.

Magnet Schools and Charter Schools

Charter schools are publicly funded schools operated like private schools by public school teachers and administrators. Freed of answering to local school boards, charter schools have the latitude to shape their own curriculum and to use nontraditional or traditional teaching methods.

In 2011, more than 5,200 charter schools served 1.8 million students in 40 states and the District of Columbia. Critics of charter schools say they hurt public schools by draining money away from them. They also criticize the quality of charter schools and worry about the lack of oversight by school boards. Charter schools vary in quality, and success is mixed. Overall, there is no evidence that they perform better than traditional public schools. In fact, a 2009 Stanford University study of charter schools found that on average, charter schools were not performing as well as public schools.

Magnet schools are public schools that attempt to achieve high standards by specializing in a certain area. One school may emphasize the performing arts while another might stress science. Magnet schools are designed to enhance school quality and to promote desegregation. Magnet schools receive praise for having a high level of academic achievement and criticism for luring the best and brightest students away from traditional community schools.

For-Profit Schools

Some reformers do not believe local or federal government is capable of improving the educational system. Government, they say, is too wasteful and ineffective. Why not look to business and market forces to solve the problems facing schools today? **For-profit schools** would be supported by government funds but run by private companies. By borrowing from modern business practices, the argument goes, these schools could be efficient, productive, and cost effective. Marketplace forces would ensure that only the best schools survive.

Critics of this approach are bothered by the idea of mixing profit and public service. What will happen to the students when their needs are weighed against the profit margin? Would for-profit schools skimp on equipment, services, and training? Another problem involves oversight. In a for-profit system, voters would lose the power to influence officials and educational policy.

✓ **READING PROGRESS CHECK**

Generalizing What is the role of competition in the school-choice movement?

These students are rehearsing a play at a magnet arts school.

▶ **CRITICAL THINKING**
Assessing What is one advantage and one disadvantage of magnet schools?

charter schools public schools that are operated like private schools by public school teachers and administrators

magnet schools public schools that focus on particular disciplines or areas, such as fine arts or science

for-profit schools schools run by private companies with government funds

---

LESSON 1 REVIEW

Reviewing Vocabulary
1. *Identifying* What is the difference between formal schooling and the open classroom?
2. *Defining* What is an integrative curriculum?

Using Your Notes
3. *Describing* Use your notes from the time line to describe the changes in educational approaches over time.

Answering the Guiding Questions
4. *Evaluating* Should schools be standardized?

5. *Exploring Issues* What are the alternatives to the bureaucratic model of education?
6. *Identifying Cause and Effect* What started the back-to-basics movement?
7. *Exploring Issues* What is the school choice movement?

Writing Activity
8. *Argument* Which education model do you think best fulfills the purposes of education? Explain.

networks

There's More Online!

- ☑ **GRAPHIC ORGANIZER** Functions of Education
- ☑ **IMAGE** Horace Mann
- ☑ **MAP** World Literacy Rates
- ☑ **SELF-CHECK QUIZ**

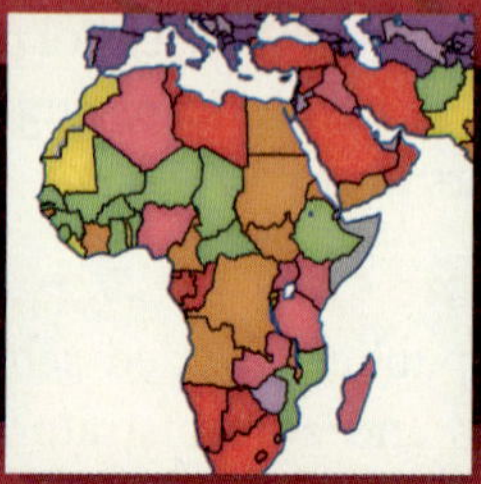

Reading HELPDESK

Academic Vocabulary
- diverse
- eventual

Content Vocabulary
- manifest function
- latent function
- tracking

TAKING NOTES:
Integration of Knowledge and Ideas

ORGANIZING Use a graphic organizer like the one below to describe examples of the manifest and latent functions of education.

Functions of Education	
Manifest	
Latent	

LESSON 2
Functionalist Perspective

ESSENTIAL QUESTION • *What purposes does education serve?*

IT MATTERS BECAUSE
Functionalists believe that schools serve to transmit culture, create a common identity, select and screen talent, and promote personal growth and development. Schools also serve other, unintended functions.

Manifest Functions of Education

GUIDING QUESTION *What purposes does the school system serve?*

According to the functionalists, social institutions develop because they meet one or more of society's basic needs. Functionalists distinguish between two different kinds of functions that institutions can provide. They can either be a **manifest function**, which is an intended and recognized result, or a **latent function**, which is an unintended and unrecognized result.

As a social institution, education performs several vital manifest functions in modern society. Obviously, schools teach academic skills, such as reading, writing, and mathematics. In addition, schools transmit culture, create a common identity for members of society, select and screen talent, and promote personal growth and development. Let's look more closely at these last four functions.

Transmitting Culture

As you know, *culture* is the beliefs, practices, values, norms, and attitudes of a society. As a social institution, a school system plays a key role in transmitting culture. It does so in two different ways.

First, through its system of education, a society manages the knowledge it wishes to pass on to the next generation. Second, by teaching children the shared values of society and the standards of behavior expected of them, the education system helps maintain order in society. It also helps ensure the continuity of the values that society holds dear. Competition, for example, is taught in American schools through emphasis on grades, sports, and school spirit. Since functionalists believe that social institutions contribute to the stability of society, teaching culture is absolutely essential if a society is to survive from one generation to the next.

Creating a Common Identity

Although television is a strong competitor, the educational system remains the major force in creating a common identity among a **diverse** population. Learning a common language, sharing in national history and patriotic themes, and being exposed to similar information all help promote a shared identity among Americans. The result is a society with homogeneous values, norms, beliefs, and attitudes.

Schools in the United States play a vital role in this process. In learning American history, students learn about the nation's values. They also learn about the contributions made by different individuals and groups to that history. In other classes, they learn how the government works and develop an idea of what it means to be an American citizen. By attending local schools, newly arrived immigrant children without the ability to speak and write English learn to participate in the American way of life.

The current debate in the United States over bilingual education touches on the role that schools play in creating a common identity. Bilingual education is the practice of giving students who are not native speakers of the English language some instruction in their native languages while they learn English.

manifest function an intended and recognized result of an action

latent function an unintended and unrecognized result of an action

diverse composed of distinct or varied elements or qualities

Connecting Sociology to History

THE NEED FOR AN EDUCATED CITIZENRY

Horace Mann was no stranger to poverty or poor education. Frustrated by the fact that he did not have access to properly trained teachers, Mann resorted to educating himself. He became an advocate for public education and believed strongly in the idea that a democratic society should provide a free education to all people. As a Massachusetts state senator, Mann pushed for free public education in his state and was integral in the formation of a state board of education. Below is an excerpt from an annual Board of Education report delivered on July 4, 1842, in which Mann expresses the importance of education in a republic.

PRIMARY SOURCE

"The establishment of a republican government, without well-appointed and efficient means for the universal education of the people, is the most rash and fool-hardy experiment ever tried by man. . . . It may be an easy thing to make a republic; but it is a very laborious thing to make republicans; and woe to the republic that rests upon no better foundations than ignorance, selfishness, and passion! . . . If such a republic be devoid of intelligence, it will only more closely resemble an obscene giant . . . whose brain has been developed only in the region of the appetites and passions, and not in the organs of reason and conscience."

— from *Annual Reports of the Secretary of the Board of Education of Massachusetts 1845–1848*

Horace Mann was known as the "Father of the Common School." He also set up schools for teacher training.

DBQ ▶ CRITICAL THINKING

1. **Making Connections** How does the excerpt illustrate the importance of establishing public schools for all people?
2. **Analyzing** Do you agree with Mann's statement about how important it is for a republic to educate its citizens? Explain.

A Global Perspective

WORLD LITERACY RATES
One of the functions of education is to promote literacy—the key to continued learning, problem solving, and information analysis. This map shows rates of literacy among adults in various countries of the world. Because of cultural norms and discrimination, even today, more men than women are able to read and write.

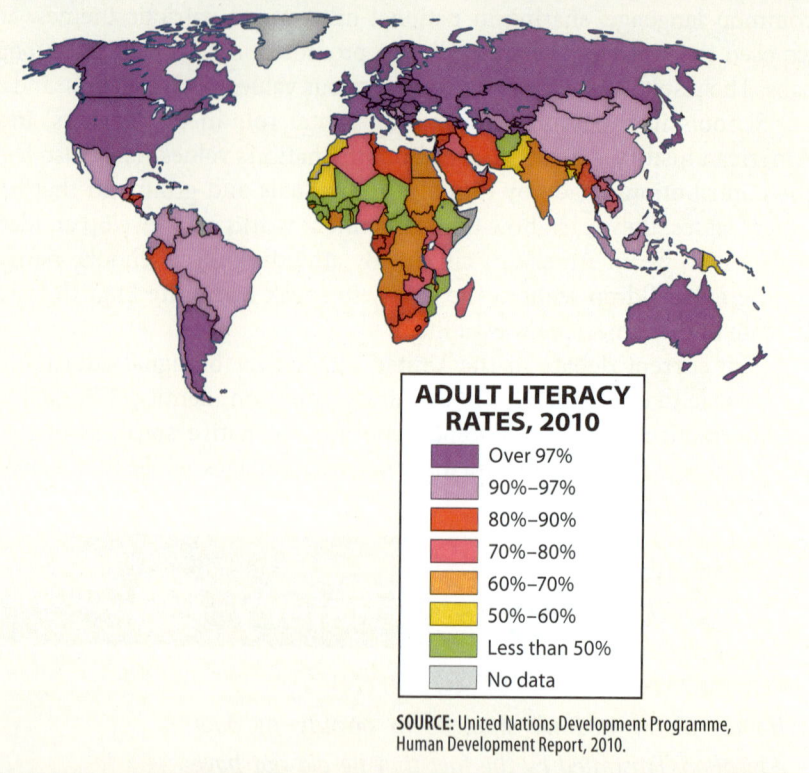

ADULT LITERACY RATES, 2010
- Over 97%
- 90%–97%
- 80%–90%
- 70%–80%
- 60%–70%
- 50%–60%
- Less than 50%
- No data

SOURCE: United Nations Development Programme, Human Development Report, 2010.

Geography Connection

1. **Places and Regions** What patterns do you see with regard to literacy rates in world regions?
2. **The Uses of Geography** How does this map help you better understand literacy rates and demographics?

The idea is that this approach allows students to keep up with their grade levels in other subjects by giving them a chance to learn the subjects in their native tongues. Without that opportunity, students would fall behind in those other curriculum areas.

People who emphasize recognizing and honoring cultural diversity usually support teaching in the student's own language, at least for some period of time. Opponents of bilingual education argue that bilingual education hinders the development of a common American identity and has not been proven to help students succeed academically.

Bilingual education has become a political as well as an educational issue. Opponents to this kind of instruction have played a major role in laws passed in 31 states that declare English as their official language. The creation of a similar law for the nation has been discussed in Congress for several years, but a majority of both houses has never approved it.

Selecting and Screening Students

For over 50 years, scores on intelligence and achievement tests have been used to group children in school. The stated purpose of testing is to identify an individual's talents and aptitudes. Test scores have also been used for **tracking**—placing students in curricula consistent with academic abilities and expectations for their **eventual** occupations. Counselors use test scores and early performance records to predict careers for which individuals may be best suited. Students are then placed in classes deemed appropriate for them in the rest of their school careers.

Tracking, though widely used, has been criticized for unfairly labeling students. It creates different expectations for different groups of students, setting children down paths they might not otherwise have been destined to follow.

tracking the placement of students in programs according to academic ability

eventual taking place at an unspecified future time

Promoting Personal Growth and Development

Schools expose students to a wide variety of perspectives and experiences. These different opportunities encourage them to develop creativity, verbal skills, artistic expression, intellectual accomplishment, and cultural tolerance. In this way, education provides an environment in which individuals can improve the quality of their lives.

In addition, schools attempt to prepare students for the world of work. Besides transmitting skills and knowledge, schools accomplish this purpose in various ways. Having students work together in teams teaches them skills they are likely to use in their careers. Schools today also teach computer skills to help prepare students for their working lives.

✅ **READING PROGRESS CHECK**

Making Connections How does education help a diverse population develop a shared identity?

Latent Functions of Education

GUIDING QUESTION What are some of the unintentional functions of the school system?

Many public school students enjoy taking part in school athletics.

▶ **CRITICAL THINKING**
Identifying What is one manifest function and one latent function of school athletics?

The educational system has latent functions as well. Some are positive; others are not. Educators do not usually think of schools as day care facilities for two-income couples or single parents, yet they serve that function. Nor do parents vote for additional school taxes so that their sons and daughters can find dates or marriage partners. Schools are not consciously designed to prevent delinquency by holding juveniles indoors during the daytime. Neither are schools intended as training grounds for athletes. Nonetheless, all these activities are latent functions of the school system.

Each of the functions mentioned also has some consequences that are negative, or dysfunctional. Tracking, for example, can perpetuate an unequal social class structure from generation to generation. In addition, evidence suggests that tracking is harmful to those placed on "slower" tracks.

✅ **READING PROGRESS CHECK**

Generalizing Why can latent functions be either positive or negative?

LESSON 2 REVIEW

Reviewing Vocabulary
1. *Identifying* What is the difference between manifest function and latent function?
2. *Defining* What is tracking?

Using Your Notes
3. *Specifying* Use your notes to give examples of manifest functions and latent functions of the school system.

Answering the Guiding Questions
4. *Finding the Main Idea* What purposes does the school system serve?
5. *Identifying* What are some of the unintentional functions of the school system?

Writing Activity
6. *Narrative* Describe some ways in which your schooling encouraged you to develop a shared identity.

networks

There's More Online!

- ☑ **CARTOON** Intelligence Tests
- ☑ **CHART** SAT Scores by Race and Ethnicity
- ☑ **GRAPHIC ORGANIZER** Barriers to Equality
- ☑ **IMAGE** No Child Left Behind
- ☑ **MAP** Dropout Rates
- ☑ **SELF-CHECK QUIZ**

Reading HELPDESK

Academic Vocabulary
- exceed
- criterion

Content Vocabulary
- meritocracy
- competition
- educational equality
- cognitive ability
- cultural bias
- school desegregation
- multicultural education
- compensatory education

TAKING NOTES:
Key Ideas and Details

ORGANIZING Use a web graphic organizer like the one below to note the barriers to equality in education.

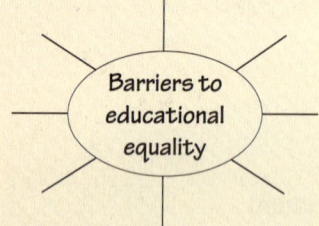

LESSON 3
Conflict Perspective

ESSENTIAL QUESTION • *What purposes does education serve?*

IT MATTERS BECAUSE
In theory, the United States is a meritocracy in which social status is achieved through individual effort. Proponents of the conflict perspective identify flaws in this model by identifying inequalities in our schools that unfairly limit the future opportunities of those who suffer these inequalities. Various methods and programs have been developed to help make education more equal.

Meritocracy

GUIDING QUESTIONS *Is the American education system a meritocracy? Why or why not?*

Conflict theorists attempt to show that popular conceptions about the relationship between schools and society are not entirely accurate. Schools and society often interact in complicated and not obvious ways.

In a **meritocracy**, social status is based on ability and achievement rather than social class background or parents' social status. In theory, all individuals in a meritocracy have an equal chance to develop their abilities for the benefit of themselves and their society. A meritocracy, then, gives everyone an equal chance to succeed. It is free of barriers that prevent individuals from developing their talents.

A meritocracy is based on competition. For this reason, sport is seen as the ultimate meritocracy. Although some sports have glaring shortcomings in this regard, sport does fit very closely with the definition of competition. For sociologists, **competition** is a social process that occurs when rewards are given to people on the basis of how their performance compares with the performance of others doing the same task or participating in the same event.

American Meritocracy
Although the United States claims to be a meritocracy, sociologists have identified several barriers to true merit-based achievement in American society. They include class, gender, race, and ethnicity. An example (greatly simplified) is how the education system creates barriers for students from poor neighborhoods and favors those from wealthy neighborhoods. Schools in wealthy neighborhoods are significantly

better than schools in economically disadvantaged areas. It follows, then, that students attending wealthier schools get a better education than students attending poorer schools. With that better education, they are better prepared to gain high-paying jobs.

Furthermore, students attending poorer schools do not learn the values, manners, language, and dress of people in more affluent schools. Because the majority of students in poorer schools are members of racial and ethnic minorities, they find themselves at a disadvantage when applying for higher-level jobs that lead to higher incomes.

College Entrance Exams

A related barrier faced by racial and ethnic minorities is lower performance on college entrance examinations. African Americans, Latinos, and Native Americans have lower average scores on the SAT, a college assessment test, than white students. Sociologists attribute this fact, in part, to the differences in school quality noted above. And both school quality and SAT performance are related to social class. Children from upper-class and upper-middle-class families attend more affluent schools. These children also have higher SAT scores. Social class clearly affects SAT performance.

The SAT, created in 1926, was originally used to identify talented youth regardless of social class background so they could attend elite colleges and universities. Yet, as we have just seen, social class is a major factor in SAT performance. Consequently, social class (through SAT performance) still influences who will attend the institutions that are the gateway to America's higher social classes.

On the surface it does seem that merit is being rewarded in the system just outlined. After all, people who perform better academically enjoy higher levels of success. There are two problems with this conclusion, however. The first is the advantage some people have because their parents' social class creates an uneven playing field. Talent in the lower social classes often does not get recognized and developed. The second is the assumption that SAT performance measures academic ability and the likelihood of success in both college and life.

meritocracy a society in which social status is based on ability and achievement

competition a social process in which rewards are based on relative performance

Social class is a strong predictor of success on the SATs.

▶ **CRITICAL THINKING**

Making Connections How is race related to social class?

AVERAGE SAT SCORES BY RACE AND ETHNICITY		
	CRITICAL READING	MATHEMATICS
All students	501	516
White	528	536
African American	429	428
Mexican American	454	467
Puerto Rican	454	452
Other Latino	454	462
Asian/Pacific Islander	519	591
Other	494	514

Source: U.S. Department of Education, National Center for Education Statistics. (2011). *Digest of Education Statistics, 2010*

CHART

SAT SCORES BY RACE AND ETHNICITY
An examination of this table reveals the gap in average SAT scores for white and Asian American students versus African American and Latino students.

▶ **CRITICAL THINKING**

1. **Applying** How would a conflict theorist explain these achievement gaps?
2. **Analyzing Visuals** Between which two groups is the performance gap widest?

exceed to surpass

educational equality the condition in which schooling produces the same results for lower-class and minority children as it does for other children

criterion (plural *criteria*) a standard on which a judgment may be based

For example, African American students who attend the most prestigious schools—including those students with lower SAT scores (below 1000)—complete college at a higher rate than African American students attending less rigorous institutions. They are also more likely to go on to graduate or professional schools. Apparently these students are succeeding because they attended better schools, even if they did not achieve high SAT scores.

At the least, these findings raise doubts about the ability of the SAT to achieve a level playing field. Recognizing this, an official at the Educational Testing Service (ETS)—developer and marketer of the SAT—announced in 1999 that ETS was creating a "strivers" score. The idea was to predict a student's SAT score based on a number of factors, including family income, parents' education level, and high-school socioeconomic mix as well as racial and ethnic characteristics. Any student whose original score **exceeded** by 200 points the score predicted for their social class, racial, or ethnic category would be considered a "striver." The strivers score would be made available to colleges and universities to use, if they desired, in their admissions decisions. The proposal was quickly withdrawn after a firestorm of criticism from both privileged and disadvantaged sources.

☑ **READING PROGRESS CHECK**

Finding the Main Idea What facts challenge the notion that the United States is a meritocracy?

Equality and Inequality in Education

GUIDING QUESTION *In what ways, if any, do schools provide educational equality?*

Achieving success can be difficult for those individuals disadvantaged by social class and racial and ethnic background. Education plays a large role in shaping an individual's future. The issue that looms largest is educational equality. **Educational equality** exists when schooling produces the same results, in terms of achievement and attitudes, for lower-class and minority children as it does for middle- and upper-class children.

Research has shown that even the best teachers may evaluate students on the basis of their social class or their racial and ethnic characteristics. This tendency to judge students on nonacademic **criteria** is especially apparent in the practice of tracking. (Tracking, remember, places students in curricula based on academic performance and expectations for their eventual occupations.) Researchers report that social class and race heavily influence student placement in college preparatory, vocational, or basic tracks regardless of their intelligence or past academic achievement.

Once students are placed on a track, their grades and test scores are influenced more by the track they have been placed on than by their current performance. Regardless of earlier school performance or intelligence, the academic performance of college-bound students increases. The performance of those on a noncollege track, however, decreases. In other words, schools fail to provide educational equality for their students.

☑ **READING PROGRESS CHECK**

Explaining What role does tracking play in school equality?

Cognitive Ability

GUIDING QUESTION *Is intelligence inherited? Explain.*

The technical term for intelligence is **cognitive ability**—the capacity for thinking abstractly. Since the turn of the twentieth century, schools have attempted to measure cognitive ability. Cognitive ability testing is used to sort and track students, and it contributes to educational inequality. Whenever cognitive ability tests are discussed, the question of inherited intelligence always arises.

cognitive ability the capacity for thinking abstractly

Inherited Intelligence Theory

In the past, some people assumed that individual and group differences in measured intellectual ability were due to genetic differences. This assumption underlies Social Darwinism. *Social Darwinism* is the theory, popular in the late 1800s and early 1900s, that the socially elite classes are at the top of society because they are biologically superior. A few researchers still take this viewpoint. More than 40 years ago, Arthur Jensen, an educational psychologist, contended that the lower average intelligence score among African American children may be due to heredity. A more recent book by Richard Herrnstein and Charles Murray, *The Bell Curve* (1994), also linked intelligence to heredity. According to these authors, humans inherit 60 to 70 percent of their intelligence level. Herrnstein and Murray further contend that inherited intelligence makes the efforts to help the disadvantaged through programs such as Head Start and affirmative action largely futile.

Arguments Against Inherited Intelligence Theory

Most social scientists oppose the genetic explanation of intelligence differences between races because it fails to consider the effects of the social, psychological, and economic environment on intelligence. Even those social scientists who believe that genetics plays an important role in intelligence criticize both the interpretations of the evidence and the public policy conclusions contained in *The Bell Curve*. They point to the body of research that runs counter to Herrnstein and Murray's thesis. More specifically, they see intelligence not as an issue of nature versus nurture but as a matter of genetics and environment.

"Walsh faked being sick while we're stuck taking this intelligence test? He's a genius!"

◁ CARTOON

INTELLIGENCE TESTS
Intelligence tests are supposed to measure the capacity for thinking abstractly, but they are not universally accepted.

▶ **CRITICAL THINKING**

1. *Analyzing Visual* What attitudes does the cartoonist seem to have toward intelligence tests?
2. *Summarizing* What criticisms are leveled at intelligence tests?

Education

We know, for example, that city dwellers usually score higher on intelligence tests than do people in rural areas, that higher-status African Americans score higher than lower-status African Americans, and that middle-class African American children score about as high as middle-class white children. We also have discovered that as people get older, they usually score higher on intelligence tests. These findings, and others like them, have led researchers to conclude that environmental factors affect performance on intelligence tests at least as much as genetic factors. One of these environmental factors is a cultural bias in the measurement of cognitive ability.

Culturally Biased Intelligence Tests

Many social scientists have argued that intelligence tests have a **cultural bias**—that is, the wording used in questions may be more familiar to people of one social group than to those of another group. Tests with cultural bias unfairly measure the cognitive abilities of people in some social categories. Specifically, intelligence tests are said to be culturally biased because they are designed for middle-class children. The tests measure learning and environment as much as intellectual ability. Consider this intelligence test item cited by Daniel Levine and Rayna Levine:

A symphony is to a composer as a book is to what?
a. paper
b. a musician
c. a sculptor
d. a man
e. an author

According to critics, higher-income children find this question easier to answer correctly than lower-income children because they are more likely to have been exposed to information about classical music.

Several studies have indicated that because most intelligence tests assume fluency in English minorities cannot do as well on them. Some researchers have suggested that many urban African American students are superior to their white classmates on several dimensions of verbal capacity, but this ability is not recognized because intelligence tests do not measure those specific areas.

Some researchers have shown that the testing situation itself affects performance. Low-income and minority students, for example, score higher on intelligence tests when tested by adult members of their own race or income group. Apparently children can feel threatened when tested in a strange environment by someone dissimilar to them. Middle-class children are frequently eager to take the tests because they have been taught the importance both of test results and of academic competitiveness. Because low-income children do not recognize the importance of tests and have not been taught to be academically competitive, they ignore some of the questions or look for something more interesting to do. Other researchers report that nutrition seems to play a role in test performance. Low-income children with poor diets may do less than their best when they are hungry or when they lack proper nutrition over long periods of time.

✓ READING PROGRESS CHECK

Determining Importance What factors besides inheritance play a role in intelligence?

---

cultural bias an unfair slant in testing or materials in favor of certain groups

The bias for English-language skills on intelligence tests can artificially lower the scores of immigrants just learning the language like these Somali Americans.

▶ CRITICAL THINKING
Assessing How effective do you think intelligence tests are? Why?

Connecting Sociology to Human Geography

DROPOUT RATES

Even though high-school dropout rates have decreased in the last 40 years from 15 to 7 percent, there is still a dropout divide. Ethnic factors contribute to the percentage of dropouts in the nation. In 2009, Latino Americans represented 18 percent of dropouts compared to 10 percent of African Americans and a mere 5 percent of non-Latino whites.

Another factor is geographic location: urban, suburban, and rural. Even though a high percentage of high-school dropouts live in urban areas, it is not just an urban problem. In 2009, 51 percent of the nation's lowest-performing schools were located in urban areas while 30 percent were in towns and rural areas and 19 percent were in suburban areas. Most of the nation's lowest-performing schools—in which the dropout rate is a factor—are located in the Southeast. African Americans make up the majority of high-school dropouts in this region.

In studying the causes that lead to high-school students quitting school, researchers have found that many dropouts begin with a low attendance in middle school. Another indicator is the challenge of ninth grade and the transition from middle school to high school. Students who feel they do not have the skills to perform at a certain level lose confidence, and many do not receive the academic support they need to succeed.

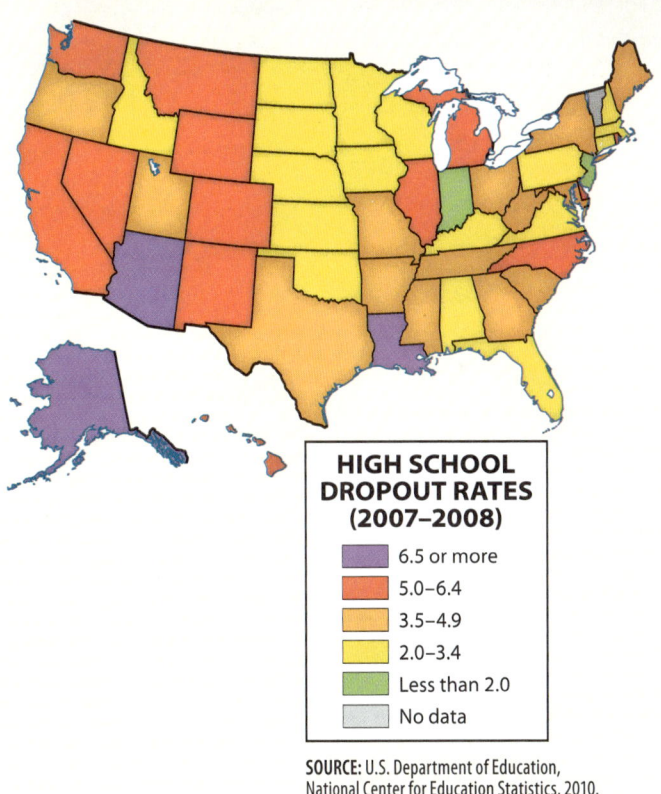

HIGH SCHOOL DROPOUT RATES (2007–2008)
- 6.5 or more
- 5.0–6.4
- 3.5–4.9
- 2.0–3.4
- Less than 2.0
- No data

SOURCE: U.S. Department of Education, National Center for Education Statistics, 2010.

In 2009 almost half of all high-school dropouts in the United States came from only 12 percent of the nation's high schools.

▶ **CRITICAL THINKING**
1. **Making Connections** How does geographic location—region, state, and area—affect a student's likelihood of dropping out of high school?
2. **Identifying Cause and Effect** How does a high dropout rate affect education and the nation?

Promoting Educational Equality

GUIDING QUESTION What methods have been used to attempt to promote equality in education?

Although it is difficult to completely overcome the barriers of economic and social class, policy makers and educators are exploring ways to promote educational equality. Three methods are *school desegregation, multicultural education,* and *compensatory education*. In recent years, education has been greatly affected by a federal law that aimed at improving poor-performing schools.

Desegregation

In this discussion, **school desegregation** refers to the achievement of a racial balance in the classroom. Desegregated classrooms can have either positive or negative effects on the academic achievement of minority children. Mere physical desegregation without adequate support may actually harm both white and African American children. But desegregated classrooms with an atmosphere of respect and acceptance improve academic performance.

school desegregation the achievement of a racial balance in the classroom

Education 349

Minority students who attend desegregated public schools get better jobs and earn higher incomes than minority students who attend segregated schools. The formal education they receive is only part of the reason. Middle-class students become models for the behavior, dress, and language often required by employers in the middle-class hiring world.

In addition, exposure to people of different backgrounds can lead to better racial and ethnic relations. This evidence leads to the reasoning behind another movement, multicultural education.

Multicultural Education

Multicultural education is a curriculum that accents the viewpoints, experiences, and contributions of minorities, including women and ethnic and racial minorities. Among minorities, school attendance and academic performance appear to increase with multicultural education. Multicultural education attempts to dispel stereotypes and to embrace the traditions of minorities as valuable assets for the broader culture.

Multicultural education has its critics, however. According to some opponents, encouraging people to think of themselves as culturally separate and unique divides rather than unites American society. Some critics point to instances in which multicultural programs, such as African American studies programs, actually promote feelings of racial separation in schools.

Compensatory Education

The term **compensatory education** refers to specific curricular programs designed to overcome an educational deficiency. Special compensatory programs provided during early childhood, it appears, can improve the school achievement of disadvantaged children. The best known attempt at compensatory education is Head Start. This federally supported program prepares disadvantaged preschoolers for public school. Its goal is to provide disadvantaged children an equal opportunity to develop their potential.

Follow-up studies report positive long-term results from participation in Head Start. One study showed that low-income students between the ages of nine and nineteen who had been in preschool compensatory programs performed better in school. They had higher achievement test scores and were more motivated academically than low-income youths who had not been in compensatory education programs. Another study found that compared to their peers, a group of children who scored lower on intelligence tests when they entered a Head Start program later had better school attendance, completed high school at a higher rate, and entered the workforce in greater proportion than comparable students who had not participated in the program.

No Child Left Behind

In an effort to improve school performance, especially for disadvantaged students, Congress passed the No Child Left Behind Act of 2001. No Child Left Behind (NCLB) represents greater involvement of the federal government in education. It requires states to give students annual standardized tests. States must meet a given level of proficiency on a schedule devised by the federal government or face certain consequences. By making states accountable, the federal government hopes to

Multicultural education seeks to embrace the traditions of all racial and ethnic groups found in a school.

▶ **CRITICAL THINKING**

Analyzing What advantages have been identified for multicultural education?

multicultural education
a curriculum that emphasizes differences among gender, ethnic, and racial categories

compensatory education
specific curricular programs designed to overcome a deficiency

President George W. Bush, who championed the No Child Left Behind Act, signed it into law in 2001.

▶ **CRITICAL THINKING**

Analyzing What was the purpose of making schools accountable under this law?

increase student performance. Proponents of the law note that, at least at first, NCLB raised the performance of minority students. Some also noted that NCLB reporting helped reveal the education gap experienced by minorities and special education students in otherwise high-performing schools. The law requires schools to report test scores according to whether students are African American, Latino, English-language learners, or learning-disabled students.

Critics, however, expressed grave concerns over the expanded federal role in education, an area traditionally left to the states. Others charged that the law actually worsens the quality of education because teachers are compelled to teach only the test topics at the expense of the full curriculum.

In 2011, almost half (49 percent) of the nation's public schools failed to make "adequate yearly progress" as defined by the law. The law requires schools to raise student achievement annually, reaching 100 percent student proficiency by 2014. Efforts to remove the 2014 deadline have failed, but the federal government has granted waivers to half the states. Opposition to the law has grown, as groups of students, parents, and teachers have called for a reduction in high-stakes standardized testing.

✓ **READING PROGRESS CHECK**

Explaining How does the No Child Left Behind Act use standardized tests?

LESSON 3 REVIEW

Reviewing Vocabulary
1. ***Identifying*** Upon what is a meritocracy based?
2. ***Explaining*** How does cultural bias affect testing?

Using Your Notes
3. ***Making Generalizations*** Use your web graphic organizer to make a generalization about the roots of educational inequality in the United States.

Answering the Guiding Questions
4. ***Drawing Conclusions*** Is the American education system a meritocracy? Why or why not?

5. ***Evaluating*** In what ways, if any, do schools provide educational equality?
6. ***Identifying Perspectives*** Is intelligence inherited? Explain.
7. ***Problem Solving*** What methods have been used to attempt to promote equality in education?

Writing Activity
8. ***Informative/Explanatory*** In your own words explain the relationship between socioeconomic status and educational achievement.

FOCUS on research
Field Research

Segregated Schools

In the case Brown v. Board of Education of Topeka, Kansas (1954), the U.S. Supreme Court ruled that segregation in public schools is unconstitutional. Jonathan Kozol, however, argues in his book The Shame of the Nation: The Restoration of Apartheid Schooling in America, *that segregation still exists in inner-city public schools. In his study of about 60 public schools in 11 states around the nation, Kozol discovered that schools in inner cities are more segregated than ever before.*

PRIMARY SOURCE

"Many Americans I meet who live far from our major cities and who have no first-hand knowledge of realities in urban public schools seem to have a rather vague and general impression that the great extremes of racial isolation they recall as matters of grave national significance some 35 or 40 years ago have gradually, but steadily, diminished in more recent years. The truth, unhappily, is that the trend, for well over a decade now, has been precisely the reverse. Schools that were already deeply segregated 25 or 30 years ago, like most of the schools I visit in the Bronx, are no less segregated now, while thousands of other schools that had been integrated either voluntarily or by the force of law have since been rapidly resegregating both in northern districts and in broad expanses of the South. . . .

Perhaps most damaging to any effort to address this subject openly is the refusal of most of the major arbiters of culture in our northern cities to confront or even clearly name an obvious reality they would have castigated with a passionate determination in another section of the nation 50 years before and which, moreover, they still castigate today in retrospective writings that assign it to a comfortably distant and allegedly concluded era of the past. There is, indeed, a seemingly agreed-upon convention in much of the media today not even to use an accurate descriptor such as 'racial segregation' in a narrative description of a segregated school. Linguistic sweeteners, semantic somersaults, and surrogate vocabularies are repeatedly employed. Schools in which as few as three or four percent of students may be white or Southeast Asian or of Middle Eastern origin, for instance—and where *every other child* in the building is black or Hispanic—are referred to, in a commonly misleading usage, as 'diverse.' Visitors to schools like these discover quickly the eviscerated meaning of the word, which is no longer a descriptor but a euphemism for a plainer word that has apparently become unspeakable.

School systems themselves repeatedly employ this euphemism in descriptions of the composition of their student populations. In a school I visited in fall 2004 in Kansas City, Missouri, for example, a document distributed to visitors reports that the school's curriculum 'addresses the needs of children from diverse backgrounds.' But as I went from class to class I did not encounter any children who were white or Asian—or Hispanic, for that matter—and when I later was provided with the demographics of the school, I learned that 99.6 percent of the students there were African-American. In a similar document, the school board of another district, this one in New York State, referred to 'the diversity' of its student population and 'the rich variations of ethnic backgrounds. . . .' But when I looked at the racial numbers that the district had reported to the state, I learned that there were 2,800 black and Hispanic children in the system, one Asian child, and three whites. Words, in these cases, cease to have real meaning; or, rather, they mean the opposite of what they say.

One of the most disheartening experiences for those who grew up in the years when Martin Luther King and Thurgood Marshall were alive is to visit public schools today that bear their names, or names of other honored leaders of the integration struggles that produced the temporary progress that took place in the three decades after *Brown*, and to find how many of these schools are bastions of contemporary segregation."

—Jonathan Kozol, *The Shame of the Nation: The Restoration of Apartheid Schooling in America*, 2005

> "Schools that were already deeply segregated 25 or 30 years ago ... are no less segregated now, while thousands of other schools that had been integrated ... have since been rapidly resegregated."

Working With the Research

1. **Comparing and Contrasting** According to Kozol, how has the ethnic makeup of inner-city schools changed over what it was as many as 40 years ago?
2. **Identifying Bias** Based on this excerpt, do you think that Kozol is biased? Use evidence to support your response.
3. **Evaluating** Do you think that Kozol uses solid evidence to support his argument? Explain.

Education 353

networks

There's More Online!

- ☑ **CHART** Theoretical Perspectives: Investigating Education
- ☑ **GRAPHIC ORGANIZER** Student-Teacher Interaction
- ☑ **IMAGE** Pygmalion
- ☑ **IMAGE** Science for Girls
- ☑ **SELF-CHECK QUIZ**

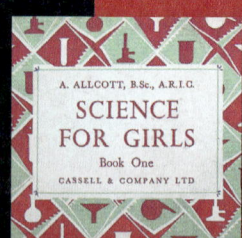

LESSON 4
Symbolic Interactionism

ESSENTIAL QUESTION • *What purposes does education serve?*

Reading HELPDESK

Academic Vocabulary
- sexist
- objective

Content Vocabulary
- hidden curriculum

TAKING NOTES:
Integration of Knowledge and Ideas

ORGANIZING Use a graphic organizer like the one below to describe how interactions between students and teachers shape a student's academic performance.

Student-Teacher Interaction	
Textbooks	
Teacher Expectations	
Sexism	

It Matters Because

Symbolic interactionists emphasize the socialization that occurs in schools. Through the hidden curriculum, children are taught values, norms, beliefs, and attitudes. Much of this socialization helps young people make the transition from home to the larger society.

The Hidden Curriculum

GUIDING QUESTION *What is the hidden curriculum?*

Symbolic interactionists are very interested in how schools transmit culture through the socialization process. Modern society places considerable emphasis on the verbal, mathematical, and writing skills an adult needs to obtain a job, read a news article, balance a checkbook, and compute income taxes. Schools teach much more than these basic academic skills, however. They also transmit a variety of values, norms, beliefs, and attitudes to children. Besides teachers and textbooks, which we will discuss later, the most important agent of this socialization process is the hidden curriculum.

The **hidden curriculum** is the nonacademic agenda that teaches children norms and values, such as discipline, order, cooperativeness, and conformity. These citizenship skills are thought to be necessary for success in modern bureaucratic society, whether one becomes a doctor, a college president, a computer programmer, or an assembly-line worker. For example, over the years, schools socialize children for the transition from their closely knit, cooperative families to the loosely knit, competitive adult occupational world. Schools provide children opportunities for systematic practice in operating independently in the pursuit of personal and academic achievement. The values of conformity and achievement are emphasized through individual testing and grading. Because teachers evaluate young people as students, not as relatives, friends, or equals, students participate in a model for future secondary relationships—such as employer-employee, salesperson-customer, or lawyer-client.

☑ **READING PROGRESS CHECK**

Finding the Main Idea What do schools teach besides academics?

354

Textbooks

GUIDING QUESTION *How do textbooks convey values and beliefs?*

A critical part of the hidden curriculum is the development of patriotism and a sense of civic duty in future adults. For this reason, courses such as history and government generally present a view of history that favors the nation where the school is located. Accounts of the American Revolution, for example, are not the same in textbooks published in the United States and in Great Britain.

Few societies are willing to admit to their imperfections, and educators may think that some negative information is not appropriate for children of young ages. As a result, schools tend to resist teaching critical accounts of history. For example, for many years U.S. history textbooks failed to portray the U.S. government's harsh treatment of Native Americans. They also presented little information about the unfair treatment of Asian Americans at different times or about the harsh conditions enslaved African Americans had to endure.

Textbooks convey values and beliefs as much by what they omit as by what they include. Although today's textbooks present a more balanced picture, surveys of primary-school textbooks written before the 1980s found that they almost always presented men in challenging and aggressive activities while portraying women as homemakers, mothers, nurses, and secretaries. Women were not only shown in traditional roles but also appeared far less frequently in the books than men did. When women did appear, they did not initiate action but instead played largely passive roles. Minority groups were rarely present in textbooks, and when they were, it was often in a negative context. History textbooks of the past had little to say about the contributions of African Americans, for instance, to American life.

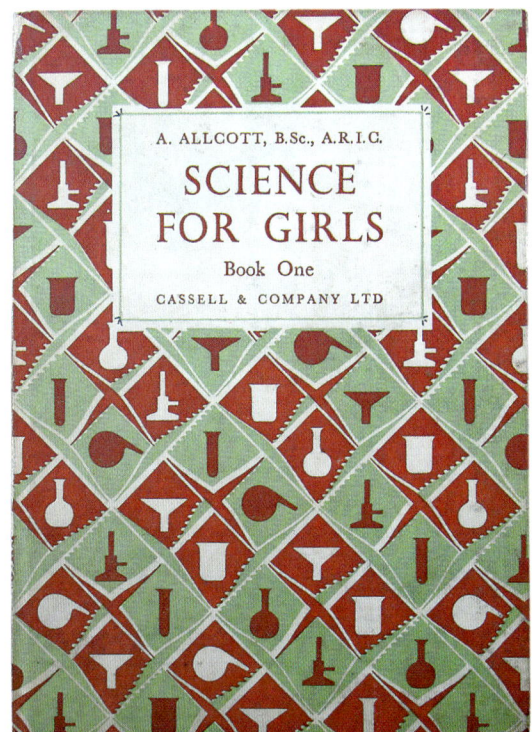

This old science textbook from Great Britain clearly shows gender bias.

▶ **CRITICAL THINKING**

Hypothesizing Based on the information in the lesson about how women used to be portrayed in textbooks, what kinds of activities might be found in this textbook?

Theoretical Perspectives

INVESTIGATING EDUCATION

This table illustrates differences in the ways the major theoretical perspectives investigate education as a social institution. It is, of course, possible for a theoretical perspective to be applied to education using one of the concepts associated in this table with another perspective. Explain, for example, how conflict theory might lead to interpretations of the hidden curriculum and tracking.

Theoretical Perspective	Social Arrangement	Example
Functionalism	Tracking	Schools shape the occupational future of children by placing them in educational programs based on test scores and early school performance.
Conflict Theory	Meritocracy	Students attending better schools have an occupational advantage over students from poorer schools.
Symbolic Interactionism	Hidden curriculum	Schools teach children the values of conformity and achievement.

▶ **CRITICAL THINKING**

1. *Making Connections* How might functionalism interpret meritocracy, and how are tracking and meritocracy related?

2. *Evaluating* Which theoretical perspective explains the factors that have the greatest influence on a student's social behavior? Why?

Similarly, textbooks of the past tended to portray all students as living in "little white houses with white picket fences" in the suburbs. That image may have been the goal of middle-class Americans of the time, but parents of low-income or inner-city children complained that such pictures of middle-class life harmed their children. Poor children who compared their homes with middle-class homes felt out of place.

Today, textbook publishers make much larger effort to present a balanced picture of society. At the same time, active parent groups, minority special-interest groups, and state boards of education comment on their publications and even work with them as books are developed to eliminate these kinds of biases. Problems may still arise, however. Conflicts can occur over which group's view of society is the most accurate.

☑ **READING PROGRESS CHECK**

Explaining Why do textbooks tend to portray the nation in a flattering light?

Teachers and Socialization

GUIDING QUESTION *How do teachers affect the socialization of students?*

Pygmalion is a figure from Greek mythology. He made a sculpture of his idea of the perfect woman and then fell in love with it.

▶ **CRITICAL THINKING**

Making Connections Why do you think the term *Pygmalion effect* was chosen to label self-fulfilling prophecy in the classroom?

hidden curriculum the nonacademic agenda that teaches discipline, order, cooperativeness, and conformity

Classroom teachers have a unique and important role in socializing children. Teachers are usually a child's first authority figures outside the family, and children spend a lot of time in school. In addition, most parents urge their children to obey teachers, in part because their children's futures are affected by school performance.

Teachers Affect Students' Performance

Clearly, all teachers affect students' performance in the academic tasks they set for them, the way they plan their lessons, and how they teach the content in those lessons. Research has shown, however, that teachers affect children unintentionally as well. In a classic 1986 study, Robert Rosenthal and Lenore Jacobson explored the impact in the classroom of the self-fulfilling prophecy—a prediction that results in behavior that makes the prediction come true. This can be a very significant factor for teachers.

In their study, elementary-school teachers were given a list of children in their classrooms who, the researchers told them, were soon to blossom intellectually. Actually, these children were picked at random from the school roster and were no different from other children in the school. At the end of the year, this randomly selected group of children significantly improved their scores on intelligence tests while their classmates as a group did not.

According to Rosenthal and Jacobson, the teachers expected the selected students to spurt academically. Consequently, the teachers treated these students as if they were special. This behavior on the part of the teachers encouraged the students to become higher academic achievers. The term *Pygmalion effect* describes the phenomenon in which some students perform better than others simply because they are expected to do so.

Quick Case Study

HOW DOES THE GENDER COMPOSITION OF A CLASSROOM AFFECT STUDENT LEARNING?

Classrooms can vary with regard to gender makeup. What effect does the gender composition of a classroom have on student participation?

Procedure

1. Ask your teacher to teach a lesson plan to both a coeducational group of classmates and a single-gender group.
2. Observe both settings and take notes on student participation, both verbal and physical. After the lesson, interview three students from each group. Ask each student to share his or her experience. Record all responses.

Analysis

As you read through the responses, consider these questions:

1. Did students feel that they received equal attention from the teacher?
2. Did students willingly choose to participate, or did the teacher call on them?
3. What conclusions can you draw from this study?

Another, earlier study published in 1969 by sociologist Eleanor Leacock found the self-fulfilling prophecy at work in a study of second and fifth graders in African American and white low- and middle-income schools. Both studies demonstrated that self-fulfilling prophecies can transmit negative self-impressions as well as positive ones.

Sexism in Education

Children are also taught to adopt the "appropriate" gender identity in school. Following a long line of earlier researchers, in a 1995 study, Myra Sadker and David Sadker contended that America's teachers are often unfair to girls.

The Sadkers say this is the case because teachers treat girls differently than boys based on assumptions and stereotypes of what is appropriate behavior. Well-meaning teachers unconsciously transmit their **sexist** expectations of how male and female students should behave. Girls, for example, learn to talk softly, to avoid certain subjects (especially math and science), to defer to the alleged intellectual superiority of boys, and to emphasize appearance over intelligence. As a result of these differences in teachers' interactions with students, in a coeducational setting boys are more likely to:

- receive the most attention from teachers.
- be praised.
- call out in class.
- be talkative in class.
- demand help or attention.
- be called on in class.

sexist describes an attitude or belief that one sex, usually male, is superior to the other

White boys are more likely to receive teacher attention than any other students.

▶ **CRITICAL THINKING**

Making Connections How do you think classroom experience might influence students once they enter the workforce?

Female students have had many more opportunities to compete in sports in recent years than they had in the past.

▶ **CRITICAL THINKING**

Making Connections What caused school officials to limit these opportunities in the past?

objective unbiased; neutral

The conclusions seem to be incontrovertible: In general boys talk more, move more, have their hands up more, do more, argue more, and receive more of the teacher's attention than do girls in classes that include students of both genders.

Contrary to the claims of some commentators, these inequalities are not gone from the educational scene but have persisted to today. Writers who paint a rosier picture have so far failed to produce convincing evidence to support it. For example, there is **objective** evidence that girls are guided in school toward traditional female jobs and away from high-paying, powerful, and prestigious jobs in science, technology, and engineering. It is true that significantly more high-school girls want to go into engineering today than in the past. Nevertheless, a huge gap between males and females still exists: Four times more men than women receive bachelor's degrees in engineering.

These gender-based discrepancies cannot be explained by ability differences between females and males. Girls perform as well as boys on math tests now that they have the opportunity to participate in advanced math classes in equal numbers. They perform nearly as well as boys in science as well. Girls score higher than boys in reading and writing at all grade levels, and they are more likely to attend college. In fact, in 2009, 56 percent of all college students were female and only 44 percent were male.

Interestingly, studies have shown that females fare better in single-gender schools and single-gender classes than they do in coeducational schools. Girls in these situations, in general, get better grades, report that they learn more and are more positive about the learning situation, and have higher self-esteem. Girls in single-gender schools also move more often to advanced courses than do girls in regular coeducational situations. These findings suggest that, when teachers no longer have boys to respond to more favorably than girls, they give their attention to female students, who respond with high levels of performance.

✓ **READING PROGRESS CHECK**

Explaining How do stereotypes affect learning?

LESSON 4 REVIEW

Reviewing Vocabulary
1. *Identifying* Give an example of the hidden curriculum.
2. *Defining* What is a self-fulfilling prophecy?

Using Your Notes
3. *Explaining* Use your graphic organizer about symbolic interactionism to explain how interactions between students and teachers shape a student's academic performance.

Answering the Guiding Questions
4. *Identifying Central Issues* What is the hidden curriculum?

5. *Making Connections* How do textbooks convey values and beliefs?

6. *Assessing* How do teachers affect the socialization of students?

Writing Activity
7. *Argument* Browse several lessons in this or another textbook and examine the images. Do you see evidence of a hidden agenda? Explain what you think that agenda might be.

CHAPTER 12 Assessment

Directions: On a separate sheet of paper, answer the questions below. Make sure you read carefully and answer all parts of the questions.

Lesson Review

Lesson 1

1 **Exploring Issues** What might a professional educator say are the benefits of the bureaucratic model of education?

2 **Making Connections** Which would be most effective for your personal learning style: the bureaucratic model, the open classroom, or cooperative learning? Explain.

Lesson 2

3 **Interpreting Significance** Why is it important to understand the distinction between manifest function and latent function in education?

4 **Defending** Select a position for or against bilingual education and support it through a short discussion that shows an understanding of both sides of the debate.

Lesson 3

5 **Assessing** A recent study revealed that high school students who had taken numerous AP courses were admitted to the elite universities but those who had taken only a few AP courses were not accepted by those schools. Does this finding support or weaken the claim that the United States is a meritocracy? Explain.

6 **Making Connections** Explain the connection between cognitive ability and inherited intelligence.

Lesson 4

7 **Theorizing** A teacher is given a list of students in the class on the first day of the school year. A number of 130 or higher appears next to each student's name. At the end of the school year, each student has shown remarkable progress. When the principal congratulates the teacher, the teacher thanks the principal for providing a class filled with students of such high IQs. The principal responds that the numbers next to students' names were not IQs, but district identifying numbers. Is this a good example of a self-fulfilling prophecy? Why or why not?

8 **Identifying Cause and Effect** Many textbooks written prior to the 1980s presented men in challenging and aggressive activities but portrayed women as homemakers, mothers, nurses, and secretaries just as many early textbooks did not provide a balanced view of different races and ethnicities. What do you think is the impact of the Digital Age on such unbalanced portrayals in educational content?

DBQ Analyzing Primary Sources

PRIMARY SOURCE

Use the document to answer the following question.

Educational Attainment by Sex: Selected Years, 1970–2010					
High School Graduate or More	Male	Female	College Graduate or More	Male	Female
1970	51.9%	52.8%	1970	13.5%	8.1%
1980	67.3	65.8	1980	20.1	12.8
1990	77.7	77.5	1990	24.4	18.4
1995	81.7	81.6	1995	26.0	20.2
2000	84.2	84.0	2000	27.8	23.6
2005	84.9	85.5	2005	28.9	26.5
2010	86.6	87.6	2009	30.3	29.6

Source: U.S. Census Bureau, *Statistical Abstract of the United States: 2012*

9 **Using Charts** In this chapter, you read about strengths and weaknesses of the American system of education. Can you draw a reasonable correlation between gender equality in the American system of education and the data represented in this table? Write a short essay to explain.

Need Extra Help?

If You've Missed Question	1	2	3	4	5	6	7	8	9
Go to page	332–333	332–339	340–343	341–342	344–346	347–348	355–356	355–358	354–358

CHAPTER 12 Assessment CCSS

Directions: On a separate sheet of paper, answer the questions below. Make sure you read carefully and answer all parts of the questions.

College and Career Readiness Skills

10 *Clear Communication* In an attempt to ensure that all students can meet a minimum standard of skills and knowledge prior to leaving high school, some states require that high school students pass a comprehensive exam. Some parents challenge these exams, claiming that students with passing high-school grades might not be accepted to good colleges if they fail the exam. Other critics argue that students who fail to pass classes might be able to pass the exam. As a college admissions officer, write an editorial that takes the position that these exams should be—or should not be—required for high school graduation. Defend your position with support from the chapter and your own knowledge and experience.

Critical Thinking

11 *Identifying Perspectives* Stakeholders are people who have a vested interest in or are directly affected by a process. Identify four stakeholders of American education, such as students. Explain the competing perceptions each stakeholder would have of the functions of education. Support your response with information from the chapter.

21st Century Skills
CREATING AND USING DIAGRAMS

12 *Time, Chronology, and Sequencing* Create a time line to show details related to education from 1647 (the year that Massachusetts started a school system) to the present. Use information from the chapter to complete your time line. Include the year whenever possible; however, the year is not essential for each entry as long as all entries are depicted chronologically.

13 *Explaining Continuity and Change* Based on your time line, summarize the changes in education in the United States since 1647, explaining cause and effect where appropriate.

14 *Understanding Relationships Among Events* Based on your time line and summary, predict the direction in which you think American education is headed. Discuss two items you think will be the same in twenty years and two items you think will change. Support your predictions with chapter content and your knowledge and experience.

Exploring the Essential Question

15 *Problem Solving* Your task is to create an ideal school of the future. Money is no object. Create a sketch that shows the layout of the school, labeling each area. Then write a report explaining how each area will serve the purpose of enhancing students' education. Provide support from the chapter and from your experience and knowledge.

Research and Presentation

16 *Formulating Questions* Check with your local school board to obtain the schedule and agenda of upcoming meetings. Based on the topics, select a meeting you would like to attend. After learning the views of board members during the meeting, select two board members to interview, preferably two with opposing viewpoints. Prepare questions in advance to learn more information about the board members' positions and the reasons for them. Using video or audio equipment, record the interviews. If you are using video equipment, you will need another person to record the video as you interview.

17 *Considering Advantages and Disadvantages* Prepare a presentation of your interviews for the class. Edit the interviews to reflect the most important points, making certain your editing does not distort each school board member's views. Create a diagram to reflect the viewpoints of both school board members you interviewed. Write a summary to explain your position on the issue you are presenting to the class. You may organize the edited interviews, diagram, and summary in any effective way you wish in order to present the information to the class.

Need Extra Help?

If You've Missed Question	10	11	12	13	14	15	16	17
Go to page	332–351	332–358	332–358	332–358	332–358	332–358	332–358	332–358

Political and Economic Institutions

ESSENTIAL QUESTION • *How does the interaction between political systems and economic systems affect society?*

netw⊕rks
There's More Online about political and economic institutions.

CHAPTER 13

Technology & Society
Politics and Technology

Lesson 1
Power and Authority

Lesson 2
Political Power in American Society

Lesson 3
Economic Systems

Lesson 4
The Modern Corporation

Lesson 5
Work in the Modern Economy

Sociology Matters...

The United States government has existed as a political institution for more than 220 years. The United States has always used a capitalist, or free-enterprise, system. There have been great differences of opinion about America's government and economy, but most of these differences have been settled peacefully because Americans share a basic set of political and economic values.

◀ People from across the country and around the world go out of their way to view the original U.S. Constitution and Bill of Rights.

National Geographic/SuperStock

361

CHAPTER 13
Technology & Society

Politics and Technology

In just a short period, the Internet and other forms of electronic communication have changed the way American politicians collect and communicate information, mobilize support, motivate voters, and raise money.

The politician seeking to win an election needs to identify possible voters, win their support, motivate them to act—and raise money to pay for these efforts. The Internet and other revolutionary technologies have created a whole new world of opportunities that politicians have only recently begun to exploit.

In the late 1990s and early 2000s, the political world was beginning to discover the power of the Internet. During this period, several groundbreaking, politically oriented online forums and communities began to appear. Some of the leading political blogs made their first appearance at this time. Republican candidate John McCain made news by following up an impressive primary win in the 2000 presidential race by raising significant amounts of money online.

The presidential election of 2004 witnessed a major advance in the sophisticated use of technology in political campaigns. The Internet emerged as a tool for everything from online voter registration to helping individuals across the country learn about campaign events in their communities.

The 2004 campaign was just the beginning. The 2008 and especially the 2012 elections highlighted the development of video-sharing websites as well as a growing understanding of how to utilize social media. These sites enable users to access and share a range of political information—as well as views and beliefs to far-flung social connections. Technology has also helped campaigns collect detailed information about users and target advertising and get-out-the-vote efforts more effectively.

Bill Clinton and his wife Hillary turned to traditional media—an interview on *60 Minutes*—to address rumors about his personal life. The interview, before the New Hampshire primary, saved his candidacy.

362

TIME LINE Explore the interactive version of the time line on Networks.

1996

The website for Republican candidates Bob Dole and Jack Kemp became the first political website to tailor content to the characteristics of Web visitors. Understanding of the Internet was limited, though—after Dole announced the website during a presidential debate, the site received so many hits it crashed.

2000

Although their campaigns for their respective party's nominations were unsuccessful, candidates John McCain (Republican) and Bill Bradley (Democrat) revolutionized campaign financing with heavy use of the Internet to raise funds. The technology story in 2000, though, was the apparent failure of punch-card ballots to register votes, throwing the outcome of the Florida vote—and the election—into doubt.

2004

Howard Dean used the Internet extensively in his losing effort to win the Democratic nomination for president. Interested citizens could use the campaign website to sign up to meet the candidate at a scheduled event, and he launched the first campaign blog.

2008

Interactivity took a new step in 2008 when YouTube joined with CNN for presidential debates in which citizens posed their questions to candidates via YouTube video.

2012

With smartphones, candidates found new ways to reach voters, like this Mitt Romney-supporting overlay that users can place over photos. However, the Romney campaign was embarrassed by this particular overlay, which misspelled "America." The gaffe, of course, received extensive comment on Twitter.

Thinking Like a Sociologist

1 Analyzing

What is it about the nature of politics that makes the Internet and other high-tech communication methods so powerful?

2 Evaluating

There is a lot of concern about the impact of money in American politics today. Do you think the role of technology increases or decreases the influence of money in politics? Explain.

networks

There's More Online!

- ☑ **GRAPHIC ORGANIZER** Power and Authority
- ☑ **IMAGE** Dr. Martin Luther King, Jr.
- ☑ **MAP** Political Freedom
- ☑ **SELF-CHECK QUIZ**

LESSON 1
Power and Authority

ESSENTIAL QUESTION • *How does the interaction between political systems and economic systems affect society?*

Reading HELPDESK

Academic Vocabulary
- inherently
- collapse

Content Vocabulary
- economic institution
- political institution
- power
- coercion
- authority
- charismatic authority
- traditional authority
- rational-legal authority
- representative democracy
- totalitarianism
- authoritarianism

TAKING NOTES:
Key Ideas and Details

ORGANIZING As you read about power and authority, use a graphic organizer like the one below to record details.

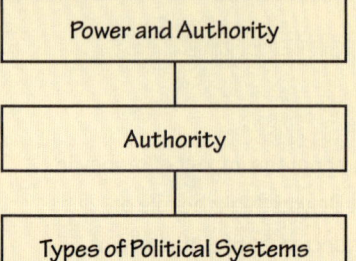

It Matters Because

Authority is the sanctioned use of power. Political systems can be based on three types of authority: charismatic, traditional, and rational-legal. Democratic, totalitarian, and authoritarian are types of political systems. In democracies, power lies with elected officials. Totalitarian political systems have absolute rulers who control all aspects of political and social life. Authoritarian rulers also possess absolute control but often permit some personal freedoms.

Definitions of Power and Authority

GUIDING QUESTION *What are power and authority?*

In October 2011, the union for some railroad workers voted to strike because it could not resolve disagreements with the railroad owners. Industry experts suggested that a rail strike would cost the U.S. economy as much as $2 billion a day. President Barack Obama quickly appointed a board to review and resolve the dispute. "Freight rail is vital to our economy and our future. It's in our national interest to make sure our freight rail system runs smoothly," declared the president in a written statement. The president's action demonstrated the close connection between business and government in modern American society.

The set of functions that concern the production and distribution of goods and services for a society is called the **economic institution**. Because economic decisions affect how valuable resources are shared between organizations and the general public, conflicts inevitably arise. The responsibility for handling these conflicts lies with the institution through which power is obtained and exercised—the **political institution**. These two institutions are so closely interrelated that it is very hard to think of them as separate.

For a beginning study of sociology, however, we can think of economics as the distribution of resources and politics as the exercise of power. This chapter will look first at how politics affects group behaviors and then at the economic scene.

364

Defining Power

Max Weber profoundly influenced sociological theory. Weber's contribution to political sociology deals with his identification of different forms of power and authority. Weber defined **power** as the ability to control the behavior of others, even against their will. Power takes various forms. Some people, for example, wield great power through their personal appeal or magnetism. John F. Kennedy, Martin Luther King, Jr., and César Chávez were able to influence others through the force of their charismatic personalities.

Weber recognized another form of power that he called *coercion*. **Coercion** is the use of physical force or threats to exert control. A blackmailer might extort money from a politician. A government might take, without compensation, the property of one of its citizens. In such cases, the victims do not believe this use of power is right. In fact, they normally are resentful and want to fight back. Weber recognized that a political system based on coercive power is **inherently** unstable; that is, the abuses of the system itself cause people to rise against it.

Defining Authority

Weber also believed that a political institution must rest on a stable form of power if it is to function and survive. This more stable form of power is *authority*. **Authority** is power accepted as legitimate by those subject to it. For example, students take exams and accept the results they receive because they believe their teachers have the right (authority) to determine grades. Most citizens pay taxes because they believe their government has the right (authority) to collect money from them.

☑ **READING PROGRESS CHECK**

Contrasting How is coercion different from authority?

economic institution the institution that determines how goods and services are produced and distributed

political institution the institution that determines how power is obtained and exercised

power the ability to control the behavior of others

coercion control through force

inherently naturally; basically

authority power accepted as legitimate by those subject to it

Forms of Authority

GUIDING QUESTION *How do charismatic, traditional, and rational-legal forms of authority differ?*

Weber identified three forms of authority—charismatic, traditional, and rational-legal. People who live under governments based on these forms recognize authority figures as holders of legitimate power.

Dr. Martin Luther King, Jr., inspired and led millions of people through the power of his ideas and personality.

▶ **CRITICAL THINKING**

Analyzing What are some of the personal characteristics of charismatic leaders?

Charismatic Authority

Charismatic authority arises from a leader's personal characteristics. Charismatic leaders lead through the power or strength of their personalities or the feelings of trust they inspire in a large number of people. Nelson Mandela and Fidel Castro also have strong personalities that made them highly charismatic leaders. For modern nation-states, however, charismatic authority alone is too unstable to provide a permanent basis of power. It is linked to an individual and is therefore difficult to transfer to another.

When charismatic leaders die, the source of power is removed. Adolf Hitler, himself a charismatic leader, made an unsuccessful attempt at the end of World War II to name his successor:

PRIMARY SOURCE

"Hitler's death brought an abrupt, absolute end to National Socialism. Without its only true leader, it burst like a bubble.... What had appeared to be the most powerful and fearsome political force of the twentieth century vanished overnight. No other leader's death since Napoleon had so completely obliterated a regime."

—John Toland, *Adolf Hitler*, 1976

Located between China and India, the small nation of Bhutan became a parliamentary democracy in 2008, but it had been ruled through traditional authority by the family of its current king, Jigme Khesar Namgyel Wangchuk, for more than a hundred years.

▶ **CRITICAL THINKING**

Speculating Why do you think most nations have replaced monarchy with a different style of government?

charismatic authority authority that arises from the personality of an individual

traditional authority the form of authority in which the legitimacy of a leader is rooted in custom

rational-legal authority the form of authority in which the power of leaders is vested in the offices they hold, not in their persons

Even governments controlled by charismatic leaders must eventually come to rely on other types of authority. The two alternatives to charismatic authority identified by Weber are traditional authority and rational-legal authority.

Traditional Authority

In the past, most states relied on **traditional authority**, in which the legitimacy of a leader is rooted in custom. Early kings often claimed to rule by the will of God, or divine right. The peaceful transfer of power was possible because only a few individuals, such as offspring or other close relatives, were eligible to become the next ruler. The kings in eighteenth-century Europe, for example, counted on the custom of loyalty to provide a stable political foundation. Tradition provided more stability than charismatic authority could have provided.

Rational-Legal Authority

Most modern governments are based on **rational-legal authority**. In this type of government, power resides in the offices rather than in the officials. Those people who hold government offices are expected to operate on the basis of specific rules and procedures that define and limit their rights and responsibilities. Power is assumed only when the individual occupies the office.

Many leaders in religious organizations fall under this category of authority. Since rational-legal authority is invested in positions rather than in individuals, persons lose their authority when they leave their formal positions of power. When a new president is elected, for example, the outgoing president becomes a private citizen again and gives up the privileges of the office. Leaders are also expected to stay within the boundaries of their legal authority. Even presidents (Richard Nixon, for example) can lose their power if their abuse of it is made public. Thus, rational-legal authority also limits the power of government officials.

✓ **READING PROGRESS CHECK**

Comparing What basic characteristic is shared by charismatic, traditional, and rational-legal authority?

Connecting Sociology to Political Science

CONSTITUTIONAL GOVERNMENT

The United States is what political scientists call a constitutional republic. At the heart of this system of government is something known as "the social contract."

Enlightenment thinkers, such as Englishman John Locke, first put forth the idea of the social contract. Writing in the 1600s, Locke argued that all human beings are born with certain basic "natural rights." To preserve these rights, people agree in a social contract to give certain powers to a government. This government, in turn, protects each person's rights. The thinking is that government serves the people and their needs and gets its power from them. Government, then, exists for no other purpose than to protect the rights of the people—people who join together voluntarily in a social contract to create it.

The Framers of the U.S. Constitution were strongly influenced by Locke and his ideas. The Preamble to the Constitution clearly states that it is "We the people" who establish the government and grant it its powers. The Constitution clearly outlines the specific offices, structures, and powers that the government will possess. It sets up procedures to ensure that chosen individuals possess those powers only for a limited period of time and then pass them on to the next elected or appointed person. It requires that officials swear to uphold the Constitution. And it provides means for removing from office those who fail to do so.

In short, the Constitution limits the power of government. It makes clear that government answers to the will of the people who created and sustain it.

The Constitution begins with the words "We the people," making clear the source of the power and authority of the U.S. government.

▶ CRITICAL THINKING
1. **Describing** What are the basic ideas behind the concept of the social contract?
2. **Explaining** How does the U.S. Constitution reflect the ideas of the social contract?

Types of Political Systems

GUIDING QUESTION *What are the different types of political systems, and what are their characteristics?*

In hunting-and-gathering societies, there was very little formal government. Political leaders were typically chosen on the basis of exceptional physical prowess or personal charisma. Formal governmental structures emerged with the development of agricultural economies and the rise of city-states. As societies became more diversified with the development of commerce, industry, and technology, government began to take the form of the national political state. The first strong modern nation-states, including France, Spain, and England, appeared in the late 1400s. Gradually, traditional authority was replaced by rational-legal authority. Contemporary nation-states can be classified into three basic types: democratic, totalitarian, and authoritarian.

Democracy

Democracy in its pure form, as practiced by the ancient Greeks, involves all citizens in self-government. This type of direct democracy is similar to that practiced in some New England town meetings, where the citizens debate and vote directly on various issues. More familiar to us today is **representative democracy**, in which elected officials are responsible for fulfilling the wishes of the majority of citizens.

representative democracy a system of government that uses elected officials to fulfill majority wishes

A Global Perspective

POLITICAL FREEDOM

Political freedom and democracy are not evenly distributed around the world. This map classifies different countries according to measures of political freedom, including open competition for political power, respect for civil liberties, an independent civic life, and a media free from government control.

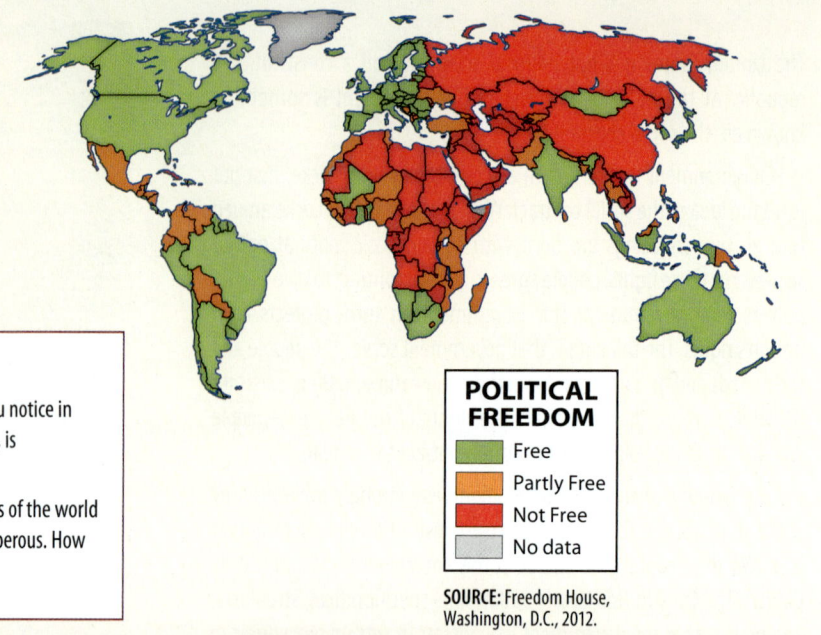

POLITICAL FREEDOM
- Free
- Partly Free
- Not Free
- No data

SOURCE: Freedom House, Washington, D.C., 2012.

Geography Connection

1. **Places and Regions** What pattern, if any, do you notice in how political freedom, as represented on this map, is distributed around the world?
2. **Making Connections** The politically free nations of the world are, by and large, also the most economically prosperous. How would you explain this connection?

Representative democracy operates under two assumptions. The first is that, realistically, not everyone in modern society can be actively involved in all political decision making. Thus, although citizens are expected to vote, most citizens are not expected to be deeply involved in politics. Second, elected officials who fail to satisfy the wishes of the majority of voters are not expected to win reelections.

With the major two-party system of the United States, we have a "winner-take-all" form of representative democracy. Here, the party with the most votes wins the election. In other countries, as in Europe, where third-party systems are common, political parties participate in the government to the extent that they win representation in general elections. For example, one party might win 40 percent of the vote and they would then control 40 percent of the legislature. Three other parties might take 20 percent each and control a combined 60 percent of the legislature. This proportional representation system seems to be more democratic, as it tends to encourage compromises and cooperation in forming governments. Governments formed under this system can be fragile, however, and shifting political alliances may be able to force new elections after short periods of time.

collapse total breakdown

The **collapse** of Soviet communism and the end of the Cold War created opportunities for more societies to adopt democratic forms of government, and in the 1990s, many countries in Eastern Europe became democracies. The uprisings in the Middle East in 2011, called the "Arab Spring," created possibilities for more political freedom in this region. It is not clear, however, that democracy and civil liberties around the world have been increasing in the first decades of the 2000s. Since 2005, the overall scores of countries for political and civil liberties have shown more countries declining than improving. Between 1981 and 2011, the percentage of free countries in the world had increased from 33 percent to 45 percent, but the percentage had remained essentially unchanged since 2001. The same trends are seen when countries that are considered "partly free" are included.

Totalitarianism

Totalitarianism lies at the opposite end of the political spectrum from democracy. In this type of political system, a ruler with absolute power attempts to control all aspects of a society. Characteristics of a totalitarian state include:

- A single political party, typically controlled by one person
- A well-coordinated campaign of terror
- Total control of all means of communication
- A monopoly over military resources
- A planned economy directed by a state bureaucracy

Examples of totalitarian states include Iraq under Saddam Hussein, the former Soviet Union, and Nazi Germany. Hitler's National Socialist (Nazi) government, which came to power in Germany in 1933, shows how a totalitarian system works. Despite presenting a false image of democracy to the world, Hitler and the National Socialist Party held all the power. The Nazis seized or shut down nearly all news media. Hitler's four-year economic plans included strategies for budgets, production, organization of factories, and forced labor. Hitler dominated the armed forces. His absolute control was strengthened by the Gestapo secret police and SS troops, who terrorized political enemies and citizens. The SS brutally and systematically put to death more than 6 million European Jews—a genocide now known as the Holocaust—and murdered between 5 and 6 million others.

Authoritarianism

For sociologists, authoritarianism is a middle category between democracy and totalitarianism, although it is closer to totalitarianism than to democracy. **Authoritarianism** refers to a political system controlled by elected or nonelected rulers who usually permit some degree of individual freedom but do not allow popular participation in government. Countless governments have leaned toward totalitarianism but have fallen short of all its defining characteristics. These governments are classified as authoritarian. Examples include certain monarchies (the dynasties of the shahs of Iran), military seizures of power (Fidel Castro's takeover of Cuba), and communist governments, such as China.

✔ **READING PROGRESS CHECK**

Making Predictions Do you think a totalitarian or authoritarian system could ever gain power in the United States? Why or why not?

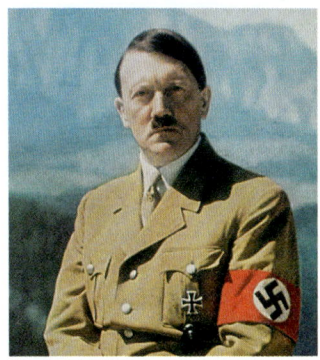

Adolf Hitler created a totalitarian government in Germany beginning in the 1930s by taking absolute power and controlling all aspects of the society.

▶ **CRITICAL THINKING**

Evaluating Which aspect of a totalitarian government do you think is most important in maintaining control of a society?

totalitarianism a political system in which a ruler with absolute power attempts to control all aspects of society

authoritarianism a political system controlled by elected or nonelected rulers who usually permit some degree of individual freedom

---

LESSON 1 REVIEW

Reviewing Vocabulary
1. *Contrasting* How are totalitarianism and authoritarianism related?
2. *Applying* Provide one example of charismatic authority not found in the text.

Using Your Notes
3. *Contrasting* Use your notes to write a few sentences that describe the current type of authority in the United States.

Answering the Guiding Questions
4. *Analyzing* What are power and authority?
5. *Explaining* How do charismatic, traditional, and rational-legal forms of authority differ?
6. *Explaining* What are the different types of political systems, and what are their characteristics?

Writing Activity
7. *Informative/Explanatory* Identify a leader whom you support, and describe what type of authority he or she has. Remember that leaders can be other students or community or family members.

networks

There's More Online!

- ☑ **CHART** Theoretical Perspectives: Two Models of Political Power
- ☑ **CHART** Types of Interest Groups
- ☑ **GRAPH** Voter Participation in Presidential Elections
- ☑ **IMAGE** Petitioner
- ☑ **MAP** Voter Turnout in Presidential Elections
- ☑ **SELF-CHECK QUIZ**

Reading HELPDESK

Academic Vocabulary
- environmental
- overlap

Content Vocabulary
- political socialization
- pluralism
- elitism
- interest group
- power elite

TAKING NOTES:
Key Ideas and Details

ORGANIZING As you read about political power in America, use a graphic organizer like the one below to record details.

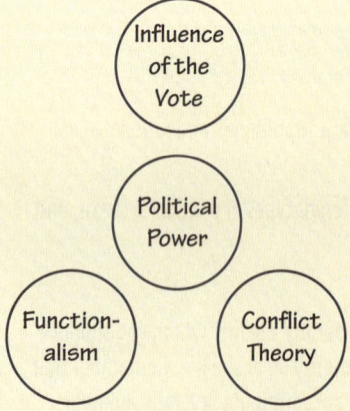

LESSON 2
Political Power in American Society

ESSENTIAL QUESTION • How does the interaction between political systems and economic systems affect society?

IT MATTERS BECAUSE
The two major models of political power are elitism and pluralism. Advocates of the conflict perspective believe American society is controlled by elites. Pluralists, whose view is associated with functionalism, depict power as widely distributed among interest groups. Voting is one means by which elites and nonelites seek to influence political decisions in the United States.

Influence of the Vote

GUIDING QUESTIONS What factors influence a voter's political beliefs?

Like all other democracies today, the United States emphasizes political participation through voting. Voting is an important source of power for citizens. It enables us to remove incompetent, corrupt, or insensitive officials from office. It also allows us to influence issues at the local, state, and national levels.

Voting Choices

In practice, the amount of real choice exercised through voting is limited. The range of candidates from which to choose is restricted because of the power of political parties. Usually, only a candidate endorsed by a major political party has a chance of winning a state or national office. To get party support, a candidate must appeal to the largest possible number of voters. As a result, candidates often resemble one another more than they differ. In addition, the cost of running a political campaign today limits the choice of candidates to those who have party backing or are independently wealthy. For example, campaign finance reports indicated that Mitt Romney and his supporters spent more than $120 million to win the Republican Party nomination for president in 2012.

Voting Influences

Most attitudes and beliefs that are expressed as political opinions are gained through a learning process called **political socialization**. This process can be formal, as in government class, or informal. The informal process interests sociologists because it involves such factors as the family, the

370

media, economic status, and educational level. Studies have shown that most political socialization is informal. A brief summary of the major agents of political socialization follows.

- **Family.** Children learn political attitudes in the same way that they learn values and norms—by listening to everyday conversations and by watching the actions of other family members. The influence of the family is strong. In one study, more high-school students could identify their parents' political party affiliation than any other of their parents' attitudes or beliefs.
- **Education.** The level of education a person has influences his or her political knowledge and participation. For example, more highly educated men and women tend to show more knowledge about politics and policy. They also tend to vote and participate more often in politics.
- **Mass media.** Television is the leading source of political and public-affairs information for most people. Television and other mass media can determine what issues, events, and personalities are in the public eye. By publicizing some issues and ignoring others and by giving some stories high priority and others low priority, the media decide the relative importance of issues. The mass media obviously play an important role in shaping public opinion, but the extent of that role is unclear. Studies indicate that the media have the greatest effect on people who have not yet formed opinions.

Political socialization helps determine the issues we feel strongly about and what actions we might take because of them.

▶ **CRITICAL THINKING**

Applying What issues do you feel strongly enough about that you would take action to support your beliefs?

A Diverse America

VOTER TURNOUT IN PRESIDENTIAL ELECTIONS

Voters may hold the power in American politics—but to exercise that power, they have to show up at the polls. This map shows the voter turnout as a percentage of eligible voters for each state in the 2008 presidential election.

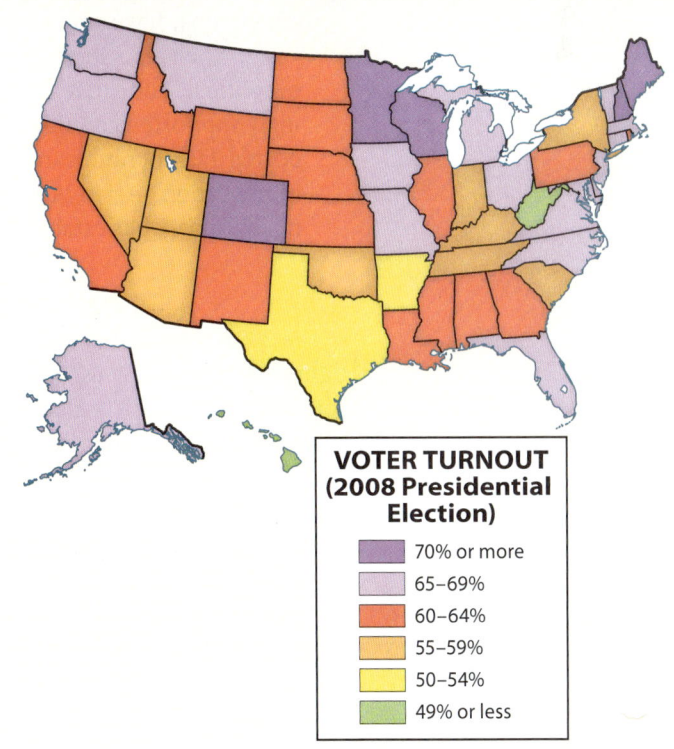

VOTER TURNOUT (2008 Presidential Election)
- 70% or more
- 65–69%
- 60–64%
- 55–59%
- 50–54%
- 49% or less

SOURCE: http://elections.gmu.edu/Turnout_2008G.html

Geography Connection

1. **Places and Regions** Which states had the highest turnout in the 2008 election? Which states had the lowest turnout?
2. **Places and Regions** How did your state perform in the election? Does this surprise you? Explain.
3. **Human Systems** What factors might explain voter turnout in a particular state or region?

Political and Economic Institutions

| GRAPH >

VOTER PARTICIPATION IN PRESIDENTIAL ELECTIONS, 1932–2008

This graph shows how voter turnout in American presidential elections has fluctuated over more than 70 years.

▶ **CRITICAL THINKING**

1. **Analyzing** What factors might affect voter turnout in different years?
2. **Hypothesizing** Why do you think voter turnout increased for the 2008 election?

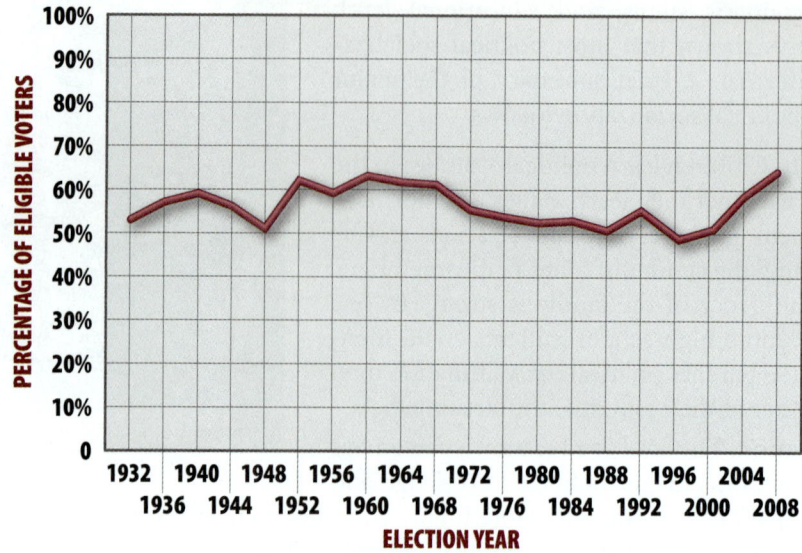

Source: U.S. Bureau of the Census, *Statistical Abstract of the United States, 2004–2005, Current Population Survey* (November 2004) and *Voting and Registration in the Election of November 2008.*

political socialization the informal and formal processes by which a person develops political opinions

- **Economic status and occupation.** Economic status clearly influences political views. Poor people are more likely to favor government-assistance programs than wealthy people, for example. Similarly, the job you hold affects how you vote. Corporate managers are more likely to favor tax shelters and aid to businesses than hourly workers in factories.
- **Age and gender.** Young adults tend to be more progressive than older persons on such issues as racial and gender equality. Women tend to be more liberal than men on such issues as abortion rights, women's rights, health care, and government-supported child care.
- **Racial and ethnic group.** African Americans, as well as Latinos and Asian Americans, have increased their political participation by voting in recent years. They also show a tendency to favor candidates with liberal positions over those considered conservative. African Americans have overwhelmingly supported candidates with liberal positions, and Latinos have also supported Democratic candidates, especially those with more liberal views on immigration. Asian Americans tend to vote Democratic as well, although neither party has established a strong base within the group.

American Voter Participation

In the 2008 presidential election, 64 percent of eligible U.S. voters exercised their right to vote, which was a small increase from 2004. About 32 percent of eligible voters voted for Barack Obama for president. In fact, the United States has among the lowest voter-turnout rates compared to other countries and regions.

The American public's interest in voting is very low, partly because of a relatively low level of confidence in political leaders. Another reason for lower voter turnout is that political parties are no longer as instrumental in getting voters to the polls as they once were. In general, minorities and the lower and working classes tend to vote in smaller proportions than whites and the middle and upper classes. Members of minorities, people with little education, and people with smaller incomes are less likely to vote in both congressional and presidential elections.

✓ **READING PROGRESS CHECK**

Describing What political socialization have you experienced that affects your views?

Two Models of Political Power

GUIDING QUESTION *How do functionalism and the conflict perspective explain political power in a democracy?*

In a democratic society, two major models of political power are evident—pluralism and elitism. According to **pluralism**, political decisions are the result of bargaining and compromise among special-interest groups. No one group holds the majority of power. Rather, power is widely distributed throughout a society or community. In contrast, according to **elitism**, a community or society is controlled from the top by a few individuals or organizations. Power is concentrated in the hands of an elite group whose members have common interests and backgrounds. The masses are very weak politically.

Functionalists think that pluralism based on the existence of diverse interest groups best describes the distribution of power in the United States. While recognizing competition among interest groups, functionalists contend that it is based on an underlying consensus regarding the goals of the entire society. Elitism is based on the conflict perspective. This theory of power distribution assumes that the elites are constantly working to maintain their hold on society's major institutions. In so doing, elites force others to help them reach their goals.

Functionalist Perspective: Pluralism

According to pluralists, major political decisions in the United States are not made by an elite few. As an example, they point to the beneficiaries of the 2001 tax cut bill. Tax breaks came not only to the wealthy, such as Microsoft's Bill Gates, but also to groups with more modest resources, such as the lower classes and mental health care facilities.

An **interest group** is a group organized to influence political decision making. Group members share one or more goals. The goals may be specific to the group's own members—as in the case of the National Rifle Association—or may involve a larger segment of society—as in the case of ecology-oriented groups like the Sierra Club. Pluralists contend that decisions are made as a result of competition among special-interest groups, each of which has its own stake in the issues.

In addition to reaching their own ends, interest groups try to protect themselves from opposing interest groups. Responsibility falls to government leaders to balance the public welfare with the desires of various special interests.

pluralism a system in which political decisions are made as a result of bargaining and compromise among special-interest groups

elitism a system in which a community or society is controlled from the top by a few individuals or organizations

interest group a group organized to influence political decision making

Interest groups try to influence political decision making in a variety of ways.

▶ **CRITICAL THINKING**

Identifying What are some ways in which interest groups might try to influence a political decision?

> **CHART >**

TYPES OF INTEREST GROUPS
A wide variety of interest groups attempts to influence political decisions in the United States. This chart shows a few of the largest, but there are thousands working to achieve their goals.

▶ **CRITICAL THINKING**

1. **Speculating** What other types of professional groups do you think might represent workers or professions?
2. **Assessing** How important do you think the size of an interest group is to its effectiveness?

Economic Groups

Organization	Membership	Objectives
Business		
U.S. Chamber of Commerce	More than 3,000,000 businesses	Lobby for businesses
Agricultural		
National Farmers Union	About 200,000 farm and ranch families	Represent family farms and ranches
Professional		
American Medical Association (AMA)	More than 200,000 members	Represent physicians and improve the medical profession
American Bar Association (ABA)	About 400,000 members	Improve the legal system
Labor		
AFL-CIO	More than 8,000,000 members through affiliates	Protect members from unfair labor practices

Noneconomic Groups

Organization	Membership	Objectives
Public Interest		
League of Women Voters	About 1,000 local leagues, more than 90,000 members	Promote voter registration and election reform
Single Issue		
Sierra Club	About 1,400,000 members	Protect the natural environment
National Rifle Association (NRA)	About 4,000,000 members	Promote and protect the rights of gun owners
Ideological		
National Organization for Women (NOW)	More than 500,000 members	Eliminate discrimination and protect the rights of women
National Association for the Advancement of Colored People (NAACP)	About 200,000 members	Eliminate discrimination and protect the rights of minorities

Interest groups are not new to American politics. In the nineteenth century, they were active in extending women's rights and promoting the abolition of slavery. The twentieth century saw such active interest groups as the Woman's Christian Temperance Union and early labor unions. During the 1960s, controversies surrounding civil rights, the Vietnam War, the environment, the women's movement, and corporate power strengthened many interest groups and led to the creation of a number of new ones.

New interest groups are born all the time. The **environmental** lobby is a good example. There were relatively few environmental-interest groups before the passage of major environmental legislation in the 1960s and early 1970s. The success of this legislation spawned additional groups, numbering three times the original total. This added clout produced additional environmental legislation—for example, the 1990 Clean Air Act Amendments—that subsequently led to the creation of other interest groups.

environmental concerned with the natural world or environment

Theoretical Perspectives

TWO MODELS OF POLITICAL POWER
This table illustrates views of the functionalist and conflict perspectives on political power. Several key features of the political system are compared.

Characteristics	Functionalist Perspective (Pluralist Model)	Conflict Perspective (Power Elite Model)
Who exercises power?	Bargaining and compromising interest groups	National political, economic, and military leaders
What is the source of power?	Resources of interest groups	Leadership positions in major institutions
Where is the power located?	Spread widely among interest groups	Concentrated in hands of elites
How much influence do nonelites have?	Nonelites have considerable influence on public policy.	Nonelites have very little influence on public policy.
What is the basis for public policy decisions?	Goals and values are shared by the general public.	Preferences of the elites

▶ CRITICAL THINKING

1. **Expressing** Which theory do you think best describes power in the United States? Explain.
2. **Constructing Arguments** Which perspective do you think comes closest to representing the intentions and beliefs of the Framers of the U.S. Constitution and the U.S. system of government? Explain.

Conflict Perspective: The Power Elite

Sociologist C. Wright Mills was a leading proponent of the elitist perspective. In the 1950s, he claimed that the United States no longer had separate economic, political, and military leaders. Rather, the key people in each area **overlapped** to form a unified group that he labeled the **power elite**.

According to Mills, members of the power elite share common interests and similar social and economic backgrounds. Members of the power elite have known one another for a long time, have mutual acquaintances of long standing, share many values and attitudes, and intermarry. All this makes it easier for them to coordinate their actions to obtain what they want.

overlap having an area, range, or other characteristics in common

power elite a unified group of military, corporate, and government leaders

✓ READING PROGRESS CHECK

Evaluating Do you think functionalism or conflict theory better describes political power in the United States? Why?

LESSON 2 REVIEW

Reviewing Vocabulary
1. **Contrasting** How are pluralism and elitism different?
2. **Applying** What is one interest group to which you might belong?

Using Your Notes
3. **Contrasting** Use your notes to describe the importance of interest groups in the United States.

Answering the Guiding Questions
4. **Listing** What factors influence a voter's political beliefs?

5. **Explaining** How do functionalism and the conflict perspective explain political power in a democracy?

Writing Activity
6. **Narrative** Write a paragraph that describes your thoughts on voting. Answer such questions as: Are you looking forward to voting? Do you know what kinds of candidates you will support? How important is it for you and others of your age to vote?

Political and Economic Institutions

FOCUS on research
Survey Research

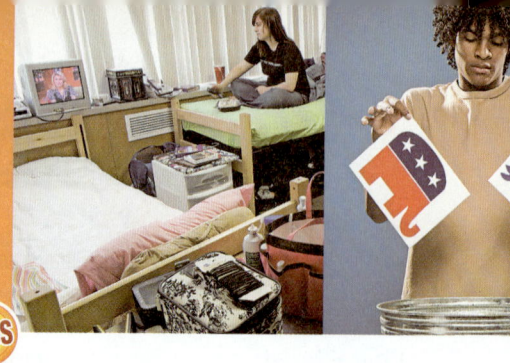

Consuming Politics: Jon Stewart, Branding, and the Youth Vote in America

Authors Dan Cassino and Yasemin Besen-Cassino surveyed young people to help identify the appeal and impact of the politically themed comedy program The Daily Show. *The survey results suggest that, for younger people, delivery of information that reflects their attitudes about and alienation from the larger society is more significant than the ideological bias present in that information.*

PRIMARY SOURCE

"It's difficult to argue that *The Daily Show* doesn't have a relatively strong liberal bias. This is not necessarily an ideological bias, but rather a comedic one. Satire works largely by deflating those in power, and for most of the time since the change in format that brought Stewart to the show and politics to the forefront in 1999, Republicans have been in the best position to be satirized.

As such, we would expect that support for, and positive images of, Stewart's program would be correlated with partisanship. Republican young people would object to a program that mocked (mostly) Republicans, and Democratic young people would appreciate a program that mirrored their stances. However, as with Fox News and NPR [National Public Radio], our respondents didn't seem to know enough about the underlying ideology of the program to embrace or reject it on those grounds. Almost none of the Republican respondents noted any liberal content, and neither did the Democratic respondents. Rather, respondents who knew about it—and it was the best known of the three media sources included in the final study—discussed it in terms of the images they associated with it.

While the content and the ideological stance of the show had little to do with how young people see it, the presentation of the material was an important part of the show's image. Many emphasized that it was a fun or humorous element, both of which made the show attractive. This quality was mentioned across the board, among all partisan groups, and respondents emphasized that it was young, hip humor, targeted specifically to young people, college students, like themselves. This aspect was particularly important for the generally alienated pessimistic youth we spoke to, who see the satire as akin to their own views and the comedy as a kind of escape from reality. As Adrian, a nineteen-year-old independent, described the average viewer, 'a teenager who is tired of all the government-filtered news that is shown on every other network and wants to hear the straight truth from someone who is as tired of our current government as they are.'

These respondents may be alienated from the political process, but the show is seen as being just as outside of the system as they are, and is thus relatable. As another put it, 'A *Daily Show* viewer is tired about hearing about the grim news all of the other stations report.' They like to hear the lighter side of the news reports and hear the reporter make some jokes. As nineteen-year-old Steve, a Republican, put it, '*Daily Show* reporters like to remind viewers they are human too by the way they act, while other reporters just read

> "These respondents may be alienated from the political process, but the show is seen as being just as outside of the system as they are, and is thus relatable."

the news and get off of the air . . . viewers like to be reminded that the reporter on the other end is also a human.' Such viewers just 'want to be entertained'; the news, therefore, 'does not necessarily have to be true.'

Perhaps most importantly, respondents noted that *The Daily Show* was more user-friendly than the other news sources mentioned in the survey. . . . The complexity of political news stories, and the generally unfamiliar nature of the rhetoric and concepts employed there, make it difficult for relatively unsophisticated viewers to get a good understanding of the topic at hand. Traditionally, partisanship has been used to simplify these stories, making it clear which side is right, and which wrong, but among young people alienated from the parties, this isn't necessarily an option. While many of the respondents voiced this concern when describing other media sources, saying that they didn't understand them, or that they were talking about obscure topics, things that no one really cares about, or has time for, such comments were missing from descriptions of *The Daily Show* and its viewers. It was not uncommon for a typical viewer to be described as someone 'that does not know anything about politics.' This is a political news program that anyone can watch and understand. 'This is because,' a female Democratic respondent tells us, 'Jon Stewart puts a comical view on real life events so it makes it easier for college students to be interested by it because they have political classes in school and this makes it perfect to relate the information that they learned. They like to watch the news but they like the satirical view that he expresses and the opinions that he has.'"

—from *Consuming Politics: Jon Stewart, Branding, and the Youth Vote in America*, 2011

Working With the Research

1. **Explaining** What qualities of *The Daily Show* allow young people to enjoy it in spite of its political content or biases?
2. **Contrasting** How did respondents say more conventional news programs differ from *The Daily Show*?
3. **Analyzing** Based on these responses, what factors do you think are most important in building a connection between providers of information and entertainment and their viewers?

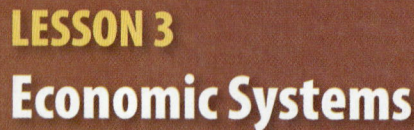

LESSON 3
Economic Systems

networks

There's More Online!

- ☑ **GRAPHIC ORGANIZER** Economic Systems
- ☑ **IMAGE** Globalized McNuggets
- ☑ **SELF-CHECK QUIZ**

Reading HELPDESK

Academic Vocabulary
- deviation
- guarantee

Content Vocabulary
- capitalism
- monopolies
- oligopolies
- socialism

TAKING NOTES:
Key Ideas and Details

ORGANIZING As you read about economic systems, use a graphic organizer like the one below to record details.

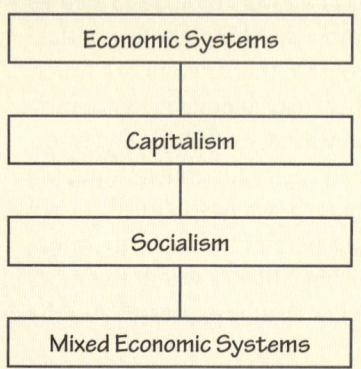

ESSENTIAL QUESTION • *How does the interaction between political systems and economic systems affect society?*

IT MATTERS BECAUSE

Capitalist economies are based on private property and the pursuit of profit, and government, in theory, plays a minor role in regulating industry. In socialist economies, the means of production are owned collectively, and government has an active role in planning and controlling the economy.

Capitalism

GUIDING QUESTIONS *How can a capitalist system benefit society?* • *What potential problems exist in a capitalist system?*

Economic systems, as suggested earlier, involve the production and distribution of goods and services. **Capitalism** is an economic system founded on two basic premises: the sanctity of private property and the right of individuals to profit from their labor. Capitalism is also known as the free-market system or the free-enterprise system.

Capitalists believe that individuals, not government, should own and control land, factories, raw materials, and the tools of production. They argue that private ownership benefits society and promotes individual initiative and growth. Capitalists also believe in unrestricted competition with minimum government interference.

How Capitalism Can Benefit Society

According to Adam Smith, an eighteenth-century Scottish social philosopher and founder of economics, a combination of the private ownership of property and the pursuit of profit brings advantages to society. Self-interest regulates the economy, Smith argued. Individual capitalists will always be motivated to provide the goods and services desired by the public at prices the public is willing and able to pay. Capitalists who produce inferior goods or who charge too much will soon be out of business because the public will turn to their competitors. The public, Smith reasoned, will benefit through economic competition.

Not only will the public receive high-quality goods and services at reasonable prices, but capitalists will always be searching for new products and new technologies to reduce their costs. As a result, capitalist societies will use resources efficiently. Actually, no pure capitalist economy exists in the world. In practice, there are important **deviations** from Smith's ideal model. One of these deviations involves the tendency to form monopolies and oligopolies.

Monopolies and Oligopolies

When capitalist organizations experience success, they tend to grow until they become giants within their particular industries. In this way, capitalism fosters the rise of **monopolies**, companies that control a particular market, and **oligopolies**, combinations of companies working together to control a market. New organizations find it difficult to enter these markets, where they have little hope of competing on an equal basis. Thus, competition is stifled. Among other problems, the creation of monopolies and oligopolies permits price fixing. Consumers must choose between buying at the "going price" set by the sellers and not buying at all.

A good recent example of alleged monopolistic practices in the U.S. economy involved the Microsoft Corporation. Microsoft produces, among other products, the Windows operating system—by far the most popular operating system for personal computers. Many computer manufacturers typically include Windows on the machines they sell. In the 1990s, Microsoft began to insist that manufacturers include its Internet browser, Internet Explorer, on their computers as well. The manufacturers were also instructed not to install another browser in addition to Internet Explorer. If they refused, Microsoft would withhold their license to sell Windows on the machines.

Because Microsoft had so much power over computer manufacturers, other makers of Internet browsers, such as Netscape, were essentially excluded from the market. Eventually, the federal government took Microsoft to court, where it was ruled that Microsoft did indeed engage in monopolistic practices. By 2005, Microsoft had settled its federal case and paid out billions of dollars in antitrust, state, and consumer claims.

The Role of Government in Capitalism

Adam Smith is often misinterpreted as saying that government should have a strictly hands-off approach where the economy is concerned. While Smith strongly opposed overregulation by government, he reserved a place for some regulation.

capitalism an economic system based on private ownership of property and the pursuit of profit

deviation a move away from the norm or what is expected

monopolies companies that have control over the production or distribution of a product or service

oligopolies combinations of companies that control the production or distribution of a product or service

The National Highway Traffic Safety Administration regulates automobile safety features as part of the government's authority over private business.

▶ **CRITICAL THINKING**

Identifying What are two other areas in which government controls or regulates private business?

Because one of the legitimate roles of government is to protect its citizens from injustice, Smith knew that the state might have to step in to prevent abuses by businesses. In fact, the U.S. government has always been involved in the workings of the economy.

Government Contributions to the U.S. Economy

The U.S. Constitution expressly provides a role for the national government in the promotion of a sound economy. Government functions include the regulation of commerce, development of a strong currency, creation of uniform standards for commerce, and the provision of a stable system of credit. In 1789, Congress supported our shipping industry through a tariff on goods imported on foreign ships.

Since this initial move into the economy, the federal government has continued to help business, labor, and agriculture. For example, the federal government aids private industry through loan **guarantees**—as in the 2008 government guarantees of $25 billion to automakers and $700 billion to financial institutions. American workers are supported by the government through regulations on such matters as minimum wages, maximum working hours, health and safety conditions, and unemployment support. Small farmers and agribusinesses receive financial assistance amounting to billions of dollars each year.

guarantee a promise

✓ **READING PROGRESS CHECK**

Explaining What did Adam Smith think the role of government should be under capitalism?

Connecting Sociology to Economics

THE FREE-ENTERPRISE SYSTEM

There are a number of theories about personality development. The general consensus is that a combination of heredity and environmental factors shape an individual's personality. Among the environmental factors that may play a role in personality development for people in this country is our free-enterprise economic system.

Think about the key features of the free-enterprise system in which American young people are raised and socialized. Americans grow up being taught that all people should have freedom to choose and make economic decisions in their own best interests. The individual, acting independently, is the driving, positive force of our economic system. Each person has the basic right to acquire property, make a profit, and take risks. We celebrate those who take risks and reap the rewards of their decisions. In effect, we socialize children to think and behave as individuals.

Our economic system also celebrates competition. Americans generally believe that playing one business off another leads to progress and prosperity for the whole. Aggressive competition in the marketplace is expected and praised.

Many sociologists believe that these prevailing cultural values and practices may shape personality development. The free-enterprise economic system certainly represents such a powerful environmental influence.

The New York Stock Exchange symbolizes the free-enterprise system: People buy stock in the hopes of gaining a profit.

▶ **CRITICAL THINKING**

1. *Identifying* What are some of the central values associated with the free-enterprise system?
2. *Evaluating* What kinds of personality traits do you think the free-enterprise system might encourage?

Socialism

GUIDING QUESTIONS *How can a socialist system benefit society?* • *What potential problems exist in a socialist system?*

Socialism is an economic system founded on the belief that the means of production should be controlled by the people as a whole. The state, as the people's representative, should own and control property. Under a socialist system, government directs and controls the economy. The state is expected to ensure that all members of society have a share in the monetary benefits.

How Socialism Can Benefit Society

Socialist theory points to important benefits for workers. Workers under capitalism receive wages below the value their labor produces and have little control over their work. In theory, workers under socialism should profit because both the state and the workplace exist for their benefit. As a result, workers should be able to exert significant control over both their work organizations and the policy directions of the society as a whole.

Socialism in Reality

Cases of pure socialism are as rare as cases of pure capitalism. Strict socialist systems have not been successful in eliminating income inequalities nor have they been able to develop overall economic plans that guarantee sustained economic growth. In the socialistic economy of the former Soviet Union, for example, some agricultural and professional work was performed privately by individuals who worked for a profit. Significant portions of housing were privately owned as well. Managers received salaries that were considerably higher than those received by workers, and managers were eligible for bonuses, such as automobiles and housing. The reality of modern socialist systems has also differed from the ideal of socialism because modern socialist systems frequently suffer from entrenched problems, such as inefficiency and corruption.

Private enterprise also existed in Poland under Soviet communist domination. Service businesses, such as restaurants and hotels, had a significant degree of private ownership. Hotels, in fact, were typically built and managed by multinational chains. Because Poles could travel abroad, they formed business relationships, learned about capitalist methods, imported goods to fill demand, and brought back hard currency. They then used the hard currency earned abroad to create private businesses.

✓ **READING PROGRESS CHECK**

Identifying Theoretically, what group is the most powerful under socialism, and what can they control?

The former Soviet Union had a socialist economy for about 70 years, but the failure of its economy was one reason for the collapse of the country.

▶ **CRITICAL THINKING**

Hypothesizing Why do you think some people in the Soviet Union were unhappy with the socialist economy?

socialism an economic system founded on the belief that the means of production should be controlled by the people as a whole

Mixed Economic Systems

GUIDING QUESTION *What is a mixed economic system?*

Most nations fall between the extremes of capitalism and socialism and include elements of both economic systems. Countries in Western Europe, for example, have developed capitalist economic systems in which both public and private ownership play important roles. In these nations, highly strategic industries (banks, transportation, communications, and some others) are owned and operated by the state.

Political and Economic Institutions

Most countries in the world today operate under a system that mixes capitalist and socialist ideas.

▶ **CRITICAL THINKING**

Making Connections What benefits do you think international fast-food chains bring to socialist countries?

Other industries are privately owned but are more closely regulated than in the United States.

As the former Soviet Union lost control over its republics and Eastern Europe, many of these formerly socialist countries began to move toward capitalism. Czechoslovakia shifted from public to private ownership of businesses. Private property that had been nationalized after the communists took over in 1948 was returned to the original owners or their heirs. The assets moved from the public to the private sector were valued at about $5 billion. Many small shops and businesses were sold in public auctions. In 1992, Czechoslovakia sold over 1,000 of its bigger state enterprises to its citizens. Today, the private sector accounts for about 80 percent of the total economic production for the Czech Republic. The same is true for Hungary, where nearly all the state-owned small businesses are now in the hands of private owners and account for 80 percent of total economic production. China has been successfully incorporating free-market reforms into its economy since the late 1970s, but it still ranks very low on scores for economic freedom.

☑ **READING PROGRESS CHECK**

Evaluating How common are mixed economic systems?

LESSON 3 REVIEW

Reviewing Vocabulary

1. *Comparing and Contrasting* How are monopolies and oligopolies similar and different?

2. *Contrasting* How are capitalism and socialism different?

Using Your Notes

3. *Describing* Use your notes to describe how capitalist and socialist ideas can contribute to a mixed economic system.

Answering the Guiding Questions

4. *Explaining* How can a capitalist system benefit society? What potential problems exist in a capitalist system?

5. *Explaining* How can a socialist system benefit society? What potential problems exist in a socialist system?

6. *Defining* What is a mixed economic system?

Writing Activity

7. *Argument* Think of an economic activity you are commonly involved in, such as purchasing or selling a product or service. Describe how that activity might be different under a socialist system and make an argument that it would be better or worse under that system.

networks

There's More Online!

- ☑ **CHART** Revenues of Multinational Corporations Compared to GDPs of Some Countries
- ☑ **GRAPHIC ORGANIZER** Modern Corporations
- ☑ **SELF-CHECK QUIZ**

Reading HELPDESK

Academic Vocabulary
- facility
- enhance

Content Vocabulary
- interlocking directorates
- conglomerates
- multinationals

TAKING NOTES:
Key Ideas and Details

ORGANIZING As you read about modern corporations, use a graphic organizer like the one below to record details.

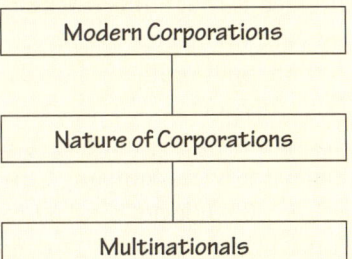

LESSON 4
The Modern Corporation

ESSENTIAL QUESTION • *How does the interaction between political systems and economic systems affect society?*

IT MATTERS BECAUSE

Corporations, especially those with multinational connections, have grown very powerful. Corporate managers affect domestic political decision making and influence the political and economic institutions of countries around the world.

The Nature of Corporations

GUIDING QUESTION *What is a corporation, and how can a corporation exert power?*

Sociologists study corporations because of their great importance in modern economic systems. Corporations in the United States, for example, not only dominate the American economic system but also influence the economies of nations around the world. Corporations represent massive concentrations of wealth. Because of their economic muscle, corporations such as Microsoft, AT&T, and General Electric command the attention of government decision makers. As a result, government policies regarding such matters as consumer safety, tax laws, and relationships with other nations usually reflect corporate influence.

A corporation is an organization owned by shareholders. These shareholders have limited liability and limited control. *Limited liability* means they cannot be held financially responsible for actions of the corporation. Shareholders are not expected to pay debts the corporation owes. At the same time, they do not have a direct voice in the day-to-day operations of the firm. Shareholders are formally entitled to vote regularly for members of the board of directors. But in practice, candidates are routinely approved as recommended by the existing board. The real control of a corporation rests with the board of directors and management.

Top corporate officials can have tremendous influence on government decisions. Because of their personal wealth and organizational connections, corporate officials are able to reward or punish elected government officials through investment decisions. For example, suppose a town depends on a single large corporation for jobs and other economic advantages.

Political and Economic Institutions

Applying Sociology

EMPLOYEE RIGHTS

The Supreme Court of the United States has historically granted employers a great deal of power over their employees. For example, in 1878, a New York company was able to require its employees to attend church on Sundays.

Even today, some employee rights are curtailed at work. For instance, employees can be prevented from printing and distributing a critical newsletter to customers of their companies. Of recent concern is the right of employers to track workers' movements with GPS technology and to read personal e-mail.

Today there is a growing employee rights movement that is pushing for greater political and legal protection. Employee rights groups are looking to secure a range of rights concerning job security, privacy on and off the job, and the ability to bring grievances against an employer.

Many of these rights already exist in some form; others need to be discussed with employers. There is one thing most employers and employees agree on: If employees take a balanced approach to pursuing their rights on the job and recognize the legitimate needs of employers, both individuals and organizations will benefit.

▶ **CRITICAL THINKING**

1. **Summarizing** What kinds of rights are employee rights groups concerned with ensuring?
2. **Finding the Main Idea** Why do you think a balanced approach to employee rights is most effective for all parties involved?

---

facility something created to serve a particular function, such as manufacturing or health care

interlocking directorates shared directorates that result when heads of corporations sit on one another's boards

enhance to improve; strengthen

conglomerate a network of unrelated businesses operating under one umbrella

Corporate officials are deciding whether to increase their operation in this town or move some of the **facilities** to another town, which would endanger local jobs. Town officials are likely to do what they can to make corporate officials happy, so that new investment will be made locally.

In 2010, the U.S. Supreme Court allowed corporations to exert even more influence on the political system by allowing them, for the first time in history, to spend their profits on political advertising. The Court ruled that they had the same right to freedom of speech (through advertising) as individual people.

The political clout of large corporations is multiplied through **interlocking directorates**. A directorate is another name for the board of directors. Directorates interlock when the heads of corporations sit on one another's boards. Although by law competing corporations may not have interlocking directorates, such directorates are legal for noncompeting corporations. For example, one study found that 13 members of the board of the financial services company Citigroup served on the boards of 25 other corporations in 2005. It is not difficult to imagine the political power created by a web of interlocking directors among already powerful corporations.

The political power of corporations can also be **enhanced** through **conglomerates**—networks of unrelated businesses operating under a single corporate umbrella. General Electric, a conglomerate, holds companies in such different areas as household appliances, airplane engines, nuclear power, solar power, health care products, software services, and water-treatment products. A listing of the company holdings stretches over several screens on their website.

✓ **READING PROGRESS CHECK**

Explaining How do interlocking directorates increase the power of corporations?

Revenues of Multinationals		GDPs of Countries
Walmart: $408 billion	vs.	Sweden: $406 billion
Exxon Mobil: $285 billion	vs.	Thailand: $263 billion
Bank of America: $150 billion	vs.	Kuwait: $148 billion
Ford Motor Company: $118 billion	vs.	Ukraine: $113 billion
Nestle: $99 billion	vs.	Vietnam: $91 billion
IBM: $95 billion	vs.	Morocco: $90 billion

Sources: World Bank and *Fortune Magazine*

◀ CHART

REVENUES OF MULTINATIONAL CORPORATIONS COMPARED TO GDPS OF SOME COUNTRIES, 2010

This chart compares revenues of some of the largest multinationals with the gross domestic product (GDP) of some countries.

▶ **CRITICAL THINKING**

1. *Analyzing Visuals* Which two multinationals have the highest revenues?
2. *Analyzing* Why are multinationals so powerful in the United States and other countries?

Multinational Corporations

GUIDING QUESTION *What are the effects of multinational corporations?*

The political influence of corporations is not confined to their countries of origin. The world is increasingly influenced by **multinationals**—firms based in highly industrialized societies with operating facilities throughout the world. Improved communication and transportation technology have allowed these companies to exert wide control over global operations.

If we combined all the political and economic units in the world and then chose the 100 largest units, 44 would be multinational corporations rather than countries. Several corporations based in the United States, including Walmart, Exxon Mobil, Chevron, General Electric, General Motors, Ford Motor Company, Bank of America, Hewlett Packard, and AT&T, have sales volumes exceeding the annual economic output of some industrialized nations.

Defenders of multinationals argue that these corporations provide developing countries with technology, capital, foreign markets, and products that would otherwise be unavailable to them. Critics claim that multinationals actually harm the economies of the foreign nations in which they operate by exploiting natural resources, disrupting local economies, introducing inappropriate technologies and products, and increasing the amount of income inequality. Multinationals, these critics note, rely on inexpensive labor or abundant raw materials in developing nations while returning their profits to shareholders in rich nations. Multinationals' domination of their industries has made it difficult for less economically developed nations to establish new companies that can compete with the multinationals.

multinationals firms based in highly industrialized societies with operating facilities throughout the world

✓ **READING PROGRESS CHECK**

Making Connections What changes in communications and transportation technology have allowed multinationals to grow?

LESSON 4 REVIEW

Reviewing Vocabulary
1. *Making Connections* What do interlocking directorates and conglomerates have in common?
2. *Identifying* Where are most multinationals based?

Using Your Notes
3. *Listing* Use your notes to list some sources of corporate power.

Answering the Guiding Questions
4. *Defining/Explaining* What is a corporation, and how can a corporation exert power?
5. *Analyzing* What are the effects of multinational corporations?

Writing Activity
6. *Informative/Explanatory* Identify one multinational corporation from which you have made a purchase. Explain how you think that product was affected by the fact that the corporation was multinational rather than just a national or local company.

Political and Economic Institutions

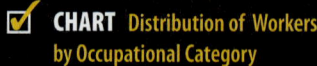

There's More Online!

- ☑ **CARTOON** Corporate Downsizing
- ☑ **CHART** Distribution of Workers by Occupational Category
- ☑ **GRAPHIC ORGANIZER** Work in the Modern Economy
- ☑ **IMAGE** Semi-Employment
- ☑ **SELF-CHECK QUIZ**

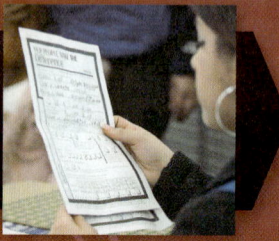

LESSON 5
Work in the Modern Economy

ESSENTIAL QUESTION • *How does the interaction between political systems and economic systems affect society?*

Reading HELPDESK

Academic Vocabulary
- capacity
- disposable

Content Vocabulary
- primary sector
- secondary sector
- tertiary sector
- occupations
- core tier
- peripheral tier
- downsizing
- contingent employment

TAKING NOTES:
Key Ideas and Details

ORGANIZING As you read about work in the modern economy, use a graphic organizer like the one below to record details.

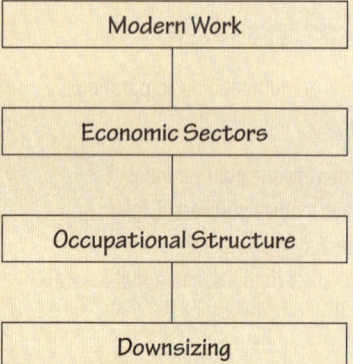

IT MATTERS BECAUSE
Workers today face a changing job structure. More corporations are downsizing and replacing full-time employees with consultants or temporary workers. Evidence indicates that this trend is having some negative consequences.

The Changing Nature of Work

GUIDING QUESTION *What are the three sectors of the economy, and how have they changed over time?*

To understand work in modern society you need to be familiar with the three basic economic sectors. They are the *primary*, *secondary*, and *tertiary* sectors.

The Economic Sectors

The **primary sector** of an economy depends on the natural environment to produce economic goods. The types of jobs in this sector vary widely—for example, farmer, miner, fisherman, timber worker, and rancher. In the **secondary sector**, manufactured products are made from raw materials. Occupations in this sector include factory workers of all types, from those who produce computers to those who turn out baseball cards. Those in the secondary sector are popularly known as blue-collar workers. Employees in the **tertiary sector** provide services. If today you went to school, filled your car with gas, stopped by the bank, and visited your doctor, you spent time and money in the tertiary (service) sector. Other service industries include insurance, real estate, retail sales, and entertainment from radio and television to sports. Many people in the service sector are white-collar workers.

Historical Changes in the Sectors

Obviously, the primary sector dominated the preindustrial economy. At that stage of economic development, goods were made by hand. This balance began to change with the mechanization of farming in the agricultural economy. Mechanical inventions (such as the cotton gin, plow,

Workers by Occupational Category, 2010

Occupational Category	Percentage of Total	Percentage Male	Percentage Female
Management, professional, and related occupations	37.2	48.5	51.5
Sales and office occupations	24.0	37.1	62.9
Service occupations	17.7	43.2	56.8
Natural resources, construction, and maintenance occupations	9.4	95.4	4.6
Production, transportation, and material-moving occupations	11.6	78.8	21.2

Source: U.S. Census Bureau, *Statistical Abstract of the United States: 2012*

◀ CHART

WORKERS BY OCCUPATIONAL CATEGORY

This table shows the percentage of American workers who are employed in each occupational category and how the category is broken down by gender.

▶ **CRITICAL THINKING**

1. **Analyzing Visuals** Which occupational category is most heavily male? Which is most heavily female?
2. **Hypothesizing** Which occupational categories would you predict will gain the most jobs in the next decade? Why?

primary sector that part of the economy producing goods directly from the natural environment

secondary sector that part of the economy engaged in manufacturing goods

tertiary sector that part of the economy providing services

Sociologists divide different types of jobs into sectors.

▶ **CRITICAL THINKING**

Making Connections To which sector do these workers belong? Why?

and tractor), along with the application of new scientific methods (including fertilization and crop rotation), dramatically increased crop yields. During the 1800s, the average farmer could feed around five workers. Today, the figure is 155. At the same time that production increased, the demand for farm labor decreased. In 1900, around 40 percent of the labor force was employed in the primary sector. By the early twenty-first century, less than 1 percent of the American labor force worked in the primary sector.

With other technological advancements in industry (power looms, motors of all types, and electrical power) came the shift of agricultural workers from farms to factories, ushering in the secondary sector. Just as in agriculture, technological developments permitted greater production with fewer workers. Since World War II, the fastest-growing occupations in the secondary sector have been white-collar—managers, professionals, sales workers, and clerical workers. In 1956, white-collar workers for the first time accounted for a larger proportion of the American labor force than blue-collar workers.

Technological progress did not end with the secondary sector. As relative growth in the proportion of workers in goods-producing jobs was decreasing, the demand for labor in the tertiary sector was increasing. Fueled by discoveries in computer science and their application to new technologies, the U.S. economy moved from a manufacturing base to a knowledge, or information, base. The current demand is for people who can manage information and deliver services. More than 80 percent of Americans now work in management, professional, service, sales, and office occupations. Scientific research also fuels new health care products and techniques, which has expanded that part of the tertiary sector. The ever-increasing number of women employed outside the home also has influenced the American workplace.

Other service jobs have increased in recent decades as well. Increases in tourism, entertainment, and professional sports have spawned jobs in hotels and restaurants.

✓ **READING PROGRESS CHECK**

Describing In which sector of the economy do you hope to work? Why?

Occupational Structure

GUIDING QUESTION What is the occupational structure in the United States?

Occupations are categories of jobs that involve similar activities at different work locations. For example, teacher, dental assistant, computer programmer, film producer, and electrician are all occupations because each position requires similar training and involves some standard operations. The United States Department of Labor has identified more than 800 occupations, with hundreds more specialties within the broader occupational categories.

The Occupational Structure

A two-tier occupational structure has developed in the United States. One level—the **core tier**—includes jobs with large firms that have dominant positions within their industries. Computer technology, pharmaceutical, and aerospace firms are examples of companies in the core tier. About 46 percent of American workers at private companies work for companies with more than 500 employees. The other level—the **peripheral tier**—is composed of jobs in smaller firms that either are competing for business left over from core firms or are engaged in less profitable industries, such as agriculture, textiles, and small-scale retail trade. Most American workers—around 54 percent—are employed by these companies.

Historically, jobs in the core tier pay more, offer better benefits, and provide longer-term employment. This is not surprising, since the firms involved are large and highly profitable. Peripheral jobs are characterized by low pay, few or no benefits, and short-term employment. These features follow from the weaker competitive position and the smaller size of the employing firms.

The industries that have supplied most of the core jobs in the United States have been scaling back during the past 20 years, laying off experienced workers and not hiring new ones. As early as the 1980s, large firms were reducing the workforce. In fact, more than 3.8 million manufacturing jobs in the United States were eliminated between just 2000 and 2008, one out of every five jobs.

The recession that began in about 2008 caused unemployment to rise to as high as 10 percent in 2009, but the rates dropped to about 8 percent by 2012. Unskilled jobs, however, are generally leaving the United States for other parts of the world, where wages are lower. In the United States, nearly all unskilled occupations are projected to see drops in employment levels in the coming years.

Middle-class jobs are also at risk. Some 300,000 office and administrative jobs disappeared from 2004 to 2008. This trend has had a profound effect on the U.S. economy and American workers. The U.S. economy has been losing higher-paying jobs, and the jobs that replace them do not pay as well. Many of the new jobs that are projected to be created in the coming years pay at or below the poverty level for a family of four. This helps explain why, since the 1970s, the majority of workers have been losing economic ground. Whereas 30 years ago one American worker alone could support a family, the two-paycheck married couple has become the norm today.

This process, known as *downwaging*, is expected to continue into the second decade of the twenty-first century. Many sociologists believe that the job loss and downwaging trends threaten the American dream.

✓ **READING PROGRESS CHECK**

Explaining How has downwaging affected American workers?

Sociologists also assign tiers to the occupational structure according to the size of the company and its position in the particular industry.

▶ **CRITICAL THINKING**

Making Connections To which tier does this worker belong?

Large firms have been cutting their workforces for many years, including both office and manufacturing jobs.

▶ **CRITICAL THINKING**

Making Connections How did the recession that began in 2008 affect unemployment rates?

Downsizing and Contingent Employment

GUIDING QUESTION Why have downsizing and contingent employment become widespread?

Clearly, the occupational structure in the United States has changed dramatically over the past few decades. *Downsizing* and *contingent employment*, two strategies used by top management, reduce employment in core industries. A discussion of these related practices will help explain why the U.S. occupational structure is changing. **Downsizing** is the process by which companies reduce the size of their full-time workforces. **Contingent employment** involves hiring people on a part-time or short-term basis. Although corporate downsizing had been going on since the late 1970s, it accelerated during the 1980s and 1990s and continued into the recession beginning in 2008.

Part of the motivation for downsizing is based on top management's belief that their companies employ a surplus of people and that, thanks to computers and other labor-saving technology, they can operate at full **capacity** using fewer employees. Top management also points to lower profits caused by increasing foreign competition. Foreign competition is held responsible for the loss of about 1 million U.S. jobs between 1991 and 2007.

Companies have responded to increased foreign competition by moving operations overseas and by replacing full-time employees with part-time workers hired to do a limited amount of work for a specified time period. Contingent employment is a cost-cutting device. Unlike full-time employees, contingent workers receive lower pay and are not entitled to expensive benefits, such as vacation time, health insurance, and retirement benefits.

Some recent research indicates that downsizing and contingent employment often do not achieve their stated goals of gaining efficiency and competitiveness. At the same time, it is clear that these approaches are creating greater polarization between those who control capital and those who do not.

occupation category of job that involves similar activities at different work locations

core tier the part of the occupational structure composed of large firms dominating their industries

peripheral tier the part of the occupational structure composed of smaller, less profitable firms

downsizing the process by which companies reduce their workforces

contingent employment the hiring of part-time, short-term workers

capacity the full size or rate

disposable unimportant; something that can be discarded or easily replaced

"I still say we're stretched dangerously thin."

◀ CARTOON

CORPORATE DOWNSIZING

Corporate downsizing is associated with higher unemployment and lower pay.

▶ **CRITICAL THINKING**

1. **Paraphrasing** How would you paraphrase the message of this cartoon?
2. **Identifying Perspectives** How do corporate managers view downsizing? How do workers see it?

Political and Economic Institutions

One way companies have responded to the new market conditions is by reducing full-time employees and increasing contingent and part-time workers.

▶ **CRITICAL THINKING**

Explaining What benefits do companies get by changing their workforces to more part-time and contingent workers?

Quick Case Study

TEENS IN THE MODERN ECONOMY
Many young people have jobs. What kind of experience do they have in the changing modern economy of the United States?

Procedure
1. Create a survey in which you ask fellow students about their work histories. Include categories for where they worked, what type of jobs they had, whether it was contingent or permanent employment, and why they left.
2. Distribute your survey to ten different students.

Analysis
As you collect the surveys and read the responses, answer the following questions:
1. Were there any patterns in the answers to your survey? Did your classmates have similar work histories?
2. Were the classmates who responded more or less likely to be employed in a core-tier or a peripheral-tier job?
3. Were the classmates who responded more or less likely to be engaged in contingent employment or permanent employment?

Some critics believe the **"disposable"** workforce is the most important trend in business today. They contend that it is fundamentally changing the relationship between American workers and their employers.

Recent surveys indicate that about half of all workers feel very satisfied with their salary and their job security and about 60 to 80 percent feel very loyal to their company. But there is a large gap between the percentage of employees who feel loyal to the company and the percentage who believe that the company is loyal to them, ranging from 18 to 33 percent below the number who felt loyal to their company. Employee trust in management has been eroding. Many workers have lost faith in management's commitment to them. Trust and loyalty are difficult to maintain when employees do not believe company policies treat them fairly. Additional research will help focus attention on the full effects of corporate downsizing and contingent employment.

✓ **READING PROGRESS CHECK**

Defining What is the "disposable" workforce?

LESSON 5 REVIEW

Reviewing Vocabulary
1. *Explaining* What is the relationship between the core tier and the peripheral tier of the occupational structure?

Using Your Notes
2. *Describing* Use your notes to write a few sentences that describe the changes in the occupational structure over the years.

Answering the Guiding Questions
3. *Identifying* What are the three sectors of the economy, and how have they changed over time?

4. *Describing* What is the occupational structure in the United States?
5. *Explaining* Why have downsizing and contingent employment become widespread?

Writing Activity
6. *Informative/Explanatory* Think of a job you have held or a family member holds. Identify the job and classify it according to sector and tier. Write an essay explaining whether it might be subject to downsizing or contingent employment.

CHAPTER 13 Assessment

Directions: On a separate sheet of paper, answer the questions below. Make sure you read carefully and answer all parts of the questions.

Lesson Review

Lesson 1

1. **Explaining** Are most modern governments based on charismatic authority? Explain.
2. **Identifying Significance** Explain the significance of agricultural economies and city-states as related to formal governmental structures.

Lesson 2

3. **Identifying Perspectives** What do you think are the causes of voter apathy?
4. **Making Predictions** Discuss the extent to which you think women and minorities are represented in the power elite. Provide a strongly supported prediction as to whether this is likely to change in the future.

Lesson 3

5. **Analyzing** Is there a pure capitalist economy in the world? Why or why not?
6. **Identifying Cause and Effect** Discuss the cause-and-effect relationship between competition and monopolies and oligopolies.

Lesson 4

7. **Categorizing** Explain why some corporations, but not others, command the attention of government decision makers. Identify at least two U.S. corporations that have commanded such attention.
8. **Identifying Perspectives** Identify two sides of the argument related to the relationship between multinational corporations and developing countries. Discuss your opinion regarding the issue.

Lesson 5

9. **Interpreting Significance** Explain the impact of the mechanization of farming on the dominance of the primary sector.

10. **Comparing and Contrasting** Create a Venn diagram to compare and contrast the core tier and the peripheral tier.

Critical Thinking

11. **Defending** Capitalism encourages the accumulation of wealth, which often affects political activity. Select a pro or con position using one of the following statements and write an editorial supported by information from the chapter:

    "The government should place limits on the amount of wealth permitted to be accumulated by an individual."
    "The government should limit the political influence of the wealthy."

DBQ Analyzing Primary Sources

PRIMARY SOURCE

Use the document below to answer the following question.

12. **Identifying Bias** What is the nature of the store that is being described and how does it fit into a discussion about the power elite of a society?

"Our goal is to make prices so low that even our employees could shop here."

Need Extra Help?

If You've Missed Question	1	2	3	4	5	6	7	8	9	10	11	12
Go to page	365–366	367	370–372	375	378	379	383	385	386–387	388	370–390	375

CHAPTER 13 Assessment

Directions: On a separate sheet of paper, answer the questions below. Make sure you read carefully and answer all parts of the questions.

College and Career Readiness Skills

13 *Critical Listening* Review the feature titled *Employee Rights* in this chapter. Then conduct online research and utilize the *Employee Rights* feature and your research to compile a list of at least seven employee rights. These can be rights that currently exist through law or rights that groups are currently advocating. After you compile your list, conduct two interviews, one of an employer or business owner, such as a restaurant or store owner or manager, and one of a student or other community member who holds a nonmanagerial position. Ask questions to determine which of these rights employees at the business currently hold. Listen carefully to the information and perspectives provided in the interviews. Then write two memos you think should be sent to employers to explain which of these rights should and should not be offered to employees. Write one memo from the perspective of the employee and the other from the perspective of the employee or business owner.

21st Century Skills
CREATING AND USING GRAPHS, CHARTS, DIAGRAMS AND TABLES

14 *Identifying Perspectives and Differing Interpretations* Use the information from the *Workers by Occupational Category, 2010* table in Lesson 5 to create a graph that depicts the same information. Then use perspectives gained from your graph to develop two editorial cartoons based on different aspects of the graph. Explain how developing the graph helped you better understand the data that gave rise to your editorial cartoons.

Exploring the Essential Question

15 *Identifying Central Issues* Suppose you are majoring in political science in college and you want to teach high school students after you graduate. For one of your college assignments, you have surveyed high school students across the nation. Some have stated that their political science classes are very interesting, but others have told you their classes are dry and dull. Before you graduate from college, you want to begin work to develop a fascinating unit on the effects of interaction between political systems and economic systems on society. You are excited about presenting this unit to your classes when you begin teaching. You plan to include Web links in your unit so students can access relevant sources. Develop an outline for your course, including an overview and at least three points from each lesson. For each entry in the outline, explain how you will make the information interesting and relevant for your high school students.

Research and Presentation

16 *Gathering Information* An ongoing American debate focuses on the responsibility of the corporation in society. One viewpoint holds that the sole responsibility of a corporation is to generate income for its shareholders. Another viewpoint holds that corporations are charged with a "social responsibility" to their own communities and to society in general. Some corporations are known for their efforts in acting with an eye toward social responsibility. Conduct online research to locate at least two of these corporations. Print out and then summarize their mission statements, and list specific actions they take to meet the mission as they improve their own communities and the nation and/or world.

17 *Simulating* As you consider the information you have gathered, formulate an idea for a corporation you would like to start. Keep in mind that corporations can be small; in fact, some types of corporations can consist of a single person acting as president, owner, and shareholder. On the computer, create a prototype of a website to showcase your corporation's name, major type of business, and mission statement. Additionally, explain specific steps your corporation will take to fulfill its social responsibility. Then share your prototype website with the class.

Need Extra Help?

If You've Missed Question	13	14	15	16	17
Go to page	384	387	364–390	383–390	383–390

Religion

ESSENTIAL QUESTION • What roles does religion play in society?

networks
There's More Online about religion and society.

CHAPTER 14

Technology & Society
Religion and Technology

Lesson 1
Religion and Sociology

Lesson 2
Religious Organization and Religiosity

Lesson 3
Religion in the United States

Sociology Matters...

Some of the earliest European settlers came to America so that they could practice their religion freely. Throughout history, religion has played a major role in American life and has been the source of both inspiration and conflict for many.

In the 1960s, during a time of social unrest, John Lennon, a member of the Beatles, was quoted as saying their musical group was "more popular than Jesus." The angry reaction from many Americans forced Lennon to apologize. Even though fewer Americans said that religion was very important in their lives, many still took their religion very seriously. The same is true today.

◀ Construction of the Washington National Cathedral, a cathedral of the Episcopal Church, was begun in 1907 and completed in 1990.

©Hisham Ibrahim/Corbis

393

CHAPTER 14
Technology & Society

Religion and Technology

Religious leaders tap into technology to connect with followers and others.

Houses of worship are one place where people usually turn off their smartphones, cell phones, tablet computers, or other gadgets. Yet religious leaders themselves are realizing how technology not only keeps them connected to current worshipers and members but also can be used to attract new followers. Consider the impact of technology on prayer requests. Instead of waiting for a phone call from a worshiper or the next religious ceremony or meeting, a religious leader can instantly retrieve prayer requests on his or her smartphone, tablet computer, or from the social-networking site for the house of worship he or she leads.

How do religious and faith-based groups get the "word" out? Televangelism was an early use of technology. It began in the 1950s when some religious leaders began to use television to spread religious ideas and maintain ties with followers. Today, video-conferencing technology can reach followers or others who are considering joining a religious group, locally or globally. Such forms of technology are much cheaper than sending missionaries around the world to spread religious beliefs. These new technologies can also reach more people. To connect with members who are shut in at home due to illness or who have transportation challenges, some religious groups have even used live streaming to transmit their religious services or prayers over the Internet. An Islamic website provides live broadcasts that can then be added to a follower's personal social media site.

Some people think that communication technology removes the one-on-one, in-person connection that religious groups have fostered for centuries. Despite this concern among some critics, the trend for religious groups to use technology continues to grow. For example, Pope Benedict XVI blessed a smartphone application that would help Roman Catholics record their sins and experience the Catholic ritual of confession without a priest. The Jewish community has created an online magazine for those who wish to find out about applications that relate to their faith.

PERCENTAGE OF RELIGIOUS INSTITUTIONS THAT USE TECHNOLOGY TO STAY CONNECTED TO FOLLOWERS AND MEMBERS

INFOGRAPHIC Explore the interactive version of the infographic on Networks.

The use of **email** by congregations more than **doubled** from 2000 to 2010.

90% email

13% BLOGS According to one study of **Christian bloggers**, most of the **writers** were males and most were members of the clergy.

A majority of **congregations** with **websites** use them to **communicate** with members. They list events on calendars, present needs for **volunteers or opportunities** for providing service, and **present news.**

WEBSITES 69%

CHURCHES AND SPIRITUAL TEACHERS USE PODCASTS TO PRESENT SERMONS, INFORMAL TALKS, OR INTERVIEWS. **12%**

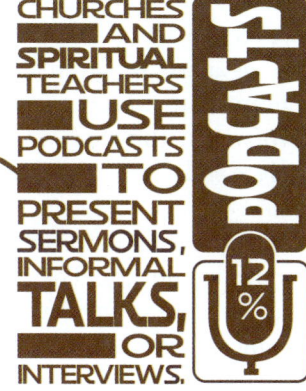

SOCIAL MEDIA 41%

Increased use of **facebook** may well signal a shift and even a **positive** trend in the use of technology by religious groups. Currently, few congregational websites are **interactive** or updated regularly. On the other hand, **facebook** pages have a **dynamic** interactive quality.

OTHER USES INCLUDE A RANGE OF TECHNOLOGIES FROM PHONE CALLING SYSTEMS TO STREAMING RELIGIOUS SERVICES.

Thinking Like a Sociologist

1 Identifying Cause and Effect
How has the use of technology affected religious and faith-based groups?

2 Speculating
Do you think that religious groups will expand their use of technology in the future to reach followers and others? Explain.

Religion **395**

networks

There's More Online!

- ☑ **CHART** Theoretical Perspectives: Religion
- ☑ **CHART** Major World Religions
- ☑ **GRAPH** World Population by Religion
- ☑ **MAP** Religions of the World
- ☑ **SELF-CHECK QUIZ**

Reading HELPDESK

Academic Vocabulary
- maturity
- thereby

Content Vocabulary
- religion
- sacred
- profane
- legitimate
- spirit of capitalism
- Protestant ethic

TAKING NOTES:
Key Ideas and Details

ORGANIZING As you read about religion and sociology, use a graphic organizer like the one below to record details.

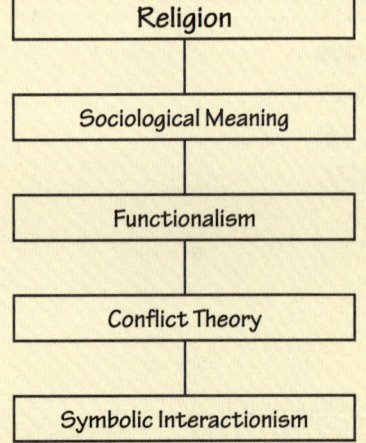

LESSON 1
Religion and Sociology

ESSENTIAL QUESTION • *What roles does religion play in society?*

IT MATTERS BECAUSE

Religion separates the sacred from the profane. Sociologists do not judge the validity of religions but study what can be measured and observed. Religion legitimates the structure of society, promotes social unity, and provides a sense of meaning and belonging. Karl Marx argued that religion is used to maintain the group in power. Max Weber believed it could promote social change.

The Sociological Meaning of Religion

GUIDING QUESTION How do sociologists interpret religion?

A **religion** is a unified system of beliefs and practices concerned with sacred things. This definition comes from Émile Durkheim, whose work was based on studies of the Australian aborigines in the late nineteenth century. According to Durkheim, every society distinguishes between the **sacred**—things and ideas that are set apart and given a special meaning that goes beyond, or transcends, immediate existence—and the **profane**, or nonsacred, aspects of life. Profane in this context does not mean unholy. It simply means commonplace and not involving the supernatural. Another word for profane is *secular*.

Sacred things take on a public character that makes them appear important in themselves; profane things do not. The particular things considered sacred vary from culture to culture. For example, Bolivian tin miners attach sacred meaning to figures of the devil and of bulls. Because Americans do not share these religious beliefs, these cultural items are part of their nonsacred, or profane, world.

Sociologists study religion without becoming involved in theological issues. By focusing on the cultural and social aspects of religion, sociologists avoid questions about the ultimate validity of any particular religion. This point is so important that it needs more explanation.

The sociological study of religion involves looking at a set of meanings and practices attached to a world beyond human observation. Because this nonphysical world cannot be directly observed, and therefore studied with scientific methods, sociologists limit their study to what can be observed: the beliefs and practices related to sacred things.

It is essential that sociologists remain objective in their study. Religion draws strong emotional responses and is filled with value systems and statements. Sociologists are not in the business of determining which religions people ought to follow. They must keep their own faith personal while investigating the *social* dimensions of religion. Like people in any other occupation, sociologists themselves follow a variety of religions. As scientists, they cannot study the unobservable, so they approach religion as a human creation and focus on social aspects of religion that can be measured and observed.

✓ **READING PROGRESS CHECK**

Summarizing In what ways do sociologists limit themselves when they study religion?

Functionalism and Religion

GUIDING QUESTION *How do functionalists view religion?*

Religion exists in some form in virtually all societies. The earliest evidence of religion and religious customs and taboos has been traced as far back as 50,000 B.C. Humans had, by then, begun to bury their dead, a practice that some scholars think was based on the belief in existence after death. Evidence of religious practices appears in many ancient cultures.

Émile Durkheim was among the first sociologists to study religion scientifically. He wondered why all societies have some form of religion. In *The Elementary Forms of Religious Life* (1912), he offered an explanation rooted in the function religion performs for society. The essential function of religion, he believed, is to provide social solidarity and cohesiveness through the use of sacred symbols and ceremonies. Through religious rituals, groups remind themselves of their shared past and future. Sociologists now identify several social functions of religion.

How the American flag should be treated has been a subject of debate in recent years.

▶ **CRITICAL THINKING**

Exploring Issues Do you consider the American flag a sacred or a profane object? Why?

religion a unified system of beliefs and practices concerned with sacred things

sacred holy; set apart and given a special meaning that goes beyond, or transcends, immediate existence

profane nonsacred

A Global Perspective

RELIGIONS OF THE WORLD

This map shows where followers of the major world religions live throughout the world. In Western democracies, Christianity dominates. In the Middle East and Africa, Islam, Judaism, and indigenous religions are practiced. In South Asia and East Asia, Hinduism, Buddhism, and Sikhism are the main religions.

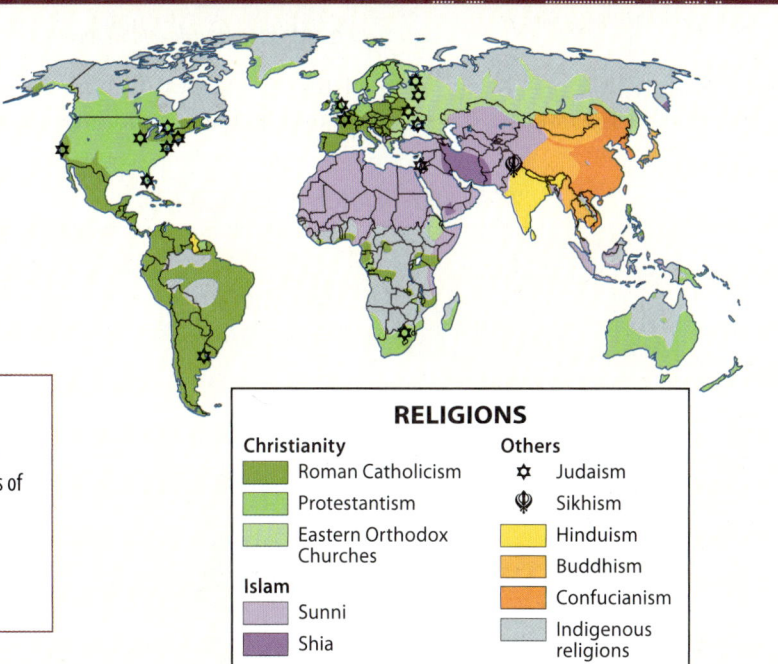

RELIGIONS

Christianity
- Roman Catholicism
- Protestantism
- Eastern Orthodox Churches

Islam
- Sunni
- Shia

Others
- Judaism
- Sikhism
- Hinduism
- Buddhism
- Confucianism
- Indigenous religions

Geography Connection

1. ***Places and Regions*** What generalizations can you make about the religions practiced in different regions of the world?
2. ***The Uses of Geography*** How has globalization affected the demographics of religion?

legitimate to justify or give official approval to

- *Religion gives formal approval to existing social arrangements.* Religious doctrines **legitimate** the status quo. Religion justifies social norms and customs. A society's religion explains why the society is—and should be—the way it is. It tells us why some people have power and others do not, why some are rich and others poor, why some are common and others elite. According to Durkheim, legitimation is the central function of religion.

- *Religion encourages a sense of unity.* Religion, according to Durkheim, is the glue that holds society together. Without religion, society would be chaotic. Durkheim suggested that all societies must have religious commitments.

- *Religion creates distinctions between things and groups.* Religion separates sacred and profane objects and divides people into those who believe and those that do not. In this respect, religion has, throughout history, also divided societies and even led to war. Today, religion divides Catholics and Protestants in Northern Ireland and Muslims and Jews in the Middle East.

- *Religion provides a sense of understanding.* Religion gives people meaning beyond day-to-day life. People mark important events in life—birth, sexual **maturity**, marriage, and death—with religious ceremonies and explain such events in religious terms. Religion gives believers a sense of their place in the cosmos and gives significance to a short, uncertain existence.

maturity adulthood

- *Religion promotes a sense of belonging.* Religious organizations provide opportunities for people to share important ideas, ways of life, and ethnic or racial backgrounds. Religion supplies a kind of group identity. People usually join religious organizations freely and feel a degree of influence within them. For many people, membership in a religious organization provides a feeling of belonging that helps counteract the depersonalization of modern society.

✓ **READING PROGRESS CHECK**

Analyzing Do you think religion in the United States today promotes social unity or social divisions? Why?

GRAPH

WORLD POPULATION BY RELIGION, 2010

This graph compares the percentage of the world population belonging to each religion.

▶ **CRITICAL THINKING**

1. **Hypothesizing** Do you think the percentages of believers in particular religions has been changing rapidly? Why or why not?

2. **Making Connections** Which area of the world do you connect with Hinduism?

Conflict Theory and Religion

GUIDING QUESTION *How do conflict theorists view religion?*

Conflict theory focuses on how religion works to either inhibit or encourage social change. Two early and important sociologists who looked at religion from these perspectives are Karl Marx and Max Weber.

Marx and Religion

Karl Marx believed that human beings created religion to justify economic and social inequalities. Once people create a unified system of beliefs and practices, they treat it as something sacred and beyond their control. They become "alienated" from the religious system and misidentify it as a binding force to which they must conform. The ruling class uses religion to justify their economic, political, and social advantages over the lower classes. In turn, the lower classes accept their poverty

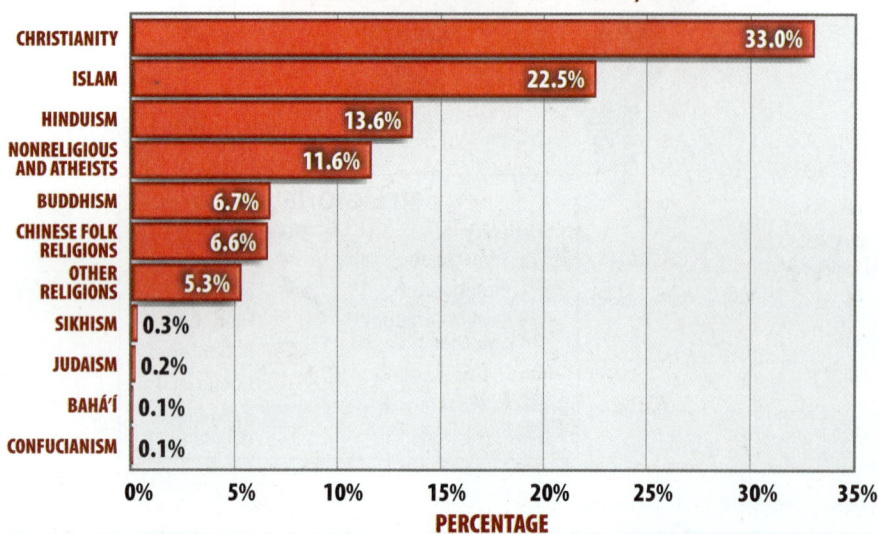

WORLD POPULATION BY RELIGION, 2010

Religion	Percentage
CHRISTIANITY	33.0%
ISLAM	22.5%
HINDUISM	13.6%
NONRELIGIOUS AND ATHEISTS	11.6%
BUDDHISM	6.7%
CHINESE FOLK RELIGIONS	6.6%
OTHER RELIGIONS	5.3%
SIKHISM	0.3%
JUDAISM	0.2%
BAHÁ'Í	0.1%
CONFUCIANISM	0.1%

Source: *Britannica Book of the Year, 2011.*

Connecting Sociology to History

RELIGIOUS-BASED CONFLICTS

Religious-based conflicts have erupted in many parts of the world. Some violence has been aimed at civilians and religious adherents and others at military personnel. In his book Terror in the Mind of God: The Global Rise of Religious Violence, *Mark Juergensmeyer uses the perspectives of symbolic interactionism and conflict theory to argue that religious followers are "actors" in a larger dramatic performance, or "Theater of War," when they commit violent actions. They connect religion with violence to promote their beliefs and to empower themselves. In his book, he describes these acts of violence from around the globe.*

Religious-based conflicts have intensified in some regions of the world in the twenty-first century.

PRIMARY SOURCE

"The catastrophic bombings of the American embassies, the World Trade Center, the Oklahoma City federal building, and the American military residence in Saudi Arabia; the burning of abortion clinics and the shooting of a clinic doctor in the face; the assassination of Israeli and Indian political leaders; the massacre of innocent worshipers at a mosque; the slaying of a busload of Hindu pilgrims in the Himalayan foothills by a band of radical Sikh youths; the agonizing effects of the nerve gas attack in a Tokyo subway; and the bloody confusion of suicide bombings on the otherwise peaceful streets of Jerusalem and Tel Aviv—all of these are not just incidents of violence. They are acts of deliberately exaggerated violence."

—from *Terror in the Mind of God: The Global Rise of Religious Violence*, 2003

DBQ ▶ CRITICAL THINKING

1. **Making Connections** How does sociology approach violent acts of terrorism by religious followers?
2. **Researching** Research one of the acts of violence listed in the excerpt and write a summary to explain how it fits into Juergensmeyer's description of actors performing in a "Theater of War."

---

and misery as God's will. Religion, Marx wrote, is an "opiate of the masses" that distracts the oppressed into serving the interests of the rich. Therefore, like Durkheim, Marx believed that religion legitimates traditions. Unlike Durkheim, however, Marx argued that religion actually undermines social unity and cohesion by reinforcing distinctions between the haves and the have-nots, **thereby** working against change and progress. Marx felt religion should be eliminated.

Weber Links Protestantism and Capitalism

Where Marx believed that religion works against social change, Max Weber suggested that religion sometimes encourages social change. He pointed to the relationship between Protestantism and the rise of capitalism. Weber wondered why capitalism emerged in northwestern Europe and America and not in other parts of the world. A possible answer lay in what he termed the *spirit of capitalism* and the *Protestant ethic*. Under capitalism, work became a moral obligation rather than a mere necessity. If businesses were to grow, money (capital) had to be put back into the businesses rather than spent. Investment for the future was more important than immediate consumption. All this Weber called the **spirit of capitalism**.

thereby by that means; because of that

spirit of capitalism the obligation to reinvest money in business rather than spend it

Religion	Number of Followers	Key Figure	Beliefs	Main Geographic Areas
Christianity	2,280,616,000	Jesus	Jesus is the son of God. People are saved and achieve eternal life by faith in Jesus.	Africa, North America, South America, Europe, Asia, Australia
Islam	1,553,188,720	Muhammad	Muhammad received the Quran (holy scriptures) from God. Central to Islamic beliefs are the Five Pillars: affirmation of the belief in Allah and his prophet Muhammad, group prayer, tithing, fasting during Ramadan, and a pilgrimage to Makkah.	North Africa, Asia
Hinduism	942,871,000	Unknown	Of many gods, Brahman is the creator of the universe. Life is determined by the law of karma (the spiritual force generated by one's actions, which determines one's next reincarnation).	South Asia
Buddhism	462,625,000	Siddhartha Gautama	Through adherence to the Eightfold Path (correct thought and behavior), one can escape from desire and suffering and achieve Nirvana (a state of bliss reached through denial of the self).	Africa, Asia, Southeast Asia
Sikhism	23,738,500	Gurū Nānak	There is one God who is formless and without qualities but can be known through meditation and heard directly.	South Asia
Judaism	14,824,000	Abraham	God has established a covenant with Jews. God, who expects them to pursue justice and live ethical lives, will one day usher in an era of universal peace.	North America, Europe, Southwest Asia

Source: *Britannica Book of the Year, 2011*

> **CHART**
>
> **MAJOR WORLD RELIGIONS**
> This chart summarizes characteristics of some of the world's major religions.
>
> ▶ **CRITICAL THINKING**
> 1. *Identifying* Which religions are widely practiced in Asia?
> 2. *Comparing* In what way does Buddhism differ from Judaism, Christianity, and Islam?

Protestant ethic a set of values, norms, beliefs, and attitudes stressing hard work, thrift, and self-discipline

Most major religions did not define hard work as an obligation or demand the reinvestment of capital for further profits, but some Protestant sects did. Theirs was a religion with values, norms, beliefs, and attitudes that favored the growth of modern capitalism. Weber referred to these values, norms, beliefs, and attitudes that stressed hard work, thrift, and self-discipline as the **Protestant ethic**.

The Protestant Ethic

The Protestant ethic is often associated with John Calvin (1509–1564), a Protestant theologian whose followers were known as Calvinists. Calvinist beliefs illustrate several features of the Protestant ethic. According to Calvin, God identifies his chosen by rewarding them in this world. Therefore, the more successful people were in this life, the more certain they were of being a member of God's select few. Consumption beyond necessity was considered sinful; those who engaged in self-pleasure were agents of the devil. Calvinists believed that the purpose of life was to glorify God on Earth through one's occupational calling. Because all material rewards were actually God's and the purpose of life was to glorify God, profits should be multiplied (through reinvestment) rather than used in the pursuit of personal pleasures.

☑ **READING PROGRESS CHECK**

Analyzing According to the Protestant ethic, how could a person tell which people were God's chosen few?

Symbolic Interactionism and Religion

GUIDING QUESTION *How do symbolic interactionists view religion?*

In 1967, sociologist Peter Berger captured the relationship between religion and symbolic interactionism in his book *The Sacred Canopy*. Berger explored the idea that humans use their religious traditions to create a canopy, or cover, based on

Theoretical Perspectives

RELIGION
This table shows that in examining religion, the three major perspectives focus on different aspects. One conclusion has been provided for each perspective's focus, but other conclusions could also be reached.

Theoretical Perspective	Focus	Conclusions
Functionalism	Look at the contributions of religion to society.	Religion legitimates social arrangements. It promotes social unity. It provides a sense of understanding. It encourages a sense of belonging.
Conflict Theory	Elites use religion to manipulate the masses. The masses accept oppression in hopes of a better existence in the afterlife.	Religion is used by the most powerful to justify their economic, political, and social advantages.
Symbolic Interactionism	People create symbolic meanings from their religious beliefs, rituals, and ideas.	People use their socially created symbolic meanings to guide everyday social interactions.

▶ **CRITICAL THINKING**
1. *Comparing and Contrasting* How are the conclusions for functionalism and symbolic interactionism similar and different?
2. *Analyzing* What is another conclusion that could be listed for the conflict theory?

symbolic meanings to "lay over" the secular world. These symbolic meanings are used to guide everyday social interactions. Religious beliefs, rituals, and ideas provide guidance by telling people the difference between the sacred and the profane and give them stability and security in a changing and uncertain existence.

Symbolic interactionism helps us understand the expression "there are no atheists in foxholes." Insecurity and uncertainty peak in the life-and-death situation of war, and the desire to regain security and certainty is a natural human response. Religious meanings, especially those related to an afterlife, can offer some relief. Japanese kamikaze pilots in World War II and some modern terrorists infuse their suicidal behavior with meaning by focusing on their reward beyond life. Less dramatically, people in troubled marriages can be strengthened by their commitment to uphold marriage vows they spoke in a place of worship.

✓ **READING PROGRESS CHECK**

Interpreting According to symbolic interactionism, what types of situations encourage people to seek certainty through religion?

LESSON 1 REVIEW

Reviewing Vocabulary
1. *Making Connections* How are the words *sacred* and *profane* related?
2. *Making Connections* How are the phrases *spirit of capitalism* and *Protestant ethic* related?

Using Your Notes
3. *Contrasting* Use your notes from the lesson to write two sentences that describe the two different views of religion within conflict theory.

Answering the Guiding Questions
4. *Analyzing* How do sociologists interpret religion?
5. *Explaining* How do functionalists view religion?
6. *Explaining* How do conflict theorists view religion?
7. *Explaining* How do symbolic interactionists view religion?

Writing Activity
8. *Informative/Explanatory* Review the functions of religion as defined by functionalists. Select one of those functions and give an example of a time when you have felt or observed religion fulfill that role.

There's More Online!

- ☑ **GRAPHIC ORGANIZER** Religious Organization and Religiosity
- ☑ **IMAGE** Charismatic Cultists
- ☑ **IMAGE** Prem Rawat
- ☑ **SELF-CHECK QUIZ**

Reading HELPDESK

Academic Vocabulary
- dimension
- commitment

Content Vocabulary
- church
- denomination
- sect
- religiosity

TAKING NOTES:
Key Ideas and Details

ORGANIZING As you read about religious organization and religiosity, use a graphic organizer like the one below to record details.

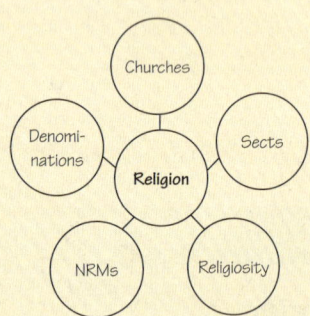

LESSON 2
Religious Organization and Religiosity

ESSENTIAL QUESTION • *What roles does religion play in society?*

IT MATTERS BECAUSE
The major forms of religious organization are churches, denominations, sects, and new religious movements. Religiosity—the ways people express their religious interests and convictions—can be analyzed in terms of five dimensions: belief, ritual, intellect, experience, and consequences.

Religious Organization

GUIDING QUESTION *How do sociologists distinguish among the basic types of religious organizations?*

In Western societies, most people practice religion through some organizational structure. For this reason, the nature of religious organization is an important component of the sociological study of religion. Scholars identified four basic types of religious organization: *church, denomination, sect,* and *new religious movements*.

Churches and Denominations

To sociologists, a **church** is a life-encompassing religious organization to which all members of a society belong. This type of religious organization exists when religion and the state are closely intertwined. For example, in Elizabethan England around 1600, Archbishop Richard Hooker of the Church of England wrote that "there is not any man of the Church of England but the same man is also a member of the commonwealth; nor any man a member of the commonwealth which is not also of the Church of England." In the early modern era, England was not the only state that had an official church. Other rulers officially adopted either Catholicism or a Protestant faith and required all subjects to follow that faith.

As you can see, the sociological definition of *church* is different from the one commonly used in American society. When most Americans talk about "churches," they have in mind organizations such as the Roman Catholic Church or one of the national Baptist organizations. But they are actually referring to what sociologists call *denominations*.

A **denomination** is one of several religious organizations that most members of a society accept as legitimate. Because denominations are not tied to the government, they are voluntary associations and competition among them for members is socially acceptable. Because it is one religious organization among many, a denomination generally accepts the values and norms of the secular society and the state, although it may at times oppose them. A denomination does not control the government or make the laws. Denominational leaders may be politically active, as is the case among many evangelical leaders in the United States. But no denomination dominates the society. As mentioned, most American "churches"—Methodist, Episcopalian, Presbyterian, Baptist, Roman Catholic, and Reform Judaism, for example—are actually denominations.

Sects

A **sect** is a religious organization formed when members of an existing religious organization break away in an attempt to reform the "parent" group. Generally, sect members believe that some valuable beliefs or traditions have been lost by the parent organization, and they form their own group to save these features. Thus, they see themselves not as establishing a new religious faith but as redeeming an existing one. The withdrawal of a sect from the parent group is usually psychological, but some sects go further and form communal groups physically apart from the larger society. One example is the group of Separatists, or Pilgrims, who landed at Plymouth in 1620. They wished to reform the Church of England from which they had separated. They questioned the church's hierarchy and its use of sacred icons and were persecuted for their beliefs.

Another example is the Amish, a sect formed in 1693 when a Swiss bishop named Jacob Amman and his followers broke from the Mennonite church in Europe. They believed that only people who could be successful in their religious beliefs should be a part of the community and all others should be disregarded and shunned. Other sects in the United States today include the Seventh-Day Adventists, the Quakers, and the Assemblies of God.

New Religious Movements

Sociologists categorize other religious groups as new religious movements (NRMs). Unlike sects, NRMs are religious organizations whose characteristics are not drawn from existing religious traditions within a society. Whether imported from outside the society or created within the society, NRMs bring something new to the larger religious environment. NRMs are sometimes referred to as *cults*.

The Roman Catholic Church is the largest single denomination in the United States, with over 70 million members.

▶ **CRITICAL THINKING**

Labeling In the history of the United States, was the Roman Catholic religious organization ever a "church" according to sociologists?

church a life-encompassing system of beliefs and practices to which all members of a society belong

denomination one of several religious organizations that most members of society accept as legitimate

sect a religious organization that arises out of a desire to reform an existing religious organization

The Amish are a sect who have had communities in the United States since the 1700s.

▶ **CRITICAL THINKING**

Defining Why are the Amish a sect rather than a denomination or a new religious movement?

Prem Rawat became the leader of the Divine Light Mission at age eight.

▶ **CRITICAL THINKING**

Analyzing Why are new religious movements often the target of anger from other religious groups?

It is easy to think of NRMs as engaging in extreme behavior. The world has been shocked several times in recent years by the actions of NRMs. In 1978 over 900 members of the Peoples Temple group, most of whom had emigrated on the instructions of their leader, Jim Jones, from the United States to the South American nation of Guyana, either committed suicide or were murdered at Jones's direction. In 1997 reports came of the ritualistic suicides of 39 members of the Heaven's Gate cult in California. In March 2000, about 1,000 members of the Ugandan group the Movement for the Restoration of the Ten Commandments of God were murdered, probably by the group's leaders.

NRMs do not, however, usually engage in such extreme behavior. Some other examples of NRMs in the United States include the Unification Church, the Divine Light Mission (now Elan Vital), and the Church of Scientology. Wiccans are an NRM who include a variety of smaller groups focusing on the power of the natural world and beliefs in a broad range of gods and goddesses.

Because of their rejection of mainstream religions and their focus on alternative approaches to religious involvement, NRMs often cultivate an outside, or fringe, status in society or have it thrust upon them. NRMs may be very active in trying to recruit new members, and they may impose harsh penalties on those who attempt to leave the group. These practices often cause tension with mainstream society as well.

☑ **READING PROGRESS CHECK**

Summarizing Identify as many denominations, sects, and NRMs in your area as you can and classify each one.

Applying Sociology

THE DANGER OF CULTS

Religious cults are groups of people who are devoted to a person or movement or even an idea. Sometimes a cult shares views that are unorthodox, which makes the group stand out, attracting followers who may have been shut out by society and are looking for a group where they feel they belong. Names in American history that have become synonymous with the word *cult* are the Peoples Temple, which started in California, and members of the Branch Davidians, who lived in a compound near Waco, Texas.

The Peoples Temple was led by Jim Jones, an ordained minister who initially gained the support of local politicians and the news media. Eventually, his unorthodox ways led to the death of hundreds of the cult's followers in 1978 in Jonestown, Guyana, where he had established a compound. David Koresh led the Branch Davidians, a group that had left the Davidian Seventh-Day Adventists Church to act independently. Koresh's unorthodox actions attracted the attention of the U.S. government and led to an unsuccessful raid on the compound by federal agents in 1993. During the siege that followed, Koresh and dozens of his followers died in a fire that erupted.

Cults such as these often attract followers by promising faith healing or a place to live a pure life. Leaders may use behavior that is inappropriate or inhumane toward their followers. Verbal and physical abuse are common, and when some followers try to leave a cult, they may be blackmailed or isolated from their family members.

David Koresh and many of his Branch Davidian followers died during a confrontation with federal agents in 1993.

▶ **CRITICAL THINKING**

1. ***Analyzing*** Why are some people attracted to cults?
2. ***Comparing and Contrasting*** How were the cult practices of the Peoples Temple and the Branch Davidians, as well as the fate of both cults, similar and different?

Religiosity

GUIDING QUESTION *How do people express religiosity?*

Charles Glock and Rodney Stark are two sociologists who have studied religion and society. Their work has focused on **religiosity**—the types of religious attitudes and behavior people display in their everyday lives. They identify five **dimensions** of religiosity: *belief, ritual, an intellectual dimension, experience,* and *consequences.*

- *Belief* refers to what a person considers to be true. People may, for example, believe that Jesus is the son of God or that there is no God but Allah. In most cases, these beliefs coincide with the teachings of their religious organization.
- A *ritual* is a religious practice that the members of a religion are expected to perform. A ritual may be private, such as personal prayer, or public, such as attending mass. Some religions have more rituals, and some religions consider rituals to be more important than do other religions.
- The *intellectual dimension* of religiosity may involve knowledge of holy or sacred texts or an interest in such religious aspects of human existence as evil, suffering, and death. Religious persons are expected to be knowledgeable about their faith. In some cases, it has been the intellectual experience of religion that has prompted sects to break away from the parent religion.
- *Experience* encompasses certain feelings attached to religious expression. This dimension is the hardest to measure. For example, religious believers may feel "close" to the deity when praying or believe that they are receiving direction or inspiration in their daily life.
- *Consequences* are the decisions and **commitments** people make as a result of religious beliefs, rituals, knowledge, or experiences. Consequences may be social, such as opposing or supporting capital punishment, or personal, as when practicing sexual abstinence before marriage or telling the truth regardless of the cost.

Some religious organizations express religiosity through distinctive dress or personal appearance.

▶ **CRITICAL THINKING**

Identifying To which dimension of religiosity do physical symbols of a religion belong?

religiosity ways in which people express their religious interests and convictions

dimension an aspect or feature of something

commitment a pledge or promise

✓ **READING PROGRESS CHECK**

Observing In what ways do students at your school display religiosity?

LESSON 2 REVIEW

Reviewing Vocabulary
1. ***Making Connections*** What is the relationship between a church, a denomination, and a sect?
2. ***Applying*** Give one example of religiosity.

Using Your Notes
3. ***Contrasting*** Use your notes from the lesson to write a sentence that contrasts sects with new religious movements.

Answering the Guiding Questions
4. ***Analyzing*** How do sociologists distinguish among the basic types of religious organizations?
5. ***Explaining*** How do people express religiosity?

Writing Activity
6. ***Informative/Explanatory*** Identify the most important or powerful religious organization you have been a part of or observed. Classify which type of organization it is and what types of religiosity members display.

FOCUS on research
Survey Research

Moral–Cultural Issues

In 2011, Kenneth D. Wald and Allison Calhoun-Brown, both political science professors, examined and analyzed the results of a survey conducted by the American National Election Studies (ANES) on the state of the nation. Based on the results, they concluded that there is a division among different religious groups in the United States on whether there should be tolerance for non-traditional lifestyles and different moral standards. Many groups agreed that maintaining their own moral values was possible in a society influenced by changes in moral standards.

PRIMARY SOURCE

"There is no doubt that the social changes of the latter part of the twentieth century have unnerved Americans. The ANES asks a series of questions about the overall state of the country and what should be done about it. Questions include whether new lifestyles are destroying society, whether society would be better off emphasizing traditional family ties, whether there should be toleration for moral differences, and whether morals should be adjusted to a changing world. . . .

Clear majorities of nearly all the religious traditions agree that new lifestyles are breaking down society. The notable exceptions to this pattern are Jews and seculars, but even near majorities of these groups agree with the statement. There is also broad support for the idea that the country would have fewer problems if there were more emphasis on traditional family ties. Overwhelming numbers of all religious groups and half of all seculars said that this would be helpful. What constitutes a traditional family tie is not defined by the ANES, so there is broad latitude in the interpretation of this question. Still, people also report that they are willing to be tolerant of those who live according to moral values that differ from their own. Seculars and Jews are most enthusiastic about the need to tolerate different standards of morality. The lowest level of agreement was found among evangelicals, but even half of them agree that it is important. On these questions, there is more unanimity of opinion in some traditions than others, but in almost every instance, the majority opinion about the threat from new lifestyles, the propriety of emphasizing traditional ties, and toleration for different moral standards was the same.

Religious groups are most divided about whether views of morality should be adjusted to a changing world. More than 60 percent of Hispanic Catholics, Jews, black Protestants, and seculars agree that morals should be adjusted. This is compared to a little more than a third of evangelical and mainline Protestants and only about a quarter of Latter-Day Saints who hold more conservative views. Hispanic Protestants and Catholics again occupied a midrange position—more supportive than the most conservative groups, less supportive than the most liberal. While in the moderate category on this issue, it is interesting that Hispanic Protestants were much less liberal than Hispanic Catholics. Hispanic Protestants are of higher status than their Catholic counterparts and often more conservative in their approach to political matters (Hunt 2001).

Not everybody appears to be enlisting in the mythical culture war. Rather, many people are best described as ambivalent (Craig et al. 2005; Craig and Martinez 2005). We found broad agreement across religious traditions about the moral and cultural challenges faced by the United States. Concerns about 'new' lifestyles and the decline of the traditional family are almost universal. Yet people also want to get along with one another, reflected by the stated willingness in all religious traditions to tolerate those who live according to different moral standards even if, in some traditions, it requires adjusting standards of morality to changing times. Because it is possible to tolerate the standards of others without rejecting your own, there is opportunity in American politics for religion to be much less divisive than many expect."

—from *Religion and Politics in the United States*, 2011

> "Concerns about 'new' lifestyles and the decline of the traditional family are almost universal. Yet people also want to get along with one another..."

Working With the Research

1. **Identifying Central Ideas** Based on the findings of Wald and Calhoun-Brown, why do you think some groups tolerate moral standards that are different from their own?

2. **Identifying Perspectives** Why do you think certain groups are resistant to tolerating changes in lifestyles and moral standards?

3. **Analyzing** What do most of the groups that were surveyed think is the biggest challenge to the traditional family, and why do you think they share this concern?

networks

There's More Online!

- ☑ **CHART** Religious Traditions in the United States
- ☑ **GRAPH** Percentage of Population Who Attend Weekly Religious Services
- ☑ **IMAGE** Angel of Judgment
- ☑ **MAP** Religiosity in the United States
- ☑ **SELF-CHECK QUIZ**

Reading HELPDESK

Academic Vocabulary
- constitute
- proportion

Content Vocabulary
- secularization
- fundamentalism

TAKING NOTES:
Key Ideas and Details

ORGANIZING As you read about religion in the United States, use a graphic organizer like the one below to record details.

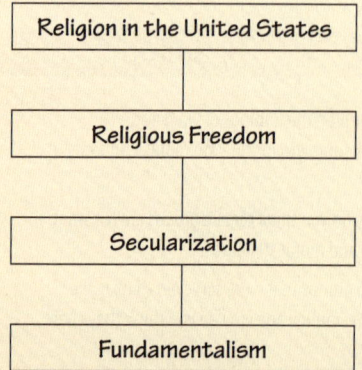

LESSON 3
Religion in the United States

ESSENTIAL QUESTION • What roles does religion play in society?

IT MATTERS BECAUSE

Through the process of secularization, the sacred and the profane tend to become intermixed. There has been a revival of religious fundamentalism in the United States. Religious faiths can be analyzed by major social characteristics such as class and political tendencies.

The Foundations of Religious Freedom

GUIDING QUESTION What were the origins of religious freedom in the United States?

The search for religious freedom was only one of many reasons Puritan colonists came to America—but it was an important one. The Puritans viewed themselves as a religious example for the world to follow and admire. Sociologist Robert Bellah has described the American religious connection this way:

PRIMARY SOURCE

"In the beginning, and to some extent ever since, Americans have interpreted their history as having religious meaning. They saw themselves as being a 'people' in the classical and biblical sense of the word. They hoped they were a people of God."

—from *The Broken Covenant*, 1975

The Framers of the U.S. Constitution seldom raised arguments against religious faith. They were sharply critical of any entanglement between religion and the state, however. Indeed, the ideas of separation of church and state and freedom of religious expression are cornerstones of American life. Religion has always been of great importance in American life, but it has played a more active role in some periods than in others. There have been several "Awakenings" in American history, when religious principles have guided the development of culture and society. The 1830s, for example, saw many religious reform movements, including that against slavery. Later, the Protestant-led temperance movement resulted in the Nineteenth Amendment, which outlawed alcohol during the 1920s and early 1930s.

☑ **READING PROGRESS CHECK**

Evaluating Does religion influence American government today? Explain.

Secularization in the United States

GUIDING QUESTION *Is secularization destroying religion in the United States? Explain.*

Countering the growth of religion in American history has been **secularization**. Through this process, the sacred loses influence over society or aspects of the sacred enter into the secular (profane) world of everyday life. For example, formal education originally was a function of religion. Most early teachers and professors were clerics and church members. Over time in the United States, this function was taken over by the state, although many schools sponsored by religious groups still exist.

Some findings from surveys indicate a decline in the importance of religion in the United States in recent years. For example, the percentage of Americans claiming that religion is very important in their lives fell from 75 percent in 1952 to 55 percent in 2011. In 1957, 14 percent of the public indicated that they believed religion was losing influence on American life. In 2008, 70 percent of the public saw a loss of influence. The trends in religious self-identification indicate that fewer people identify themselves with a particular denomination in recent years as well. According to one study, 15.0 percent of Americans in 2008 did not identify as members of any type of religion, up from 8.2 percent in 1990.

Still, the United States appears to be a religious nation when compared with other industrialized countries. About 35 percent of Americans attend weekly religious services on a regular basis. This is about twice the rate of the people of Great Britain and three times or more the rate for industrial countries such as Germany, France, Japan, and Sweden.

Religious life in the United States has become much more diverse in recent years. About 81 percent of Americans identified themselves as Christians in 2010, compared to about 96 percent in 1900. There are now more than 200 denominations in the United States. Furthermore, although the proportion of Americans belonging to a church, synagogue, or mosque has declined from a high of 76 percent in 1947 to 61 percent in 2008, church attendance has declined less.

secularization the process through which the sacred loses influence over society

GRAPH

PERCENTAGE OF POPULATION WHO ATTEND WEEKLY RELIGIOUS SERVICES

This graph shows how the United States compares to other countries in the percentage of people who attend religious services at least once a week.

▶ **CRITICAL THINKING**

1. **Contrasting** How does attendance at religious services in the United States compare to that in European countries?

2. **Contrasting** How does attendance at religious services in the United States compare to that in other countries in North America and in South America?

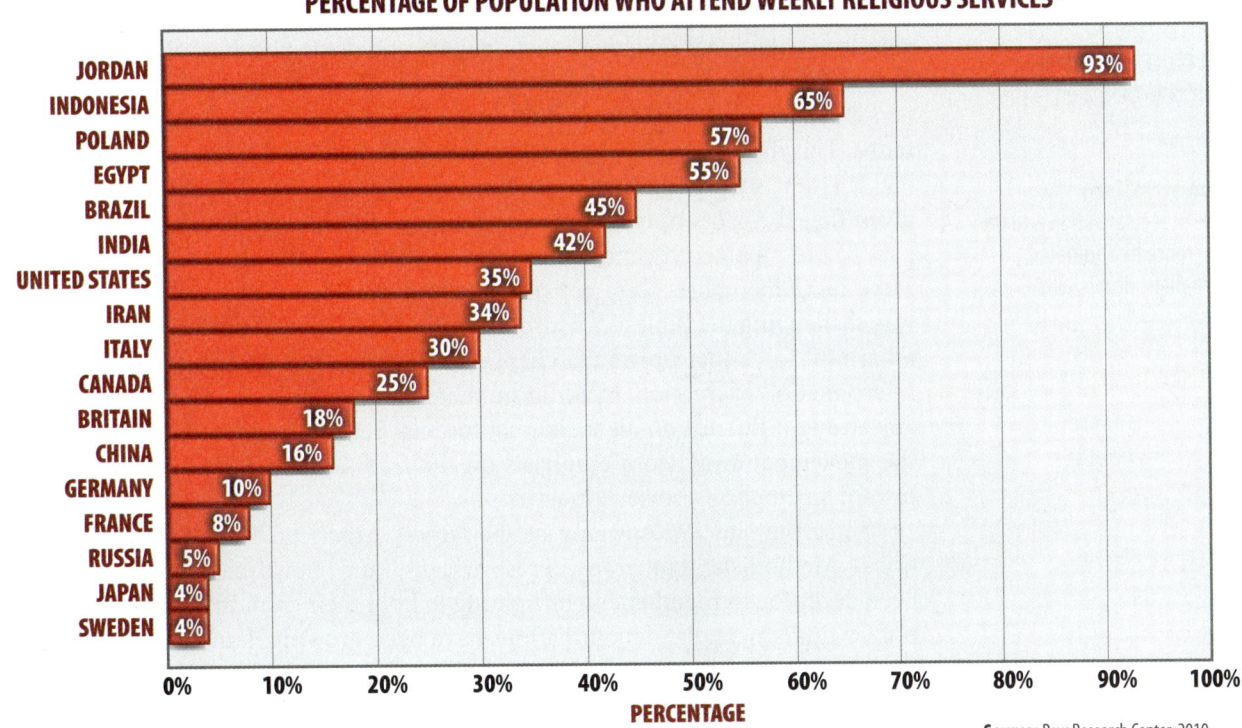

PERCENTAGE OF POPULATION WHO ATTEND WEEKLY RELIGIOUS SERVICES*

- JORDAN: 93%
- INDONESIA: 65%
- POLAND: 57%
- EGYPT: 55%
- BRAZIL: 45%
- INDIA: 42%
- UNITED STATES: 35%
- IRAN: 34%
- ITALY: 30%
- CANADA: 25%
- BRITAIN: 18%
- CHINA: 16%
- GERMANY: 10%
- FRANCE: 8%
- RUSSIA: 5%
- JAPAN: 4%
- SWEDEN: 4%

*Estimated Percentage

Source: Pew Research Center, 2010.

Although fewer Americans identify religion as very important in their lives, most still support traditional religious beliefs.

▶ CRITICAL THINKING

Making Connections How does Americans' belief in angels and demons reflect the country's basic religious orientation?

constitute to make up; account for

proportion percentage; fraction or ratio compared to the whole

fundamentalism the resistance of secularization and the rigid adherence to traditional religious beliefs, rituals, and doctrines

Weekly attendance at religious services in the United States has dropped from 41 percent in 1939 to 35 percent in 2010.

Americans also tend to support traditional religious beliefs. Ninety-two percent of the American population believes in God or a universal spirit, 74 percent believes in life after death, the same percentage believes in heaven, and 59 percent believes in hell. Sixty-eight percent believes in the existence of angels and demons.

✓ **READING PROGRESS CHECK**

Contrasting How important is religion in the United States compared to other industrialized countries?

Religious Preferences in the United States

GUIDING QUESTION *What are the trends in religion in the United States?*

Although there are hundreds of religious denominations and sects in the United States, half of all Americans in 2008 were Protestant, and a significant share of the population belonged to just a few major denominations—Baptist (16 percent), Methodist (5 percent), Lutheran (4 percent), Presbyterian (2 percent), and Episcopalian/Anglican (1 percent). Fourteen percent belonged to various other Protestant denominations. Catholics **constituted** a relatively large **proportion** of the American population (25 percent) and Jews a relatively small proportion (1 percent). Americans who have no religious preference formed 15 percent of the population.

Fundamentalism in America

Any careful observer of religion in the United States over the past ten years or so will have noted the rise of religious *fundamentalism* in the country, especially among Protestant denominations. The percentage of fundamentalists nearly doubled from about 0.5 percent of the population in 2000 to about 0.9 percent in 2008. **Fundamentalism** is based on the desire to resist secularization and to adhere closely to traditional religious beliefs, rituals, and doctrines. It is, of course, incorrect to think that fundamentalism is limited to Protestants alone. Fundamentalism is found in all religions, including the Roman Catholic, Jewish, and Muslim faiths. This discussion, however, will focus on Protestant fundamentalism.

It is not surprising that most fundamentalists are politically conservative, given that the roots of contemporary religious fundamentalism are in the latter part of the nineteenth century. Two issues disturbed the early fundamentalists. First, fundamentalists were concerned about the spread of secularism. Science was challenging the Bible as a source of truth. Marxism was portraying religion as a harmful force that prevented change. Darwinism was challenging the biblical interpretation of creation. In addition, religion in general was losing its traditionally strong influence on all social institutions. Second, fundamentalists rejected the movement away from emphasis on the traditional message of Christianity toward an emphasis on social service.

Since the late 1960s, many of the largest American Protestant denominations—Methodists, Lutherans, Presbyterians, and Episcopalians—have either been declining in membership or fighting to hold their own. In contrast, contemporary fundamentalist denominations have been growing. Fundamentalists exist in all Protestant organizations, but they are predominantly found in such religious bodies as the Assemblies of God, the Seventh-Day Adventists, the Baptists, and the Jehovah's Witnesses.

Ridolfo di Arpo Guariento/The Bridgeman Art Library/Getty Images

The theological agenda of today's fundamentalists is very close to that of their forebears in the nineteenth century. Fundamentalists believe in the literal truth of the Christian Bible. Protestant fundamentalism involves being "born again" through acceptance of Jesus as the son of God, who was sent to redeem mankind through his sacrifice. Fundamentalist doctrine includes belief in the responsibility of all believers to give witness for God, the presence of Satan as an active force for evil, and the destruction of the world prior to the Messiah's return to establish his kingdom on Earth.

Religious organizations that share much of the fundamentalist theology vary in their beliefs and practices. An example is neo-Pentacostalism—or the *charismatic movement*, as it is sometimes called—which has occurred for the most part within traditional religious organizations, particularly the Roman Catholic and Episcopal churches. Those involved in this movement often speak of receiving "the baptism of the Holy Spirit." But central to most neo-Pentecostal groups is the experience of "speaking in tongues," which believers claim is a direct gift of the Holy Spirit.

Several reasons for the rise of fundamentalism have been proposed. Many Americans feel their world is out of control. The social order of the 1950s was shattered by a string of traumatic events beginning with the civil rights movement and progressing through campus violence, political assassinations, and the Vietnam War.

Sociologists think that traumatic events and social trends have encouraged people to seek certainty in religious beliefs.

▶ **CRITICAL THINKING**

Explaining How can religious beliefs help people respond to traumatic events and trends?

Connecting Sociology to Human Geography

RELIGIOUS BELIEFS AROUND THE GLOBE

People practice many different religions in the United States and around the world; some are monotheistic, or believe in one God, and others are polytheistic, or believe in many gods. The three major monotheistic religions are Judaism, Christianity, and Islam. An example of a polytheistic religion is Hinduism. Some religions are animistic, focused on the belief that animals, plants, and objects are spiritual beings.

Many monotheistic and polytheistic religions have key figures, but not all of them do. For example, Jesus is a key figure in Christianity; Muhammad is a key figure in Islam. In Judaism, there is no single key figure. As in Judaism, Hinduism is not linked to one key figure but, rather, developed over a period of time, as people migrated onto the Indian subcontinent over thousands of years. In Buddhism, which is neither monotheistic nor polytheistic, the Buddha (Siddhartha Gautama) is the key figure.

People practice their religions in different ways, but in some aspects their practices are similar. For example, in monotheistic religions people may pray to their God. They may have different methods of praying or distinct rituals that they follow to pray. Many followers of the world's major religions attend weekly or daily religious services. They read from or listen to the reading of sacred texts, such as the Hebrew Bible in Judaism, the Christian Bible in Christianity, the Quran in Islam, the Vedas in Hinduism, and the Tripitaka in Buddhism.

Religion	Belief	Major Region
Buddhism	----	Africa, Asia, Southeast Asia
Christianity	monotheism	Africa, North and South America, Europe, Asia, Australia
Hinduism	polytheism	South Asia
Islam	monotheism	North Africa, Asia
Judaism	monotheism	North America, Europe, Southwest Asia
Sikhism	monotheism	South Asia

Source: *Britannica Book of the Year, 2011*

▶ **CRITICAL THINKING**

1. *Comparing and Contrasting* How are the monotheistic religions alike and different? How are they similar and different to the polytheistic religions?

2. *Identifying Central Issues* Why are the religions practiced in the United States also practiced elsewhere in the world?

Many people saw increases in substance abuse, single motherhood, divorce, and crime as signs of moral decline. The threat from terrorists after the events of September 11, 2001, added more uncertainty.

Fundamentalist religion, with its absolute answers and promise of eternal life, provides a strong anchor in a confusing, bewildering world. Fundamentalist churches provide solace to people who are witnessing and experiencing the weakening of family and community ties by emphasizing warmth, love, and caring. Mainline churches tend to be more formal and impersonal.

Fundamentalist churches offer what they consider a more purely sacred environment in contrast to mainline denominations that fundamentalists see as accommodating to secular society. The electronic church, in its role as part of the mass media, has been an important contributing factor in the growth of religious fundamentalism.

Religion, Education, Politics, and Race

Religious affiliation is related to education. There are marked differences when adherents are classified by the percentage of college graduates among the more traditional religions in the United States. Generally speaking, Jews and members of Asian religions have the greatest percentages of college graduates while Baptists and Pentecostal/Charismatic religions are at the lowest end.

Political affiliation, too, is related to religion. Among those that classify themselves as highly religious, 49 percent say they are Republicans or lean toward the Republican Party, with only 37 percent saying they are Democrats or lean toward the Democratic Party. The trend is that as people identify themselves as less religious, they are more likely to identify themselves as Democrats or leaning toward the Democratic Party. Those identifying themselves as not religious are strongly Democratic, 56 percent, while 26 percent are Republican.

This does not hold true for African Americans and Latinos, however. About 80 percent of African Americans identify with the Democratic Party no matter how they identify their religiosity, and about 50 percent of Latinos identify with the Democratic Party at all religious intensity levels. The percentages for whites change dramatically, with 62 percent of highly religious people favoring the Republican Party to 28 percent Democratic. Conversely, whites who are not religious favor the Democratic Party over the Republican Party by 56 percent to 28 percent.

CHART >

RELIGIOUS TRADITIONS IN THE UNITED STATES, 2008
This chart compares the number of adherents, or believers, in the largest religious traditions in the United States.

▶ **CRITICAL THINKING**

1. **Analyzing Visuals** How does the number of Catholics in the United States compare to that of other denominations?

2. **Hypothesizing** Which religious traditions do you think will gain the most new adherents in the near future? Why?

United States Adult Population by Religious Tradition	
Religious Tradition	Number of Adherents
Christian	**173,400,000***
Catholic	57,199,000
Baptist	36,148,000
Methodist	11,366,000
Lutheran	8,674,000
Pentecostal/Charismatic	7,948,000
Presbyterian	4,723,000
Mormon/Latter Day Saints	3,158,000
Episcopalian/Anglican	2,405,000
Jewish	**2,680,000**
Muslim	**1,349,000**
Buddhist	**1,189,000**

* Not all Christian traditions are listed below.
Source: American Religious Identification Survey, 2008

A Diverse America

RELIGIOSITY IN THE UNITED STATES

Gallup Research conducted a poll in 2011 to determine which state in the country had the most religious population. The results indicated that Mississippi was the most religious state while Vermont and New Hampshire tied for the least religious. The overall results proved that religion is still an important part in the lives of many Americans.

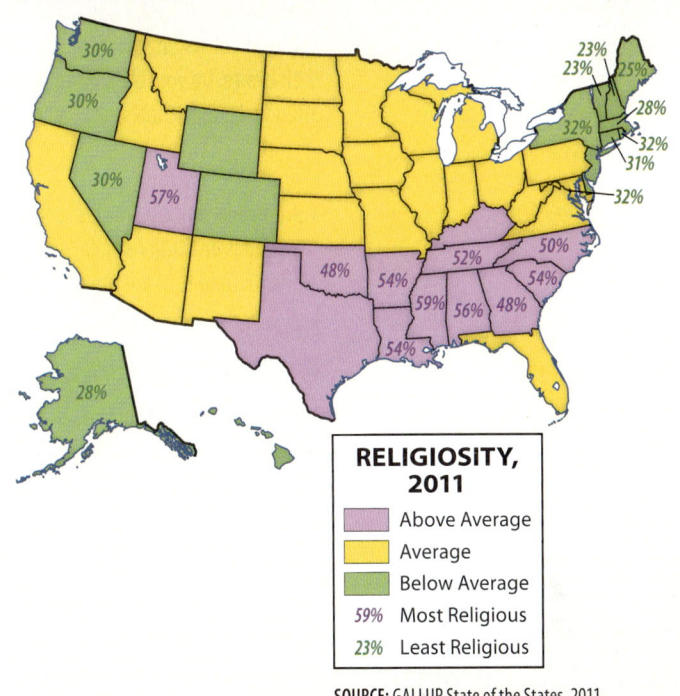

Geography Connection

1. **Places and Regions** Based on the map, which regions are the least and most religious?
2. **Environment and Society** What influence do you think culture has on how religious a state's population is?
3. **The Uses of Geography** How could the data on this map be used to make connections between religion, social class, and politics?

These kinds of analyses grow out of conflict theory and have their roots in the Marxist view that religion contributes to the stratification of society by reinforcing distinctions and advantages.

Religion, Science, and Society

Both science and religion examine humanity's relationship to the world, but they examine it in very different ways. Religion involves matters beyond human observation while science is solely about the observable. These fields of endeavor are not mutually exclusive. Many scientists are religious, and many professional clergy appreciate and support the intellectual achievements of science.

Sometimes, however, these two institutions can appear to be in conflict. Depending on the values and norms of the culture, society may favor religious or scientific explanations. In the United States, following the principle of separation of state and church, it has been common to keep religion apart from government-sponsored institutions. Scientific explanations for natural phenomena, when commonly accepted, have been taught in the schools, leaving religious groups free to teach other interpretations within their organizations.

Strict fundamentalists do not believe that scientific theories, such as evolution and the Big Bang theory of creation, should be presented in public schools as facts while Christian Bible-based explanations, such as creationism and intelligent design, are not even discussed. In 1999, fundamentalists convinced the Kansas Board of Education to remove any questions about evolution from the state high-school exit examination. Until the decision was repealed in 2001, Kansas teachers were not required to teach the theory of evolution.

In 2005, a federal district court heard a case brought against the Dover County, Pennsylvania, School Board, which required high-school biology teachers to read students a statement questioning Darwin's theory of evolution before discussing it.

Quick Case Study

SHOULD TAXPAYERS FUND RELIGIOUS SCHOOLS?
Some school systems have established voucher programs that allow students to attend the school of their choice. Do your classmates believe taxpayers should pay for vouchers that allow students to attend religious schools?

Procedure
1. Interview your classmates to find out if they think voucher programs that give public money to religious institutions violate the First Amendment to the U.S. Constitution. Why or why not?
2. Invite them to share their responses with the class. Record their responses.

Analysis
As you read through their responses, consider these questions:
1. How absolute should the separation of church and state be?
2. Do you believe voucher programs that fund religious schools are constitutional? Why or why not?

The U.S. Supreme Court has often been called upon to make decisions related to the separation of church and state.

▶ **CRITICAL THINKING**

Speculating How do you think the Framers of the U.S. Constitution would have felt about teaching scientific research and not religious theories in public schools?

The district court ruled that teaching "intelligent design" in public schools was unconstitutional because it was a form of creationism, which contradicts scientific thought and research. Currently, scientists are fighting against state laws such as a 2008 Louisiana law that requires teachers to identify scientific information on evolution as "controversial." A group of 42 Nobel Prize-winning scientists are backing this effort for repeal. Similarly worded legislation was introduced in Florida, Texas, Kentucky, and Oklahoma. None of them passed. A bill passed the Tennessee House of Representatives in 2011 and in April 2012 was voted into law.

Today, many people are questioning whether "pure science" can remain independent of cultural or social norms, as some scientists believe. Scientific discoveries and processes, such as cloning and gene therapy, are moving into ever more ethically debatable areas. The result appears obvious: The interface and conflict between science and religion are sure to increase. Society, in particular government, will need to learn how to deal constructively with apparent contradictions in these two areas.

☑ **READING PROGRESS CHECK**

Summarizing What functions do fundamentalist religions serve in American society today?

LESSON 3 REVIEW

Reviewing Vocabulary
1. **Making Connections** What is the relationship between secularization and fundamentalism?

Using Your Notes
2. **Describing** Use your notes from the lesson to write a few sentences describing the importance of religious freedom in American society.

Answering the Guiding Questions
3. **Analyzing** What were the origins of religious freedom in the United States?

4. **Evaluating** Is secularization destroying religion in the United States? Explain.

5. **Describing** What are the trends in religion in the United States?

Writing Activity
6. **Informative/Explanatory** Consider the rise of fundamentalism in American religion. Write a paragraph that explains why you think this increase has occurred.

CHAPTER 14 Assessment

Directions: On a separate sheet of paper, answer the questions below. Make sure you read carefully and answer all parts of the questions.

Lesson Review

Lesson 1

1. **Analyzing** Some people believe modern communications technology removes the one-on-one, in-person connections that religious groups have fostered for centuries. Do you agree or disagree? Explain what you believe to be the overall impact of today's technology on religious observance.

2. **Explaining** Explain why you think this statement is true or not: "It is important for sociologists to interject personal religious beliefs into their work, as this allows them to develop understanding and compassion."

Lesson 2

3. **Discussing** Is it a major goal of sect members to establish a new religion? Why or why not?

4. **Comparing and Contrasting** Compare and contrast new religious movements (NRMs) that engage in extreme behaviors and those that do not. Provide examples of each.

Lesson 3

5. **Speculating** What role do you think the Internet and other types of modern technology have had on the recent rise of fundamentalism in the United States?

6. **Identifying Central Issues** Suppose a religious group is demanding that schools state that evolution is a theory—and that the group's views of humans being created through stars and the moon is another theory. Discuss whether these ideas can legally be taught in a public school. In your discussion, include reference to creationism and a ruling from a court case.

Critical Thinking

7. **Applying** Many people appear to be less interested in religion during their teenage years. This might be seen in falling church attendance for this age group. Using your sociological imagination, suggest some reasons for this apparent lack of interest. Consider developmental (age) and social factors. Depending on your answers, what suggestions might you make to religious organizations looking for ideas on how to keep teenagers involved and active?

DBQ Analyzing Primary Sources

PRIMARY SOURCE

Use the document to answer the following question.

8. **Analyzing** Which aspect of religiosity is demonstrated by the man in the cartoon? Why do you think so?

Need Extra Help?

If You've Missed Question	1	2	3	4	5	6	7	8
Go to page	396–401	396–397	402–404	403–404	410–412	413–414	402–414	404

Religion 415

CHAPTER 14 Assessment

Directions: On a separate sheet of paper, answer the questions below. Make sure you read carefully and answer all parts of the questions.

College and Career Readiness Skills

9 *Clear Communication* As a project for a college class, you have been assigned the task of developing a charitable organization. Choose a purpose for your charity such as collecting food for the economically disadvantaged or providing tutoring services. These are just a few suggestions. You may use one of these activities or choose one of your own. Your professor has explained that religious organizations in your area are usually very supportive of charitable endeavors. Devise promotional material that will appeal to a variety of denominations and inspire them to contribute to your organization. Your promotional materials should consist of at least two of the following: a prototype for webpage, a flyer, an email, a poster, and a speech to be presented at a religious service. After you create your promotional materials, explain why you have developed them in the way you have—and why they will appeal to a variety of religious groups.

21st Century Skills

CREATING AND USING GRAPHS, CHARTS, DIAGRAMS AND TABLES

10 *Creating Diagrams* Create a Venn diagram to compare and contrast the views of Max Weber, Karl Marx, and Émile Durkheim regarding religion.

Exploring the Essential Question

11 *Organizing* Imagine you attend a public school in a district where large groups of immigrants from a variety of regions have recently settled. Many of the new students have come to the United States from locations where a religious group in power controlled the government and schools. Teachers and administrators in your district believe it would be very helpful for these students, as they acclimate to a new school, to be able to understand religion and its impact on public schools in the United States. You are one of several students on a committee assembled to provide a sociological overview of religion in the United States for these students, including an explanation of the separation of church and state and the impact of this separation on public schools. Prepare a report to outline the major points you would include in the overview for these new students. At the end of your report, explain the most important point the new students need to know in order to understand what they should expect, in terms of the impact of religion, as they attend their new schools.

Research and Presentation

12 *Gathering Information* As this chapter explained, it is difficult to determine whether one person is "more religious" than another, or considers religion more important than another, as there is no authoritative definition for terms such as *religious*. Similarly, it is difficult to rank states as more or less religious than one another; however, various entities, such as the Pew Forum, have conducted studies to determine the importance of religion in states across the nation. Conduct online research to locate information about a study that ranks states in terms of the importance of religion to their residents. Explain the criteria used by the group to determine the importance of religion. Note where your state ranks in terms of the importance of religion. Select two other states and note where those states rank.

13 *Evaluating* Using a computer, create a graphic that compares and contrasts your state to the two other states you have selected in terms of importance of religion. Below your graphic, provide a credit for the group or organization that conducted the research. Develop a class presentation to display your graphic and explain the following: the criteria used by the study to determine the importance of religion, where your state and the two states you have selected rank in relation to other states, where your state ranks in relationship to the other two states, and your conclusions regarding why the three states rank as they do.

Need Extra Help?

If You've Missed Question	9	10	11	12	13
Go to page	396–414	396–414	396–414	396–414	396–414

Population and Urbanization

ESSENTIAL QUESTION • What is demography and why do we study demographics?

networks
There's More Online about population and urbanization.

CHAPTER 15

Technology & Society
Food, Hunger, and Technology

Lesson 1
The Dynamics of Demography

Lesson 2
World Population

Lesson 3
The Urban Transition

Lesson 4
Urban Ecology

Sociology Matters...

There are more people alive today than have lived and died throughout all the previous years of human history, and our numbers continue to grow. How will we and future generations cope with the large numbers of people competing for limited space and nonrenewable resources? How can we best curb population growth while respecting individual freedom? How can we build cities that meet the needs of their citizens while preserving the natural environment?

Sociology can help identify problems, predict consequences, and offer solutions for a crowded planet.

◄ Sociologists are concerned with the nature of life in urban areas.

©Igors Sinitsyn/Demotix/Corbis

CHAPTER 15
Technology & Society

Food, Hunger, and Technology

The dilemma is acute: Too many people in the world are hungry. The processes for growing food are environmentally harmful in many cases. Yet one possible solution to this problem may come, some say, with the threat of worldwide disaster.

There may be nearly 1 billion people on the planet who suffer from hunger—nearly one out of every seven human beings. Hunger, and related problems, is the world's number-one health concern. At the same time, agriculture—the industry that holds the answer to the world's hunger problem—is a major source of environmental degradation around the world.

One proposed solution to this problem is the use of genetically modified (GM) crops. These crops are the product of genetic engineering, in which scientists insert genes for certain desirable characteristics—such as the ability to produce higher yields, resist pests, or require less water—into the genetic material of different organisms. Genetic modification offers the hope of growing more food while using less energy, pesticides, water, and land.

The problem is that the long-term impact of changing the genetic structure of organisms is not fully understood. Many observers worry that efforts to solve the hunger problem could unleash threats to human health that dwarf the danger they are intended to combat. Critics warn that genetic material released into the environment might lead to illness or environmental damage that scientists have not anticipated and might be powerless to stop. These and other concerns over GM foods have led some nations to limit their use.

Other nations, such as the United States, have been more willing to allow GM crops. The debate is certain to continue in the years to come as concerns over hunger and environmental degradation loom large over the planet.

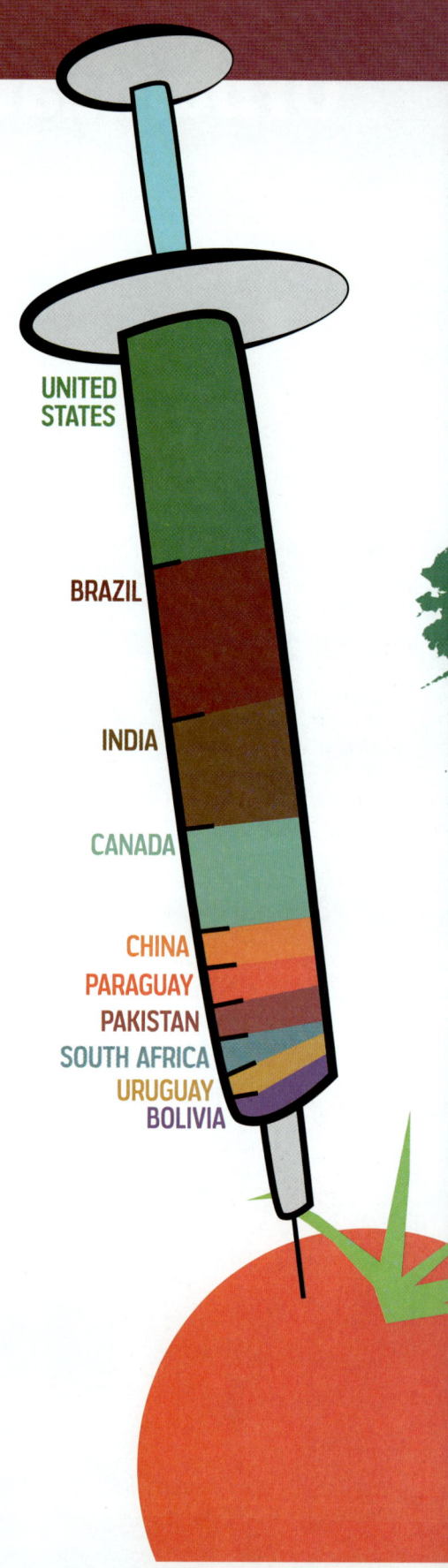

COUNTRIES WITH THE MOST LAND PLANTED WITH GENETICALLY MODIFIED CROPS (millions of hectares) 2011

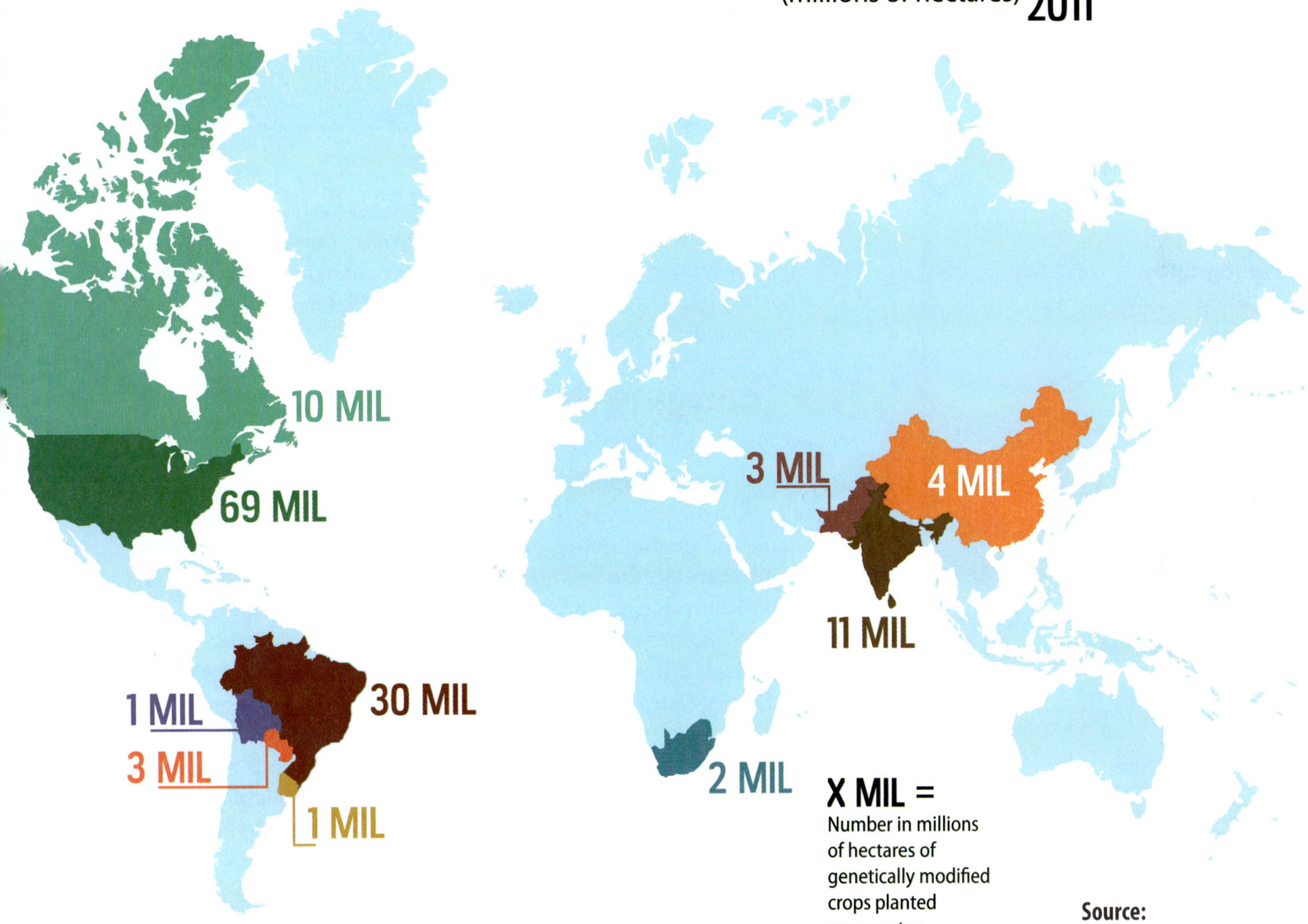

- 10 MIL
- 69 MIL
- 1 MIL
- 3 MIL
- 30 MIL
- 1 MIL
- 3 MIL
- 4 MIL
- 11 MIL
- 2 MIL

X MIL = Number in millions of hectares of genetically modified crops planted per country

Source: *The Guardian*, 2012

Thinking Like a Sociologist

1 Assessing
Do you think the benefits of GM foods outweigh the potential risks they pose? Why or why not?

2 Formulating Questions
What is the key question that would allow some resolution to the debate over whether we should raise more or fewer genetically modified crops?

Population and Urbanization

networks

There's More Online!

- ☑ **CHART** Nonmetropolitan Population Change
- ☑ **MAP** The Fertility Rate in the United States
- ☑ **SELF-CHECK QUIZ**

Reading HELPDESK

Academic Vocabulary
- controversial
- migration

Content Vocabulary
- population
- demography
- fertility
- fecundity
- crude birthrate
- fertility rate
- total fertility rate
- mortality
- lifespan
- life expectancy
- crude death rate
- infant mortality rate
- gross migration rate
- net migration rate

TAKING NOTES:
Key Ideas and Details

ORGANIZING As you read about demography, use a graphic organizer like the one below to record the various factors that demographers study.

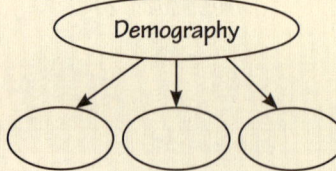

LESSON 1
The Dynamics of Demography

ESSENTIAL QUESTION • *What is demography and why do we study demographics?*

IT MATTERS BECAUSE
Demography is the scientific study of population. Demographers collect and analyze data on fertility, mortality, and migration. This data is used not only by sociologists but by governments, industries, and world health and human services organizations.

The Changing Population

GUIDING QUESTION *How do sociologists define population?*

Sociologists study **population** because it affects social structure, especially in crowded areas. They look for patterns that will help them understand and predict how groups of people will behave. For example, they might examine the relationship between population growth and politics. We know that, historically, the growth of minority groups in the United States has benefited Democrats more than Republicans. But the situation today is different with respect to Latinos. Now the largest minority in the United States, Latinos are not firmly aligned with either political party. Regardless of political affiliation, the growth of minority populations affects how congressional districts are drawn and is one reason that census taking can be a **controversial** topic. Sociologists might also study trends in population shifts, such as the aging baby boomers, to help future planning for hospitals and long-term nursing facilities.

A population is a group of people living in a particular place at a specified time. The scientific study of population is called **demography** (*demos* is a Greek word that means "people"). To study population, demographers look at many factors, including the number of people (size), how and where they are located (distribution), what groups make up the population (composition), and the ages represented in the population (age structure). Demographers also analyze three processes: birth (*fertility*), death (*mortality*), and movement from one place to another (*migration*). Major changes in population come from one or all of these three processes. In the following sections, we look at the factors and processes that affect populations.

☑ **READING PROGRESS CHECK**

Identifying What factors and processes are used to study population?

Fertility

GUIDING QUESTIONS *How is fertility measured? What other factors influence the birthrate?*

Fertility measures the actual number of children born to a woman or to a population of women. **Fecundity** is the potential number of children that could be born if every woman reproduced as often as biology allowed. Obviously, fertility rates are much lower than fecundity rates. The highest realistic fecundity rate you could expect from a society would be about fifteen births per woman. The record fertility rate for a group is likely held by the Hutterites, who migrated a century ago from Switzerland to North and South Dakota and Canada. Hutterite women in the 1930s were giving birth to an average of more than 12 children each. The Hutterites give us a good estimate of fecundity, because they are the best example of *natural fertility*—the number of children born to women in the absence of conscious birth control.

The **crude birthrate** is the annual number of live births per 1,000 members of a population. The crude birthrate varies considerably from one country to another. The crude birthrate for the United States is 13 per 1,000. Niger, in West Africa, experiences a very high crude birthrate of 48 per 1,000 and Germany a very low rate of 8 per 1,000.

To calculate the crude birthrate, divide the annual number of live births by the total population and multiply that number by 1,000.

$$\text{Crude Birthrate} = \frac{\text{Number of Live Births}}{\text{Total Population}} = N \times 1{,}000$$

population a group of people living in a particular place at a specified time

controversial disputed

demography the scientific study of population

fertility the actual number of children born to a woman or a population of women

fecundity the maximum rate at which women can physically produce children

crude birthrate the annual number of live births per 1,000 members of a population

A Diverse America

THE FERTILITY RATE IN THE UNITED STATES

For the United States as a whole, the number of births per 1,000 women has been dropping steadily since 1960. Today, the national fertility rate, which measures the annual number of babies born per 1,000 women between the ages of 15 and 44, stands at nearly 67 babies per year. But it varies by state, as the map shows.

Geography Connection

1. **Places and Regions** Which states had the highest fertility rate? Which states had the lowest?
2. **Places and Regions** What was the fertility rate in your state? Does this surprise you? Explain.
3. **Human Systems** What factors might explain differences in fertility rate by state?

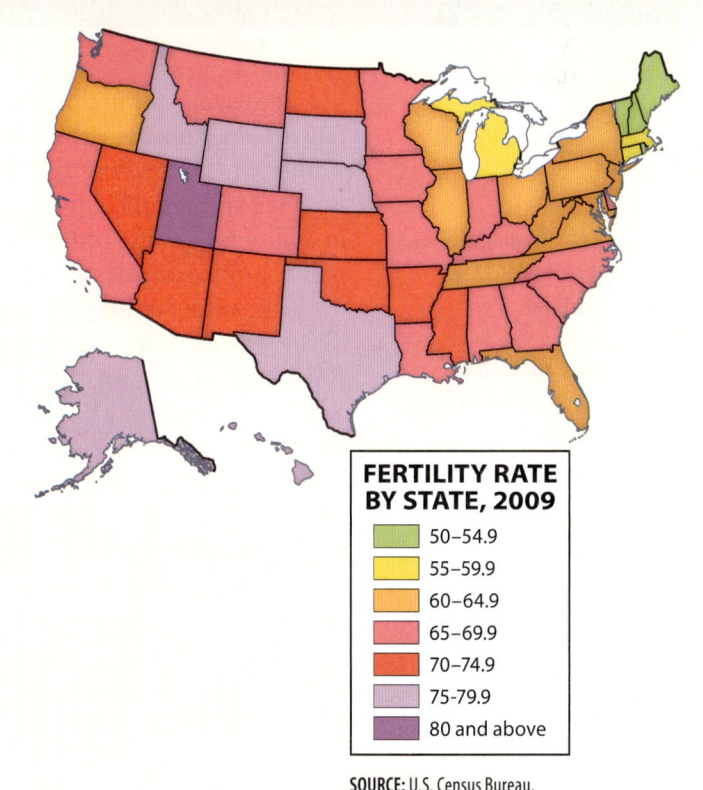

FERTILITY RATE BY STATE, 2009
- 50–54.9
- 55–59.9
- 60–64.9
- 65–69.9
- 70–74.9
- 75–79.9
- 80 and above

SOURCE: U.S. Census Bureau, *Statistical Abstract of the United States: 2012*

Applying Sociology

BUSINESS AND DEMOGRAPHICS

Businesses are intensely interested in demographic information about their communities and about the people who consume their goods and services. Knowing who their actual and potential customers are—for example, their ages and racial makeup, as well as income levels and other demographic information—can enable businesses to target their marketing and advertising more effectively.

For example, if you had a business selling clothing, knowing who lives and shops in your community might help you decide what products to stock. Knowing which specific customers are actually coming to your store and buying your goods is even more valuable information.

Businesses acquire demographic information from many sources. The U.S. Census makes available large amounts of detailed demographic data about communities throughout the United States. The federal government's Small Business Administration helps guide businesses to this and other information. There are also many businesses—market research firms—dedicated to collecting and providing detailed demographic data to other businesses.

Have you ever wondered why social networking sites are so valuable? It is because these sites are able to collect huge amounts of information about their members, including demographic data and personal preferences. This information is tremendously valuable to businesses.

Businesses value demographic information because it helps them target advertising and promotions at likely customers.

▶ **CRITICAL THINKING**

Finding the Main Idea What are two reasons businesses may want to use demographic data?

---

fertility rate the annual number of live births per 1,000 women aged 15 to 44

total fertility rate the average number of children born to a woman during her lifetime

The term *crude* in this case means "rough" or "approximate." The crude birthrate is approximate because it is based on the entire population rather than just women of childbearing age. It also ignores the age structure of the population. Both sex and age affect the number of live births in any given year. Consequently, in addition to crude birthrate, demographers use the **fertility rate**—the annual number of live births per 1,000 women aged 15 to 44. The rate that is easiest to use is the **total fertility rate**, or the average number of children born to a woman during her lifetime. Currently, total fertility rates in the world range from 7.0 in Niger to 0.9 in Taiwan.

The birthrate of a population is influenced by both health and social factors. For example, widespread disease (especially rubella, or German measles) causes the birthrate to decline because many pregnancies end in miscarriages. Social factors affecting the birthrate include the average age at marriage, the level of economic development, the availability and use of contraceptives and abortion, the number of women in the labor force, the educational status of women, and social attitudes toward reproduction. The U.S. birthrate in recent years has shown a steady decline. Work patterns have affected the birthrate as well. More American women today are postponing having children until their late twenties and early thirties. As a result, American women are having fewer children overall.

☑ **READING PROGRESS CHECK**

Predicting Can you make predictions about the fertility rate in the United States in the future—will it increase or decrease? Why?

Mortality

GUIDING QUESTION *How is mortality measured?*

Mortality refers to death. To analyze patterns of mortality within a population, sociologists look at *lifespan* and *life expectancy*. **Lifespan** is the most advanced age to which humans can survive. We know for sure of a Japanese man who lived nearly 121 years, but few people even approach this age. **Life expectancy** is the average number of years that persons in a given population, born at a particular time, can expect to live. Life expectancy around the world ranges from 83 years in Japan to 44 years in Afghanistan.

The **crude death rate** is figured by dividing the annual number of deaths by the total population and multiplying by 1,000. Like the crude birthrate, the crude death rate varies widely throughout the world. The worldwide average crude death rate is 9 per 1,000 persons. Looking at specific regions of the world, the death rate varies from a low of 1 per 1,000 in Qatar to a high of 17 per 1,000 in the Democratic Republic of the Congo. The death rate in the United States is about 8 per 1,000. Demographers are also interested in the variations in death rates for specific groups. They have devised *age-specific death rates* to measure the number of deaths per 1,000 persons in a specific age group, such as 15- to 19-year-olds or 60-to-64-year-olds. This allows demographers to compare the risk of death to members of different groups. Although death eventually comes to everyone, the rate at which it occurs depends on many factors, including age, sex, race, occupation, social class, standard of living, and health care.

The **infant mortality rate**—the number of deaths among infants under one year of age per 1,000 live births—is considered a good indicator of the health status of any group. This is because infants are the first to suffer from a lack of good medical care and sanitation. Infants in developing countries are almost ten times more likely to die before their first birthday than infants in developed nations. Working together, birthrates, fertility rates, and mortality rates determine world population growth.

✓ **READING PROGRESS CHECK**

Making Inferences What factors might increase life expectancy in a given population?

mortality death

lifespan the most advanced age to which humans can survive

life expectancy the average number of years that persons in a given population born at a particular time can expect to live

crude death rate the annual number of deaths per 1,000 members of a population

infant mortality rate the annual number of deaths among infants under one year of age per 1,000 live births

Women with their infants wait for health care at a clinic in Mogadishu, Somalia. Infant mortality is a key measure of the overall health and quality of life in a country.

▶ **CRITICAL THINKING**

Analyzing Cause and Effect Why is infant mortality considered a key measure of a society's health and well being?

Migration

GUIDING QUESTION *How is migration measured?*

migration *the movement of people from one geographic area to another*

Migration refers to the movement of people from one geographic area to another. Migration can occur within a country or between countries. An example of migration from country to country is the resettlement of African refugees from Somalia and Sudan in countries around the world. Many of the people who come to the United States from another country and settle in one particular city or region later move to another region, thus becoming internal migrants. Anyone who moves from one part of the country to another—say, from New York to Arizona—is engaging in internal migration.

People migrate for many different reasons, and those reasons can be seen in the several waves of immigration to the United States over the years. In the late nineteenth century, millions of people from southern and eastern Europe migrated to the United States. Many came for economic reasons. Living in poverty and often with no land of their own, they sought opportunity in America's industrializing economy. Some, like Jews from Poland and Russia, were also escaping persecution. Earlier in the nineteenth century, liberal-minded reformers migrated from Germany to the United States after conservative governments suppressed a revolution in their homeland. In recent years, hundreds of thousands of immigrants have come to the United States seeking jobs or the chance to start their own businesses. Others have fled political or social unrest in their homelands.

How Migration Is Measured

gross migration rate *the number of persons per 1,000 members of a population who enter or leave a geographic area*

net migration rate *the annual increase or decrease per 1,000 members of a population resulting from migration into and out of the population*

The **gross migration rate** into or out of an area is the number of persons per 1,000 members of a population who enter or leave a geographic area in a given year. *Net migration* is the difference between the number of people entering and leaving an area. Thus, the **net migration rate** is the annual increase or decrease per 1,000 members of a population resulting from movement into and out of the population. Between April 1, 2010, and July 1, 2011, for example, the United States had a net migration rate of about 2.3. That is, 2.3 more persons per 1,000 people in the total population entered the country than left the country. It is also possible, of course, to have a negative net migration rate, showing more people overall left an area than entered it.

When the U.S. Census Bureau reports migration rates, it refers only to the number of legal immigrants. Many people violate immigration laws to enter the United States. In the 1970s, the issue of illegal immigration—primarily from Latin American and Caribbean countries—became a major concern, and it continues to be a hot topic today. There are no precise statistics on either the illegal immigration rate or the total number of undocumented immigrants living in the United States. Currently, the U.S. Census Bureau estimates that there are about 7 million unauthorized immigrants living in the United States.

Rural-to-Urban Migration in the United States

When people move from rural to urban areas, this is called *rural-to-urban migration*. Migration to urban areas occurs often because people are seeking economic and career opportunities. For instance, a young man or woman might be unable to find a good job in a rural area or may want to follow a career path only available in urban areas.

A mass, long-term migration of this type began in the United States during World War I. Many African American men and women did not want to work in agriculture because the sharecropping system that had replaced slavery was still oppressive. Booming wartime factories in northern cities offered new economic

Nonmetropolitan Population Change Among 55–74-Year-Olds (recent and projected)							
	Nonmetropolitan Population Ages 55–74				Population Growth Rate		
U.S. Region	1990	2000	2010	2020	1990s	2000s	2010s
	Millions				Percentage		
Northeast	0.9	0.9	1.3	1.7	4.4	37.9	32.1
Midwest	2.6	2.7	3.2	3.9	2.0	20.5	21.9
South	3.5	3.9	5.0	6.3	11.2	28.5	26.1
West	1.0	1.2	1.7	2.3	20.3	48.2	31.8
Total*	8.0	8.6	11.2	14.2	8.5	29.7	26.5

*Totals may vary from the sum of regions' populations due to rounding.

Source: John Cromartie and Peter Nelson, *Baby Boom Migration and Its Impact on Rural America* (USDA, Economic Research Service, 2009)

◀ CHART

NONMETROPOLITAN POPULATION CHANGE
With the aging of the baby boomer generation, the migration from urban to rural, or nonmetropolitan, areas is increasing.

▶ **CRITICAL THINKING**

1. **Differentiating** In which regions of the country will the population of older adults living in nonmetropolitan areas grow faster than the national average?

2. **Theorizing** Why might older adults want to move to nonmetropolitan areas?

---

opportunities. The North also promised a more tolerant racial atmosphere compared to the South. This migration of African Americans from the rural South to the urban centers of the North was called "the Great Migration." During the roughly five decades of the Great Migration, approximately 7 million African Americans migrated from southern rural to northern urban areas.

Migration from rural to urban areas still occurs today, especially among certain groups. For instance, migrants are more likely to be young, and females migrate to urban areas more than males, probably due to the types of jobs available.

Urban-to-Rural Migration

Recently, migration in the other direction—urban to rural—has increased. In fact, it may continue to do so as more and more baby boomers reach retirement age and choose to move to small towns and rural areas, in search of recreation and scenic landscapes. This migration pattern is expected to create new demands for goods and services and different economic opportunities in affected rural areas in the coming years. In addition, such urban-to-rural migration will doubtless change the character of many areas that experience the influx of these new migrants.

✓ **READING PROGRESS CHECK**

Generalizing What causes people to migrate from one place to another?

LESSON 1 REVIEW

Reviewing Vocabulary
1. **Differentiating** What is the difference between lifespan and life expectancy?
2. **Identifying** What is the scientific study of population called?

Using Your Notes
3. **Analyzing** Use your notes from the lesson to name three factors demographers study.

Answering the Guiding Questions
4. **Defining** How do sociologists define population?
5. **Analyzing** How is fertility measured? What other factors influence the birthrate?
6. **Explaining** How is mortality measured?
7. **Explaining** How is migration measured?

Writing Activity
8. **Narrative** Write a science-fiction narrative set 100 years in the future. The plot of your narrative should focus on some aspect of demographics. For instance, the story could center around a dramatic increase or decrease in the birthrate or mortality rate, or it could tell the tale of a great migration—perhaps to another planet.

networks

There's More Online!

- ☑ **GRAPH** Long-Range Projections of World Population
- ☑ **GRAPH** Population Indicators in 2011
- ☑ **GRAPH** The Demographic Transition
- ☑ **IMAGE** A Dense Population
- ☑ **SELF-CHECK QUIZ**

LESSON 2
World Population

ESSENTIAL QUESTION • *What is demography and why do we study demographics?*

Reading HELPDESK

Academic Vocabulary
- phenomenon
- predict

Content Vocabulary
- census
- doubling time
- exponential growth
- demographic transition theory
- zero-population growth
- population momentum
- replacement level
- population control
- family planning
- population pyramid
- dependency ratio

TAKING NOTES:
Key Ideas and Details

Organizing As you read about world population, use a graphic organizer like the one below to record details about its growth and efforts to control that growth.

World Population	
Growth	Control

IT MATTERS BECAUSE
While the rate of world population growth is slowing, the world's population will continue to increase for many years. Population control has become a concern of many governments worried about providing for their future citizens.

The Problem of Population Growth

GUIDING QUESTION *Why is the world's population growing so fast?*

No organization has actually ever counted all the people in the world. World population figures are a composite of best estimates and national **census** figures, where available. While many countries count and categorize people living in those countries, the quality of census data varies a great deal and can be very unreliable. Nevertheless, world-population growth patterns can be identified.

Rapid world population growth is a relatively recent **phenomenon**. In fact, your grandparents have seen more population growth during their lifetimes than occurred during the preceding 4 million years. An estimated 250 million people were on Earth in A.D. 1. It was not until 1650 that the world's population doubled to half a billion. The second doubling occurred in 1800, bringing the world population to 1 billion. By 1930, another doubling had taken place. Less than 50 years after that, in 1976, a fourth doubling raised the world's population to 4 billion. In 2011, the world population reached 7 billion. At the current growth rate, the world's population is expected to be about 8 billion by 2025. As you can see, the number of years between each doubling of the population—called, for obvious reasons, the **doubling time**—has gotten much shorter in modern times. Interestingly, though, the doubling time from 1976 to 2025 is about the same as the previous doubling time. This is because of slower population growth in some parts of the world. The graph Projected Populations looks at key demographic statistics for a few countries.

The population has increased so dramatically in part because of the way population increases. We are accustomed to thinking in terms of *linear growth*, whereby amounts increase arithmetically (as in the progression 1, 2, 3, 4, 5, and so on). Population, however, does not grow linearly. It follows the principle of **exponential growth** and increases geometrically (as in the progression 2, 4, 8, 16, 32). With exponential growth, the amount of increase is greater each time period even though the rate of increase remains the same. This is because each increase is added to the base amount and becomes part of the calculation for the next rise.

A classic example of exponential growth goes as follows: A clever adviser presented a beautiful chess set to his king. In return, he asked only that the king give him one grain of rice for the first square on the chessboard; two grains, or double the amount, for the second square; four (doubling again) for the third; and so forth. The king, not being mathematically minded, agreed and ordered the rice brought forth. The eighth square required 128 grains and the twelfth took more than a pound of rice. Long before reaching the sixty-fourth square, the king's entire store of rice was depleted in the attempt to fulfill his promise to his adviser. Even today, the world's richest king could not produce enough rice to fill the final square. The reason is that to do so would require more than 200 billion tons of rice, or the equivalent of the world's current annual production of rice for the next 653 years.

The same kind of exponential growth seen in the rice example can be observed in population growth. If a population is growing at 1 percent per year, it takes 70 years to double. For example, suppose the population of a city was 50,000 in 1800. At a growth rate of 1 percent, that population would grow to 100,000 in 1870. By 1940, it would reach 200,000; by 2010, 400,000. Recalling the chessboard example, you can see that even a 1 percent growth rate can have serious consequences. The number of people added each year becomes part of the total population, which then increases by another 1 percent in the next year. When population grows faster than 1 percent a year, of course, the doubling time is much shorter.

✓ **READING PROGRESS CHECK**

Explaining What is exponential growth?

census regularly occurring count of a particular population

phenomenon an unusual or unaccountable fact or event

doubling time the number of years needed to double the base population size

exponential growth growth in which the amount of increase is added to the base figure at each time period

⌄ **GRAPHS**

PROJECTED POPULATIONS

China, India, and the United States are currently the three most populous countries in the world.

▶ **CRITICAL THINKING**

1. *Analyzing Visuals* Which country's population is expected to grow at the fastest rate? Which countries are expected to see a decline in population?

2. *Hypothesizing* Which problem do you think is more serious, rapid population growth or population decline? Why?

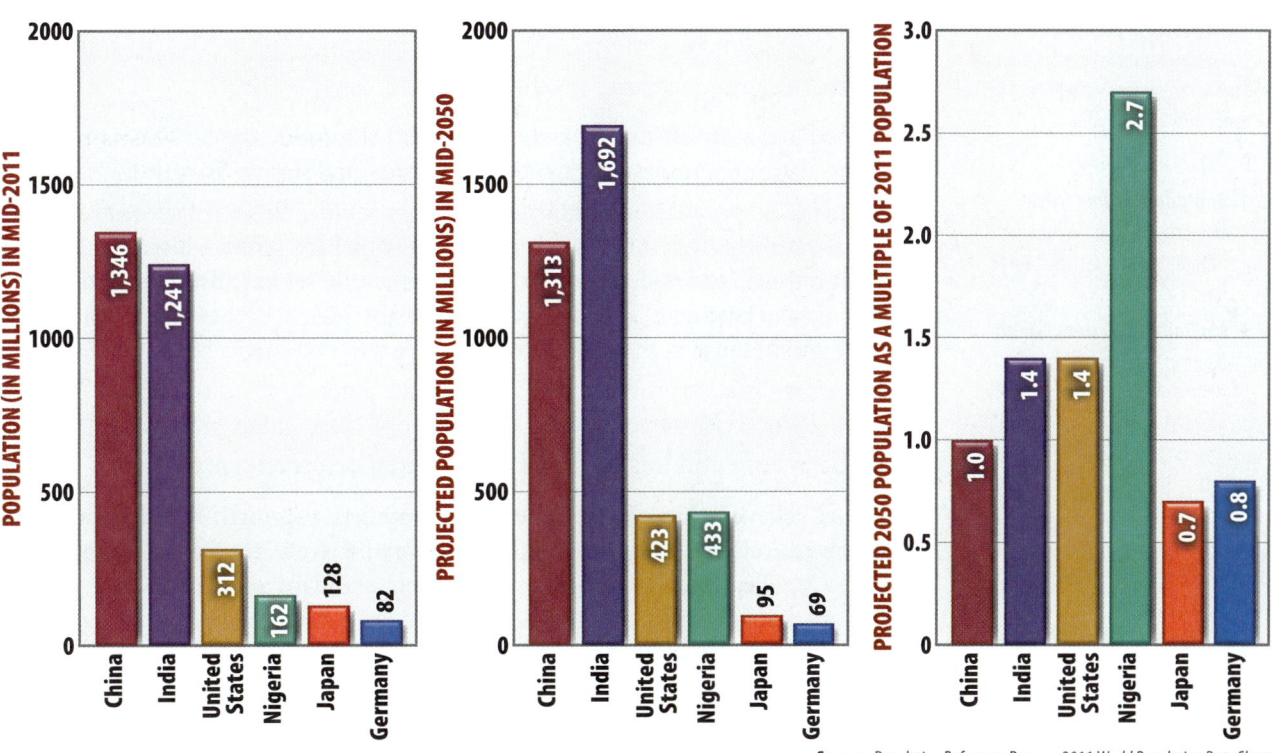

Source: Population Reference Bureau, *2011 World Population Data Sheet*

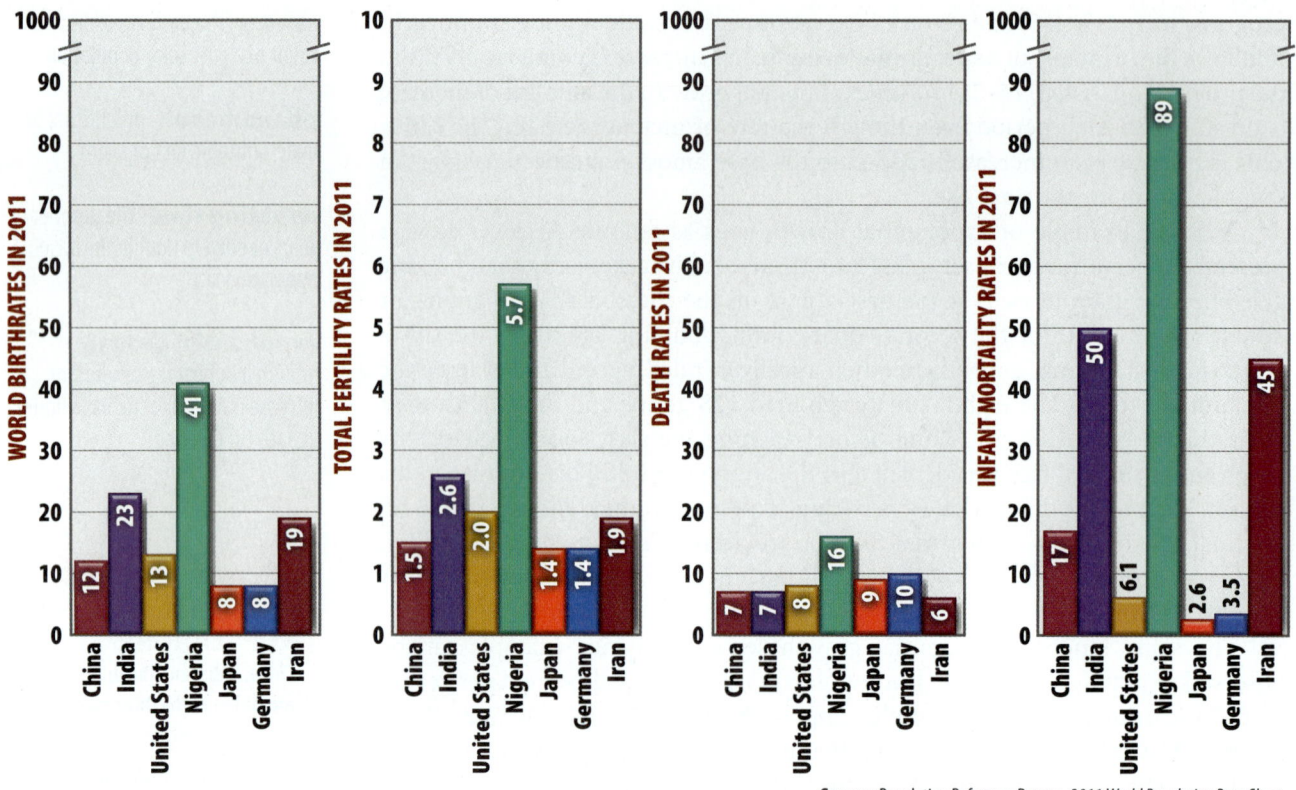

Source: Population Reference Bureau, *2011 World Population Data Sheet*

GRAPHS

POPULATION INDICATORS IN 2011

The fertility rate is the average number of children to which a woman gives birth. The birthrate and the death rate are the number of births or deaths per year per 1,000 people in the population. The infant mortality rate is the number of infants who die out of every 1,000 live births.

▶ **CRITICAL THINKING**

1. **Analyzing Visuals** What connection is there between birthrates and infant mortality rates?
2. **Making Connections** Which figure in these graphs explains Nigeria's high rate of population growth?

Theories of Population Growth

GUIDING QUESTIONS *What theories explain population growth? How do they explain population growth?*

Study of population growth began in 1798 when Thomas Malthus, an English minister and economist, published *An Essay on the Principle of Population*. Malthus described relationships between population growth and economic development. Other thinkers have contributed different views in more recent times.

Malthus recognized the exponential nature of population growth. He set this growth against the availability of food to conclude that there were natural limits. Here are the key concepts of his theory:

- Population, if left unchecked, will exceed the food supply. This is because population increases exponentially, and the food supply does not.
- Checks on population can be *positive* or *preventive*. Positive factors are events or conditions that increase mortality. They include famine, disease, and war. Preventive factors decrease fertility and include sexual abstinence and marrying at a later age. (Malthus emphasized abstinence because he was a minister and because at the time he wrote there was no reliable birth control.)
- For the poor, improvements in income are eaten up by more births, leading to less food per person, lower standards of living, and eventually death.
- The wealthy and well educated already exercise preventive checks.

Malthus believed that positive checks on population growth could be avoided through education of the poor. With education, he wrote, the poor would choose to have smaller families and thus raise their standard of living. That part of Malthus's theory is not generally known, however, because he is most remembered for his dire predictions that overpopulation would result in famine and poverty.

Although wrong in some of his key assumptions, Malthus had a lasting impact on population studies. His is not the only theory, however. Developed nations have followed a pattern of population growth different from that

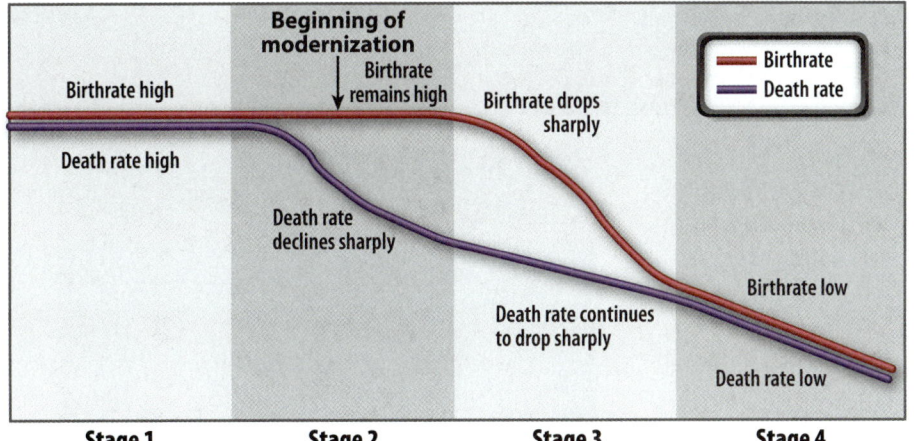

GRAPH

THE DEMOGRAPHIC TRANSITION

According to demographic transition theory, population growth is affected by economic development.

▶ **CRITICAL THINKING**

1. **Making Connections** Based on what other graphs in this lesson show about Nigeria, in what stage is that nation? Why do you think so?

2. **Identifying Cause and Effect** What factors can cause death rates to decline?

predicted by Malthus's theory. The **demographic transition theory** looks at the stages of economic development in a country to make predictions about population growth. This theory takes into consideration two things Malthus did not **predict**—increased agricultural productivity and reliable methods of birth control. Demographic transition theory describes four stages of population growth:

- Stage 1. Both the birthrate and the death rate are high. Population growth is slow. No countries are at this stage today.
- Stage 2. The birthrate remains high, but the death rate drops sharply because of modernizing factors, such as sanitation, increased food production, and medical advances. The rate of population growth is very high. Most African countries south of the Sahara are currently at this stage.
- Stage 3. The birthrate declines sharply, but because the death rate continues to go down, population growth is still rapid. Many Latin American countries are currently at this stage.
- Stage 4. Both the birthrate and the death rate are low, and the population grows slowly, if at all. The United States, Europe, and Japan are at this stage today.

World population growth has reached a turning point. After increasing for more than two centuries, the rate of annual population growth rate is declining.

demographic transition theory the theory that population growth is a function of the level of economic development in a country

predict to foretell what will happen

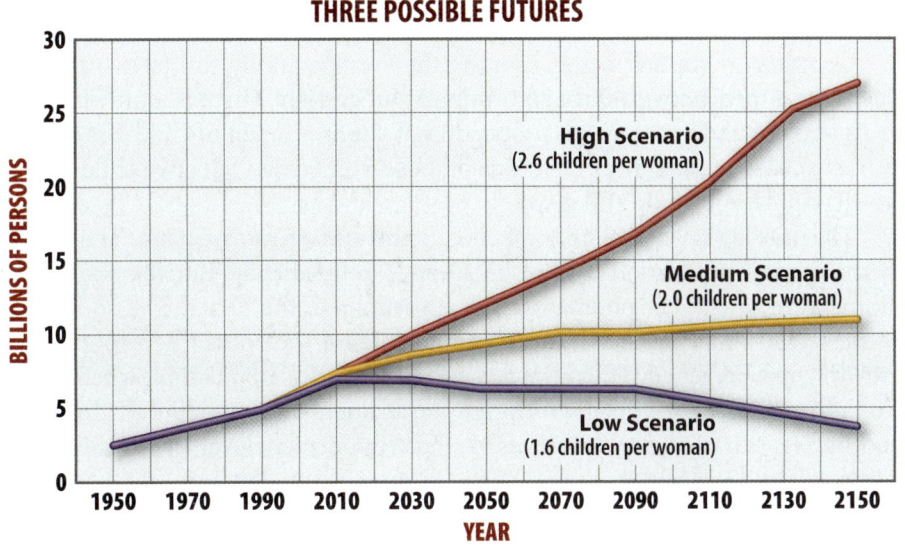

GRAPH

LONG-RANGE PROJECTIONS OF WORLD POPULATION, 2000–2150

Projections of the number of people in the world in 2150 vary tremendously depending on women's fertility rates.

▶ **CRITICAL THINKING**

1. **Analyzing Visuals** What are the three projected population levels in 2150?

2. **Making Predictions** Which scenario is more likely to lead to conflict between countries? Why?

Population and Urbanization

Connecting Sociology to Economics

THOMAS MALTHUS: ECONOMIST

The common perception of Thomas Malthus is of a gloomy prophet of doom. His theoretical models that seemed to promise a sharp crash in population present an arresting and alarming picture.

Malthus was interested in this problem from the perspective of an economist. Economists study the production, distribution, and consumption of goods, and the choices involved in those processes. Malthus, therefore, was not so much predicting population decline as he was examining the choices that prevent it.

In particular, Malthus was interested in promoting economic policies that would improve conditions in England. His ideas, however, were controversial. He did not believe it was possible to eliminate the miseries of poverty, and he viewed attempts to do so as misguided.

For example, Malthus opposed "poor laws," a welfare system that provided income to the poor. In his mind, such laws encouraged the irresponsible poor to have more children than they could support. Instead, he sought ways to encourage smaller family size among the poor. For his ideas, which accepted as unavoidable a certain level of poverty, Malthus was regarded by some as an enemy of the working classes.

Malthus believed that irresponsible biological reproduction among the poor of England was an economic issue.

▶ **CRITICAL THINKING**
1. **Contrasting** How did Malthus's ideas about poverty contrast with those who supported giving welfare to the poor?
2. **Identifying Central Issues** What made Malthus, to some people, an enemy of the working classes?

---

zero-population growth
a situation in which births are balanced by deaths so the population does not increase

population momentum
the inability to stop population growth immediately because of the previous high rate of growth

replacement level the birthrate at which a couple replaces themselves without adding to the population

In 2011, the growth rate was 1.2 percent, compared with the peak of 2.0 percent in the late 1960s. Moreover, the rate is projected to drop to zero by the year 2100. Yet despite the reduction in the annual growth rate and birthrate, the world's population will continue to increase and some 8 billion people are expected to inhabit the globe by 2025. Throughout the first half of this century, however, the annual growth rate is expected to decline until world population stabilizes at about 11 billion people. At this point, the world will have reached **zero-population growth**—when births are balanced by deaths so that the population does not increase.

Contrary to popular belief, limiting the average family size to two children does not immediately produce zero-population growth. There is a time lag of 60 to 70 years because of the high proportion of young women of child-bearing age in the world's population. Even if each of these women had only two children, the world population would still grow.

The time lag is what demographers call **population momentum**. The growth of the world's population cannot be stopped immediately. But the sooner the momentum of current population growth is halted, the better. The sooner the world fertility rate reaches the **replacement level** the sooner zero-population growth will be reached. The ultimate size of the world's population, when it does stop growing, depends greatly on when replacement level is achieved. To state it another way, for each decade it takes to reach replacement level, the world's population will increase by 15 percent.

✓ **READING PROGRESS CHECK**

Identifying What are two theories of population growth?

Population Control

GUIDING QUESTIONS *What strategies have been used to control population growth? Why have they been effective or ineffective?*

Since the death rate in both less developed and more developed nations has already dropped dramatically, any significant progress in curbing world population growth must concentrate on lowering birthrates. **Population control** refers to the conscious attempt to regulate population size through national birth control programs.

Government-Sponsored Population Control

Historically, most societies were more concerned with increasing the population than with overpopulation. Many births were needed to offset the high death rates from disease and poor hygiene. With surplus populations, aggressive nations were able to maintain larger armies. Agricultural societies needed large numbers of people to work the land. Aging parents wanted many children to help them feel more secure in old age. High birthrates were also encouraged in countries with religious laws against birth control.

Since the middle of the twentieth century, however, more (but certainly not all) governments have come to view high birthrates as a threat to their national well-being. By 1990, most countries had in place formal programs to reduce birthrates. Government policies for population control range from voluntary to compulsory.

Voluntary Population Control

The voluntary use of population control methods is generally known as **family planning**. Governments that support family planning provide information and services that help couples have only the number of children they want. Voluntary government policies range from indirect means, such as family planning education, to direct means, such as distributing birth control materials at health clinics.

Even when effective, however, family planning programs merely enable families to achieve their *desired* family size. Unfortunately for effective population control, the desired family size in many nations is quite high. For instance, the average preferred family size (number of children) in African nations is 7.1, and it is 5.1 in western Asian nations.

Effectiveness of Voluntary Population Control

Family planning has succeeded in Taiwan, where the birthrate fell below replacement level in the 1980s and has declined further since. Taiwan's family planning efforts were launched under very favorable conditions. When the Japanese withdrew from Taiwan after World War II, they left behind a labor force trained for industrial work. Consequently, the Taiwanese were able to use this advantage to build an expanding economy. With economic development came a decline in both birth- and death rates. In short, the Taiwanese went through the demographic transition fairly rapidly.

India was a different story. Family planning efforts failed because government officials and family planners did not take the broader social context into account. India did not have Taiwan's advantage of relatively rapid economic development. In addition, Indian officials and planners did not make enough of an effort to overcome cultural and religious opposition to birth control. Nor did they find ways to effectively communicate birth control information and technology. Finally, the national birth control program was left in the hands of individual state governments to implement.

population control attempts by government to control the birthrate

family planning the voluntary use of population control methods

China has used heavy advertising and various incentives to promote its "one-child" policy.

▶ **CRITICAL THINKING**

Making Predictions What are the benefits of the "one-child" policy?

Effectiveness of Compulsory Population-Control Methods

Both China and Singapore have forced population-control policies that have been effective. China has reduced its total fertility rate from 7.5 in 1963 to 1.6 in 2012 through a system of rewards and punishments that includes a "one-child" policy. One-child families receive a larger retirement pension and enjoy preference in housing, their child's school admission, and employment. Families with more than one child are subject to an escalating tax on each child, and they get no financial aid from the government for the medical and educational costs of their extra children.

Singapore began formally discouraging large families in 1969. The government passed laws that penalized parents with large families. These measures included denial of a paid eight-week maternity leave, loss of an income-tax allowance, diminished access to public housing, and increased maternity costs for each additional child. These policies worked so well that the total fertility rate in Singapore dropped from 4.5 children per woman to 1.4 between 1966 and 1987. In fact, the government became worried about the reduction in population size and, in 1986, reversed some of its earlier policies. The government of Singapore now supports three or more children for people able to afford them. Despite this effort, in 2012 Singapore's total fertility rate was only 0.8, far below replacement level.

The Importance of One Child

The importance of limiting family size, even by one child, can be illustrated by population projections for the United States. The hypothetical American case can help us understand the importance of population control. The U.S. Population Projections graph, based on data from 2000, contrasts the projected population in the year 2070 for an average family of two children and an average family of three children.

When small decreases in the death rate and net migration were assumed, an average two-child family was projected to result in a population of 300 million in 2015. With the hypothetical average family of three children, the U.S. population was projected to grow to 400 million by 2015. Over time, the difference of one extra child per family assumes added significance. By 2070, the two-child family would produce a population of 350 million, but the three-child family would push the population close to 1 billion.

The consequences of limiting population in less developed regions become clearer when the effect of even one child added to the average number of children in a family is recognized. Moreover, the addition of one child per family has a greater effect as the population base gets larger; not only is one extra person added,

GRAPH >

U.S. POPULATION PROJECTIONS

This graph projects population growth in the United States based on an average of either two children per family or three children per family.

▶ **CRITICAL THINKING**

1. *Analyzing Visuals* What is the population difference between the two sets of assumptions in 2015? What is the difference in 2070?

2. *Identifying Central Issues* What problems might the higher population level cause?

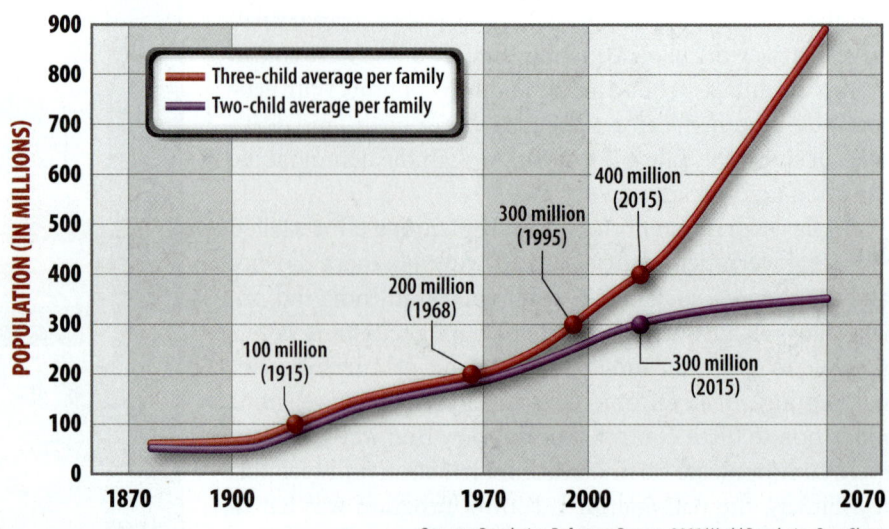

Source: Population Reference Bureau, *2000 World Population Data Sheet*

but theoretically that one person will be involved with the reproduction of yet another three, and on it goes. The largest populations are found in less developed countries, which also have the largest average number of children per family.

✓ **READING PROGRESS CHECK**

Evaluating Do you think compulsory population control is a good idea? Why or why not?

Population Pyramids

GUIDING QUESTION *Why is the dependency ratio important?*

Population pyramids allow you to see the age and sex composition of a population. Age and sex are key indexes to fertility and mortality rates, which in turn are used to project school and housing needs, health resources, and other key social services. Population pyramids illustrate the *dependency ratio* that results from different rates of population growth. The **dependency ratio** is the ratio of persons in the dependent ages (under 15 and over 64) to those in the "economically active" ages (15 to 64). The two aspects of the dependency ratio are *youth dependency* and *old-age dependency*. Less developed nations have much higher youth dependency than more developed nations. More developed nations have significantly higher old-age dependency. The population pyramids in the graphs show typical age sex data for more developed and less developed nations.

For less developed countries, such as Iran, a high youth dependency means that national income must be diverted from economic development to provide food, housing, and education for its high numbers of youths. In more developed countries, such as the United States, rising old-age dependency creates a different set of problems. With a larger number of older persons, there are fewer younger people in the labor force to support them.

✓ **READING PROGRESS CHECK**

Summarizing What do the two aspects of the dependency ratio mean?

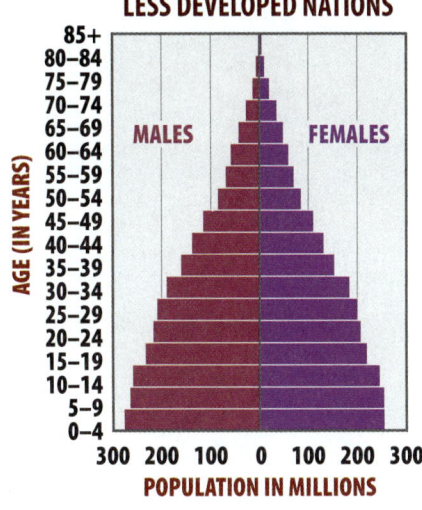

Source: United Nations Population Division

△ GRAPHS

POPULATION PYRAMIDS
These pyramids compare populations of countries grouped by economic development.

▶ **CRITICAL THINKING**

1. **Analyzing Visuals** What do these two population pyramids show?
2. **Making Connections** Which population pyramid shows a better dependency ratio? Why?

population pyramid a graphic representative of the age and sex composition of a population

dependency ratio the ratio of dependent persons to economically active persons

---

LESSON 2 REVIEW

Reviewing Vocabulary
1. ***Defining*** What is meant by the term *doubling time*?
2. ***Identifying*** What is family planning?

Using Your Notes
3. ***Summarizing*** Use your notes from the lesson to summarize key ideas about population growth and control.

Answering the Guiding Questions
4. ***Explaining*** Why is the world's population growing so fast?

5. ***Identifying*** What theories explain population growth? How do they explain population growth?
6. ***Analyzing*** What strategies have been used to control population growth? Why have they been effective or ineffective?
7. ***Explaining*** Why is the dependency ratio important?

Writing Activity
8. ***Argument*** Write an argument either for or against compulsory population control. Support your argument with reasons and evidence from this textbook and from your own experience.

Population and Urbanization **433**

networks

There's More Online!

- ✓ **CHART** Theoretical Perspectives: Urban Society
- ✓ **GRAPH** Ten Largest Cities
- ✓ **IMAGE** City Life
- ✓ **MAP** Urbanization
- ✓ **SELF-CHECK QUIZ**

LESSON 3
The Urban Transition

ESSENTIAL QUESTION • What is demography and why do we study demographics?

Reading HELPDESK

Academic Vocabulary
- transportation
- concentration

Content Vocabulary
- city
- urbanization
- over-urbanization
- suburbanization
- central-city dilemma
- gentrification
- edge city

TAKING NOTES:
Key Ideas and Details

ORGANIZING As you read about the urban transition, use a graphic organizer like the one below to record details about the growth of cities, urbanization, and suburbanization.

Growth of Cities
Urbanization:
Suburbanization:

IT MATTERS BECAUSE

With the Industrial Revolution came a major increase in the rate of urbanization. Today a large percentage of the world's population lives in or near a large urban area.

Urbanization

GUIDING QUESTION What is urbanization?

When does a village become a city? In Denmark and Sweden, an area with 200 inhabitants officially qualifies as a city. Populous Japan uses a much higher number—30,000. The U.S. Census Bureau defines an urban area as a place with a population of 2,500 or more. This number was set in the early 1900s, when urbanization had just begun and population concentrations were small. It is obviously too low for modern times. Recognizing that this standard is inadequate, the Census Bureau now distinguishes between two types of urban areas: *urbanized areas*, which have 50,000 people or more, and *urban clusters*, which have from 2,500 to 50,000 people.

A city is more than just a reasonably large number of people, however. Cities are also long lasting. The periodic Woodstock rock festivals gather a large number of people in one place but only for short periods. Clearly, large gatherings alone do not make a city. Cities also have a centralized economic focus. That is, they provide people with a chance to work in commerce, industry, or service. In summary, a **city** is a dense and permanent concentration of people living in a limited geographic area who earn their living primarily through nonagricultural activities.

The world has been greatly changed by **urbanization**—the process by which an increasingly larger portion of the world's population lives in or very near cities. Urbanization has been so common that it is now taken for granted in many parts of the world. Today, almost as many people live in urban areas as in rural areas. This is a fairly recent development in human history.

✓ **READING PROGRESS CHECK**

Paraphrasing In your own words, define the word *city*.

434

The History of Cities

GUIDING QUESTION *How have cities changed through history?*

The first cities appeared about five or six thousand years ago and were quite small by modern standards. One of the world's first major cities was Ur, located at the point where the Tigris and Euphrates Rivers meet (in modern-day Iraq). At its peak, Ur held only about 24,000 people. Later, during the time of the Roman Empire, only a few cities had populations over 100,000. The population of Rome itself was probably between 500,000 and 1 million.

In addition to their small sizes, the cities of ancient and medieval periods held only a small portion of the world's population. As recently as 1800, less than 3 percent of the world's population lived in cities of 20,000 or more. In contrast, more than 51 percent of the world's population lived in urban areas in 2011. In the United States, the 2010 census showed that 81 percent of the population lived in urban areas. Why have cities replaced rural living for most people?

city a dense and permanent concentration of people living in a specific area and working primarily in nonagricultural jobs

urbanization the process by which an increasingly larger portion of the world's population lives in cities

Preindustrial Cities

Many of the first urban settlements were located in what is known as the Fertile Crescent and were established around 3500 B.C. This was after people learned how to cultivate plants and domesticate animals, a period known as the *agricultural revolution*. The Fertile Crescent region is among the world's most fertile areas, and the farmers in the area were able to provide enough surplus food to feed people in the cities. A surplus food supply is necessary for urbanization to occur.

Once a surplus food supply was available, however, there were other reasons that people gathered in cities. Cities tended to attract four basic types of people: elites, functionaries, craftspeople, and the poor and destitute.

A Global Perspective

URBANIZATION

As you have learned, the Industrial Revolution encouraged the rapid growth of cities. This map shows that many countries now have urban populations that make up 60 percent or more of their total population. In other countries, however, most of the population still lives in rural areas.

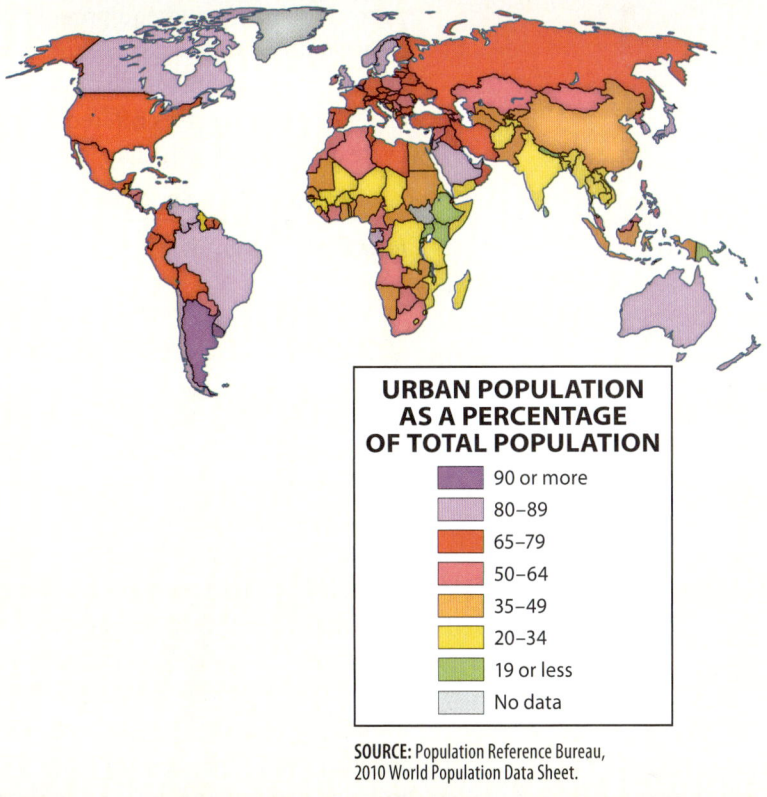

URBAN POPULATION AS A PERCENTAGE OF TOTAL POPULATION
- 90 or more
- 80–89
- 65–79
- 50–64
- 35–49
- 20–34
- 19 or less
- No data

SOURCE: Population Reference Bureau, 2010 World Population Data Sheet.

Geography Connection

1. **Human Systems** Consider the high rate of urbanization of a larger country, such as Argentina. What are some possible explanations for this phenomenon?
2. **Places and Regions** Study the data for the more developed countries and regions of the world, including Europe, the United States, and Canada. What generalization can you make about the degree of urbanization in these places?

Population and Urbanization

Many cities in India have some preindustrial characteristics as shown in this photograph of apartments in Mumbai.

▶ **CRITICAL THINKING**

Drawing Conclusions What elements can you identify in this photograph that have a preindustrial quality?

transportation the conveyance of passengers, goods, or materials

For elites, the city provided a setting for consolidating political, military, or religious power. The functionaries were the political or religious officials who carried out the plans of the elites. Their lives were undoubtedly easier than those of the peasant farmers in the countryside. Craftspeople, still lower in the stratification structure, came to the city to work and sell their products to the elites and functionaries. The poor came hoping to find work but were seldom able to improve their condition.

Africa, Asia, and Latin America are only partly industrialized. For this reason, many of their cities still have some preindustrial characteristics. This is particularly true in capital cities because they are a magnet for the rural poor seeking a better life. Rural migrants are attracted to these cities because there are limited opportunities for making a living in the rural areas, and the city promises a better life. Unfortunately, most of those who migrate to the cities are disappointed, because the expected employment opportunities do not exist. The migrants end up living in slums. Disease is commonplace, and epidemics are frequent.

The Rise of the Modern City

Beginning in the 1700s, the Industrial Revolution created major changes in **transportation**, agriculture, commerce, and industry. Technological developments led to better agricultural productivity and more efficient transportation systems. Farmworkers were free to leave rural areas and move into cities. More important, however, was the spread of factories.

Factories were not established to encourage the growth of cities, but they did. Factory owners tended to build in the same area to share raw materials and to take advantage of natural features, such as water power and river transport or ports. Machinery and equipment makers located their plants next to the factories they would be supplying. All these businesses in turn attracted retailers, innkeepers, entertainers, and a wide range of other people offering services to city dwellers. The more services offered, the more people were attracted, maintaining the cycle of urban growth. The industrial world was becoming an urbanized world.

✓ **READING PROGRESS CHECK**

Identifying Causes Why did people begin to gather in cities?

World Urbanization

GUIDING QUESTION *What are the differences in the patterns of world urbanization?*

Urbanization is a worldwide development. From 1800 to the mid-1980s, the number of urban dwellers increased 100 times while the population increased only about fivefold. In 2011, the United Nations reported that at least 50 percent of the world's population was living in urban areas. By 2030, that number is projected to rise to nearly 60 percent. This explosion of the urban population threatens to severely damage natural resources and ecosystems. For instance, 8 percent of the world's vertebrate species are considered endangered due to rapid urbanization. Furthermore, growing urban populations threaten the quality, and even the availability, of fresh water supplies. Fortunately, there is hope. If governments, urban planners, and conservationists work together, they may be able to mitigate some of the damage by shaping and controlling the growth of cities.

The Patterns of Urbanization

More developed and less developed countries have distinct patterns of urbanization. Most of the urban growth in less developed countries before the turn of the century occurred through colonial expansion. Western countries, which had been involved in colonial expansion since the late fifteenth century, held half the world under colonial rule by the latter part of the nineteenth century. It has been only since World War II that many of these colonial countries have become independent nations.

Since gaining independence, these former colonies have been experiencing rapid urbanization and industrialization. In fact, urbanization in these areas is now proceeding nine times faster than it did in the West during its urban expansion period. The rate of urbanization for major industrial nations in the West was 15 percent each decade throughout the nineteenth century. In the 1960s, the rate of urbanization in major less developed countries was 20 percent per decade.

Other Differences in Patterns of Urbanization

Industrialization in less developed countries, unlike the Western experience, has not kept pace with urbanization. Cities of North America and Europe had jobs for most migrants from rural areas. In the cities of less developed nations, the supply of labor from the countryside is greater than the demand for labor in the cities. A high rate of urban unemployment is the obvious result. The term **over-urbanization** has been created to describe a situation in which a city is unable to supply adequate jobs and housing for its inhabitants.

Another difference between urbanization in more developed and less developed countries is the number and size of cities. When grouped by size, cities in more developed countries form a pyramid: a few large cities at the top, many medium-sized cities in the middle, and a large base of small cities. In contrast, many less developed countries have one tremendous city that dwarfs a large number of villages. Kolkata, India, and Mexico City, Mexico, are examples.

over-urbanization a situation in which a city cannot supply adequate jobs and housing for its inhabitants

GRAPHS

TEN LARGEST CITIES, 1950 AND 2010
The size and regional location of the ten largest cities in the world has changed dramatically in the last six decades.

▶ **CRITICAL THINKING**

1. **Analyzing Visuals** What four cities were among the world's ten largest cities in both years? How much had they grown?
2. **Solving Problems** India had three of the ten largest cities in 2010. If you were India's leader, what would you do about that situation? Why?

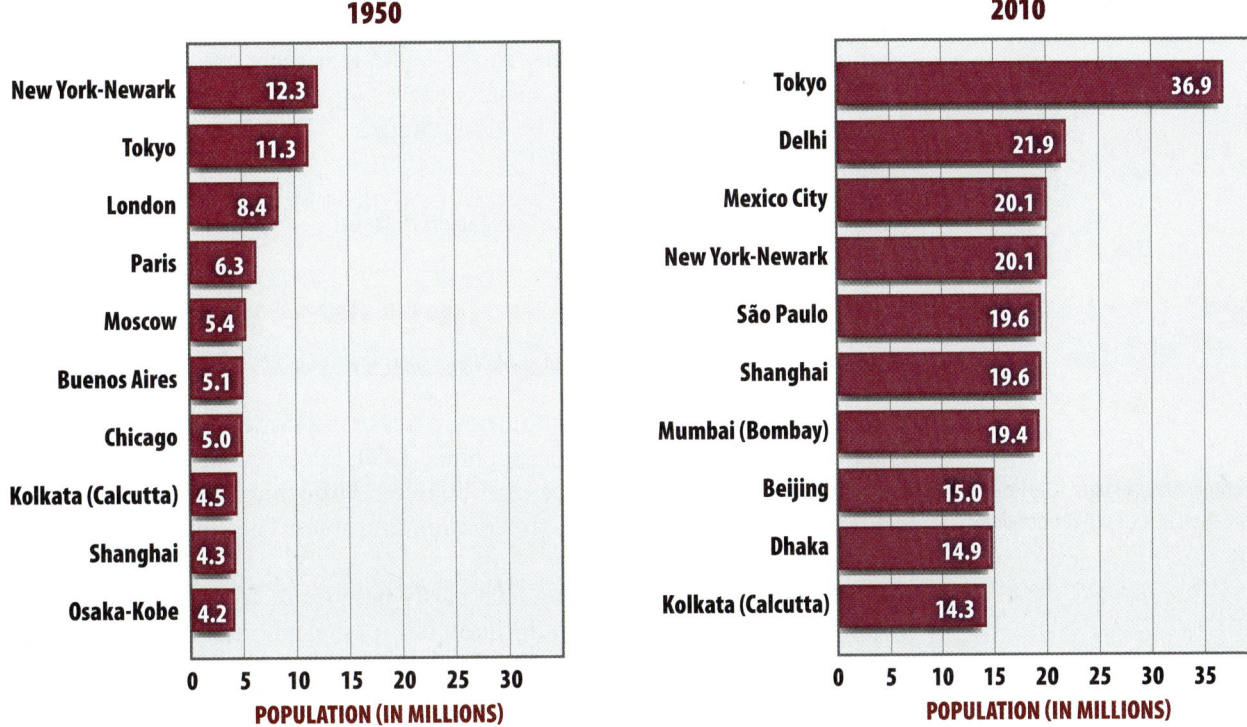

Source: United Nations, Department of Economic and Social Affairs, Population Division, *World Urbanization Prospects: The 2011 Revision*, 2012

Theoretical Perspectives

URBAN SOCIETY
This table illustrates how functionalism and conflict theory might approach the study of urban society.

Theoretical Perspective	Concepts	Sample Research Topic
Functionalism	Urbanization	Study the relationship between population density and the suicide rate
Conflict Theory	Over-urbanization	Identify the relationship between the distribution of scarce resources and social class

▶ **CRITICAL THINKING**

1. **Identifying** Why do you think symbolic interactionism was not included in this table?
2. **Constructing Arguments** Can you think of a research topic in urbanization for which symbolic interactionism would be appropriate?

Of the world's ten largest cities, only three—Shanghai, Buenos Aires, and Kolkata—were in less developed countries in 1950. By 2003, as you can see in the graph on the previous page, seven of the top ten largest urban areas were in less developed countries. By the year 2025, it is predicted that there will be 37 "megacities," with populations of 10 million or more. Over three-fourths of these new "megacities" will be in less developed countries, including the most impoverished societies in the world.

"Push" and "Pull" Factors

In explaining why people in less developed countries move to large cities with inadequate jobs and housing, sociologists point to the operation of "push" and "pull" factors. People are pushed out of their villages because expanding rural populations cannot be supported by the existing agricultural economy. They are forced to migrate elsewhere, and cities are at least an alternative. Poor people are also attracted, or pulled, to cities in the belief that there are opportunities for better education, employment, social welfare support, and good medical care. Unfortunately, they are likely to be disappointed.

☑ **READING PROGRESS CHECK**

Analyzing Why have patterns of urbanization differed?

Suburbanization in the United States

GUIDING QUESTION What is the central-city dilemma, and can it be solved?

Unlike cities in less developed countries, cities in the United States have recently been losing population, not gaining. Since 1950, the proportion of the population living in suburbs has more than doubled. **Suburbanization** occurs when central cities lose population to the surrounding areas. The United States is now predominantly suburban.

Suburbanization became possible partly because of technological developments. Improvements in communication (such as telephones, radios, television, and, later, computers, fax machines, and the Internet) have allowed people to live away from the central city. Developments in transportation (especially trains, highways, and automobiles) have made it possible both for people to commute to work and for many businesses to leave the central city for suburban locations.

suburbanization the loss of population of a city to surrounding areas

New technology is not the only cause of suburbanization, however. Some Americans prefer urban life, but most report that they would rather live in a rural setting. Even those who choose to live in the city believe they are giving up some advantages. Suburbs, with their low-density housing, have allowed many people to escape the problems of urban living without leaving the urban areas completely. Suburbs are attractive because of decreased crowding and traffic congestion, lower taxes, better schools, less crime, and reduced pollution.

The scarcity and high cost of land in the central city also encourage suburbanization. Finally, government policy has often increased the impact of economic forces. Federal Housing Administration regulations, for example, have favored the financing of new houses (which can be built most cheaply in suburban locations) rather than the refurbishing of older houses in central cities. Among other things, this has led to the *central-city dilemma*.

In the 1930s, only the upper and middle classes could afford to leave the central city. Not until the 1950s did the white working class follow them. Despite federal legislation prohibiting housing discrimination, the suburbs remained largely white until the 1970s. Businesses have followed the more affluent people to the suburbs, where they can find lower tax rates, less expensive land, and less congestion. Accompanying the exodus of the middle class, manufacturers, and retailers is the shrinking of the central-city tax base. This has created the **central-city dilemma**—the **concentration** of a large population in need of public services but without the tax base to provide them.

Some countertrends exist. Some city governments now require certain public employees to live in the city and encourage others to do so through incentives. Some parts of inner cities are being restored through **gentrification**—the development of low-income areas by middle-class home buyers, landlords, and professional developers. Finally, there is a fairly significant movement of middle-class people back to the central city.

Since increasing numbers of businesses and jobs have followed people to the suburbs, "suburban downtowns" are changing the face of urban America. An **edge city** is a smaller, more focused suburban version of an urban downtown, often specializing in a particular economic activity, such as computer technology or health care. Another recent trend is *new urbanism*. This trend involves new housing and shopping areas built to mimic old-style neighborhoods.

✅ **READING PROGRESS CHECK**

Analyzing Why have patterns of urbanization differed over time?

Edge-city development, with low-rise buildings in close proximity to metropolitan downtowns of major cities, is a growing trend.

▶ **CRITICAL THINKING**

Hypothesizing What are the benefits of living in an edge city?

central-city dilemma the concentration of people in need of public services without the tax base-generated funds to provide for them

concentration something that has been gathered together

gentrification the development of low-income areas by middle-class home buyers, landlords, and professional developers

edge city a suburban unit specializing in a particular economic activity

---

LESSON 3 REVIEW

Reviewing Vocabulary
1. *Defining* What is over-urbanization?
2. *Differentiating* How is suburbanization different from urbanization?

Using Your Notes
3. *Summarizing* Use your notes to summarize key ideas about the growth of cities, urbanization, and suburbanization.

Answering the Guiding Questions
4. *Defining* What is urbanization?
5. *Identifying* How have cities changed through history?
6. *Analyzing* What are the differences in the patterns of world urbanization?
7. *Predicting* What is the central-city dilemma, and can it be solved?

Writing Activity
8. *Narrative* Write a chronological narrative in which you trace the evolution of the city from its beginnings to its most recent manifestations, such as the edge city.

FOCUS on research
Field Research

Gang Leader for a Day: A Rogue Sociologist Takes to the Street

Sudhir Venkatesh, a sociologist who studies urban populations, describes the plight of poor African American residents of a massive urban housing project, the Robert Taylor Homes in Chicago. The project, which was home to thousands of residents, was torn down amid promises of improved opportunities for project residents—promises that Venkatesh found proved mostly empty.

PRIMARY SOURCE

"Politicians . . . promised that tenants would be relocated to middle-class neighborhoods with good schools, safe streets, and job opportunities. But reliable information was hard to come by. Nor would it be so easy to secure housing outside the black ghetto. The projects had been built forty years earlier in large part because white Chicagoans didn't want black neighbors. Most Robert Taylor tenants thought the situation hadn't changed all that much.

. . . In the media all you heard were politicians' promises to help CHA [Chicago Housing Authority] tenants forge a better life. On the ground, meanwhile, the lowest-ranking members of society got pushed even lower, thanks to a stingy and neglectful city agency and the constant hustling of the few people in a position to help. In the coming months, the place began to take on the feel of a refugee camp, with every person desperate to secure her own welfare, quite possibly at the expense of a neighbor.

Not everyone, however, was so selfish or fatalistic. For some tenants demolition represented a chance to start fresh with a better apartment in a safer neighborhood. It was particularly inspiring to watch such tenants work together toward this goal while their elected leaders mainly looked out for themselves.

One such optimist was Dorothy Battie, a forty-five-year-old mother of six who had spent nearly her entire life in the projects. . . .

'See here's the problem,' Dorothy explained. 'I know what it's like out there in the private market. You end up in some apartment, with no one around, no one to help you. And you're scared. At least if a few people can move with each other, stay together, they can help each other. Lot of people out there don't like us because we come from the projects. They may not answer the door if we knock for help. So I want to make sure people don't get stuck in the cold.' . . .

. . . Despite her perseverance, she was able to help only four [families]. . . move out together, to neighboring apartments in Woodlawn and South Shore. . . . As it turned out Dorothy's success rate was easily as good as that of the various social-services agencies contracted by the CHA, each of which was awarded hundreds of thousands of dollars to carry out the job. Dorothy herself would stay in Robert Taylor until it was demolished, and then she joined her daughter Lee-Lee in Englewood, a high-crime predominantly black neighborhood a few miles away.

> "For some tenants demolition represented a chance to start fresh with a better apartment in a safer neighborhood. It was particularly inspiring to watch such tenants work together toward this goal while their elected leaders mainly looked out for themselves."

Dorothy's move to Lee-Lee's house was, unfortunately, a typical outcome for many tenants who left Robert Taylor and other CHA projects. While the goal of the demolition was to move families to safer, integrated communities, the CHA was so inept that nearly 90 percent of the relocated tenants wound up living in poor black areas that left them as badly off as being in the projects, or worse.

In place of the projects, the city began to build market-rate condominiums and town houses, three-story structures tucked cozily together instead of the sixteen-story high-rises separated by vast expanses. Robert Taylor tenants had been promised the right to return to the community once construction was done, but fewer than 10 percent of the units were set aside for public-housing families. It is little wonder that the prevailing wisdom in Chicago is that the Daley administration and the powerful real-estate interests, rather than creating new and improved low-income housing, in fact knocked down the projects to initiate a land grab."

—from *Gang Leader for a Day*, 2008

Working With the Research

1. **Summarizing** Describe the events that take place in the excerpt.
2. **Contrasting** What is the difference, as described by the author, between resident Dorothy Battie and the paid city officials involved in these events?
3. **Analyzing** What does this excerpt suggest about the challenges of the urban poor in the United States?

networks

There's More Online!

- ☑ **DIAGRAM** Theories of City Growth
- ☑ **GRAPHIC ORGANIZER** Urban Ecology
- ☑ **IMAGE** Roadside Motels
- ☑ **SELF-CHECK QUIZ**

LESSON 4
Urban Ecology

ESSENTIAL QUESTION • What is demography and why do we study demographics?

Reading HELPDESK

Academic Vocabulary
- transition
- core

Content Vocabulary
- urban ecology
- concentric-zone theory
- sector theory
- multiple-nuclei theory
- peripheral theory

TAKING NOTES:
Key Ideas and Details

Organizing As you read about urban ecology, use a graphic organizer like the one below to record details about the theories of city growth.

Theories of the Growth of Cities
Concentric-Zone:
Sector:
Multiple-Nuclei:
Peripheral:

It Matters Because

Urban ecologists have developed four major theories of city growth: concentric-zone theory, sector theory, multiple-nuclei theory, *and* peripheral theory. *Combining insights from all four theories is useful to our understanding of how humans relate to city environments.*

The Nature of Urban Ecology

GUIDING QUESTION *What is urban ecology?*

Although every city is unique, patterns have been found in the way humans interact within the cities they inhabit. **Urban ecology** is the study of the relationships between humans and their city environments. Sociologists today argue that human behavior determines the layout and landscape of the urban environment. In turn, the urban environment affects human behavior.

In the 1920s and 1930s, sociologists at the University of Chicago studied the effects of the city environment on city residents. They asked such questions as: Why are there differences between areas of a city? How do different areas affect one another? What processes change an area? To answer these and other questions, the University of Chicago sociologists developed theories of urban ecology, including theories of city growth.

Today, sociologists, urban planners, city leaders, ecologists, and others interested in urban growth understand that the health of the physical environment is closely connected to the physical, social, and mental well-being of residents. Urban ecologists and their partners study the trees, plants, rivers, wildlife, and other natural resources to understand how they are affected by development, pollution, and other human activities. In response to their findings, scientists, urban planners, conservationists, leaders, and ordinary citizens are taking action around the world to protect urban environments and ecosystems, thereby also protecting the quality of life of urban residents.

✓ **READING PROGRESS CHECK**

Identifying What relationships do urban ecologists study?

Theories of City Growth

GUIDING QUESTIONS *What theories explain urban growth? How do they differ?*

Sociologists focus on four major theories of city growth. *Concentric-zone theory* describes urban growth in terms of circular areas that grow from the central city outward. *Sector theory* emphasizes the importance of transportation routes in the process of urban growth. *Multiple-nuclei theory* focuses on specific geographic or historical influences. *Peripheral theory* emphasizes the growth of suburbs around the central city. The four approaches lead to quite different images of urban space.

No city exactly fits any of these images, however. Indeed, the theories tell us more when considered together than they tell us separately. To understand why this is so, we must first examine each theory.

Concentric-Zone Theory

Ernest Burgess, like other early sociologists at the University of Chicago, was interested in the causes and consequences of Chicago's growth. His work led to the **concentric-zone theory**, which describes city growth in terms of distinctive zones—zones that develop from the central city outward in circles. Many northern cities that experienced a great deal of immigration and rapid growth developed this way.

As illustrated in the diagram below, the innermost circle is the *central business district*, the heart of the city. This district contains major government and private office buildings, banks, retail and wholesale stores, and entertainment and cultural facilities. Because land values in the central city are high, space is at a premium. The central business district contains a large proportion of a city's important businesses, partly because the less important ones are unable to compete for the expensive space there.

The central business district strongly influences other parts of a city. Its influence is especially clear in the zone immediately surrounding it. Because this zone is undergoing **transition**, or a process of change, Burgess called this the *zone in transition*.

urban ecology the study of the relationship between humans and city environments

concentric-zone theory the theory that describes urban growth in terms of circular areas that grow from the central city outward

transition the process of changing from one state to another

▽ DIAGRAMS

THEORIES OF CITY GROWTH

These diagrams show the four major theories of urban growth.

▶ **CRITICAL THINKING**

1. **Synthesizing** For each theory, state one contribution that adds to our understanding of urban growth.

2. **Drawing Conclusions** Does the term *urban sprawl* fit into any of these models? Why or why not?

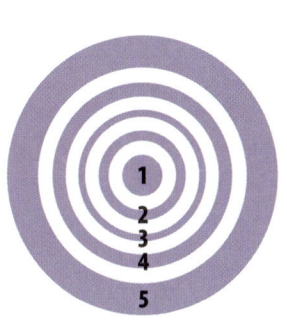

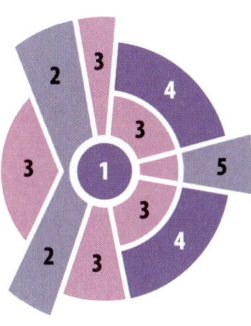

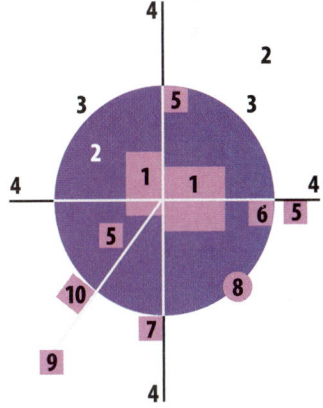

CONCENTRIC-ZONE THEORY
1. Central business district
2. Zone in transition
3. Zone of workingmen's homes
4. Residential zone
5. Commuter's zone

SECTOR THEORY
1. Central business district
2. Wholesale, light manufacturing
3. Lower-class residential
4. Middle-class residential
5. Upper-class residential

MULTIPLE-NUCLEI THEORY
1. Central business district
2. Wholesale, light manufacturing
3. Lower-class residential
4. Middle-class residential
5. Upper-class residential
6. Heavy manufacturing
7. Outlying business district
8. Residential suburb
9. Industrial suburb

PERIPHERAL THEORY
1. Central city
2. Suburban residential area
3. Circumferential highway
4. Radial highway
5. Shopping mall
6. Industrial district
7. Office park
8. Service center
9. Airport complex
10. Combined employment and shopping center

Source: Adapted from Chauncy D. Harris, *Urban Geography*, 1997

Connecting Sociology to Human Geography

THE INFORMAL HOUSING SECTOR

In terms of economic development, housing is a central factor. Housing is a basic human need, but it is also a means of encouraging saving and investment and a source of capital. Home ownership is also a means of promoting political stability. In many developing cities, however, large numbers of residents—almost all of them poor—are forced to live in what observers call "informal housing." This term refers to housing that is built on land that the occupants do not own. Informal housing is often clustered in large settlements that are not planned and do not receive basic city services. The scale of the problem is massive—and likely to get worse as more and more rural poor move to the cities. Sadly, this account about an informal settlement in Nairobi, Kenya, is not unusual.

In an informal settlement, residents often live without many basic city services.

PRIMARY SOURCE

"As his peers in Korogocho, an informal settlement in Nairobi, leave for school, 15-year-old John Kinuthia sets off too. But instead of heading to school, he walks half a kilometer to the city's largest dump site to eke out a living.

At the dump, John joins men, women and children scurrying about the garbage. None of them have protective clothing, gloves or masks. All they have are hooks, which they use to fish out items, and gunny bags to bring their wares to buyers.

'I rummage through the mounds of garbage for plastics, clothes, shoes . . . anything that I can sell for a little money,' John said. The items either make it to factories for recycling or, in the case of clothes, cutlery, electronics and the household goods, they are re-sold in the streets.

Between 1980 and 2009, the population of Nairobi, the capital, ballooned from 862,000 to about 3.4 million—a growth accompanied by increasing rates of poverty and poor health outcomes. Around two thirds of the city's population now lives in crowded informal settlements, often with poor access to basic services.

John dropped out of school in 2010, when his mother could no longer afford it. Although primary education is free, parents are expected to buy uniforms and desks for their children and contribute to school projects.

His mother, Jemima Wambui, wishes he could go back to school. But her earnings, from selling chapati bread on the roadside, are simply not enough. 'I have to fend for John and his sister, and her four children. I have to clothe them, feed them and pay the rent. They all rely on me,' she said.

. . . According to local priest and educator John Webootsa, the area has only two public primary schools. 'These schools serve only a small fraction of the population of this area. . . . Other parents have to struggle to send their children to the informal schools, which are privately run.'

As a result, about 30 per cent of children in this informal settlement don't go to school at all, Mr. Webootsa said.

'Most of them will end up at the dumpsite, because they must earn a living somehow. In fact, child prostitution and child marriage are so common here,' he said.

Where available, urban data reveal wide disparities in children's rates of survival and nutritional status, the result of unequal access to services. Yet even this information is often hard to find. Further data and analysis are needed to address the needs of these impoverished and excluded urban children.

Mr. Webootsa is advocating for the government to allocate more resources for children in informal settlements. UNICEF's flagship report, 'The State of the World's Children 2012' also calls on governments to direct resources and services to these children. . . .," and to help understand the scale of urban poverty so officials and partner organizations can better address children's needs."

—Pamela Sittoni, "The State of the World's Children, 2012"

DBQ ▶ CRITICAL THINKING

1. **Identifying Central Issues** What defines "informal housing"?
2. **Identifying Cause and Effect** How has rapid urbanization contributed to the development of informal settlements?

As new businesses and activities enter the central business district, the district expands by invading the next zone. This area may have been a residential area inhabited by middle- or upper-class families who left because of the invasion of business activities. Most of the property in this zone is bought by those with little interest in the area. Rather than investing money in building maintenance, landowners simply extract rent from the property or sell it at a profit after the area has become more commercialized. Until the zone in transition is completely absorbed into the central business district (which may never occur), it is used for slum housing, warehouses, and marginal businesses that are unable to compete economically for space in the central business district. In short, the invasion of business activities creates deterioration for the zone in transition.

Surrounding the zone in transition are three zones devoted primarily to housing. The *zone of workingmen's homes* contains modest but stable neighborhoods populated largely by blue-collar workers. In the northern United States, the zone of workingmen's homes is often inhabited by second-generation immigrants who have had enough financial success to leave the deteriorating zone in transition. Next comes a *residential zone* containing mostly middle-class and upper-middle-class neighborhoods. Single-family dwellings dominate this zone, which is inhabited by managers, professionals, white-collar workers, and some well-paid factory workers. On the outskirts of the city, often outside the official city limits, is the *commuter's zone*, which contains upper-class and upper-middle-class suburbs.

Sector Theory

Not everyone agreed with Burgess's theory of how cities grow. The sociologist Homer Hoyt offered another model—**sector theory**. Hoyt's work indicated that growth patterns do not necessarily spread out in rings from the central business district. Instead, he believed that growth is more strongly affected by major transportation routes.

As the "Theories of City Growth" diagram shows, sectors tend to be pie shaped, with wedges radiating from the central business district to the city's outskirts. Each sector is organized around a major transportation route. Once a given type of activity is organized around a transportation route, its nature tends to be set. Thus, some sectors will be predominantly industrial, others will contain stores and professional offices, others will be "neon strips" with motels and fast-food restaurants, and still others will be residential sectors, each with its own social class and ethnic composition.

As in concentric-zone theory, cities are generally circular. But because of the importance of transportation routes extending from the central business district, the boundaries of many cities form a star-like pattern, rather than a uniformly circular shape. The exact shape of a city, however, is not a major issue in sector theory. Emphasis here is on how patterns of growth are organized around transportation routes. Cities that follow this pattern include Seattle, Richmond, and San Francisco.

Multiple-Nuclei Theory

Many cities have areas that cannot be explained by either concentric-zone or sector theory. Geographers Chauncy Harris and Edward Ullman suggested that cities do not always follow a pattern dependent on a central district. The **multiple-nuclei theory** states that a city may have several separate centers. These specialized centers can develop because of the availability of automobiles and highways. They reflect such factors as geography, history, and tradition. The city of Boston fits this model.

sector theory the theory that emphasizes the importance of transportation routes in the process of urban growth

multiple-nuclei theory the theory that focuses on specific geographic or historical influences on urban growth

"Neon strips" with motels and fast-food restaurants are common along transportation routes.

▶ **CRITICAL THINKING**

Analyzing Visuals What type of sector does the photograph suggest?

Quick Case Study

HOW DO URBAN ENVIRONMENTS AFFECT PEOPLE?
Cities present a number of different types of environments. These different environments have different effects on people.

Procedure
1. Collect photographs or illustrations of different types of urban spaces—recreational, residential, commercial, rich, and poor.
2. Create a questionnaire that measures individuals' reactions to the different photographs. For example, the questionnaire could ask viewers to rate, on a scale, whether they would like to visit the place pictured.
3. Show the pictures to ten people and collect their responses.

Analysis
As you collect the responses, answer the following:
1. Were there any patterns in the answers to your questionnaire? Did people respond similarly to the same pictures?
2. Can you draw any conclusions about urban environments based on your survey?

core the innermost or most important part of something

peripheral theory the theory that emphasizes the growth of suburbs around the central city

Peripheral Theory
The three theories of urban growth just discussed were originally developed more than 60 years ago. The insights of each theory still help us understand how cities have expanded from the center outward. This is especially the case for older cities, such as Chicago and San Francisco. Many cities today, however, no longer have a central city **core**. Dependence on shipping, railroads, and heavy manufacturing has been replaced by more flexible means of transportation, such as cars and trucks. And large urban areas are now encircled by highways. New technologies are also loosening the ties of most parts of the city to the central-city core. As a result, many cities are now oriented *away* from the older urban core.

Chauncy Harris formulated the **peripheral theory**. The dominant feature of this model is the growth of suburbs (and edge cities) around and away from the central cities. Peripheral theory brings urban growth research up to date.

Contributions by Each Theory
As suggested earlier, no single theory covers the dynamics of city growth for all cities. But each theory emphasizes the importance of certain factors that cannot be overlooked by anyone interested in city growth. Concentric-zone theory emphasizes the fact that growth in any one area of a city is largely influenced by politics and economics. Sector theorists note that decisions about the placement of railroad lines had important effects on the growth of cities in the nineteenth and early twentieth centuries, and highways have an even larger impact now. Although multiple-nuclei theory is vague in its predictions, the types of geographic and historical factors it emphasizes are also important for understanding any specific city. Finally, peripheral theory has brought urban growth research up to date by emphasizing the development of suburbs around the central city.

☑ **READING PROGRESS CHECK**

Identifying Which theory seems most applicable to the city you live in or the city with which you are most familiar? Explain.

LESSON 4 REVIEW

Reviewing Vocabulary
1. *Defining* Which theory focuses on the growth of suburbs?
2. *Identifying* What does sector theory emphasize in the growth of cities?

Using Your Notes
3. *Summarizing* Use your notes from the lesson to summarize the key ideas of the four theories of the growth of cities.

Answering the Guiding Questions
4. *Defining* What is urban ecology?
5. *Identifying* What theories explain urban growth? How do they differ?

Writing Activity
6. *Informative/Explanatory* Research the growth of a city of your choice, either in this or another country. Report your findings as a research paper or as a multimedia presentation.

CHAPTER 15 Assessment

Directions: On a separate sheet of paper, answer the questions below. Make sure you read carefully and answer all parts of the questions.

Lesson Review

Lesson 1

1. **Analyzing** Define fertility and fecundity and explain why fertility rates are much lower than fecundity rates.

2. **Contrasting** How does the crude death rate in the United States differ from that of the Democratic Republic of Congo? What do you believe to be the reasons for this difference? Explain whether you believe that people in the United States, as long as they have the resources to care for themselves and their own families, should be concerned about applying their time, energy, and/or economic resources to aid in lowering death rates, such as infant mortality rates, in less developed nations.

Lesson 2

3. **Identifying Cause and Effect** Would limiting the average family size to two children immediately produce zero population growth? Explain.

4. **Considering Advantages and Disadvantages** What is a population pyramid? Discuss the advantages and the disadvantages of sociologists utilizing population pyramids.

Lesson 3

5. **Diagramming** Create a flowchart to depict the relationships among the four basic types of people attracted to preindustrial cities.

6. **Making Connections** Within what context are sociologists likely to refer to "push" and "pull" factors? Explain.

Lesson 4

7. **Formulating Questions** At the beginning of Lesson 4, note the questions asked by sociologists at the University of Chicago regarding the effects of the city environment on city residents. Why do you think the sociologists chose these questions? List at least two additional questions you think would have been helpful—and explain why.

8. **Interpreting Significance** Why is the central-business district referred to as the "heart of the city"? Why is real estate so expensive in this area?

DBQ Analyzing Primary Sources

Use the document to answer the following question.

PRIMARY SOURCE

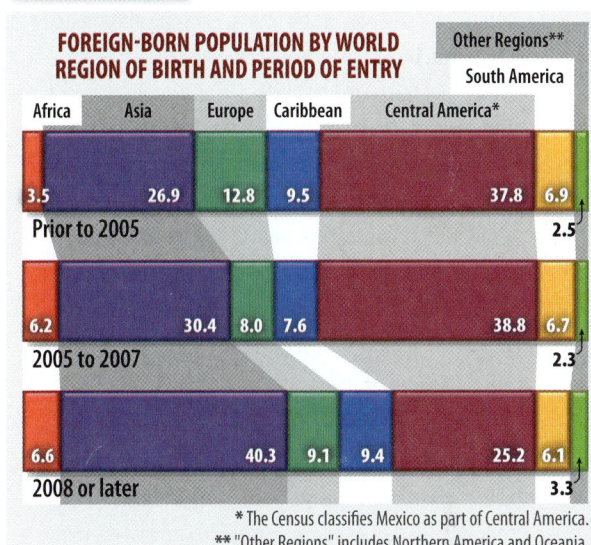

* The Census classifies Mexico as part of Central America.
** "Other Regions" includes Northern America and Oceania.
Source: U.S. Census Bureau, 2010 American Community Survey

9. **Drawing Conclusions** In this chapter, you read about demographic transition theory. This graph provides data regarding immigration to the United States. What conclusions can you reasonably draw from the graph about the United States and the countries of origin as related to demographic transition theory?

Need Extra Help?

If You've Missed Question	1	2	3	4	5	6	7	8	9
Go to page	421–422	423	430	433	435	437	442	443	429

CHAPTER 15 Assessment

Directions: On a separate sheet of paper, answer the questions below. Make sure you read carefully and answer all parts of the questions.

Exploring the Essential Question

10. *Summarizing* Imagine you have been hired by the U.S. Census Bureau to train new researchers. You know it is important for the researchers to understand population and urbanization in order to perform their job duties effectively. You also know that these new employees will be assimilating a great deal of new information, so you will need to provide a reference resource that will "hit the high points" and still provide an overview of the information they need. Due to their strong qualifications, you are aware that they will be able to perform additional research on their own, if necessary, after they have been apprised of the general information you provide. To provide this general information for them, you will create a reference resource that summarizes each lesson in this chapter, "hitting the high points" as you go. Remember that your summaries will need to focus on the most important points.

College and Career Readiness Skills

11. *Research and Methods* You have been hired to develop a new marketing campaign for a business in your community. Your employer has asked you to determine—based on the demographics of your community—how to reach and influence the maximum number of community members. If you are successful, the business will draw in more customers and greater profits. For this task, you may select the type of business. Then you will develop an overview for a marketing campaign, which may consist of online, print, and other methods of reaching potential customers. In your overview, identify the methods you have chosen to use, and explain why these methods will be beneficial based on the demographics of your community and the customers your employer wishes to reach.

Critical Thinking

12. *Exploring Issues* Émile Durkheim was concerned about the changes brought about by the Industrial Revolution. He studied suicide rates and found them to be higher in urban areas than in rural areas. What factors might contribute to higher suicide rates in urban areas? Do you think Durkheim's findings hold true today, or is the likelihood of suicide just as great in rural and suburban areas in today's society?

21st Century Skills

CREATING AND USING GRAPHS, CHARTS, DIAGRAMS AND TABLES

13. *Creating Diagrams* Create a diagram to compare and contrast the effectiveness of voluntary population control and compulsory population control methods.

Research and Presentation

14. *Gathering Information* You have just landed a contract to head up the Urban Planning Board of Planned Lovelyville, U.S.A. Your primary responsibility is to redevelop the city design. Determine which theory or combination of theories you will utilize as you design the city.

15. *Evaluating* Using a computer, create the city design you will use. Consider options such as a blueprint, a chart, an artist's rendering, or a combination of these. Write a report to the city council, explaining the theory or theories you have chosen to utilize and the reason for your choice. Present the explanation and visual to the class, who will serve as your city council.

Need Extra Help?

If You've Missed Question	10	11	12	13	14	15
Go to page	417–446	422	443–446	431–432	442–446	442–446

Social Change and Collective Behavior

ESSENTIAL QUESTIONS • What influences collective behavior?
• What factors influence social change?

networks
There's More Online about social change and collective behavior.

CHAPTER 16

Technology & Society
Social Movements and Technology

Lesson 1
Social Change

Lesson 2
Theoretical Perspectives on Social Change

Lesson 3
Collective Behavior

Lesson 4
Social Movements

Sociology Matters...

Have you ever found yourself swept up in the excitement of a crowd? Some sociologists study how members of a crowd influence each other, changing the character of the crowd as a whole. The behavior of groups can have a powerful effect on a society, bringing about change. Social processes such as the spread of ideas and factors like technology can also change a society in profound ways.

◀ This crowd is enjoying a music festival in England.

Naki Kouyioumtzis/age fotostock

CHAPTER 16
Technology & Society

Social Movements and Technology

Technology and globalization have influenced social movements and change.

Think about the following social movements: the "Arab Spring" in North Africa and western Asia, the "Occupy Wall Street" protests in New York City, strikes and protests in Greece, and the Counter-NATO Summit in Chicago. What do they have in common? They all are either pro-democracy rebellions or antiwar demonstrations, influenced by globalization, and fueled by the Internet and social-media technology.

Organizers of these and other movements understood the power of social media. They used technology to enable their movements to gain support, to grow, and eventually to go global. Social-media technology also broke down barriers. It meant the movements could reach the masses unedited. In some countries the government controls the news media and all other information that reaches the public. This allows the government to issue propaganda, or manipulate public opinion through the media and distort the truth. Social-networking sites and other social media are not controlled and can independently influence public opinion. They enable the user to experience the events during a protest in real time.

The Arab Spring resulted in the removal of the leaders in Egypt, Tunisia, and Libya. The movements caused these changes to happen very quickly. Tunisia's leader fled about a month after protests broke out. Without the technology of social media, the movement could have taken years to achieve or failed to incite real change. Historically, movements for change have taken much longer. The French Revolution, for example, lasted about a decade, from 1789 to 1799. Today, social movements benefit from the use of technology, maximizing the Internet and social media to further their quest for change.

Source: Racha Mourtada and Fadi Salem, *Arab Social Media Report, Vol. 1, No. 2 Dubai School of Government,* May 2011

THE INFLUENCE TECHNOLOGY AND GLOBALIZATION HAVE ON SOCIAL MOVEMENTS AND CHANGE.

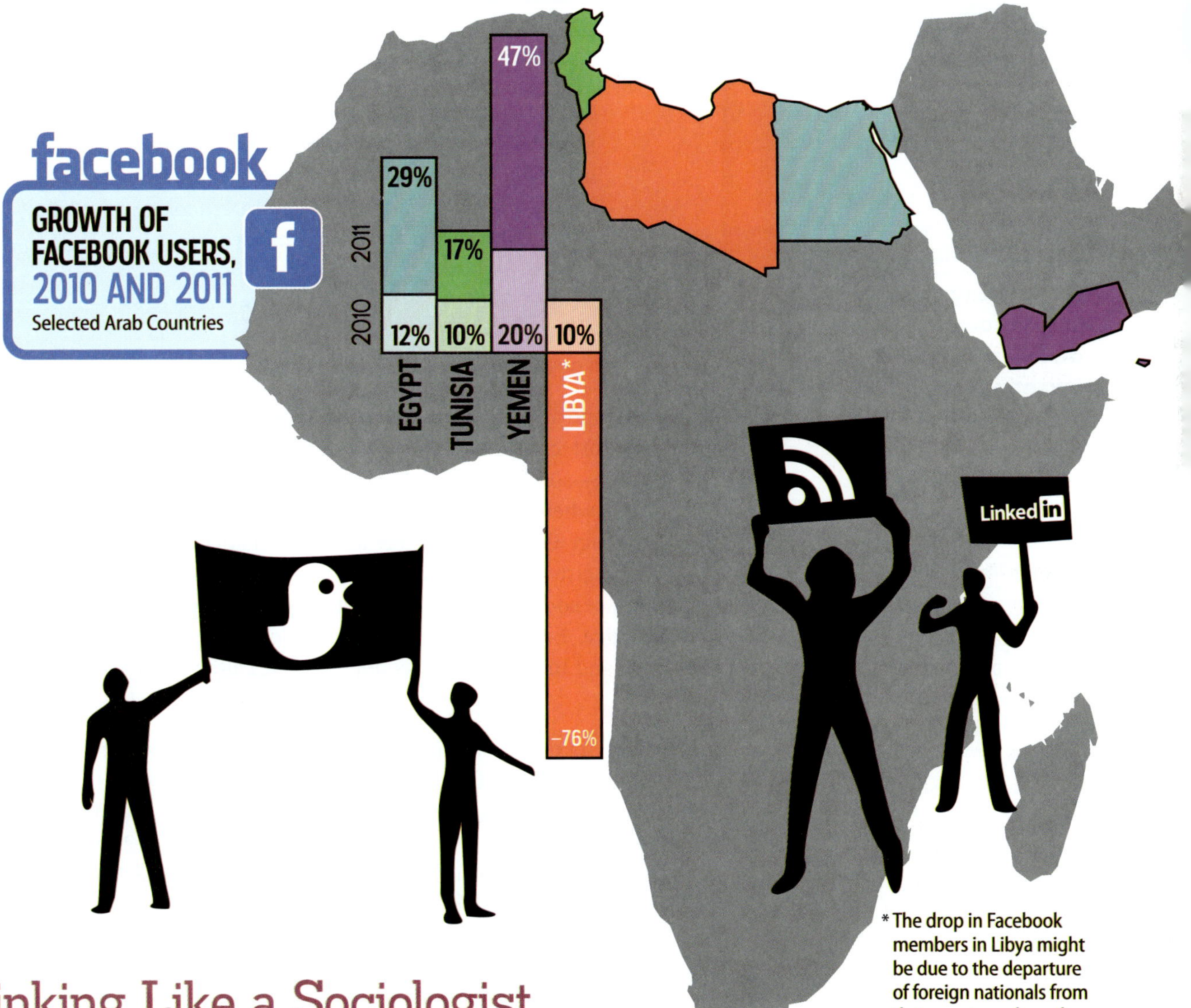

facebook
GROWTH OF FACEBOOK USERS, 2010 AND 2011
Selected Arab Countries

	2010	2011
EGYPT	12%	29%
TUNISIA	10%	17%
YEMEN	20%	47%
LIBYA*	10%	–76%

*The drop in Facebook members in Libya might be due to the departure of foreign nationals from that country or by a change in users' Facebook locations.

Thinking Like a Sociologist

1 Identifying Cause and Effect
How have technological innovations influenced social movements and social change?

2 Explaining Continuity and Change
Why do you think social movements continue to use social media as a tool?

Social Change and Collective Behavior

networks

There's More Online!

- ☑ **CHART** Alexis de Tocqueville's Key Assumptions in Predicting Social Change in the United States
- ☑ **GRAPHIC ORGANIZER** Processes and Factors of Social Change
- ☑ **MAP** Geographic Mobility
- ☑ **SELF-CHECK QUIZ**

Reading HELPDESK

Academic Vocabulary
- technology
- revolution

Content Vocabulary
- social change
- social processes
- discovery
- invention
- diffusion
- war

TAKING NOTES:
Key Ideas and Details

ORGANIZING As you read about social change, use a graphic organizer like the one below to record the processes and factors of social change.

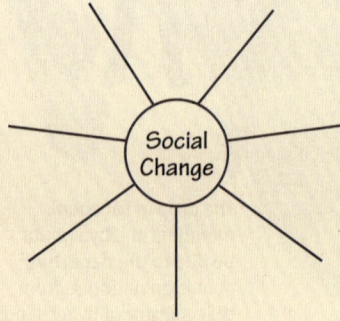

LESSON 1
Social Change

ESSENTIAL QUESTIONS • *What influences collective behavior?* • *What factors influence social change?*

IT MATTERS BECAUSE

Social change *refers to new behaviors that have long-term and relatively important consequences. Discovery, invention, and diffusion are the major social processes through which social change occurs. Important agents of social change are technology, population, the natural environment, revolution, and war.*

Defining Social Change

GUIDING QUESTION *What is the pace of social change?*

The importance of **social change** cannot be overstated. Change is one of the most constant features of American society. In fact, all societies change—some rapidly, others more slowly. For sociologists, social change occurs when many members of the society adopt new behaviors. The role of change is to allow society a means to adapt to new conditions. Some sociologists go as far as to say that the role of change is to develop and advance society. Others argue that social change can be either positive or negative. Either way, the new behaviors people adopt must have long-term and important consequences to be called social change.

The Pace of Social Change

Scientists use an analogy to help people understand the pace of social change. Imagine for a moment the entire history of Earth as a single 365-day year. Midnight of January 1 is the starting point. Today's date is December 31. Each Earth "day" represents about 12 million years. The first form of life, a simple bacterium, appeared in February. More complex life, such as fish, appeared about November 20. On December 10, the dinosaurs appeared; by Christmas they were extinct. The first recognizable human beings did not appear until the afternoon of December 31. Modern humans *(homo sapiens)* emerged shortly before midnight of that day. All of recorded history occurred in the last 60 seconds of the year. In the scheme of history, then, human social changes occur in the "blink of an eye." Only when we look at social change from the perspective of the human lifespan does it sometimes seem to be a slow process.

452

Alexis de Tocqueville's Key Assumptions in Predicting Social Change in the United States

- Major social institutions (such as the family, religion, and the state) would continue to exist.
- Human nature would remain the same.
- Equality and the trend toward centralized government would continue.
- The availability of material resources (such as land, minerals, and rich soils) limits and directs social change.
- Change is affected by the past, but history does not strictly dictate the future.
- There are no social forces aside from human actions.

Source: Adapted from Theodore Caplow, *American Social Trends* (New York: Harcourt Brace Jovanovich, 1991)

CHART

Alexis de Tocqueville's *Democracy in America*, published in the 1830s, displayed an amazing grasp of American society. De Tocqueville was one of the most accurate predictor of trends in the United States.

▶ **CRITICAL THINKING**

1. **Evaluating** Do you think that any of these assumptions are less important today in predicting social change?
2. **Hypothesizing** What new assumption would you add to this list to describe social change today?

social change alteration in a society's makeup or norms that occurs when many members of a society adopt new behaviors

Predicting Social Change

It is difficult to predict how a society will change. This is partly because the course of change in a society depends on the nature of the existing culture. For example, two societies that adopt a democratic form of government may develop in very different ways. Both Britain and the United States are democracies. But their histories prior to becoming democracies were different, since Britain has a royal tradition and the United States developed out of a colonial past. As a result, democratic government took different forms in these two nations.

In addition, change does not merely "happen" to people. People in a society can consciously decide for themselves how change will occur. They can, for example, deliberately avoid a predicted state of affairs.

A Diverse America

GEOGRAPHIC MOBILITY

People move or remain in the same location where they were born for their entire lives for a variety of reasons. Jobs, health, family needs, and other reasons can affect whether residents come or go. This map shows the percentage of Americans who were living in the same state in which they were born in 2010.

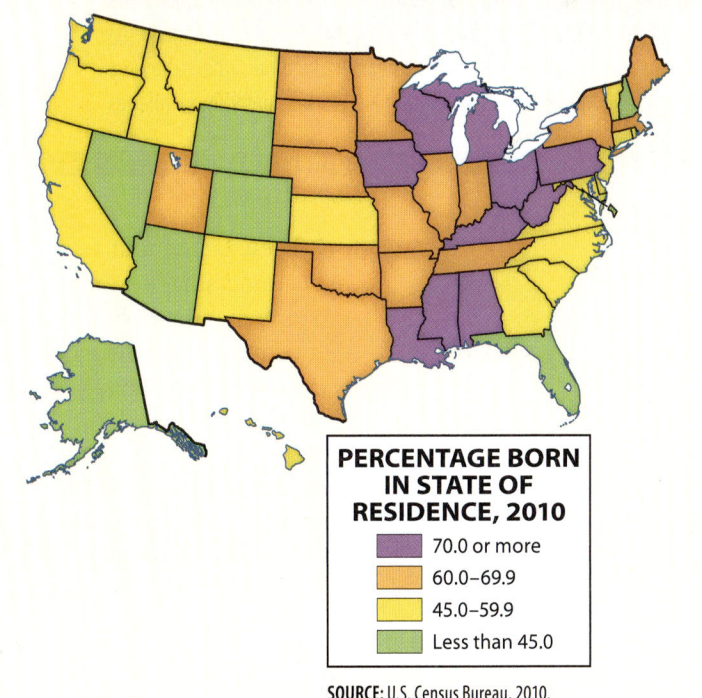

PERCENTAGE BORN IN STATE OF RESIDENCE, 2010
- 70.0 or more
- 60.0–69.9
- 45.0–59.9
- Less than 45.0

SOURCE: U.S. Census Bureau, 2010.

Geography Connection

1. **Places and Regions** Which regions show the lowest geographic mobility? The greatest?
2. **Environment and Society** What are the other reasons that might influence people to remain in the state in which they were born?
3. **The Uses of Geography** How does geographic mobility affect society?

Connecting Sociology to Economics

GLOBALIZATION OF THE ECONOMY

Globalization has made the world smaller by connecting people and places and integrating cultural, economic, and political awareness. Globalization has produced social change, and the results are both positive and negative. According to world systems theory, there is an international division of labor in which the more developed (or core) nations concentrate on higher-skill manufacturing and less developed (or periphery) nations focus on lower-skill manufacturing.

Economics has been a force in globalization that has affected social change. For example, increased global trade and new markets have made products more available to more people around the world. Check the label of your favorite shirt or outfit. Where was it made? Much of the clothing that we wear today is made outside the United States, often because it could be produced more economically elsewhere. This also produces a negative effect, however. Many Americans have lost their jobs because of this type of outsourcing.

On the other hand, the people who are making the clothing in other countries are affected by globalization, too. Many young women, age eighteen to twenty-five, who work in textile manufacturing plants in South and Southeast Asian countries, such as Sri Lanka, feel exploited, working long hours for low wages. They are referred to as "Juki girls"—*Juki* is the name of a common Japanese brand of sewing machine used by the young women—because they are working on foreign-brand clothing and outside their traditional roles.

The young female workers in Sri Lanka have not necessarily benefited from the effects of globalization. These women need the work and rely on boardinghouses and other living arrangements because their families do not live near the factories where they are employed. Most of these young female workers grew up in villages with their families and now they are living in poor, crowded accommodations in cities with other Juki girls. Because many of them are not married, rumors associated with lax moral behavior of Juki girls have circulated, creating a social stigma against them.

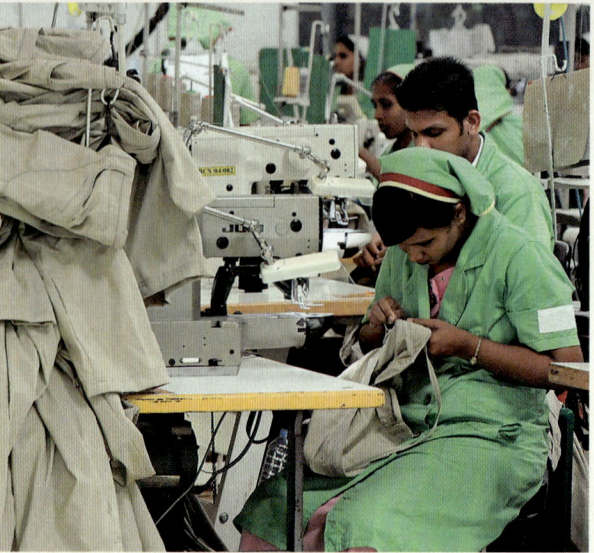

The textile industry in Sri Lanka has exploded under globalization, and its workforce is 90 percent female.

▶ **CRITICAL THINKING**

1. **Identifying Cause and Effect** How has globalization affected the economy and caused social change?
2. **Evaluating** Is economic expansion through globalization worth its effects on social change? Explain.
3. **Identifying Cause and Effect** How has globalization affected social norms for many young women in Sri Lanka?

These facts about social change should not discourage people from attempting to understand changes in their society or other societies. Alexis de Tocqueville was a Frenchman who published a remarkably penetrating study of American democracy and society after he toured the United States in the early 1830s. The accuracy of his predictions was based upon sound assumptions he made about American society.

Variations in the Pace of Social Change

Understanding why some societies change faster than others is another difficult task. Sociologists have identified several important social processes that influence the pace of social change. In addition, several specific factors play important roles. In the remainder of the lesson, we will turn first to the social processes and then to the specific agents, or factors, that affect rates of change.

✓ **READING PROGRESS CHECK**

Explaining When can we say that social change has occurred?

Social Processes

GUIDING QUESTION *Why are discovery, invention, and diffusion important social processes?*

A *process* is a series of steps that lead gradually to a result. As you get closer to graduation from high school, you may decide to continue your formal education. You will then begin a process of applying for admittance to various colleges. If you follow all the steps in the necessary order and meet the colleges' criteria for entrance, the end result of your application process will be an acceptance letter.

Cultures and societies experience **social processes** that result in significant changes. Three important social processes are *discovery, invention,* and *diffusion.*

social processes a series of steps leading to change on a societal level

Discovery

In the **discovery** process, something is either learned or reinterpreted. When early ocean explorers did not fall off the end of the Earth, they changed what all but a few people believed about its shape. With this geographical knowledge came new patterns of migration, commerce, and colonization. Salt, another early discovery, was first used to preserve food. Because it was so highly valued, it also came to be used as money in Africa and as a religious offering among early Greeks and Romans. Fire was used first by prehistoric peoples for warmth and cooking. Later, people discovered that fire could be used to clear fields, to create ash for fertilizer, and to melt ores to combine into new metals.

discovery the process by which something is learned or reinterpreted

Scientific exploration is a path to discovery. It can bring us to new understandings of the world around us, and beyond. The work of early astronomers, such as Nicolaus Copernicus and Galileo Galilei, for example, led to the abandonment of the long-held belief that Earth was the center of the cosmos.

invention the creation of something new from previously existing items or processes

Discovery can also shake up society, as it sometimes challenges both authority and people's beliefs. Galileo's evidence of a sun-centered cosmos angered the Catholic Church, for it brought into question the Church's teachings. He was brought before the Inquisition, the Church court that tried and punished heretics (people who reject Church teachings). To avoid torture, he recanted his position. Nonetheless, the idea took root and paved the way for the Age of Reason, the Enlightenment, and the loosening of the grip of the Catholic Church over the intellectual development of Europe.

Invention

Invention is the creation of something new from items or processes that already exist. Examples of physical inventions come easily to mind. Consider the airplane. It was not so much the materials Orville and Wilbur Wright used—most of the parts were available—but the way the brothers combined these materials that enabled them to make their successful flight at Kitty Hawk, North Carolina.

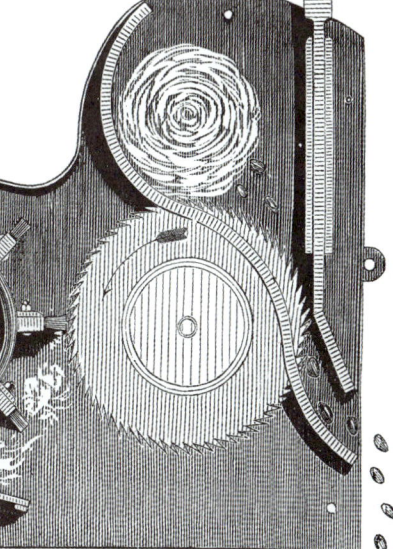

The cotton gin, designed by Eli Whitney in 1793, greatly increased the rate at which a worker could clean the seeds out of a cotton boll. Its use led to increased cotton production—and the institutionalization of slavery in the American South.

▶ **CRITICAL THINKING**

Making Connections Which social process is illustrated by the cotton gin?

The pace of social change through invention is closely tied to how complex the society or culture already is. The greater the number of existing items, or elements, the more ways they can be combined into inventions. Thus, the more complex and varied a society, the more rapidly it will change. This helps explain why people reached the moon less than 70 years after the Wright brothers' first flight, even though several million years had passed between the appearance of the human species and the invention of the airplane. NASA was able to reach the moon relatively quickly because the United States had become advanced in such areas as physics, aerodynamics, and the manufacturing of specialized materials.

Social Change and Collective Behavior **455**

Food courts in malls and other settings with many eating establishments often offer a variety of foods from different cultures.

▶ CRITICAL THINKING

Assessing What type of social change does this image exemplify?

diffusion the process by which one culture or society borrows from another culture or society

Diffusion

When one group borrows something from another group—knowledge, religion, values, foods, styles of architecture, and other cultural traits—change occurs through the process of **diffusion**. The extent and rate of diffusion depend on the degree of social contact. The more contact a group has with another group, the more likely it is that objects or ideas will be exchanged. In other words, social contact has the same effect on diffusion that complexity has on invention.

In recent decades, globalization has been an agent of diffusion. *Globalization* is the development of an increasingly integrated global economy. More broadly, it is a process that also results in increasingly integrated political, cultural, and environmental systems. Social scientists refer to the process by which less developed nations adopt the characteristics of more developed nations as *modernization*.

As the world becomes more integrated, individual societies can experience great change that may seem unrelated to the economic forces linking the world. For example, globalization has resulted in the rise of obesity throughout the globe. The opening of global markets has brought down the price of food, and the spread of technology has changed the nature of work for many people, making them more sedentary and less active. What's more, the influence of Western media and the incursion of Western fast food have brought about a change in the way people eat, particularly in rapidly developing societies.

☑ **READING PROGRESS CHECK**

Defining What are social processes?

Factors Influencing Social Change

GUIDING QUESTION What other forces lead to social change?

Besides the three processes for social change, sociologists have identified some major forces that often lead to social change. These five major forces include technology, population, the natural environment, revolution, and war.

Technology

Technology includes the knowledge and hardware (tools) that are used to achieve practical goals. The appearance of new technology in a society is generally a sign that social change will soon follow.

technology the knowledge and tools used to achieve practical goals

Technology is a prime promoter of social change. *TIME* magazine's selection of Albert Einstein as the person of the century reflected the magazine's conclusion that the twentieth century will be remembered most for its advances in science and technology.

The creation of the silicon chip, which led to the computer revolution, has brought about technological change at an astounding rate. It took over a century for telephones to spread to 94 percent of the homes in the United States. In contrast, in less than five years the Internet had reached over 25 percent of Americans.

The changes that resulted from the use of computers are almost impossible to list. At the turn of the millennium, social historian Francis Fukuyama described the workplace as undergoing a transformation. The effects of these changes, he claims, will be as great as those of the Industrial Revolution. Telecommunications technology, for example, will allow many to work from their homes, but it will result in far less human interaction.

In the field of medicine, computer technology has radically changed many surgical techniques. Robotic surgery, for example, allows surgeons to operate with greater precision in small places and, sometimes, remotely. Drivers in Germany can get real-time computer-generated information on traffic problems on the autobahn, the national highways in that country, by using cell phones or electronic consoles in their cars.

Population

Changing demographics are another important factor for creating social change. Demographers study the growth, size, composition, distribution, and movement of human populations. As a result of industrialization, for example, the nation became urbanized. Factories drew people away from the countryside and to smaller, densely settled areas—cities. These concentrations of people also became centers of economic, political, and cultural control.

Another example is the huge increase in the birthrate that followed the return of American soldiers at the end of World War II (the so-called baby boom). Americans born between 1946 and 1964 caused the expansion of child health care facilities and created the need for more teachers and schools in the 1950s and 1960s. On the other hand, the generation following the baby boomers, now in their forties, is experiencing increased competition for jobs and fewer opportunities to move up the career ladder. As the baby boomers retire, problems of health care and Social Security loom large. Longer working hours, retraining programs, and reeducation for older people will probably become political issues in future elections. As the population of the United States continues to age, more attention is being paid to senior citizens. Already, there are more extended-care homes, an increase in geriatric emphasis in medicine, and more television advertising targeting the aging population.

The Natural Environment

Interaction with the natural environment has, from the earliest times, also transformed American life. The vast territory west of the original thirteen colonies permitted the nation to expand, ultimately to the Pacific Ocean. This westward movement helped shape America's cultural identity and values. It also caused countless changes, most tragically the destruction of many Native American cultures.

Alzheimer's disease usually begins after age 60, then the risk doubles every five years. It is currently untreatable and incurable. To realize the impact the disease might have on society, keep in mind that some 10,000 Americans turn 65 each day.

▶ **CRITICAL THINKING**

Hypothesizing What kind of changes to society do you think might come about in response to the rise of Alzheimer's disease?

The environment continues to shape historical events, especially when disasters occur. Some can be natural disasters, such as extreme weather events. Others can be human made. The disaster known as the "dust bowl" that hit the Midwestern plains states in the 1930s was a combination of both. A long drought devastated a region where overplanting and plowing had upset the fragile ecosystem. The disaster contributed to the Great Depression of the 1930s and resulted in the emigration of thousands of families from the region.

In the early 1970s, OPEC (an organization of oil-producing nations) launched an oil embargo, refusing to sell its oil to other countries. Because of the short supply of oil without the contribution of these oil-rich countries, oil products became scarce and expensive, contributing to inflation in the United States in the 1970s and early 1980s. As a result, Americans began driving smaller, more fuel-efficient automobiles.

Revolution and War

Revolution and war are related factors that lead to social change. A **revolution** involves the sudden and complete overthrow of an existing social or political order. A revolution is often, but not always, accompanied by violence. Most revolutionaries expect that the revolution will bring about fundamental changes. Karl Marx, for example, expected workers' revolutions to eliminate class-based inequality and therefore to have a profound effect on the social and economic structures of the societies in which they occurred.

The year 2011 was a year of revolutions. A wave of pro-democracy uprisings, known as the Arab Spring, swept North Africa and the Middle East. It began in Tunisia, where a movement sparked by the dramatic suicide of a young protester forced Tunisia's president to give up power. Egypt soon followed suit. With the aid of social media, thousands of protesters took to the streets of major cities to protest unemployment and government corruption. By the spring of 2012, Egyptians lined up to cast ballots in the country's first free presidential election. In Libya, what began as anti-government protests turned into an armed revolt. By September 2011, Libya's former military dictator was dead, and a new transitional government was in place. In Syria, antigovernment protests beginning in March of 2011 resulted in a violent crackdown. After a year of violence, the country appeared headed toward civil war fueled in part by Syria's ethnic divisions.

revolution a sudden and complete overthrow of a social or political order

In June 2012, Egyptians voted for the first time for their nation's president. The ink spot on the woman's finger showed that she had cast her ballot.

▶ **CRITICAL THINKING**

Making Connections How do you think free elections might change Egyptian society?

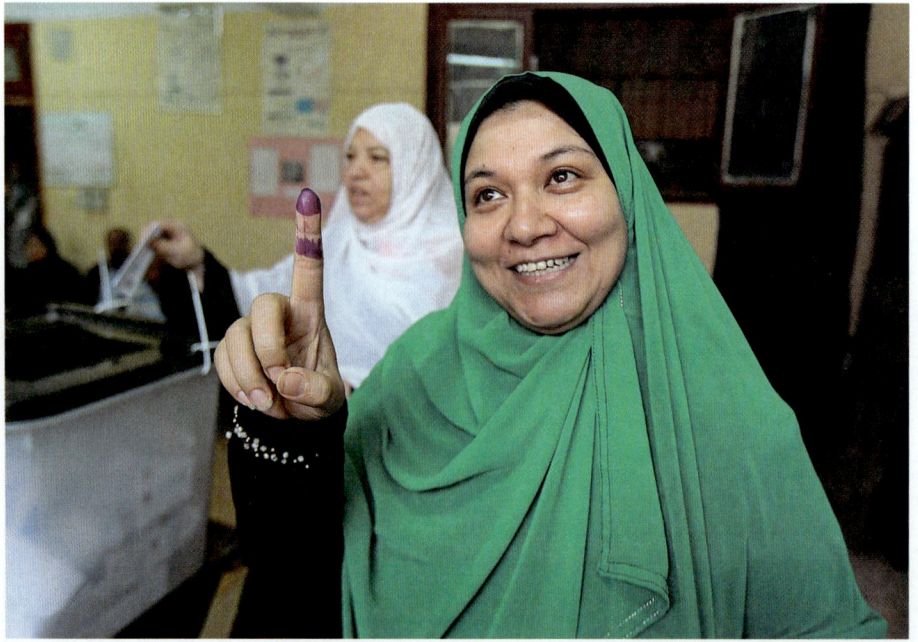

According to sociologist Charles Tilly, a revolution results in the replacement of one set of power holders by another. In the view of another respected sociologist, a postrevolutionary society is eventually replaced by a society that looks much like the original one. Radical changes are rarely permanent because people tend to revert to more familiar customs and behaviors.

In most cases, the new social order created by a successful revolution is likely to be a compromise between the new and the old. Consider the example of China, where a communist revolution took place in 1949. The revolution did not result in the wholesale changes promised by its leaders. One of the revolutionary reforms, for example, promised liberation from sexism. The situation for Chinese women has improved, but sexual equality is a far-distant dream in that country.

War is organized, armed conflict that occurs within a society or between nations. War can bring about social change in many ways. Iraq, for example, was ruled by a series of strongmen for half a century until the United States overthrew its leader Saddam Hussein. Iraq drafted a new constitution and instituted democratic reforms. Unfortunately, the war aggravated conflicts between different groups within the country. Social instability resulted from competing factions struggling for control of the new government. In addition, terrorist activity in the country increased sharply, and its Kurdish minority faces renewed discrimination and persecution.

Sociologist Robert Nisbet described how war also brings about social change through diffusion, discovery, and invention. Social change is created through diffusion because wars break down barriers between societies, bringing people from different societies together. This association leads to the adoption of new ways of thinking, feeling, and behaving.

Wars also promote invention and discovery. For example, during World War II (1939–1945), the pressure of war enabled the U.S. government to promote and finance the development of such technologies as the atomic bomb, synthetic rubber, and antibiotics. Each contributed to a cultural revolution after the war. In addition, American culture, both during and after World War II, was imported by societies all over the world.

Tensions between factions in Iraq's postwar government were played out in Diyala province, where bombings became a daily occurrence.

▶ **CRITICAL THINKING**

Making Connections How did war change society in Iraq?

war organized, armed conflict that occurs within a society or between nations

✓ **READING PROGRESS CHECK**

Identifying Central Issues What is the aim of revolution?

LESSON 1 REVIEW

Reviewing Vocabulary
1. ***Defining*** What is discovery?
2. ***Explaining*** How does revolution differ from war?

Using Your Notes
3. ***Explaining*** Use your web diagram from the lesson to write a paragraph explaining how social change occurs.

Answering the Guiding Questions
4. ***Describing*** What is the pace of social change?

5. ***Drawing Conclusions*** Why are discovery, invention, and diffusion important social processes?
6. ***Identifying*** What other forces lead to social change?

Writing Activity
7. ***Narrative*** What changes would you like to see in society? Identify some processes or factors that would be needed to bring about this change. Next, suppose that you are a historian from the future describing these changes. Use the processes and factors to explain how your supposed change occurred.

Social Change and Collective Behavior

FOCUS on research

Case Study

Globalization and Work

How are outsourcing, downsizing, and globalization affecting American workers and the workplace? Sociologist and labor activist Tom Juravich wanted to understand the social impact of it all. In his study, Juravich interviewed workers in four distinct workplaces, for a total of 85 interviews. He learned not only that the workers had found themselves in situations in which they were expected to work overtime but that they were working in fear of being laid off or losing their jobs and were expected to produce more for less pay and fewer benefits.

PRIMARY SOURCE

"In each of the four sites, employers and the industries they were part of adapted to growing competition, the globalization of production, and a crisis in profitmaking by expanding through mergers and acquisitions. Verizon gobbled up its competitors; Boston City Hospital merged with Boston University Hospital to become the Boston Medical Center; and Jones Beloit became part of the global firm Harnischfeger. Even the fish-processing industry in New Bedford went through no less consolidation. Such consolidation, driven by the search for increased profits, fundamentally altered the way work was done in the four sites. Each employer in a different way turned up the heat on its workers, leaving some workers feeling stressed and others exhausted, exploiting some and abandoning others.

As we step back from the specific details of the four case studies, it is clear that a series of paradoxes is emerging in the contemporary American workplace which are hard to reconcile within our postwar thinking about work. At some very basic level it is becoming difficult to distinguish between good jobs and bad jobs. For most of the postwar era, good jobs were the ones at major firms that provided decent wages, working conditions, and benefits in what economists called the primary labor market. Bad jobs were the ones in the secondary labor market at the periphery of the economy—jobs with little security, poor wages, and few benefits. The line between good jobs and bad ones is not so easy to draw anymore.

From the pay and benefits of the call center reps at Verizon or the nurses at Boston Medical, it would be difficult to conclude that they have anything but good, very good jobs. Yet do good jobs require employees to ask permission to go to the bathroom, or employers to discipline employees for being sick, as at Verizon? Or do good jobs require a professional worker with twenty-five years of experience to work weekends or overnight shifts, like nurses at Boston Medical?

> "At some very basic level it is becoming difficult to distinguish between good jobs and bad jobs."

It should be noted that the sixty-hour weeks and twelve-hour shifts at Verizon and Boston Medical Center are part of a trend among major employers—the kinds of firms we expected more from in past decades. After World War II, large, established employers such as General Motors and Ford were innovators in labor relations and employment policy, offering working conditions far removed from the cruelty encountered in jobs in the secondary market. Today, however, working conditions normally associated with small, marginal firms are becoming commonplace among some of the nation's largest and most respected companies. The historical link between large, profitable firms and the creation of good jobs in the United States has been broken.

There are no fewer contradictions in Dalton or New Bedford. In Dalton the workers at Jones Beloit had a series of record-breaking years in terms of productivity, excellent equipment, and a seasoned, highly trained workforce. The plant was abruptly closed nonetheless, and all efforts by the workers and their union to keep work going in Dalton were thwarted by the company and government regulations that were supposed to help them."

—from *At the Altar of the Bottom Line: The Degradation of Work in the 21st Century,* 2009

Working With the Research

1. **Identifying Central Ideas** What general trends does Juravich describe as becoming prominent in the workplace?
2. **Contrasting** How have work and workers' benefits changed since the post-World War II era?
3. **Evaluating** Why do you think there were similarities rather than differences in the situations that workers faced?

networks

There's More Online!

- ☑ **CHART** Theoretical Perspectives: Social Change
- ☑ **GRAPHIC ORGANIZER** Theoretical Perspectives on Social Change
- ☑ **IMAGE** Sharing the City
- ☑ **SELF-CHECK QUIZ**

Reading HELPDESK

Academic Vocabulary
- instability
- dynamic

Content Vocabulary
- equilibrium
- urbanism

TAKING NOTES:
Key Ideas and Details

IDENTIFYING As you read about social change, use a graphic organizer like the one below to identify the key ideas of the different theoretical perspectives.

Functionalist	
Conflict	
Symbolic Interactionism	

LESSON 2
Theoretical Perspectives on Social Change

ESSENTIAL QUESTIONS • What influences collective behavior?
• What factors influence social change?

IT MATTERS BECAUSE
The functionalist perspective depicts societies as relatively stable, always seeking a return to equilibrium. Conflict theory views societies as unstable systems that are constantly undergoing change. Symbolic interactionism identifies decreasing shared values as a source of social instability.

The Functionalist Perspective

GUIDING QUESTIONS *How does functionalism explain social change?*

Functionalism emphasizes social stability. How, then, do functionalists address social change? Two functionalist sociologists, William Ogburn and Talcott Parsons, based their theories on the concept of equilibrium. Just as a tightrope walker continually makes adjustments to maintain equilibrium, or balance, so too does society. When used by sociologists, **equilibrium** describes a society's tendency to react to changes by making small adjustments to keep itself in a state of balance.

A society in the process of change will move from stability to temporary **instability** and back to stability. Sociologists refer to this as a **dynamic**, or moving, equilibrium. For example, in 1972, a broken dam led to the destruction of Buffalo Creek, West Virginia. Despite the ensuing chaos, residents slowly pulled their lives together again. Although things were not the same as before, a new equilibrium was achieved. More recently, we can watch how this tendency toward equilibrium unfolds as New Orleans, which was devastated by a hurricane in 2005, continues to rebuild. The devastation disproportionately affected African Americans, who were more likely to live in low-lying areas that were most vulnerable to flooding. Evacuation plans, which relied mainly on personal transportation, also disproportionately disadvantaged African Americans. For these reasons and more, New Orleans is often cited as an example of environmental racism, or racial discrimination in practices that subject minority communities to disproportionate environmental risks. The 2010 federal census revealed that 25 percent of New Orleans residences were vacant. The city has been razing these properties to sell to developers. Only time will tell how long the city will take to return to equilibrium.

Ogburn noted that one social change might bring about another. For example, an obesity epidemic in the United States is putting a strain on the nation's health and economy. By 2010, 36 percent of American adults and 17 percent of American children were obese. By some estimates, the medical costs associated with obesity have reached a staggering $147 billion. Obesity also results in a loss of productivity at work, costing employers billions of dollars. Experts are looking to the past to determine what changes in society led Americans to gain so much weight. They found several factors that increased obesity rates: Moving to the suburbs made Americans more dependent on cars, rather than walking, for transportation; the use of many labor-saving devices; the reliance on convenience foods; and eating much larger portions than in the past. Experts hope to use these findings to recommend lifestyle changes that return the United States to a better and less costly state of health.

☑ **READING PROGRESS CHECK**

Making Connections Why do you think functionalists stress equilibrium?

The Conflict Perspective

GUIDING QUESTION *How does the conflict theory explain social change?*

According to the conflict perspective, social change is the result of struggles between groups for scarce resources. Social change is created as these conflicts are resolved. Many of the basic assumptions of the conflict perspective emerge from the writings of Karl Marx about class conflicts.

Sociologists such as Ralf Dahrendorf have adapted many of Marx's ideas. Dahrendorf believes that the resources at stake are more than economic. The quest for power is the source of social change, in his view. Whereas Marx saw conflict between two opposing social classes, Dahrendorf sees conflict between groups at all levels of society. Social change, thus, comes from a multitude of competing interest groups. These groups can be political, economic, religious, racial, ethnic, or gender based. Society changes as power relationships between interest groups change.

A Pennsylvania woman ignites the water coming out of her faucet, a phenomenon made possible because natural gas, being drilled near her home by the controversial process called "fracking," leached into the home's water supply.

▶ **CRITICAL THINKING**

Differentiating Does the fracking debate support Marx's view or Dahrendorf's view of conflict? Explain.

equilibrium a state of functioning and balance maintained by a society's tendency to make small adjustments to change

instability the quality or state of being unstable; unsteady

dynamic marked by continuous and productive activity or change

Theoretical Perspectives

SOCIAL CHANGE
This table provides one example each of how the functionalist, conflict, and symbolic interactionist perspectives view social change. The conflict perspective differs from the others, as it focuses on how social change is caused by struggle among groups.

Theoretical Perspective	Focus	Conclusions
Functionalism	Equilibrium	Continuity is the nature of the presidency, despite scandals in the Nixon and Clinton administrations.
Conflict Theory	Interest groups	Enactment of civil rights laws in the 1960s was a result of the struggle over racial equality.
Symbolic Interactionism	Urbanism	The smaller proportion of social interaction in a large city compared to a small town is based on a decrease in the number of shared meanings.

▶ **CRITICAL THINKING**

1. **Analyzing** Which perspective emphasizes stability? Why do you think so?

2. **Interpreting** What conclusion could you draw from the conflict theory perspective on social change?

Social Change and Collective Behavior

New York City's population is renowned for its ethnic diversity.

▶ CRITICAL THINKING

Analyzing Visuals Does this photograph suggest the fragmentation of urban life or the shared meaning of a subgroup? Why do you think so?

urbanism the distinctive way of life shared by the people living in a city

History seems to favor Dahrendorf's viewpoint over Marx's. Social classes have not been polarized into major warring factions. Rather, capitalist societies are composed of countless competing groups. In America, racial groups struggle over the issue of equal economic opportunity, environmentalists and industrialists argue about environmental protection and economic development, and so on. Ecofeminists, for example, link the domination of men over women with the exploitation of the ecosystem by industrial capitalism. They claim that the environment can be saved only through political action that promotes the equality of all species.

✓ **READING PROGRESS CHECK**

Analyzing How does Dahrendorf's view differ from that of Marx?

Symbolic Interactionism

GUIDING QUESTION *How does symbolic interactionism explain social change?*

Humans, according to symbolic interactionism, interact on the basis of commonly shared symbols. The nature and frequency of social interactions are affected by the extent to which people share meanings. As shared interpretations of the world decrease, social ties weaken and interactions become more impersonal.

The relationship between shared meanings and the nature of social interaction can be illustrated within the context of the transitions from an agricultural economy to an industrial economy to an information-based economy. Accompanying the shift to an industrial economy was the emergence of urbanization and its distinctive way of life. This distinctive way of life is known as **urbanism**.

According to German sociologist Ferdinand Tönnies, social interaction prior to the Industrial Revolution was based on shared tradition. Daily life revolved around family, common norms and values, and an interest in the welfare of all community members. Tönnies thought that urbanization created a very different way of life. In urban society, he wrote, social interaction is impersonal and fragmented because most people with whom one interacts are strangers.

Tönnies's critics say that the urban way of life is more varied than he described. While some urbanites may have hardly any shared meanings on which to base social interaction with others, many others belong to subgroups with which they share meanings, such as ethnic neighborhoods or artistic subcultures.

✓ **READING PROGRESS CHECK**

Analyzing Why is social interaction impersonal and fragmented in urban society?

LESSON 2 REVIEW

Reviewing Vocabulary
1. *Explaining* How do societies achieve equilibrium?
2. *Defining* What is urbanism?

Using Your Notes
3. *Identifying* Use your notes to describe how the three theoretical perspectives view social change.

Answering the Guiding Questions
4. *Explaining* How does functionalism explain social change?

5. *Explaining* How does the conflict theory explain social change?
6. *Explaining* How does symbolic interactionism explain social change?

Writing Activity
7. *Narrative* Use one of the perspectives on social change to describe a social change you have witnessed or about which you have learned.

networks

There's More Online!

- ✓ **CARTOON** Rumors
- ✓ **DIAGRAM** Contagion Theory
- ✓ **GRAPHIC ORGANIZER** Types of Collective Behavior
- ✓ **SELF-CHECK QUIZ**

Reading HELPDESK

Academic Vocabulary
- insecurity
- aggregate

Content Vocabulary
- collective behavior
- rumor
- urban legend
- fashion
- fad
- mass hysteria
- panic
- crowd
- mob
- riot
- contagion theory
- emergent-norm theory
- convergence theory

TAKING NOTES:
Key Ideas and Details

IDENTIFYING As you read about collective behavior, use a web graphic organizer to identify various types of collective behavior.

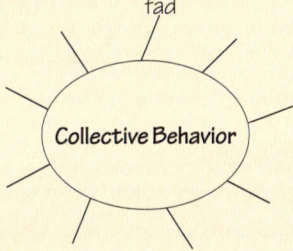

LESSON 3
Collective Behavior

ESSENTIAL QUESTIONS • What influences collective behavior?
• What factors influence social change?

IT MATTERS BECAUSE

Collective behavior describes how people behave when they are united by a single short-term goal. Rumors, fads, fashions, mass hysteria, and panics are all examples of collective behavior. Crowds gather and behave in different ways depending on the stimuli and conditions present.

Defining Collective Behavior

GUIDING QUESTION Why is the study of collective behavior problematic?

The term **collective behavior** refers to the spontaneous behavior of people who are responding to similar stimuli. When sociologists use the term *collective*, they are referring to a large number of people who do not normally interact and who do not necessarily share clearly defined norms. Sociologists call such a gathering of people a *collectivity*. Stimuli are any outside events or persons that cause a response. Collective behavior, therefore, involves spontaneous social interaction in which loosely connected participants influence one another's behavior.

For example, people may gather on a street to watch a fire burning at a neighbor's house. Stimuli can also be remote, however. Acts of terrorism committed around the world, for example, have increased Americans' anxiety about their safety. As a result, Americans are not only more cautious when they travel, but we have become more tolerant of surveillance and routine searches of our baggage.

The study of collective behavior poses a problem. Sociologists often study structured behavior. How are researchers going to investigate a social phenomenon that occurs spontaneously? Sociologists have developed fascinating theories of collective behavior. It turns out that collective behavior involves more structure and rationality than may seem to be the case on the surface.

Sociologists have been able to identify several types of collective behavior. In the more structured forms, such as crowds and social movements, people are in physical proximity to one another. In a dispersed collectivity, on the other hand, the people in the collective are widely scattered.

Social Change and Collective Behavior

collective behavior the spontaneous behavior of people responding to similar stimuli

rumor a widely circulating piece of information that is not verified as being true or false

insecurity state of fear, anxiety, or uncertainty

urban legend a moralistic tale that focuses on current concerns and fears of the city or suburb dweller

Nevertheless, they are in some way following common rules or responding to common stimuli. Behavior among members of dispersed collectivities is not highly individualized:

PRIMARY SOURCE

"When people are scattered about, they can communicate with one another in small clusters of people; all of the members of a public need not hear or see what every other member is saying or doing. And they can communicate in a variety of ways—by telephone, letter, Fax machine, computer linkup, as well as through second-, or third-, or fourth-hand talk in a gossip or rumor network."

—Erich Goode, from *Collective Behavior*, 1992

✓ READING PROGRESS CHECK

Defining What is a collectivity?

Rumors, Legends, Fads, and Fashions

GUIDING QUESTION *How are rumors, legends, fads, and fashions examples of collective behavior?*

People will typically respond to certain information in similar ways, even when physically separated. Rumors, fads, and fashions are collective behaviors characteristic of dispersed collectivities.

Rumor

A **rumor** is a widely circulating story of questionable truth. Rumors are usually spread by people about events or other people that are of great interest to themselves. The mass media exploit the public's fascination with rumors. Entertainment magazines devote themselves to rock idols and movie stars; tabloid newspapers are loaded with suggestive guesswork, half-truths, and innuendos. Even mainstream news publications offer accounts of the rich, famous, and offbeat. As these examples suggest, rumors and gossip are closely related.

In 1999, rumors circulated about what would happen when the clock struck midnight on the last day of the year. According to these rumors, power grids would fail, elevators would stop working, and the stock market would crash as the year 2000 began. According to another rumor, a fast-food restaurant chain was increasing the protein content of its hamburgers by adding ground worms.

The media reported murders, rapes, and beatings in the New Orleans Superdome following Hurricane Katrina. There were also rumors of anthrax, monkey pox, and various rashes. None of these rumors proved true, but they were spread and believed, in part, because they touched on people's **insecurities** and anxieties.

Urban Legends

Related to rumors are what Jan Harold Brunvand calls urban legends. **Urban legends** are moralistic tales passed along by people who swear the stories happened to someone they know or to an acquaintance of a friend or family member. Unlike fairy tales set in the far-distant past, urban legends are set in

CARTOON

RUMORS
Sociologists have observed that people separated by geographical and cultural distances react similarly to certain types of information.

▶ **CRITICAL THINKING**
Analyzing Visuals What is the cartoonist's point in naming the media trucks for a news crew?

shopping malls, on city subways, and in schools. The tales often focus on current concerns and fears, such as AIDS and inner-city gangs. A typical story tells about a man who woke up in a hotel room to discover his kidney had been stolen by a gang of illegal organ traffickers. Another describes alligators roaming the sewer systems of big cities. As cautionary tales, urban legends warn us against engaging in risky behaviors by pointing out what has supposedly happened to others who did what we might be tempted to try. Like rumors, urban legends permit us to play out some of our hidden fears and guilt by being shocked and horrified at others' misfortune.

Fashions

Fashion is a way of dressing or behaving that is widely accepted but continually changing. Fashion changes are seen most often in items that involve personal appearance, such as clothing, jewelry, and hairstyles. Automobile design, home decorating, architecture, and politics are also subject to fashion. Advertising and the mass media are prime agents of fashion change.

fashion a widely accepted behavior pattern that changes periodically

Fads

A **fad** is a fashion, mannerism, or activity that spreads rapidly, is embraced zealously, and then disappears after a short time. The widespread popularity of a fad rests largely on its novelty. Students in the early 1970s introduced the "streaking" fad—running naked across college grounds or through classrooms. More recently, planking (lying rigid and facedown in an odd place) and flash mobs (groups that assemble briefly at an appointed time to perform a public prank) have taken the place of streaking. Consumer-related fads come and go and can be as intense as they are short-lived. Small plush toys, bottle caps, and silicon bracelets have each taken their turn as the latest consumer craze.

fad a fashion, mannerism, or activity that spreads rapidly and disappears quickly

Fads may seem trivial, but they can have profound economic effects. A tulip craze in Europe in the seventeenth century, for example, caused a fury of speculative economic activity in Holland. When the fad ended, many Dutch found themselves in economic ruin.

mass hysteria a collective anxiety created by the acceptance of one or more false beliefs

☑ **READING PROGRESS CHECK**

Comparing In what ways are rumors and urban legends similar?

New technologies have changed how people communicate across the globe and how they form communities.

▶ **CRITICAL THINKING**

Analyzing Visuals How is a virtual community an example of a mass and a dispersed collectivity?

Mass Hysteria and Panics

GUIDING QUESTION *What is the difference between mass hysteria and a panic?*

To understand mass hysteria and panics, we must distinguish between a mass and a crowd. Unlike a crowd, the members of a mass are not in the same physical location. When people react to world events, such as terrorism, disease, or natural disasters, they may share a common pattern of behavior even though they are in different places.

Mass hysteria exists when collective anxiety is created by acceptance of one or more false beliefs. In 1938, Orson Welles's famous "Men from Mars" radio broadcast, which was based entirely on H. G. Wells's novel *The War of the Worlds*, caused nationwide hysteria.

Social Change and Collective Behavior 467

Wild rumors of strange blood-sucking creatures known as chupacabras attacking livestock began circulating in Puerto Rico, Mexico, and the American Southwest in the 1990s.

▶ **CRITICAL THINKING**

Making Connections How would a sociologist describe the fear of the chupacabra?

panic reaction to a real threat in fearful, anxious, and often self-damaging ways

crowd a temporary collection of people who share an immediate common interest

aggregate a gathering of people that is considered as a whole simply because they happen to be in the same place at the same time

Thousands of listeners mistakenly believed they were being attacked by Martian invaders. Telephone lines were jammed as people shared rumors, anxieties, fears, and escape plans. Some took to the roads to escape, while others hid in their cellars.

A tragic example of mass hysteria took place in seventeenth-century Salem, Massachusetts. Accusations of witchcraft resulted in 22 people being hanged. The mass hysteria dissipated only after the false beliefs were discredited.

In the 1980s and into the 1990s, the United States witnessed some mass hysteria regarding AIDS. A 1987 Gallup Poll showed that a substantial proportion of Americans held false beliefs regarding the spread of AIDS—30 percent believed insect bites could spread the disease, 26 percent related the spread to food handling or preparation, 26 percent thought AIDS could be transmitted via drinking glasses, 25 percent saw a risk in being coughed or sneezed upon, and 18 percent believed that AIDS could be contracted from toilet seats. These mistaken ideas persisted on a widespread basis despite the medical community's conclusion that AIDS is spread only through sexual contact, by sharing hypodermic needles, and by transfusion of infected blood. By the late 1990s a better understanding of AIDS had reduced the frequency of these rumors.

More recently, hysteria revolves around illegal immigration. Vigilante groups, for example, now patrol the United States–Mexico border. They use rallies, websites, and media attention to whip up anti-immigration sentiment. Anti-immigration groups prey on people's fears of crime, unemployment, and other social ills, claiming that immigrants are causing the collapse of American society.

While mass hysteria is based upon false beliefs, a **panic** occurs when people react to a real threat in fearful, anxious, and often self-damaging ways. Panics usually occur in response to such unexpected events as fires, invasions, and ship sinkings. Over 160 people, for example, died in the Kentucky Beverly Hills Supper Club in 1977 when a panic reaction to a fire caused a jamming of the escape routes. Interestingly enough, people often do not panic after natural disasters, such as earthquakes and floods. Although panics may occur at the outset, major natural catastrophes usually lead to highly structured behavior.

✓ **READING PROGRESS CHECK**

Explaining How is mass hysteria an example of collective behavior?

Crowds

GUIDING QUESTIONS *What are the different types of crowds? How have sociologists explained their behavior?*

A **crowd** is a temporary collection of people who share an immediate common interest. The temporary residents of a large campground, each occupied with his or her own activities, would not be considered a crowd. Sociologists would call this kind of gathering an **aggregate**. But if some stimulus, such as the landing of a hot-air balloon or the sudden appearance of a bear, drew the campers together, the aggregate would become a crowd.

People in a crowd often have no predefined ideas about the way they should behave. They do, however, share the urgent feeling that something either is about to happen or should be made to happen.

Types of Crowds

Sociologist Herbert Blumer has distinguished four basic types of crowds: *casual, conventional, expressive,* and *acting*. His classification takes into account what links the members of the group to one another and the degree of emotion involved in the experience.

1. A casual crowd is the least organized, least emotional, and most temporary type of crowd. Although the people in a casual crowd share some point of interest, it is minor and fades quickly. A casual crowd may gather momentarily to observe the aftermath of an accident or to listen to a street performer.

Applying Sociology

THE 9/11 TERRORIST ATTACKS

Sociologists define a disaster as an event that causes extensive property damage, great loss of human life, and massive disruption and that strikes unpredictably and suddenly. Researchers typically divide disasters into "natural disasters," such as floods, earthquakes, and hurricanes, and "technological accidents," such as airline crashes, nuclear plant meltdowns, and the sinkings of ships.

But how can we classify the September 11, 2001, attacks on the World Trade Center in New York City and the Pentagon in Washington, D.C.? Although the attacks had all the characteristics of a disaster, they were neither natural nor accidents. In fact, terrorist attacks are a new type of disaster—one that involves technology and is intentionally caused by humans. The 9/11 attacks met the criteria of a disaster and also exposed as false three such myths about how people act in a disaster.

- *Victims of disasters panic.* Contrary to this myth, disaster victims do not generally panic. Some inside the World Trade Center did respond with incapacitating emotion. One secretary in shock, for example, had to be carried out by a fellow worker. Some people jumped from the towers. But the disaster failed to set off a widespread panic. Many who heeded the first building-wide instructions died after calmly remaining in their offices.

- *Disaster victims respond as isolated individuals.* According to research, people immediately engaged in group efforts to help others. People in the World Trade Center with cell phones offered them to other victims desperate to call family or friends. Scores of New York City police and more than 300 firefighters died while working together to rescue trapped victims.

- *Disaster victims leave the scene as soon as possible.* Contrary to this myth, the majority of victims remained near the disaster site. Large numbers of volunteers and off-site emergency personnel rushed to the scene. Bellevue Hospital, at one point, had five doctors for each emergency ward patient. Four firefighters who were playing golf on Staten Island saw the first plane hit the north tower. Three of those

Pedestrians flee as one of the towers of the World Trade Center collapses.

four lost their lives in rescue efforts. They were just a few of the hundreds of firefighters who died while trying to help. Ironworkers, many of whom had built the World Trade Center, worked 12-hour volunteer shifts clearing away twisted steel.

▶ **CRITICAL THINKING**

1. **Identifying Central Issues** Why is it difficult to classify the 9/11 terrorist attacks?

2. **Analyzing** Why are there myths associated with human behavior in disasters?

Shoppers intent on finding bargains during the holiday season sometimes form dangerous crowds at large retail stores.

▶ CRITICAL THINKING

Evaluating What type of crowd is depicted in this photograph? Explain.

mob an acting crowd that is ready to use violence to achieve a purpose

riot an episode of largely random destruction and violence carried out by a crowd

2. A conventional crowd has a specific purpose and follows accepted norms for appropriate behavior. People watching a film or taking a flight form conventional crowds. As in casual crowds, there is little interaction.

3. An expressive crowd has no significant or long-term purpose beyond unleashing emotion. Its members are collectively caught up in the drama of the moment. They yell, cry, laugh, and jump. Screaming fans at a rock concert or sports event, for example, are an expressive crowd.

4. An acting crowd takes some action toward a target. It concentrates intensely on some objective and engages in aggressive behavior to achieve it. For example, some violent protesters attempted to disrupt the 2005 Group of Eight economic summit in Edinburgh, Scotland.

A conventional crowd may become an acting crowd, as when European soccer fans abandon the guidelines for spectators and attack the officials. Similarly, an expressive crowd may become an acting one, as in the case of celebrating Super Bowl fans who overturn cars and damage property.

Mobs and Riots

Mobs are acting crowds, as are crowds engaging in riots. A **mob** is an emotionally stimulated, disorderly crowd that is ready to use destructiveness and violence to achieve a purpose. A mob knows what it wants to do and considers all other things distractions. In fact, individuals who are tempted to deviate from the mob's purpose are pressured to conform. Strong leadership keeps the mob focused on the main event.

Mobs have a long and violent history. Many students are familiar with the scenes of mob actions described by Charles Dickens in his classic novel *A Tale of Two Cities*. The formation of mobs is not limited to revolutions, however. During the American Civil War, hundreds of people were killed or injured as armed mobs protested against the federal draft. Mobs in the United States have acted as judge, jury, and executioner in the lynchings of African Americans (as well as some whites) from the end of the nineteenth century through the 1960s.

Some acting crowds, although engaged in deliberate destructiveness and violence, do not have the mob's sense of common purpose. These episodes of crowd destructiveness and violence are called **riots**. Riots involve a much wider range of activities than mob action. Whereas a mob might surge to burn a particular building, to lynch an individual, or to throw bombs at a government official's car, rioters often direct their violence and destructiveness at targets simply because they are convenient. People who participate in riots typically lack power and engage in destructive behavior as a way to express their frustrations.

A riot, usually triggered by a single event, is best understood within the context of long-standing tensions. In Los Angeles in 1992, four white police officers charged in the beating of an African American man named Rodney King were acquitted by an all-white jury. The trial highlighted the suspicion and hostility between the city's police force and the African American and Latino communities. In the aftermath of the acquittal, Los Angeles experienced America's deadliest riots in 25 years. The city's mayor imposed a curfew and the governor deployed the National Guard to help restore order. President George H. W. Bush sent federal troops to assist. The rioting left at least 53 dead, more than 2,000 injured, more than 16,000 arrested, and an estimated $800 million in damage from looting and burning. A few days later the city quieted down, the troops withdrew, and the mayor lifted the curfew.

Contagion Theory

Theories have been developed to explain crowd behavior. The three most important are *contagion theory*, *emergent norm theory*, and *convergence theory*.

Contagion often refers to the spread of disease from person to person. Accordingly, **contagion theory** focuses on the spread of emotion in a crowd. As emotional intensity in the crowd increases, people temporarily lose their individuality to the "will" of the crowd. This makes it possible for a charismatic or manipulative leader to direct crowd behavior, at least initially.

Contagion theory has its roots in the classic 1895 work of Gustave Le Bon. Le Bon was a French aristocrat who disdained crowds made up of the masses. People in crowds, Le Bon thought, were reduced to a nearly subhuman level.

By the mere fact that he forms part of an organized crowd, said Le Bon, a man descends several rungs on the ladder of civilization. Isolated, he may be a cultivated individual; in a crowd, he is a barbarian—that is, a creature acting by instinct. He possesses the spontaneity, the violence, the ferocity, and also the enthusiasm and heroism of primitive beings.

In the late 1960s, Herbert Blumer offered another version of contagion theory. Blumer avoided Le Bon's elitist bias but still implied that crowds are irrational and out of control. For Blumer, the basic process in crowds is a "circular reaction"—people mutually stimulating one another. This process includes three stages. In milling, the first stage, people move around in an aimless and random fashion, much like excited herds of cattle or sheep. Through milling, people become increasingly aware of and sensitive to one another; they enter something akin to a hypnotic trance. All of this prepares the crowd to act in a concerted and spontaneous way.

The second stage, collective excitement, is a more intense form of milling. At this stage, crowd members become impulsive, unstable, and highly responsive to the actions and suggestions of others. Individuals begin to lose their personal identities and take on the identity of the crowd.

The last stage, social contagion, is an extension of the other stages. Behavior in this stage involves rigid, unthinking, and nonrational transmission of mood, impulse, or behavior. We see such behavior, for example, when fans at soccer games in Europe launch attacks on referees that disrupt games and leave people injured or even dead.

contagion theory the theory stating that members of crowds stimulate each other to higher and higher levels of emotion and irrational behavior

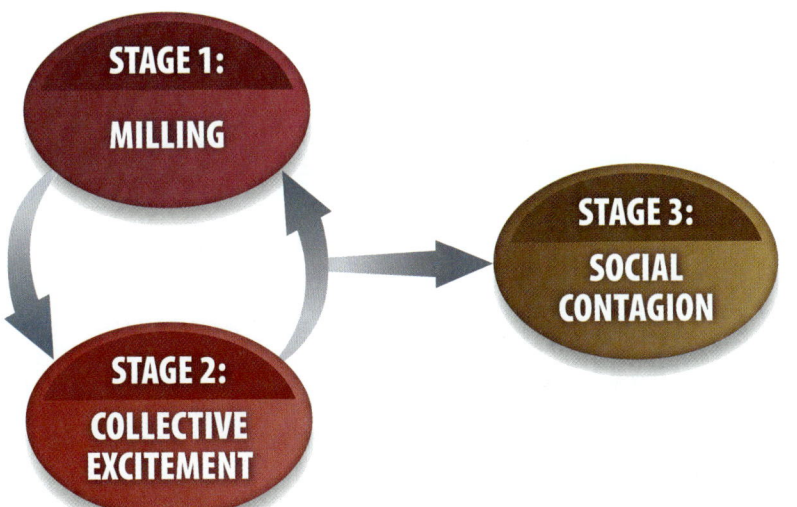

◁ DIAGRAM
CONTAGION THEORY
Contagion theory holds that people in a crowd affect one another emotionally as they mill about.

▶ **CRITICAL THINKING**
1. *Analyzing* Why does the diagram show a circular movement between Stage 1 and Stage 2?
2. *Making Connections* At what point does a crowd move into Stage 3?

Soccer, or football, hooligans engage in violent behavior while attending matches. They often make trouble with the intention of starting riots.

▶ **CRITICAL THINKING**

Evaluating What theory or theories of crowd behavior do you think help explain this behavior?

emergent-norm theory the theory stating that norms develop to guide crowd behavior

convergence theory the theory that states that crowds are formed by people who deliberately congregate with like-minded others

Taking a less extreme case, people at auctions can find themselves buying objects of little or no value to them because they have become caught up in the excitement of bidding.

Emergent-Norm Theory

Sociologists today realize that much crowd behavior, even in mobs, is actually very rational. **Emergent-norm theory** stresses the similarity between daily social behavior and crowd behavior. In both situations, norms guide behavior. So even within crowds, rules develop. These rules are emergent norms because the crowd participants are not aware of the rules until they find themselves in a particular situation. The norms develop on the spot as crowd participants pick up cues for expected behavior. Contagion theory proposes a collective mind that motivates members of the crowd to act. According to emergent-norm theory, people in a crowd are present for a variety of reasons. Hence they do not all behave in the same way. Conformity may be active (some people in a riot may loot) or passive (others may simply not interfere with the looters, although they take nothing for themselves). In Nazi Germany, for instance, some people destroyed the stores of Jewish merchants, while others watched silently.

Convergence Theory

Both the contagion and emergent-norm theories of crowd behavior assume that individuals are merely responding to those around them. It may be a more emotional response (as in contagion theory) or a more rational response (as in emergent-norm theory). In other words, the independent variable in crowd behavior is the crowd itself. In contrast, in **convergence theory** crowds are formed by people who deliberately congregate with others who they know are like-minded. According to convergence theory, the independent variable in crowd behavior is the desire of people with a common interest to come together.

There have been many instances of crowds gathering near clinics to discourage abortions. This behavior, say convergence theorists, does not occur because people happened to be at the same place and were influenced by others. Such a crowd is motivated to form because of shared values, beliefs, and attitudes.

☑ **READING PROGRESS CHECK**

Identifying What is a conventional crowd?

LESSON 3 REVIEW

Reviewing Vocabulary

1. ***Differentiating*** What is the difference between fashion and fad?

2. ***Defining*** What is a crowd?

Using Your Notes

3. ***Describing*** Use the notes in your graphic organizer to write a paragraph describing collective behavior.

Answering the Guiding Questions

4. ***Identifying*** Why is the study of collective behavior problematic?

5. ***Identifying*** How are rumors, legends, fads, and fashions examples of collective behavior?

6. ***Differentiating*** What is the difference between mass hysteria and a panic?

7. ***Identifying*** What are the different types of crowds? How have sociologists explained their behavior?

Writing Activity

8. ***Narrative*** Use one theory of crowd behavior to write an account of a crowd transforming into a mob.

networks

There's More Online!

- ☑ **CHART** Selected Subjects of Social Movements
- ☑ **GRAPHIC ORGANIZER** Value-Added Theory of Social Movements
- ☑ **IMAGE** Three Leaders of Social Movements
- ☑ **MAP** Internet Users
- ☑ **SELF-CHECK QUIZ**

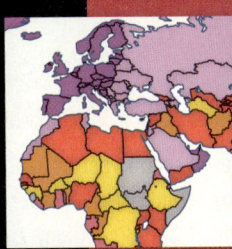

LESSON 4
Social Movements

ESSENTIAL QUESTIONS • *What influences collective behavior?* • *What factors influence social change?*

Reading HELPDESK

Academic Vocabulary
- advocate
- ambiguity

Content Vocabulary
- social movement
- revolutionary movement
- reformative movement
- redemptive movement
- alternative movement
- value-added theory
- resource-mobilization theory

TAKING NOTES:
Key Ideas and Details

ORGANIZING Complete a graphic organizer like the one below to organize your notes about social movements.

Type	Characteristics

It Matters Because

Social movements are more permanent and more organized than other types of collectivities. Theories that sociologists have developed to explain how social movements develop include value-added theory and resource-mobilization theory.

The Nature of Social Movements

GUIDING QUESTION *What is the purpose of a social movement?*

A **social movement** is the most highly structured, rational, and enduring form of collective behavior. Several defining elements characterize social movements:

- A large number of people
- A common goal to promote or prevent social change
- A structured organization with commonly recognized leaders
- An activity sustained over a relatively long time period

Most social movements set out to stimulate change. The civil rights movement of the 1950s and 1960s, for example, was a mass protest movement to secure federal protection of equal rights for African Americans. Civil rights groups such as the National Association for the Advancement of Colored People (NAACP) and the Student Nonviolent Coordinating Committee (SNCC) organized marches, demonstrations, and other protest activities around the nation. Martin Luther King, Jr., a Baptist minister, emerged as one of the movement's foremost leaders. Most famously he led the peaceful 1963 march on Washington, D.C., where he delivered his "I Have a Dream" speech. The movement resulted in the passage of the Civil Rights Act of 1964—sweeping legislation prohibiting discrimination based on race, color, religion, or national origin.

Contrast this structured, organized movement with the race riots of the same era. In Los Angeles, a riot erupted in the mostly African American Watts neighborhood over charges of police brutality. After nearly a week of violence in August of 1965, 34 people were dead, more than 1,000 were injured, and more than 600 buildings were damaged or destroyed.

Social Change and Collective Behavior **473**

Connecting Sociology to History

LEADERS OF SOCIAL MOVEMENTS

Historians and sociologists would most likely agree that, in history, there have been a number of notable leaders of social movements and that those leaders used different methods to achieve desired results. Sociologists would examine how the movements and methods affected the behavior of society.

Mohandas Gandhi started a nationalist Indian social movement against Britain, racism, and colonialism in general. He practiced nonviolence and often fasted to further his cause. Many British people did not want colonialism to end. They viewed themselves as superior to the Indian people. Over time, however, Gandhi's movement led to British recognition of India's independence in 1948.

While in the seminary, Martin Luther King, Jr., learned about Gandhi's use of nonviolence; it later served as his most valuable tool in his mission to end racism and gain civil rights for African Americans. American society was resistant to the civil rights movement and often responded with violence to the nonviolent actions of King and his followers. He led peaceful marches, such as the march on Washington, D.C., in 1963. After he was assassinated in April 1968, race riots broke out across the nation.

About a century before Gandhi's and King's movements, Susan B. Anthony became a major leader in the woman suffrage movement in the United States. Anthony championed her cause through civil disobedience, breaking laws (she voted in an election, which was illegal for women at the time), and speaking publicly to gain national attention. Despite her efforts, many Americans were not ready for women's roles to change. They did not want women to be involved in politics. In fact, women did not gain the right to vote until fourteen years after Anthony's death.

Although some social movements do not bring about positive change, they are still powerful. Adolf Hitler quickly rose to power in Germany as leader of a mass movement under the Nazi Party and took control of every aspect of German society. He gained popularity through a campaign to unite the German people in part by blaming the Jews for Germany's problems, making it his mission to destroy them. Germany society embraced Hitler because Germans were demoralized and felt punished by the countries that defeated Germany in World War I. Hitler began a campaign of genocide against Europe's Jews and started World War II.

---

social movement a movement whose goal is to promote or prevent social change; the most structured collective behavior

revolutionary movement a social movement that attempts to change the total structure of society

reformative movement a social movement that attempts to make limited changes in society

redemptive movement a social movement that seeks to change individuals completely

alternative movement a social movement that focuses on bringing about limited changes in individuals

advocate to plead in favor of

A government study blamed the violence on the community's poor socioeconomic condition. Despite the study and its recommendations to improve the community, little was accomplished.

As the definition indicates, however, the purpose of a social movement may also be to oppose change. An example is the National Rifle Association (NRA), an organization for sport shooting enthusiasts, gun collectors, and others interested in firearms. It is also an effective lobbying organization. In recent years, it has focused its resources on opposing gun control legislation.

✓ **READING PROGRESS CHECK**

Differentiating Why would a riot not be considered a social movement?

Primary Types of Social Movements

GUIDING QUESTIONS What are the four basic types of social movements? How do they differ?

Despite commonalities, various social movements have unique characteristics. It is difficult to compare the civil rights movement with the environmental movement. This has led sociologists to study differences between social movements. Anthropologist David Aberle identified four basic types of social movements:

- A **revolutionary movement** attempts to change a society totally. The American Revolution was one of the most successful revolutionary movements in history. Another example is the revolutionary movement led by Mao Zedong in China. As a result of Mao's revolutionary movement, a communist government was instituted, and Chinese society was radically transformed.

Mohandas Gandhi led the movement for Indian independence.

Martin Luther King, Jr., was a leader of the modern civil rights movement.

Susan B. Anthony was a leading figure in the woman suffrage movement.

▶ CRITICAL THINKING

1. **Comparing and Contrasting** How were the social movements of Gandhi, King, Anthony, and Hitler similar and different?

2. **Analyzing** How do historians and sociologists examine leaders of social movements?

- A **reformative movement** aims to effect more limited changes in a society. The Woman's Christian Temperance Union (an antialcohol organization founded in 1874) and the antiwar movement of the 1960s illustrate this type of social movement.

- A **redemptive movement** focuses on making a radical change within individuals. It is limited in scope but profound in the degree of change. Alcoholics Anonymous, an organization dedicated to helping its members achieve and maintain sobriety, is one such movement. The born-again Christian movement is another. A born-again Christian is a Christian who has experienced a dramatic renewal of his or her faith.

- An **alternative movement**, like a redemptive movement, is focused on individuals. An alternative movement, however, seeks only limited changes in people. Zero Population Growth (renamed Population Connection), an organization that began in the late 1960s, illustrates such a movement. It attempts to persuade people to limit the sizes of their families. It actively supports access to health information for women who are interested in limiting sizes of their families. It does not **advocate** sweeping lifestyle changes or legal penalties for large families, though.

Social Movement	Example
Technology	Protect online privacy
Government	Reduce the influence of money in politics
Health Care	Improve the health care system
Environment	Stop global warming
GLBT Rights	Secure marriage rights

∧ CHART

SELECTED SUBJECTS OF SOCIAL MOVEMENTS
A wide variety of hot-button topics drives today's social movements.

▶ CRITICAL THINKING

1. **Making Connections** How would a sociologist compare these movements?

2. **Speculating** Choose one of these topics and suggest the type of social movement that you think might be most effective in reaching the stated goal.

✓ READING PROGRESS CHECK

Explaining Why do sociologists study differences between social movements?

Social Change and Collective Behavior

Theories of Social Movements

GUIDING QUESTIONS *What is value-added theory? What is resource-mobilization theory?*

value-added theory the theory holding that certain conditions must exist for social movements to occur

ambiguity a state of being uncertain, doubtful, or open to more than one meaning

Sociologists have been able to analyze social movements because this form of collective behavior is highly structured. They have devised two major theories in an effort to gain a better understanding of how social movements grow and develop. One is value-added theory, and the other is resource-mobilization theory.

The Value-Added Theory

Before discussing value-added theory, we need to understand the concept of adding value. In the value-added process, each step in the creation of a product contributes, or adds value, to the final entity. Neil Smelser, the sociologist who originated the value-added theory of social movements, gives an example involving automobile production:

> **PRIMARY SOURCE**
>
> "An example of [the value-added process] is the conversion of iron ore into finished automobiles by a number of stages of processing. Relevant stages would be mining, smelting, tempering, shaping, and combining the steel with other parts, painting, delivering to retailer, and selling. Each stage 'adds its value' to the final cost of the finished product. The key element in this example is that the earlier stages must combine according to a certain pattern before the next stage can contribute its particular value to the finished product, an automobile. Painting, in order to be effective as a 'determinant' in shaping the product, has to 'wait' for the completion of the earlier processes. Every stage in the value-added process, therefore, is a necessary condition for the appropriate and effective addition of value in the next stage."
>
> —from *Theory of Collective Behavior*, 1962

Smelser used this process as a model to understand social movements. The **value-added theory** identifies six conditions that must exist in order for social movements to occur.

1. *Structural conduciveness.* The environment must be conducive to, or supportive of, the formation and growth of a social movement. In the 1960s and 1970s, millions of college students demonstrated against the war in Vietnam. The environment was supportive of this movement in two ways. First, the war itself provided a reason for the movement to form. Second, the antiwar movement formed initially among college students because most college campuses had convenient sites for rallies and protest meetings.

2. *Structural strains.* Conflicts, **ambiguities**, and discrepancies must be present within a society. Without some form of strain, there is no stimulus for change. The antiwar movement was stimulated by the government's aggressive prosecution of the Vietnam War, which many protesters saw as a violation of American values of self-determination for people around the world. College students also came into conflict with the government over the policy of drafting individuals to serve in the army and thus fight the war.

3. *Generalized beliefs.* Generalized beliefs include a general recognition that there is a problem and agreement that something should be done to fix it. Two shared beliefs were crucial to the antiwar movement: the belief that the Johnson and the Nixon administrations were not telling the truth about the war and the belief that the Vietnam War was morally wrong.

4. *Precipitating factors.* One or more significant events must occur to galvanize people into action. The ongoing deaths caused by the war were the precipitating factors for many antiwar protests and mass marches. While some of these actions were months in the planning, some more spontaneous protests arose in response to particular events. On April 30, 1970, President Nixon ordered the

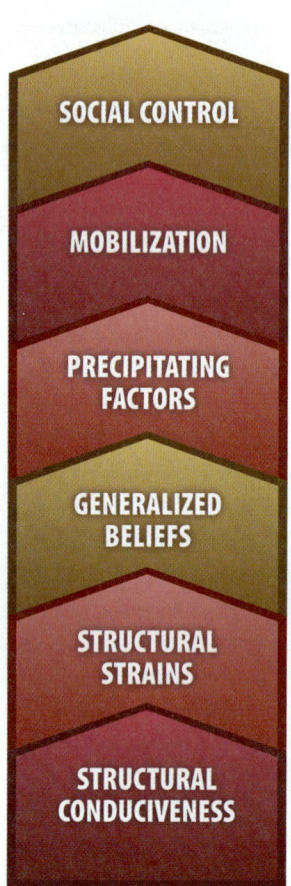

GRAPHIC ORGANIZER

VALUE-ADDED THEORY OF SOCIAL MOVEMENTS
Neil Smelser identified six conditions necessary for a social movement.

▶ **CRITICAL THINKING**

1. *Making Connections* What is a value-added process?
2. *Evaluating* What do you think would happen if one of these conditions was removed?

- SOCIAL CONTROL
- MOBILIZATION
- PRECIPITATING FACTORS
- GENERALIZED BELIEFS
- STRUCTURAL STRAINS
- STRUCTURAL CONDUCIVENESS

A Global Perspective

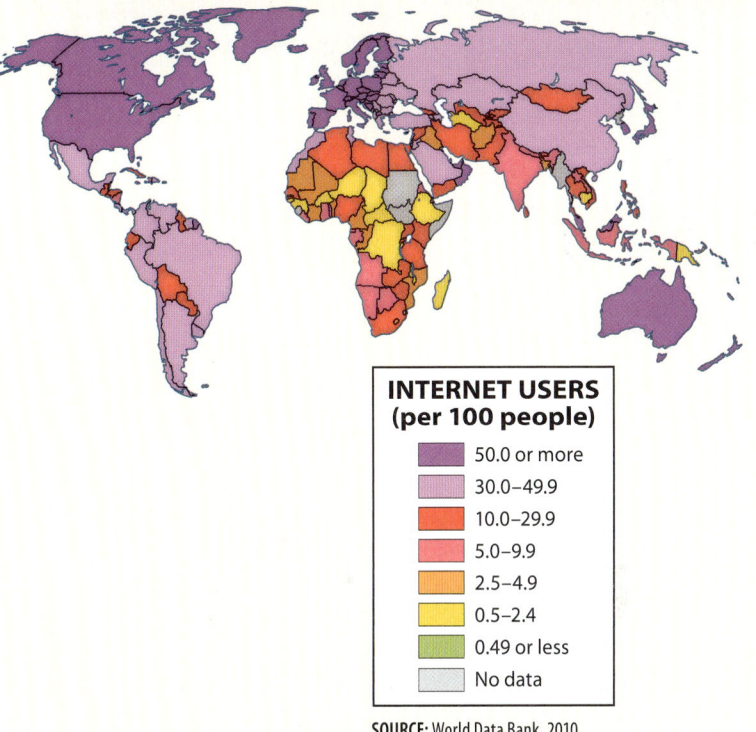

INTERNET USERS

As this map indicates, the number of people connected to the Internet varies widely from country to country. This map shows the number of computers connected to the Internet per 100 people in each nation. There has been significant growth in the past decade, but some countries still have few users.

INTERNET USERS (per 100 people)
- 50.0 or more
- 30.0–49.9
- 10.0–29.9
- 5.0–9.9
- 2.5–4.9
- 0.5–2.4
- 0.49 or less
- No data

SOURCE: World Data Bank, 2010.

Geography Connection

1. **Places and Regions** Which continent or continents have the most Internet connectivity? The least?
2. **Environment and Society** How might the number of Internet users in a country affect social change?

---

invasion of the neutral country of Cambodia. The government used this show of force to try to convince the North Vietnamese government, with which it was negotiating, to end the war. That action provoked renewed protests.

5. *Mobilization of participants for action.* Once the first four conditions exist, the only remaining step is to get the people moving. The invasion of Cambodia provoked massive demonstrations, and student strikes forced hundreds of colleges across the country to close. Students were angry at what they saw as Nixon's escalation of the war through the invasion.

6. *Social control.* The sixth factor is ineffective social control. Actions of the media, police, courts, community leaders, and public officials can lead to the success or failure of a social movement. If the right kind of force is applied, a potential social movement may be prevented even if the first five determinants are present. Efforts to control the situation may block the social movement or minimize its effects. Of course, such efforts can also make matters worse. During the student protests against the invasion of Cambodia, the governor of Ohio mobilized the National Guard and sent units to Kent State University, where protests were taking place. Jittery soldiers fired into the crowd, killing four students and wounding at least nine others. Such heavy-handedness only stimulated further antiwar protests.

Resource Mobilization Theory

Resource-mobilization theory focuses on the process through which members of a social movement secure and use the resources needed to advance their cause. Mobilization theory contends that social movements compete with one another for these resources.

Several days after the killing of four white students at Kent State University in 1970, two African American students were killed during an antiwar protest at Jackson State University in Mississippi.

resource-mobilization theory a temporary collection of people who share an immediate common interest

Social Change and Collective Behavior **477**

Organizations that promote social change compete for donations and volunteers.

▶ CRITICAL THINKING

Speculating What do you think will convince this passerby to commit her personal resources to the cause?

Quick Case Study

HOW WOULD YOU CHANGE THE WORLD?
Student activists have been inspired to action since the 1960s. How would your classmates change the world?

Procedure
1. Interview five classmates who have participated in a social movement. This could include such activities as signing a petition, attending a rally, or raising funds for a cause.
2. Invite them to share why they chose that cause. Record their responses.

Analysis
As you read through their responses, consider these questions:
1. Why did your classmates feel that they wanted to be part of the social movement? How did the cause they supported reflect their values or priorities?
2. How did their participation in the movement make them feel? Did they feel proud or more self-confident as a result of their participation?
3. How did the rest of the class react to the shared responses?

This competition can happen among social movements, as they compete with one another for resources, or within a social movement, as different groups seek leadership of the movement's direction or goals. The resources needed include human skills such as leadership, organizational ability, and labor, as well as material goods such as money, property, and equipment.

Resource-mobilization theorists believe that a social movement cannot begin until it has sufficient resources. The civil rights movement of the 1960s succeeded primarily because of the leadership and commitment of African Americans, but white Americans also contributed time, money, and energy to the cause. In recent years, members of the gay, lesbian, bisexual, and transgender (GLBT) community, too, have achieved greater equality. This achievement can be traced to active support from a broad segment of American society. Today, many more Americans support equal rights for members of the GLBT community than did in the 1950s.

☑ **READING PROGRESS CHECK**

Comparing What do value-added and resource-mobilization theories have in common?

LESSON 4 REVIEW

Reviewing Vocabulary
1. **Defining** What is a social movement?
2. **Differentiating** What is the difference between a revolutionary movement and a reformative movement?

Using Your Notes
3. **Finding the Main Idea** Review your graphic organizer on social movements. What do you think is the defining feature of a social movement?

Answering the Guiding Questions
4. **Identifying** What is the purpose of a social movement?

5. **Contrasting** What are the four basic types of social movements? How do they differ?
6. **Explaining** What is value-added theory? What is resource-mobilization theory?

Writing Activity
7. **Argument** Think about a change you would like to see in your school or community. Which type of social movement do you think would be best suited to bring about that change? Craft a brief argument to defend your choice.

CHAPTER 16 Assessment

Directions: On a separate sheet of paper, answer the questions below. Make sure you read carefully and answer all parts of the questions.

Lesson Review

Lesson 1

1. **Understanding Historical Interpretation** Is it easy or difficult to predict how a society will change? Use the United States and Britain as examples in your explanation.

2. **Explaining** Why did Galileo recant his position regarding a sun-centered cosmos? Should he have refused to do so? Why or why not?

Lesson 2

3. **Synthesizing** Which perspective's explanation of social change do you find most convincing—the functionalist perspective, the conflict perspective, or symbolic interactionism? Why? Support your response with information from this chapter.

4. **Diagramming** Create a Venn diagram to compare and contrast Dahrendorf and Tönnies's ideas on social change.

Lesson 3

5. **Synthesizing** Define the terms *fashion* and *fad*. Provide examples of at least one current fashion and one current fad that are common in your generation.

6. **Drawing Conclusions** What happened when Orson Welles's famous "Men from Mars" radio broadcast occurred in 1938? If this same broadcast were to occur today, would the same effect probably occur? Explain why or why not.

Lesson 4

7. **Comparing and Contrasting** Is it accurate to say that virtually all social movements have the same characteristics? Discuss four primary types of social movements in your response.

8. **Identifying Central Issues** Explain why, according to value-added theory, conflicts, ambiguities, and discrepancies must be present within a society.

DBQ Analyzing Primary Sources

PRIMARY SOURCE

Use the document to answer the following question.

"Why don't the women's movement and the men's movement get together and form a women-and-men's movement?"

9. **Drawing Conclusions** Look at the cartoon. Why is the joining together of two social movements not as simple a process as the woman suggests? Use information from the chapter in your explanation.

College and Career Readiness Skills

10. **Clear Communication** Television dramas and comedies often mirror social changes. Sometimes, these changes have yet to reach the mainstream culture. You are a network executive who has been asked to write a broadcast segment to explain the role of broadcast networks in changing society. Write a short, two-minute talk to explain the issue. Deliver it to the class.

Need Extra Help?

If You've Missed Question	1	2	3	4	5	6	7	8	9	10
Go to page	452–454	455	462–464	463–464	467	467–468	473–475	476	473–478	452–459

CHAPTER 16 Assessment

Directions: On a separate sheet of paper, answer the questions below. Make sure you read carefully and answer all parts of the questions.

DBQ Analyzing Primary Sources

PRIMARY SOURCE

Use the document to answer the following question.

> "Discrimination against women solely on the basis of their sex, is so widespread that it seems to many persons normal, natural and right. . . . It is time we act to assure full equality of opportunity to those citizens who, although in a majority, suffer the restrictions that are commonly imposed on minorities, to women.
>
> The argument that this amendment will not solve the problem of sex discrimination is not relevant. If the argument were used against a civil rights bill—as it has been used in the past—the prejudice that lies behind it would be embarrassing. Of course laws will not eliminate prejudice from the hearts of human beings. But that is no reason to allow prejudice to continue to be enshrined in our laws—to perpetuate injustice through inaction."
>
> —U.S. Representative Shirley Chisholm, speech before Congress, August 10, 1970

11 *Drawing Conclusions* This is an excerpt from a speech by U.S. Representative Shirley Chisholm in support of the Equal Rights Amendment. Explain how the excerpt supports the goal of the women's movement.

Critical Thinking

12 *Drawing Conclusions* Read the fable below. Explain how it provides a metaphor for society. Identify a question the children in the fable do not ask but likely would ask in the real world.

> Once upon a time, a family decided to grow orange trees. After several years of hard work, the first oranges appeared. During each successive year, when the oranges appeared, the mother would say, "Everyone is entitled to choose one orange from the crop." The business thrived and expanded. The children grew puzzled that even though the orange grove had grown, they were still allowed only one orange each year. Finally, when there were grandchildren, one of them said, "Grandmother, every year we produce hundreds of thousands of oranges, and every year, you tell us we can have only one orange. Why is that?" The grandmother replied, "Because that is the way it has always been."

21st Century Skills

CREATING AND USING GRAPHS, CHARTS, DIAGRAMS AND TABLES

13 *Creating Diagrams* New technology has produced a variety of methods to disseminate information. For example, blogs and Internet news sites provide instant information. Use a diagram to identify benefits and drawbacks of at least three of these methods.

Exploring the Essential Questions

14 *Identifying Central Issues* You have been hired by a publisher to explain how each of the lessons in this chapter helped you answer these questions: *What influences collective behavior? What factors influence social change?* Write a memo to provide a brief explanation.

Research and Presentation

15 *Gathering Information* Jan Harold Brunvand coined the term *urban legend* to describe a type of rumor that is long lasting and widely believed. Many Internet sites contain examples of these legends. Select three of these sites, noting the URLs, and write summaries of at least three urban legends from each site.

16 *Exploring Issues* Answer these questions: *What common elements do these urban legends share? What role do you think the Internet plays in spreading urban legends? Do you think reading urban legends creates a danger that someone will actually perform the action they describe? If so, should the sites that include them be censored?* Use a computer to create a visual that will illustrate the elements the urban legends you have identified have in common. In a presentation to the class, discuss your visual and your responses to the questions.

Need Extra Help?

If You've Missed Question	11	12	13	14	15	16
Go to page	473–474	452–459	452–459	449–478	466–467	466–467

Analyzing Readings in Sociology

CHAPTER 1 The **Promise** of **Sociology**
C. Wright Mills — **482**

CHAPTER 2 The **Sociology** of Ethics and the Ethics of **Sociologists**
Gideon Sjoberg and Ted R. Vaughan — **483**

CHAPTER 3 **Yąnomamö**
Napoleon A. Chagnon — **484**

CHAPTER 4 **Power** at **Play**
Michael A. Messner — **486**

CHAPTER 5 **Community** and **Society**
Ferdinand Tönnies — **488**

CHAPTER 6 The **McDonaldization** of **Society**
George Ritzer — **490**

CHAPTER 7 On Being **Sane** in **Insane** Places
D. L. Rosenhan — **492**

CHAPTER 8 **Richistan**
Robert Frank — **493**

CHAPTER 9 **Living** with **Racism**
Joe R. Feagin and Melvin P. Sikes — **494**

CHAPTER 10 **Half** the **Sky**
Nicholas D. Kristof and Sheryl WuDunn — **496**

CHAPTER 11 Life **Without** Father
David Popenoe — **498**

CHAPTER 12 The "**Rationalization**" of **Education** and **Training**
Max Weber — **500**

CHAPTER 13 The Uses of **Poverty**
Herbert J. Gans — **501**

CHAPTER 14 **Habits** of the **Heart**
Robert N. Bellah, et al. — **502**

CHAPTER 15 **Sidewalk**
Mitchell Duneier — **503**

CHAPTER 16 **Networked**
Lee Rainie and Barry Wellman — **504**

CHAPTER 1
An Invitation To Sociology

The Promise of Sociology

Reader's Dictionary

welter: turmoil
degradation: lowering of rank or esteem

In his classic 1959 work, The Sociological Imagination, *American sociologist C. Wright Mills put forth his assertion that the life of an individual cannot be understood unless it is considered in the context of society as a whole. At the same time, society cannot be fully understood unless we consider the role of the individual in shaping it. This insight is what Mills dubbed the sociological imagination. In the following passage, Mills describes the value of this perspective.*

PRIMARY SOURCE

"The sociological imagination enables its possessor to understand the larger historical scene in terms of its meaning for the inner life and the external career of a variety of individuals. It enables him to take into account how individuals, in the **welter** of their daily experience, often become falsely conscious of their social positions. Within that welter, the framework of modern society is sought, and within that framework the psychologies of a variety of men and women are formulated. By such means the personal uneasiness of individuals is focused upon explicit troubles and the indifference of publics is transformed into involvement with public issues.

The first fruit of this imagination—and the first lesson of the social science that embodies it—is the idea that the individual can understand his own experience and gauge his own fate only by locating himself within his period, that he can know his own chances in life only by becoming aware of those of all individuals in his circumstances. In many ways it is a terrible lesson; in many ways a magnificent one. We do not know the limits of man's capacities for supreme effort or willing **degradation**, for agony or glee, for pleasurable brutality or the sweetness of reason. But in our time we have come to know that the limits of 'human nature' are frighteningly broad. . . .

The sociological imagination enables us to grasp history and biography and the relations between the two within society. That is its task and its promise. To recognize this task and this promise is the mark of the classic social analyst. . . .

No social study that does not come back to the problems of biography, of history, and of their intersections within a society has completed its intellectual journey. . . .

Whether the point of interest is a great power state or a minor literary mood, a family, a prison, a creed—these are the kinds of questions the best social analysts have asked. They are the intellectual pivots of classic studies of man in society—and they are the questions inevitably raised by any mind possessing the sociological imagination. For that imagination is the capacity to shift from one perspective to another—from the political to the psychological; from examination of a single family to comparative assessment of the national budgets of the world; from the theological school to the military establishment; from considerations of an oil industry to studies of contemporary poetry."

—from *The Sociological Imagination*

DBQ Document-Based Questions

1. **Finding the Main Idea** What is the purpose of the sociological imagination?
2. **Explaining** How does Mills view the relationship between the individual and society?
3. **Synthesizing** How does possessing a sociological imagination aid the individual?

CHAPTER 2
Sociological Research Methods

The Sociology of Ethics and the Ethics of Sociologists

Reader's Dictionary

legitimize: to give authority or respectability to
self-actualization: the realization of one's full potential

In this 1971 essay, Gideon Sjoberg and Ted R. Vaughan address the struggle of sociologists to form ethical codes to guide them as they conduct their research. The authors are particularly concerned about the role of nationalism in the scientific method. In the modern era, nationalism has replaced religion as the basis for ethical conduct in science. But a commitment to nationalism, they argue, limits the scope and freedom of research. It also prevents sociologists from being able to make generalizations about humanity as a whole. By what standard, then, should sociologists justify and evaluate their actions? What should form the moral foundation of their conduct?

PRIMARY SOURCE

"Our argument is that sociologists must strive to **legitimize** their actions in terms of their contributions to 'the dignity of man' principle. That is, the idea of the dignity of man is the ultimate source of justification for the scientific enterprise, not tradition, not the legal-rational principle enunciated by [Max] Weber. For the idea of man's dignity cannot be defined within the context of any one nation-state but only in terms of some trans-national category.

Immediately we are confronted with the problem of defining or specifying the meaning of 'the dignity of man.' We must proceed beyond [George A.] Lundberg's orientation which stresses survival and biological needs and we should emphasize man's unique features—his sociocultural environment. Therefore, we define man's dignity in terms of his ability to pursue alternative courses of action—to have available significant choices. The idea of alternatives, when defined in terms of significant structural choices, emphasizes man's effort to control his own destiny. In these terms, freedom is not to be equated, as some sociologists do, with adherence to norms. Many persons in Hitler's Germany and Stalin's Russia thought they were free. Nor is freedom in this sense to be equated with the psychological freedom of **self-actualization** irrespective of its implications for others. The dignity of man is enhanced when he is free to participate meaningfully in the construction of socially meaningful choices.

It would follow that sociologists are interested in attaining objective knowledge in order to help men to attain control over their life chances—their destiny. And it is not enough for sociologists merely to examine existing courses of action: they must also examine alternative courses of action for man. Again, these alternatives cannot be defined by adherence to the perspective of any given society or nation-state. . . .

. . . We believe that although sociologists must strive to attain objective knowledge and must be concerned with exploring the alternatives in human action, sociologists must also moralize in defense of their own commitment, the scientific method. . . .

. . . Thus, while scientists need not become politicians, they nonetheless cannot be committed to a particular nation–state structure if they are to build a body of knowledge which can be applicable to, or useful for, all of mankind."

—from "The Sociology of Ethics and the Ethics of Sociologists,"
The Phenomenon of Sociology: A Reader in the Sociology of Sociology

DBQ Document-Based Questions

1. **Finding the Main Idea** According to the authors, on what principle should sociologists base their conduct?
2. **Explaining** Why do the authors argue that the concept of the "dignity of man" be applied across all cultures?
3. **Analyzing** How do the authors justify moralizing in favor of an open society?

CHAPTER 3
Culture

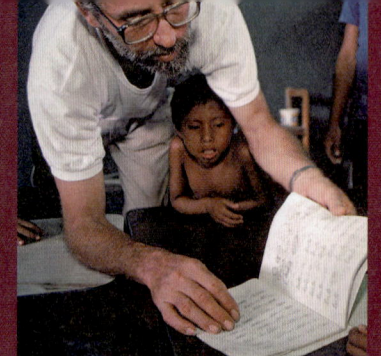

Yąnomamö

Reader's Dictionary

indelible: unable to be removed, washed away, or erased
proficiency: advanced level of skill

Between 1964 and 1995, anthropologist Napoleon A. Chagnon spent 64 months living among the Yąnomamö in their remote, isolated villages located along the border between Brazil and Venezuela. Chagnon found adapting to life in the rain forest very challenging. An even more daunting challenge was to adapt to the values and norms of this traditional South American people.

PRIMARY SOURCE

"The hardest thing to learn to live with was the incessant, passioned, and often aggressive demands they would make. It would become so unbearable at times that I would have to lock myself in my hut periodically just to escape from it. Privacy is one of our culture's most satisfying achievements, one you never think about until you suddenly have none. It is like not appreciating how good your left thumb feels until someone hits it with a hammer. But I did not want privacy for its own sake; rather, I simply had to get away from the begging. Day and night for almost the entire time I lived with the Yąnomamö I was plagued by such demands as: 'Give me a knife, I am poor!'; 'If you don't take me with you on your next trip to Widokaiyateri, I'll chop a hole in your canoe!'; 'Take us hunting up the Mavaca River with your shotgun or we won't help you!'; 'Give me some matches so I can trade with the Reyaboböwei-teri, and be quick about it or I'll hit you!'; 'Share your food with me, or I'll burn your hut!'; 'Give me a flashlight so I can hunt at night!'; 'Give me all your medicine, I itch all over!'; 'Give me an ax or I'll break into your hut when you are away and steal all of them!' And so I was bombarded by such demands day after day, month after month, until I could not bear to see a Yąnomamö at times.

It was not as difficult to become calloused to the incessant begging as it was to ignore the sense of urgency, the impassioned tone of voice and whining, or the intimidation and aggression with which many of the demands were made. It was likewise difficult to adjust to the fact that the Yąnomamö refused to accept 'No' for an answer until or unless it seethed with passion and intimidation—which it did after a few months. So persistent and characteristic is the begging that the early 'semi-official' maps made by the Venezuelan Malaria Control Service (*Malarialogía*) designated the site of their first permanent field station, next to the village of Bisaasi-teri, as *Yababuhii*: 'Gimme.' I had to become like the Yąnomamö to be able to get along with them on their terms: somewhat sly, aggressive, intimidating, and pushy.

It became **indelibly** clear to me shortly after I arrived there that had I failed to adjust in this fashion I would have lost six months of supplies to them in a single day or would have spent most of my time ferrying them around in my canoe or taking them on long hunting trips. As it was, I did spend a considerable amount of time doing these things and did succumb often to their outrageous demands for axes and machetes, at least at first, for things changed as I became more fluent in their language and learned how to defend myself socially as well as verbally. More importantly, had I failed to demonstrate that I could not be pushed around beyond a certain point, I would have been the subject of far more ridicule, theft, and practical jokes than was the actual case. In short, I had to acquire a certain **proficiency** in their style of interpersonal politics and to learn how to imply subtly that certain potentially undesirable, but unspecified, consequences might follow if they did such and such to me. They do this to each other incessantly in order to establish precisely the point at which they cannot goad or intimidate an individual

484

any further without precipitating some kind of retaliation. As soon as I realized this and gradually acquired the self-confidence to adopt this strategy, it became clear that much of the intimidation was calculated to determine my flash point or my 'last ditch' position—and I got along much better with them. Indeed, I even regained some lost ground. It was sort of like a political, interpersonal game that everyone had to play, but one in which each individual sooner or later had to give evidence that his bluffs and implied threats could be backed up with a sanction. I suspect that the frequency of wife beating is a component in this syndrome, since men can display their *waiteri* (ferocity) and 'show' others that they are capable of great violence. Beating a wife with a club is one way of displaying ferocity, one that does not expose the man to much danger—unless the wife has concerned, aggressive brothers in the village who will come to her aid. Apparently an important thing in wife beating is that the man has displayed his presumed potential for violence and the intended message is that other men ought to treat him with circumspection, caution, and even deference. . . .

For the most part, my own 'fierceness' took the form of shouting back at the Yanomamö as loudly and as passionately as they shouted at me, especially at first, when I did not know much of the language. As I became more fluent and learned more about their political tactics, I became more sophisticated in the art of bluffing and brinksmanship. For example, I paid one young man a machete (then worth about $2.50) to cut a palm tree and help me make boards from the wood. I used these to fashion a flooring in the bottom of my dugout canoe to keep my possessions out of the water that always seeped into the canoe and sloshed around. That afternoon I was working with one of my informants in the village. The long-awaited mission supply boat arrived and most of the Yanomamö ran out of the village to see the supplies and try to beg items from the crew. I continued to work in the village for another hour or so and then went down to the river to visit with the men on the supply boat. When I reached the river I noticed, with anger and frustration, that the Yanomamö had chopped up all my new floor boards to use as crude paddles to get their own canoes across the river to the supply boat. I knew that if I ignored this abuse I would have invited the Yanomamö to take even greater liberties with my possessions in the future. I got into my canoe, crossed the river, and docked amidst their flimsy, leaky craft. I shouted loudly to them, attracting their attention. They were somewhat sheepish, but all had mischievous grins on their impish faces. A few of them came down to the canoe, where I proceeded with a spirited lecture that revealed my anger at their audacity and license. I explained that I had just that morning paid one of them a machete for bringing me the palmwood, how hard I had worked to shape each board and place it in the canoe, how carefully and painstakingly I had tied each one in with vines, how much I had perspired, how many *bareto* bites I had suffered, and so on. Then, with exaggerated drama and finality, I withdrew my hunting knife as their grins disappeared and cut each one of their canoes loose and set it into the strong current of the Orinoco River where it was immediately swept up and carried downstream. I left without looking back and huffed over to the other side of the river to resume my work.

They managed to borrow another canoe and, after some effort, recovered their dugouts. Later, the headman of the village told me, with an approving chuckle, that I had done the correct thing. Everyone in the village, except, of course, the culprits, supported and defended my actions—and my status increased as a consequence."

—from *Yanomamö*

DBQ Document-Based Questions

1. **Explaining** Which of his own cultural values or norms did Chagnon most long for, and why?

2. **Analyzing** What led Chagnon to the conclusion that he must adopt Yanomamö norms?

3. **Describing** How did Chagnon earn the respect of the Yanomamö? Cite a passage from the text to support your answer.

CHAPTER 4
Socialization

Power at Play

Reader's Dictionary

dearth: inadequate supply
endemic: characteristic or prevalent in a particular people, country, or environment

Upon becoming a sociologist, Michael A. Messner, a sports enthusiast, began looking at sport through the lens of the social construct of masculinity. In his book, Power at Play: Sports and the Problem of Masculinity, *Messner examines the world of sport as a social institution and the role it plays in the socialization of men and women in our culture.*

PRIMARY SOURCE

"For most people, 'the sportsworld' is an escape from the pressures and problems of everyday life. For decades, this perspective led to a **dearth** of social scientific studies of sport, which in turn reinforced the perception of sport as the realm of the 'natural,' separate from society. But research over the past two decades has shown convincingly that sport is indeed a social institution. As sociologists began to argue in the 1970s, the perception that sport is separate from the rest of society masks the fact that the values and structure of sport have always been closely intertwined with dominant social values, power relations, and conflicts between groups and between nations.

Historical analyses of sport reveal that ruling groups have shaped and utilized sport to maintain control, but subordinate groups at times have also used sport to contest that control. For instance, historian J. A. Mangan has demonstrated that in the late nineteenth and early twentieth centuries, the British consciously developed sport in their public schools as a means of preparing boys to one day administer the Empire. Team sports, based as they were on the twin values of dominance over others and deference to the authority of leaders, were valued as a means to inculcate 'initiative and self-reliance,' along with 'loyalty and obedience.' In short, the British promoted, developed, and used sport to socialize boys to a certain kind of 'manliness' whose raison d'etre was the administration of domination over (mostly nonwhite) colonized peoples. . . .

As in Britain, sport in the United States (as we now know it) originated in the nineteenth century mostly with upper- and middle-class whites who were concerned with 'building character' in an expanding entrepreneurial environment. Blue-collar workers and people of color were largely denied access to major sporting institutions. By the turn of the century, historians have argued, the expansion of organized sport into widespread 'recreation for the masses' was seen by the upper classes as a means of integrating immigrants and the growing industrial working class into an expanding capitalist order where work was becoming routinized and leisure time was increasing. Though the extension of sport to workers and blacks was viewed by elites as a means of control, underprivileged and oppressed groups eventually learned to utilize sport for self-expression, and—especially for blacks in the twentieth century—as a means to attain status and mobility in an otherwise limited structure of opportunity. . . .

The recognition that sport is an institution in which colonial, class, and racial power relations are played out is important. But feminist historians and sociologists of the 1970s and 1980s point to another fact that, in its apparent obviousness, had been largely ignored: The struggles over power and meanings within sport have been struggles fought almost exclusively between men. The divide between men and women in sport is much wider, much more fundamental and sharply defined, than the divide between men of different nationalities, social classes, and races. . . .

With no frontier to conquer, with physical strength becoming less relevant in work, and with urban boys being raised and taught by women, it was feared that males were becoming 'soft,' that society itself was becoming 'feminized.' Many men responded to these fears with a defensive insecurity which manifested itself in the creation of new organizations such as the Boy Scouts of America (founded in 1910) as a separate cultural sphere of life where 'true manliness' could be instilled in boys by men. The rapid rise and expansion of organized sport during this same era can similarly be interpreted as the creation of a homosocial institution which served to counter men's fears of feminization in the new industrial society.

But it was more than simply modernization and changes in the organization of men's work that led to a crisis in gender relations. The late nineteenth and early twentieth centuries were also characterized by dramatic cultural and political changes among American women. An active and vibrant women's movement began to challenge men's institutional power. As historian Carroll Smith-Rosenberg has documented, by the 1880s, the United States had seen the rise of a new phenomenon: 'the single, highly educated, economically autonomous New Woman,' who repudiated the Cult of True Womanhood and 'threatened men in ways her mother never did.' As Smith-Rosenberg demonstrates, 'for the next half a century, American women and men bitterly debated the social and sexual legitimacy of the New Woman. Through her, they argued about the naturalness of gender and legitimacy of the bourgeois order. They agreed on one point: The New Woman challenged existing gender relations and the distribution of power.'

That the modern institution of sport was shaped during the time when women were challenging existing gender relations helps to explain the particular forms that sport eventually took. A number of feminist analyses have suggested that one of the key elements in maintaining men's overall power over women is the elevation of the male-body-as-superior through the use (or threat) of violence. Susan Brownmiller, for instance, argues that although various forms of control (psychological, ideological, etc.) are utilized, ultimately men's control of women rests on violence. According to sociologist Eric Dunning, historical and cross-cultural evidence shows that the balance of power tips more strongly toward men when violence and fighting are **endemic** parts of social life. With industrialization and modernization, social life became more rule-governed and 'civilized,' more controls were placed on the interpersonal use of violence, and the balance of power thus shifted more toward women. British men responded to this threat to their power by instituting 'combat sports' such as boxing and rugby: 'Such games were justified ideologically, partly as training grounds for war, partly in terms of their use in the education of military and administrative leaders in Britain's expanding empire, and partly as vehicles for the inculcation and expression of "manliness."'

Similarly, historian E. J. Gorn has interpreted the rapid rise in popularity of bare-knuckle prize fighting in late nineteenth-century America as, in large part, a masculine backlash against feminism. Sport, especially in its more violent forms, supported male dominance not simply through the exclusion or marginalization of females, but also, according to sociologist Lois Bryson, 'through the association of males and maleness with valued skills and the sanctioned use of aggression, force, and violence.' In promoting dominance and submission, in equating force and aggression with physical strength, modern sport naturalized the equation of maleness with power, thus legitimizing a challenged and faltering system of masculine domination.'

—from *Power at Play: Sports and the Problem of Masculinity*

DBQ Document-Based Questions

1. **Finding the Main Idea** Why does Messner consider sport to be a social institution?

2. **Analyzing** According to Messner, how has sport been used to control changes in society brought on by industrialization?

3. **Explaining** How does sport socialize us to accept the system of masculine domination of our society?

CHAPTER 5
Social Structure and Society

Community and Society

Reader's Dictionary

weal: state of well-being
abominable: deserving of or causing disgust or hatred

The German sociologist Ferdinand Tönnies is considered one of the founders of the field of sociology. He first introduced the influential concepts of gemeinschaft (community) and gesellschaft (society or association), in 1887. We experience each type of these social relationships in our daily lives. Tönnies observed, however, that gemeinschaft is characteristic of preindustrial society, with a social system based on tradition, kinship, common values, and close social ties. By contrast, gesellschaft, representing rationalized, impersonal, and superficial social relationships, is characteristic of urban industrial and post-industrial societies. In the excerpt below, he underscores the difference between the two as experienced by the individual.

PRIMARY SOURCE

"Human wills stand in manifold relations to one another. Every such relationship is a mutual action, inasmuch as one party is active, or gives, while the other party is passive, or receives. These actions are of such a nature that they tend either toward preservation or destruction of the other will or life; that is, they are either positive or negative. This study will consider as its subject of investigation only the relationships of mutual affirmation. Every such relationship represents unity in plurality or plurality in unity. It consists of assistance, relief, services, which are transmitted back and forth from one party to another and are to be considered as expressions of wills and their forces. The group which is formed through this positive type of relationship is called an association *(Verbindung)* when conceived of as a thing or being which acts as a unit inwardly and outwardly. The relationship itself, and also the resulting association, is conceived of either as real and organic life—this is the essential characteristic of the Gemeinschaft (community); or as imaginary and mechanical structure—this is the concept of Gesellschaft (society).

Through the application of these two terms we shall see that the chosen expressions are rooted in their synonymous use in the German language. But to date in scientific terminology they have been customarily confused and used at random without any distinction. For this reason, a few introductory remarks may explain the inherent contrast between these two concepts.

All intimate, private, and exclusive living together, so we discover, is understood as life in Gemeinschaft (community). Gesellschaft (society) is public life—it is the world itself. In Gemeinschaft with one's family, one lives from birth on, bound to it in **weal** and woe. One goes into Gesellschaft as one goes into a strange country. A young man is warned against bad Gesellschaft, but the expression bad Gemeinschaft violates the meaning of the word. Lawyers may speak of domestic *(häusliche)* Gesellschaft, thinking only of the legalistic concept of social association; but the domestic Gemeinschaft, or home life with its immeasurable influence upon the human soul, has been felt by everyone who ever shared it. Likewise, a bride or groom knows that he or she goes into marriage as a complete Gemeinschaft of life *(communio totius vitae)*. A Gesellschaft of life would be a contradiction in and of itself. One keeps or enjoys another's Gesellschaft, but not his Gemeinschaft in this sense. One becomes a part of a religious Gemeinschaft; religious Gesellschaften (associations or societies), like any other groups formed for given purposes, exist only in so far as they, viewed from without, take their places among the institutions of a political body or as they represent conceptual elements of a theory; they do not touch upon the religious Gemeinschaft as such. There exists a Gemeinschaft of language, of folkways or mores, or of beliefs; but, by way of contrast, Gesellschaft exists in the realm of business, travel, or sciences. So of special importance are the commercial Gesellschaften; whereas, even though a certain familiarity and Gemeinschaft may exist among business partners, one could indeed hardly speak of commercial Gemeinschaft. To make the word combination "joint-stock Gemeinschaft" would be **abominable**. On the other hand, there exists a Gemeinschaft of ownership in fields, forest, and pasture. The Gemeinschaft of property between man and wife cannot be called Gesellschaft of property. Thus many differences become apparent.

In the most general way, one could speak of a Gemeinschaft comprising the whole of mankind, such as the Church wishes to be regarded. But human Gesellschaft is conceived as mere coexistence of people independent of each other. Recently, the concept of Gesellschaft as opposed to and distinct from the state has been developed. This term will also be used in this book, but can only derive adequate explanation from the underlying contrast to the Gemeinschaft of the people.

Gemeinschaft is old; Gesellschaft is new as a name as well as a phenomenon. This has been recognized by an author who otherwise taught political science in all its aspects without penetrating to its fundamentals. 'The entire concept of Gesellschaft (society) in a social political sense, says Bluntschli (*Staatswörterbuch IV*), 'finds its natural foundation in the folkways, mores, and ideas of the third estate [common class]. It is not really the concept of a people (*Volks-Begriff*) but the concept of the third estate . . . Its Gesellschaft has become the origin and expression of common opinion and tendencies. . . Wherever urban culture blossoms and bears fruits, Gesellschaft appears as its indispensable organ. The rural people know little of it.' On the other hand, all praise of rural life has pointed out that the Gemeinschaft among people is stronger there and more alive; it is the lasting and genuine form of living together. In contrast to Gemeinschaft, Gesellschaft is transitory and superficial. Accordingly, Gemeinschaft should be understood as a living organism, Gesellschaft as a mechanical aggregate and artifact."

—from *Community and Society*

DBQ Document-Based Questions

1. **Identifying** According to Tönnies, how do our private lives and our public lives relate to gemeinschaft and gesellschaft?
2. **Analyzing** Why does Tönnies say that gemeinschaft is "lasting and genuine," but gesellschaft is "transitory and superficial"?
3. **Inferring** Why does Tönnies call the word combination "joint-stock Gemeinschaft" abominable?

CHAPTER 6
Groups and Formal Organizations

The McDonaldization of Society

Reader's Dictionary

efficiency: the quality of being able to produce the desired results, especially without waste (as of time or energy)

innovation: new idea, method, or device

In 1993, George Ritzer took Max Weber's concept of rationalization and applied it to modern society. Increasingly, Ritzer argues, various types of organizations are adopting the same rationalized methods of operation that have made the fast-food chain McDonald's so successful: efficiency, calculation, predictability, and control through non human technology (that is, technology that controls people rather than technology that people control). He dubbed this process "the McDonaldization of society." In the following selection, Ritzer introduces the reader to the effects of McDonaldization on higher education and health care.

PRIMARY SOURCE

"Higher Education: Just Fill in the Box

The educational system, specifically the contemporary university (now often dubbed 'McUniversity'), offers many examples of the pressure for greater **efficiency**. One is the machine-graded, multiple-choice examination. In a much earlier era, students were examined individually in conference with their professors. This method may have been a good way to find out what students knew, but it was highly labor intensive and inefficient. Later, the essay examination became popular. Grading a set of essays was more efficient than giving individual oral examinations, but it was still relatively time consuming. Enter the multiple-choice examination, the grading of which was a snap.

In fact, graduate assistants could grade it, making evaluation of students even more efficient for the professor. Now computer-graded examinations maximize efficiency for both professors and graduate assistants. They even offer advantages to students, such as making it easier to study and limiting the effect of the subjective views of the grader on the grading process.

Other **innovations** in academia are further streamlining the educational process. Even the multiple-choice examination leaves the professor saddled with the inefficient task of composing the necessary sets of questions. Furthermore, at least some of the questions have to be changed each semester to foil new students who gain possession of old exams. To ease the burden, textbook publishers started providing professors with manuals (free of charge) loaded with multiple-choice questions to accompany the textbooks required for use in large classes. The professor, however, still had to retype the questions or have them retyped. Now, publishers often provide these sets of questions on computer disks. All the professor needs to do is select the desired questions and let the printer do the rest. Another advance is the advent of computer-based programs to grade essay examinations and term papers. Professors may thus soon be able to return to assigning these more traditional types of schoolwork without any loss in efficiency. Indeed, with these great advances, professors can now choose to have very little to do with the entire examination process, from composing questions to grading, freeing up time for activities that many professors, but few students, value more highly, such as writing and research.

Publishers have provided other services to streamline teaching for those professors who adopt best-selling textbooks. A professor can receive many materials with which to fill class hours—lecture outlines, computer simulations, discussion questions, DVDs, movies, even ideas for guest lecturers and student projects. Professors who choose to use all these devices need do little or nothing on their own for their classes.

Another advance in efficiency in academia is the development of a relatively new type of service on college campuses. For a nominal fee, students may purchase lecture notes for their courses written by instructors, teaching assistants, and top-notch students. No more inefficient note taking; in fact, no more inefficient class attendance. Students are free to pursue more valuable activities, such as poring over arcane academic journals in the graduate library or watching the 'soaps.'

One last academic efficiency worth noting is the ability of students to purchase already completed term papers online. There are a variety of Web sites that now promise to deliver original, made-from-scratch research papers on any topic for a 'low, low fee' of, say, $34.95 for a complete paper, or a per-page charge of $8.99. They even have quick service and express delivery available ($14.99 per page if you need the paper in 48 hours) for those students who have put off academic dishonesty to the last moment. Beware, however, for there is also a host of other Web sites popping up that help professors detect plagiarism, thereby combating efficiency with efficiency.

Health Care: Docs-in-a-Box

It might be assumed that modern medicine is immune to the drive for efficiency and invulnerable to rationalization more generally. However, medicine has been McDonaldized. In fact, instances of what may be termed 'assembly-line medicine' have been reported. One example is Dr. Denton Cooley (his 'fetish is efficiency'), who gained worldwide fame for streamlining delicate open-heart surgery in a 'heart surgery factory' that operated 'with the precision of an assembly-line.' . . . Such assembly lines are not yet the norm in medicine, but one can imagine that they will grow increasingly common in the coming years.

What is increasing is the use of robots to perform advanced forms of surgery. Perhaps the best known is the Da Vinci system that is revolutionizing various forms of surgery (e.g., for prostate cancer). This minimally invasive system not only makes an operation more efficient but also makes the process more efficient from a patient's point of view. Because only small incisions are made, hospital stays are reduced to perhaps a day, and postoperative recovery time is relatively brief.

Perhaps the best example of the increasing efficiency of medical practice in the United States is the growth of walk-in/walk-out surgical or emergency centers. 'McDoctors' or 'Docs-in-a-box' serve patients who want medical problems handled with maximum efficiency. Each center handles only a limited number of minor problems but with great dispatch. Although the patient with a laceration cannot be stitched as efficiently as a customer in search of a hamburger can be served, many of the same principles shape the two operations. For instance, it is more efficient for the patient to walk in without an appointment than to make an appointment with a regular physician and wait until that time arrives. For a minor emergency, such as a slight laceration, walking through a McDoctors is more efficient than working your way through a large hospital's emergency room. Hospitals are set up to handle serious problems for which efficiency is not (yet) the norm, although some hospitals already employ specialized emergency room physicians and teams of medical personnel.

From an organizational point of view, a McDoctors can be run more efficiently than a hospital emergency room. Docs-in-a-box can also be more efficient than private doctors because they are not structured to permit the kind of personal (and therefore inefficient) attention patients expect from their private physicians."

—from *The McDonaldization of Society 5*

DBQ Document-Based Questions

1. **Identifying** According to Ritzer, in what ways have universities and health care become more efficient?

2. **Analyzing** How does Ritzer say technology helped both professor and student become more efficient?

3. **Inferring** Do you think Ritzer believes efficiency improves higher education and health care? Explain.

CHAPTER 7
Deviance and Social Control

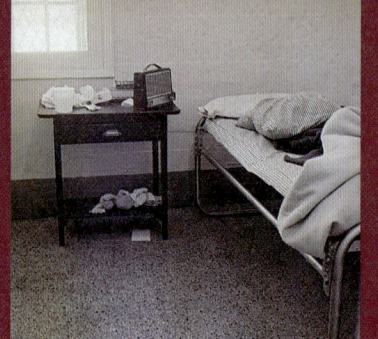

On Being Sane in Insane Places

Reader's Dictionary

capricious: impulsive, seemingly unmotivated
aberrant: unusual, deviant
substantive: real rather than apparent

In 1973, D. L. Rosenhan published "On Being Sane in Insane Places," an account of an experiment he conducted, whereby eight mentally healthy people falsely gained admission to hospitals that treat the mentally ill. Once admitted, the false patients provided staff with honest information and answers to their questions, barring their real names, profession, and place of work. Rosenhan wanted to know: "If sanity and insanity exist, how shall we know them?"

PRIMARY SOURCE

"The question is neither **capricious** nor itself insane. However much we may be personally convinced that we can tell the normal from the abnormal, the evidence is simply not compelling. It is commonplace, for example, to read about murder trials wherein eminent psychiatrists for the defense are contradicted by equally eminent psychiatrists for the prosecution on the matter of the defendant's sanity. More generally, there are a great deal of conflicting data on the reliability, utility, and meaning of such terms as 'sanity,' 'insanity,' 'mental illness,' and 'schizophrenia.' Finally, as early as 1934, [Ruth Fulton] Benedict suggested that normality and abnormality are not universal. What is viewed as normal in one culture may be seen as quite **aberrant** in another. Thus, notions of normality and abnormality may not be quite as accurate as people believe they are.

To raise questions regarding normality and abnormality is in no way to question the fact that some behaviors are deviant or odd. Murder is deviant. So, too, are hallucinations. Nor does raising such questions deny the existence of the personal anguish that is often associated with 'mental illness.' Anxiety and depression exist. Psychological suffering exists. But normality and abnormality, sanity and insanity, and the diagnoses that flow from them may be less **substantive** than many believe them to be.

At its heart, the question of whether the sane can be distinguished from the insane (and whether degrees of insanity can be distinguished from each other) is a simple matter: do the salient characteristics that lead to diagnoses reside in the patients themselves or in the environments and contexts in which observers find them? From [Paul Eugen] Bleuler, through [Ernst] Kretchmer, through the formulators of the recently revised *Diagnostic and Statistical Manual* of the American Psychiatric Association, the belief has been strong that patients present symptoms, that those symptoms can be categorized, and, implicitly, that the sane are distinguishable from the insane. More recently, however, this belief has been questioned. Based in part on theoretical and anthropological considerations, but also on philosophical, legal, and therapeutic ones, the view has grown that psychological categorization of mental illness is useless at best and downright harmful, misleading, and pejorative at worst. Psychiatric diagnoses, in this view, are in the minds of the observers and are not valid summaries of characteristics displayed by the observed."

—from "On Being Sane in Insane Places," *Science* 179 (January 1973)

DBQ Document-Based Questions

1. **Identifying Central Issues** What is the central sociological problem or problems identified by Rosenhan in this piece?
2. **Identifying Perspectives** Does Rosenhan believe that deviance can be defined or determined? Explain.
3. **Making Connections** According to Rosenhan, what role does culture play in normality and aberration?

CHAPTER 8
Social Stratification

Richistan

Reader's Dictionary

lag: to stay or fall behind
immerse: to plunge into something that surrounds

In 2003, as a reporter for the Wall Street Journal, *Robert Frank began studying the lifestyles of the New Rich. What he found was that there are now so many extremely rich people in the United States, living in an economy and enjoying a lifestyle so different from the majority of Americans, that they virtually live in their own country.*

PRIMARY SOURCE

"This book began with the discovery of a single, remarkable statistic.

In 2003, while writing a routine article about Wall Street bonuses, I stumbled onto a chart from the Federal Reserve Board. It showed that the number of millionaire households had more than doubled since 1995 to more than eight million.

Granted, a million dollars doesn't mean what it used to. But no matter how far up I looked on the wealth ladder—to households worth $10 million, $20 million, $50 million—all the populations were doubling.

Even more surprising was the fact that the United States was minting millionaires long after the tech bust, recession and terrorist attacks of 2001. The wealth boom, as the numbers showed, went far beyond the 20-something dot-commers in Silicon Valley and Wall Streeters in New York. It stretched across the country, to all age groups and to almost every industry. Never before had some many Americans become so rich, so quickly. The United States is now the world leader in producing millionaires—even if it **lags** behind China and India in other types of manufacturing. For the first time in history, we now have more millionaires than Europe.

After seeing the Fed numbers, I started to wonder about all these rich people. Who were they? How did they get rich? How was money changing their lives? Most importantly, how were they changing life for the rest of us? . . .

To answer these questions . . . I **immersed** myself in their world, hanging around yacht marinas, slipping into charity balls, loitering in Ferrari dealerships. . . .

. . . Today's rich had formed their own virtual country. They were, in fact, wealthier than most nations. By 2004, the richest 1 percent of Americans were earning about $1.35 trillion a year—greater than the total national incomes of France, Italy or Canada.

And with their huge numbers, they had built a self-contained world unto themselves, complete with their own health-care system (concierge doctors), travel network (Net Jets, destination clubs), separate economy (double-digit income gains and double-digit inflation), and language ('Who's your household manager?'). . . . The rich weren't just getting richer; they were becoming financial foreigners, creating their own country within a country, their own society within a society, and their economy within an economy.

They were creating Richistan."

—from *Richistan: A Journey Through the American Wealth Boom and the Lives of the New Rich*

DBQ Document-Based Questions

1. **Identifying** What did Frank find so surprising about the composition of the wealth boom he describes?
2. **Inferring** In what way did Frank explore a foreign culture in his research?
3. **Making Connections** According to Frank, how have the very rich used social structures to create what he sees as a virtual separate country?

CHAPTER 9
Inequalities of Race and Ethnicity

Living with Racism

Reader's Dictionary

racialize: to assign racial distinction to
deference: respect

In this work from 1994, social scientists Joe R. Feagin and Melvin P. Sikes explore how recurring racism affects middle-class African Americans. Middle-class African Americans as a group, they write, have been held up as a model of achievement. They have also had the most widespread interactions with whites—desegregating government, corporations, colleges, white neighborhoods, and upscale businesses and restaurants. Many white Americans may see the presence of an African American middle class as evidence that discrimination is not widespread. In extended interviews with middle-class African Americans, however, the authors provide an intimate look at the "reality and pain" of persistent discrimination.

PRIMARY SOURCE

"The motivations, stereotypes, and prejudices lying behind the white discrimination we examine in this book are often not clear. Still, some accounts provide some insight into white attitudes. White opinion surveys reviewed in two major books, *Racial Attitudes in America* and *A Common Destiny*, have shown that in certain subject areas white attitudes toward blacks have improved in recent decades. Nonetheless, recent opinion surveys also indicate that large proportions of whites candidly express racial prejudices and stereotypes. Judging from the overtly antiblack responses to questions in 1990s opinion surveys, somewhere between 20 and 35 percent of whites are very negative and exclusionary in their attitudes toward black Americans, in regard to such matters as supporting anti-intermarriage laws and keeping blacks out of white neighborhoods. These percentages are very significant, especially if they do not include, as seems likely, the large proportion of whites who more or less share the same views but are unwilling to say so to a pollster. Yet if only a third or so of whites hold the most hostile antiblack views, then perhaps fifty million whites over eighteen years of age today fall into this category. This number is far greater than the total of all black men, women, and children in the United States. In addition to those whites with very hostile views, the majority of whites interviewed in recent NORC surveys have shown that they accept some racial stereotypes, such as that blacks are less hardworking and more violent than whites.

In fact, in recent years social scientists have conducted few systematic, in-depth research studies of white racial attitudes or of white discriminatory actions in particular settings. Brief responses to short poll questions do not necessarily signal the true feelings of many whites. Most whites share a common historical and cultural heritage of racism centered on African Americans. While much anti-black thinking is conscious, some is so deeply embedded in white assumptions and perspectives as to be half-conscious or even unconscious. It appears that a majority of whites think in racial terms when they make important choices—choosing neighborhoods, employees, business partners, places to go in the city, and mates for themselves and their children. Indeed, the negative reactions that at least two thirds of whites in recent surveys have shown toward interracial marriages are evidence of the depths of this racial heritage. Without having to think much about it, the majority of whites seem to have a racial consciousness that is more than a few prejudices, but rather a broader framework of **racialized** thought, a way of organizing information about black and white Americans.

Another aspect of discrimination is its lasting impact. In the immediate situation or over the long haul, discrimination can generate determination, embarrassment, frustration, bitterness, anger, rage, and any combination of these feelings. Discrimination is an energy-consuming, life-consuming experience. The enduring, cumulative impact of white racism has rarely been understood by white Americans...."

Even to empathetic whites discrimination appears as discrete and isolated events. For blacks, the thick skin necessary for survival may make a given individual unaware at the conscious level, or only barely conscious, of the damage some of these instances inflict. As we noted earlier, an individual's own negative experiences are frequently shared with family and friends, relieving the victim's pain but also spreading the psychological costs....

Surprisingly few recent analyses pay much attention to another important dimension of racial discrimination, the responses and strategies for coping of African Americans. Before desegregation in the 1960s, 'old-fashioned racism,' especially in the South, routinely took the form of an asymmetrical encounter in which blacks were expected to treat whites with **deference**. Examples included the obsequious words and gestures, the etiquette of race relations, that many black people used to survive segregation and informal mistreatment. Racially deferential behavior can still be found on the part of African Americans, especially when there is the threat of force (for example, during police harassment) or in work situations not far removed from the old segregation. For example, [Judith] Rollins found in a study northeastern study that black domestic workers were commonly very deferential to white female employers. Today, however, most discriminatory interactions no longer seem to involve an open show of old-fashioned deference by the black victims. Even when whites still expect it, black Americans usually do not oblige.

While many whites assert that blacks jump much too quickly to a cry of 'racism,' in reality the opposite reaction is more likely the case. Our interviews suggest that black middle-class people frequently respond to possible discrimination by taking a 'long look,' by evaluating a situation carefully before judging it discriminatory and taking action. One respondent, a clerical employee, described the 'second eye' she uses: 'I think that it causes you to have to look at things from two different perspectives. You have to decide whether things that are done or slights that are made are made because you are black or they are made because the person is just rude, or unconcerned and uncaring. So it's kind of a situation where you're always kind of looking to see with a second eye or a second antenna just what's going on.' The term 'second eye' suggests that she and others like her look carefully at the white-black interaction through a distinctive lens colored by accumulating personal and group experience. We have noted in our interviews the willingness of many black respondents, using this 'second eye,' to give whites the benefit of the doubt in many interracial encounters.

Once a black person has spent mental energy in evaluating the situation, the active response to it may vary greatly. One strategy is to leave rather than engage in explicit conflict. Another is to ignore the discrimination and continue with the interaction, a strategy similar to the one Carol Brooks Gardner has reported in her research on women who deal with harassing remarks from men on the street. In some situations resigned acceptance may be the only realistic response. More confrontational responses to hostile white actions include verbal reprimands and sarcasm, physical counterattacks, and lawsuits.

Most people want to be legitimate in the eyes of others, and this includes many white discriminators. This concern for legitimacy can give black victims some leverage in certain discriminatory situations. In subsequent chapters numerous respondents articulate an ideal of 'liberty and justice for all.' What is especially significant is that the equal rights ideology of these middle-class black Americans is based on this American creed, the basic American principles accepted in the abstract, if not in practice, by most whites. The American creed and the legal system are often silent partners in black battles with an often hostile white world."

—from *Living with Racism: The Black Middle-Class Experience*

DBQ Document-Based Questions

1. **Making Connections** How does the historical context of an act of discrimination affect perception, according to the authors?

2. **Explaining** According to the authors, how is the "second eye" used to evaluate white-black interactions?

3. **Analyzing** What do the authors portray as the psychological toll of discrimination on the African American middle class?

CHAPTER 10
Inequalities of Gender and Age

Half the Sky

Reader's Dictionary

ebullient: cheerful, lively
paramount: superior to all others
empowerment: the realization of one's full potential
ineluctable: inescapable

The title of Half the Sky: Turning Oppression into Opportunity for Women Worldwide, *by Nicholas D. Kristof and Sheryl WuDunn, comes from a Chinese proverb: Women hold up half the sky. In the book, they chronicle the global oppression of women, particularly in poor and underdeveloped nations where women face the greatest gender inequity. They argue that giving women the opportunity to "hold up the sky," or fully participate in society, is the key to ending global poverty.*

PRIMARY SOURCE

"Amartya Sen, the **ebullient** Nobel Prize-winning economist, has developed a gauge of gender inequality that is a striking reminder of the stakes involved. 'More than 100 million women are missing,' Sen wrote in a classic essay in 1990 in *The New York Review of Books*, spurring a new field of research. Sen noted that in normal circumstances women live longer than men, and so there are more females than males in much of the world. Even poor regions like most of Latin America and much of Africa have more females than males. Yet in places where girls have a deeply unequal status, they *vanish*. China has 107 males for every 100 females in its overall population (and an even greater disproportion among newborns), India has 108, and Pakistan has 111. This has nothing to do with biology, and indeed the state of Kerala in the southwest of India, which has championed female education and equality, has the same excess of females that exists in the United States.

The implication of the sex ratios, Professor Sen found, is that about 107 million females are missing from the globe today. Follow-up studies have calculated the number slightly differently, deriving alternative figures for 'missing women' of between 60 million and 101 million. Every year, at least another 2 million girls worldwide disappear because of gender discrimination.

In the wealthy countries of the West, discrimination is usually a matter of unequal pay or underfunded sports teams or unwanted touching from a boss. In contrast, in much of the world discrimination is lethal. In India, for example, mothers are less likely to take their daughters to be vaccinated than their sons—that alone accounts for one fifth of India's missing females. . . .

The global statistics on the abuse of girls are numbing. It appears that more girls have been killed in the last fifty years, precisely because they were girls, than men were killed in all the battles of the twentieth century. More girls are killed in this routine 'gendercide' in any one decade than people were slaughtered in all the genocides of the twentieth century.

In the nineteenth century, the central moral challenge was slavery. In the twentieth century, it was the battle against totalitarianism. We believe that in this century the **paramount** moral challenge will be the struggle for gender equality in the developing world. . . .

. . . For many years we have regularly trod the mud paths of the Taishan region [of southern China] to Shunshui, the hamlet in which Sheryl's paternal grandfather grew up. China traditionally has been one of the more repressive and smothering places for girls. . . .

Something bothered us each time we explored Shunshui and the surrounding villages: Where were the young women? Young men were toiling industriously in the paddies or fanning themselves indolently in the shade, but young women and girls were scarce. We finally discovered them when we stepped into the factories that were spreading throughout Guangdong Province, the epicenter of China's economic eruption.

... Eighty percent of the employees on the assembly lines in coastal China are female, and the proportion across the manufacturing belt of East Asia is at least 70 percent. The economic explosion in Asia was, in large part, an outgrowth of the economic **empowerment** of women. . . .

Women are indeed a linchpin of the region's development strategy. Economists who scrutinized East Asia's success noted a common pattern. These countries took young women who previously had contributed negligibly to gross national product (GNP) and injected them into the formal economy, hugely increasing the labor force. The basic formula was to ease repression, educate girls as well as boys, give the girls the freedom to move to the cities and take factory jobs, and then benefit from a demographic dividend as they delayed marriage and reduced childbearing. The women meanwhile financed the education of younger relatives, and saved enough of their pay to boost national savings rates. This pattern has been called 'the girl effect.' . . .

Evidence has mounted that helping women can be a successful poverty-fighting strategy anywhere in the world, not just in the booming economies of East Asia. . . .

In the early 1990s, the United Nations and the World Bank began to appreciate the potential resource that women and girls represent. 'Investment in girls' education may well be the highest-return investment available in the developing world,' Lawrence Summers wrote when he was chief economist of the World Bank. 'The question is not whether countries can afford this investment, but whether counties can afford not to educate more girls.' In 2001 the World Bank produced an influential study, *Engendering Development Through Gender Equality in Rights, Resources, and Voice*, arguing that promoting gender equality is crucial to combat global poverty. UNICEF issued a major report arguing that gender equality yields a 'double divided' by elevating not only women but also their children and communities. The United Nations Development Programme (UNDP) summed up the mounting research this way: 'Women's empowerment helps raise economic productivity and reduce infant mortality. It contributes to improved health and nutrition. It increases the chances of education for the next generation.' . . .

Concerns about terrorism after the 9/11 attacks triggered interest in these issues in an unlikely constituency: the military and counterterrorism agencies. Some security experts noted that the countries that nurture terrorists are disproportionally those where women are marginalized. The reason there are so many Muslim terrorists, they argued, has little to do with the Koran but a great deal to do with the lack of robust female participation in the economy and society of many Islamic countries. . . .

We will try to lay out an agenda for the world's women focusing on three particular abuses: sex trafficking and forced prostitution; gender-based violence, including honor killings and mass rape; and maternal mortality, which still needlessly claims one woman a minute. We will lay out solutions such as girls' education and microfinance, which are working right now. . . .

Honor killings, sexual slavery, and genital cutting may seem to Western readers to be tragic but inevitable in a world far, far away. In much the same way, slavery was once widely viewed by many decent Europeans and Americans as a regrettable but **ineluctable** feature of human life. It was just one more horror that had existed for thousands of years. But then in the 1780s a few indignant Britons, led by William Wilberforce, decided that slavery was so offensive that they had to abolish it. And they did. Today we see the seed of something similar: a global movement to emancipate women and girls."

—from *Half the Sky: Turning Oppression into Opportunity for Women Worldwide*

DBQ Document-Based Questions

1. **Contrasting** According to the authors, how does discrimination against women and girls in the West differ from discrimination in other parts of the world?

2. **Explaining** What, according to the authors, is at the center of the economic boom in China?

3. **Identifying** What do the authors identify as some of the overall benefits to society that can be achieved with the empowerment of girls and women?

CHAPTER 11
The Family

Life Without Father

Reader's Dictionary

second shift: household and childcare responsibilities that, due to gender stratification, often fall to women despite their hours in the workplace outside the home

ominous: foreshadowing evil

In this 1996 book Life Without Father, *David Popenoe describes what he sees as a path of social decline in the United States. He believes that a weakening of family relationships has contributed to a society plagued by crime, personal and social mistrust, greed, crumbling communities, and a confused morality. Children growing up typically have two important role models in their lives, but one of them is increasingly missing.*

PRIMARY SOURCE

"'Fathers should be neither seen nor heard,' Oscar Wilde once wrote. 'That is the only proper basis for family life.' With each passing year, American society has increasingly become an immense social testing ground for this proposition. Unfortunately for Wilde's reputation as a social analyst, to say nothing about the health of our society, the results have proved highly unsupportive. American fathers are today more removed from family life than ever before in our history. And according to a growing body of evidence, this massive erosion of fatherhood contributes mightily to many of the major social problems of our time. . . .

The print pages and airwaves have been filled with discussions of fatherhood in recent decades. Yet most discussions have focused on just one issue—how to get fathers to share their traditional breadwinner role and take up a new (for them) child-care-provider role. The call from younger women has been loud and clear: We need a new conception of fatherhood, a 'new father,' one who will help equally in the home just as women now strive to help equally in the workplace; one who will share the **'second shift'** with his mate.

The father's role—what society expects of fathers—has indeed changed enormously in recent years. Fathers are expected to be more engaged with their children and involved with housework—if not nearly as much as most women would like, certainly far more than the past generation of fathers would have thought possible.

This role change has been highly positive in most respects. But with all the concentration on 'role equality' in the home, the larger and more **ominous** trend of modern fatherhood has been mostly overlooked. We have been through many social revolutions in the past three decades—sex, women's liberation, divorce—but none more significant for society than the startling emergence of the absent father, a kind of pathological counterpart to the new father.

While the new father has been emerging gradually for most of this century, it is only in the past thirty years that we have witnessed the enormous increase in absent fathers. In times past, many children were left fatherless through his premature death. Today, the fathers are still alive and out there somewhere; the problem is that they seldom see much, if anything, of their children.

The main reason for contemporary father absence is the dramatic decline of marriage. . . . What this means, in human terms, is that about half of today's children will spend at least a portion of their growing-up years living apart from their fathers.

As a society, we can respond to this new fatherlessness in several ways. We can, as more and more of us seem to be doing, simply declare fathers to be unnecessary, superfluous. This is the response of 'single parents by choice.' It is the response of those who say that if daddies and mommies are expected to do precisely the same things in the home, why do we need both? It is the response of those who declare that unwed motherhood is a woman's right, or that single-parent families are every bit as good as two-parent families, or that divorce is generally beneficial for children.

In my view, these responses represent a human tragedy—for children, for women, for men, and for our society as a whole.... Fathering is different from mothering; involved fathers are indispensable for the good of children and society; and our growing [trend in] national fatherlessness is a disaster in the making....

No one predicted this trend, few researchers or government agencies have monitored it, and it is not widely discussed, even today. But its importance to society is second to none. Father absence is a major force lying behind many of the attention-grabbing issues that dominate the news: crime and delinquency; premature sexuality and out-of-wedlock teen births; deteriorating educational achievement; depression, substance abuse, and alienation among teenagers; and the growing number of women and children in poverty. These issues all point to a profound deterioration in the well-being of children. Some experts have suggested, in fact, that the current generation of children and youth is the first in our nation's history to be less well-off—psychologically, socially, economically, and morally—than their parents were at the same age. Or as Senator Daniel Patrick Moynihan has observed, 'the United States... may be the first society in history in which children are distinctly worse off than adults.'

Along with the growing father absence, our cultural view of fatherhood is changing. Few people have doubts about the fundamental importance of mothers. But fathers? More and more the question is being raised, are fathers really necessary? Many would answer no, or maybe not. And to the degree that fathers are still thought necessary, fatherhood is said by many to be merely a social role, as if men had no inherent biological predisposition whatsoever to acknowledge and to invest in their own offspring. If merely a social role, then perhaps anyone is capable of playing it....

The decline of fatherhood and of marriage cuts at the heart of the kind of environment considered ideal for childrearing. Such an environment, according to a substantial body of knowledge, consists of an enduring two-parent family that engages regularly in activities together, has many of its own routines and traditions, and provides a great deal of quality contact time between adults and children. The children have frequent contact with relatives, active neighboring in a supportive setting, and contact with their parents' world of work. In addition, there is little concern on the part of children that their parents will break up. Finally, each of these ingredients comes together in the development of a rich family subculture that has lasting meaning and strongly promulgates such family values as responsibility, cooperation, and sharing....

What the decline of fatherhood and marriage in America really means, then, is that slowly, insidiously, and relentlessly our society has been moving in an ominous direction—toward the devaluation of children. There has been an alarming weakening of the fundamental assumption, long at the center of our culture, that children are to be loved and valued at the highest level of priority. Nothing could be more serious for our children or our future."

—from *Life Without Father: Compelling New Evidence That Fatherhood and Marriage Are Indispensable for the Good of Children and Society*

DBQ Document-Based Questions

1. **Explaining** Why does Popenoe disagree with Wilde's quip that "fathers should be neither seen nor heard"?

2. **Identifying** What structural change in society does Popenoe blame for the absence of fathers in the lives of children?

3. **Finding the Main Idea** What does Popenoe identify as the ultimate cost of absent fathers for society?

CHAPTER 12
Education

The "Rationalization" of Education and Training

Reader's Dictionary

indispensable: absolutely necessary
concomitant: occurring at the same time
ambivalent: possessing simultaneous and contradictory attitudes or feelings toward something

In his classic essay "The 'Rationalization' of Education and Training," Max Weber notes that modern bureaucracy is increasingly dependent upon trained experts. As educational institutions strive to produce trained experts, they are increasingly turning to special examinations. Weber outlines the effects of this bureaucratization of education on the quality of education and on democracy.

PRIMARY SOURCE

"Educational institutions . . . are dominated and influenced by the need for the kind of 'education' that produces a system of special examinations and the trained expertness that is increasingly **indispensable** for modern bureaucracy.

The 'special examination,' in the present sense, was and is found also outside of bureaucratic structures proper; thus, today it is found in the 'free' professions of medicine and law and in the guild-organized trades. Expert examinations are neither indispensable to nor **concomitant** phenomena of bureaucratization. . . .

'Democracy' also takes an **ambivalent** stand in the face of specialized examinations, as it does in the face of all the phenomena of bureaucracy—although democracy itself promotes these developments. Special examinations, on the one hand, mean or appear to mean a 'selection' of those who qualify from all social strata rather than a rule by notables. On the other hand, democracy fears that a merit system and educational certificates will result in a privileged 'caste.' Hence, democracy fights against the special-examination system. . . .

The modern development of full bureaucratization brings the system of rational, specialized, and expert examinations irresistibly to the fore. . . .

The development of the diploma from universities, and business and engineering colleges, and the universal clamor for the creation of educational certificates in all fields make for the formation of a privileged stratum in bureaus and in offices. . . . When we hear from all sides the demand for an introduction of regular curricula and special examinations, the reason behind it is, of course, not a suddenly awakened 'thirst for education' but the desire for restricting the supply for these positions and their monopolization by the owners of educational certificates. Today, the 'examination' is the universal means of this monopolization, and therefore examinations irresistibly advance. As the education prerequisite to the acquisition of the educational certificate requires considerable expense and a period of waiting for full remuneration, this striving means a setback for talent (charisma) in favor of property. For the 'intellectual' costs of educational certificates are always low, and with the increasing volume of such certificates, their intellectual costs do not increase, but rather decrease."

—from *The Structure of Schooling: Readings in the Sociology of Education*

DBQ Document-Based Questions

1. **Identifying Central Issues** Does Weber believe that bureaucracies require special examinations?
2. **Explaining** What, according to Weber, does democracy have to fear from the rationalization of education?
3. **Inferring** What effect does the rise of special examinations and certificates have on the quality of education according to Weber? Cite the passage or passages that support your answer.

CHAPTER 13

Political and Economic Institutions

The Uses of Poverty

Reader's Dictionary

subsidize: to assist by furnishing money
dysfunction: impaired or abnormal functioning

In 1971, Herbert J. Gans applied functional theory to poverty. While he identified the positive functions of poverty, he also provided functional alternatives to poverty. By doing so, he hoped to show that functionalism is not necessarily conservative in its approach to sociology.

PRIMARY SOURCE

"Poverty and the poor may well satisfy a number of positive functions for many nonpoor groups in American society. I shall describe 13 such functions—economic, social, and political—that seem to me most significant.

First, the existence of poverty ensures that society's 'dirty work' will be done....

Second, because the poor are required to work at low wages, they **subsidize** a variety of economic activities that benefit the affluent. For example . . . because the poor pay a higher proportion of their income in property and sales taxes, among others, they subsidize many state and local governmental services that benefit more affluent groups....

Third, poverty creates jobs for a number of occupations and professions that serve or 'service' the poor, or protect the rest of society from them....

Fourth, the poor buy goods others do not want and thus prolong the economic usefulness of such goods—day-old bread [for example].... They also provide incomes for doctors, lawyers, teachers and others who are too old, poorly trained, or incompetent to attract more affluent clients....

Ninth, the poor also aid the upward mobility of groups just above them in the class hierarchy....

Eleventh, the poor, being powerless, can be made to absorb the costs of change and growth in American society. During the nineteenth century, they did the backbreaking work that built the cities; today, they are pushed out of their neighborhoods to make room for 'progress.'... They have provided many of the foot soldiers for Vietnam and other wars....

Thirteenth, the role of the poor in upholding conventional norms . . . also has a significant political function. An economy based on the ideology of laissez-faire requires a deprived population that is allegedly unwilling to work or that can be considered inferior....

This analysis is not intended to suggest that because it is often functional, poverty *should* exist, or that it *must* exist. For one thing, poverty has many more **dysfunctions** than functions; for another it is possible to suggest functional alternatives.

For example, society's dirty work could be done without poverty, either by automation or by paying 'dirty workers' decent wages.... This would, however, drive up the costs of these activities . . . "

—from "The Uses of Poverty," *Social Policy* (July/Aug. 1971)

DBQ Document-Based Questions

1. **Identifying Central Issues** According to Gans, who reaps the functional benefits of poverty?
2. **Explaining** Why does Gans claim that, despite its functions, poverty need not exist?
3. **Identifying** According to Gans, what must happen for society to adopt functional alternatives to poverty?

CHAPTER 14
Religion

Habits of the Heart

Reader's Dictionary

isolation: the state of being apart from others
republican: relating to or characteristic of a republic (a government in which supreme power resides in citizens entitled to vote for representatives)

In Habits of the Heart: Individualism and Commitment in American Life, *first published in 1985, Robert N. Bellah, along with coauthors Richard Madsen, William M. Sullivan, Ann Swidler, and Steven M. Tipton, explored the role of religion in American life and how it relates to American individualism and republicanism.*

PRIMARY SOURCE

"Religion is one of the most important of the many ways in which Americans 'get involved' in the life of their community and society. Americans give more money and donate more time to religious bodies and religiously associated organizations than to all other voluntary associations put together. Some 40 percent of Americans attend religious services at least once a week (a much greater number than would be found in Western Europe or even Canada) and religious membership is around 60 percent of the total population.

In our research, we were interested in religion not in **isolation** but as part of the texture of private and public life in the United States. Although we seldom asked specifically about religion, time and again in our conversations, religion emerged as important to the people we were interviewing, as the national statistics just quoted would lead one to expect.

For some, religion is primarily a private matter having to do with family and local congregation. For others, it is private in one sense but also a primary vehicle for the expression of national and even global concerns. Though Americans overwhelmingly accept the doctrine of the separation of church and state, most of them believe, as they always have, that religion has an important role to play in the public realm. . . .

To remind us of what is possible, we may call to mind one of the most significant social movements of recent times, a movement overwhelmingly religious in its leadership that changed the nature of American society. Under the leadership of Martin Luther King, Jr., the Civil Rights movement called upon Americans to transform their social and economic institutions with the goal of building a just national community that would respect both the differences and the interdependence of its members. It did this by combining biblical and **republican** themes in a way that included, but transformed, the culture of individualism."

—from *Habits of the Heart: Individualism and Commitment in American Life*

DBQ Document-Based Questions

1. **Identifying** What evidence do the authors cite to back up their claim that religion is a vehicle for community participation?

2. **Analyzing** According to the authors, how is religion both a private and public matter?

3. **Explaining** According to the authors, how did religion assist the civil rights movement?

CHAPTER 15
Population and Urbanization

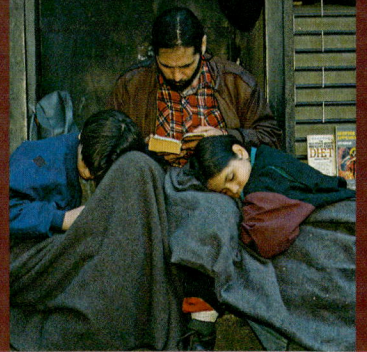

Sidewalk

Reader's Dictionary
dependable: reliable
violation: infringement, transgression

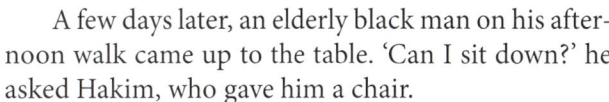

Sidewalk is an ethnographic study of street vendors in New York City's Greenwich Village neighborhood. In this excerpt, sociologist Mitchell Duneier, who spent several years working with the street vendors, describes an exchange with book vendor Hakim Hasan, who had earned the respect of the other street vendors and other members of the "sidewalk" community.

PRIMARY SOURCE

"'It is not hard to understand why Hakim Hasan came to see himself as a public character. Early one July morning, a deliveryman pulled his truck up to the curb behind Hakim's vending table on Greenwich Avenue off the corner of Sixth Avenue and carried a large box of flowers over to him.

'Can you hold these until the flower shop opens up?' the deliveryman asked.

'No problem,' responded Hakim as he continued to set up the books on his table. 'Put them right under there.'

When the story opened for business, he brought them inside and gave them to the owner.

'Why did that man trust you with the flowers?' I later asked.

'People like me are the eyes and ears of this street,' he explained, echoing [sociologist] Jane Jacobs again. 'Yes, I could take those flowers and sell them for a few hundred dollars. But that deliveryman sees me here everyday. I'm as **dependable** as any store-owner.'

A few days later, an elderly black man on his afternoon walk came up to the table. 'Can I sit down?' he asked Hakim, who gave him a chair.

The man was panting and sweating, so Hakim went to the telephone on the corner and called 911.

As they waited for the paramedics to arrive, the man said he was going into the subway.

'It's too hot for you down there,' Hakim replied. 'You wait right here for the ambulance!'

Soon an ambulance arrived, and the crew carried away the old man. It turned out he had suffered an asthma attack.

Another day, I was present at the table when a traffic officer walked by to give out parking tickets.

'Are any of these your cars?' she asked Hakim.

'Yes, that one and that one,' said Hakim, pointing.

'What is that all about?' I asked.

'The day I met her, we got into an argument,' he explained. 'She was getting ready to give the guy across the street a ticket. I say, "You can't do this!" She said, "Why not?" I say, "'Cause I'm getting ready to put a quarter in." She said, "You can't do that." I guess that, because of the way I made my argument, she didn't give out the ticket, and from that point onward we became friends. And when she comes on the block, she asks me, for every car on the block that has a **violation** sign, "Is that your car?" Meaning, "Is it someone you know?" And depending on whether I say yes or no, that's it—they get a ticket.'"

—from *Sidewalk*

DBQ Document-Based Questions

1. **Using Context Clues** What does Hakim Hasan mean when he refers to himself as a "public character"?
2. **Interpreting** Why do you think Hasan is respected by the other street vendors?
3. **Making Connections** What kind of neighborhood subcultures can you identify in your community?

Analyzing Readings in Sociology **503**

CHAPTER 16
Social Change and Collective Behavior

Networked

Reader's Dictionary

cohesion: the act of sticking together tightly
recede: to diminish; to decrease

In the 2012 book, Networked: The New Social Operating System, *Lee Rainie and Barry Wellman explore how digital technology is not isolating individuals or undermining social structures. Rather, they argue that the rise of what they call "networked individualism" means that people have increasingly become networked as individuals rather than as part of groups.*

PRIMARY SOURCE

"We wonder about the folks who keep moaning that the internet is killing society. They sound just like those who worried generations ago that TV or automobiles would kill sociability, or sixteenth-century fears that the printing press would lead to information overload. . . . The evidence in our work is that none of these technologies are isolated—or isolating—systems. They are being incorporated into people's social lives much like their predecessors were. People are not hooked on gadgets—they are hooked on each other. When they go on the internet, they are not isolating themselves. They are conversing with others—be they emailers, bloggers, Facebookers, Wikipedians, or even organizational web posters. When people walk down the street texting on their phones, they are obviously communicating. Yet things are different now. In incorporating gadgets into their lives, people have changed the ways they interact with each other. They have become increasingly networked as individuals. . . . It is the person who is the focus: not the family, not the work unit, not the neighborhood, and not the social group.

. . . However, some analysts fear that people's lesser involvement in local community organizations—such as church groups and bowling leagues—means that we live in a socially diminished world where trust is lower, societal **cohesion** is reduced, loneliness is widespread, and people's collective capacity to help one another is at risk. . . .

The evidence suggests that those with such fears have been looking at the new world through a cloudy lens. Our research supports the notion that small, densely knit groups like families, villages, and small organizations have **receded** in recent generations. A different social order has emerged around social networks that are more diverse and less overlapping than those previous groups. . . .

A key reason why these kinds of networks function effectively is that social networks are large and diversified thanks to the way people use technology. To some critics, this seems to be a problem. They express concern that technology creates social isolation, as people rely on tech-based communication rather than face-to-face encounters. We find a different story. Technologies such as the internet and mobile phones help people manage a larger, more diverse set of relationships. . . . The lesson is this: Rather than the internet or mobile phones luring people away from in-person contact, extensive internet use is associated with larger, more diverse, and growing networks. For example, one study of internet users shows that between 2002 and 2007, there was an increase of more than one-third in the number of friends seen in person weekly."

—from *Networked: The New Social Operating System*

DBQ Document-Based Questions

1. **Identifying Central Issues** According to Rainie and Wellman, what is "networked individualism"?
2. **Explaining** Why do the authors argue that the Internet and social media are not undermining society?
3. **Making Inferences** Why do you think that there is an association between Internet use and larger networks?

Sociology Handbook

Contents

Thinking Like a Sociologist 505	**Analyzing Graphics** 513
Study and Writing Skills 506 Study Skills The Writing Process	Line Graphs and Bar Graphs Circle Graphs and Tables Maps
Critical Thinking Skills 509 Identifying Central Issues Determining Cause and Effect Separating Fact From Opinion Making Generalizations	**Interpreting Data** 518 Percentages Mean, Median, and Mode

Thinking Like a Sociologist

Why Should You Study Sociology?

If someone in the United States is asked why he or she acted in a certain way, most of us would expect the person to provide an explanation that described the causes of the behavior in terms of his or her *individual* choices. Americans are generally taught to think that they totally determine their own thoughts, feelings, and actions. Sociologists recognize, however, that the groups, or social structures, to which one belongs have a profound influence over the way individuals think, feel, and act. Sociology provides tools to understand what these social structures are, how they affect our beliefs and behaviors, and how individuals relate to each other. Developing a sociological imagination—the mind-set that enables individuals to see the relationship between events in their personal lives and events in their society—will help you see how social forces affect your life in a way that a more individualistic perspective does not.

What Should You Expect?

As you begin your study of sociology, you will probably find that it is very different from other classes you have taken. This is because sociology looks at groups rather than at individuals. It is this focus on groups, rather than on individuals, that distinguishes sociology from psychology, the study of individual behavior. Although sociology employs a distinct perspective, it does share some common features with other social sciences, including anthropology, psychology, economics, human geography, political science, and history. You will find elements of all of these disciplines in this sociology textbook. You will also find that you will begin to look at your life and your interactions with other people and with social institutions in a different way as you proceed through this course.

Sociologists as Scientists

In your study of sociology, you will learn to think like a social scientist. Scientists constantly question their own assumptions and look for alternative evidence and conclusions. All scientists—including sociologists—use the scientific method as a problem-solving tool. It teaches them to think critically by encouraging open-mindedness, intellectual curiosity, and evaluation of reasons. Using the scientific method will help you think critically and be objective when applying sociological principles to everyday events, issues, and problems.

Study and Writing Skills

Study Skills

To get the most out of any course you take, you must be active in learning the material. All fields of study have their own terminology, and sociology is no different in that respect. In sociology, however, understanding the central concepts is confounded by the fact that many of the terms used by sociologists are often also used in everyday language with different meanings. Because it is important for you to understand such definitional differences, sociological concepts are carefully defined throughout the textbook.

Learning the Skill
To understand the central concepts used in sociology:

- identify the terms that sociologists use to represent specific scientific concepts. You must be careful at this point because many of the words that sociologists use are also used in everyday language. You may mistakenly think that you already understand a word when, in fact, its scientific meaning is different.
- be sure that you understand the words that are used to define a sociological term.
- try to put the definition in your own words. If you cannot do this at first, keep working at it until you can. Be careful not to lapse back into everyday usage of the term.
- understand the context in which the term is used, not just its specific definition.
- practice using sociological terms with their scientific meanings.

CARTOON >

Words can have different meanings depending upon context.

"O.K. What part of 'malignant regression and pathogenic reintrojection as a defense against psychic decompensation' don't you understand?"

Discrimination and prejudice come in many forms and have many targets.

Practicing the Skill
Read the following paragraph and then answer the questions below.

"Prejudice is a widely held preconception of a group and its individual members. These preconceptions are often based on strong emotions and unchallenged ideas. Consequently, they are difficult to change, even in the face of overwhelming evidence to the contrary. Prejudice involves an either/or type of logic: a group is either good or bad, and it is assumed that each of the members of that group possesses the characteristics attributed to the group. Prejudice, then, involves an overgeneralization based on biased or insufficient information. While prejudice refers to an attitude, discrimination describes unequal treatment of others. Prejudice does not always result in discrimination, but it often does."

1. Define *prejudice* in its sociological meaning. Do the same for *discrimination*.
2. Based on their sociological meanings, are prejudice and discrimination always negative?
3. Based on their sociological meanings, can discrimination occur without prejudice?

Applying the Skill
1. Look up the sociological definitions of *culture* and *society*. How are these meanings different from everyday usage?
2. How are these terms similar to each other?
3. How are they different?

Sociology Handbook **507**

The Writing Process

Researching and writing allow you to organize your ideas in a logical manner. Actually, writing a paper is only the final step in a process that involves using other skills you have already learned, such as identifying central issues, distinguishing fact from opinion, and making generalizations.

Learning the Skill

Use the following guidelines in the writing process:

- select an interesting topic. As you identify possible topics, focus on resources that are available. Do preliminary research to determine whether your topic is too broad or too narrow.
- write a thesis statement that defines what you want to prove, discover, or illustrate in your writing. This will be the focus of your entire paper.
- research your topic. First, formulate a list of central questions. Prepare note cards on each question and list the information sources.
- organize your information by building an outline. Then follow your outline in writing a rough draft of your report.
- a report should have three main parts: the introduction, the body, and the conclusion. The introduction briefly presents the topic and gives your topic statement. In the body, follow your outline to develop the important ideas in your argument. The conclusion summarizes and restates your findings.
- each paragraph should express one main idea in a topic sentence. Additional sentences support or explain the main idea by using details and facts.
- revise the draft into a final report. Wait for a day, then reread and revise it.

Practicing the Skill

Suppose you are writing a report on the role family income plays in the children's educational attainment. Answer the following questions about the writing process.

1. How could you narrow the topic?
2. Write a thesis statement.
3. What are the main ideas?
4. What are three possible sources of information?

Applying the Skill

Use research resources in your library to find information on the role of the family in society. Narrow the topic and write a short report on it.

Practice paraphrasing when you take notes. It will help you understand the topic better and avoid plagiarism.

Critical Thinking Skills

Identifying Central Issues

Identifying central issues will help you organize information and assess the most important concepts to remember.

Learning the Skill

To identify a central issue, follow these steps:

- Understand the context in which the reading was written.
- Skim the material to identify its general subject. Look at headings and subheadings.
- Read the information carefully to pinpoint the ideas and the details that support the subject.
- Identify the central issue. Ask what part of the reading conveys the main idea.

Read the following excerpt from *The New Jim Crow: Mass Incarceration in the Age of Colorblindness*, by Michelle Alexander.

PRIMARY SOURCE

"An extraordinary percentage of black men in the United States are legally barred from voting today, just as they have been throughout most of American history. They are also subject to legalized discrimination in employment, housing, education, public benefits, and jury service, just as their parents, grandparents, and great-grandparents once were.

What has changed since the collapse of Jim Crow has less to do with the basic structure of our society than with the language we use to justify it. In the era of colorblindness, it is no longer socially permissible to use race, explicitly, as a justification for discrimination, exclusion, and social contempt. So we don't. Rather than rely on race, we use our criminal justice system to label people of color 'criminals' and then engage in all the practices we supposedly left behind. Today it is perfectly legal to discriminate against criminals in nearly all the ways it was once legal to discriminate against African Americans. Once you're labeled a felon, the old forms of discrimination—employment discrimination, housing discrimination, denial of the right to vote, denial of educational opportunity, denial of food stamps and other public benefits, and exclusion from jury service—are suddenly legal. As a criminal, you have scarcely more rights, and arguable less respect, than a black man living in Alabama at the height of Jim Crow. We have not ended racial caste in America; we have merely redesigned it."

—*The New Jim Crow: Mass Incarceration in the Age of Colorblindness*, 2012

A first step in identifying the central issue is to find out who wrote the piece and understand the author's purposes in writing it. Michelle Alexander is a civil rights lawyer, legal scholar, and advocate. She is the former director of the Racial Justice Project for the Northern California chapter of the American Civil Liberties Union, where she focused her efforts on criminal justice reform. In her book, she hopes to convince people concerned about racial justice that our criminal justice system operates like the old system of Jim Crow.

Practicing the Skill
Read another paragraph from Alexander's book and answer the questions that follow.

PRIMARY SOURCE

"The stark racial disparities [of incarceration] cannot be explained by rates of drug crime. Studies show that people of all colors *use and sell* illegal drugs at remarkably similar rates. If there are significant differences in the surveys to be found, they frequently suggest that whites, particularly white youth, are more likely to engage in drug crime than people of color. That is not what one would guess, however, when entering our nation's prisons and jails, which are overflowing with black and brown drug offenders. In some states, black men have been admitted to prison on drug charges at rates twenty to fifty times greater than those of white men. And in major cities, wracked by the drug war, as many as 80 percent of young African American men now have criminal records and are thus subject to legalized discrimination for the rest of their lives. These young men are part of a growing undercaste, permanently locked up and locked out of mainstream society."

—*The New Jim Crow: Mass Incarceration in the Age of Colorblindness*, 2012

1. According to Alexander, is greater drug use the reason so many African American males face incarceration compared to white males?
2. Summarize the central issue of this paragraph in one sentence.

Applying the Skill
1. Bring to class three editorials from your local newspaper, national newspaper, or a newsmagazine. Try to find examples written by professional writers and the publications' readers.
2. Identify the central issue in each editorial.
3. Discuss how clearly each writer made his or her main point(s).

Determining Cause and Effect

Understanding cause and effect involves determining why an event occurred. A cause is the action or situation that produces an event. What happens as a result of a cause is an effect. Despite the seeming simplicity of this relationship, determining the true cause of an event is often very difficult. This is the case because there is seldom a single cause of any effect. Like other scientists, sociologists realize that almost all events occur as a result of several factors operating in combination. This viewpoint is known as the principle of multiple causation.

Learning the Skill
Just because two things happen at nearly the same time, or they seem to occur regularly together, does not mean that they have a causal relationship. To identify cause-and-effect relationships, follow these steps:

- identify two or more events.
- decide whether one event caused the other. Look for clue words such as *because, led to, brought about, produced, as a result of, so that, since*, and *therefore*.
- Look for logical relationships between events, such as "She overslept, and then she missed her bus."
- Identify the outcomes of events. Remember that some effects have more than one cause, and some causes lead to more than one effect. Also, an effect can become the cause of yet another effect.

Practicing the Skill

Sociologists have studied the relationship between violence on television and violent behavior for many years. For decades, no one was willing to conclude that there was a cause-and-effect relationship between the two. In 1968, President Lyndon B. Johnson established the National Commission on the Causes and Prevention of Violence to investigate the reasons behind the growth of violence in American society. The report issued by the commission in 1969 established a causal link between viewing violence on television and increased levels of violent behavior among viewers.

PRIMARY SOURCE

"We believe it is reasonable to conclude that a constant diet of violent behavior on television has an adverse effect on human character and attitudes. Violence on television encourages violent forms of behavior, and fosters moral and social values about violence in daily life which are unacceptable in a civilized society."

—National Commission on the Causes and Prevention of Violence, 1969

1. Why do you think the commission concluded that a cause-and-effect relationship exists between violence on television and violence in society?
2. Do you agree that their conclusion is reasonable? Explain.

Applying the Skill

1. Do some research on the causes of criminal behavior. Prepare a short report that summarizes your findings.
2. Discuss how the principle of multiple causation applies to criminal behavior.
3. What other questions does your research raise?

Separating Fact From Opinion

Being able to distinguish fact from opinion can help you make reasonable judgments about what others say and write. Unfortunately, fact and opinion are often confused with each other, and separating them can be difficult. Facts must be verified by evidence. Opinions are simply based on people's differing values and beliefs.

Learning the Skill

The following steps will help you distinguish facts from opinions:

- Read or listen to the information carefully. Identify the facts by asking: Can these statements be proved? Where would I find information to verify them?
- If a statement can be verified, it is factual. Check the sources for the facts. Often statistics sound impressive, but they may come from an unreliable source.
- Identify opinions by looking for statements of feelings or beliefs. If a statement refers to situations that are desirable or undesirable, important or unimportant, or likely or unlikely, then the statement is an opinion. Opinions may also contain words like *should, would, could, best, greatest, all, every,* or *always*.

Even when listening to experts and trusted sources, you must be able to separate fact from opinion.

Sociology Handbook

Practicing the Skill
Read the following passage, and then answer the questions below it.

PRIMARY SOURCE

"In my experience, relinquishment of cars or licenses came years after elderly folks should have stopped driving. It often happens after an accident or other traumatic driving event, such as getting lost while driving. That's too late.

Current law in Wisconsin requires no special testing or limits on elderly drivers, in spite of the fact that one of three drivers is over age 55. While 60 may be the new 50, our bodies continue to go south with diminished vision and peripheral vision, muted hearing, decreased mobility, increased medications and other unwelcome changes, all of which directly affect our driving skills.

It is time to change Wisconsin's licensing laws. I believe that drivers over the age of 70 should be required to take an annual driving test as rigorous as that for new drivers. As a community, we need to expand a network of convenient, safe and inexpensive transit services to replace the loss of independent driving for elderly citizens. The costs of failure to change can be measured in preventable deaths and injuries, and that is too high a cost."

—Nancy Ettenheim, *Milwaukee Journal Sentinel,* February 20, 2012

1. Which of the statements in the preceding paragraph are facts? How did you identify the facts?
2. Which of the statements are opinions? How did you identify them?

Applying the Skill
1. Watch a television interview. List three facts and three opinions that were stated.
2. Can you verify the facts?
3. How did you identify the opinions?
4. What statements, if any, seemed to contain both fact and opinion?

Making Generalizations

Generalizations are statements believed to be true by those who make them. If you say, "People who work hard make more money," you are making a generalization.

Learning the Skill
To make a valid generalization, you must first collect factual information relevant to the topic. Follow these steps:
- Identify the subject matter.
- Gather related facts and examples.
- Identify similarities among these facts.
- Use these similarities to form some general conclusions about the subject.

Practicing the Skill
Read this paragraph, and then answer the questions below:

Many people believe that the poor are poor because they lack the motivation to succeed in a competitive marketplace. In a survey, most Americans blamed poverty on the poor themselves. Yet in studies of those receiving welfare, researchers have consistently found that a majority want to work and to get off the welfare rolls.

1. Based on the preceding paragraph, what generalizations are made about the poor?
2. Is the generalization about the poor based on facts?
3. Is the generalization accurate? If so, how does that influence our policies regarding the poor? If not, why does the generalization persist?

Applying the Skill
Read newspaper editorials for a week. Then write a list of generalizations about the newspaper's position on issues such as economic policy or the environment.

Analyzing Graphics

Line Graphs and Bar Graphs

A graph, like a picture, may present information in a more concise way than words. Line graphs and bar graphs are drawings that compare numerical values. They often are used to compare changes over time or differences between places, groups of items, or other related events. Both types of graphs can be used to display the same information, and the choice between the two is often at the discretion of the author. In general, however, line graphs are used to show trends over time related to one type of data (e.g., percentage of the population that believes in God, average age at first marriage, or number of households headed by a single woman). Bar graphs may be used to show trends over time or to compare different types of information, such as median income for men and women or age groups of a population.

Learning the Skill

Follow these steps to learn how to understand and use line and bar graphs:

- Read the title of the graph. This should tell you what to expect or to look for.
- Note the information on the left side of the graph—the vertical axis. The information being compared usually appears on this axis.
- Note the information along the bottom of the graph—the horizontal axis. Time often appears along this axis.
- Determine what the line(s) or bar(s) symbolizes.
- Select a point on the line or bar, then note the date below this point on the horizontal axis and the quantity measured on the vertical axis.
- Analyze the movement of the line (whether increasing or decreasing over time), or compare bars to determine the point being made.

Practicing the Skill

Review the graphs, and then answer the questions. Note that both graphs present the same information.

1. About what percentage of families with children under 18 were headed by single parents in 1980? In 2010?
2. How would you describe the general trend shown by these graphs?
3. Based on the data for the last ten years shown, can you state what the current trend is for families headed by single parents?
4. Which graph represents this data in a more meaningful way?

Applying the Skill

1. Create line and bar graphs that show the number and percent of children living in poverty in the United States from 1980 through 2010.
2. Pose two questions that the graphs you created raise in your mind.
3. Answer the questions you pose.
4. Which graph do you think is easier to understand and presents the information more meaningfully?

PERCENTAGE OF SINGLE-PARENT HOUSEHOLDS, 1980–2010 BAR GRAPH

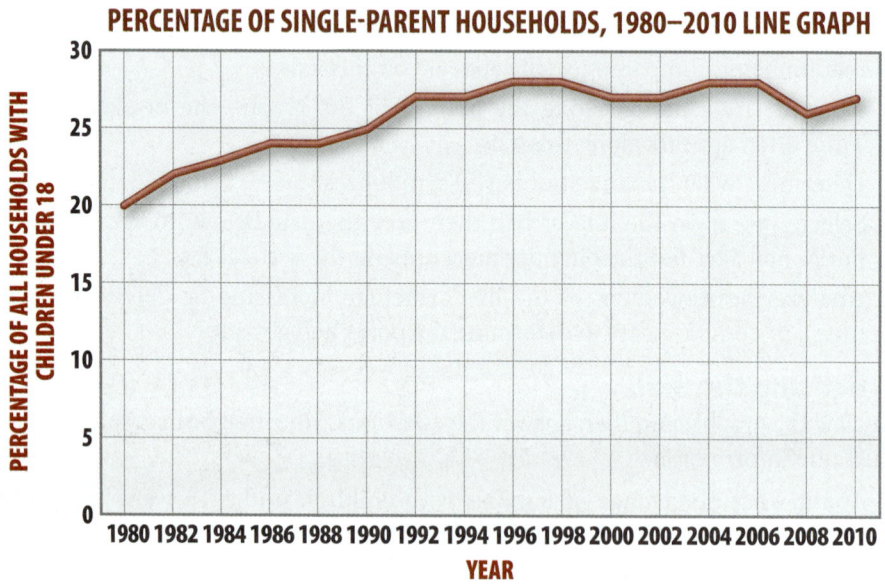

Source: U.S. Bureau of the Census, Current Population Survey-Families and Living Arrangements, Historical Tables

PERCENTAGE OF SINGLE-PARENT HOUSEHOLDS, 1980–2010 LINE GRAPH

Source: U.S. Bureau of the Census, Current Population Survey-Families and Living Arrangements, Historical Tables

GRAPHS

Drawing Conclusions Read the horizontal and vertical axis labels of both graphs. The labels will tell you what the graph is measuring and the units of measurement. What are the years with the highest percentage of children under the age of 18 in a single-parent household?

Circle Graphs and Tables

Circle graphs (also called pie charts) are often used to present information that shows the proportions of a whole. The particular data being presented can vary widely, but the common element in circle graphs is to show how the entire population is divided into subgroups. The same information can be presented in tables but in numerical, rather than graphic, form. Tables have the advantage of being able to present multiple categories of data in one location, whereas circle graphs are limited to one type of data.

Learning the Skill

Follow these steps to learn how to understand and use circle graphs and tables:

- Read the graph or table title to determine the content being presented.
- Read the labels (on circle graphs) or row headings (in tables). These will tell you what information is to be compared.
- For tables, examine the labels in the left-hand column. They describe ranges or subgroups and are often organized chronologically or alphabetically.
- Note the source of the data. It may tell you about the reliability of the data or where to go for further information.
- Compare the data presented to discover the relationships among categories.

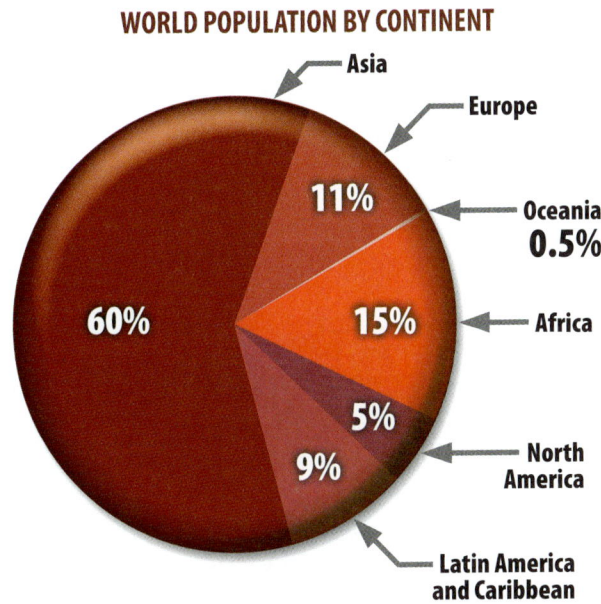

WORLD POPULATION BY CONTINENT

- Asia 60%
- Europe 11%
- Oceania 0.5%
- Africa 15%
- North America 5%
- Latin America and Caribbean 9%

Source: Population Reference Bureau, *2011 World Population Data Sheet*

GRAPH AND CHART

Comparing To have a high quality of life, a country or region usually has a population it can support, a high life expectancy rate, and a low deaths-at-birth ratio. By comparing the circle graph and the table, can you determine which part of the world offers the best quality of life statistics?

	Population (in millions)	Life expectancy (in years)	Births per 1,000 population	Infant mortality rate (infant deaths per 1,000 live births)
World	6,987	70	8	44
Africa	1,051	58	36	74
North America	346	78	13	6
Latin America and Caribbean	596	74	18	19
Asia	4,216	70	18	39
Europe	740	76	11	6
Oceania	37	77	18	24

Source: Population Reference Bureau, *2011 World Population Data Sheet*

Practicing the Skill

Study the table and circle graph, and then answer the following questions.

1. Which medium presents more information to the reader?
2. If you were interested solely in the world's population distribution, which would you prefer—the graph or the table? Why?

Applying the Skill

1. Gather information on the demographics (for example, age, sex, parental income) of high school students in your state.
2. Present selected information in a table and in circle graphs.

Maps

Maps are visual tools that show the relative size and location of specific geographic areas. There are political maps, which show human-made boundaries; physical maps, which show physical features of an area; and special purpose maps that can show historical change, cultural features, population, climate, land use, resources, or any other information of interest. Regardless of type, all maps use symbols to convey information.

Learning the Skill

Follow these steps to learn how to understand and use maps:

- Read the title to determine the map's content.
- Examine the map's scale, which indicates the ratio between the map's size and the actual area being represented. For many special purpose maps, this information will not be provided and is not relevant to the information being presented.

MAPS >

There are two basic types of maps—reference maps and thematic maps. We use reference maps, such as road maps, to navigate physical space. Sociologists are most interested in thematic maps, such as population density maps, which they use to show and interpret various kinds of information.

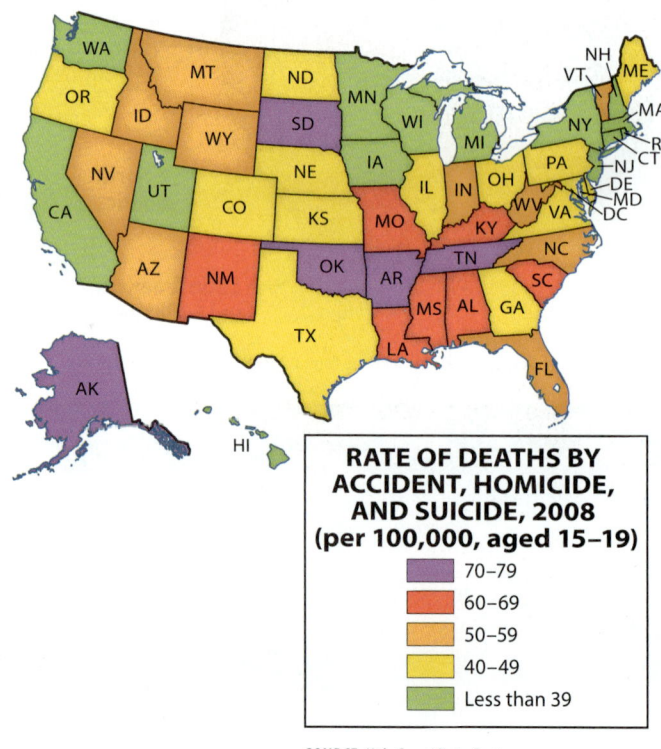

RATE OF DEATHS BY ACCIDENT, HOMICIDE, AND SUICIDE, 2008 (per 100,000, aged 15–19)

- 70–79
- 60–69
- 50–59
- 40–49
- Less than 39

SOURCE: Kids Count Data Center, The Annie E. Casey Foundation

- Read the legend, or key, to interpret any shapes, colors, boundary lines, or symbols. This step is, in many ways, the most important to sociologists for maps of interest.
- Interpret the information being presented. Determine patterns or other interesting points of interest. What questions does the map raise in your mind?

Practicing the Skill
1. What information does this map present to the reader?
2. Do you see any patterns in the information?
3. What questions does the map raise for you?
4. Where could you find the answers to the questions you posed?

Applying the Skill
1. Research the participation of high school students in school-sponsored music programs by state.
2. Summarize your findings by preparing a map of the United States that depicts the information you found.

Interpreting Data

Percentages

Sociologists use the concept of percentages quite often in their work on groups and social structures. Percent means "parts per hundred." So when a sociologist notes that, say, 18 percent of a group has a certain trait, she means that 18 out of 100 members of that group possess the trait in question. Changes in the size or number of a particular item (usually over time) can be expressed in percentages also. Stating the amount of change as a percentage allows you to analyze the relative size of the change. For example, if you knew that the populations of two states each increased by 250,000 people, you would have some information. But knowing that the percentage change in one state was 1 percent, while in the other state it was 15 percent, would provide you with substantially more information about the relative size of the increase and would allow you to infer some of the possible consequences for the states.

Learning the Skill
Follow these steps to learn how to calculate and use percentages:

- Calculate the percentage by dividing the number of the subgroup or change by the number of the original group population. Multiply your answer by 100 to express it as a percentage.
- Compare the percentage you calculated with other relevant measures.
- Remember that numbers or percentages by themselves tell you very little. This type of information is most useful when compared to other, similar types of information so that you can put it into its proper context.

The individuals in this group can be categorized in many different ways. A sociologist might ask: What percentage are on the honor roll? What percentage come from single-parent homes? What percentage belong to a club or play a sport?

School	2000			2010		
	Total Number of Students	Number of Students Studying Sociology	Percentage of Students Studying Sociology	Number of Students	Number of Students Studying Sociology	Percentage of Students Studying Sociology
Cave Spring	928	83	8.9%	1,008	164	
Glenvar	316	40		421	44	10.5%
Northside	745	52		763	79	
Patrick Henry	866	54	6.2%	940	30	
William Byrd	643	37		715	55	
William Fleming	872	91		948	116	

Practicing the Skill
Complete the table by calculating the missing percentages. Then answer the questions below the table.

1. Look at the percentages of students studying sociology at each school. Do you see a pattern? Does sociology seem to be more popular at some schools than others?
2. Now look at the differences between the percentages studying sociology in 2000 and 2010 at each school. Do you see a pattern of change during the ten-year period?
3. What might account for the changes you noticed?

Applying the Skill
1. Survey 50 students at your high school to determine their favorite style of music. Based on the results of your survey, determine the percentages of your sample that listed each kind of music as their favorite.
2. Do the results of your survey surprise you? Why or why not?
3. How did you categorize students who named more than one style of music as their favorite?

Mean, Median, and Mode

The most commonly used summary statistic is the average. Generally speaking, an average is a measure of central tendency, indicating where the middle of a series of number lies. There are three ways to compute the average: the mean, median, and mode. The mean is the arithmetic average of a series of items. Using the mean to represent the average can sometimes be misleading. This generally occurs when a few of the numbers in the series are much higher or lower than the others, resulting in a skewed or biased mean. When this happens, using the median or mode to represent the average may be more meaningful. The median is the midpoint in a series of numbers when they are arranged in order from low to high. The mode is the number that appears most frequently in the series.

Learning the Skill
Follow the steps below to learn how to determine and use measures of central tendency:
- To find the mean, add all of the numbers in the series. Then divide the sum by the number of observations in the series.
- Locate the median by arranging all of the numbers in the series from lowest to highest. Then find the number that is the midpoint in the series.

When an even number of figures is in the series, the median is the mean of the two middle numbers.
- The mode is the number in the series that appears most frequently. Simply look at the series and count which number appears the most.
- Compare the mean, median, and mode. Determine which one or combination is the most accurate in a particular case.

Practicing the Skill
Read the paragraph below and answer the questions.

An academic department at a major university conducts a survey each year of its recent graduates. One of the questions on the survey asks the respondents to report their annual income. Suppose this question drew the following responses from some graduates:

$23,500
$26,750
$26,750
$18,760
$28,410
$34,500
$43,000
$32,400
$1,466,980
$27,600
$24,580

1. Determine the mean, median, and mode for these earnings figures.
2. Which measure of central tendency would you recommend using for this series? Why?

Applying the Skill
1. What are some data that you would want to know?
2. Which of the three measures of central tendency would you use for each type of data?
3. Explain your choices.

Suppose a group of your friends wanted to compare scores on a college entrance exam. How would you calculate the group's mean score? Its median score? Its mode score? Which measure would be most meaningful?

GLOSSARY/GLOSARIO

- Content vocabulary are words that relate to Sociology content.
- Words that have an asterisk (*) are academic vocabulary. They help you understand your school subjects.
- All vocabulary words are **boldfaced** or highlighted in yellow in your textbook.

abandon • agricultural society

A

ENGLISH

*abandon to suddenly leave a person or activity (p. 321)

absolute poverty the absence of enough money to secure life's necessities (p. 216)

*abstract expressing a quality or characteristic apart from any specific object or instance (p. 29)

*accommodation a choice by a minority group to maintain its own culturally unique way of life independent of the dominant culture (p. 241)

*accompany to go along with someone engaging in an activity (p. 144)

achieved status a position in a social structure that is earned or chosen (p. 133)

*adaptive being able to change behavior as necessary (p. 271)

*adjacent situated next to or nearby (p. 74)

adolescence stage of development between childhood and adulthood (p. 119)

adolescent person between the ages of 12 and 17 (p. 322)

*advocate to plead in favor of (p. 475)

age stratification the unequal distribution of scare resources based on age (p. 288)

ageism a set of beliefs, attitudes, norms, and values used to justify age-based prejudice and discrimination (p. 288)

*aggregate a gathering of people that is considered as a whole simply because they happen to be in the same place at the same time (p. 468)

agricultural society a society that uses plows and draft animals to grow food (p. 145)

ESPAÑOL

*abandonar dejar repentinamente una actividad o a una persona (pág. 321)

pobreza absoluta falta del dinero suficiente para cubrir las necesidades de la vida (pág. 216)

*abstracto que expresa una cualidad o característica que no se ajusta a ningún objeto u ocasión específicos (pág. 29)

*acomodación decisión de un grupo minoritario de mantener la forma de vida propia de su cultura independientemente de la cultura dominante (pág. 241)

*acompañar participar con alguien en una actividad (pág. 144)

estatus alcanzado posición que se gana o elige dentro de una estructura social (pág. 133)

*adaptivo capaz de modificar el comportamiento según sea necesario (pág. 271)

*adyacente situado cerca o en los alrededores (pág. 74)

adolescencia etapa del desarrollo que ocurre entre la niñez y la adultez (pág. 119)

adolescente persona que tiene entre 12 y 17 años (pág. 322)

*abogar declarar a favor de (pág. 475)

estratificación por edad distribución desigual de recursos escasos basada en la edad (pág. 288)

discriminación por edad conjunto de creencias, actitudes, normas y valores que son utilizados para justificar los prejuicios y la discriminación basados en la edad (pág. 288)

*aglomeración grupo de personas considerado como una unidad simplemente porque están en el mismo lugar en el mismo momento (pág. 468)

sociedad agrícola sociedad que usa arados y animales de tiro para cultivar alimentos (pág. 145)

alternative movement • blended family

alternative movement a social movement that focuses on bringing about limited changes in individuals (p. 475)

*ambiguity a state of being uncertain, doubtful, or open to more than one meaning (p. 476)

*ambiguous unclear (p. 321)

anomie a social condition in which norms are weak, conflicting, or absent (p. 185)

*anticipate to expect or predict (p. 107)

anticipatory socialization the voluntary process of preparing to accept new norms, values, attitudes, and behaviors (p. 126)

*appropriateness suitability; correctness (p. 186)

ascribed status a position in a social structure that is neither earned nor chosen to be assigned to a person (p. 133)

*aspect a particular trait or feature of something (p. 290)

*assign to give someone a particular social position (p. 133)

assimilation the blending or fusing of a minority group into the dominant society (p. 240)

*assumption the act of taking for granted or supposing (p. 18)

authoritarianism a political system controlled by elected or nonelected rulers who usually permit some degree of individual freedom (p. 369)

authority the legitimate or socially approved use of power (p. 171); power accepted as legitimate by those subject to it (p. 365)

movimiento alternativo movimiento social que se enfoca en provocar cambios limitados en los individuos (pág. 475)

*ambigüedad cualidad de incierto, dudoso o con más de un significado (pág. 476)

*ambiguo poco claro (pág. 321)

anomia condición social en la que las normas son débiles, contradictorias o inexistentes (pág. 185)

*anticipar esperar o predecir (pág. 107)

socialización anticipatoria proceso voluntario en el que alguien se prepara para aceptar nuevas normas, valores, actitudes y comportamientos (pág. 126)

*adecuación conveniencia; corrección (pág. 186)

estatus adscrito posición que una persona ocupa dentro de una estructura social y que no ha ganado ni elegido (pág. 133)

*aspecto rasgo o característica particular de algo (pág. 290)

*asignar dar a alguien una determinada posición social (pág. 133)

asimilación la mezcla o fusión de un grupo minoritario con la sociedad dominante (pág. 240)

*suposición acto de dar por sentado o conjeturar (pág. 18)

autoritarismo sistema político controlado por gobernantes, electos o no, que generalmente permiten cierto grado de libertad individual (pág. 369)

autoridad uso legítimo o socialmente aprobado del poder (pág. 171); poder aceptado como legítimo por quienes están sometidos a él (pág. 365)

B

belief an idea about the nature of reality (p. 85)

*bias negative or positive preconceptions (p. 246)

biological determinism the principle that behavior differences are the result of inherited physical characteristics (p. 268)

blended family type of family in which at least one of the partners has a child or children from a previous marriage (p. 320)

creencia idea acerca de la naturaleza de la realidad (pág. 85)

*sesgo preconceptos negativos o positivos (pág. 246)

determinismo biológico principio que establece que las diferencias de comportamiento son el resultado de características físicas heredadas (pág. 268)

familia ensamblada tipo de familia en la que al menos uno de los cónyuges tiene uno o más hijos de un matrimonio anterior (pág. 320)

boomerang kid a young adult who stays at home or returns home to live with parents (p. 325)

bourgeoisie the class owning the means for producing wealth (pp. 14, 206)

bureaucracy a formal organization based on rationality and efficiency (p. 171)

joven de la generación búmeran joven adulto que no se marcha de la casa de sus padres o que regresa a ella (pág. 325)

burguesía clase que posee los medios para producir riqueza (págs. 14, 206)

burocracia organización formal basada en la racionalidad y la eficiencia (pág. 171)

C

*capacity the full size or rate (p. 389)

capitalism an economic system based on private ownership of property and the pursuit of profit (p. 379)

capitalist person who owns or controls the means for producing wealth (p. 14)

case study intensive study of a single group, incident, or community (p. 41)

caste system a stratification structure that does not allow for social mobility (p. 224)

*category a defined group (p. 224)

causation the belief that events occur in predictable ways and that one event leads to another (p. 46)

census regularly occurring count of a particular population (p. 427)

central-city dilemma the concentration of people in need of public services without the tax base-generated funds to provide for them (p. 439)

charismatic authority authority that arises from the personality of an individual (p. 366)

charter schools public schools that are operated like private schools by public school teachers and administrators (p. 339)

church a life-encompassing system of beliefs and practices to which all members of a society belong (p. 402)

*cite to quote as an authoritative source (p. 193)

city a dense and permanent concentration of people living in a specific area and working primarily in nonagricultural jobs (p. 434)

*capacidad contenido total o tasa (pág. 389)

capitalismo sistema económico que se basa en la posesión privada de la propiedad y en la búsqueda de ganancias (pág. 379)

capitalista persona que posee o controla los medios para producir riqueza (pág. 14)

estudio de caso estudio intensivo de un único grupo, incidente o comunidad (pág. 41)

sistema de castas estructura de estratificación que no permite la movilidad social (pág. 224)

*categoría grupo definido (pág. 224)

causalidad creencia de que los sucesos ocurren de manera predecible y que un suceso lleva a otro (pág. 46)

censo recuento periódico de una población en particular (pág. 427)

dilema de ciudad principal concentración de personas que necesitan servicios públicos pero que no cuentan con los fondos provenientes de los impuestos para poder brindarlos (pág. 439)

autoridad carismática autoridad proveniente de la personalidad de un individuo (pág. 366)

escuelas públicas experimentales escuelas públicas que funcionan como las privadas pero cuyos maestros y administradores son empleados del Estado (pág. 339)

iglesia sistema de creencias y prácticas que constituye una forma de vida y al que pertenecen todos los miembros de una sociedad (pág. 402)

*citar mencionar como fuente autorizada (pág. 193)

ciudad área específica donde vive una concentración densa y permanente de personas con empleos que, en su mayoría, no son agrícolas (pág. 434)

class conflict the ongoing struggle between the bourgeoisie (owners) and the proletariat (working) classes (p. 14)

class consciousness identification with the goals and interests of a social class (p. 212)

closed-ended questions questions a person must answer by choosing from a limited, predetermined set of responses (p. 38)

coercion interaction in which individuals or groups are forced to behave in a particular way (p. 166); control through force (p. 365)

cognitive ability the capacity for thinking abstractly (p. 347)

cohabitation a marriage-like living arrangement without the legal obligations and responsibilities of formal marriage (p. 324)

***collapse** total breakdown (p. 368)

***colleague** associate, fellow worker (p. 161)

collective behavior the spontaneous behavior of a group of people responding to similar stimuli (p. 465)

collegial mutually respectful (p. 59)

***commit** to do or to perform (p. 189)

***commitment** a pledge or promise (p. 405)

compensatory education specific curricular programs designed to overcome a deficiency (p. 350)

competition a social process in which rewards are based on relative performance (p. 344)

***complex** complicated (p. 147)

***concentration** something that has been gathered together (p. 439)

concentric-zone theory the theory that describes urban growth in terms of circular areas that grow from the central city outward (p. 443)

***concept** an idea (p. 185)

***conception** idea (p. 239)

confidential private (p. 61)

conflicto de clases lucha permanente entre la burguesía (los propietarios) y el proletariado (los trabajadores) (pág. 14)

conciencia de clase identificación con las metas y los intereses de una clase social (pág. 212)

preguntas cerradas preguntas que una persona debe contestar eligiendo una respuesta de un conjunto limitado y predeterminado (pág. 38)

coerción interacción en la que se obliga a los individuos o grupos a actuar de una manera determinada (pág. 166); control mediante la fuerza (pág. 365)

habilidad cognitiva capacidad de pensar en forma abstracta (pág. 347)

concubinato un acuerdo de vida en pareja sin las obligaciones ni responsabilidades legales de un matrimonio formal (pág. 324)

***colapso** crisis total (pág. 368)

***colega** asociado, compañero de trabajo (pág. 161)

comportamiento colectivo comportamiento espontáneo de un grupo de personas que responden a estímulos similares (pág. 465)

compañerismo respeto mutuo (pág. 59)

***cometer** hacer o perpetrar (pág. 189)

***compromiso** convenio o promesa (pág. 405)

educación compensatoria programas específicos de educación diseñados para superar una deficiencia (pág. 350)

competencia proceso social en el que las recompensas se basan en desempeños relativos (pág. 344)

***complejo** complicado (pág. 147)

***concentración** algo que se ha acumulado (pág. 439)

teoría de las zonas concéntricas teoría que describe el crecimiento urbanístico en términos de áreas circulares que crecen desde la ciudad principal hacia afuera (pág. 443)

***concepto** idea (pág. 185)

***concepción** idea (pág. 239)

confidencial privado (pág. 61)

conflict interaction aimed at defeating an opponent (p. 164)

conflict perspective approach emphasizing the role of conflict, competition, and constraint within a society (p. 27)

***conformity** behavior that matches group expectations (pp. 7, 166)

conglomerates networks of unrelated business operating under one corporate umbrella (p. 384)

***consensus** a broad agreement (p. 149)

***considerably** substantially; to a significant degree (p. 256)

***constitute** to make up; account for (p. 410)

contagion theory the theory stating that members of crowds stimulate each other to higher and higher levels of emotion and irrational behavior (p. 471)

contingent employment the hiring of part-time, short-term workers (p. 389)

***contrary** the opposite of what was previously stated (p. 196)

***contrast** dissimilar attributes among things with common natures (p. 85)

control theory the theory that compliance with social norms requires strong bonds between individuals and society (p. 186)

***controversial** disputed (p. 420)

convergence theory the theory that states that crowds are formed by people who deliberately congregate with like-minded others (p. 472)

cooperation interaction in which individuals or groups combine their efforts to reach a goal (p. 163)

cooperative learning an instructional method that relies on cooperation among students (p. 334)

***core** the innermost or most important part of something (p. 446)

core tier the part of the occupational structure composed of large firms dominating their industries (p. 388)

conflicto interacción que tiene como objetivo vencer a un oponente (pág. 164)

perspectiva de conflicto enfoque que pone el énfasis en el papel del conflicto, la competencia y la restricción dentro de una sociedad (pág. 27)

***conformidad** comportamiento que se ajusta a las expectativas de un grupo (págs. 7, 166)

conglomerados redes de firmas no relacionadas que operan bajo la protección de una corporación (pág. 384)

***consenso** acuerdo amplio (pág. 149)

***considerablemente** sustancialmente; de manera significativa (pág. 256)

***constituir** conformar; componer (pág. 410)

teoría del contagio teoría que afirma que los miembros de una multitud se estimulan mutuamente para alcanzar niveles cada vez más altos de emoción y comportamiento irracional (pág. 471)

empleo contingente la contratación de empleados a medio tiempo por periodos cortos (pág. 389)

***contrario** lo opuesto a lo que se afirmó previamente (pág. 196)

***contraste** atributos diferentes entre cosas de naturaleza común (pág. 85)

teoría del control teoría que afirma que el ajuste a las normas sociales requiere que haya lazos fuertes entre los individuos y la sociedad (pág. 186)

***controversial** discutido (pág. 420)

teoría de la convergencia teoría que afirma que las multitudes están formadas por personas que se juntan a propósito con otras que tienen una forma de pensar similar (pág. 472)

cooperación interacción en la que los individuos o grupos combinan sus esfuerzos para alcanzar una meta (pág. 163)

aprendizaje cooperativo método de instrucción que se basa en la cooperación entre los estudiantes (pág. 334)

***centro** la parte más profunda o importante de algo (pág. 446)

primera línea estructura ocupacional compuesta de grandes firmas que dominan a sus industrias (pág. 388)

*corporation a large legal business group with its own duties, powers, and liabilities (p. 171)

correlation a measure of the relationship between two variables (p. 48)

*correspond to align with or match (p. 158)

counterculture a subculture deliberately and consciously opposed to certain central beliefs or attitudes of the dominant culture (p. 89)

crime an act committed in violation of the law (p. 196)

criminal justice system a system comprising institutions and processes responsible for enforcing criminal statutes (p. 197)

*criterion a standard on which a judgment may be based (p. 346)

crowd a temporary collection of people who share an immediate common interest (p. 468)

crude birthrate the annual number of live births per 1,000 members of a population (p. 421)

crude death rate the annual number of deaths per 1,000 members of a population (p. 423)

cultural bias an unfair slant in testing or materials in favor of certain groups (p. 348)

cultural particular the way in which a culture expresses universal traits (p. 93)

cultural pluralism the desire of a group to maintain some sense of identity separate from the dominant group (p. 241)

cultural universal general cultural trait that exists in all cultures (p. 93)

*culture knowledge, values, customs, and physical objects that are shared by the members of a society (p. 69)

*corporación gran grupo legal de negocios con sus propios deberes, poderes y responsabilidades (pág. 171)

correlación medida de la relación entre dos variables (pág. 48)

*corresponder alinearse o coincidir con algo (pág. 158)

contracultura subcultura que se opone de manera deliberada y consciente a ciertas creencias o actitudes centrales de la cultura dominante (pág. 89)

delito acto cometido en violación de la ley (pág. 196)

sistema de justicia penal sistema que comprende las instituciones y los procesos responsables de hacer respetar los estatutos penales (pág. 197)

*criterio estándar en el que puede basarse una opinión (pág. 346)

multitud grupo temporal de personas que comparten un interés común inmediato (pág. 468)

tasa bruta de natalidad número anual de nacimientos vivos por cada 1,000 miembros de una población (pág. 421)

tasa bruta de mortalidad número anual de muertes por cada 1,000 miembros de una población (pág. 423)

sesgo cultural enfoque injusto de evaluaciones o materiales que favorece a determinados grupos (pág. 348)

particularidad cultural manera en la que una cultura expresa características universales (pág. 93)

pluralismo cultural deseo de un grupo de mantener cierto sentido de identidad distinto al del grupo dominante (pág. 241)

universal cultural característica cultural general que existe en todas las culturas (pág. 93)

*cultura conocimiento, valores, costumbres y objetos físicos que comparten los miembros de una sociedad (pág. 69)

D

*data facts or statistics (p. 36)

de facto segregation the denial of equal access based on common prejudice (p. 242)

*datos hechos o estadísticas (pág. 36)

segregación de facto negación de la igualdad de acceso basada en un prejuicio común (pág. 242)

de jure segregation the denial of equal access based on the law (p. 242)

demographic transition theory the theory that population growth is a function of the level of economic development in a country (p. 429)

demography the scientific study of population (p. 420)

denomination one of several religious organizations that most members of society accept as legitimate (p. 403)

dependency ratio the ratio of dependent persons to economically active persons (p. 433)

dependent variable a characteristic that reflects a change (p. 48)

desocialization the process of giving up old norms, values, attitudes, and behaviors (p. 125)

deterrence discouraging criminal acts by threatening punishment (p. 197)

deviance behavior that departs from societal or group norms (p. 182)

deviant a person who breaks significant societal or group norms (p. 182)

***deviation** a move away from the norm or what is expected (p. 379)

differential association theory the theory that individuals learn deviance in proportion to the number of deviant acts and norms in which they are exposed (p. 188)

diffusion the process by which one culture or society borrows from another culture or society (p. 456)

***dimension** an aspect or feature of something (p. 405)

***diminished** reduced; limited (p. 291)

discovery the process by which something is learned or reinterpreted (p. 455)

***discrimination** unfair treatment of a minority by the dominant group (p. 247)

***disposable** unimportant; something that can be dissolved or easily replaced (p. 390

segregación de iure negación de la igualdad de acceso basada en la ley (pág. 242)

teoría de la transición demográfica teoría que afirma que el aumento de la población depende del nivel de desarrollo económico de un país (pág. 429)

demografía el estudio científico de la población (pág. 420)

confesión una de varias organizaciones religiosas que la mayoría de los miembros de la sociedad consideran legítimas (pág. 403)

tasa de dependencia relación de las personas dependientes con respecto a las personas económicamente activas (pág. 433)

variable dependiente característica que refleja un cambio (pág. 48)

desocialización proceso en el que se renuncia a antiguas normas, valores, actitudes y comportamientos (pág. 125)

disuasión acción de desalentar actos delictivos mediante amenazas de castigo (pág. 197)

desviación comportamiento que se aparta de las normas sociales o grupales (pág. 182)

individuo de conducta desviada persona que quebranta normas importantes de la sociedad o grupo (pág. 182)

***anomalía** alejamiento de la norma o de lo que es esperado (pág. 379)

teoría de la asociación diferencial teoría que establece que la proporción de individuos que incurren en conductas desviadas guarda relación con el número de actos y normas desviados a las que están expuestos (pág. 188)

difusión proceso por el cual una cultura o sociedad toma algo prestado de otra cultura o sociedad (pág. 456)

***dimensión** aspecto o característica de algo (pág. 405)

***disminuido** reducido; limitado (pág. 291)

descubrimiento proceso por el que se aprende o reinterpreta algo (pág. 455)

***discriminación** trato injusto de una minoría por parte del grupo dominante (pág. 247)

***descartable** sin importancia; algo que se puede desechar o remplazar fácilmente (pág. 390)

*distort to twist out of the true meaning (p. 107)

*diverse composed of distinct or varied elements or qualities (p. 341)

*diversity the condition of being made up of different elements, such as a racial identity, ethnicity, religious beliefs, and so on (p. 88)

divorce rate the number of divorces per year for every thousand members of the population (p. 314)

*domesticated tamed (p. 145)

*dominant having power over others (p. 310)

doubling time the number of years needed to double the base population size (p. 427)

downsizing the process by which companies reduce their work forces (p. 389)

dramaturgy approach that depicts human interaction as theatrical performance (p. 30)

drive impulse to reduce discomfort (p. 70)

*dynamic marked by continuous and productive activity or change (p. 463)

dysfunction negative consequences of an aspect of society (p. 25)

*distorsionado cambiado respecto del significado verdadero (pág. 107)

*diverso compuesto por elementos o cualidades diferentes o variadas (pág. 341)

*diversidad la condición de estar formado por diferentes elementos, como la identidad racial, la pertenencia a una etnia, las creencias religiosas, etcétera (pág. 88)

tasa de divorcios número de divorcios al año por cada mil miembros de la población (pág. 314)

*domesticado domado (pág. 145)

*dominante que tiene poder sobre otros (pág. 310)

tiempo de duplicación número de años necesarios para duplicar el tamaño de la población base (pág. 427)

reducirse el proceso mediante el cual las empresas reducen su fuerza laboral (pág. 389)

dramaturgia enfoque que describe las interacciones humanas como representaciones teatrales (pág. 30)

impulso iniciativa para reducir el malestar (pág. 70)

*dinámico caracterizado por actividades o cambios continuos y productivos (pág. 463)

disfunción consecuencias negativas de un aspecto de la sociedad (pág. 25)

E

economic institution the institution that determines how goods and services are produced and distributed (p. 364)

edge city a suburban unit specializing in a particular economic activity (p. 439)

educational equality the condition in which schooling produces the same results for lower-class and minority children as it does for other children (p. 346)

egalitarian when authority is split evenly between a man and a woman (p. 303)

elitism a system in which a community or society is controlled from the top by a few individuals or organizations (p. 373)

institución económica institución que determina cómo se deben producir y distribuir los bienes y servicios (pág. 364)

ciudad periférica unidad suburbana que se especializa en una actividad económica en particular (pág. 439)

igualdad educacional condición en la que la enseñanza produce los mismos resultados en los niños de las clases sociales más bajas y de las minorías que en los demás niños (pág. 346)

igualitario cuando la autoridad se distribuye de manera equitativa entre un hombre y una mujer (pág. 303)

elitismo sistema en el que unos pocos individuos u organizaciones controlan desde arriba a una comunidad o sociedad (pág. 373)

emergent-norm theory the theory stating that norms develop to guide crowd behavior (p. 472)

*encounter to come across or meet (pp. 85, 140)

*enhance to improve; strengthen (p. 384)

*environmental concerned with the natural world or environment (p. 374)

*equilibrium a state of functioning and balance maintained by a society's tendency to make small adjustments to change (p. 463)

*ethics rules of conduct that distinguish between acceptable and unacceptable human actions (p. 56)

ethnic minority group identified by cultural, national, or religious characteristics (p. 238)

ethnocentrism judging others in terms of one's own cultural standards (p. 91)

*eventual taking place at an unspecified future time (p. 342)

*evolution a process of change from one point of development to another (p. 71)

*exceed to surpass (p. 346)

*exclusive limited to possession, control, or use by a single individual or group (p. 213)

*exhibit to show or display (p. 113)

*exploit to take unfair advantage of (p. 206)

exponential growth growth in which the amount of increase is added to the base figure at each time period (p. 427)

*exposure the state of being made known (p. 74)

extended family two or more adult generations of the same family whose members share economic resources and live in the same household—and sometimes close relatives such as grandparents, grandchildren, aunts, uncles, and cousins (p. 301)

teoría de la norma emergente teoría que afirma que las normas se desarrollan para guiar el comportamiento de las multitudes (pág. 472)

*encontrar dar con algo o alguien (págs. 85, 140)

*aumentar mejorar; reforzar (pág. 384)

*ambiental relacionado con el mundo natural o el medioambiente (pág. 374)

*equilibrio estado de funcionamiento y armonía que se mantiene gracias a la tendencia de una sociedad a cambiar mediante pequeños ajustes (pág. 463)

*ética reglas de conducta que distinguen las acciones humanas aceptables de las inaceptables (pág. 56)

minoría étnica grupo identificado por características culturales, nacionales o religiosas (pág. 238)

etnocentrismo juzgar a los demás en términos de los propios estándares culturales (pág. 91)

*finalmente que ocurrirá en algún momento indeterminado del futuro (pág. 342)

*evolución proceso de cambio desde un punto del desarrollo a otro (pág. 71)

*exceder sobrepasar (pág. 346)

*exclusivo que se limita a la posesión, el control o el uso limitado por parte de un individuo o grupo (pág. 213)

*exhibir mostrar o exponer (pág. 113)

*explotar aprovecharse injustamente (pág. 206)

crecimiento exponencial crecimiento en el cual la cantidad aumentada se suma a la cifra base en cada período (pág. 427)

*exposición estado de haberse dado a conocer (pág. 74)

familia ampliada dos o más generaciones adultas de la misma familia cuyos miembros comparten los recursos económicos y la vivienda; puede incluir familiares cercanos como abuelos, nietos, tíos y primos (pág. 301)

facility something created to serve a particular function, such as manufacturing or health care (p. 384)

instalaciones algo creado para servir a una función en particular, como la manufactura o los servicios de salud (pág. 384)

fad a fashion, mannerism, or activity that spreads rapidly and disappears quickly (p. 467)	**furor** moda, peculiaridad o actividad que se extiende rápidamente y que desaparece enseguida (pág. 467)
false consciousness according to Karl Marx, working-class acceptance of capitalist ideas and values (p. 210)	**falsa conciencia** según Karl Marx, la aceptación de las ideas y los valores capitalistas por parte de la clase trabajadora (pág. 210)
family planning the voluntary use of population control methods (p. 431)	**planificación familiar** uso voluntario de métodos de control de la población (pág. 431)
fashion a widely accepted behavior pattern that changes periodically (p. 467)	**moda** patrón de comportamiento ampliamente aceptado que cambia periódicamente (pág. 467)
fecundity the maximum rate at which women can physically produce children (p. 421)	**fecundidad** tasa máxima en la que las mujeres pueden físicamente tener niños (pág. 421)
feminization of poverty a trend in U.S. society in which women and children make up an increasing proportion of the poor (p. 217)	**feminización de la pobreza** tendencia de la sociedad estadounidense en la que las mujeres y los niños representan una proporción cada vez mayor del número de pobres (pág. 217)
fertility the actual number of children born to a woman or a population of women (p. 421)	**fertilidad** número real de niños nacidos de una mujer o de una población de mujeres (pág. 421)
fertility rate the annual number of live births per 1,000 women aged 15 to 44 (p. 422)	**tasa de fertilidad** número anual de nacimientos vivos por cada 1,000 mujeres de entre 15 y 44 años de edad (pág. 422)
field research research that takes place in a natural (nonlaboratory) setting (p. 41)	**investigación de campo** investigación realizada en un entorno natural (no en el laboratorio) (pág. 41)
folkway norm that lacks moral significance (p. 76)	**costumbre popular** norma que carece de significado moral (pág. 76)
formal organization a group deliberately created to achieve one or more long-term goals (p. 171)	**organización formal** grupo creado específicamente para alcanzar una o más metas a largo plazo (pág. 171)
formal sanction a sanction imposed by persons given special authority (p. 78)	**sanción formal** sanción impuesta por personas a quienes se ha dado una autoridad especial (pág. 78)
formal schooling education that is provided and regulated by society (p. 333)	**educación formal** educación proporcionada y regulada por la sociedad (pág. 333)
for-profit schools schools run by private companies with government funds (p. 339)	**escuelas privadas con subsidio estatal** escuelas administradas por empresas privadas con fondos gubernamentales (pág. 339)
functionalism approach that emphasizes the contributions made by each part of society (p. 25)	**funcionalismo** enfoque que enfatiza las contribuciones de cada parte de la sociedad (pág. 25)
fundamentalism the resistance of secularization and the rigid adherence to traditional religious beliefs, rituals, and doctrines (p. 410)	**fundamentalismo** resistencia a la secularización y adhesión estricta a las creencias, los rituales y las doctrinas tradicionales de una religión (pág. 410)

G

game stage Mead's third stage in the development of role taking; children anticipate the actions of others based on social rules (p. 108)

gemeinschaft a preindustrial society based on tradition, kinship, and close social ties (p. 148)

gender identity a sense of being male or female based on learned cultural values (p. 269)

gender socialization the social process of learning how to act as a boy or girl (p. 275)

generalized other integrated conception of the norms, values, and beliefs of one's community or society (p. 109)

genocide the systematic effort to destroy an entire population (p. 243)

gentrification the development of low-income areas by middle-class home buyers, landlords, and professional developers (p. 439)

gesellschaft an industrial society characterized by weak family ties, competition, and impersonal social relationships (p. 149)

global stratification the unequal distribution of wealth, power, and resources among the countries of the world (p. 226)

globalization the development of an increasingly integrated global economy (p. 230)

gross migration rate the number of persons per 1,000 members of a population who enter or leave a geographic area (p. 424)

group at least two people who have one or more goals in common and share ways of thinking and behaving (p. 157)

groupthink self-deceptive thinking that is based on conformity to group beliefs and created by group pressure to conform (p. 167)

***guarantee** a promise (p. 380)

etapa de juego tercera etapa de Mead en el desarrollo del juego de roles; los niños anticipan las acciones de otros según las reglas sociales (pág. 108)

comunidad (*gemeinschaft*) sociedad preindustrial basada en la tradición, el parentesco y los lazos sociales estrechos (pág. 148)

identidad de género sentido de ser hombre o mujer basado en valores culturales aprendidos (pág. 269)

socialización de género proceso social en el que se aprende a actuar como un niño o una niña (pág. 275)

otro generalizado concepción integrada de las normas, los valores y las creencias de la propia comunidad o sociedad (pág. 109)

genocidio campaña sistemática para destruir una población completa (pág. 243)

aburguesamiento desarrollo de áreas de bajos recursos debido a compradores de clase media que adquieren casas, rentistas y promotores inmobiliarios (pág. 439)

sociedad (*gesellschaft*) sociedad industrial caracterizada por la ausencia de lazos familiares fuertes, la competencia y las relaciones sociales impersonales (pág. 149)

estratificación global distribución desigual de la riqueza, el poder y los recursos entre los países del mundo (pág. 226)

globalización desarrollo de una economía global cada vez más integrada (pág. 230)

tasa bruta de migración número de personas que entran o salen de un área geográfica por cada mil miembros de una población (pág. 424)

grupo dos o más personas que tienen al menos una meta común y que comparten maneras de pensar y comportarse (pág. 157)

pensamiento de grupo pensamiento surgido del autoengaño que se basa en la conformidad con las creencias del grupo y que se genera por la presión ejercida por el mismo grupo para actuar en conformidad (pág. 167)

***garantía** promesa (pág. 380)

H

hate crime a criminal act motivated by extreme prejudice (p. 249)

hidden curriculum the informal and unofficial aspects of culture that children are taught in school (p. 112); the nonacademic agenda that teaches discipline, order, cooperativeness, and conformity (p. 356)

hidden unemployment unemployment that includes people not counted in the traditional unemployment rate (p. 256)

horizontal mobility a change in occupation within the same social class (p. 222)

horticultural society a society that survives primarily through using simple tools to grow plants (p. 144)

hunting and gathering society a society that survives by hunting animals and gathering edible plants (p. 144)

hypothesis testable statement of relationships among variables (p. 55)

hypothesis of linguistic relativity theory stating that our idea of reality depends largely upon language (p. 73)

crimen de odio acto criminal motivado por prejuicios extremos (pág. 249)

currículum oculto aspectos informales y extraoficiales de la cultura que se enseñan a los niños en la escuela (pág. 112); contenidos no académicos que enseñan disciplina, orden, cooperación y conformidad (pág. 356)

desempleo oculto desempleo que toma en cuenta a las personas que no se consideran en la tasa de desempleo tradicional (pág. 256)

movilidad horizontal cambio en la ocupación dentro de la misma clase social (pág. 222)

sociedad hortícola sociedad que sobrevive principalmente mediante el cultivo de plantas con herramientas simples (pág. 144)

sociedad cazadora y recolectora sociedad que sobrevive gracias a la caza de animales y la recolección de plantas comestibles (pág. 144)

hipótesis enunciación de las relaciones entre las variables que puede ponerse a prueba (pág. 55)

hipótesis de la relatividad lingüística teoría que establece que nuestra idea de la realidad depende en gran medida del lenguaje (pág. 73)

I

"I" the part of the self that accounts for unlearned, spontaneous acts (p. 109)

ideal culture cultural guidelines that group members claim to accept (p. 86)

*ideology ideas characteristic of a person, group, or political party (p. 332)

imitation stage Mead's first stage in the development of role taking; children begin to imitate behaviors without understanding why (p. 108)

incarceration a method of protecting society from criminals by keeping them in prison (p. 198)

incest taboo a rule against marriage between certain kinds and degrees of relatives (p. 305)

"ello" parte del ser que es responsable de los actos instintivos o espontáneos (pág. 109)

cultura ideal pautas culturales que los miembros de un grupo dicen aceptar (pág. 86)

*ideología ideas características de una persona, grupo o partido político (pág. 332)

etapa de imitación primera etapa de Mead en el desarrollo del juego de roles; los niños comienzan a imitar los comportamientos sin saber por qué (pág. 108)

encarcelamiento método de proteger a la sociedad de los delincuentes manteniéndolos en prisión (pág. 198)

tabú de incesto regla que prohíbe el matrimonio entre personas con ciertos tipos y grados de parentesco (pág. 305)

*income amount of money received by an individual or group over a specific time period (p. 206)	***ingreso** cantidad de dinero que recibe un individuo o grupo durante un período específico (pág. 206)
*incompatible unable to be reconciled (p. 142)	***incompatibles** que no pueden reconciliarse (pág. 142)
independent variable a characteristic that causes something to occur (p. 48)	**variable independiente** característica que hace que se produzca algo (pág. 48)
*indicator a measurement, based on some standard or system, taken to gauge the status of the whole (p. 229)	***indicador** medida, basada en algún estándar o sistema, que se toma para calcular el estado del todo (pág. 229)
industrial society a society that depends on science and technology to produce basic goods and services (p. 147)	**sociedad industrial** sociedad que depende de la ciencia y la tecnología para producir bienes y servicios básicos (pág. 147)
industrialization the movement from an economy based on agriculture to one based on manufacturing (p. 227)	**industrialización** el movimiento de una economía basada en la agricultura a otra basada en la manufactura (pág. 227)
*industry a group of productive enterprises or organizations that produce or supply goods or services (p. 227)	***industria** grupo de empresas u organizaciones productivas que fabrican o suministran bienes o servicios (pág. 227)
infant mortality rate the annual number of deaths among infants under one year of age per 1,000 live births (p. 423)	**tasa de mortalidad infantil** número anual de muertes de niños menores de un año por cada 1,000 nacimientos vivos (pág. 423)
informal organization a group within a formal organization in which personal relationships are guided by norms, rituals, and sentiments that are not part of the formal organization (p. 173)	**organización informal** grupo dentro de una organización formal en el que las relaciones personales están guiadas por normas, rituales y sentimientos que no forman parte de la organización formal (pág. 173)
informal sanction a reward or punishment that can be applied by most members of a group (p. 78)	**sanción informal** recompensa o castigo que puede ser aplicado por la mayoría de los miembros de un grupo (pág. 78)
in-group exclusive group demanding extreme loyalty (p. 161)	**endogrupo** grupo exclusivo; que demanda lealtad extrema (pág. 161)
*inherently naturally; basically (p. 365)	***intrínsecamente** naturalmente; básicamente (pág. 365)
*initiation a ceremony marking entry into a group (p. 161)	***iniciación** ceremonia que marca el ingreso a un grupo (pág. 161)
*insecurity state of fear, anxiety, or uncertainty (p. 466)	***inseguridad** estado de miedo, ansiedad o incertidumbre (pág. 466)
*instability the quality or state of being unstable; unsteady (p. 463)	***inestabilidad** cualidad o estado de falta de equilibrio; poco firme (pág. 463)
instincts innate (unlearned) patterns of behavior (p. 69)	**instinto** patrones de comportamiento innatos (no aprendidos) (pág. 69)
institutionalized discrimination unfair practices that grow out of common behaviors and attitudes and that are a part of the structure of a society (p. 253)	**discriminación institucionalizada** prácticas injustas que surgen de comportamientos y actitudes comunes y que forman parte de la estructura de una sociedad (pág. 253)
*integrate to mix; to blend (p. 308)	***integrado** mezclado; fusionado (pág. 308)

integrative curriculum an approach to education based on student-teacher collaboration (p. 335)

programa integrador enfoque educativo que se basa en la colaboración entre el estudiante y el maestro (pág. 335)

*intelligence the ability to learn or understand or to deal with new or difficult situations; the ability to apply knowledge (p. 335)

*inteligencia capacidad de aprender, comprender o enfrentar situaciones nuevas o difíciles; capacidad de aplicar los conocimientos (pág. 335)

*interact to relate with other people (p. 133)

*interactuar relacionarse con otras personas (pág. 113)

*interaction meaningful contact (p. 157)

*interacción contacto significativo (pág. 157)

interest group a group organized to influence political decision making (pp. 294, 373)

grupo de interés grupo organizado para influir en la toma de decisiones políticas (págs. 294, 373)

intergenerational mobility a change in status or class from one generation to the next (p. 222)

movilidad intergeneracional cambio de estatus o clase de una generación a la siguiente (pág. 222)

interlocking directorates shared directorates that result when heads of corporations sit on one another's boards (p. 384)

directorios entrelazados los directorios que resultan cuando las cabezas de algunas corporaciones forman parte de los directorios de otras (pág. 384)

intervening variable a variable that changes the relationship between an independent and a dependent variable (p. 48)

variable interviniente variable que cambia la relación entre una variable independiente y otra dependiente (pág. 48)

*intervention intervening action taken to influence the outcome of a particular event, condition, or process (p. 48)

*intervención acto de mediación para influir en el resultado de un suceso, condición o proceso en particular (pág. 48)

interview a survey method in which a trained researcher asks questions and records the answers (p. 37)

entrevista método de encuesta en el cual un investigador entrenado hace preguntas y registra las respuestas (pág. 37)

invention the creation of something new from previously existing items or processes (p. 455)

invento creación de algo nuevo a partir de elementos o procesos preexistentes (pág. 455)

iron law of oligarchy the theory that power increasingly becomes concentrated in the hands of a few members of any organization (p. 174)

ley de hierro de la oligarquía teoría que afirma que el poder va centralizándose cada vez más en las manos de unos pocos miembros de toda organización (pág. 174)

*isolation the condition of being set apart from others (p. 101)

*aislamiento condición de encontrarse separado de otros (pág. 101)

J

jeopardize to put at risk (p. 59)

poner en riesgo comprometer (pág. 59)

L

*label a descriptive term or identification (p. 188)

*rótulo término o identificación descriptivos (pág. 188)

labeling theory the theory that society creates deviance by identifying particular members as deviant (p. 188)

teoría del etiquetado teoría que afirma que la sociedad crea la desviación identificando a ciertos miembros como individuos de conducta desviada (pág. 188)

latent function an action that produces an unintended and unrecognized result (pp. 25, 340)

latent functions unintended and unrecognized consequences of an aspect of society (p. 25)

legitimate to justify or give official approval to (p. 398)

law a norm that is formally defined and enforced by officials (p. 77)

life cycle the stages of development individuals pass through between birth and death (p. 119)

life expectancy the average number of years that persons in a given population born at a particular time can expect to live (p. 423)

lifespan the most advanced age to which humans can survive (p. 423)

looking-glass self an image of yourself based on what you believe others think of you (p. 106)

función latente acción que produce un resultado no buscado ni reconocido (págs. 25, 340)

funciones latentes consecuencias no buscadas ni reconocidas de un aspecto de la sociedad (pág. 25)

legitimar justificar o aprobar oficialmente (pág. 398)

ley norma definida formalmente e impuesta por los funcionarios públicos (pág. 77)

ciclo de vida etapas de desarrollo que atraviesan los individuos desde su nacimiento hasta su muerte (pág. 119)

expectativa de vida número promedio de años al que pueden aspirar vivir las personas de una población determinada nacidas en un momento en particular (pág. 423)

período de vida la edad más avanzada que pueden alcanzar los seres humanos (pág. 423)

espejo de sí mismo imagen de uno mismo basada en lo que se cree que los demás piensan de uno (pág. 106)

M

magnet schools public schools that focus on particular disciplines or areas, such as fine arts or science (p. 339)

manifest function an action that produces an intended and recognized result (pp. 25, 340)

marriage rate the number of marriages per year for every thousand members of the population (p. 314)

mass hysteria a collective anxiety created by the acceptance of one or more false beliefs (p. 467)

mass media means of communication designed to reach the general population (p. 114)

master status a position that strongly influences most other aspect of a person's life (p. 135)

material culture the concrete, tangible objects of a culture (p. 85)

matriarchy when authority in a family is assigned to the oldest woman (p. 303)

*****maturity** adulthood (p. 398)

escuelas especializadas escuelas públicas que se enfocan en disciplinas o áreas específicas, como las bellas artes o las ciencias (pág. 339)

función manifiesta acción que produce un efecto buscado y reconocido (pág2. 25, 340)

tasa de matrimonios número de matrimonios al año por cada mil miembros de la población (pág. 314)

histeria colectiva ansiedad colectiva surgida de la aceptación de al menos una creencia falsa (pág. 467)

medios de comunicación masiva medios de comunicación diseñados para llegar a la población general (pág. 114)

estatus principal posición que tiene una gran influencia en casi todos los otros aspectos de la vida de una persona (pág. 135)

cultura material los objetos concretos y tangibles de una cultura (pág. 85)

matriarcado cuando la autoridad de una familia se asigna a la mujer de mayor edad (pág. 303)

*****madurez** adultez (pág. 398)

"me" the part of the self formed through socialization (p. 109)

mechanical solidarity social dependency based on a widespread consensus of values and beliefs and dependence on tradition and family (p. 15); a type of social unity achieved by people doing the same type of work and holding similar values (p. 149)

mechanization the process of replacing animal and human power with machine power (p. 147)

meritocracy a society in which social status is based on ability and achievement (p. 344)

*migration the movement of people from one geographic area to another (p. 424)

*minority pertaining to a racial, religious, national, or other group regarded as different from the larger group of which it is a part (p. 193); a group of people who, because of physical or cultural traits, are differentiated from the dominant group in a society and treated unequally (p. 236)

mob an acting crowd that is ready to use violence to achieve a purpose (p. 470)

monogamy marriage between one person and one other person (p. 304)

monopolies companies that have control over the production or distribution of a product or service (p. 379)

more norm that has moral dimension and that should be followed by members of the society (p. 76)

mortality death (p. 423)

*motivation a factor that causes movement, change, or action (p. 313)

multicultural education a curriculum that emphasizes differences among gender, ethnic, and racial categories (p. 350)

multinationals firms based in highly industrialized societies with operating facilities throughout the world (p. 385)

multiple causation the belief that an event occurs as a result of several factors working in combination (p. 47)

multiple-nuclei theory the theory that focuses on specific geographic or historical influences on urban growth (p. 445)

"yo" la parte de uno mismo que se forma mediante la socialización (pág. 109)

solidaridad mecánica dependencia social basada en un consenso generalizado de valores y creencias, y en la dependencia de la tradición y la familia (pág. 15); tipo de unidad social que logran personas que hacen el mismo tipo de trabajo y tienen valores similares (pág. 149)

mecanización proceso en el que se reemplazan la fuerzas animal y humana con la fuerza mecánica (pág. 147)

meritocracia sociedad en la que el estatus social se basa en las capacidades y los logros (pág. 344)

*migración movimiento de personas de un área geográfica a otra (pág. 424)

*minoritario relativo a un grupo racial, religioso, nacional o de otro tipo que se considera diferente del grupo más grande del que forma parte (pág. 193); grupo de personas que, debido a rasgos físicos o culturales, se diferencian del grupo dominante de una sociedad y reciben un trato desigual (pág. 236)

turba multitud activa que está dispuesta a usar la violencia para lograr un objetivo (pág. 470)

monogamia matrimonio entre una persona y otra (pág. 304)

monopolios empresas que controlan la producción o distribución de un producto o servicio (pág. 379)

moralidad objetiva norma de dimensión moral que deben obedecer los miembros de la sociedad (pág. 76)

mortalidad muerte (pág. 423)

*motivación factor que causa un movimiento, un cambio o una acción (pág. 313)

educación multicultural programa que enfatizaba las diferencias de género, etnia y categorías raciales (pág. 350)

firmas multinacionales basadas en sociedades altamente industrializadas con instalaciones operativas en todo el mundo (pág. 385)

causalidad múltiple la creencia de que un suceso ocurre como resultado de la operación de varios factores en conjunto (pág. 47)

teoría de los núcleos múltiples teoría que se enfoca en las características geográficas o históricas específicas que influyen sobre el crecimiento urbano (pág. 445)

*mutual shared (p. 300)

N

negative deviance behavior that underconforms to accepted norms (p. 181)

net migration rate the annual increase or decrease per 1,000 members of a population resulting from migration into and out of the population (p. 424)

nonmaterial culture ideas, knowledge, and beliefs that influence people's behavior (p. 85)

*norm rule determining appropriate and inappropriate behavior (p. 76)

nuclear family a group that includes a parent or parents and any children (p. 301)

O

*objective not distorted by personal feelings (p. 112); unbiased; neutral (p. 357)

obligation a behavior that individuals are expected to perform toward others (p. 138)

*occupation one's business or profession (pp. 195, 222); category of job that involves similar activities at different work locations (p. 388)

occupational sex segregation the concentration of women in lower-status positions (p. 279)

oligopolies combinations of companies that control the production or distribution of a product or service (p. 379)

open classroom a nonbureaucratic approach to education based on democracy, flexibility, and noncompetitiveness (p. 334)

open-class system a system in which social class is based on merit and individual effort; movement is allowed between classes (p. 224)

open-ended questions questions a person is to answer in his or her own words (p. 39)

*mutuo compartido (pág. 300)

desviación negativa comportamiento que no llega a ajustarse a las normas aceptadas (pág. 181)

tasa neta de migración aumento o disminución anual por cada 1,000 miembros de una población a causa del ingreso o la salida de personas de dicha población (pág. 424)

cultura inmaterial ideas, conocimientos y creencias que influyen en el comportamiento de las personas (pág. 85)

*norma regla que determina el comportamiento adecuado o inadecuado (pág. 76)

familia nuclear grupo que incluye a un padre o a los padres y a los hijos (pág. 301)

*objetivo que no está distorsionado por sentimientos personales (pág. 112); imparcial; neutral (pág. 357)

obligación comportamiento que se espera de los individuos hacia los demás (pág. 138)

*ocupación negocio o profesión de una persona (págs. 195, 222); categoría de trabajo que incluye actividades semejantes en diferentes lugares de trabajo (pág. 388)

segregación ocupacional de la mujer concentración de las mujeres en las posiciones de menor importancia (pág. 279)

oligopolios combinación de empresas que controlan la producción o distribución de un producto o servicio (pág. 379)

educación abierta enfoque no burocrático de la educación que se basa en la democracia, la flexibilidad y la ausencia de competencia (pág. 334)

sistema social abierto sistema en el que las clases sociales se basan en el mérito y el esfuerzo individual; se permite el movimiento entre las clases (pág. 224)

preguntas de final abierto preguntas que una persona debe contestar con sus propias palabras (pág. 39)

Glossary/Glosario

organic solidarity social interdependency based on a high degree of specialization of roles (p. 15); a type of social unity in which members' interdependence is based on specialized functions and statuses (p. 149)

*orientation direction, place, or relative location (p. 300)

out-group group targeted by an in-group for opposition, antagonism, or competition (p. 161)

*overlap having an area, range, or other characteristics in common (p. 375)

over-urbanization a situation in which a city cannot supply adequate jobs and housing for its inhabitants (p. 437)

solidaridad orgánica interdependencia social basada en un alto grado de especialización de los diferentes roles (pág. 15); tipo de unidad social en la que la interdependencia de los miembros se basa en los estatus y las funciones especializados (pág. 149)

*orientación dirección, lugar o ubicación relativa (pág. 300)

exogrupo grupo seleccionado por un grupo endógeno para fines de oposición, antagonismo o competencia (pág. 161)

*superponerse tener un área, rango u otra característica en común (pág. 375)

sobreurbanización situación en la que una ciudad no logra proporcionar empleos y viviendas adecuados para sus habitantes (pág. 437)

P

panic reaction to a real threat in fearful, anxious, and often self-damaging ways (p. 468)

participant observation a case study in which the researcher becomes a member of the group being studied (p. 42)

*passive accepting what happens without active response or resistance (p. 269)

pastoral society a society in which goods are obtained primarily by raising and taking care of animals (p. 145)

patriarchy when authority in a family is assigned to the oldest man (p. 303)

peer group set of individuals of roughly the same age and interests (p. 113)

peripheral theory the theory that emphasizes the growth of suburbs around the central city (p. 446)

peripheral tier the part of the occupational structure composed of smaller, less profitable firms (p. 388)

*perspective a particular point of view (p. 4)

*phenomenon an unusual or unaccountable fact or event (p. 426)

play stage Mead's second stage in the development of role taking; children act in ways they imagine other people would (p. 108)

pánico reacción temerosa, ansiosa y a menudo autodestructiva frente a un amenaza real (pág. 468)

observación participante estudio de caso en el cual el investigador pasa a formar parte del grupo estudiado (pág. 42)

*pasivo que acepta lo que sucede sin una respuesta o resistencia activa (pág. 269)

sociedad pastoril sociedad en la que los bienes se obtienen principalmente por medio de la cría y el cuidado de animales (pág. 145)

patriarcado cuando la autoridad de una familia se asigna al hombre de mayor edad (pág. 303)

grupo de pares conjunto de individuos que tienen aproximadamente la misma edad y los mismos intereses (pág. 113)

teoría periférica teoría que enfatiza el crecimiento de los suburbios de una ciudad central (pág. 446)

teoría periférica estructura ocupacional compuesta por firmas más pequeñas con menores ganancias (pág. 388)

*perspectiva punto de vista en particular (pág. 4)

*fenómeno dato o suceso inusual o inexplicable (pág. 426)

etapa de juego segunda etapa de Mead en el desarrollo del juego de roles; los niños actúan como creen que otras personas actuarían (pág. 108)

pluralism a system in which political decisions are made as a result of bargaining and compromise among special-interest groups (p. 373)

political institution the institution that determines how power is obtained and exercised (p. 364)

political socialization the informal and formal processes by which a person develops political opinions (p. 370)

polyandry marriage of one woman to more than one man at a time (p. 304)

polygamy marriage of one person to multiple partners at the same time (p. 304)

polygyny marriage of one man to more than one woman at a time (p. 304)

population a group of people with certain specific characteristics (p. 37); a group of people living in a particular place at a specified time (p. 420)

population control attempts by government to control the birthrate (p. 431)

population momentum the inability to stop population growth immediately because of the previous high rate of growth (p. 430)

population pyramid a graphic representative of the age and sex composition of a population (p. 433)

positive deviance behavior that overconforms to social expectations (p. 181)

positivism the belief that knowledge should be derived from scientific observation (p. 12)

postindustrial society a society in which the economic emphasis is on providing services and information (p. 150)

power the ability to control the behavior of others, even against their will (pp. 27, 171, 207, 365)

power elite a unified group of military, corporate, and government leaders (p. 375)

*predict to foretell what will happen (p. 429)

*predictability when something can be foretold or predicted (p. 167)

pluralismo sistema en el que se toman decisiones políticas a partir de negociaciones y acuerdos de los grupos de intereses especiales (pág. 373)

institución política institución que determina cómo se obtiene y cómo se ejerce el poder (pág. 364)

socialización política procesos formales e informales mediante los que una persona elabora sus opiniones políticas (pág. 370)

poliandria matrimonio de una mujer con más de un hombre al mismo tiempo (pág. 304)

poligamia matrimonio de una persona con más de una pareja al mismo tiempo (pág. 304)

poliginia matrimonio de un hombre con más de una mujer al mismo tiempo (pág. 304)

población grupo de personas con ciertas características específicas (pág. 37); grupo de personas que viven en un lugar determinado en un momento específico (pág. 420)

control de la población intentos del gobierno de controlar la tasa de natalidad (pág. 431)

ímpetu demográfico incapacidad de detener el crecimiento de la población en forma inmediata porque anteriormente hubo una alta tasa de crecimiento (pág. 430)

pirámide de la población representación gráfica de la composición de una población por edad y sexo (pág. 433)

desviación positiva comportamiento que supera las expectativas sociales (pág. 181)

positivismo creencia de que el conocimiento debe derivar de la observación científica (pág. 12)

sociedad posindustrial sociedad en la que la economía se enfoca en brindar servicios e información (pág. 150)

poder capacidad de controlar el comportamiento de otros, incluso contra su voluntad (págs. 27, 171, 207, 365)

elite de poder grupo unificado de líderes militares, empresariales y gubernamentales (pág. 375)

*predecir anunciar con anterioridad lo que ocurrirá (pág. 429)

*previsibilidad cuando algo se puede pronosticar o predecir (pág. 167)

prejudice deeply held negative attitudes toward a group (minority or majority) and its individual members (p. 246)

prestige recognition, respect, and admiration attached to social positions (p. 208)

primary deviance deviance involving occasional breaking of norms that is not a part of a person's lifestyle or self-concept (p. 189)

primary group people who are emotionally close, know one another well, and seek one another's company (p. 157)

primary relationship interaction that is intimate, personal, caring, and fulfilling (p. 157)

primary sector that part of the economy producing goods directly from the natural environment (p. 386)

profane nonsacred (p. 396)

*professional relating to a job requiring specialized knowledge and academic preparation (p. 214)

*prohibit to prevent by rule or law (p. 274)

proletariat working class; those who labor for the bourgeoisie (p. 14); the class that labors without owning the means of production (p. 206)

*proportion percentage; fraction or ratio compared to the whole (p. 410)

proscribed forbidden (p. 60)

Protestant ethic a set of values, norms, beliefs, and attitudes stressing hard work, thrift, and self-discipline (p. 400)

prejuicio actitudes negativas muy arraigadas contra un grupo (minoritario o mayoritario) y sus miembros individuales (pág. 246)

prestigio reconocimiento, respeto y admiración relacionados con las posiciones sociales (pág. 208)

desviación primaria desviación que comprende un quebrantamiento ocasional de las normas que no forma parte del estilo de vida de una persona o su concepto de sí misma (pág. 189)

grupo primario personas emocionalmente cercanas, que se conocen bien y buscan la compañía de los otros (pág. 157)

relación primaria interacción íntima, personal, afectuosa y satisfactoria (pág. 157)

sector primario la parte de la economía que produce bienes procedentes del medio ambiente natural (pág. 386)

profano no sagrado (pág. 396)

*profesional relativo a un trabajo que requiere de conocimientos específicos y preparación académica (pág. 214)

*prohibir impedir mediante una regla o ley (pág. 274)

proletariado clase trabajadora; aquellos que trabajan para la burguesía (pág. 14); la clase que trabaja sin ser propietaria de los medios de producción (pág. 206)

*proporción porcentaje; fracción o tasa en comparación al total (pág. 410)

proscrito vedado (pág. 60)

ética protestante conjunto de valores, normas, creencias y actitudes que ponen énfasis en el esfuerzo, el ahorro y la autodisciplina (pág. 400)

Q

qualitative variable a characteristic that is defined by its presence or absence in a category (p. 47)

quantitative variable a characteristic that can be measured numerically (p. 47)

questionnaire a written set of questions to be answered by a research participant (p. 37)

variable cualitativa característica definida por la presencia o ausencia de una categoría (pág. 47)

variable cuantitativa característica que puede medirse en términos numéricos (pág. 47)

cuestionario conjunto de preguntas escritas que debe contestar la persona que participa en una investigación (pág. 37)

R

race people sharing certain inherited physical characteristics that are considered important within a society (p. 237)

racism an extreme form of prejudice that assumes superiority of one racial group over others (p. 246)

rational-legal authority the form of authority in which the power of leaders is vested in the offices they hold, not in their persons (p. 366)

rationalization the mind-set emphasizing knowledge, reason, and planning (p. 16); a mind-set that emphasizes knowledge, reason, and planning (p. 172)

real culture actual behavior patterns of members of a group (p. 86)

recidivism a repetition of, or return to, criminal behavior (p. 198)

redemptive movement a social movement that seeks to change individuals completely (p. 475)

reference group group whose norms and values are used to guide behavior; group with whom you identify (p. 126); group used for self-evaluation and the formation of attitudes, values, beliefs, norms, and mores (p. 161)

reflex automatic reaction to physical stimuli (p. 70)

reformative movement a social movement that attempts to make limited changes in society (p. 474)

rehabilitation the process of changing or reforming a criminal through socialization (p. 198)

*reinforce to strengthen an existing structure, belief, or behavior (p. 276)

relative property a measure of poverty based on the economic disparity between those at the bottom of a society and the rest of the society (p. 216)

religion a unified system of beliefs and practices concerned with sacred things (p. 396)

religiosity ways in which people express their religious interests and convictions (p. 405)

*reorientation a change in attitudes and beliefs (p. 121)

raza personas que comparten ciertas características físicas que se consideran importantes dentro de una sociedad (pág. 237)

racismo forma extrema de prejuicio que supone la superioridad de un grupo racial sobre otros (pág. 246)

autoridad racional legal forma de autoridad en la que el poder de los líderes corresponde a los cargos que ocupan, no a las personas (pág. 366)

racionalización modo de pensar que enfatiza el conocimiento, la razón y la planificación (pág. 16); modo de pensar que enfatiza el conocimiento, la razón y la planificación (pág. 172)

cultura real patrones de comportamiento reales de los miembros de un grupo (pág. 86)

reincidencia repetición de un comportamiento delictivo o su regreso a él (pág. 198)

movimiento redentor movimiento social que busca cambiar completamente a los individuos (pág. 475)

grupo de referencia grupo cuyas normas y valores se usan para guiar el comportamiento; grupo con el que uno se identifica (pág. 126); grupo que se usa para la autoevaluación y para la formación de actitudes, valores, creencias, normas y moralidad objetiva (pág. 161)

reflejo reacción automática a los estímulos físicos (pág. 70)

movimiento reformista movimiento social que intenta efectuar cambios limitados en la sociedad (pág. 474)

rehabilitación proceso en el que se cambia o reforma a un delincuente mediante la socialización (pág. 198)

*reforzar fortalecer una estructura, creencia o conducta existentes (pág. 276)

propiedad relativa medida de la pobreza que se basa en la disparidad económica que existe entre quienes se encuentran en la parte inferior de la sociedad y el resto (pág. 216)

religión sistema unificado de creencias y prácticas relacionadas con lo sagrado (pág. 396)

religiosidad formas en las que las personas expresan sus convicciones e intereses religiosos (pág. 405)

*reorientación cambio de actitudes y creencias (pág. 121)

replacement level the birthrate at which a couple replaces themselves without adding to the population (p. 430)	**nivel de reemplazo** tasa de natalidad en la que las parejas se reemplazan a sí mismas sin que haya un aumento de la población (pág. 430)
representative democracy a system of government that uses elected officials to fulfill majority wishes (p. 367)	**democracia representativa** sistema de gobierno en el que los funcionarios elegidos cumplen los deseos de la mayoría (pág. 367)
representative sample a sample that accurately reflects the characteristics of the population as a whole (p. 37)	**muestra representativa** muestra que refleja de manera precisa las características de la población en su conjunto (pág. 37)
***research** investigation or experimentation aimed at the discovery and interpretation of facts (p. 13)	**investigación** estudio o experimentación destinados al descubrimiento y la interpretación de hechos (pág. 13)
resocialization the process of adopting new norms, values, attitudes, and behaviors (p. 125)	**resocialización** proceso en el que se adoptan nuevas normas, valores, actitudes y conductas (pág. 125)
resource-mobilization theory a temporary collection of people who share an immediate common interest (p. 477)	**teoría de la movilización de recursos** grupo temporal de personas que comparten un interés común inmediato (pág. 477)
restitution punishment intended to make criminals pay monetary compensation to make up for the financial damage caused by their acts (p. 198)	**restitución** castigo que tiene como objetivo que los delincuentes paguen una compensación monetaria por el daño económico que causaron sus actos (pág. 198)
retribution punishment intended to make criminals pay compensation for their acts (p. 197)	**retribución** castigo que tiene como objetivo que los delincuentes paguen una compensación por sus actos (pág. 197)
***revolution** a sudden and complete overthrow of a social or political order (p. 458)	***revolución** derrocamiento repentino y complejo de un orden social o político (pág. 458)
revolutionary movement a social movement that attempts to change the total structure of society (p. 474)	**movimiento revolucionario** movimiento social que intenta cambiar toda la estructura de la sociedad (pág. 474)
right a behavior that individuals expect from others (p. 138)	**derecho** comportamiento que los individuos esperan de otros (pág. 138)
riot an episode of largely random destruction and violence carried out by a crowd (p. 470)	**disturbio** episodio de destrucción y violencia, mayormente al azar, llevado a cabo por una multitud (pág. 470)
rites of passage rituals marking the passage from one status to another (p. 120)	**ritos de pasaje** rituales que marcan el paso de un estatus a otro (pág. 120)
role an unexpected behavior associated with a particular status (p. 138)	**rol** comportamiento inesperado asociado con un estatus particular (pág. 138)
role conflict the situation that exists when expectations for or performance of a role in one status clash with expectations for or performance of a role in another status (p. 141)	**conflicto de roles** situación que se produce cuando las expectativas o el desempeño de un rol en un estatus chocan con las expectativas o el desempeño de un rol en otro estatus (pág. 141)
role performance the actual conduct, or behavior, exhibited by people as they carry out a role (p. 139)	**desempeño de roles** la conducta, o comportamiento, real de las personas mientras representan un rol (pág. 139)

role strain the situation that occurs when a person has trouble meeting the many roles connected with a single status (p. 141)

role taking assuming the viewpoint of another person and using that viewpoint to shape the self-concept (p. 107)

rumor a widely circulating piece of information that is not verified as being true or false (p. 466)

tensión de roles situación que se produce cuando una persona tiene dificultades para cumplir con todos los roles relacionados con un único estatus (pág. 141)

juego de roles asumir el punto de vista de otra persona y usarlo para formar el concepto de sí mismo (pág. 107)

rumor dato muy difundido que no se ha verificado como verdadero o falso (pág. 466)

S

sacred holy; set apart and given a special meaning that goes beyond, or transcends, immediate existence (p. 396)

sample a group of people who represents a larger population (p. 37)

sanction a reward or punishment used to encourage people to follow rules (p. 78)

school desegregation the achievement of a racial balance in the classroom (p. 349)

scientific method the recognition and formulation of a problem, the collection of data through observation and experiment, and the formulation and testing of hypotheses (p. 55)

secondary analysis using precollected information for data collection and research purposes (p. 40)

secondary deviance deviance in which an individual's life and identity are organized around breaking society's norms (p. 189)

secondary groups people who share only part of their lives while focusing on a goal or task (p. 159)

secondary relationship impersonal interaction involving limited parts of personalities (p. 159)

secondary sector that part of the economy engaged in manufacturing goods (p. 386)

sect a religious organization that arises out of a desire to reform an existing religious organization (p. 403)

sector theory the theory that emphasizes the importance of transportation routes in the process of urban growth (p. 445)

sagrado santo; algo considerado único y con un significado especial que supera, o trasciende, la existencia inmediata (pág. 396)

muestra grupo de personas que representa a una población más grande (pág. 37)

sanción recompensa o castigo que se utiliza para estimular a las personas a seguir las reglas (pág. 78)

integración escolar logro de un equilibrio racial en el salón de clases (pág. 349)

método científico el reconocimiento y la formulación de un problema, la recopilación de datos mediante la observación y la experimentación, y la formulación y comprobación de hipótesis (pág. 55)

análisis secundario usar información recopilada previamente con el objetivo de recolectar datos e investigar (pág. 40)

desviación secundaria desviación en la que la vida y la identidad de un individuo están organizadas en torno al quebrantamiento de las normas de la sociedad (pág. 189)

grupos secundarios personas que comparten solo una parte de su vida mientras se enfocan en una meta o tarea (pág. 159)

relación secundaria interacción impersonal que involucra partes limitadas de las personalidades (pág. 159)

sectores secundarios aquella parte de la economía que se ocupa de los bienes manufacturados (pág. 386)

secta organización religiosa que surge del deseo de reformar una organización religiosa preexistente (pág. 403)

teoría de la sectorización teoría que enfatiza la importancia de las rutas de transporte en el proceso de crecimiento urbanístico (pág. 445)

secularization the process through which the sacred loses influence over society (p. 409)

self-concept an image of yourself as having an identity separate from other people (p. 106)

self-fulfilling prophecy an expectation that leads to behavior that causes the expectation to become a reality (p. 252)

sex the classification of people as male or female based on biological characteristics (p. 268)

sexism a set of beliefs, attitudes, norms, and values used to justify sexual inequality (p. 278)

***sexist** an attitude or belief that one sex, usually male, is superior to the other (p. 357)

significant others those people whose reactions are most important to your self-concept (p. 107)

***similarity** the quality of being alike (p. 94)

social aggregate people temporarily in the same place at the same time (p. 157)

social category people who share a social characteristic (pp. 88, 156)

social change alteration in a society's makeup or norms that occurs when many members of a society adopt new behaviors (p. 453)

social class a segment of society whose members have similar economic circumstances, norms, and status (p. 204)

social control ways to encourage conformity to society's norms (p. 182)

social dynamics the study of social change (p. 12)

social exchange a voluntary action performed in the expectation or getting a reward in return (p. 164)

social interaction any of the processes by which people influence one another as they interrelate (p. 139)

social mobility the movement of individuals or groups between social classes (p. 222)

secularización proceso por el que lo sagrado pierde influencia sobre la sociedad (pág. 409)

concepto de sí mismo imagen de uno mismo como alguien que tiene una identidad diferente a la de otras personas (pág. 106)

profecía autocumplida predicción que produce un comportamiento que hace que lo esperado se haga realidad (pág. 252)

sexo clasificación de las personas en masculino o femenino basada en sus características biológicas (pág. 268)

sexismo conjunto de creencias, actitudes, normas y valores usados para justificar la desigualdad de los sexos (pág. 278)

***sexista** actitud o creencia de que un sexo, generalmente el masculino, es superior al otro (pág. 357)

otros significativos aquellas personas cuyas reacciones son las más importantes para el concepto de sí mismo (pág. 107)

***semejanza** cualidad de parecerse (pág. 94)

agregado social personas que se encuentran por un tiempo determinado en el mismo lugar y en el mismo momento (pág. 157)

categoría social personas que comparten una característica social (págs. 88, 156)

cambio social alteración en la composición o en las normas de una sociedad, que ocurre cuando muchos miembros de la sociedad adoptan nuevos comportamientos (pág. 453)

clase social segmento de la sociedad cuyos miembros tienen circunstancias económicas, normas y estatus similares (pág. 204)

control social maneras de estimular la conformidad con las normas sociales (pág. 182)

dinámica social el estudio del cambio social (pág. 12)

intercambio social acción voluntaria realizada con la esperanza de obtener una recompensa (pág. 164)

interacción social cualquiera de los procesos por los que las personas influyen unas sobre otras al interrelacionarse (pág. 139)

movilidad social el movimiento de individuos o grupos de una clase social a otra (pág. 222)

social movement a movement whose goal is to promote or prevent social change; the most structured collective behavior (p. 473)

social network a web or social relationships that join a person to other people and groups (p. 161)

social processes a series of steps leading to change on a societal level (p. 455)

social sanctions rewards or punishments that encourage conformity to social norms (p. 183)

social solidarity the degree to which a society is unified (p. 149)

social statics the study of social stability and order (p. 12)

social stratification the ranking of people or groups according to their unequal access to scarce resources (p. 204)

social structure the patterned interaction of people in social relationships (p. 4); the pattern of social relationships within a group (p. 133)

socialism an economic system founded on the belief that the means of production should be controlled by the people as a whole (p. 381)

socialization the process of learning to participate in a group (p. 101)

society a specific territory inhabited by people who share a common culture (p. 69); a group of a people living within defined territorial borders and sharing a common culture (p. 144)

sociobiology the study of how biology influences human behavior (p. 70)

socio-emotional maintenance the provision of acceptance and emotional support (p. 309)

sociological imagination the ability to see the link between society and self (p. 9)

sociological perspective a view that looks at the behavior of groups, not individuals (p. 4)

sociology the scientific study of social structure; patterned social behavior (p. 4)

*somewhat partially; in a limited way (p. 279)

movimiento social movimiento cuya meta es promover o evitar los cambios sociales; la forma más estructurada del comportamiento colectivo (pág. 473)

red social red o relaciones sociales que unen a una persona con otras personas y grupos (pág. 161)

procesos sociales serie de pasos que conducen a un cambio social (pág. 455)

sanciones sociales recompensas o castigos que estimulan la conformidad con las normas sociales (pág. 183)

solidaridad social el grado de unificación que existe en una sociedad (pág. 149)

estática social el estudio de la estabilidad y el orden de la sociedad (pág. 12)

estratificación social clasificación de las personas o grupos según su acceso desigual a los recursos escasos (pág. 204)

estructura social la interacción, según un patrón, de las personas en las relaciones sociales (pág. 4); patrón de relaciones sociales dentro de un grupo (pág. 133)

socialismo sistema económico fundado en la creencia de que los medios de producción deben estar bajo el control de la población en su conjunto (pág. 381)

socialización proceso en el que se aprende a participar en un grupo (pág. 101)

sociedad territorio específico habitado por personas que comparten una cultura común (pág. 69); grupo de personas que viven dentro de límites territoriales definidos y que comparten una cultura común (pág. 144)

sociobiología el estudio de cómo influye la biología en el comportamiento humano (pág. 70)

apoyo socioemocional acción de brindar aceptación y respaldo emocional (pág. 309)

imaginación sociológica la capacidad de ver el vínculo entre la sociedad y uno mismo (pág. 9)

perspectiva sociológica visión que se enfoca en el comportamiento de los grupos, no de los individuos (pág. 4)

sociología estudio científico de la estructura social; comportamiento social que sigue un patrón (pág. 4)

*de alguna manera parcialmente, en forma limitada (pág. 279)

***sphere** a defined area or subject (p. 278)	***esfera** área o materia definida (pág. 278)
spirit of capitalism the obligation to reinvest money in business rather than spend it (p. 399)	**espíritu del capitalismo** obligación de reinvertir el dinero en negocios en lugar de gastarlo (pág. 399)
spurious correlation a relationship between two variables that is actually caused by a third factor (p. 49)	**correlación espuria** relación entre dos variables que, en realidad, es causada por un tercer factor (pág. 49)
***stability** reliability; resistance to sudden change (p. 182)	***estabilidad** fiabilidad; resistencia al cambio repentino (pág. 182)
standard of living the necessities, comforts, and luxuries enjoyed by an individual or group (p. 226)	**estándar de vida** necesidades, comodidades y lujos que disfruta un individuo o grupo (pág. 226)
status a position a person occupies within a social structure (p. 133)	**estatus** posición que ocupa una persona dentro de una estructura social (pág. 133)
status set all the statuses a person occupies at any given time (p. 134)	**conjunto de estatus** todos los estatus que ocupa una persona en determinado momento (pág. 134)
stereotyping a labeling of a group based on distorted, exaggerated, or oversimplified images of that group (p. 247)	**estereotipado** rotulación de un grupo sobre la base de imágenes distorsionadas, exageradas o simplistas de ese grupo (pág. 247)
stigma an undesirable label that is used to deny a deviant social acceptance (p. 189)	**estigma** rótulo no deseable que se usa para negar la aceptación social a un individuo de conducta desviada (pág. 189)
strain theory the theory that deviance is more likely to occur when a gap exists between cultural goals and the ability to achieve them (p. 185)	**teoría de la tensión** teoría que establece que es más probable que se produzcan desviaciones si existe una brecha entre las metas culturales y la capacidad de alcanzarlas (pág. 185)
subculture a group that is part of the dominant culture but that differs from it in some important respects (p. 88)	**subcultura** grupo que forma parte de la cultura dominante, pero que difiere de esta en algunos aspectos importantes (pág. 88)
subjugation the process by which a minority group is denied equal access to the benefits of a society (p. 242)	**subyugación** proceso por el cual se niega a un grupo minoritario el acceso igualitario a los beneficios de una sociedad (pág. 242)
***submit** to yield or to surrender to the authority of another (p. 171)	***someterse** ceder o rendirse a la autoridad de otro (pág. 171)
suburbanization the loss of population of a city to surrounding areas (p. 438)	**suburbanización** pérdida de población de una ciudad porque sus habitantes se trasladan a los alrededores (pág. 438)
***survey** research method in which people respond to questions (p. 36)	***encuesta** método de investigación en el que las personas contestan preguntas (pág. 36)
***symbol** anything that stands for something else and has an agreed-upon meaning attached to it (p. 29)	***símbolo** todo aquello que representa otra cosa y tiene un significado que le ha sido otorgado de manera consensuada (pág. 29)
symbolic interactionism approach that focuses on the interactions among people based on their mutually understood symbols (p. 29)	**interacción simbólica** enfoque que se centra en las interacciones entre las personas basadas en los símbolos que comprenden entre sí (pág. 29)

taboo a rule of behavior, the violation of which calls for strong punishment (p. 76)

*****technology** the knowledge and tools used to achieve practical goals (p. 456)

*****terminal** leading ultimately to death (p. 122)

tertiary sector that part of the economy providing services (p. 386)

theoretical perspective a set of assumptions about an area of study accepted as true (p. 22)

*****thereby** by that means; because of that (p. 399)

total fertility rate the average number of children born to a woman during her lifetime (p. 422)

total institution place in which people are separated from the rest of society and controlled by officials in charge (p. 125)

totalitarianism a political system in which a ruler with absolute power attempts to control all aspects of society (p. 369)

tracking the placement of students in programs according to academic ability (p. 342)

traditional authority the form of authority in which the legitimacy of a leader is rooted in custom (p. 366)

*****transition** the process of changing from one state to another (p. 443)

transitional adulthood a period after high school when young adults have not yet assumed the responsibilities usually associated with adulthood (p. 120)

*****transmission** the act or process of conveying information from one person to another (p. 101)

*****transportation** the conveyance of passengers, goods, or materials (p. 436)

two-income marriage a marriage in which both spouses work outside the home (p. 323)

tabú regla de comportamiento cuya violación exige un castigo severo (pág. 76)

*****tecnología** conocimientos y herramientas utilizados para alcanzar metas prácticas (pág. 456)

*****terminal** que en última instancia provocará la muerte (pág. 122)

sector terciario la parte de la economía que proporciona servicios (pág. 386)

perspectiva teórica conjunto de suposiciones sobre un área de estudio que se aceptan como verdaderas (pág. 22)

*****de ese modo** por ese motivo; por eso (pág. 399)

tasa de fertilidad total número promedio de hijos que una mujer da a luz durante su vida (pág. 422)

institución absoluta lugar en el que las personas están separadas del resto de la sociedad y controladas por los funcionarios a cargo (pág. 125)

totalitarismo sistema político en el que un gobernante con poderes absolutos trata de controlar todos los aspectos de una sociedad (pág. 369)

clasificación división de los estudiantes en programas acordes a sus capacidades académicas (pág. 342)

autoridad tradicional forma de autoridad en la que la legitimidad de un líder proviene de la costumbre (pág. 366)

*****transición** proceso de cambio de un estado a otro (pág. 443)

transición a la adultez período posterior a la escuela secundaria, cuando los jóvenes adultos aún no han asumido las responsabilidades que suelen asociarse con la adultez (pág. 120)

*****transmisión** el acto o proceso de transferir información de una persona a otra (pág. 101)

*****transporte** traslado de pasajeros, bienes o materiales (pág. 436)

pareja de doble ingreso matrimonio en los que ambos esposos trabajan fuera de casa (pág. 323)

U

underclass people typically unemployed who come from families that have been poor for generations (pp. 215, 256)

clase marginada personas generalmente desempleadas que provienen de familias que han sido pobres durante varias generaciones (págs. 215, 256)

*underlying important but not obvious (p. 291)

*subyacente importante, pero no obvio (pág. 291)

*uniformity consistency; without variation (p. 166)

*uniformidad coherencia; sin variaciones (pág. 166)

*unique like no other, distinct (p. 125)

*único que no tiene igual, distinto (pág. 125)

urban ecology the study of the relationship between humans and city environments (p. 443)

ecología urbana estudio de la relación entre los seres humanos y los medioambientes de las ciudades (pág. 443)

urban legend a moralistic tale that focuses on current concerns and fears of the city or suburb dweller (p. 466)

leyenda urbana relato moralizador que se centra en las preocupaciones y temores actuales de los habitantes de una ciudad o suburbio (pág. 466)

urbanism the distinctive way of life shared by the people living in a city (p. 464)

urbanismo forma de vida distintiva que comparten los habitantes de una ciudad (pág. 464)

urbanization the shifting of the population from farms and villages to large cities (p. 147); the process by which an increasingly larger portion of the world's population lives in cities (p. 434)

urbanización el paso de la población de las granjas y aldeas a las grandes ciudades (pág. 147); proceso por el cual una porción cada vez mayor de la población mundial vive en las ciudades (pág. 434)

*utilize to use (p. 289)

*utilizar usar (pág. 289)

V

value broad idea about what is good or desirable shared by people in a society (p. 79)

valor concepto amplio acerca de lo que es bueno o deseable que comparten las personas en una sociedad (pág. 79)

value-added theory the theory holding that certain conditions must exist for social movements to occur (p. 476)

teoría del valor agregado teoría que afirma que deben darse condiciones determinadas para que se produzcan movimientos sociales (pág. 476)

*variable a characteristic that is subject to change (p. 47)

*variable característica que puede cambiar (pág. 47)

verstehen understanding social behavior by putting yourself in the place of others (p. 16)

comprensión (verstehen) entender el comportamiento social poniéndose en el lugar de otros (pág. 16)

vertical mobility a change upward or downward in occupational status or social class (p. 222)

movilidad vertical ascenso o descenso del estado ocupacional o la clase social (pág. 222)

victim discounting the process of reducing the seriousness of the crimes that injure people of lower status (p. 193)

clasificación de víctimas proceso en el que se reduce la gravedad de los delitos que dañan a las personas de las clases sociales más bajas (pág. 193)

*violation the breaking of a rule or law (p. 76); the act of breaking or discarding (p. 182)

*violación el acto de romper una regla o ley (pág. 76); el acto de romper o descartar (pág. 182)

*virtually almost; for all practical purposes (p. 255)

*voluntary done by free choice (p. 126)

voucher system a system in which public school funds may be used to support public, private, or religious schools (p. 336)

*virtualmente casi; a todos los efectos (pág. 255)

*voluntario hecho con libertad de elección (pág. 126)

sistema de comprobantes sistema por el que los fondos de las escuelas públicas pueden usarse para financiar escuelas públicas, privadas o religiosas (pág. 336)

W

war organized, armed conflict that occurs within a society or between nations (p. 459)

wealth total economic resources held by a person or group (p. 206)

white-collar crime job-related crimes committed by high-status people (p. 194)

*widespread commonly found; frequently occurring (p. 315)

working poor people employed in low-skill jobs with the lowest pay who do not earn enough to rise out of poverty (p. 215)

guerra conflicto armado organizado que se produce dentro de una sociedad o entre diferentes naciones (pág. 459)

riqueza el total de los recursos económicos de una persona o grupo (pág. 206)

delitos de cuello blanco delitos en el ámbito laboral cometidos por personas de clase alta (pág. 194)

*generalizado común, que ocurre con frecuencia (pág. 315)

clase trabajadora pobre personas con trabajos poco calificados que reciben los sueldos más bajos y no ganan lo suficiente como para salir de la pobreza (pág. 215)

Z

zero-population growth a situation in which births are balanced by deaths so the population does not increase (p. 430)

crecimiento cero de la población situación en la que los nacimientos están equilibrados con las muertes, de modo que la población no crece (pág. 430)

INDEX

abandonment ... **assumption**

Page numbers with *c* indicate charts; *crt* indicates cartoons; *g* indicates graphs; *m* indicates maps, *p* indicates photographs, and *q* indicates quotes.

A

abandonment, 321
Aberle, David, 474
Abraham, *c400*
abstract, 29
abuse, 316–317
acceptance, as stage of grief, 123
accommodation, 241
acculturation, 240
achieved status, *c133*, 133–134
achievement, 80
acting crowd, 470
activity, 80
adaptive evolutionary responses, 271
Addams, Jane, *p3*, 3, 17, *p17*, 20–21, *q21*
adjacent, 74
adolescence, 119, 126, 134; cyberbullying and, 154–155; failure of schools and parents and, 82–83; gender and, 52–53; gender socialization and, 277; juvenile crime and, 196; single-parent families and, 322
adoption, Internet, 203
adulthood: mature, 134; milestones in the transition to, *c121*; transitional, 120–121; young, 134
adult literacy rates, *m342*
affirmative action, 347
Affordable Health Care Act (2010), 282
Afghanistan, elderly population in, 122
AFL-CIO, *c374*
African Americans, *p238*, 254–256; assessing progress for, 256; average SAT scores by, *c346*; barriers to assimilation for, 254–255; college entrance exams and, 345; cultural bias and, 348; discrimination against, 156, 193, 233; employment of, 255–256; hate crimes and, 249; high-school graduates, *g334*; income of, 255; intelligence scores of children, 347–348; juvenile crime and, 196; as minority group, 236; politics and, 242, 412; poverty rate for, 216; single-parent families in, *g322*; stereotyping and, 248–249; treatment of, 193; urban housing and, *p440*, 440–441; voting by, 242, 372; world of, 233
African diaspora, *m237*
age: as agent of socialization, 372; as ascribed master status, 135; distribution in a population, *m122*; poverty and, 217; stereotyping and, *p290*; suicide rates by, *g289*; technology and, 266–267
ageism: conflict theory and, 289–290; defined, 288; functionalism and, 288–289; symbolic interactionism and, 290
age-specific death rates, 423
age stratification, 288
aggravated assault, 195
aggregate, 468
agricultural economics, 367
agricultural employment, 149, *m149*
agricultural revolution, 435
agricultural societies, 145
AIDS, 468
Aid to Families with Dependent Children (AFDC), 218, 219
Alaska Natives, 261–262
Albright, Madeleine, 282
Alcoholics Anonymous, 475
Alger, Horatio, 225
Alien Land Bill (1913), 260
Allport, Gordon, 251
alternative movement, 475
Alzheimer's disease, *p457*
ambiguities, 476
ambiguous roles, 321
America. *See* United States.
American Association of Retired Persons (AARP), 294
American Bar Association, *c374*
American flag, *p397*
American Medical Association, *c374*
American meritocracy, 344–345
American National Election Studies (ANES), 406
American Sociological Association, 79; Code of Ethics of, 57, 58–62
Amish, 241, 403, *p403*
Amman, Jacob, 403
anger as stage of grief, 122–123
Anglo-conformity, 240
Angola, elderly population in, 122
***Animal Farm* (Orwell),** 204
animism, 411
anomie, 185
Anthony, Susan B., 474, *p475*
anthropology, *c5*; connecting sociology to, 73, 120, 146, 181, 223, 270; defined, 146
anticipation, 107
anticipatory socialization, 126
Anti-Defamation League (ADL), 234
antisocial behavior, dealing with, 198
anti-Vietnam war protests, 90, *p477*
apartheid, 223–224; gender, 274
Arab Spring, 450, 458
Arapesh, 271
Aristotle, 165–166, *q166*
Arkwright, Richard, *p2*
Army War College, 274
arson, 195
Aryan migration, 223
Asch, Solomon, 169; experiment of, 166–167
ascribed status, *c133*, 133–134
Asian Americans, *p238*, *p260*, 260–261; average SAT scores by, *c346*; hate crimes and, 249; high-school graduates, *g334*; politics and, 242; stereotyping and, 248; voting by, 242, 372
assault, 196
Assemblies of God, 410
assigned status, 133
assimilation: barriers to, for African Americans, 254–255; defined, 240; patterns of, 240–241
assumption, 18

550

A

atheism, g398
attachment, 186
authoritarianism, 369
authority, 171; charismatic, 366; defined, 364–365; forms of, 365; hierarchy of, 171; rational-legal, 366; traditional, 366, 367
automobile safety, p379
average, 43–44
awakenings, 408

B

baby boom, 90, 457
back-to-basics movement, 335–336
Bahá'í, g398
Baker, Charisse, 116–117
Bandura, Albert, 316
banishment, 181
Banks, Curt, 137
Baptists, 410, c412
bargaining as stage of grief, 122–123
Barrow, Georgia M., 290
Barton, Clara, 274
Becker, Howard, q188
behavior: antisocial, 198; biology, culture and, 68, 270–272; collective, 465; effect of heredity on, 69–70; of gangs, 190–191; gender-related, 270, 271–272; group versus individual, 7; social, 132, 271; unethical, 248
beliefs, 405; defined, 84; generalized, 476; importance of, 84–85; physical objects and, 84–85
Bell, Alexander Graham, p3
Bell, Daniel, 150
Bellah, Robert, 408
The Bell Curve **(Herrnstein and Murray),** 347
Benedict XVI, 394
Berger, Peter, 6, 400–401
Besen-Cassino, Yasemin, 376–377
Bhutan, 366
bias: cultural, 348; defined, 246; in law, 282–283
Big Bang theory of creation, 413
Bigelow, Kathryn, 278
bilineal families, 302–303, 312
bilingual education, 341–342
Bill of Rights, p361
biological determinism, 268–269, 271
biological differences, social behavior and, 271
biology: culture, behavior and, 270–272; influence on behavior, 68
Birom people, 144
birth cohorts, 126
birthrates: crude, 421–422; decline in, 422; world, g428
Black Like Me **(Griffin),** 42
Black Picket Fences **(Patillo),** 116–117
Black Power movement, 249
Blau, Francine, 282
blended families, 320–321, p321
blogs, 66
Blumer, Herbert, 29, 471
Bobo doll experiment, 316, p316
Boehner, John, p286
boomerang kids, 325, crt325
born-again Christian movement, 475
bourgeoisie, 14, 206
Bradley, Bill, 363
Brahmins, 224
Brajuha, Mario, 57
Branch Davidians, 404
Brazil, norms and customs of, c77
Brinkerhoff, David, 276
broadcast media, 98
Brown v. Board of Education of Topeka, 242, 352
Buddhism, m397, c400, 411
Bulgaria, norms and customs of, c77
bullying, 154
bureaucracies: advantages of, 172; characteristics of, 171; in education, 332–333; efficiency as goal of, 333; in protecting people, 172–173; rules in, crt172
bureaucratic model, criticisms of, 333
Burgess, Ernest, 443, 445
Bush, George H. W., 470
Bush, George W., 351
business: careers in, 10; demographics and, 422, p422
Byrd, James, Jr., 89, 247, 249
bystander effect, 167

C

Calhoun-Brown, Allison, 406, q407
Calvin, John, 400
Canasatego, 8, q8
capitalism, 14, 210, 378–380; benefits to society, 378–379; defined, 378; link between Protestantism and, 399–400; role of government in, 379–380
capital punishment, 197; legal status of, m196
Carter, Jimmy, 284
cartograms, 228
case studies, 33, c40, 41; *Black Picket Fences,* 116–117; Family Violence, 318–319; Globalization and Work, 460–461; on isolated children, 102–104; psychological, 100; Saints and Roughnecks, 190–191; *School Talk: Gender and Adolescent Culture,* 52–53.
Casler, Lawrence, 101
Cassino, Dan, 376–377
caste system, 223–224
Castro, Fidel, 257, 366, 369
casual crowd, 469
Catholic Church, m397, 403, p403, c412; teachings of, 455
causation, 46–51; defined, 46; multiple, 46; nature of, 46; standards for showing, 49–51
celebrations, 65, p65
cell phones: ownership of, c99; use of, m47, 266–267, 298
Census, 426
Census Bureau, U.S., 41, 43, 422, 424
Center for New Community, 234
Center for the Study of Hate and Extremism, 234
central business district, 443, 445
central-city dilemma, 439
ceremonies, initiation, 160
Chagnon, Napoleon, 146
Chambliss, William, 190–191, q191
change: cultural, 88–89; voluntary, 126. See also social change.
charismatic authority, 366
charismatic movement, 411
charter schools, 339
Chávez, César, 365
Cherokee people, 302; Trail of Tears for, 243
Cheyenne people, 181, p181
Chicago, University of, 17; sociology department at, 3, 17, 19
childhood, 118–119, 134
childless marriages, 322–323
children: attitudes of, p252; boomerang, 325, crt325; case studies on isolated, 102–104; limiting number of, in controlling population, 432–433; peer group socialization and, 113; socializing of, 307. See also adolescence.

China, socialism and, 382
Chinese Americans, 260
Chinese Exclusion Act (1882), 260
Chinese folk religions, g398
chiseling, 173
Christianity, 397, m397, g398, c400
chupacabras, p468
church, 402; separation of state and, p393, p414. See also religion.
Church of England, 402
Church of Scientology, 404
circular reaction, 471
cities: defined, 434; edge, 439; history of, 435–436; preindustrial, 435–436; rise of the modern, 436; theories of growth, c443, 443–446
citizenry, need for educated, 341
Civil Rights Act (1964), 473; Title VII of the, 281
civil rights movement, 92
class conflict, 14
class consciousness, 212
class structure, in the U.S., c214
Clean Air Act Amendments, 374
Clinton, Bill, 285, p362
Clinton, Hillary, 284, p362
closed-ended questions, 37, 38; samples of, p38
coercion, 165–166
cognitive ability, 347–348
cohabitation, 324
Cohen, David, q332
colleagues, 161
collective behavior, 465
collective excitement, 471
collectivity, 465
college entrance exams, 345–346
college settings, careers in, 10
Collins, Eileen, 278
Columbine High School, school violence at, p161
commitment, 189
communism, 14; collapse of, in Soviet Union, 368
community service in dealing with antisocial behavior, 198
community work, careers in, 10
commuter's zone, 445
compact disc players, p114
compensatory education, 350
competition, 344

complex technologies, 147
computers: commercial sale of, p114; in education, 330; high-tech crime and, 178–179; ownership of, c99
Comte, Auguste, 2, p3, 12, 13, 46
concentration, 439
concentric-zone theory, 443, c443, 445
conception, 239
conflict, 164; patterns of, 242–243; reducing, in two-career families, 141; religious-based, 399, p399; role of, 27; strikes as form of, p164
conflict theory, 23, 27–28; ageism and, 289–290; assumptions of, 26; comparing functionalism and, 28; culture and, 69; deviance in, 192, 193; discrimination and, 250–251; domination and, 166–167; education and, 344–351; families and, 310; feminist writers and, 310; gender and, 274–275, 310; power elite and, 375; religion and, 398–400; role of conflict and constraint, 27; school violence, school funding and, 41; social change and, 27, 463–464; social interactions and, 165; socialization and, 105, 107; social stratification and, 210, 211; social structure and, 142
conformity, 7–8, 166–167, 177; encouraging, as function of primary groups, 158
Confucianism, g398
Congo, elderly population in, 122
consensus, 149
consequences, 405
Constitution, U.S., p361, p367, 380
Constitutional government, 367
constraint, role of, 27
contagion theory, 471, c47W, 472
contrast, 84
control: self-, 111; social, 182–183
control theory, deviance and, 186
conventional crowd, 469, 470
Cooley, Charles Horton, 29, 106
cooperation, 163
cooperative learning, 334–335
Copernicus, 50, 455
corporations, 170
corrections, careers in, 10
correlations, 48; defined, 48; negative, 48, g48; positive, 48, g63; spurious, 49, c51; variables and, 47–48
correspondence, 158
cotton gin, p455
countercultures, 89, 90; prison, 89; youth, 89

Counter-NATO Summit, 450
Cowgill, Donald, 288–289
Creole culture, 241
crime(s): controlling, p197, 197–198; defined, 195; hate, 195, 249, p249; high-tech, and deviance, 178–179; involving the Internet, 178–79; juvenile, 196; measurement of, 195; relationship between race, ethnicity and, 193; violent, 182, m182; white-collar, 194
crime index offenses, 195
criminal justice system, 197; sociology and, 79
criminology, 46
crisis situations, cooperation in, 163
criteria, 346
crowds, 449, p449, 468, p470, p472; types of, 469–470
crude birthrate, 421–422
crude death rate, 423
Cubans, 241, 257. See also Latinos.
cults, 403; dangers of, 404, p404
cultural bias, 348
cultural change, 87–88
cultural diversity, 88–89
culturally biased intelligence tests, 348, p348
cultural norms, 140
cultural particulars, 93
cultural pluralism, 241
cultural relevance, 88
cultural transmission, 72
cultural universals, 93–94, c94; accounting for, 94
culture, 24, 65–94; biology, behavior and, 270–272; conflict theory on, 69; counter, 89, 90; Creole, 241; defined, 68, 340; enforcing rules in, 78; ethnocentrism and, 91–92; folk, 88; functionalism on, 69; gender and adolescent, 52–53; heredity and, 69–70; ideal, 86; importance of, 68; versus instinct, 69; links between social structure and, c140; material, 84–86; Nacirema, 73; nonmaterial, 84, 85; norms and, 75–78; popular, 66–67, 88; prison, 89; real, 86; in shaping social behavior, 132; society and, 68; sociobiology and, 70–71; sub, 88–89; symbolic interactionism on, 69; symbols, language and, 72; Tejano, 241, p241; transmitting, 340; values and, 79–81; youth, 89
culture shock, 88

curiosity, 111
curriculum: hidden, 112, 329, 354; integrative, 335
customs, c77
cyberbullying, 154–155
Czechoslovakia, socialism and, 382

D

Dahrendorf, Ralf, 463
The Daily Show, p376, 376–377
Darwin, Charles, p3, 13, 16, 70, 71, 413
Darwinism, 410; social, 347
data, 36; analysis of, 35, 55; collecting, 35, 55; descriptive, 36; numerical, 36; precollected, 36, 40–41, c42
dating, interracial, 87
Davidian Seventh-Day Adventists Church, 404
Davis, Kingsley, 102–103
Dean, Howard, 363
death and dying, 122–123, p123
death rate: crude, 423; age-specific, 423
de facto segregation, 243
de jure segregation, 243
democracy, 81, 367–368, 453; direct, 367; representative, 367–368
Democracy in America (de Tocqueville), 205
Democratic Party, 412–413; growth of minorities and, 420
democratic reforms in the classroom, 334–335
demographics, 45; business and, 422, p422
demographic transition, 428–429
demography, 420
denial as stage of grief, 122–123
denomination, 402–403
dependency ratio, 433; significance of, 433
dependent variables, 48, 51
depression as stage of grief, 122–123
descriptive data, 36
desegregation, 349–350
desktop computers, ownership of, c99
desocialization, 124–125
determinism, biological, 268–269
deterrence, 197
de Tocqueville, Alexis, 205, p205, q205, 453
developed economy, 148

developed nations, 226
developing nations, 226; elderly population in, 122
deviance, 177; beneficial effects of, 184–185; conflict theory and, 193; control theory and, 186; defined, 180; defined by the individual, 188–189; degrees of, 189; in functionalism, 193; high-tech crime and, 178–179; in industrial society, 192; learning, 187; nature of, 180–182; negative, 181, 184; positive, 181; primary, 189; secondary, 189; strain theory and, 185–186; in symbolic interactionism, 193; types of youth, c185
deviant, 182
deviations, 379
Dewey, John, 334
Dickens, Charles, 13, 470
Dickson, William, 173
differential association theory, 187
diffusion, 75, 87–88; as a social change, 456
digital audio players, ownership of, c99
digital communications, 66
diminished capacities, 291
direct democracy, 367
disability, poverty and, 217
discovery, 75, 87; as a social change, 455
discrimination, 239; conflict theory on, 250, 251; functionalism on, 250; institutionalized, 253–262; racial, 233; studies of, and formation of policy, 254; symbolic interactionism on, 250, 251–252
discriminatory groups, groups that monitor, 234
distance learning, 338, p338
distortion, 107
diverse, 341
diversion, 198
diversity: cultural, 88–89; defined, 88; ethnocentrism and, 91
Divine Light Mission, 404
divorce, 121; causes of, 314–315; rates of, 27, 314, g315
DNA, double helix model of, p70
Dr. Seuss, 204
Dole, Bob, 363
Dole, Elizabeth, 282
domestication, 145, 301
Domhoff, William, 285
domination, 166–167
doubling time, 426

downward mobility, 225
dowry, 303
dramaturgy, 30
drives, 70
dropout rates, 349, m349
Du Bois, W. E. B., 1, p1, 18, p18, q18
Durkheim, Émile, 2, 7, 15, q15, 26, 40–41, 46, 55, 149, 184, 186, 396, 398, 399
dynamic equilibrium, 462
dysfunctions, 25–26

E

earnings: comparison of women's and men's, g280; effect of race and ethnicity of, g281
earnings gap, 280, 282; of women, 279–280
e-book readers, ownership of, c99
Eccles, Jacquelynne, 82–83, q83
Eckstein, Daniel, 166
ecology, urban, 42
economics, c5; as agent of socialization, 372; agricultural, 367; connecting sociology to, 148, 239, 282, 380, 430, 454; as dimension of social stratification, 206–207; elderly and, 291–292, p292; as a function of families, 309; inequality of women and, 279–280; institutions in, 364; non-Internet users and, 202
economic systems: capitalism as, 378–380; mixed, 381–382; socialism as, 381;
economy: globalization of the, 454, p454
Eder, Donna, 52–53, q53
edge cities, 439
Edison, Thomas Alva, p3, p114
education, 329–358; as agent of political socialization, 371; alternatives to the public school system, 336–339; back-to-basics movement in, 335–336; bilingual, 341–342; bureaucracy in, 332–333; changes in, p333; classrooms in, p333, p336; cognitive ability and, 347–348; compensatory, 350; computers in, 330; in dealing with antisocial behavior, 198; debate over bilingual, 341–342; democratic reforms in the classroom in, 334–335; distance learning and, 338; dropout rates and, 349, m349; equality and inequality in, 346; hidden curriculum in, 112, 329, 354; high-school graduates and, g334; homework and, 330; institutionalized discrimination in, 253; latent functions of, 343; of Latinos, 258; manifest functions of, 340–343; median

earnings by, *g44*; meritocracy and, 344–346; multicultural, 350; No Child Left Behind Act and, 350–351, *p351*; non-Internet users and, 202; number of high-school graduates and, 334; politics, race, religion and, 412–413; promoting equality in, 349–350; religious affiliation and, 412; sexism in, 357–358, *p357*, *p358*; teachers and socialization and, 357–358; technology and, 330–331; textbooks and, 355–356; tracking in, 342, 343, 346; vouchers in, 336–339, *crt337*. See also schools.

Educational Testing Service (ETS), 346

efficiency, 80; as goal of a bureaucracy, 333

egalitarian families, 303, 312

Ehrenreich, Barbara, 42, 220–221, *q221*

Einstein, Albert, 22, 457

Elan Vital, 404

elderly, *m293*; economics and, 291–292, *crt292*; politics and, *p294*; support for, 122; voting turnout among, 293

The Elementary Forms of Religious Life **(Durkheim),** 397

elitism, 373

emails, 130, 299; numbers sent, 131; surveys in, 39

Ember, Carol, *q303*

Ember, Melvin, *q303*

embezzlement, 194

emergent-norm theory, 472

emotional support as function of primary groups, 158

employment, 121; of African Americans, 255–256; agricultural, 149, *m149*; hidden, 256

encounters, 85, 140

endogamy, 306

Engels, Friedrich, 3, 14

environmental lobby, 374

Episcopalians, 410–411

equality, 80–81; in education, 346; promoting, in education, 349–350

equilibrium, 462

Erikson, Erik, 120–121

An Essay on the Principle of Population **(Malthus),** 428

ethics: defined, 56; in social research, 56–57

ethnic cleansing, 243

ethnic groups: as agents of socialization, 372; good and not good places to live, *g239*; other, 262; socioeconomic indicators for, 259, *c259*; in the U.S., *c255*. See also specific ethnic groups.

ethnicity, 238–239; as ascribed master status, 135; effects of, on earnings, 281; population by, *g257*; relationship between crime, race and, 193; women's wages compared to men's by, *g281*

ethnic minority, 238, 240

ethnocentrism, 91–92, 238–239; advantages and disadvantages of, 92; defined, 91; examples of, 91; extreme, 92; globalism, diversity and, 91; racial, 92

Evans, Jean, *q110*

evolution, 71, 413–414

exchange relationships, 164–165

exclusivity, 213

Executive Order 9066, 260

exhibit, 113

exogamy, 305

experience, 405

experiments, *c40*; Adopting Statuses in a Simulated Prison, 136–137; of Asch, Solomon, 166–167; Bobo doll, 316, *p316*; Group Pressure and Obedience, 168–169; Stanford Prison, 57

expert knowledge, 207

exploitation, 206

exponential growth, 426–427

exposure, 74

expressive crowd, 469, 470

extended family, 301, *p301*

external social control, 183

F

Facebook, 395, 451, *p467*; percentage of state population with accounts, *m162*; users of, 131

fads, 467

false consciousness, 210

families, 121, *p297*, 297–326, *crt314*; as agent of political socialization, 371; bilineal, 302, 312; blended, 320–321, *p321*; changing roles of, 148; conflict theory and, 310; defined, 297, 300–301; economic function of, 309; egalitarian, 303, 312; extended, 301, *p301*; farm, *p25*; functionalism and, 307–309; future of, 326; median income for majority and minority groups, *g258*; monogamous, 312; nature of the American, 312; neolocal, 303, 312; nuclear, 301, 312; of orientation, 300; of procreation, 300; reducing conflict in two-career, 141; regulation of sexual activity and, 309; reproductive function of, 308–309; single-parent, 321–322, *g322*; socialization and, 110–111, 307; socio-emotional function of, 307–308; structure of, 301, 302–304; symbolic interactionism and, 310–311; technology and, 298–299; transmittal of social status, 309; two-income, 323–324; types of, 301; varieties of, *c303*, 320–326

Family and Medical Leave Act (1993), 282

family planning, 431

family violence, 315–317; among siblings, 317; case study of, 318–319; frequency of, 315–317; physical abuse as, 316; statistics on, *g317*

fashions, 467

fathers, grading of, by children, *c308*

fecundity, 421

Federal Bureau of Investigation's *Uniform Crime Reports*, 195

Federal Government dollar, spending of, *g219*

females. *See* women.

feminist writers, conflict theory and, 310

feminization of poverty, 217

Ferraro, Geraldine, 282

fertility, 421–422; defined, 420, 421; natural, 421

fertility rate, 422; total, 422; in the U.S., 421, *m421*

field research, 36, 41–42; Gang Leader for a Day: A Rogue Sociologist Takes to the Street, 440–441; Nickel and Dimed, 220–221; The Objective Value of a Social Settlement, 20–21; Segregated School, 352–353

Fiorina, Carly, 278

first world, 226

folk culture, 88

folkways, 75, 76, 77

food, genetically modified, 418–419, *p418*–419

forcible rape, 195

Ford, Henry, 225

formal organizations, 170

formal sanctions, 78

formal schooling, 333

for-profit schools, 339

Franklin, Benjamin, 8

fraud, 194
free-enterprise system, 380, *p380*
French Revolution, 2, 12
Fukuyama, Francis, 150, 457
functional integration, 23
functionalism, 23, 25–26; ageism and, 288–289; assumptions of, 26; comparing to conflict theory, 28; on culture, 69; deviance and, 184–186, 193; discrimination and, 250; education and, 340–343; families and, 307–309; gender and, 273; nature of functions, 25–26; pluralism and, 373–374; religion and, 397–398, 401; role of values in, 26; on school violence and school funding, 41; social change and, 25, 462–463; social interactions and, 165; socialization and, 105, 107; social stratification and, 209–210, 211; social structure and, 142
functions: latent, 25; manifest, 25; nature of, in functionalism, 25
fundamentalism, 410–412, *p411*

G

Galileo, 50, 455
Gallup Poll, 37, 55
Galton, Francis, 16
game stage, 108
gaming, impact on Native Americans, 261–262
gaming console, ownership of, *c99*
Gandhi, Mohandas (Mahatma), 208, 474, *p475*
***Gang Leader for a Day* (Venkatesh),** 440–441
gangs, 89, 440–441; behavior of, 190–191; case study of, 190–191; juvenile crime and, 196; urban, 161
García, Alma, 244–245
Gates, Bill, 373
Gautama, Siddhartha, *c400*
gay, lesbian, bisexual, and transgender (GLBT) community, 478
gay couples, 325
gays and lesbians, hate crimes and, 248
Gemeinschaft, 148–149
gender: adolescent culture and, 52–53; as agent of socialization, 372; as ascribed master status, 135; conflict theory and, 274–275; functionalism and, 273; median earnings by, *g44*; poverty and, 217; suicide rates by, *g289*; symbolic interactionism and, 275–277; technology and, 266–267
gender apartheid, 274
gender behavior, 271–272
gender identity, 268–269, *p269*, *crt271*
gender inequality, 284, *m284*
gender relations, 27; sociologists and, 271–272
gender relationships, conflict theory and, 310
gender socialization, 115, 275; parents and, 275–276; peers and, 277; schools and, 276–277
gender stereotyping, *p272*
generalized beliefs, 476
generalized other, 109
genetically modified food, 418–419, *p418*–419
genocide, 243
gentrification, 439
geographic mobility, 453, *m453*
geography: connection to sociology, 9, 23, 43, 47, 74, 80, 122, 125, 139, 149, 162, 173, 182, 196, 217, 228, 237, 248, 284, 293, 304, 313, 337, 342, 368, 371, 397, 413, 421, 435, 453, 477; human, *c5*; connecting sociology to, 241, 302, 349, 411, 444
Germany: culture in, 74; elderly population in, 122
Gesellschaft, 149
Ghana, norms and customs of, *c77*
Ginsburg, Ruth Bader, 285
glass ceiling, 275, 282
globalism, ethnocentrism and, 91
globalization: defined, 230, 456; of the economy, 454, *p454*; work and, *p460*, 460–461
A Global Perspective, 23, 47, 74, 122, 149, 173, 196, 228, 237, 284, 304, 342, 368, 397, 435, 477
global stratification, 226–230, *g229*
Goffman, Erving, 30, 189
Goode, Erich, *q466*
Google+, 362
government: careers in, 10; contributions to U.S. economy, 380; population control and, 431; role of, in capitalism, 379–380
GPS technology, 299
graphs, 43; line, 43; reading, 45

Gray Panthers, 294
Great Migration, 424
grief, stages of, 122–123
Griffin, John Howard, 42
gross migration rate, 424
Gross National Income (GNI), 226, 228
group behavior: versus individual behavior, 7; predicting, 8
group norms, 173
group pressure: conforming to, 167; obedience and, *p168*, 168–169
groups: boundaries between, 156; coercion and, 165–166; conflict in, 164; conformity and, 7–8, 167; cooperation between, 163; defined, 156; pressure and obedience and, 168–169; primary, 157–158; reasons for forming, *p159*; reference, 160–161; secondary, 159
group superiority, 81
groupthink, 166, 167
gun control, 161

H

Haney, Craig, 137
Hanunóo, 144
Harlow, Harry, 101
Harlow, Margaret, 101
Harris, Chauncy, 445
Harris Poll, 37, 55
hate, high-tech, 234–235
hate crimes, 195, 249, *p249*
Hate Crimes Statistics Act (1990), 249
hate groups, 28; groups that monitor, 234; in the U.S., 248, *m248*
Head Start, 347, 350
health care, poverty and, 218
health services, careers in, 10
Heaven's Gate cult, 404
heredity: culture and, 69–70; effect on behavior, 69–70
Herrnstein, Richard, 347
heterogamy, 306
hidden curriculum, 112, 329, 354
hidden employment, 256
high-income countries, 226–227
high school, dropout rates from, *m349*
high-school graduates, *g334*
high-tech crime, deviance and, 178–179
high-tech hate, 234–235

Hiller, Susan, 290
Hinduism, *m397, g398,* 411, *c400,* polygyny and, 302
Hindu people, 223, *p223*
hippies, 89, 90
Hirschi, Travis, 186
Hispanics. *See* Latinos.
history, *c5;* connecting sociology to, 8, 50, 90, 188, 341, 399, 474
Hitler, Adolf, 92, 243, 366, 369, *p369,* 474
Hoebel, E. Adamson, *q181*
Holmes, Lowell, 288–289
Holocaust, 243, 369
Holt, John, 112–113
home schooling, 338
homework, 330
homogamy, 306
Hooker, Richard, 402
horizontal mobility, 222
horticultural societies, 144–145
hospice movement, 123
households, female-headed, 217
housing sector, informal, 444, *p444*
Howe, Elias, *p3*
Hoyt, Homer, 445
Hull House, 17, 20–21
human behavior: sociology and, 71; study of, 4, 6
human development, 173
Human Development Index (HDI), *m173*
human-development indicators, 229
human geography, *c5;* connecting sociology to, 241, 302, 349, 411, 444. *See also* geography.
human resources, careers in, 10
Hungary, socialism and, 382
hunger, technology and, 418–419
hunting and gathering societies, 144
Hussein, Suddam, 369
Hutterites, fertility of, 421
hypothesis: defined, 55; formulating, 55; of linguistic relativity, 73

I

"I," 109
ideal culture, 86
identity, creating a common, 341
ideology, 332
illegal immigration, 424, 468
imitation stage, 108
immigration, 80; from China, 260; illegal, 424, 468; from Japan, 260–261; Latinos and, 257–258; statistics on, *m80*
impression management, 30
imprisonment, rates of, 125, *m125*
incarceration, 197
incest taboos, 305–306
income: of African Americans, 255; extremes of, in United States, 206–207; growth in after-tax, *c206;* of Latinos, 258–259; median family for majority and minority groups, *g258;* versus wealth, 206–207. *See also* wealth.
incompatibility, 142
independent variables, 48, 51
India: caste system in, 224; norms and customs of, *c77*
indicators, 229; socioeconomic, for racial and ethnic groups, 259
individual, deviance defined by the, 188–189
individual behavior versus group behavior, 7
individual problems versus societal problems, 6
industrialization, 118, 170, 227
Industrial Revolution, 12, 13, 25, 227, 435, 457; impact of, 2
industrial societies, 143; deviance in, 192; features of, 147–150
industry, growth of, 227
inequality in education, 346
infant mortality rate, 423
informal housing sector, 444, *p444*
informal sanctions, 78
informal structures within organizations, 173–174
in-groups, 160
inherited intelligence theory, *347;* arguments against, 347–348
initiation ceremonies, 160
innovation, 185
insecurities, 466
insider trading, 194
instability, 462
instinct, culture versus, 69
institutionalized discrimination, 253–262; defined, 253; in education, 253
institutions: economic, 364; political, 364; total, 124
integrative curriculum, 335
intellectual dimension, 405
intelligence: defined, 335; inherited theory of, 347–348
intelligence tests, culturally biased, 348
interactions, 132; defined, 157
interest groups, 294, *p373,* 373–374; types of, *c374*
intergenerational mobility, 222, 224, *g224*
internal social control, 183
Internet, 130; access to, *m66*–67, 330; adoption of the, 203; crimes involving, 178–179; cyberbullying and, 154–155; evaluating resources on, 44–45; high-tech crime and, 178–179; high-tech hate and, 234–235; politics and, 362; social networking and, 161; use of, 202–203, *m477*
interracial dating, 87
intervening variables, 48
intervention, 48
interviews, 37
introspection, 16
Inuit societies, 144
invention, 75, 87; as a social change, 455
invisible religion, 112
Iraq, war in, 459, *p459*
iron law of oligarchy, 174, *crt174*
Iroquois, 93
Islam, *m397, g398, c400*
Isolation, social, 101
Italy, elderly population in, 122

J

Jackson State University, antiwar protest at, 477
Jacobson, Lenore, 356
Jaffe, Dave, 137
James, William, 16
Janis, Irving, 167
Japan: culture in, 74; elderly population in, 122; norms and customs of, *c77*
Japanese Americans, *p260,* 260–261
Jehovah's Witnesses, 410
Jensen, Arthur, 347
Jesus, *c400*
Jews, hate crimes and, 249
Johnson, Lyndon, 218
Jones, Jim, 404

journalism, careers in, 10
Judaism, p76, m397, g398, c400, 411
Juergensmeyer, Mark, q399
Juravich, Tom, 460–461, q461
jury, p166
Just, Peter, 223
juvenile crime, 196
juvenile justice system, emergence of, 119

K

Kagan, Elena, 285
Kahn, Lawrence, 282
Kaska, 144
Kemp, Jack, 363
Kennedy, John F., 167, 218, 365
Kent State University, antiwar protest at, 477, p477
Kenya, elderly population in, 122
Khoi-San (Bushmen), 144
King, John, 89
King, Martin Luther, Jr., 353, 365, p365, 473, 474, p475
King, Rodney, 470
knowledge, expert, 207
Kohn, Melvin, 111
Koresh, David, 404, p404
Kozol, Jonathan, 352–353, q353
Kübler-Ross, Elisabeth, 122–123

L

labeling, 188, 189
labeling theory, 188
labor force, composition of by sex, g279
Land Ordinance (1785), 334
language, 72; English as dominant, 66; families of, 74, m74; non-English speaking at home, m43; symbols, culture and, 72
Lapps, 145
laptop computers, ownership of, c99
Lareau, Annette, 318–319, q319
latent functions, 25; defined, 340; of education, 343
Latinos, 257–259, p258; average SAT scores by, c346; education of, 258; groups in, 257–258; hate crimes and, 249; high-school graduates, g334; income of, 258; politics and, 242, 258, 412; poverty rate for, 216; single-parent families in, g322; stereotyping and, 248; treatment of, 193; voting by, 242, 372
Latter-Day Saints, c412
laws, 75, 77; bias in, 282–283
Lazerson, Marvin, q332
Leacock, Eleanor, 357
League of Women Voters, c374
learning; cooperative, 334–335; deviance, 187; distance, 338, p338. See also education.
Le Bon, Gustave, 471
legal inequality of women, 282–285
legitimate, 398
Lemert, Edwin, 189
Lennon, John, 393
Levine, Daniel, 348
Levine, Rayna, 348
Li, Jun, 84
Liebow, Elliot, 42
life cycle: defined, 118; socialization through the, 118–123
life expectancy, 423
lifespan, 423
Lincoln, Abraham, 225
linguistic relativity, hypothesis of, 73
literacy rates, 47; world, 342, m342
live streaming, 394
Locke, John, 367
Lombroso, Cesare, 46
looking-glass self, 106
love, romantic, and marriage, 313–314
Lovedu, 93
Lowell, Francis, 3
low-income countries, p229, 229–230
Luckmann, Thomas, 112
Lutherans, 410, c412

M

Madoff, Bernard, p194
magnet schools, 339
mail surveys, 39
majority groups, median family income for, g258
males: brains in, 271; defining, 268–270; earnings of, 279–280, g280, g281; in the labor force, g279
Malthus, Thomas, 428, 430
Mandela, Nelson, 366
manifest functions, 25; defined, 340; of education, 340–343
Mann, Horace, 341, p341
Manus, 93
Mao Zedong, 474
Marconi, Guglielmo, p114
marriage, 133, crt314; arrangements for, 303; childless, 322–323; choosing a spouse, 71, 305–306; formation of family units through, p297; forms of, 304; future of, 315; norms and, 306; rates of, m304, 313, g315; romantic love and, 313–314; two-income, p310, 323–324; varieties of, c303
Marshall, Thurgood, 353
Martineau, Harriet, 13, p13
Marx, Karl, 2, p3, 3, 14, 204, 206, 207, 210, 398–399, 458, 463, 464
Marxism, 410
Masai, 145
mass hysteria, 467–468
mass media: as agent of political socialization, 371; defined, 114; socialization and, 98–99, 114
master status, occupation as a, 135
material culture, 84–86
matriarchy, 303
matrilineal arrangements, 302
matrilocal pattern, 303
mature adulthood, 134
maturity, 398
Mbuti, 93
McCain, John, 362, 363
"me," 109
Mead, George Herbert, 17, 19, 29, 106, 108, 109
Mead, Margaret, q270, p270, 271–272
mean, 44
mechanical solidarity, 15, 149
mechanization, 147
median, 44
median earnings: in dollars, g44; by gender, race, and education, g44
Medicare, 294
megacities, 438
melting pot, 240
meritocracy, 344–346; American, 344–345
Merton, Robert, 25, 54, 185
Methodists, 410, c412
Mexican American Graduate Studies Program, 19
Mexican Americans, 241, 257; narratives of women, p244, 244–245. See also Latinos. narratives of women, p244, 244–245
Mexican Border Studies Project, 19

Michels, Robert, 174
Microsoft, 373, 379
middle class, 111, 213–214; in America, 201; income and living standards of, 228
middle-income countries, 228–229
middle-middle class, 214
middle years, 121
migration, 145, 424–425, c425; defined, 420, 424; measurement of, 424; net, 424; rural-to-urban in the U.S., 424; urban-to-rural, 425
migration rate: gross, 424; net, 424
Milgram, Stanley, 168–169
military, women in the, 274, p274
milling, 471
Mills, Charles Wright, 6, 9, 11
Miner, Horace, q73
minorities, 80; attitudes toward, 239, g239; defined, 236; ethnic, 238, 240; growth of, and politics, 420; hatred toward, 234–235; key features of, 236–237; median family income for, 258, g258; population growth of, 257, g257; portrayal of, in textbooks, 355; racial and ethnic in U.S., c255; treatment of, 193; voting and, 242, p242; women as, 236, 278. See also specific minorities.
Mitchell, David H., 166
mixed economic systems, 381–382, p382
mobility: downward, 225; geographic, 453, m453; horizontal, 222; intergenerational, 222, 224, g224; social, 222; vertical, 222, 223
mobilization of participants for action, 476
mobs, 470
mode, 44
Model T Ford, p3
Monaghan, John, 223
monogamy, 304, 312
monopolies, 379
monotheistic religions, 411
Moore, Brenda, 274
moral-cultural issues, 406
morality, 76
morals, 76
mores, 75, 76, 77
Mormons, c412
Morse, Samuel F. B., p3
mortality: defined, 420, 423; infant, 423
mothers: grading of, by children, c308; working, crt323
motor vehicle theft, 195

Movement for the Restoration of the Ten Commandments of God, 404
Muhammad, c400, 411
multicultural education, 350
multiple causation, 46
multiple-nuclei theory, 443, c443, 445
multiple statuses, 134–135
Mundugumor, 272
murder, 195, 196
Murdock, George, 93
Murray, Charles, 347
Muslims, polygyny and, 302
mutual rights and obligations, 300

— N —

Nacirema culture, 73
Nānak, Gurū, c400
NASA, 455
National Association for the Advancement of Colored People (NAACP), c374, 473
National Commission on Excellence in Education, 335
National Farmers Union, c374
National Highway Traffic Safety Administration, 379
National Organization for Women, c374
National Rifle Association, 373, c374, 474
National Socialist Party, 369
A Nation at Risk, 335
Native Americans, p238, p261, 261–262; impact of gaming on, 261–262; stereotyping and, 248
natural environment in defining social change, 457–458
natural fertility, 421
natural rights, 367
Navajo, 93
negative correlations, 48, g48
negative deviance, 181
neocolonialism, 230
neolocal families, 303, 312
Neo-Nazis, 249, p249
neo-Pentacostalism, 411
net migration rate, 424
new religious movements, 402, 403–404
new urbanism, 439

New Zealand, norms and customs of, c77
Nickel and Dimed: On (Not) Getting By in America **(Ehrenreich),** 42, 220–221
The Nicomachean Ethics **(Aristotle),** 164
9/11 terrorist attacks, 469, p469
Nisbet, Robert, 17, 459
Nixon, Richard, 366, 476–477
No Child Left Behind Act (2001), 350–351, p351
nongovernment agencies, 227, p227
nonmaterial culture, 84, 85
norms, c77; conflict and, 164; defined, 75; deviance and, 181; group, 173; marriage and, 306; sexual activities and, 309; social, 75; values as basis for, 79
Norway, norms and customs of, c77
nuclear family, 301, 312
numerical data, 36
Nuremberg trials, 56

— O —

Obama, Barack, 242, p256, 284, 285, 364
Obedience, group pressure and, p168, 168–169
objective evidence, 358
objective standards, 112
obligations, 138–139
occupation(s): as achieved status, 133; as agent of socialization, 372; defined, 195, 222; inequality of women and, 279–280; as a master status, 135; prestige rankings of selected in the U.S., c208; sex segregation and, 280; typical, c214
Occupy Wall Street, 450
O'Connor, Sandra Day, 283
Ogburn, William, 462–463
old age, 121, 134. See also elderly.
oligarchy, 174; iron law of, 174, crt174
oligopolies, 379
one-child policy, 432–433
online search engines, 130
online surveys, 39–40
online video-sharing sites, 130
OPEC, 458
open classroom, 334
open-class system, 224

open-ended questions, 37, 39; samples of, *p38*
orderliness, 166
organic solidarity, 15, 149
organizations: formal, 170; informal, 173–174
orientation, family of, 300
Orwell, George, 204
out-groups, 160
over-urbanization, 437
Oxfam International, 227

——— P ———

Palin, Sarah, 282
Pan-African movement, 18
panics, 468
parents: gender socialization and, 275–276; grading of, by children, *c308*
Park, Robert Ezra, 17, 19
Parker, Steve, 52–53
parliaments, women in national, 284, *m284*
Parsons, Talcott, 462
participant observation, 42
The Passion of the Western Mind **(Tarnas),** 50
passivity, 268
pastoral societies, 145
patriarchy, 303, 310
patrilineal arrangements, 302, 310
patrilocal pattern, 303
patterns, importance of, 7–8
Pattillo, Mary, 116, *q117*
Pearl Harbor, attack on, 260
peer group: defined, 113; socialization and, 113, 277
Pelosi, Nancy, 284, *p286*
Pennsylvania Human Relations Commission, 234
Peoples Temple, 404
people with disabilities, *p202*; education for, *p338*; hate crimes and, 249; poverty rate for, 217–218
peripheral theory, 443, *c443*, 446
personal growth and development, promoting, 343
personality, socialization and, 100–101
perspective, 4; sociological, 4

Pew Internet and American Life Project, 202
Pew Research Center, 233, 286
phenomenon, 426
The Philadelphia Negro **(Du Bois),** 18
physical objects, beliefs and, 84–85
Pilgrims, 403
pink-collar jobs, 280
plays, roles in, 139–140
play stage, 108
pluralism, 373–374
podcasts, 66
Poland, socialism and, 381
political affiliation, religion and, 412–413
political blogs, 362
political freedom, 368, *m368*
political inequality of women, 282–285
political institutions, 364
political parties, 370
Political Parties **(Michels),** 174
political power: models of, 373–375; voting and, 294
political science, *c5*; connecting sociology to, 158, 242, 367
political socialization, 370–371, *p371*, 372
political sociology, 365
political systems: types of, 367–369
politics: of African Americans, 242; of Asian Americans, 242; of Latinos, 242, 259; population growth and, 420; race, religion, education and, 412–413; technology and, 362–363; women in, 284–285, *p286*, 286–287
polyandry, 304
polygamy, 304
polygyny, 302, 304
polytheistic religions, 411
popular culture, 66–67, 88
population, 37; age distribution of, *m122*; aging, 293; changes in, *m9*, 420; consequences of limiting, 432–433, *g433*; defined, 420; in defining social change, 457; growth of, and politics, 420; long-range projections of world, *g429*; percentage, living in poverty, *m228*; by race and ethnicity, 257, *g257*; reasons for studying, 420; urban, as a percentage of total, 435, *m435*
Population Connection, 475

population control, 431–433; defined, 431; effectiveness of compulsory, 432; effectiveness of voluntary, 431; government-sponsored, 431; one-child policy, 432–433; voluntary, 431
population growth: future world, 430; Malthus on, 428–429; problem of, 426–427; theories of, *g427*, 428–430; zero, 430
population momentum, 430
population pyramids, 433
population transfer, 243
positive correlations, 48, *g48*, *g63*
positive deviance, 181
Positive Philosophy **(Comte),** 12, 13
positivism, 12
postindustrial societies, 143; features of, 150
poverty, 48; absolute, 216; age and, 288; chronic, 228; distribution of, in the U.S., *g216*, 216–219; feminization of, 217; health care and, 218; living in, 217, *m217*; measuring, for the elderly, 291–292, *g293*; percentage of population living in, *m228*; relative, 216
power, 24, 81, 171; defined, 27, 207, 364–365; models of political, 373–375; social control and, 183; social stratification and, 207–208; voting and political, 294; voting as source of, 370
power elite, 375
practicality, 80
precipitating factors, 476
precollected data, 36, 40–41
predictability, 166
pregnancy, teenage, 188–189
preindustrial cities, 435–436
preindustrial societies, 143
prejudice, 239; defined, 246; forms of, 246–247
Presbyterians, 410, *c412*
presentation of self, 30
presidential elections: of 1996, 363; of 2000, 363; of 2004, 362, 363; of 2008, 363; of 2012, 363; voter turnout in, 371, *m371*, *g372*
prestige, 208–209
price fixing, 194
primary deviance, 189
primary groups, 157–158; defined, 157; development of, 157; functions of, 159
primary relationships, 157; secondary groups and, 159

The Principles of Psychology (James), 16
print media, 98
prisons, *p177*; adopting statuses in a simulated, 136–137; counterculture in, 89; as schools for crime, 125
probation, shock, 198
problems, individual versus societal, 6
procreation, family of, 300
profane, 396, 397
program evaluations, 42
progressive education movement, 334
proletariat, 14, 206
propaganda, 115
Protestant ethic, 399–400
The Protestant Ethic and the Spirit of Capitalism **(Weber),** 15
Protestantism, *m397*; link to capitalism, 399–400
psychological case studies, 100
psychology, *c5*; connecting sociology to, 16, 56, 108, 166, 316
public relations, careers in, 10
public schools: alternatives to, 336–339; bureaucracy at, *c171*; expenditures in, *m337*; first, 334. *See also* schools.
publishing, careers in, 10
Pueblo people, 302
Puerto Ricans, 257. *See also* Latinos.
pull factors in urbanization, 438
punishment, 112, 125; for white-collar crime, 194
punk, 89
Puritans, 334, 408
push factors in urbanization, 438
Pygmalion, *p356*
Pygmalion effect, 356

Q

Quakers, 403
qualitative research, 36, 41, 42
qualitative variables, 47
quantitative research, 36, 42
quantitative variables, 47
questionnaires, 37

R

race: as ascribed master status, 135; average SAT scores by, *c346*; defined, 237–238; effects of, on earnings, 280; median earnings by, *g44*; population by, 257, *g257*; relationship between ethnicity, crime and, 193; religion, education, politics and, 412–413; women's wages compared to men's by, *g281*
racial discrimination, 18, 233
racial ethnocentrism, 92
racial groups: as agents of socialization, 372; good and not good places to live, *g239*; socioeconomic indicators for, *c259*; suicide rates by, *g289*; in the U.S., *c255*
racism, 246–247
radio stations, first, *p114*
random numbers, table of, 37
rape, 196
Rape of Nanking, 243
rationalization, 16, 172
rational-legal authority, 366
Rawat, Prem, *p404*
Reagan, Ronald, 282
real culture, 86
real life, roles in, 139–140
rebellion, 186
recession, 292
recidivism, 198
redemptive movement, 475
reference groups, 126, 160–161
reflexes, 70
reformative movement, 474–475
rehabilitation, 197–198
reinforcement, 276
relationships: exchange, 164–165; primary, 157, 159; secondary, 159
relevance, cultural, 88
religion, 393–414, conflicts based on, 399, *p399*; conflict theory and, 398–400, *c401*; defined, 396; education, politics, race and, 412–413; functionalism and, 397–398, *c401*; moral-cultural issues for, *p406*, 406–407; organization of, 402–404; percentage of population attending weekly services, *g409*; preferences in the U.S., *p410*, 410–411; science, society and, 413–414; socialization and, 112; sociological meaning of, 396–397; symbolic interactionism and, 400–401, *c401*; technology and, 394–395; of the world, 397, *m397*, *g398*. *See also* specific religions.
religiosity, 405, *p405*; in the U.S., 413, *m413*
religious freedom, foundations of, 408
religious organizations, *c412*
reorientation, 121
replacement level, 430
representative democracy, 367–368
representative sample, 37
reproductive function of families, 308–309
Republican Party, 412–413; growth of minorities and, 420
research: methods of, *c40*; process of, 54–55, *p55*; qualitative, 36, 41, 42; quantitative, 36, 42; social, 56–57. *See* field research.
residential zone, 445
resource mobilization theory, 477–478
restitution in dealing with antisocial behavior, 198
retreatism, 185
retribution, 197
revolutionary movement, 474
revolution in defining social change, 458–459
rewards, 112
rights, 138–139; defined, 138
riots, 470
rites of passage, 120
ritualism, 185
rituals, 405
robbery, 195, 196
Rocco, Johnny, 110
Rockefeller, John D., 213
role conflict, role strain and, 141
role diversity, problems created by, 141
role performance, 139–140
roles: defined, 138; in real life versus in plays, 139–140
role strain, role conflict and, 141
role taking, 107–108
Roman Catholicism. *See* Catholic Church.
Romney, Mitt, 363
Roosevelt, Franklin, 260
Rosenthal, Robert, 356
rubella, birth rate and, 422
rules, 97; enforcing, 78
rumors, 466
rural-to-urban migration, 424
Rwanda, genocide in, 243

S

Saami, 145
The Sacred Canopy **(Berger),** 400–401
sacred objects, 396
Sader, David, 276–277
Sader, Myra, 276–277
safety, automobile, p379
Salem witchcraft trials, 468
same-sex domestic partners, 325
Samora, Julian, 17, 19
sample, 37; representative, 37
sanctions, 78; formal, 78; informal, 78; negative, 183; positive, 183
sandwich generation, 121
Sapir, Edward, 73–74
Sapir-Whorf hypothesis, 73–74
SAT, 345–346; scores on, p345, c346
Saudi Arabia, norms and customs of, c77
school choice movement, 336
schools: administration of, 332; athletics at, p343; charter, 339; desegregation of, 349–350, 352–353; expenditures on, 337; formal, 333; for-profit, 339; gender socialization and, 276–277; magnet, 339; public, 334, 336–339; segregated, p352, 352–353; socialization in, 112–113; social networks and violence in, 161, p161. *See also* education.
science, society, religion and, 413–414
scientific method, 50; steps in, 54–55
scientific observation in studying social behavior, 12
secondary analysis, c40, 40–41; advantages and disadvantages of, c42
secondary deviance, 189
secondary groups, 170; primary relationships and, 159
secondary relationships, 159
sect, 403
sector theory, 443, c443, 445
secularization in the U.S., 409–410
segregation: de facto, 243; de jure, 243; occupational sex, 280; in schools, p352, 352–353
self, sense of, 19
self-concept, 106
self-control, 111
self-esteem, symbolic interactionist view of, 211
self-expression, 111
self-fulfilling prophecy, 252
Serbia, ethnic cleansing and, 243
Seventh-Day Adventists, 403, 411
sex, 268
Sex and Temperament in Three Primitive Societies **(Mead),** 270
sexism, 278; in education, 357–358, p357, p358; in textbooks, 355
sexual activity, regulating, in families, 309
Shakers, 94
Shakespeare, William, 138
The Shame of the Nation: The Restoration of Apartheid Schooling in America **(Kozol),** 352–353
Shepard, Matthew, 247, 249
shock probation, 198
sibling violence, 317
Sierra Club, 373, c374
significant others, 107
Sikhism, g398, c400
similarity, 94
Simmel, Georg, 164
Simmons, J. L., 180, q180
single life, 324
single-parent families, 321–322, g322
slavery, abolishment of, 254
slave trade, 237
slum housing, 445
Small Business Administration, 422
smartphones, 202, 235, 298, 394
Smelser, Neil, q476
Smith, Adam, 378, 379–380
social action, 24
social aggregate, 156
social behavior: biological differences and, 271; culture in shaping, 132
social categories, 88, 156
social change: conflict theory and, 27, 463–464; defined, 452; factors influencing, 456–459; functionalism and, 25, 462–463; pace of, 452–453; predicting, 453, c453; symbolic interactionism and, 464; variations in the pace of, 454
social class, 14, 24; as changeable, 212; defined, 204; effect on adolescents, 119; middle class, 213–214; social stratification and, 204–205; underclass, 215; upper class, 213; in the U.S., 212–215; working class, 214; working poor, 215
social contagion, 471
social control, 182–183, 477; external, 183; internal, 183; power and, 183
Social Darwinism, 13, 347
social dynamics, 12, 146
social environment, proper, 157
social exchange, p165, 165–166
social groups in shaping our perceptions, 1
social inequities, conflict and, 164
social institutions, 24
social interactions, 139–140; conflict theory and, 165; functionalism and, 165; symbolic interactionism and, 165
socialism, 381, p381; benefits to society, 381; defined, 381; in reality, 381
social isolation, 101; researching the effects of, 101
socialization, 97–126; agents of, 110–115; anticipatory, 126; conflict theory and, 105, 107; defined, 100; family and, 110–111; functionalism and, 105, 107; as function of primary groups, 158; gender, 115, 275–277; importance of, 100–101; mass media and, 98–99, 114–115; peer group, 113; personality and, 100–101; political, 370–371, p371, 372; processes of, 124–126; religion and, 112; in schools, 112–113; symbolic interactionalism and, 106–109; teachers and, 356–358; through the life cycle, 118–123
social life, cooperation in, 163
social media, power of, 450
social mobility: defined, 222; types of, 222
social modeling, 316
social movements, 90; defined, 473; leaders of, 474; nature of, 473–474; resource mobilization theory of, 477–478; selected subjects of, g475; technology and, 450–451; theories of, 476–478; types of, 474–475; value-added theory of, g476, 476–477
social networks, 161–162, 235, 422; defined, 161; school violence and, 161; sites for, 161
social norms, 75
social processes: defined, 455; diffusion as, 456; discovery as, 455; invention as, 455
social relationships, influences of, 1
social research, ethics in, 56–57
social sanctions, 183

social sciences: doing research in, 36–45; sociology and, c5. *See also* specific social sciences.

Social Security, 218, 294

social services, careers in, 10

social settlement, objective value of, 20–21

social solidarity, 149

social stability, 12

social statics, 12

social status: as hierarchical, 134; transmitting, in families, 309

social stratification, 201–230; conflict theory of, 210, 211; defined, 204; economic dimension of, 206–207; functionalist theory of, 209–210, 211; global, 226–230; Internet and, 202–203; poverty and, 216–219; power dimension of, 207–208; prestige dimension of, 208–209; social classes and, 204, 205, 213–215; social mobility and, 222–225; symbolic interactionism and, 210–211; theories of, 209–211

social structure, 23–24; conflict theory and, 142; defined, 4, 132; functionalism and, 142; links between culture and, c140; public issues of, 6; symbolic interactionism and, 142

societal problems versus individual problems, 6

society: agricultural, 145; culture and, 68; defined, 68, 143; horticultural, 144–145; hunting and gathering, 144; industrial, 143, 147–150; pastoral, 145; postindustrial, 143, 150; preindustrial, 143; religion, science and, 413–414; types of, 143

Society in America (Martineau), 13

sociobiology, 70–71; criticisms of, 71; on human behavior, 71

socioeconomic indicators for racial and ethnic groups, c259

socio-emotional maintenance, 307–308

sociological imagination: acquisition of, 9, 11; defined, 9; promise of, 11; using, 9, 11

sociological perspective, 4, 6, 36

sociological research, 33–62; causation in, 46–51; closed-ended questions in, 38; correlations in, 47–48; ethics in, 56–57, 58–62; field research in, 41–42; Internet resources in, 44–45; open-ended questions in, 39–40; program evaluations in, 42; secondary analysis in, 40–41; statistical methods in, 43–44; steps in, 54–55; surveys in, 36–40; tables and graphs in, 45; technology in, 34–35; variables in, 47–48

sociologists: conversation with two, 148–149; gender-related behavior and, 271–272

sociology: applying, 10, 39, 79, 114, 141, 161, 227, 254, 274, 305, 338, 384, 404, 422, 469; careers in, 10; coining of term, 12; connecting to anthropology, 73, 120, 146, 181, 223, 270; criminal justice system and, 79; defined, 4; to economics, 148, 239, 282, 380, 430, 454; European origins of, 12–16; geography and, 9, 23, 43, 47, 74, 80, 122, 125, 139, 149, 162, 173, 182, 196, 217, 228, 237, 248, 284, 293, 304, 313, 337, 342, 368, 371, 397, 413, 421, 435, 453, 477; to history, 8, 50, 90, 188, 205, 302, 341, 399; to human geography, 241, 349, 411; key concepts of, 23–24; nature of, 4–6; to political science, 158, 242, 367; to psychology, 16, 56, 108, 166, 316; key concepts of, 23–24; nature of, 4–6; social sciences and, c5; in United States, 17–19; uses of, 1

solidarity: mechanical, 15, 149; organic, 15, 149; social, 149

Sotomayor, Sonia, 285

Southern Poverty Law Center (SPLC), 234

Soviet Union: collapse of communism in, 368; economy of, 381, p381

special-interest groups, 158

specialization, division of labor based on, 171

Spencer, Herbert, 2, 13–14

spheres: defined, 279; of society, 278

spirit of capitalism, 399–400

Spitz, René, 101

Spitzer, Steven, 192

spouse, choosing a, 305–306

spurious correlation, 49, c51

stability, 182

standardization, purpose of, 332–333

standardized achievement tests, 335–336

standard of living, 226

standards, objective, 112

Stanford Prison Experiment, 57

Starr, Ellen Gates, 20

state, separation of church and, p393, p414

statistical methods, using basic, 43–44

status(es): achieved, c133, 133–134; adopting, in a simulated prison, 136–137; ascribed, c133, 133–134; assigned, 133; defined, 133; master, 135; multiple, 134–135; studying, 135

status set, 134

stereotyping, 247–249; age and, 290, p290; effects of, 92; gender, p272

Stewart, Jon, p376, 376–377

stigma, 189

strain: deviance and, 185; responding to, 185–186

strain theory, deviance and, 185–186

stratification, global, g229

strikes, p164

structural conductiveness, 476

structural strains, 476

Student Nonviolent Coordinating Committee (SNCC), 473

students: effect of teachers on performance of, 356; selecting and screening, 342

subcultures, 88–89

subjugation, 242

submit, 171

suburbanization in the U.S., 438–439

success, 80

Sudan, elderly population in, 122

sudra caste, 224

Suicide: A Study in Sociology (Durkheim), 15

suicide, ritualistic, 404

suicide rates: by age, gender, and racial group, 289, g289

Sumner, William Graham, 75–76

superstition, 188

survey research: Consuming Politics: Jon Stewart, Branding, and the Youth Vote in America, 376–377; How Do Schools and Parents Fail Teens? 82–83; Moral-Cultural Issues, 406–407; Narratives of Mexican American Women, p244, 244–245; Obstacles to Female Political Leadership, 286–287

surveys, 33, 36–40, c40; email, 39; evaluating, 39; mail, 39; online, 39–40

Sutherland, Edwin, 194

symbolic interactionism, 23, 29–30; ageism and, 290; assumptions of, 26, 29–30; on culture, 69; defined, 29; deviance in, 193; and discrimination, 250–252; dramaturgy and, 30; education and, 354–358; families and, 310–311; gender and, 275–277; religion and, 401; on school violence and school funding, 41; significance of symbols and, 29; on social change, 464; social interactions and, 165; socialization and, 106–109; social stratification and, 210–211; social structure and, 142

symbols, 65, 72; defined, 29; for in-groups, 161; language, culture and, 72; significance of, 29

T

tables, 43; reading, 45
tablets, ownership of, *c99*
taboos, 76, 397; incest, 305–306
Taliban, 274–275
Tarnas, Richard, *q50*
tax evasion, 194
Taylor, Robert, Homes, *p440,* 440–441
Tchambuli tribe, 272
teachers: effect of, on student performance, 356; socialization and, 356–358
teaching, careers in, 10
technology: age and gender and, 266–267; defined, 456; in defining social change, 456–457; education and, 330–331; families and, 298–299; food, hunger, and, 418–419; politics and, 362–363; religion and, 394–395; social movements and, 450–451; in sociological research, 34–35; suburbanization and, 439
teenage pregnancy, 188–189
Tejano culture, 241, *p241*
televangelism, 394
television: color, *p114*; early, *p114*
Temporary Assistance for Needy Families (TANF), 219
terminal illness, 122
textbooks, *p355,* 355–356
texting, 266–267, 299
theft, 196
theoretical perspectives: conflict theory as, 27–28; defined, 22; on discrimination, 250–251; functionalism as, 25–26; role of, 22–24; symbolic interactionism as, 29–30. *See also* specific perspectives.
therapy in dealing with antisocial behavior, 198
third world, 226
Thirteenth Amendment, 254

Three Strikes Law, 197
Tilly, Charles, 459
time intervals, 73
Toland, John, *q366*
Tönnies, Ferdinand, 148–149, 464
total fertility rate, 422
total institutions, 124
totalitarianism, 369
Toynbee Hall, 20
tracking, 342, 343
traditional authority, 366, 367
transition, 443
transmission, 100
trust, deviance and, 184
Tudor, Mary, 56
Tuskegee Institute, 19
twin studies, 70
Twitter, 363
two-career families, reducing conflict in, 141
two-income marriages, *p310,* 323–324

U

Ullman, Edward, 445
underclass, 215, 256
underlying causes, 291
unemployment rates, 139, *m139*
Unequal Childhoods: Class, Race, and Family Life (Lareau), 318–319
unethical behavior, stereotyping in justifying, 248
Unification Church, 404
uniformity, 166
uniqueness, 125
United States: basic values in, 80–81; class structure in, *c214*; composition of the labor force by sex, *g279*; extremes of income and wealth in, 206–207; fertility rate in the, 421, *m421*; hate groups in, 248, *m248*; immigration to the, 80, *m80*; imprisonment rates in, 125, *m125*; intergenerational mobility in, *g224*; poverty in, *g216,* 216–219; prestige rankings of selected occupations in, 208; racial and ethnic minority groups in, *c255*; religiosity in the, 413; religious preferences in the, 410–411; rural-to-urban migration in, 424; secularization in the, 409–410; social classes in the, 212–215; sociology in, 17–19; suburbanization in the, 438–439; unemployment in, *m139*

universals, cultural, 93–94
Untouchables, 224
upper class, 213, *p213*
upper-middle class, 213–214
upward mobility, 224–225
urban ecology: defined, 442; nature of, 442
urban housing, life in, 440–441
urbanism, 464
urbanization, 147, 170, 434; defined, 434; differences in patterns of, 437–438; patterns of, 437, *g437*; push and pull factors in, 438; world, 436–438
urban legend, 466–467
urban population, 435, *m435*
urban-to-rural migration, 424–425
U.S. Chamber of Commerce, *c374*
usury, 78
utilization, 289

V

Vaisyas, 224
value-added theory of social movements, *g476,* 476–477
values: basic, in the United States, 80–81; as basis for norms, 79; conflict and, 164; role of, in functionalism, 26
Vanderbilt, Cornelius, 213
variables, 46; correlations and, 47–48; defined, 47; dependent, 48, 51; independent, 47, 51; intervening, 48; qualitative, 47; quantitative, 47; types of, 47–48
Venkatesh, Sudhir, 440–441, *q441*
verstehen, 16
vertical mobility, 222, 223
victim discounting, 193
videoconferencing, 394
violations, 75–76, 182
violence: case study of, 318–319; crime and, 182, *m182*; family, 315–317, *g317*; school, 41, 161, *p161*; sexual, 316–317; at soccer match, *p472*
violent crime, 182, *m182*
virtual, 254
voluntary change, 126
voluntary population control, 431; effectiveness of, 431–432
voter turnout, 371, *m371,* 372, *g372*; among the elderly, 293–294
voting: choices in, 370; influences of, 370–371; political power and, 294; youth, 376–377

W

voucher system, 336–339, crt337

wages. See earnings.
Wald, Kenneth D., 406, q407
Wangchuk, Jigme Khesar Namgyel, p366
war, 458–459, p459
War on Poverty, 218–219
Washington, Booker T., 17, 19, p19
Watt, James, p2
wealth: distribution of, c206; extremes of, in United States, 206–207; versus income, 206. See also income.
Weber, Max, p3, p15, 15–16, 24, 172, q172, 204, 207, 365, 366, 398–399
weddings, 65, p65
welfare reform, 219
Wells, H. G., 467
Western Electric, 173
White, Lynn, 276
white-collar crime, 194; punishment for, 194
whites: poverty rate for, 216; treatment of, 193; world of, 233
Whitney, Eli, p2
Whorf, Benjamin, 73–74
Wiccans, 404
wikis, 66
Williams, Robin, 80, 81
Wirth, Louis, 236, q236
Woman's Christian Temperance Union, 374, 475
women: brains in, 271; characteristics of, 268–270; earnings of, g280, 281, g281; in elective offices, 285; feminist writers and, 310; glass ceiling and, 275, 282; legal and political inequality of, 282–285; in the military, 274, p274; minimum legal age of marriage for, m304; as a minority group, 236, 278; narratives of Mexican American, p244, 244–245; in national parliaments, 284, m284; obstacles to political leadership by, 286–287; occupational and economic inequality of, p265, 279–281; in politics, 284–285, p286, 286–287; portrayal of, in textbooks, 355, p355; sexual abuse against, 317; types of jobs for, 280
women's liberation movement, 90
work, 80; globalization and, p460, 460–461
working class, 111, 206, 214
working mothers, crt323
working poor, 215
World Bank, 226
world birthrates, g428
world literacy rates, 342, m342
world urbanization, 436–438
Wright, Orville, 455
Wright, Wilbur, 455
Wundt, Wilhelm, 16, p16

Y

Yanomamö, 144, 146, p146
Yemen, elderly population in, 122
youth counterculture, 89
youth deviance, types of, c185
You Tube, 66, 363; viewers of, 131
Yugoslavia, ethnic cleansing in, 243

Z

Zero Population Growth, 430, 475
Zimbardo, Philip, 136–137, q137
zone of workingmen's homes, 445
Zweigenhaft, Richard, 285